Visual Basic for DOS
Inside & Out

David Schneider
Gary Cornell

Visual Basic for DOS
Inside & Out

Osborne **McGraw-Hill**

Berkeley New York St. Louis San Francisco
Auckland Bogotá Hamburg London Madrid
Mexico City Milan Montreal New Delhi Panama City
Paris São Paulo Singapore Sydney
Tokyo Toronto

Osborne **McGraw-Hill**
2600 Tenth Street
Berkeley, California 94710 U.S.A.

For information on translations and book distributors outside of the U.S.A., please
write to Osborne **McGraw-Hill** at the above address.

Visual Basic for DOS Inside & Out

1234567890 DOC 998765432

ISBN 0-07-881829-X

Publisher
Kenna S. Wood

Acquisitions Editor
William Pollock

Associate Editor
Vicki Van Ausdall

Editorial Assistant
Judy Kleppe

Technical Editor
Ethan Winer

Project Editor
Kathy Krause

Copy Editors
Kathy Hashimoto
Carl Wikander
Toni Murray

Proofreaders
Katja Amyx
Audrey Baer Johnson

Indexer
Richard Shrout

Computer Designer
Peter F. Hancik

Cover Designer
Bay Graphics, Inc.

Contents at a Glance

Contents

Acknowledgments

One of the best parts of writing a book is when the authors get to thank those who have helped them, for rarely (and certainly not, in this case) is a book truly produced by the authors alone. First and foremost, we have to thank the team at Osborne/McGraw-Hill. Their patience, dedication, help, cheerfulness, you name it—went way beyond the call of duty. To Vicki Van Ausdall, Kathy Krause, Cindy Brown, Jeff Pepper, Bill Pollock, Larry Robinson, Kathy Hashimoto, Carl Wikander, Toni Murray, Katja Amyx, and Audrey Baer Johnson—Thanks!

Next we have to thank those people at Microsoft (whose names, unfortunately, we don't know) who created Visual Basic for DOS. It's a great product. Troy Strain and Bill Nelson coordinated the beta program; their patience with strange requests and general all-around helpfulness also went way beyond the call of duty.

Ethan Winer did the technical review of the manuscript, carefully and patiently pointing out ways to make this book better. John Tralka helped with many of the gritty details. He contributed especially to the numerous screen captures that (we hope) make for clarity and understanding.

Special thanks go to Fred Mosher who helped in so many ways. In particular, his deep understanding of programming contributed to making this book complete.

Introduction

The Visual Basic Programming System for MS-DOS (this book will usually refer to it as Visual Basic or VBDOS, for short) makes it simple—and often fun—to develop modern menu-driven windowing programs for the 80 million or so MS-DOS users who do not use Microsoft Windows.

Visual Basic for DOS is essentially as capable and functional as Visual Basic for Windows. Visual Basic for Windows was described by Bill Gates, Chairman of the Board of Microsoft, as "awesome." Stewart Alsop said in *The New York Times* that Visual Basic for Windows is "the perfect programming environment for the 1990s." And now Visual Basic for DOS is the perfect programming environment for the millions of non-Windows users!

So what is all the hype about? Exactly what is Visual Basic for DOS, and what can it do for you? Visual Basic for DOS is an easy-to-use, yet powerful, tool for developing modern menu-driven windowing applications. This doesn't seem like enough to justify all the hoopla—until you realize that developing windowing applications often took an expert C programmer supplied with around 20 pounds of documentation, and at least 20 or 30 megabytes of hard disk space for the needed C compiler and the essential add-ons.

About This Book

This book is a comprehensive hands-on tutorial for Visual Basic for DOS programming. Yet we don't assume you've ever programmed before (although people familiar with QuickBasic or another structured programming language will, of course, have an easier time of it). You'll start at the beginning and quickly move along the road to mastery. Soon you'll be writing sophisticated menu-driven windowing programs that take full advantage of Visual Basic's exciting and powerful event-driven nature.

We've tried hard to stress the new ways of thinking needed for Visual Basic programming. We hope that even expert programmers can benefit from this. This is because trying to force Visual Basic into the framework of older programming languages is ultimately self-defeating—you can't take advantage of its power if you continue to think in an older paradigm.

How This Book is Organized

This book can be used in a variety of ways, depending on your background and needs. People familiar with structured programming techniques can skim the complete discussions of the programming constructs, like loops and Sub procedures, that Visual Basic inherited from QuickBasic 4.5. Beginners will want to work through this material carefully.

Here are short descriptions of what the chapters cover:

☐ Chapters 1 and 2 show you how to install Visual Basic and help you become familiar with the Visual Basic environment.

☐ Chapters 3 and 4 start you right off with the notion of a customize-able window (called a form) that is the heart of every windowed (and so Visual Basic) application. You'll see how to add command buttons, text boxes, and labels to your windows.

☐ Chapters 5 through 9 cover the core programming techniques needed to make full use of Visual Basic's powers. You'll see how to best take advantage of Visual Basic's many built-in functions as well as learn how to add your own. You'll begin to learn how to isolate bugs (programming errors) and then eradicate them. You'll see how to sort and search through data and use modular programming techniques to make your programs more flexible, powerful, and easier to debug.

☐   Chapter 10 takes you through most of the rest of the controls you can add to your windows. You'll see how to add list boxes, option buttons, check boxes, scroll bars, and all the other controls that users expect and that make modern applications so much easier to use then their old-fashioned counterparts.

☐   Chapter 11 shows you the debugging techniques that become vital as your program becomes more sophisticated.

☐   Chapter 12 shows you how to analyze how a user is manipulating his or her mouse.

☐   Chapter 13 shows you how to handle files within Visual Basic including practical encrypting methods for keeping files confidential and safe from casual probes.

☐   Chapter 14 introduces you to a world of very advanced topics, including multiple form applications using Microsoft's MDI (multiple document interface).

☐   Chapter 15 is a full-fledged, user-friendly home finance program. This chapter clearly shows the power of Visual Basic to improve your productivity as a programmer. Following our model, you can easily add the few additional features needed to make this program into a business and home finance program that has all the functionality and simplicity of commercial programs that have generated millions of dollars in sales.

☐   Chapter 16 introduces you to the world of graphics and sound.

☐   Chapter 17 shows you the features available in the professional edition of Visual Basic, including an extensive treatment of ISAM (Indexed Sequential Access Method) that makes writing professional-quality database managers a snap.

☐   There are also extensive appendices, including one that gives a concise but thorough reference to all of Visual Basic's commands.

Conventions Used in This Book

Keys are set like this, using small caps: CTRL or HOME. Arrow and other direction keys are also spelled out with small caps. For example, if you need to press the right arrow key, you'll see: "Press RIGHT ARROW".

When you need to use a combination of keys to activate an item, we'll use a plus sign and put the whole key combination in small caps. For example, "Press CTRL+A" means you should hold down the key marked "Ctrl" on your keyboard while pressing an "A." On the other hand, "Press ALT F P" means press "Alt," then press "F," and then press "P"—you don't need to hold down the ALT key.

DOS commands, file names and file extensions are given in all caps: COMMAND.COM, .TXT, and so on. Keywords in Visual Basic for DOS use all caps as well: PRINT, IF, FOR, and so on. The syntax for a command in Visual Basic is set in ordinary type, except that items that the programmer can change are given in italics. For example, the NAME command used to rename a file would appear as:

NAME *OldFileName* AS *NewFileName*

Finally, programs are set in a monospaced font, as in the following example:

```
SUB Form_Click ()
  PRINT "Hello world!"
END SUB
```

The Companion Disk

A companion disk containing all the programs in this book, in addition to many useful procedures, can be obtained by sending a check or money order for $25.00 (Connecticut residents please add sales tax) to

Gary Cornell: Books On Science
128 Moulton Road
Storrs, CT 06268

Please use the order form provided following this introduction.

Disk Order Form

The companion disk contains all the programs in *Visual Basic for DOS Inside & Out* that have more than two lines of code. In addition, the disk contains more than 50 bonus procedures with full source code. Here's a sample of what this disk has to offer:

General Interest Procedures for...

- ☐ Performing graphic screen dumps for many different combinations of adapter cards and printers
- ☐ Ordering the elements of an array with Quicksort or Merge sort
- ☐ Saving the contents of the screen (any monitor and graphics mode) to disk
- ☐ Creating banners on a dot-matrix printer

Business Procedures for...

- ☐ Calculating internal rate of return
- ☐ Analyzing a loan or annuity
- ☐ Determining straight-line, sum-of-digits, or double-declining balance depreciations
- ☐ Drawing a bar, line, or pie chart

Mathematics Procedures for...

- ☐ Inverting a matrix
- ☐ Drawing the graph of a function
- ☐ Performing numeric integration

To order your disk, send your name, address, and the disk size you require (5 1/4-inch or 3 1/2-inch) along with check or money order for **$25.00** payable to Gary Cornell: Books on Science (CT residents add sales tax) to:

Gary Cornell: Books on Science
128 Moulton Road
Storrs, CT 06268

.... (cut here) ....

Please rush one companion disk for *Visual Basic for DOS Inside & Out* to

Name _____

Address _____

City_____State_____ZIP_____

we also offer a 30-day money-back guarantee.

CHAPTER

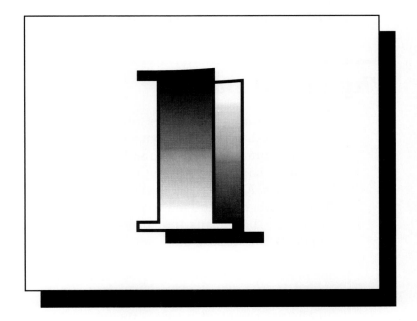

Getting Started

*T*his chapter gives you an overview of what the Visual Basic Programming System for DOS is all about. The full name is something of a mouthful, so we'll use "Visual Basic" for short. You'll learn what equipment you need to run Visual Basic, how to set it up, and how to use the built-in tutorial. Although you certainly don't need to be an expert at working with a modern, menu-driven, mouse-capable user interface to learn Visual Basic, you should be comfortable with mouse manipulations. If you don't know the difference between clicking and double-clicking or between dragging and dropping, Appendix D provides explanations of these and other terms. However, there is no better way to master what modern, user friendly program design is all about than to write applications that are modern, menu driven, and mouse capable—and making that easy to do is what Visual Basic is all about.

Why Visual Basic?

Concentrating on the user interface has revolutionized the microcomputer industry. Programs have traditionally required mastery of lots of cryptic commands and arcane keystrokes to do anything. This is now seen as a barrier preventing users from taking full advantage of their computers. Also, the *feel* that applications have has become important. Modern programs are moving more and more toward a consistent user interface. This means that users can spend more time mastering the application and less time worrying about which keystrokes do what. Users have come to know they can open a File menu by clicking a mouse (or pressing ALT F) and then look for the operations that will work with files there.

All this comes at a price, though; before Visual Basic, developing menu-driven, mouse-capable applications was much harder than developing older style DOS applications. Without add-ons, programmers had to worry about too much; what the mouse was doing, where the user was inside a menu, whether he or she was clicking or double-clicking at a given place, and so on. Visual Basic has changed this completely. Sophisticated applications can now be developed in a fraction of the time previously needed. Programming errors (bugs) don't happen as often— and if they do, they're a lot easier to detect and fix. Programming menu-driven, user-friendly windowing applications has become (at least most of the time) fun. And, you don't have to pay much of a performance penalty: applications developed under Visual Basic run quickly.

How You Develop a Visual Basic Application

The first step in developing a Visual Basic application is to plan what the user sees—in other words, to design the screens. What menus do you want? How large a window should the application use? How many windows should there be? Should the windows be resizeable by the user? Where will you place the "buttons" that the user can click on to activate the applications? (Such buttons are called *command buttons*.) Will the applications have places to enter text (*text boxes*)? Will there be lists of items to choose from (*list boxes*)? Visual Basic programs derive their user friendliness from these and other objects (called *controls*) that you place inside the windows the users see.

What makes Visual Basic different from almost any other programming tool is the ease with which you can design the screen. You literally draw the user interface, much like using a paint program. And when you're done drawing the interface, the command buttons, text boxes, and other controls that you have placed in a blank window will automatically recognize user actions such as mouse movements and button clicks. Visual Basic also comes with a menu design feature that makes creating menus a snap.

Only after you design the interface does anything like traditional programming occur. Objects in Visual Basic *will* recognize events like mouse clicks; how the objects respond to them depends on the code you write. You will always need to write code in order to make controls respond to events. This makes Visual Basic programming fundamentally different from conventional programming.

Programs in conventional programming languages run from the top, down. For older programming languages, execution starts at the first line and moves with the flow of the program to different parts as determined by the original programmer (who may not have taken all that the user wants into account). A Visual Basic program works completely differently. The core of a Visual Basic program is a set of independent pieces of code that are *activated* by, and so respond to, only the events they have been told to recognize. This is a fundamental shift. Now, instead of having to adapt to a program that reflects what the programmer thinks should happen, the user is more in control. Instead of program that asks questions and then goes off to do a calculation, a Visual Basic program allows a user to fill in boxes with information that controls what the program will do. When he or she is happy with what is entered, a click on a command button or a menu item will start the ball rolling.

Most of the programming code in Visual Basic that responds to events like mouse clicks occurs in what Visual Basic calls *event procedures*. Essentially, everything executable in a Visual Basic program is either in an event procedure or is used by an event procedure to help the procedure carry out its job. In fact, the fundamental difference between Visual Basic and ordinary programming languages is reflected in its documentation's use of the term *project* rather than *program* to refer to the combination of programming code and user interface that goes into making a Visual Basic application possible.

Here is a summary of the steps you take to design a Visual Basic application:

1. Customize the windows that the user sees.

2. Decide what events the controls on the window should recognize.

3. Write the event procedures for those events and whatever "helper" routines the event procedures need.

Here is what happens when the application is running:

1. Visual Basic monitors the windows and the controls in each window for *all* the events that each control can recognize (mouse movements, clicks, keystrokes, and so on).

2. When Visual Basic detects an event, it examines the application to see if you've written an event procedure for that event.

3. If you have written an event procedure, Visual Basic executes the code that makes up that event procedure and goes back to step 1.

4. If you have not written an event procedure, Visual Basic waits for the next event and goes back to step 1.

These steps cycle continuously until the application ends. Of particular significance is that an event *must* happen before Visual Basic will do anything. Event driven programs are *reactive* more than *active*—and that makes them more user friendly.

The Features of Visual Basic

Visual Basic lets you add menus, text boxes, command buttons, option buttons (for making exclusive choices), check boxes (for nonexclusive choices), list boxes, scroll bars, and file and directory boxes to blank windows. You can have multiple windows on a screen.

The programming language (an extension of the one in QBasic or QuickBASIC) built into Visual Basic has easy-to-use graphics statements, powerful built-in functions for mathematics and string manipulations, and sophisticated file-handling capabilities.

Moreover, Visual Basic makes it easy to build up large programs by allowing modern *modular programming techniques.* This means you can break down a program into easier-to-handle (and therefore less error-prone) modules. (A *module* is a manageable, relatively small piece of programming code.) Modules ideally accomplish one task and have a well-defined interface with the rest of the program so that they can be coded and tested independently. This way you can concentrate on how each module does its job and how the pieces of your program communicate with each other inside your application.

Visual Basic also provides sophisticated error handling for the all-too-common task of preventing new users from bombing an application. (*Bombing* is computer jargon for ending a program abruptly and abnormally.) Visual Basic has an intelligent interpreter/editor that often detects errors and can even suggest the changes needed to correct routine programming and typographical errors that are common when you begin building an application. It has an extensive on-line help system for quick reference while you're developing an application.

What You Need to Run Visual Basic

Visual Basic is a sophisticated program—the more powerful your hardware the better. But it theoretically can run on any IBM PC-compatible with at least 2 megabytes of hard disk space and MS-DOS or PC-DOS version 3.1 or higher.

To take full advantage of Visual Basic system, you'll need the following:

☐   A hard disk with at least 4 megabytes free (A minimal system needs 2MB)

☐   A mouse or other pointing device compatible with a mouse

☐   A graphics monitor and card. EGA or higher resolution is best

☐   At least 2MB of RAM with EMS/XMS support

☐   A chip at least as powerful as an Intel 80286

Visual Basic is power hungry: the more memory and speed your computer has, the better.

Setting Up Visual Basic

As with all programs, the first thing you should do is make backup copies of the original distribution disks. Although the Visual Basic files are compressed, the disks themselves are not copy protected. You can make copies to a blank disk with the DISKCOPY command from DOS. You can also use COPY *.* to transfer the files to a formatted disk.

Send in the registration card. It's true that you'll get a certain amount of junk mail as a result, but it also will be easier to get support and notices of upgrades from Microsoft.

Running the Setup Program

The first of the disks that Visual Basic comes on contains an auto-mated Setup program to install Visual Basic. You can run the Setup program as many times as you want, which means you are not tied into the options you choose the first time. (It is a good idea for first-time users to use the default options.) The first time you install Visual Basic, the Setup program asks for your name or the name of the company or person that bought this copy of Visual Basic. It keeps track of this information and uses it to remind you to whom the program is licensed—every time you start Visual Basic.

To set up Visual Basic from the A drive follow these steps:

1. Place disk 1 in drive A.

2. Type **A:SETUP**.

3. Press ENTER.

After a short wait, your screen will look something like the one in Figure 1-1. Press ENTER to begin installation of Visual Basic.

After a short delay, during which a screen appears asking for your name or your company's name, you are presented with a dialog box like the one shown in Figure 1-2. This dialog box indicates that the Setup program will install Visual Basic in a new directory called C:\VBDOS. If you are not satisfied with this, make changes in the box and then press ENTER. If you want to leave the Setup program, press CTRL+C.

Suppose you accept the defaults and choose the Continue option. You are next shown a sequence of dialog boxes that ask you where you want

FIGURE 1-1 Visual Basic's Setup screen

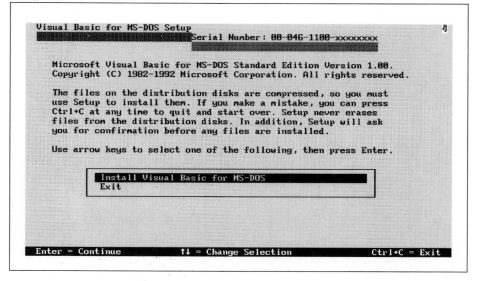

```
Visual Basic for MS-DOS Setup                                              ▯
███████████████████████████Serial Number: 00-046-1100-xxxxxxxx
                                    ████████████████████████████

   Microsoft Visual Basic for MS-DOS Standard Edition Version 1.00.
   Copyright (C) 1982-1992 Microsoft Corporation. All rights reserved.

   The files on the distribution disks are compressed, so you must
   use Setup to install them. If you make a mistake, you can press
   Ctrl+C at any time to quit and start over. Setup never erases
   files from the distribution disks. In addition, Setup will ask
   you for confirmation before any files are installed.

   Use arrow keys to select one of the following, then press Enter.

          ┌───────────────────────────────────────────────┐
          │ Install Visual Basic for MS-DOS                │
          │ Exit                                           │
          └───────────────────────────────────────────────┘



   Enter = Continue          ↑↓ = Change Selection        Ctrl+C = Exit
```

FIGURE
1-2
The first screen for copying files in Setup

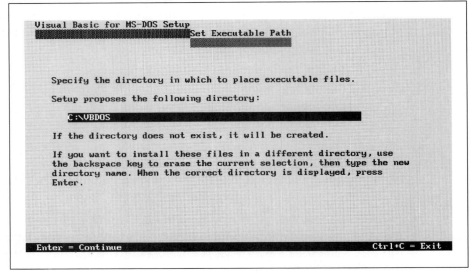

to store various types of files. A typical one looks like Figure 1-3. It's easiest to just accept the defaults that Visual Basic suggests.

FIGURE
1-3
Screen suggesting where to place Help files

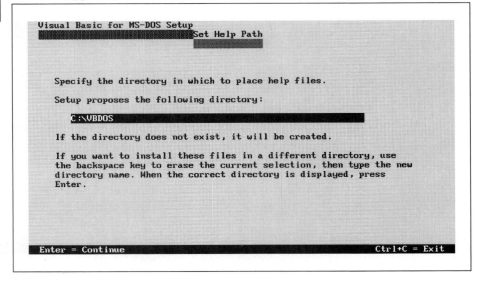

Once you've specified where you want to place everything, Visual Basic gives you one more opportunity to change your mind by presenting you with the options shown in Figure 1-4. If you decide to continue with the installation, keep in mind that installing Visual Basic takes a fair amount of time—around five minutes on a 386 machine. This is partly because of the size of Visual Basic and partly because of the decompression needed for such a large program compressed into so few disks. As the Setup program copies the file, you are told how many files are left to copy. When Visual Basic needs another disk, it will tell you. If you try to use the wrong disk at any time, it will tell you that too.

When the Setup program finishes its job, you're presented with a screen like the one in Figure 1-5 that will allow you to choose to run the Visual Basic tutorial directly or to exit the Setup program.

If there are any corrections or additions to the documentation, you'll find them in files called READNOW.TXT and README.TXT. (Look at the one called READNOW.TXT first if one appears.) If one or both of these files are on the distribution disks, the Setup program automatically copies them to the same directory that holds Visual Basic. The file named PACKING.TXT contains a list of all the files that are supplied with Visual Basic. It's worth looking at to make sure you have everything you need.

FIGURE 1-4   Confirm Install Options screen

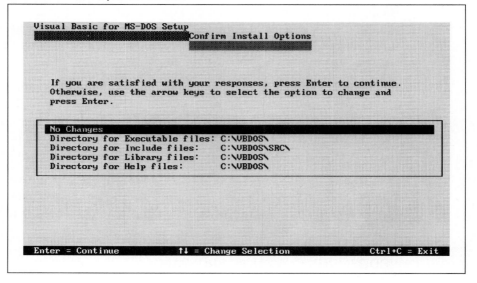

FIGURE
1-5
Screen when finished installing Visual Basic

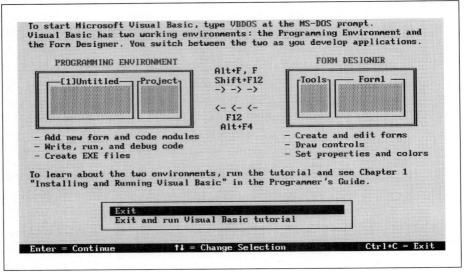

```
To start Microsoft Visual Basic, type VBDOS at the MS-DOS prompt.
Visual Basic has two working environments: the Programming Environment and
the Form Designer. You switch between the two as you develop applications.

      PROGRAMMING ENVIRONMENT           Alt+F, F        FORM DESIGNER
                                        Shift+F12
  ┌─[1]Untitled──┐ ┌Project┐           -> -> ->     ┌Tools┐ ┌── Form1 ──┐
  │░░░░░░░░░░░░░░│ │░░░░░░░│                         │░░░░░│ │░░░░░░░░░░░│
  │░░░░░░░░░░░░░░│ │░░░░░░░│            <- <- <-      │░░░░░│ │░░░░░░░░░░░│
  │░░░░░░░░░░░░░░│ │░░░░░░░│               F12        │░░░░░│ │░░░░░░░░░░░│
  └──────────────┘ └───────┘            Alt+F4       └─────┘ └───────────┘

  - Add new form and code modules              - Create and edit forms
  - Write, run, and debug code                 - Draw controls
  - Create EXE files                           - Set properties and colors

To learn about the two environments, run the tutorial and see Chapter 1
"Installing and Running Visual Basic" in the Programmer's Guide.

            ┌─────────────────────────────────────────┐
            │ Exit                                     │
            │ Exit and run Visual Basic tutorial       │
            └─────────────────────────────────────────┘

 Enter = Continue          ↑↓ = Change Selection       Ctrl+C = Exit
```

Starting Visual Basic

You can run Visual Basic by moving to the VBDOS directory and entering **VBDOS**. On the other hand, if you want to be able to start Visual Basic from any directory, then you have to add the appropriate directory (usually: C:\VBDOS) to your path. (Consult the DOS documentation for how to do this.) Visual Basic comes with a batch file called NEW_VARS.BAT to make the necessary adjustments.

Visual Basic has various switches you can set when you start it up. These are summarized in Table 1-1. Most of these are probably not of great interest to you at this point, but, if you have a limited amount of memory, the /S:1 option is one that will let you (at a great performance penalty, unfortunately) run Visual Basic in the least amount of memory.

A more common use of a startup switch is to run a specific Visual Basic project when you start it up. As Table 1-1 indicates, you need only give the (full) path name of the Visual Basic application after typing **/RUN**. For example, type

VBDOS /RUN C:\VBDOS\SRC\CALC

TABLE 1-1   Visual Basic Switches

Option	Result
/?	Displays all the options for starting Visual Basic.
/L [*library*]	Loads the specified Quick library (See Chapter 14).
/Ah	Enables huge dynamic arrays.
/B	Allows use of a monochrome monitor with a color graphics card.
/MBF	Supports MS binary-format numbers.
/NOHI	Allows the use of a monitor without high-intensity support.
/C:n	Sets default COM buffer size.
/S:n	Sets Programming Environment use of memory ($n=1$ is minimum, $n=640$ maximum).
/E:n,m	Limits expanded memory usage to for code and overlay caching to n and m kilobytes, respectively.
/X:n	Limits extended memory usage for overlay caching to n kilobytes.
/Ea	Allows arrays in expanded memory.
/RUN	Runs the specified program before displaying it in the Programming Environment.
/Es	Enables EMS sharing.
/G	Updates (fast) a CGA screen.
/CMD *string*	Passes a string to the COMMAND$ function. Must appear as the last option.
/H	Displays the maximum number of lines possible for your hardware.

This starts up Visual Basic and runs the sample Calculator program. Or, if you just want to load the application without running it, do not type **/RUN**. Simply type

VBDOS C:\VBDOS\SRC\CALC

This loads the Calculator but doesn't run the Calculator program.

FIGURE
1-6

Visual Basic opening screen

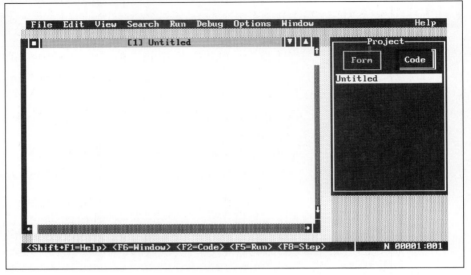

The Tutorial

When you start up Visual Basic, you see a copyright screen telling you to whom the copy of Visual Basic is licensed. After that you see a screen like the one in Figure 1-6.

The next chapter explains all the parts of this screen. For now, though, you might want to work through the on-line tutorial. Doing this will complement and reinforce the information presented in the next chapter.

To start the tutorial press ALT H. This opens the Help menu. Now press U to select the tutorial. Another way to get to the tutorial is to use the mouse. Click the Help item on the main menu bar and then click the item marked Tutorial. The following illustration shows the Help menu dropped down from the main menu bar:

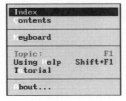

Assuming you've installed the tutorial, selecting these items will usually take you directly to the tutorial. The main screen for the tutorial looks like the one shown in Figure 1-7.

Don't be alarmed if you are instead presented with this message box:

You may see a screen like this if you do something (a mouse click in the wrong place, for example) that Visual Basic interprets as the start of developing an application. Since Visual Basic never loads a new application without trying to save the current one, you have to clear this dialog box. To do this, do *not* press ENTER (which would tell Visual Basic to save your work). Instead, press ESC to close the dialog box, then go to the File menu and choose New Project (ALT F N), and press ALT+N to tell the program that you don't want to save your work. Now you can run the tutorial by pressing ALT H U.

FIGURE 1-7   Visual Basic initial tutorial screen

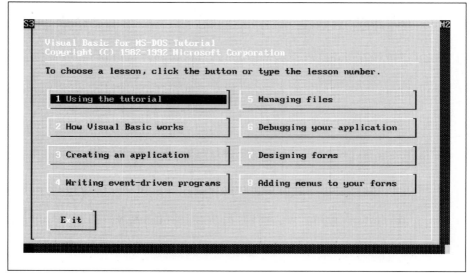

FIGURE
1-8
The control menu for the tutorial

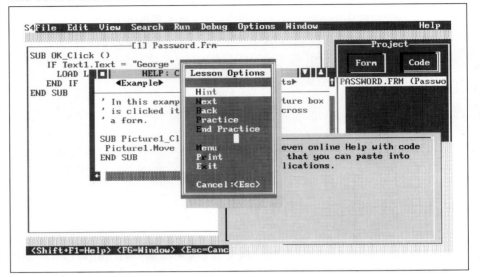

The tutorial is not hard to use. Before you begin, you might want to click the Instructions button. To do this type a **1** or click the first item. Here you will find instructions for using the Visual Basic tutorial. When you are done with this screen, click the Return to Menu button or press the SPACEBAR. You can press ALT+X to leave the tutorial whenever you're at the initial screen. The tutorial takes control of the keyboard and mouse so that you can't really go far wrong—even if you want to. You don't have to cover the lessons in any order, and you can return to them as often as you want. Once installed, the tutorial is always available to you.

Each lesson covers various topics that you may or may not be interested in; you can skip around. You double-click a heading or topic to open it, and the easiest way to move from screen to screen is to press PGDN or PGUP. (You can also click the Next or Back buttons.) To go back to the main screen at any time, press CTRL+M (pressing and releasing the CTRL key alone brings up an overlapping control menu like the one shown in Figure 1-8). Some people find the on-line tutorial too detailed to start with. If you find this is so, you might want to work through the next three chapters before returning to it. At that point you can approach it with a better perspective.

CHAPTER

The Visual Basic Environment

This chapter shows you how to use the menus and windows that make up the Visual Basic environment. This chapter will also help to familiarize you with the look and feel of a modern, menu-driven, mouse-sensitive, windowing environment. Since Visual Basic is itself a well designed windowing application, the way its menus and windows respond are typical of programs you'll be writing. Experienced users of these types of applications may want to skim much of this material. Until you are familiar with how an application should look and feel, you can't take full advantage of the power of Visual Basic.

It isn't essential to conform to the interface standards when you are developing an application with Visual Basic for your own personal use. However, following the standards shortens the learning curve when other people are using your application. For example, users will expect a single *click* (a short press and release) of the left mouse button to select an item and a *double-click* (clicking quickly twice in succession) to activate the item (if you are unfamiliar with "mice," please see Appendix D).

The default settings built into the design process of a Visual Basic application make it easy to deliver what users have grown to expect. The windows in Visual Basic default so they can be moved and resized in standard ways, and menus respond as users expect. Of course, Visual Basic doesn't lock you into these defaults, but it is not a good idea to make changes casually.

In addition to seeing how Visual Basic *feels,* this chapter will make you more comfortable with the on-line help, editing tools, and file-handling utilities built into Visual Basic.

Finally, the first lesson in the on-line tutorial discussed in Chapter 1 is a good complement to the material presented here.

An Overview of the Main Screen

As mentioned in Chapter 1, the first time you start Visual Basic, you are presented with a copyright screen indicating to whom the copy of Visual Basic is licensed. After a short delay, you are automatically dropped into the Visual Basic *programming environment,* as shown in Figure 2-1. [As mentioned in the previous chapter, Visual Basic divides

FIGURE
2-1

The Visual Basic programming environment

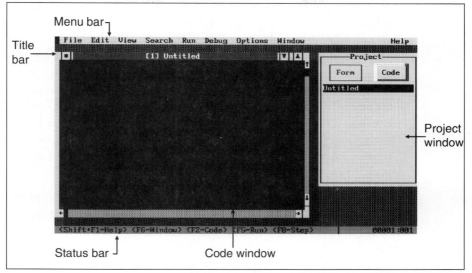

Status bar ⌐   Code window

into two different environments: one for programming and one for form design (interface design).]

The screen is certainly crowded with multiple windows and detailed menus, and you may feel overwhelmed at first by the power of Visual Basic. To help reduce any confusion, this chapter gives you a detailed description of what the programming environment has to offer.

Following is a brief description of the program environment's main screen. Subsequent sections of this chapter cover the most important parts in depth.

The Menu Bar   Selecting items from the pull-down menus listed on a *menu bar* is one of the most common ways to unleash the power of a modern application. The same is true for Visual Basic itself.

The File menu contains the commands for working with the files that go into your application. The Edit menu contains many of the editing tools that will help you write the code that activates the form you design for your application. The View menu lets you look at the different parts of your application; it's also one of the ways to switch to the form designer. The Search menu contains the search-and-replace editing tools and gives you fast access to the different parts of your program and to the help system when you are inside it. The Run menu lets you test out your application while developing it. The Debug menu gives you access to the tools you'll use to correct (debug) problems (bugs) in your programs (Chapter 11 offers a detailed discussion). The Options menu lets you customize Visual Basic's look and feel as well as locate certain files used in program development. The Window menu gives you quick access to the different windows that make up the Visual Basic environment. Finally, you use the Help menu to gain access to the detailed on-line help system provided with Visual Basic.

Press ALT to activate the menu bar. Notice that all the menus have one letter highlighted (for example, the "H" in the Help menu) and File is highlighted by a box. You can use the arrow keys to move around the bar and highlight a menu to open. To open a desired menu, press ENTER, DOWN ARROW, or the highlighted letter for that menu. You can also press the ALT key and the highlighted letter simultaneously—for example, ALT+F for the File menu, ALT+E for the Edit menu, and so on. A menu can also be opened by using the mouse pointer and clicking the left mouse button. If a menu is open and you press RIGHT ARROW or LEFT ARROW, you move to the right or left adjacent menu.

Once a menu is opened, all you need is a single key, called an *accelerator key* (some people call it an *access key* or *hotkey*), to select a menu option. For example, if the Help menu is open, pressing U brings up the tutorial. Accelerator keys are not case sensitive.

In Visual Basic, if an item on a menu has a lighter shading and the accelerator key is not highlighted, then that option is currently *disabled,* meaning it has no current function or is deliberately made inoperative by the application. For example, the item marked Paste on the Edit menu is meaningful only if you have previously cut some text, so the "P" doesn't always stand out.

Many menu items have *shortcut keys.* A shortcut key is usually a combination of keys the user can press to perform an action without having to open a menu. For example, pressing ALT+F4 exits Visual Basic without the use of the File menu. The shortcut keys are listed next to the item on the menu.

The Code Window   The initial *code window* takes up much of the left side of the screen. This is where you will write code for your program. Visual Basic allows multiple overlapping code windows.

Title Bar   The title bar gives the name or a short description of the application. The title bar also contains the controls needed to size and move the window. (A detailed section on the title bar follows.)

Status Bar   The bottom line of the screen is reserved for the status bar, which lists shortcut keys. The numbers on the far right of the bar tell you where you are in the window: the first number indicates the line, the second indicates the column.

The Project Window   At the far right of the screen, the *Project window* contains a list of all the customizeable windows (forms) and general code (modules) that make up your application.

Components of the Title Bar

This is what the title bar for the Visual Basic code window looks like:

```
[■]                    [1] Untitled                    [▼][▲]
```

As you can see, the title bar starts out by displaying

[1] Untitled

This is typical of Visual Basic applications. Usually, the title bar gives the name or a short description of the application. In sophisticated programs (like Visual Basic) that have multiple states, the title bar usually changes accordingly. For example, when moving from entering data to looking at the data, a program might change the title bar from "Data Entry" to "Data Lookup."

The title bar has three other items that will prove very important: the minimize and maximize buttons and the control box.

The Minimize and Maximize Buttons

At the far right of the title bar are the *minimize* and *maximize* buttons. Click the down arrow, and an application is shrunk to an icon (a little box with a name). Click the up arrow, and it's enlarged to take up the whole screen. Once you've enlarged a window to fill the screen, the up arrow is replaced by a two-sided arrow. Clicking that restores the screen to its original size.

The Control Box

To the far left of Visual Basic's title bar is a small rectangle with a smaller square inside of it. This rectangle is called the *control box,* which derives from Microsoft Windows applications. It is most useful for users who prefer keyboard shortcuts to a mouse. Visual Basic applications will usually need a control box in order for them to be used without a mouse.

Move the mouse pointer to the control box and click, and Visual Basic reveals a menu called the *system menu* or *control menu,* shown in Figure 2-2. This menu contains the essential commands for manipulating the window.

All of the items on the control menu have shortcut keys. For example, when a user presses CTRL+F4, if possible, the window will close. Similarly, CTRL+F10 maximizes a window. The shortcut keys for these items are listed in the specific sections that follow.

Note   This is different than in Visual Basic for Windows which uses ALT+F4 to close windows. Visual Basic for DOS uses ALT+F4 only to exit Visual Basic.

Tip   ALT+ – (minus) is a quick way to open the control box for the active window and double-clicking with the mouse on the control box is a quick way to close a window. You close the control menu by pressing the ALT key alone.

The control menu also has accelerator keys for most of the items. For example, if the control menu is open, pressing C closes the window if this

FIGURE
2-2

The control menu

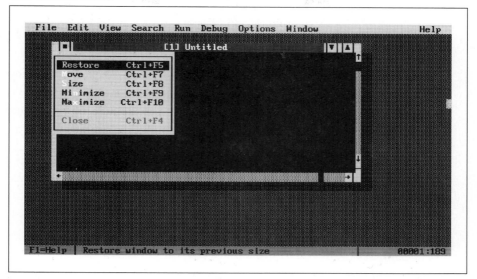

is possible. (Again, if an option is temporarily useless, then the accelerator key is not highlighted.)

The features of the control menu are:

Restore   Restore brings a window back to its previous size if it has been *minimized* (shrunk to an icon) or *maximized* (fills the screen). Open the control menu and press R to select this option or use the CTRL+F5 shortcut. Double clicking on the icon also restores it.

Move   Select the Move option and you can use the keyboard to move the window to another place using the arrow keys. Press ENTER when you're done. Open the control menu and press M to select this option or use the CTRL+F7 shortcut.

Size   Size allows you to resize a window with the arrow keys. For example, press RIGHT ARROW and the window increases in width, press LEFT ARROW and it decreases. Press ENTER when you're satisfied. Open the control menu and press S to select this option or use the CTRL+F8 shortcut.

Minimize   Choosing Minimize shrinks the active window to an icon (a small box). This has the same effect as clicking the minimize button (down arrow) on the far right of the title bar. Open the control menu and press N to select this option or use the CTRL+F10 shortcut.

Maximize   Maximize enlarges the window to full size. This has the same effect as clicking the maximize button (up arrow) at the far right of the title bar. Open the control menu and press X to select this option or use the CTRL+F10 shortcut.

Close   Use this option to close the code window. CTRL+F4 closes the current window at any time. If the control menu is open, press C to select this option.

Generalities on Window Manipulations

Visual Basic (and your Visual Basic application) uses one or more windows to display the interface. Windows can be moved, sized, or closed at will. You can shrink a window to a small box with just its name visible or enlarge it to take up the whole screen.

Visual Basic allows you to use the mouse or the keyboard to manipulate windows. The following table summarizes window manipulation with a mouse.

To Achieve This	Do This
Minimize a window	Click the minimize arrow
Restore a minimized window	Double click the icon
Maximize a window	Click the maximize button or double click in the title bar
Restore a maximized window	Click the double headed arrow to the far right of the title bar or double click in the title bar
Size a window	Click either left corner and drag the mouse
Close a window	Double click the control box

Of course, you can use the keyboard for all these operations by opening up the control box (ALT+ –).

Only one window can be active at any one time. You make the window active using the Window menu or clicking in any part of the window that's visible. The active window has a thicker border than the other windows.

Suppose you've closed a window in the Visual Basic environment and want to open the window again. Activate the Window menu and click the name of the window you want to open. Choosing a window from this menu also brings the item to the forefront of the environment if the window is hidden or obscured.

The Help System

The Setup program that installs Visual Basic automatically installs the more than 1MB of help information that comes with Visual Basic. The on-line help system contains essentially all of the information in the *Language Reference* that came with Visual Basic. In addition, there are hundreds of example programs and dozens of useful tables.

The on-line help system contains a very useful feature: it is *context-sensitive* for help. This means that you can press F1 (or the right mouse button) at the appropriate time, and you bypass the help menus to go directly to the needed information. You can get information about any keyword in the Visual Basic programming language, about an error message, about the variables in your program, or about the parts of the Visual Basic environment.

Once you've found the information you're looking for, the Edit menu on the menu bar lets you copy a topic to the Visual Basic *clipboard*. Once you have done so, you can copy the information to your Visual Basic application or save it to a file.

For example, the screen in Figure 2-3 shows you what happens when you press F1 after typing the keyword PRINT, which is used to display text. The screen in Figure 2-4 shows what you would see if you pressed F1 while you were in the Project window.

Once you start up the help system, you can move the help window anywhere you want. You can resize it or shrink it to an icon as necessary. (When you shrink it to an icon it will usually be hidden by the code window unless you've resized or moved the code window.)

FIGURE 2-3

The help screen for the keyword PRINT

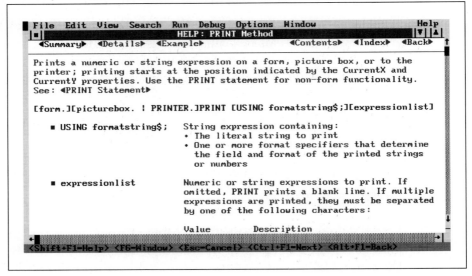

FIGURE 2-4

The help screen for the Project window

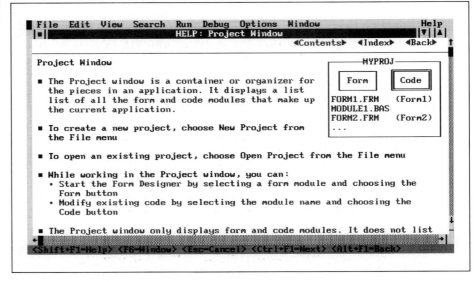

The Help Menu

Following is a description of each of the Help menu features.

Tutorial   You've already seen how choosing the Tutorial option starts the on-line tutorial. (ALT H T are the accelerator keys if the Help menu isn't open; press T if it is.)

Index   The Index option, activated by pressing ALT H I, tells you how the Visual Basic help system is organized.

Contents   The Contents option gives you the entire table of contents for the Help system.

Keyboard   The Keyboard option, activated by pressing ALT H K, gives all the shortcut key combinations. This information is organized by topic, such as the shortcut keys for editing, the keys for entering code, and so on (see Appendix B).

Using Help   The Using Help option, activated by pressing ALT H H, gives you an on-line refresher in how to use the help system. If you press F1 when you are in the help system, you'll be taken here.

Topic   This item is another way to get at context-sensitive help.

About   The About option gives you the copyright notice and tells you to whom the copy of Visual Basic is licensed.

Getting into the Help System

Although you can always use the context-sensitive help feature built into Visual Basic to get into the help system, it is more common to select Index or Contents from the Help menu. This sends you to the initial help screens as shown in Figure 2-5 (for the index) and 2-6 (for the contents). In each screen you see an independent window with a title bar containing a control box and minimize and maximize buttons, which lets you move,

FIGURE 2-5

The initial index help screen

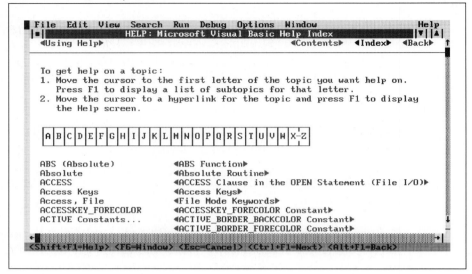

maximize, minimize, or close the window as you see fit. The help window also has scroll bars that let you move easily through the information.

FIGURE 2-6

Table of contents for the help system

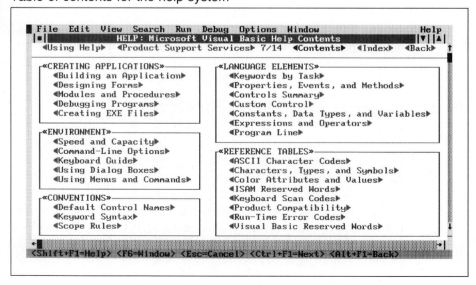

Tip Once you have pressed SHIFT+F1 you can use ALT S F to search for a particular topic or phrase, bypassing many menu steps.

As the screen in Figure 2-5 shows, there is an alphabet in the middle of the initial index screen. Pressing a letter key and hitting ENTER takes you to the part of the index starting with that letter. (You can also move the mouse pointer to the letter and double click.) If you press ENTER or double click on a letter, the help system finds all the topics that pertain to that keyword.

As you can see, the Visual Basic help system has hundreds of topics that are enclosed in solid arrows like this:

◄ Keyboard Guide ►

These are called *hyperlinks* in the Visual Basic manuals. The idea is that you use these as gateways to new information. If you move the mouse pointer to a hyperlink and click the left mouse button, you are immediately taken to the topic indicated. You can also use the TAB key to move forward between hyperlinks and press SHIFT+TAB to move back. Press ENTER to choose the highlighted topic.

When you jump around via these hyperlinks, Visual Basic keeps track of where you were. You can click on the Back hyperlink to go back.

You can also always move through index pages with the UP ARROW and DOWN ARROW keys, PGUP and PGDN, or the scroll bars. Once you've decided on a topic you want to look at, double click on the hyperlink or move the cursor to the link and press ENTER.

The help system contains lots of examples of code that illustrate how to use the commands and functions built into Visual Basic. You can use the ordinary cutting and pasting techniques described in "Editing and the Edit Menu" later in this chapter to copy the example code into your programs.

The Main File Menu

The File menu on the main menu bar allows you to work with the files that make up your project. This menu includes commands for saving, loading, and printing files. It also lets you exit Visual Basic. The File menu is shown in Figure 2-7.

File menu

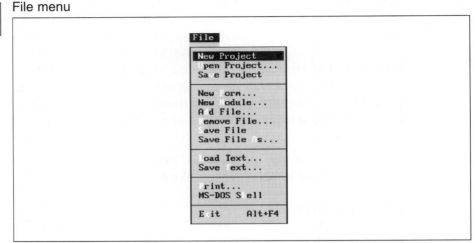

One action that can be performed from the File menu is saving an ASCII representation of your forms, which are usually stored in a binary format not readable by other applications. By storing your application in ASCII format, it is then readable by most word processors' file browsers and the DOS TYPE command. (Files saved in ASCII form are often called *text-only files*.) ASCII files can also be imported into most other programming languages. (See the section on ASCII forms in Chapter 4 for more on this.)

Most of the items on the File menu are useful only when you've started developing your own applications. What follows is a brief discussion of each of the items, to help orient yourself.

New Project   The New Project option unloads the current project. Press ALT F N to select the New Project option. If you've made any changes to a project since you've last saved it, the following dialog box pops up, asking you if you want to save your work:

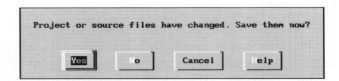

If you answer Yes by pressing ENTER or ALT+Y, you are led to another dialog box for saving files (see Chapter 3 for details on how to use this dialog box). Press ALT+N to tell the program you do not want to save your work.

Open Project   The Open Project option lets you work with an existing Visual Basic application. Since the "O" is highlighted, the shortcut for selecting this option is to press O when the File menu is open or to press the accelerator keys ALT+F O when it is not. As the ellipsis after the item indicates, choosing this option opens a dialog box. The Open Project dialog box is shown in Figure 2-8. As in any Visual Basic dialog box, you move around either with the mouse or by pressing TAB (SHIFT+TAB to move backward). You can also move directly to any location that has an accelerator key (the underlined letter) by holding down the ALT key and pressing the letter. You can close the Open Project dialog box by clicking the Cancel button or pressing ESC. Notice in Figure 2-8 that no files are shown. This is because Visual Basic keeps track of the files that make up a project in a file by looking for files with a .MAK extension (for "make file"), and the Setup program copied the sample programs to the \SRC directory, which is not currently being searched. To switch to the \SRC directory, move to the directory list box in the center of the box and double click on the SRC item.

The Open Project dialog box

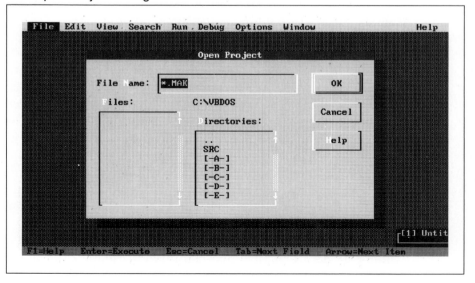

Save Project   The Save Project option saves all the files that make up the current project. The first time you choose this, a dialog box opens asking for the name of the *project file*. Project files are ordinary DOS text (ASCII) files that contain the names of the pieces of the project. They must always have a .MAK extension. Press V if the File menu is open; press ALT F V if it is not.

New Form   This is how you will add a form (a customizeable window) to your projects. When you choose this option, a dialog box asks you for a name of the file that will hold the form information. After you supply one, you are immediately switched to the form designer. (See the next chapter for more on this option.) Press F if the File menu is open; press ALT F F if it is not.

New Module   New Module allows you to add a specialized code to your projects by adding programming code that you'll want to share among all the parts of the application you develop. In Visual Basic, code is attached to a specific form unless you place it in a module. Press M to select this option when the File menu is open; when the File menu is not open, press ALT F M. (See Chapter 14 for more on this option.)

Add File   The Add File option opens a dialog box that lets you incorporate into your application work that was done previously. You can add already finished forms or general-purpose code (modules). To select this option, press D when the File menu is open; press ALT F D when it is not (again, see Chapter 14 for more on this option).

Remove File   Remove File opens up a dialog box to let you delete part of your Visual Basic application that you're currently working with. This option does not delete the file from the disk where it was stored. For that, you'll need to use ordinary DOS commands. To select the Remove File option, press R if the File menu is open; press ALT F R when it is not.

Save File   The Save File option saves the active window (form) to disk. The first time you choose this option, Visual Basic opens a dialog box identical to the one for the Save File As option. To select this option, press S when the File menu is open; press ALT F S when it is not.

Save File As   The Save File As option presents a dialog box that lets you save what you are working with, with a new name or to a new directory. Use this option to keep backup copies of a specific piece of a project on a different disk or to save different versions. You also use this option when part of your current application will be useful in other projects (in this case, use the Add File option to add the file to a different project). To select Save File As, press A when the File menu is open; press ALT F A when it is not. By making the appropriate choices in the dialog box you can save a file in either ASCII (readable by other programs) or a fast-load format that only Visual Basic can read.

Load Text   This option lets you load information saved in ASCII (text) format into your programs. You are given the choice of replacing what is in the active text window or merging it with what is already there. Press L if the File menu is open; press ALT F L if it is not.

Save Text   This option lets you save the code in the current module window in ordinary ASCII (text) format into your programs. Press T if the File menu is open; press ALT F T if it is not.

Print   Choosing the Print option opens the following dialog box:

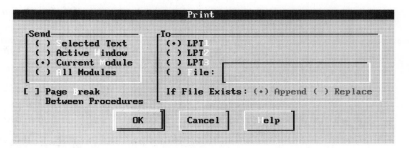

This lets you print either selected text, the current active window, the whole project, just the module (code) that you are working with, or all forms and modules in your application. You can also print everything to a file—that would then be an ordinary ASCII (text) file. To select the Print option, press P when the File menu is open; press ALT F P when it is not.

As with all dialog boxes, you can use the TAB key or the mouse to move the focus around the box. As the focus moves, you'll see the cursor move.

The Print dialog box contains two sets of four option buttons each. Choose what you want to print from the first set of four choices and where you want to send them from the second set. Click the OK button if you are satisfied with the options; click the Cancel button if you decide not to print anything. You can press ENTER if one of the buttons is selected, and you can always press ESC to close this box.

MS DOS Shell   This lets you move back to the DOS prompt temporarily to execute ordinary DOS commands like COPY or FORMAT—or (theoretically at least) any executable file. In practice, memory concerns will probably restrict what you can do from the DOS shell to simple operations. Still, don't overlook the ability of shelling to DOS to format a disk while working with Visual Basic. Press H if the File menu is open; press ALT F H if it is not.

Exit   Choosing the Exit option is the usual way to leave Visual Basic. If you've made any changes to the current project, Visual Basic asks if you want to save before ending the session. You'll see the same dialog boxes as for the New Project option discussed earlier. To select the Exit option, press X when the File menu is open; press ALT F X when it is not.

Any Visual Basic application you write that handles files should have a File menu like that of Visual Basic. The usual convention for applications is that the last item on this menu should be the Exit command.

Editing and the Edit Menu

Visual Basic comes with a full-screen editor similar to the one used in most Microsoft word processing products and programming languages. However, since it is a programming editor, it lacks features like wordwrap and print formatting that even primitive word processors have. On the other hand, it does add features like syntax checking that can spot certain common programming typos.

Many times, when editing a program, you'll be presented with a dialog box that looks like the one in Figure 2-9. If you choose Edit In Active, then Visual Basic moves the file to the active code window. If you choose Edit In New, Visual Basic opens up a new code window (that usually overlays the previous one) for your editing.

The cursor marks where you are in the code (usually called the *insertion point*). You move the insertion point around with the arrow keys

FIGURE
2-9

The editing dialog box

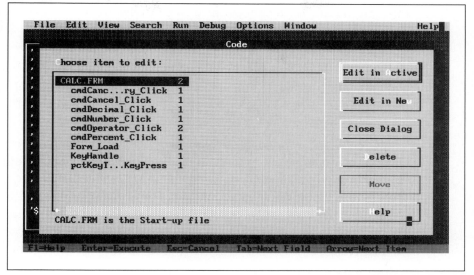

or by moving the mouse pointer and clicking. What you type appears where the insertion point was.

As with any editor, you have two choices when typing: you can be in either insert mode or overstrike mode. When you are in insert mode (the default), any text you type pushes the text that follows to the right. In overstrike mode, the text replaces the old text one character at a time. You switch between these modes by pressing INS. The cursor changes to a block when you're in overstrike mode. In both modes, you have two ways of deleting a character: BACKSPACE deletes the character to the left of the cursor, and DEL deletes the character at the cursor.

When you want to work with a block of text, whether to move it, duplicate it, or just delete it, you have to select the text. To select text, first move the cursor to the start or end of the text you want to select. Then hold down SHIFT and use the arrow keys to select the text.

For example, as you hold down SHIFT and then press the LEFT ARROW key, the selection grows (or shrinks) by one character to the left. Once you've selected text, you can delete it completely by pressing DEL. More common, however, is to cut (or copy) the selected text to the Visual Basic clipboard. The clipboard can hold only one piece of text. Once text is in the clipboard, you can paste it repeatedly to different parts of your program. To cut text, press SHIFT+DEL or open the Edit menu and choose Cut by pressing ALT E T. To place a copy of the text in the clipboard, press CTRL+INS or choose Copy from the Edit menu by pressing ALT E C.

To paste text, move the insertion point to where you want the text to be and press SHIFT+INS. (A copy remains in the clipboard until you place new text there.)

If you've cut, pasted, or deleted selected text, you can undo the action. To do this, choose Undo from the Edit menu. To select this option when the Edit menu is open, press U; press CTRL+Z when it is not. The U will not be highlighted if there is nothing that can be undone.

Here is a summary of the editing commands:

If You Want To	Use
Move left one character	LEFT ARROW
Right one character	RIGHT ARROW
Left to start of word	CTRL+LEFT ARROW
Move right to start of word	CTRL+RIGHT ARROW
Left to start of line	HOME
Right to end of line	END
Up one line	UP ARROW
Down one line	DOWN ARROW
Up to first line in program	CTRL+HOME
Down to last line in program	CTRL+END
Up to a new page	PGUP
Down to a new page	PGDN
Scroll up one line in program	CTRL+W
Scroll down one line in program	CTRL+Z
Delete character left of cursor	BACKSPACE
Delete character at cursor	DEL
Delete from cursor to end of word	CTRL+T
Delete from cursor to end of line	CTRL+Q/Y
Delete entire line	CTRL+Y

Of course, many of the shortcuts can be replaced by combinations of selecting and deleting text. For example, to delete to the end of a line, you can first select the rest of the line and then press DEL.

The Search Menu

This menu lets you search and replace text within your projects or in the help system if you are in it. Here are short descriptions of the items on this menu:

Find Choosing the Find option displays a dialog box in which you enter the text (string) you want Visual Basic to search for. Depending on what options you choose, Visual Basic searches the entire project for the string (see Chapter 14) or just the piece you are working on. As you see here, you can choose to match capitalization, or search for whole words or arbitrary strings of characters. (There is a slightly different Find box if you are inside the help system.)

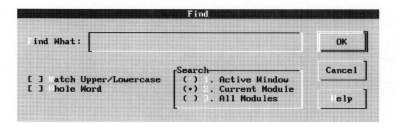

Selected Text This option lets you select text in the active code window and then search for other occurrences of it. The shortcut is CTRL+\.

Repeat Last Find This option repeats the previous search. Another way to select this option is to press F3.

Change This option opens a dialog box with two text boxes. The first is for the text to be found, and the second is for what should replace it. The other options are essentially the same as for the Find dialog box.

The Project Window

Located at the far right of the screen, the *Project window* contains a list of all the customizeable windows (forms) and general code (modules) that make up your application (see Chapter 14). Since it is quite common for Visual Basic applications to share code or already customized windows, Visual Basic organizes applications into what it calls *projects* (a fancy name for a complete program). Each project can have multiple forms the user can work with. The code that activates the controls on a window is stored with the form in separate files.

Although Visual Basic stores separately all the files that go into making up the project, it keeps track of where they are. It creates a file, called the *project make file,* that tells it where the individual files that make up a project are located so that it can put this information together when you run the project. You create the project make file whenever you choose Save Project from the File menu.

Right below the title bar of the Project window are two *command buttons.* As you'll see in Chapter 3, clicking on these produce message boxes that give you access to the forms and code for your project.

Loading and Running Programs

This chapter ends by leading you through the procedures needed to run an existing Visual Basic program. Visual Basic comes with a wide variety of full-blown sample programs that you can use and study. The one described in this section is the calculator. This program gives you a simple four-function calculator and is a good example of Visual Basic programming techniques.

Choose the Open Project option on the File menu (ALT F O). When the Open Project dialog box appears (possibly after a message box asking you if you want to save your work), switch to the SRC directory by double-clicking on it and then double click on the CALC.MAK item listed in the Files list box.

After a short delay (possibly interrupted by a dialog box asking you if you want to save your current work), you are presented with the code for the calculator project. Since this program (written completely in Visual Basic) dramatically demonstrates the power that will soon be at your fingertips, you might want to press SHIFT+F5 to run this program (see Figure 2-10).

FIGURE
2-10

The Calculator

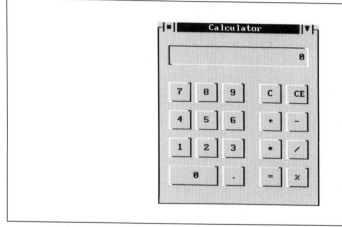

CHAPTER

Customizing a Form

Visual Basic makes it easy to build a program with the features a sophisticated windowing environment demands. Using list boxes, dialog boxes, message boxes, and command buttons inside a window will become routine. The purpose of this chapter is to show you how to work with a blank form, including how to adjust its size, shape, and color (as mentioned in Chapter 2, Visual Basic uses the term "form" for a customizeable window).

This chapter shows you how to design forms with a given size and location. You learn how to place text on a form or print an image of a form on your printer. Most important, you see how to make a form respond to events such as the user clicking or double-clicking a mouse within the form. The event-driven nature of Visual Basic is the primary reason it is both extraordinarily powerful and easy to use.

Starting a New Project

When you start up Visual Basic, after a short delay your screen will look something like the one in Figure 3-1. This screen shows the *Visual Basic programming environment* that you saw in Chapter 2. This is where you will write the code that controls how your program responds to the user's actions. In general, when you want to start a new *project* (the name Visual Basic uses for a program that is being developed), you need only to open the File menu and select New Project (ALT+F N). You can also open an existing project by choosing Open Project from the File menu (ALT+F O).

Since the user interface is so important in working with Visual Basic, the usual first step in building a program is to design the form. This is done with the Visual Basic form designer. The environment for designing a form is similar but not identical to the programming environment. You'll see the differences shortly.

You can also invoke the form designer as a stand-alone program by entering **FD** from the DOS prompt. The stand-alone form designer lets you develop only the interface for programs.

 Tip   Using the form designer as a stand-alone program is occasionally needed when working with limited memory. This lets you develop larger programs that would otherwise be impossible.

The Visual Basic programming environment

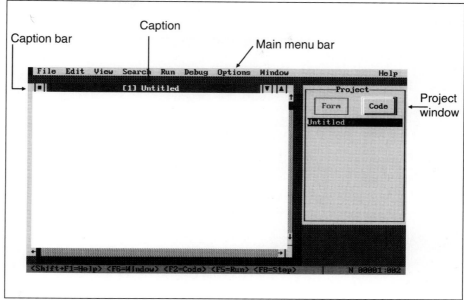

Open the File menu and select New Form (Alt+F F). This opens a dialog box that looks like Figure 3-2. To follow this example, click the OK button (or press TAB twice and then press ENTER). This action accepts the default name "Form1" that Visual Basic has proposed for this new form. The screen will blank for a few seconds before a screen like the one in Figure 3-3 appears.

Note the large box filling most of the screen and containing a grid of dots in Figure 3-3. This is the form, which you can customize with objects such as command buttons and text boxes. The form is what the user sees and interacts with when running your program. You use the grid to align objects on the screen; the grid will not be visible to the user.

At the top of the form is the caption bar. *Caption bar* is the term used in Visual Basic for the title bar of the customizeable form. Similarly, *caption* is the Visual Basic term for the title of a form. You'll see how to customize the caption bar shortly so you can give meaningful titles to your forms.

FIGURE
3-2

New Form dialog box

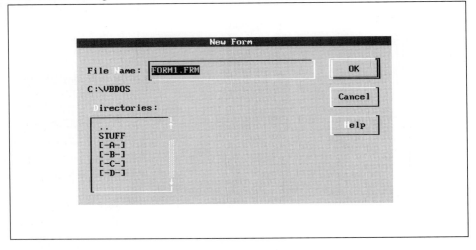

FIGURE
3-3

Form designer environment

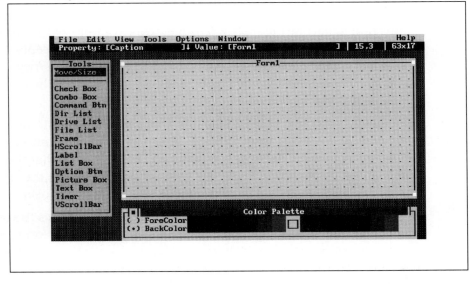

Note   The name of the form (aka FormName) is used by the programmer to refer to the form, whereas the caption is the title of the form that the user will see. Although these values start out the same by default, they can be manipulated independently.

To the left of the form is the *toolbox.* This is where you go to select command buttons, text boxes, and other controls to place on the form. (The toolbox is covered extensively in Chapters 4, 10, and 13.) Just below the main menu bar is the *properties bar.* (See the section "Form Properties" in this chapter for more on this.) Color properties can be set from the properties bar or, in a more visual way, with the *Color Palette* at the bottom of the screen. (See the section "Color Properties" in this chapter.)

The Form Designer Menus

There are seven menus on the main menu bar in the form designer. Most of the menus work in the same fashion as they do in the programming environment that you saw in Chapter 2. For example, the File menu contains options to save and remove forms or print the current form (rather than the current file).

The Edit Menu   The Edit menu lets you cut and paste controls on your form. Choosing the Event Procedures option from this menu takes you back to the programming environment. (See the section "Making a Window Responsive" in this chapter.)

The View Menu   Choosing the Code option from the View menu also moves you back to the programming environment. Select the Form option when you use multiple forms in your programs (see Chapter 14). The Menu option hides the menu bar and the properties bar. If you want to make the menu and properties bar visible again, press the ALT key or press F10. The Grid Lines option controls whether the rows of dots on the form appear (the dots never appear while the program is being run).

The Tools Menu   As you'll see in Chapter 4, the Tools menu is another way, besides the toolbox, to access the controls you place on forms. (Controls are covered in Chapters 4, 10, and 13.)

The Options Menu   The items on this menu are the same as those for the programming environment, including the very important Backup option available from the Save dialog box.

The Windows Menu   This menu gives you access to the various windows in the Form designer. For example, use the Color Palette to choose colors for controls and forms. The Menu Design Window option lets you build menus into your programs (see Chapter 10). The Toolbox option controls whether the toolbox on the far left of the screen is visible.

The Help Menu   This Help menu has the same items as the Help menu in the programming environment.

Altering a Form

For now, concentrate on the form named Form1 on your screen. It's best to be completely comfortable with the methods for changing the size and location of this form before you move on. In many Visual Basic programs, the size and location of the form at the time you finish the design (usually called *design time*), is the size and shape that the user sees (usually called *run time*). This is not to say that Visual Basic doesn't let you change the size and location of forms as a program runs. An essential property of Visual Basic is its ability to make dynamic changes in response to user events.

One way to resize a form is to first move the mouse to one of the hot spots on the form. The *hot spots* are the sides or corners of the form and appear as a square within a small rectangle. While in a hot spot, you can drag the form to change its size. Similarly, to move the form, place the mouse anywhere in the caption bar and then drag the form to a new location.

    Tip   You can also move and resize forms using the keyboard alone.

If you haven't moved away from the form, pressing an arrow key will move the form in that direction. Press SHIFT plus an arrow key, and the form will either shrink or enlarge accordingly. Many people find it easier to use the arrow keys to move and resize forms and other Visual Basic objects. For many, the keyboard seems to give finer control than the mouse.

Form Properties

The name, size and location of a form are examples of what Visual Basic calls *properties* of the form. These can be changed from the properties bar, which is located above the form:

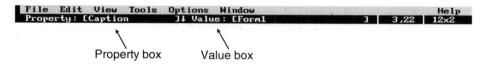

Property box   Value box

The properties bar is divided into four parts. The leftmost pair of brackets enclose the *Property box*. The *Value box* displays the current value assigned to the property named in the Property box. Next are a pair of numbers, separated by a comma, that indicate the location, by column and row, of the upper left corner of the form. (Each column is one character wide and each row is one line high. The full screen is 25 lines high and each line is 80 columns wide.) Finally, at the right end of the properties bar are a pair of numbers, separated by the "×," indicating the size of this form, measured as number of columns by number of rows.

Notice that the Property box contains the word "Caption" and the Value box contains the word "Form1." (Assuming you chose the default name for the form in the programming environment.) As mentioned before, the caption is initially the same as the FormName selected in the programming environment.

In this case, the value of the Caption property is Form1, which also appears at the top of the form as its title. This caption changes as soon as you enter new text into the Value box.

There are two ways to customize a form's caption. The easiest way is to click in a blank part of the form. At this point, whatever you type replaces the previous caption. Another method is to move the mouse to the Value box, click, and edit the caption as desired. The first method immediately erases the previous caption, while the second method allows you to edit it.

Using the second method, move the mouse to the Value box, select the entire text, and type **First Application**. Notice that the caption bar on the form changes instantly to reflect what you've typed. However, if you didn't do this exactly in the order suggested or you inadvertently clicked where you shouldn't have, this method might not work. It is easier to get used to a more general method for choosing and changing properties using the list box for properties, as described in the following section.

The Properties List Box

If you move the mouse until the pointer is at the down arrow to the right of the Property box and click, a list box drops down that looks like this:

(You can also press F2 to move to the properties bar, press TAB to move to the Property box, and then press F4 to open the list box.)

No matter what object you are trying to manipulate in Visual Basic, when the properties bar is visible, either one of the two methods just described opens the Properties list box for that object. Scroll through the box by using the arrow keys or your mouse. You'll see 19 properties you can set for a form. Although this chapter doesn't explain all nineteen, the next few sections take you through the most useful ones.

You can scroll through the Properties list box by clicking the arrows that appear at the top and bottom of its right edge. A shortcut for moving through this list (which works with all Visual Basic list boxes) is to press the first letter of the item you want to select; you may have to press the letter repeatedly to scroll past other items that begin with the same letter. For example, press M once, selecting the item MaxButton. Notice that the word "MaxButton" replaces the word "Caption" in the Property box and that the word "True" is located in the Value box:

Press ENTER (or click the mouse on the property) to indicate to Visual Basic that this is the property you want to change.

That this property is True means that the form you are designing will have a maximize button. A maximize button appears in the upper right corner of a form and lets you maximize the form by clicking the mouse there once.

As an experiment, for your first program, change this property to False. There are two ways to do this. The first method is to move the mouse pointer to the word "True," click it, and type F for False. The second method is to click the down arrow to the immediate right of the Value box. A list box drops down with the two options, True and False, as shown here:

Click False to remove the maximize button from Form1.

A general feature in Visual Basic is that whenever a property has only a fixed list of values, a down arrow appears at the right end of the Value box. Clicking the arrow (or pressing F4) gives you a list of the settings available for the selected property.

Let's also change the MinButton property to False—this property controls whether a form will have a minimize button. Reopen the Properties list box. Notice that the MaxButton property is still highlighted. Press M once more and Visual Basic highlights the MinButton property. Click on the Value box down arrow to display the available settings. Finally, select the False option.

With both of these properties set to False, run this program and see what happens. Applications cannot be tested or run from inside the form designer, so you must return to the Visual Basic programming environment. One way to return to the programming environment is to open the View menu and select the Code option (ALT+V C is the shortcut). A dialog box that asks you whether you want to return to the programming environment pops up. Click the OK button. Visual Basic opens up another dialog box that looks like this:

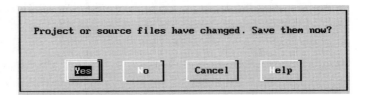

This dialog box protects you by asking if you want to save your work before returning to the programming environment. If you do not save the work you have just completed in the form designer, it will be lost when you exit to the programming environment.

Tip   You can use the Save item on the Options menu to have Visual Basic save your work automatically—with or without creating a backup file.

Once you've saved your work, Visual Basic blanks the screen for a moment before switching back to the programming environment. You'll be presented with a screen that looks like Figure 3-4. The Code selection window becomes important when you want to make your form responsive to user actions (see the section called "Making Your Forms Responsive" in this chapter.) For now though, hit ENTER.

There are three ways to run your Visual Basic program:

☐   Open the Run menu and select the Start option by using the mouse,

☐   Press ALT+R S, or

☐   Press SHIFT+F5 (pressing F5 alone also works, although the primary purpose of this key is to continue programs that you've stopped).

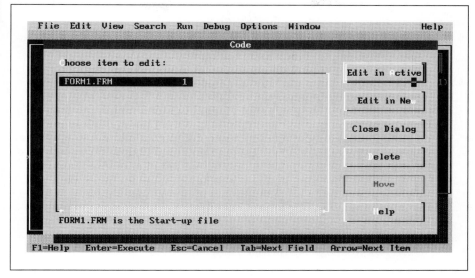

FIGURE
3-4

Code selection window

After a short delay, your screen will blank for a moment and then you'll see something like Figure 3-5. Notice the size, position, and caption of the form. Note also that this form has neither a minimize nor a maximize button.

To go back to developing a program, click the control button in the upper left corner of the form. This opens a control menu that looks like this:

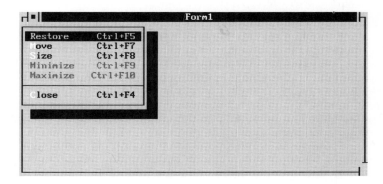

FIGURE
3-5 A form without maximize and minimize buttons

Select the Close option, then press any key. After a short delay, this brings you back to the programming environment for the program you've just developed.

 Tip You can hold down the CTRL key and press BREAK to stop any program while it is running in the development environment.

To further customize Form1, click the Form button in the Project window to the right of the screen. Then respond to all message boxes by clicking the OK button. (Message boxes appear if you've edited the code for this project since it was last saved.)

Designing a form that lacks both minimize and maximize buttons may not seem like much, but it does illustrate the absolutely essential process of changing the properties of a Visual Basic object.

Here is a summary of the general method for changing the properties on a Visual Basic form:

1. Move to the properties bar and click the down arrow to the right of the Property box to display the Properties list box.

2. Select the property you want to modify.

3. Click in the Value box, type the new setting for the property, and press ENTER, or, if a down arrow appears at the right of the Value box, click the down arrow, then select the desired setting for the property.

The following table contains the keyboard shortcuts for moving about the Properties and Value list boxes.

Key	Action
A letter key	Moves to the next item beginning with that letter
RIGHT ARROW/DOWN ARROW	Moves down one item
LEFT ARROW/UP ARROW	Moves up one item
PGDN	Moves down to show items currently just out of view
PGUP	Moves up to show items currently just out of view
END	Moves to the last item in list
HOME	Moves to the first item in list
F4	Closes (or opens) the list box
ENTER, TAB, Clicking on item	Accepts the item

The Most Common Properties of a Form

What follows is a list of some of the most common properties of forms, which you are likely to want to set in the early stages of mastering Visual Basic.

Much of this material will recur time and time again. As you'll see in later chapters, a single property may pertain to many different objects. For example, the height and width properties obviously should be (and, in fact, can be) set for text boxes, command buttons, and the like.

AutoRedraw Keeping all the elements of your interface on a Visual Basic form takes memory. This property controls whether the text you place on a form is *persistent*—which will require even more memory. For example, the default setting of False means that any time the user resizes a form while the program is running, information that was on the form will be lost. If this property is set to True, your program will need more memory (because text is preserved in memory), but text will reappear intact when the form is resized. (See the section in this chapter on "What Happens When a Visual Basic Application Runs" for more on this important property.)

BorderStyle   BorderStyle is an example of a property with only a fixed number of choices. Because of this, the arrow appears to the right of the value box for this property. There are seven values you can choose from for this property. The default value, 2, allows the user to size and shape the form via the hot spots located on the boundary of the form. Change this setting to 1 (called a *fixed single*), and the user will no longer be able to resize the form. All he or she will be able to do is minimize or maximize the form (unless, of course, you turned off those options as well when you designed the program).

Set BorderStyle value to 0, and the program will show no border whatsoever and therefore no minimize button, maximize button or control box. Because of this, a form created without a border cannot be moved, resized, or reshaped. This setting is useful when you want your forms to be inviolate.

The other four possible settings for the BorderStyle property provide for sizeable and non-sizeable, double-lined and solid borders. Double-lined borders are not often used for ordinary forms, but are quite common for dialog boxes (forms you use to display messages to the user—see Chapter 14 for more on them.)

Caption   As you've already seen, the Caption property controls the title of the form. Captions can help the user by quickly explaining what the form will do.

ControlBox   ControlBox is another property that goes into effect only when a user runs the program. All Visual Basic forms can have a control box located just to the right of the upper left corner of the form. Clicking the box gives you a list of common tasks that manipulate a form, like minimizing, maximizing, and closing the form, along with the keyboard equivalents when they exist. (The keyboard shortcut to open a control box for your forms, just like for windows in Visual Basic, will always be ALT+ -.)

You have only two choices: you can either have a control box or not. And, as always when a property has a fixed set of possible values, a value list box can be opened showing the possible settings. In this case there are two allowed settings for the ControlBox property: True if the form is to have a control box, False otherwise.

 Note If your program doesn't have a control box, a user without a mouse is in trouble. He or she won't be able to minimize, maximize, or close the program. Control boxes are generally not a good thing to remove.

Enabled Enabled is another property you do not want to change casually. Set Enabled to False, and the form cannot respond to any events. Usually you toggle this property back and forth in response to some event. To make your forms respond dynamically, you must write code. The properties bar is for setting the startup properties (and most often the properties that aren't going to change) of your objects.

Height, Width Since Visual Basic uses text mode and not graphics mode to display forms, it measures objects by how many character-sized boxes you'll need to "draw" them.

Move to the properties bar and choose the Height property. Notice that the current value is 17 characters. This means that the default size for a form is 17 text rows high. Now choose the Width property. Notice that the current value is 63 (the default size for a form is 63 characters wide):

```
 File  Edit  View  Tools  Options  Window                        Help
 Property: [Caption        ]↕ Value: [Form1              ] │ 15,3 │ 63x17
```

Next, notice that on the far right of the properties bar is the value 63×17. This tells you the current value in characters of the width and height of the form. Now use the mouse to change the width and height. Notice that when you change the size of the form, the value at the far right of the properties bar changes to reflect the new size. The setting in the Value box changes as well.

Of course, using the mouse and dragging to set the height and width is less precise than you might need. Luckily, since Height and Width are properties, their values can be changed directly via the properties bar. Just enter the measurements you want in the Value box. For example, if you changed the Width property to 32, you would have cut the form in half (at least, as accurately as the screen can possibly display it). As mentioned before, many users find the keyboard a more accurate way to move and size Visual Basic objects.

Like the Caption property, any changes you make to the height and width of the form immediately go into effect—they do not wait until the program runs.

Note   Unless you change the value of the BorderStyle property to a fixed border (a value of 1, 3, or 5), users can size and reshape the various forms in the program regardless of how you set them at design time.

Left, Top   The Left and Top settings determine the distance between the left or top of the form and the left or top of the screen. Set the value of the Left property to 0, and the form moves flush with the left of the screen. Set the Top property to 0, and the form you're designing is flush with the top of the screen.

These settings work in much the same way as the Height and Width properties. You change them by dragging the form with the mouse or by entering new values in the Value box. They are also measured in characters, and changes go into effect when you reset the values, not when the user runs the program.

MousePointer   MousePointer is an amusing (and occasionally useful) property that sets the shape of the mouse pointer. The default value is 0, but as the pull-down menu indicates, there are 12 additional values. A setting of 4, for example, turns the mouse pointer into a rather intriguing face. The setting you will use most often is 11. This value changes the mouse pointer to an "X" to imitate an hourglass, which customarily tells a user that he or she has to wait until the computer finishes what it is doing. A complete list of the values for the MousePointer property is available on line by pressing F1 when you've selected the MousePointer property.

Visible   Visible is another dangerous property to change by mistake. Set the value of this property to False, and the form will no longer be visible (and, therefore, it will be a bit difficult for the user to manipulate!).

The usual reason for making a form invisible is when you are designing a program with multiple forms. You will often want to hide one or more of the forms by resetting the Visible property. However, you will almost always reset it by using code and not at the time you design the program.

WindowState This property determines how the form will look at run time. There are three possible settings. A setting of 1 reduces the form to an icon (box); a setting of 2 maximizes it. A setting of 0 is the normal default size. This property is often changed in code.

Color Properties

The colors you use in a program can have a dramatic effect on how easy and pleasurable the program is to use and, as a result, how well it is received. You can specify the background color (BackColor) and the foreground color (ForeColor) in which text shows up on the form. Visual Basic also allows the colors of a program to be changed dynamically by using code. See the section in Chapter 5 on "Assigning to Properties" or Appendix C for more information on using code to do this.

Accessing BackColor and ForeColor via the Color Palette

Suppose you try to set the BackColor property. If you open the Properties list box and select BackColor, you'll see the following:

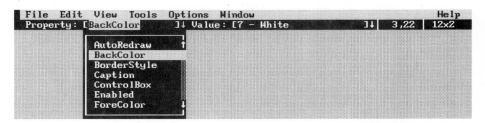

The setting is 7 — White. Visual Basic describes color codes by using a code inherited from QuickBasic. Although one can always look up the color codes on line or click the down arrow to view a list of the different colors, it is more common to use the *color palette.* If the color palette isn't showing, open the Window menu and select it (ALT+W C is the key combination). Here's what the color palette looks like:

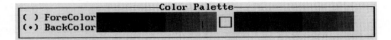

Although you cannot see the colors here, you can get an idea of what the color palette looks like. One reason for using the color palette rather than the color codes is that you can see how the colors show up on your screen.

Notice, to the left of the palette, two option buttons. Choose the top one to change the foreground color and the bottom one to change the background color.

To change the foreground color, click the top button and then click any of the colored boxes displayed. Text always shows up in the foreground color. To change the background color, click the bottom button and then click any of the colored boxes displayed. Obviously, the foreground color should be sufficiently different from the background color to allow some contrast.

Making a Window Responsive

By this point, you should be comfortable with designing Visual Basic forms. The essence of a Visual Basic program is to make your forms responsive to user actions. Visual Basic objects can recognize many different events (forms can recognize 16 different events.) For example, if a user clicks in an area on the screen, you may want to display a message; if the user clicks a command button, you may want to perform an action. To do this, you write programs in Visual Basic's modern structured programming language.

Although Visual Basic objects can recognize many different events, the objects will sit there totally inert unless you've written code to tell them what to do when an event happens. Thus, for any event that you want a Visual Basic object to respond to, you must write an event procedure telling Visual Basic what to do. Event procedures are nothing more than the lines of programming code that tell Visual Basic how to respond to a given event.

The Event Procedure Selection Window

In this section, you will make the form titled First Application respond to a mouse click. If you are still in the form designer rather than the programming environment, you'll need to switch back. ALT+E V will take you to the Event Procedures selection window (after some dialog boxes to save your work). Or, if you're in the programming environment, open the Edit menu and choose Event Procedures (ALT+E V or F12 is the shortcut). You'll see a screen like Figure 3-6. Notice that Figure 3-6 has three list boxes. The box on the left lists the forms (files) that hold the information Visual Basic is working with, the middle box lists the objects that exist on the form highlighted in the first box, and the box on the right lists the names of all the events that can be recognized by the object highlighted in the middle box. Make sure that the Click event is highlighted in the rightmost box. Notice the four buttons on the bottom of the screen. For now, choose the button marked "Edit in Active." Once you choose this editing option, Visual Basic opens up a code window that looks like Figure 3-7.

The code that follows is the first example of an *event procedure template.*

```
SUB Form_Click()

END SUB
```

Like any template, this gives you a framework in which to work. You'll enter the code that tells Visual Basic how to respond to a click here. The chapters that follow will cover in detail how to write code for Visual Basic, so don't worry if you are a novice programmer. (Experienced programmers can move through these chapters that much more quickly.)

No matter what event you want the form to respond to, the event procedure code for a form in Visual Basic begins with something that looks like this:

SUB Form_*NameOfTheEvent* ( )

FIGURE
3-6

Event Procedures selection window

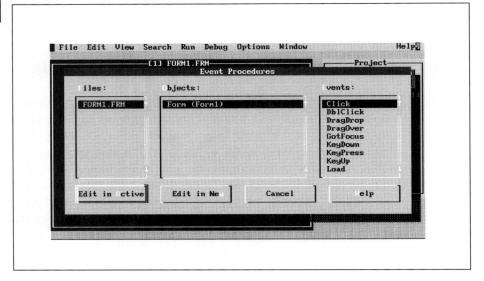

FIGURE
3-7

Event procedure template

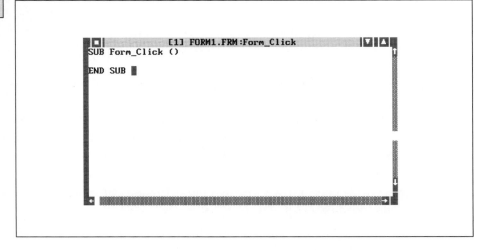

Some examples are shown in the following table:

Event Procedure	Tells the Form to respond to
SUB Form_DblClick( )	a double-click
SUB Form_GotFocus( )	receiving the focus
SUB Form_LostFocus( )	losing the focus
SUB Form_KeyPress( )	a user pressing a key

A Simple Event Procedure

As an example of how easy it is to make a Visual Basic form responsive, suppose you want to write a procedure for a single click. In this case, you need to write the code necessary for Visual Basic to respond with a message to a mouse click. You can use all the normal editing keys to enter code (for example, you can switch between insert mode and overstrike when you type, or you can select text and copy or cut it).

Move the cursor between the SUB and END SUB lines by clicking the blank line. Press SPACEBAR twice (this indentation will improve readability), and type **PRINT "You clicked the mouse once."** Your code window will look something like the one in Figure 3-8.

Now press SHIFT+F5 to run the program. As soon as the form appears, click once inside the form. You'll see something like this:

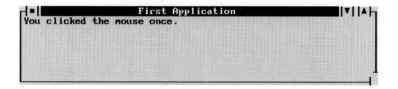

As you've probably guessed, PRINT sends the exact text found between the quotes directly to the form. The default position for text is the upper left corner of the form, but you'll soon see how to change this.

Monitoring Multiple Events

Visual Basic is always monitoring your program screen for events, but unless you write code for the event, nothing happens. For example, you

**FIGURE
3-8**

Click event procedure

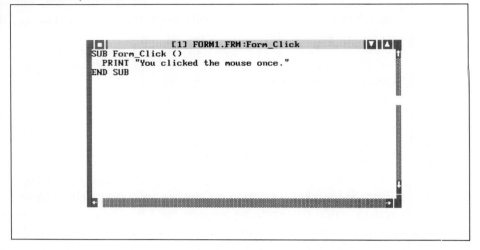

```
┌─────────────────────────────────────────────────────────────┐
│[■]               [1] FORM1.FRM:Form_Click        [▼][▲]│
│SUB Form_Click ()                                               │
│  PRINT "You clicked the mouse once."                           │
│END SUB                                                         │
└─────────────────────────────────────────────────────────────┘
```

can add more code to monitor (and display a message) when the user
double-clicks.

To do this, end the previous program by going to the control box on
the form, clicking Close, then pressing any key (CTRL+F4 followed by any
key is the shortcut.) Now press F12 to move to the Event Procedures
selection window. Notice that Visual Basic still highlights the Click event
in the box on the right. (Visual Basic displays CLICK in all caps as an
indication that code already exists for this event.) To write code for the
DblClick event, move the mouse to the DblClick item, and double-click
or use the cursor keys to highlight the DblClick item and then press
ENTER. Your code window should look something like this:

```
┌─────────────────────────────────────────────────────────────┐
│[■]               [1] FORM1.FRM:Form_DblClick      [▼][▲]│
│SUB Form_DblClick ()                                            │
│                                                                │
│END SUB                                                         │
└─────────────────────────────────────────────────────────────┘
```

A new event procedure template for the DblClick event opens. Just as before, you can type between the beginning and ending lines of the template. For example, type **PRINT "I said to click once, not twice!"** The code window will look like this:

```
┌──┬─────────────────[1] FORM1.FRM :Form_DblClick──────────────┬─┬─┐
SUB Form_DblClick ()
    PRINT "I said to click once, not twice!"
END SUB
```

Now run the program (SHIFT+F5) and double-click inside the form. What you'll see will look something like this:

```
┌─■─┬──────────────────First Application──────────────────┬─▼─┬─▲─┐
You clicked the mouse once.
I said to click once, not twice!
```

Notice that both lines of text appear on the screen. This is because in monitoring for a double click, Visual Basic also detected the single click and activated the code for that event as well.

If all you want to do is clear the screen before displaying the second message, you need only make the first line of the DblClick procedure the CLS statement, which clears any text in the form. The DblClick event procedure would now look like this:

```
SUB Form_DblClick ()
  CLS
  PRINT "I said to click once, not twice!"
END SUB
```

PRINT and CLS are the first examples you've seen of what Visual Basic calls *methods*. Roughly speaking, methods are Visual Basic statements that affect what Visual Basic objects *do* (as opposed to properties, which affect what they *are*).

There is another syntax for the PRINT or CLS method that you can use. It is the one used for other Visual Basic objects, and it follows the general framework of *Object.Method* (discussed further in Chapter 4). This syntax uses the name of the object, followed by a period, followed by the method, followed by (if applicable) what the method should do. The general form is

ObjectName.Method WhatToDo

Since the default name for the first form created in a Visual Basic project is Form1, the double click procedure in this syntax would be written as follows:

```
SUB Form_DblClick ()
  Form1.CLS
  Form1.PRINT "I said to click once, not twice!"
END SUB
```

You will need to use the longer version when your projects involve more than one form (see Chapter 14) because it lets Visual Basic know which form to apply the method to.

Printing a Form

To dump the entire contents of a form to the printer in Visual Basic requires only a single command: PRINTFORM. Since this also affects what the form does, as opposed to what it is, it is another example of a Visual Basic method. PRINTFORM tries to send to your printer a character-by-character image of the entire form. (Visual Basic forms use block characters to draw borders, for example.)

 Tip To get an accurate representation of a form, you may need to configure your printer before loading Visual Basic.

Forms use high-order ASCII codes which may not be available to your printer without the proper configuration.

Typos

Nobody types completely accurately all the time. Visual Basic points out many typing errors when you try to run your program. Suppose you had made a typo when you were writing the Click event procedure given earlier and had misspelled the command word "PRINT" by typing **PRINTF** instead. Your code window would look like this:

```
┌─■──────────[1] FORM1.FRM:Form_Click──────────▼ ▲─┐
│SUB Form_Click ()                                  ↑│
│  PRINTF "You clicked the mouse once."             │
│END SUB                                            │
│                                                   │
│                                                   │
│                                                   │
│                                                   ↓│
│                                                   │
│◄                                                 ►│
└───────────────────────────────────────────────────┘
```

If you were to run the program, your code window would look like the one in Figure 3-9. Notice that the offending word is highlighted and that the message box tells you that you have a syntax error. This means that what you've entered doesn't conform to the grammar of a Visual Basic program. If you press ENTER or click the OK button, the offending word remains highlighted, and you can either type the correct replacement or move the mouse pointer to the "F", click, and then press DEL. After you make the correction, the program can be run as before.

If you need some help on what may be causing the error, just press F1 or click the right mouse button for context-sensitive help when the cursor is on the offending word or when the word is highlighted. Visual Basic opens the help window and gives you some general information on the error. For example, if you activate help while the misspelled word "PRINTF" is still highlighted and the error message box is on the screen, then Visual Basic will offer the explanation shown in Figure 3-10.

Visual Basic can even find some syntax errors before you run your program. The default is that this feature (called *syntax checking*) is on. You can check by opening the Options menu and seeing if there is a bullet next to the Syntax Checking option. To toggle this feature on or off, press ALT+O S.

FIGURE
3-9
Syntax error message box

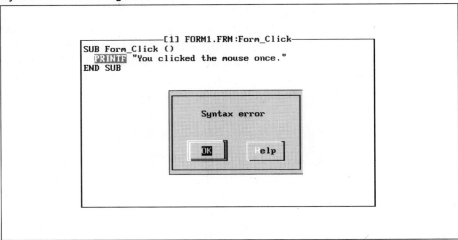

FIGURE
3-10
Context-sensitive help window for a syntax error

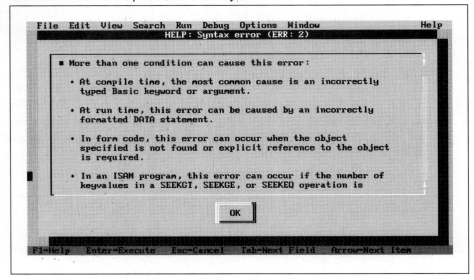

Saving Your Work

Obviously, you should get into the habit of saving your work frequently. Visual Basic will in fact not let you leave it without asking if you want to save your work. Most of the ways to save your work are found on the File menu both in the programming environment and the form designer (the accelerator keys begin with ALT+F). Since much of a Visual Basic program is made up of form information, it usually saves your work as a special binary pattern that is accessible only to Visual Basic. You can, however, save much of the information in text form—where it can be viewed by ordinary text editors and word processors. Saving a file in text form also increases the chances of recovering all or part of your work if something damages your disk or drive.

Many programmers like to have Visual Basic save their work automatically without prompting. The following three options are available from the programming environment:

☐   Save your work automatically before Visual Basic runs your program.

☐   Save your work when you switch from the programming environment to the form designer.

☐   Automatically create backup files when you save a file with any changes.

All these possibilities are controlled from the Options menu. If you open the Options menu and choose Save (ALT+O V) you'll see a dialog box with various options. This is the dialog box you'll see in the programming environment:

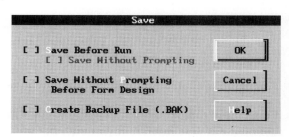

Now you can choose or cancel an option by clicking the mouse or moving with the TAB key and pressing SPACEBAR. When you are happy with your choices, press ENTER to accept them.

Saving from the File Menu

The following sections describe the four methods for saving a project that can be found on the File menu in the programming environment and form designer.

Save Project (Both Environments)   Save Project saves the entire project. To select this option, press ALT+F V. When you first try to save a project with this option, Visual Basic opens a dialog box with a suggested name—the name you gave the primary form, with a .MAK extension. This is called a project or make file and contains the names of all the forms and code modules that make up your project. It is essentially what shows up in the Project window while you are developing the program.

The next time you choose the Save Project option, a dialog box won't appear. Instead, Visual Basic saves the files automatically, updating the *project file* or *make file* as needed. Therefore you cannot rename a project from within the Visual Basic environment (to do this, rename the project (.MAK) file from DOS using the RENAME command.)

The .MAK file is a short housekeeping file that Visual Basic uses to tell itself where the various files that make up your program are located. When you create a stand-alone program, Visual Basic combines all the files (looking for them where the .MAK file tells it to) into one. Here's an example of the .MAK file for the application, NOTEPAD.FRM, that comes with Visual Basic:

```
NOTEPAD.FRM
CMNDLG.BAS
CMNDLGF.FRM
```

Note the three file names. In Visual Basic, file names with a .FRM extension contain forms and whatever code you've attached to the form. Files with a .BAS extension are used to hold general programming code (see Chapter 14). The Notepad has two forms and one module for code.

On the other hand, here's the .MAK file for the finance program from Chapter 15:

FINANCE.FRM
CHECKS.FRM
REPORTS.FRM
DEPOSITS.FRM
ESTATS.FRM
STATS.FRM
RESULTS.FRM
ACCOUNTS.FRM
GENPROCS.BAS

As you can see, this more sophisticated program uses eight forms and one module for special code.

When you open a project by choosing the .MAK file from the Open Project dialog box, Visual Basic looks for the file names in the .MAK file, loads them into the programming environment and combines them together to run your program. (This means that if these files are in directories not contained in your path, the .MAK file would contain the full pathname.)

Note When you save a form by using the Save Project option, Visual Basic does not keep a backup of the previous version unless you've set the backup option as described in the previous section.

Save Form (Form Designer), Save File (Programming Environment)
You use Save Form (Save File) when you start writing a program that uses more than one form or code module. This option lets you save only the current form or code module. To select this option, press ALT+F S. You can also use this option to save the form alone—along with all the code attached to it. If you choose to do this, Visual Basic does not create a make (.MAK) file. Instead, Visual Basic saves everything in the form (.FRM) file, and you can reopen the program by choosing the .FRM file alone.

Save Form As (Form Designer), Save File As (Programming Environment) The Save Form As (Save File As) option does much the same as Save Form and Save File except it allows you to rename the current form or module, make a backup, or store a copy of the current form on another disk. This is done from the dialog box shown in Figure 3-11 (taken from the programming environment). To select this option, press ALT+F A. Visual Basic updates the .MAK file to reflect the new name. (For more on the "Text" option in this dialog box please see the section on "The ASCII Representation of Forms" in Chapter 4.)

Saving Text Only (Programming Environment Only)   There is one more method for saving some of the information contained in your project. To use this method, choose the Save Text option from the File menu (ALT+F T) in the programming environment. This opens a dialog box that looks like Figure 3-12. This option lets you save the code for the current project in normal text (ASCII) form but drops any of the form's visual properties. The default name for the text is always the name of the project with a .TXT extension—the default is FORM1.TXT.

As your projects become more sophisticated, you will find yourself reusing code fragments more and more. To effectively do this, you need to save the code in ordinary text (ASCII) format. When you save the code using the Save Text option, Visual Basic creates an ordinary file containing all the event procedures that are attached to a form that an ordinary word processor or text editor (like Edit, the one supplied with DOS 5.0) can read and write. (For more on reusing code, see Chapter 14.)

FIGURE 3-11   Save File As dialog box

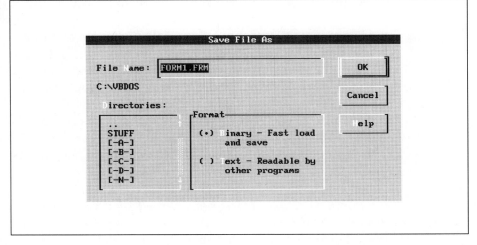

Save Text dialog box

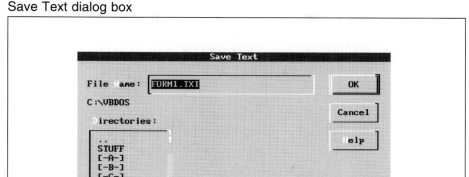

Making Stand-alone Programs

In addition to saving your projects, you can change them into stand-alone programs that you can distribute at will, with no royalties due to Microsoft. In order to do this, all you have to do is return to the programming environment, open the Run menu and choose the Make EXE File option (ALT+R X is the shortcut). If you haven't yet saved all your work, a message box appears telling you that one or more loaded files haven't been saved, and asking if they should be saved now.

After going through the steps to save your program, you'll come to a dialog box that looks like Figure 3-13. (If you have the Professional Edition of Visual Basic, the dialog box will ask some more questions. As you can see, this dialog box asks you for a name for the .EXE (executable) file.

As Figure 3-13 shows, there are two types of .EXE files you can create from Visual Basic projects. The first,

Stand-Alone EXE file

FIGURE

3-13 Make EXE dialog box

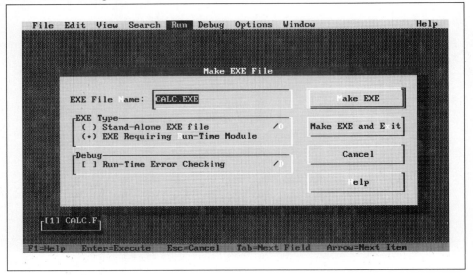

means that someone can run the program completely independent of any supporting program—it can truly stand alone. The second option:

EXE Requiring Run-Time Module

means that users will need access to a file called the run time module (the name of this file is probably VBDRT10.EXE. Check the PACK-ING.TXT file to be sure) for this type of Visual Basic executable program to run. Choosing this option leads to much smaller programs because the large run time module file isn't included. No matter how many different stand-alone Visual Basic programs users have, they need only one copy of this file in a directory accessible to the PATH command. This file contains various support routines that a Visual Basic program needs in order to handle the screens, numbers, and other parts of the program. Microsoft freely allows you to distribute the run time module.

If you are satisfied, hit ENTER to start the process of making the executable file. Visual Basic will exit temporarily to DOS and begin the process of creating the stand-alone program. This takes a bit of time and you'll see some cryptic messages. However, the process is automatic (unless you have an error in your program) so you don't need to worry about them very often.

Don't be shocked when you look at the size of the resulting EXE file—it's going to be more than 140,000 bytes! (If you chose the stand-alone file that needed the run-time module option it would be about 5000 bytes.) A stand-alone program contains an awful lot of overhead that is needed for all Visual Basic programs—whether or not they are used in your program.

What Happens When a Visual Basic Application Runs

When the user runs an application developed with Visual Basic, he or she sees the initial form that you've designed. However, much more than that is going on in the background. When Visual Basic loads a form, it checks whether you've written an event procedure for initializing the form. This event procedure is called the Form_Load procedure. The most common use of this procedure is to initialize form level variables and change the default settings for controls. Some people even prefer to use the Form_Load procedure to set the properties for a form rather than use the properties bar. In fact, it is often easier to set properties this way (see the section in Chapter 5 on resetting properties). You write code for the Form_Load procedure the same way as for any event that a form recognizes:

1. Activate the Event Procedures selection window with ALT+E V.

2. Select the form to be edited from the Files list and select Load from the Events list.

3. Either press ENTER or click the Edit in Active button.

Now you enter a procedure that looks like this:

```
SUB Form_Load ()
  'Initialize form level variables
  'Initialize properties
  ' etc
END SUB
```

Right after Visual Basic processes the Form_Load procedure, Visual Basic calls two other event procedures—if you've written code for them. Here they are in the order they are called:

The Form_Resize procedure
The Form_Paint procedure

Generally speaking, initial information you want printed to the form should be done by placing PRINT statements in the Form_Paint procedure rather than in the Form_Load procedure. This is because unless the AutoRedraw property is set to True, nothing will show up!

Visual Basic generates the Form_Resize event whenever the user resizes a form. For this reason, the most common use of this event procedure is to recalculate (and rescale if necessary) the size and position of any objects on your form. For example, suppose you spent a lot of time positioning controls on a form symmetrically. Without the Form_Resize procedure, a user can, all too easily, spoil your hard work!

The Form_Paint procedure is where you put PRINT methods when the AutoRedraw property is set to False. Visual Basic calls this event whenever the form is moved, enlarged, or newly uncovered. The event procedure then redraws the information on the form. However, when the AutoRedraw property is set to True, this event is *not* called. (Please see the REFRESH method in Appendix C for more on this.)

CHAPTER

The Toolbox:
Command Buttons,
Text Boxes, and Labels

C hapter 3 showed you how to customize a blank form. You saw how to use the properties bar to make a form more visually appealing, as well as how to write simple event procedures to make them responsive to a user. This chapter shows you how to use the toolbox to add controls to a form. You'll see three controls in this chapter: command buttons to initiate actions, text boxes to accept or display data, and labels to identify controls and data. You'll create and manipulate controls and write event procedures for them. You'll also see how message boxes can make applications more friendly, for example, by warning users of irreversible steps they may be taking.

The techniques for using the properties bar that you saw in Chapter 3 will appear again; it's a good idea to make sure you are completely comfortable with the techniques for setting properties before you continue.

Finally, this chapter will show you how to save an ASCII representation of your form, which will prove extremely helpful when debugging.

The Toolbox

As the name suggests, the toolbox is a set of tools you use to embellish a blank form with the controls needed for sophisticated windowing programs. Visual Basic comes with 16 different tools. One of the more exciting features of Visual Basic is its extendability. You can buy custom tools from third-party developers that can extend Visual Basic in even more dramatic ways. And once you install a custom control, it becomes just as much a part of your version of Visual Basic as the tools supplied by Microsoft with Visual Basic.

Figure 4-1 shows the toolbox supplied with Visual Basic. The toolbox is available only when you are in the form designer; it is not accessible from the programming environment. When the toolbox is visible, it's usually located on the far left of the Visual Basic screen. To hide the toolbox, click the control box to the left of its title bar and choose Close. To open the toolbox, go to the Window menu on the main menu bar and select Toolbox or press ALT W T. You can hide, move, or display the toolbox as you see fit. All the tools are also available from the Tool menu on the main menu bar.

FIGURE 4-1   The toolbox

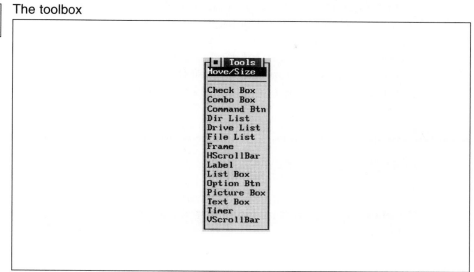

Move/Size   *Move/Size*, the first item on the toolbox in Figure 4-1, is used to manipulate controls after you create them. Click here when you want to resize or move an existing control. It is automatically activated after you place a control on a form.

Command Buttons   *Command buttons* (Command Btn on the toolbox) are sometimes called push buttons. The idea is that when the user moves the mouse (or tabs) to the command button and clicks, something interesting should happen—and will, once you've written the event procedure code that tells Visual Basic how to respond to the Click event (covered later in this chapter). You can control the background color of command buttons.

Text Boxes   *Text boxes* are sometimes called edit fields. You use text boxes to display text or to accept user input. Most of the code you write for text boxes is for processing the information users enter into them. You can use all the editing tools that users expect in a text box, such as cutting and pasting capabilities for entering information. Text boxes can word-wrap and may have scroll bars for moving through the text. Scroll bars are occasionally vital because text boxes can accept large amounts of text. The theoretical limit is slightly more than 32,000 characters, but in practice the limit is less. You can also control the background color of a text box and the color of its text.

Labels   *Labels* are for information that users can't change. They identify objects and occasionally are used to display output. As with text boxes, you can control the color of a label and its text.

Creating Controls

Suppose you want to place a command button at the bottom center of a blank form. If you haven't started up a new project, you might want to do so now. That way you can work with a fresh form, one that is not attached to any project. (Recall from Chapter 3 that you start a new project by choosing New Project from the File menu or by pressing ALT F N; both work whether you are in the programming environment or the form designer.) Next, move to the form designer if you are not already in it by choosing New Form from the File menu and giving a name for the .FRM file. Now follow these steps:

1. Move the mouse pointer to Command Btn in the toolbox and click. Visual Basic highlights this item.

2. Move the mouse pointer to the place on the form where you want the command button to be, then click and hold the left mouse button. (Move/Size on the toolbox should now be highlighted, and will remain highlighted until you select another item on the toolbox.)

 Note   The dotted grid can help you pinpoint the location of the control, if it's turned on (to make the grid visible, select the Grid Lines option from the View menu if it is not already selected).

The command button begins to appear at this point; now you must decide on its size and shape. As you hold down the left mouse button and drag the mouse, the command button takes form. Its size and ending point (the opposite corner from where you started) depend on when you release the left mouse button. When you release the mouse, the command button appears with the centered default caption Command1 (or Command2, and so on). You'll see how to change captions later in this chapter.

In theory you can have more than 200 controls on a single form, but you will rarely use this many. One reason to limit the number of controls is that Visual Basic is limited in the number of controls and forms it can handle at any one time. If you start adding too many controls or menus to a form, your program will slow down dramatically.

Working with Existing Controls

The last section showed you how to create a command button on a blank form. Now you'll see how to move and resize the command button. In Visual Basic, you are never forced to keep a control at its original size or at its original location—don't worry if you've overshot or undershot. The techniques needed for moving or resizing controls are the same for all Visual Basic controls.

Resizing an Existing Control

Notice that the command button has four small bars on the corners. These are called *sizing handles.* You use these to resize a control after you've created it. Controls always move vertically to the next grid mark and by one half of a grid mark horizontally. (Think of each box in the grid as being one character high and two characters wide.) Figure 4-2 shows you a command button with its four sizing handles on an otherwise blank form.

 Note In order to resize or move an existing control, be sure that Move/Size on the toolbox is activated. If this tool is *not* highlighted, use the mouse or the TAB key to select Move/Size.

If the sizing handles no longer appear, you make them reappear by moving the mouse pointer to the command button and clicking once. When the sizing handles are visible, you know that control has been selected. The four corner handles let you change the height and width at the same time.

Command button with sizing handles

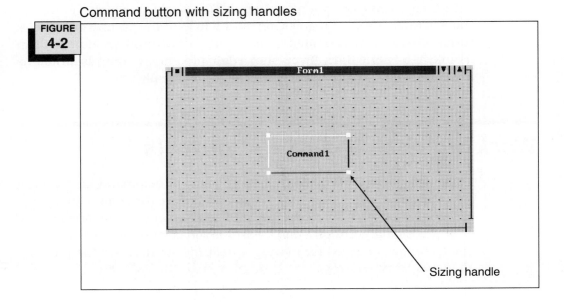

Sizing handle

To resize the command button:

1. Move the mouse pointer to a sizing handle and click and hold down the left mouse button.

2. Drag the mouse until the command button is the size you want.

For example, if you want to shrink the command button in from the top left side while keeping the right side fixed, move the mouse pointer to the sizing handle in the top left corner, click and hold down the left mouse button. Then drag the mouse over to the right.

 Tip You can also resize controls from the keyboard. To do this select the control either via the mouse or by pressing the TAB key as needed. Next, hold down the SHIFT key while pressing an arrow key. The control will be resized accordingly, in increments shown by the grid.

Moving an Existing Control

As mentioned in the previous section, in order to move an existing control, you have to activate the Move/Size control in the toolbox.

1. Move the mouse pointer to the command button, then click and hold down the left mouse button.

2. Drag the mouse until the command button is at the location you want it to be and then release the left button.

 Tip   You can also use the arrow keys to move a selected control around by selecting the control and using the arrow keys for character-sized increments.

Deleting, Cutting, and Pasting Controls

You may end up with too many controls on your form—especially if you use the double-click method a lot (see the next section). To delete a control:

1. Move the mouse pointer to the control and click the left mouse button to select it.

2. Press DEL or open the Edit menu and choose Delete (or you can press ALT E D).

 Tip   Remember you can use the TAB key to navigate around the form.

Sometimes you don't want to delete a control or move it using the techniques described earlier. You want to use the cut and paste options from the editing menu to quickly move it around a form. (Copying controls is also possible—please see Chapter 9 for the consequences of this.) To cut and paste an individual control

1. Move the mouse pointer to the control and click the left mouse button to select it.

2. Open the Edit menu and choose Cut (or press ALT E T).

3. Move the mouse pointer to where you want the control to appear and choose the Paste option by pressing ALT E P.

Shortcuts for Creating Controls

Now that you know how to move controls, you may prefer a shortcut for creating them. If you double-click any of the toolbox items, or choose that item from the Tools menu on the main menu bar, that control appears in the center of the screen in its default size. The more controls you create by these methods, the higher they get stacked on the center of the screen.

 Tip The advantage of the toolbox over the Tools menu is that you can (if you have good control of your mouse) position and size the tool at the same time. The advantage of the Tools menu is that you can create controls quickly—although you'll have to resize and position them later.

For example, suppose you want to create an application with five command buttons symmetrically dispersed, as shown in Figure 4-3. You have these options to create all five items quickly:

☐ Double-click Command Btn on the toolbox five times.

or

☐ Go to the Tools menu and select Command button five times (or press ALT T C five times).

All of these methods stack five command buttons on the center of the form. Then you can easily use the methods described in the previous section to move the buttons to the locations indicated in Figure 4-3.

(You may have noticed in Figure 4-3 that the captions on the command buttons are more informative then the usual Command1, Command2, and so on. You will see how to do this in the section "Properties of Command Buttons" later in this chapter.)

FIGURE
4-3

Form with multiple command buttons

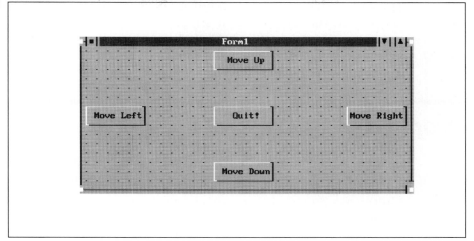

Working with Multiple Controls

Occasionally you'll want to move a group of controls in the same direction. For example, you may have three command buttons and two text boxes lined up and want to keep them aligned but move them up a couple of grid marks. To move multiple controls at the same time:

1. Select the first control by moving to it and clicking the left mouse button

2. Move to the next control, and hold down the CTRL key while clicking the left mouse button. (Each control is outlined with sizing handles.) Now both controls are selected simultaneously. Continue this until you've selected all the controls you want.

3. Move the mouse pointer to any one of the controls you've selected and drag it to its new location. The other controls move along with it by equal amounts in the desired direction.

To undo the selection process for multiple controls, move the mouse pointer outside the selected controls and click the left mouse button. You cannot use this method to unselect just one of the controls. If you press DEL when you've selected multiple controls, all the controls will be deleted.

Properties of Controls

Now that you've seen the techniques for positioning and resizing controls, you'll want to adjust their properties to suit your requirements.

Just as you use the properties bar to customize the size and shape of blank forms (as discussed in Chapter 3), you can use the properties bar to customize controls. For example, if you don't like the default values for a control's property, you can open the properties bar and change it.

Properties of Command Buttons

The next few sections take you through what are the most useful properties of command buttons. But you also may want to scroll through the list of properties and use the on-line help feature for any property with a name that intrigues you, even if that property is not covered in this chapter.

The Caption Property

As you learned in Chapter 3, the Caption property of a form determines the title that the user will see in the title bar. Similarly, the Caption property on a command button determines the message the user will see on the button. Any text you use for the caption on a command button is automatically centered within the button. However, keep in mind that command buttons don't automatically resize to fit the caption you choose—you have to do that yourself (see an earlier section in this chapter on resizing controls).

Command buttons always start out with the captions Command1, Command2, and so on. The number indicates the order in which the buttons were created. Let's create a simple command button like the one shown in Figure 4-4. The caption you see in Figure 4-4 will not fit inside the default size of a command button. Luckily, you can create a caption first via the properties bar and then resize the control to fit it. More of the message shows up as you enlarge the control, so it's easy to judge when to stop.

First, double-click Command Btn on the toolbox (or use the ALT+T C shortcut that selects the Command button item on the Tools menu) to create the button in the center of the screen. Look at the properties bar. The default property for command buttons is always the Caption property. If for some reason the Caption property isn't showing, use the procedure introduced in the previous chapter:

1. Move to the properties bar and click the down arrow of the Properties list box to reveal the list of properties for command buttons.

2. Go to the Caption property by using the mouse, the UP ARROW and DOWN ARROW keys, the TAB key, or simply by pressing C.

3. Click the left mouse button or press ENTER.

Now you can just type the new caption—in other words, change the value of the *Caption property*. What you type replaces what was there.

FIGURE 4-4   A long caption on a command button

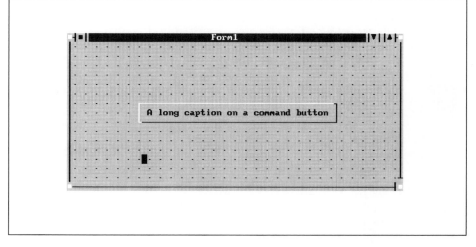

Designing a long caption

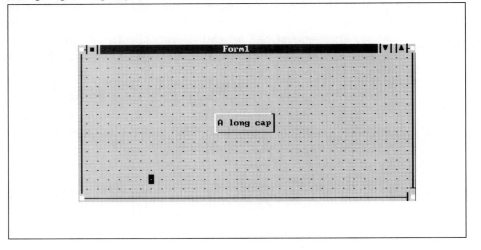

Figure 4-5 shows what you'll see if you enter the caption shown in Figure 4-4 without enlarging the default size. Suppose you want to modify part of the current setting. Make sure the Caption property is selected, and follow these steps:

1. Move the mouse pointer to the Value box in the center of the properties bar.

2. Select part or all of the old caption by holding down the left mouse button and dragging until all the text you want to use is highlighted.

3. Overwrite the old caption by typing the new one.

Tip   You may find it faster to use the TAB key to move around.

The CtrlName (Control Name) Property

The CtrlName property is very important when you start writing event procedures for controls. It is never seen by the user; it is only used by the programmer for command buttons. The default control name is the same as the default setting for the Caption property: Command1, Command2, and so on. This property determines the name Visual Basic uses for the event procedures you write to make a control respond to the user. Picking meaningful names for controls goes a long way toward making application development and its inevitable debugging process easier. For example, suppose you are writing the code to make clicking a command button move a window to the left, like the Move Left command button in the form in Figure 4-3. When you have five command buttons in an application, writing code that looks like this:

```
SUB Command4_Click ()

END SUB
```

to make a form move left is very confusing, while a clearer control name is much more useful:

```
SUB LeftButton_Click ()

END SUB
```

Don't go overboard; the setting you use for a control's name should be meaningful but not ridiculous. The limits on a control name in Visual Basic are as follows:

☐ A control name must begin with a letter. (After that, you can use any combination of letters, numbers, and underscores.)

☐ The name cannot be longer than 40 characters.

Microsoft's documentation uses an abbreviation of the type of control as a prefix to the control name (for example, btnHelp rather than HelpButton).

Other Useful Properties for Command Buttons

Of the 19 properties available for a command button, 17 of them can be set at design time. The other two are set by code at run time (see Chapter 5). Many of them are similar to the ones you saw for a form in Chapter 3. For example, command buttons have BackColor, Height and

Width, and Visible properties. What follows is a short discussion of the most useful ones.

BackColor   As with forms, the BackColor property sets the background color for the button. You can set the background color directly from the list of colors or use the color palette as described in Chapter 3. Command buttons do not have a ForeColor property, so you must accept the default color for this.

Height, Width   The Height and Width properties measure the height and width of the command button in terms of character-sized units. You can change the settings for these properties directly from the properties bar or by using the sizing handles. As with a form, the current values for the size of the command button are displayed at the far right of the properties bar.

Left, Top   The Left and Top properties determine the distance between the command button and the left edge and top of the surrounding container (usually the form but see Chapter 10 for other possibilities). As with the Height and Width properties, these properties use characters for the scale. You can change these properties by dragging, and, as with forms, the values are displayed to the right of the Value box on the properties bar.

Visible   The Visible property determines whether the command button is visible to the user. It's quite common to have code to alternately make a command button visible and invisible, depending on the situation. Just like the Visible property for forms, this property can only be set to True or False.

Enabled   The Enabled property determines if the button can respond to any event whatsoever. If you set this property to False, Visual Basic will not respond to any event concerning that button. Unlike the Visible property, the button remains on the form but is inert. The Enabled property is more often temporarily toggled on or off via code in order to maintain flexibility in your program.

MousePointer   Setting the mouse pointer to something different than the usual arrow is a good way to give a user feedback that he or she has moved the focus to the command button. ("Having the focus" is the phrase used in Visual Basic to describe that a control is primed to receive input.) The same 13 settings that are available for the MousePointer property on a form are available for a command button (see Chapter 3).

A Shortcut for Setting Properties

If you have many controls on a form, the process of setting their properties starts to get tedious. Visual Basic has a shortcut for setting properties that is worth remembering. Suppose you want to set the Caption property for all the command buttons and labels on your form. If you set it once and immediately select another command button, the Caption property for the new control is the one that appears on the properties bar. In general then, Visual Basic remembers the property just set for a control and, if possible, brings up the same property for the next control you select on the properties bar.

Simple Event Procedures for Command Buttons

Controls, like forms, remain inert until you write event procedures to tell them how to respond. Moreover, the techniques for writing event procedures for controls are similar to the way you write them for a form. For example, to have clicking a command button initiate an action requires writing an event procedure almost identical to the one that made a blank form respond to a click.

Writing an event procedure for a command button is similar to writing one for a form. You first must move from the form designer back to the programming environment. Whenever you move back to the programming environment after creating controls on a form, Visual Basic sends a message box asking if you want to save your work before switching back.

If you move back to the programming environment by choosing Event procedures from the Edit menu (ALT+E V), Visual Basic presents you with the Event Procedures selection window. Figure 4-6 shows you what you'll see for the form introduced in Figure 4-3. Notice that the Object list box

FIGURE
4-6

Event procedures selection window for Figure 4-3

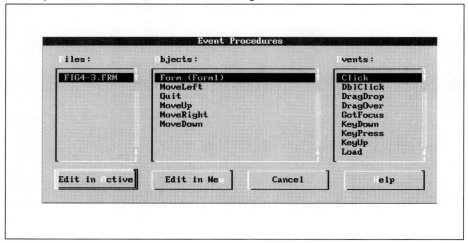

in the middle of this selection window gives all the command buttons listed by their control name right below the form itself. If you choose one of the command buttons by double clicking, Visual Basic gives you a template for the most common event procedure (usually the Click event) for that object. You can also choose a specific event procedure by clicking in the Events box on the right. Visual Basic always keeps track of all the objects in your project, and you can write event procedures for any of them.

Suppose you've set up on a form a command button with the caption "Click here for help!" and a control name of HelpButton. Figure 4-7 shows what you will see after you choose the Click event procedure from the Event procedures selection window. Notice that the event procedure template is similar to the ones you saw in Chapter 3. The only difference is that the control name for the object is used, followed by an underscore, followed by the name of the event. This is the general form for the event procedure template for controls:

SUB *CtrlName_EventName* ()
END SUB.

FIGURE
4-7

Template for the Help button Click event procedure

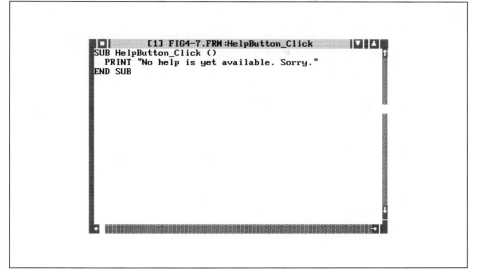

Suppose we add a simple statement using the PRINT method to this event procedure, as shown here:

```
SUB HelpButton_Click ()
  PRINT "No Help is yet available. Sorry."
END SUB
```

Now if you run this program (by pressing SHIFT+F5) and click the button, you should see something like what is shown in Figure 4-8.

In general, you have to be aware of the problems of using the PRINT method with a form that has controls on it already. If a control is located where the text wants to appear, the information printed to the form appears behind the control. Figure 4-9 shows an example of this.

The usual way to handle help information (or any other information you don't want obscured) is to use a message box or even a separate window (form). You then can have the user close the message box or help window when he or she has digested the information. (Chapter 14 shows you how to do this.) Also, you should be aware that if you move another window so that it temporarily covers a form with text on it, the text will

Result of clicking the Help button

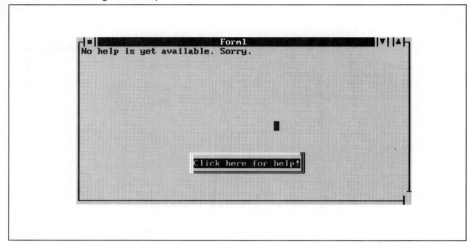

disappear—unless the AutoRedraw property of the form is set to True. (See Chapter 3 for more information on this.)

Text obscured by existing control

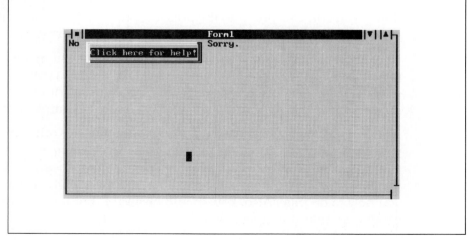

Other Events for Command Buttons

Command buttons can respond to eight events, but clicking is by far the most common. Two others you may find useful are GotFocus and LostFocus. Naive users are often inattentive to just where the focus is and become confused if what they type or click seems to be having no effect. (The Visual Basic designers have tried to help by changing the outlines of controls when they receive the focus—for example, command buttons receive thicker borders.) Controls in Visual Basic can monitor whether the focus has been moved. You can then remind users that they've moved the focus (and ask if they really want to do that). An event procedure that looks like:

```
SUB CommandButton_LostFocus ()

END SUB
```

lets you write the code to respond to users moving the focus away from that button—for example, by asking them if they really want to move. That is, Visual basic calls this procedure automatically when the user moves the focus away from the command button.

Similarly, code like this

```
SUB CommandButton_GotFocus ()

END SUB
```

might include code to generate help about that command button.

Command buttons can also respond to the user pressing specific keys (see Chapters 6 and 7) and to mouse events (see Chapter 12).

Some Final Points on Command Buttons

Usually, the user of the program you develop will choose a command button by moving the mouse pointer to the button and clicking. Sometimes, however, you will want more flexibility. One other method for activating a command button is common to many windowing applications (it's inherited from Microsoft Windows): Move the focus along by pressing TAB, and then press the SPACEBAR when the focus is at the command button you want to activate. (Visual Basic also lets the user move the focus to the button and press ENTER.) The user knows a button has received the focus when it has a thicker border and gives the appearance of being even more three-dimensional than in their non-focused state. All these methods generate the Click event for that button. In other words, all these methods make Visual Basic activate the Click event procedure if one is available for that command button.

In addition, sometimes you want to give people an escape button for an action. This button cancels an action or otherwise extricates the user from some sort of situation he or she doesn't want to be in. The user activates this command button (one to a form) by pressing ESC on the keyboard. A command button that does this is called the *default cancel button* in Visual Basic manuals.

You usually use the properties bar to asign a command button as the default cancel button, although you can use code as well. If you have scrolled through the list of properties available for a command button, you may have noticed the Cancel property. If you set the Cancel property to True, you ensure that pressing ESC generates the Click event for this button, regardless of where the user has moved the focus. Setting the Cancel property to True for one button automatically sets it to False for all the other command buttons on the form.

Another possibility—but one that has its problems for novice users—is to set up a default command button for the form. This generates the Click procedure for the chosen (default) button whenever someone presses ENTER. This can be a problem because unsophisticated users are apt to press ENTER unpredictably. In any case, if you want to use this option, set the Default property of the button to True. As with the default cancel button, you can have at most one default command button to a form.

Access Keys for Controls

Many applications, including Visual Basic, use a modern windowing interface that allows pressing ALT and one other key, the *access key*, to quickly activate a control or a menu item. These shortcut letters are highlighted in the caption or name of the menu item.

It's easy in Visual Basic to set up an access key for any object that has a caption property. When you set the caption, all you have to do is place an ampersand (&) in front of the letter you want to make the access key. For example, look at Figure 4-10. Notice that the "C" in the Caption property for this command button is highlighted. You could run this application either by pressing the ALT+C combination or by clicking the button.

While it is possible to have the same access key for more than one control on a form, doing so is unusual. What happens in this situation is that the focus moves to the next control with that access key, but the control is not activated until the user clicks the mouse or presses the SPACEBAR.

Text Boxes and Labels

Text boxes are the primary method for accepting input and displaying output in Visual Basic. Text boxes always treat what a user types as text; this means that getting numeric information to a Visual Basic program

Caption allowing access key for control

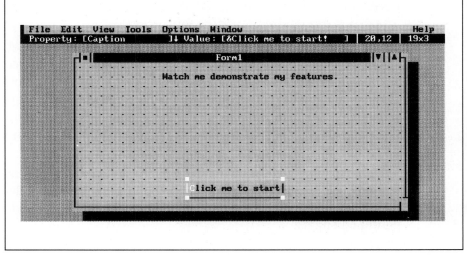

requires transforming a string of digits into a number by using a built-in function (see Chapter 5).

You use labels to display information you don't want the user to be able to change. Probably the most common use for labels is to identify a text box or other control by describing its contents. Another common use is to display help information.

Creating Text Boxes and Labels

You create a text box in the same way you do a command button: Move to the form designer and either double-click on Text box or select the item from the Tools menu. All the methods discussed for moving, sizing, and manipulating command buttons apply here. You also create and work with labels in the same way.

Standard Properties of Text Boxes

There are 23 properties for text boxes, but only 19 can be set at design time and appear in the properties bar (the others are available only via code). Many of them should be familiar to you. For example, the control name (CtrlName) property is used only for the code you write; the user never sees it. As with command buttons, the Height, Width, Left, and Top properties use character widths for the scale.

Unlike command buttons (but like forms), you can set both the BackColor and Forecolor properties for a text box. The ForeColor property affects the color of the text that is displayed. BackColor affects the rest of the text box. Both of these can be set independent of the surrounding container. You can use the color palette to set the color properties (see the section on color properties and the methods for setting them in Chapter 3).

As with command buttons, the Enabled property affects whether the text box will respond to events. In particular, if a text box is disabled, the user cannot enter text inside it. When a text box is disabled, its text is lightened slightly.

Also, as mentioned before with command buttons, it is quite common to toggle the Visible property between True and False with code in order to make a text box appear and disappear on the form.

The MousePointer property has the same 13 possible settings as for forms; you often change this property to dramatize that the focus is now within the control.

Some Special Properties for Text Boxes

Text boxes have three properties you have not seen before and one property that behaves differently when applied to text boxes. The three new properties are Text, ScrollBars, and MultiLine, and they are very important for mastering text boxes. The BorderStyle property was introduced in Chapter 3 but works differently for text boxes than for forms.

Text The Text property is the analog of the Caption property for a command button. The Text property controls the text the user sees. When you create a text box, the default value for this property is set to the default value for the CtrlName property for that control—Text1, Text2, and so on. Because text boxes do not have a Caption property, you will need a trick to give the user an access key for them; you'll see how to do this later in this chapter. If you want a text box to be empty when the application starts up, select the Text property and blank out the original setting.

ScrollBars The ScrollBars property determines if a text box has horizontal or vertical scroll bars. These are useful because Visual Basic allows you to accept long or multiple lines of data from a single text box; 32,768 characters (around 5,000 words) is the theoretic limit but in practice the limits will be less. Without scroll bars, it becomes much harder for the user to move through the data contained in the text box, thus making editing the information that much more difficult.

There are four possible settings for the ScrollBars property:

Value	Meaning
0	This is the default value. The text box lacks both vertical and horizontal scroll bars

Value	Meaning
1	The text box has horizontal scroll bars only
2	The text box has vertical bars only
3	The text box has both horizontal and vertical bars

MultiLine   The MultiLine property determines if a text box can accept more than one line of text when the user runs the application, and it is usually combined with resetting the value of the ScrollBars property. In any case, if you set the MultiLine property to True, a user can always use the standard editing methods described in Chapter 2 to move through the text box: the arrow keys, HOME, CTRL+HOME, END, and CTRL+END. You can only set one line of a text box at design time (via the Text property). To add multiple lines to a text box—especially those involving line breaks—requires code (see Chapter 5).

Visual Basic automatically word wraps when a user types more then one line of information into a text box—unless you've added horizontal scroll bars to the text box. Also, users can use the ENTER key to separate lines unless you've added a default command button to the form (yet another reason to be careful of creating default command buttons). If you have a default command button, the user has to press CTRL+ENTER to break lines.

BorderStyle   There are only two possible settings for the BorderStyle property for a text box, unlike the seven that are available for forms (see Chapter 3). The default value is 1, which gives you a single width border, called a fixed single. If you change the value of this property to 0, the border disappears.

Event Procedures for Text Boxes

Text boxes can recognize eight events. Events like GotFocus and LostFocus work exactly as described with command buttons. Three others—KeyDown, KeyUp, and KeyPress—are for monitoring exactly what the user types. For example, you would use these events to write a program that allows someone to use dollar signs when entering amounts that ultimately need to be treated as numbers. This type of data processing requires a fair amount of code, which you'll see in Chapters 6 and 7.

Although the Change event lacks the flexibility of the key events you'll see in Chapters 6 and 7, you may find it very useful. Visual Basic monitors the text box and calls this event procedure whenever a user makes any changes in the text box. No matter what the user types, Visual Basic will detect it. One of the most common uses of this event procedure is to warn people that they should not be entering data in a specific text box, blanking out what they typed.

Useful Properties for Labels

There are 19 properties for labels, 18 of which appear in the properties bar. Most of them overlap with the properties for text boxes and forms, and many of them should be familiar to you by now. Like command buttons, labels have a Caption property that determines what they display. This property is originally set to be Label1 for the first label on your form, Label2 for the second, and so on. At design time you can have at most one line of text as the caption for a label. With code (see Chapter 5) you can add multiple lines of text to a caption. As before, the CtrlName property is used only for the code you write; the user never sees it.

As with text boxes, you can set the BackColor and ForeColor properties for a text box. The ForeColor property affects the color of the text that is displayed. BackColor affects the rest of the label. Both of these can be set independent of the surrounding container.

The Enabled property is not often used for labels. Its primary role is to determine if the user can move the focus to the label or not. As before, it is quite common to toggle, using code, the Visible property between True and False to make a label appear and disappear on the form.

The MousePointer property uses the same 13 possible settings. This is rarely changed for labels, with the one possibility of changing the icon when the user moves from the label to the control that is being labeled.

There are two useful properties for labels that you have not seen before: Alignment and AutoSize. Also, the BorderStyle property has one neat use that can give more polish to your applications.

Alignment   The Alignment property has three possible settings. The usual (default) value is 0, which means the text in the label is left justified (flush left). If you set the value of this property to 1, the text inside the label will be right justified; if you set the value to 2, the text is centered.

Autosize   Unlike command buttons, labels can be made to grow automatically to encompass the text you place in them by using the AutoSize property. The default value for this property, though, is set to False, and you need to change it to True to take advantage of it.

BorderStyle   The BorderStyle property has three possible values—one more than for text boxes. The difference is that the default value is 0, so labels do not start out with a border. If you set the value to 1, though, the label resembles a text box. This is occasionally very useful when your program needs to display results. Using labels with a border property value of 1 for displaying output avoids the problem of text boxes being changed by the user. Your form will have a control that looks like a text box, but it will not be responsive to the user. The alternative, which is to set the Enabled property of the text box to False, has the disadvantage that the shading changes and the text box loses the three dimensional effect, an often less-than-perfect solution. You can also set the BorderStyle property to 2, which gives a double-width border around the label.

Event Procedures for Labels

Labels respond to eight events. For example, they can respond to clicking, double-clicking or the Change event. The most common event procedures for a label are mouse events (see Chapter 12), for example, to provide context-sensitive help. One problem to be aware of is that labels do not respond to key events or detect whether the user has shifted the focus. This dramatically restricts the use of event procedures for labels. Labels in Visual Basic remain primarily descriptive and not responsive.

Navigating with the TAB Key

Using the mouse is the most common way to move from control to control in a Visual Basic application, but your applications have to allow for using the TAB key as well. *Tab order* is the term used in a Visual Basic application for the sequence of controls that pressing TAB moves you through. In a Visual Basic application, the order in which you create the controls is the order used for the tab order; the first control you create at design time is the one that receives the focus when the application starts up. If you press TAB once when the application is running, you move to the second control you created at design time, and so on. If you press TAB when the focus is at the last control you've created, the focus moves back to the first one.

It's possible to change the setting for the tab order via the properties bar or by writing code. The property you need to set is the TabIndex property. If you set this value to 0 for a control, this control automatically becomes the first control in tab order, and all the other controls move upward in tab order. What used to be the first control in tab order is now the second, the second is now the third, and so on. If you change a control with a higher tab index, then only controls with tab indexes larger than it are affected. If you create a control and set the TabIndex property at design time, the settings for the TabIndex property are moved higher to make way for the new control. You can also change the TabIndex via code (see Chapter 5).

Access Keys for Text Boxes

Earlier in this chapter, you learned how to assign access keys to the captions of command buttons. Text boxes lack a Caption property, so you need a trick to allow users to quickly move the focus to them via an access key. The trick works because labels have captions, so you can place an ampersand (&) in front of the letter you want to designate as the access key for the label. However, labels do not respond to the GotFocus or LostFocus events. So what happens when you use the access key? If you press the access key for a control that does not respond to focus events, the focus moves to the next control in tab order that will accept it.

This makes it easy to set up access for a text box. You create a label for the text box, set up the access key for the label, and then create the text box. (Doing this ensures that the text box follows the label in tab order.)

Message Boxes

Message boxes display information in a dialog box superimposed on the form. They wait for the user to choose a button before returning to the application. Users cannot switch back to any windows (forms) in your application as long as Visual Basic is displaying a message box. Message boxes should be used for short messages or to give transient feedback; you would not generally use them to provide a help screen, for example. A good time to display a message box is when the user moves the focus away from a text box before placing information inside it.

The simplest form of the message box command looks like this:

MsgBox "*The message goes in quotes*"

Message boxes can hold a maximum of 1024 characters, and Visual Basic automatically breaks them at the right of the dialog box. You can set line breaks yourself, as you will see in Chapter 5. For example, suppose you wrote an application and thought the user needed to be reminded that nothing would happen until he or she clicked a command button. You might add a LostFocus event procedure that looks something like this:

```
SUB Command1_LostFocus ()
  MsgBox "You have to click the button for anything to happen"
END SUB
```

When you run this application and move the focus away from the command button, you will see something that looks like the screen in Figure 4-11.

Notice in Figure 4-11 that the title bar of the message box is blank and so isn't particularly informative. You can add your own, more meaningful, title to a message box. To do this, you have to use the full form of the message box statement by adding two options to it. The complete syntax for the MsgBox command is:

MsgBox *MessageInBox, TypeOfBox, TitleOfBox*

You have already seen the item called MessageInBox—this gives the text in the box. The last item, TitleOfBox, is where you type your desired

FIGURE 4-11

Message box demonstration

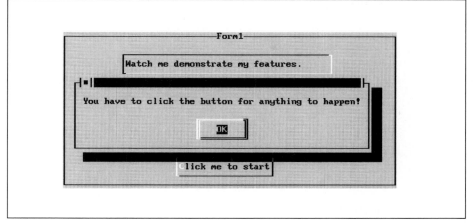

title. The middle item, TypeOfBox, requires adding together two different numbers to specify the type of message box. For this reason, the numbers are usually divided into two groups. Each group determines a different aspect of the message box functionality. The first group of numbers controls the type of buttons that appear in the box.

Value	Meaning
0	Displays an OK button only
1	Displays OK and Cancel buttons (pressing ESC works like clicking it)
2	Displays Abort, Retry, and Ignore buttons
3	Displays Yes, No, and Cancel buttons
4	Displays Yes and No buttons only
5	Displays Retry and Cancel buttons

The next group determines the default button (pressing ENTER clicks them):

Value	Default Button
0	First button
256	Second button
512	Third button

You can combine these options by adding the values together. For example, the statement

```
MsgBox "Example of buttons", 258, "Button Example"
```

displays a message box that looks like this:

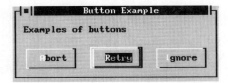

Since 258 = 2+256, this box contains Abort, Retry, and Ignore buttons, and the second, the Retry button, would be the default button for this box.

Although message boxes do not have event procedures associated with them, it is possible to determine which button was pressed, using the techniques you will see in Chapter 6.

The ASCII Representation of Forms

One of the most exciting innovations in Visual Basic for DOS over the first version of Visual Basic for Windows is the capability of getting an ASCII representation of a form. The ASCII representation of a form is an extremely useful debugging tool. Using it, you can easily check that the properties of the various controls and forms are exactly what you want. To see what the ASCII representation of a form looks like, do the following:

1. Start up a new project

2. Add a form using the name ASCII for both the FormName and the Caption property.

3. In the form designer add a command button in the default size, default location and using the default name of Command1

4. Return to the programming environment and add a Click procedure to the command button with the single line of code: PRINT "You clicked me!"

5. Choose the "Save File As" option from the file menu in the programming environment.

6. Choose the name ASCII.TXT and choose the "Text - Readable by other programs" option.

Now, if you examine the file in another word processor, text editor, or via the DOS type command, here's what you would see. (Don't be intimidated by the length of the following listing, we will go over the pieces step by step.)

```
Version 1.00
BEGIN Form ASCII
    AutoRedraw   = 0
    BackColor    = QBColor(7)
    BorderStyle  = 2
    Caption      = "ASCII"
    ControlBox   = -1
    Enabled      = -1
    ForeColor    = QBColor(0)
    Height       = Char(17)
    Left         = Char(15)
    MaxButton    = -1
    MinButton    = -1
    MousePointer = 0
    Tag          = ""
    Top          = Char(3)
    Visible      = -1
    Width        = Char(63)
    WindowState  = 0
    BEGIN CommandButton Command1
        BackColor    = QBColor(7)
        Cancel       = 0
        Caption      = "Command1"
        Default      = 0
        DragMode     = 0
        Enabled      = -1
        Height       = Char(3)
        Index        =
        Left         = Char(24)
        MousePointer = 0
```

```
        TabIndex      = 0
        TabStop       = -1
        Tag           = " "
        Top           = Char(6)
        Visible       = -1
        Width         = Char(12)
    END
END
SUB Command1_Click ()
PRINT "You clicked me!"
END SUB
```

The idea of the ASCII form representation is simple: It begins with the description of the form's properties. The listing begins with the version of Visual Basic used, followed by the name of the form. Then comes the current settings of all the properties associated to the form. For example, the new caption is reflected by the line of code that looks like this:

```
    Caption      = "ASCII"
```

because this is what we reset the Caption property to be.

Height and width properties are measured in characters. For example, as you've already seen in Chapter 3, the default height of a form is 17 characters high. This is reflected in the line in the above listing that looks like this:

```
    Height       = Char(17)
```

After the properties of the form comes the various controls on the forms in the same format, indented slightly for readability. The ASCII format for a control is the following:

Begin *ControlType ControlName*

In our example this is

```
    BEGIN CommandButton Command1
```

Then comes the properties of the control. For example, since we didn't change the control name or any of the other properties, the above listing shows the default values for a command button. Finally, whatever code is attached to the form is listed after all the controls are described.

CHAPTER

First Steps in Programming

*B*y now you've gotten a feel for what a Visual Basic application looks like. You've seen how to customize forms by adding controls, and you've started writing the event procedures that are the backbone of a Visual Basic application. But as you've probably realized, the event procedures you've seen didn't do much. To do more, you must become comfortable with the sophisticated programming language built into Visual Basic.

If you are familiar with QBasic, QuickBASIC, Pascal, or C, you'll have an easier time of it, and the next four chapters will go pretty quickly. If you are familiar only with the interpreted BASIC found on PCs (GW-BASIC, BASICA), you'll want to read these chapters much more carefully. In any case, there are subtle differences between Visual Basic programming and conventional programming that can trip up even experienced programmers, so you probably don't want to skip these chapters.

The Anatomy of a Visual Basic Program

It can't be stressed enough that the key to Visual Basic programming is in recognizing that Visual Basic processes code in response to events. If you think of a Visual Basic program as containing independent pieces that "wake up" only in response to events they have been told to recognize, you won't go far wrong. Don't think that every program must have a starting line and an ending line and move from top to bottom. For illustration purposes, this book may show you fragments of a program, but they are not meant to (nor often can they even) work independently.

Basically, even if you know a more conventional programming language very well, you shouldn't try to force your Visual Basic programs into its framework. If you impose programming habits learned from older programming languages on your Visual Basic programs, you're likely to run into problems.

The Code Windows

You always write code in a code window. As you have seen, a code window opens whenever you start a new project, open an existing project, or edit an event procedure. You can also choose the Code option from the View menu or press F2 to open the Code selection window (labeled Code). The Code selection window allows you to select from a list the procedure you want to edit and whether you want to edit it in a new window or not.

To create a new event procedure and start editing it once you have designed the form, first open the Event Procedures selection window by pressing ALT+E V. Figure 5-1 shows the Event Procedures selection window for the calculator application that comes with Visual Basic. Note that the list box on the left shows the single form that makes up this application (CALC.FRM), and the middle box lists the seven controls and the form itself.

Since our applications only use one form at this point, you first will want to select the object by moving to the Objects list box (ALT+O is the shortcut) and then choosing the control whose event procedures you'll want to work with. When you make a selection from the Objects list box, the Event list box on the right changes to reflect the events recognized by the object. If you have already written an event procedure, it shows up fully capitalized in the Events list box, such as the LOAD procedure for the calculator application, as shown in Figure 5-1.

Statements in Visual Basic

When you enter a statement in Visual Basic, Visual Basic uses the same advanced technology pioneered in QuickBASIC to analyze and process it. This happens immediately after you press ENTER or move off the line with an arrow key. Many typos are detected by Visual Basic at this stage. If a statement you enter can't be analyzed, a message box pops up that often helps you find out what caused the problem.

Except within quotes, case and spacing are ignored by Visual Basic. Nonetheless, Visual Basic does try to impose its own conventions. It capitalizes keywords and often adds extra spaces for readability. For example, no matter how you capitalize the command word PRINT—Print, PRint, print, and so on—pressing ENTER will change it to PRINT. It's a good idea to stick to a standard method of spacing and capitalization in your code for non-keywords as well.

FIGURE 5-1

Event procedure selection window for the calculator project

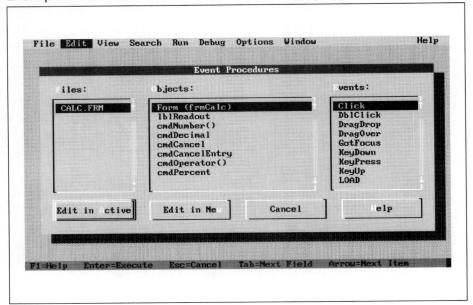

Statements in Visual Basic rarely use line numbers, and each statement generally occurs on its own line. You can combine statements on one line by placing a colon (:) between statements. Lines are limited to 255 characters and can't be extended to the next line. If you use a line with more characters than can fit in the window, Visual Basic scrolls the window toward the right as needed.

Sometimes in this book you'll see lines that easily fit this limit but are longer than can fit on one line of a printed page. If this happens and the statements are meant to be on one line, either that will be explicitly stated, an underscore will be used, or the parenthesis or quotes will be closed on the next line. For example:

```
PRINT "This is an example of a line that won't fit on a
single line of the page."
MSGBOX "You have to click button for anything to happen",_
306,"Test"
```

If you were entering this procedure in Visual Basic, you'd continue typing the first line until you reached the closing quotes and you would type the second line continuously, omitting the underscore before "306."

REMARK Statements

REMARK (or REM) statements are put into programs to explain what code does. It's easy to question why comments are important—until you try to modify (or fix) a program someone else wrote or even a program you wrote months ago. REMARK statements are neither executed nor processed by Visual Basic. As a result, they do not take up any room in the compiled code.

There are two ways to indicate a REMARK statement. The first is to use the REM keyword:

```
SUB Command1_Click ()
   REM    Comments describing the procedure would go here
   REM
END SUB
```

As usual, the programming lines are indented to improve readability. The second method to indicate a REMARK statement is to use a single quote ('), which is not the apostrophe found below the tilde (~) but is usually found below the double quote (") on your keyboard:

```
SUB Command1_Click ()
   'A comment describing the procedure would go here
   '
END SUB
```

You can also add comments to the ends of lines. In this case it is easier to use the single quote because REM requires a colon before it. For example:

```
PRINTFORM 'Dump the current window
```

or

```
PRINTFORM :REM A bit more cumbersome
```

Everything on a line following a REM statement is ignored, whether or not it is an executable Visual Basic statement. Commenting out executable statements that may be causing problems is a common technique to help debug your programs.

The END Statement

When Visual Basic processes an END statement, the program stops. If you are developing a program, you are dumped back into the development environment. In a stand-alone program, after the END statement, control returns to the DOS prompt.

You can have as many END statements within a Visual Basic program as you want, but it is good programming practice to restrict the number of events that end a program.

Assignment and Property Settings

Giving values to variables and resetting properties are two of the most common tasks in Visual Basic code. Visual Basic uses an equal sign for both these tasks. For example,

variable = value

gives the variable on the left side the value on the right side. You can also use the optional keyword LET that was common in earlier versions of BASIC:

LET *variable = value*

The value always occurs on the right and the variable occurs on the left. Visual Basic *must* be able to obtain a value from the right-hand side of an assignment statement. It will do any processing needed for this to happen.

You could consider an assignment statement as a way in which a variable gets a (new) value, but some people prefer to think of the assignment statement as copying information from a source to a destination.

Assigning to Properties

If you want to change a property setting for a Visual Basic object, place the object's name followed by a period and then the name of the property on the left side of the equal sign, and put the new value on the right-hand side:

object.property = value

For example, suppose you have a text button (CtlName = Text1) and want to change the text property directly rather than use the properties bar. You need only have lines like this in an event procedure:

```
Text1.Text = ""
Text1.Text = "This is the new text."
```

In the first case, since there is nothing between the quotes, the text assigned to this property is blank. In the second case, the string "This is the new text" will appear in the text box. Similarly a line like

```
Text1.Forecolor = 15
```

assigns high intensity white to the foreground color of the Text1 textbox. (The complete list of colors is available by looking at the possible settings for the ForeColor or BackColor property (or see Chapter 16.)

You can change the setting of a property via code as often as you need to. For example, if you wanted to change the caption on a command button called Command1, you would place a line like this in an event procedure:

```
Command1.Caption = "Put new caption here."
```

Similarly, if you wanted to make a button called Command5 the first button in tab order, you would add a line like this to an event procedure:

```
Command5.TabIndex = 0
```

Now suppose you want a form called Form1 to move around when various command buttons are clicked. Here is an example of one of the event procedures you could use:

```
SUB LeftButton_Click ()
  Form1.Left = Form1.Left - 5
END SUB
```

Look at the key line "Form1.Left = Form1.Left - 5". On the left-hand side of the assignment statement is the property that gets the value, but it seems that the property occurs on the right-hand side as well. What happens is that Visual Basic first analyzes the right-hand side of any assignment to extract a value from it. In this case, it looks at the current position of the left side of the form and calculates the number of columns it is from the left. It then subtracts 5 from this number. Only after it has done this does it look to the left side. Visual Basic now changes the old value of the "Left" property to a new one.

All this can be a little confusing. Some people find it helpful to remember that right-hand sides of assignment statements are there only for the values they yield, and only the left-hand side gets changed.

Boolean Properties

Properties that take only the value True or False are called *Boolean properties*, after the English logician George Boole. You've seen lots of these properties already. Whether a command button is visible, enabled, or serves as the cancel button are all Boolean properties.

Visual Basic uses the value zero for False and –1 for True. A statement in an event procedure like

```
Command1.Visible = 0
```

hides the command button. The control stays hidden until Visual Basic processes another statement:

```
Command1.Visible = -1
```

If you want to arrange for the TAB key to skip over a control while a program is running, change the TabStop property to False. For example:

```
Command.TabStop = 0
```

The usual way to toggle between Boolean properties is with the *NOT* operator. Suppose you have a statement in an event procedure like

```
Command1.Visible = NOT Command1.Visible
```

This statement works as follows: Visual Basic finds the current value of Command1.Visible, and then the NOT operator reverses it; that is, if it was True it goes to False, and vice versa.

Note   You will find that Visual Basic treats 0 as False and any other value as True. For example, the statement Command1.Visible = 123 will make the Command1 button visible. However, in order for the NOT operator to work properly in toggling a Boolean property between on and off or off and on, a value of -1 must be used for True. (For an explanation, see the section on "Bit Twiddling" in Chapter 7.)

Variables

Variables in Visual Basic hold information (values). Whenever you use a variable, Visual Basic sets up an area in the computer's memory to store the information. Variable names in Visual Basic can be up to 40 characters long and, provided the first character is a letter, can include any combination of letters, numbers, and underscores. The following table lists some possible variable names and whether they are acceptable.

Base1_Ball	Acceptable
1Base_Ball	Not acceptable—first character is not a letter
ThisIsLongButStillOK	Acceptable—only 19 characters long
Base.1	Not acceptable—uses a period (unlike QuickBasic or QBasic. Actually this seems to be acceptable for variables but it's not a good idea, as the documentation says it isn't acceptable.)

All characters in a variable name are significant, but case is irrelevant. BASE is the same variable as base. On the other hand, Base is a different variable from Base1, and both are different from Base_1. However, Visual Basic always changes the style of the names of your variables to reflect the capitalization pattern you last used. If you use Mortgageinterest, mortgageinterest, and MortgageInterest successively as variable names, then Visual Basic will automatically change all occurrences to MortgageInterest because this was the last one you used.

This feature is often useful in detecting typos in variable names. If you think a misspelled variable name is causing a problem, change one occurrence to all caps, press ENTER, and scan the program to see if all the occurrences of the variable name have been changed. If you find one that didn't change, then that's where a typo is. When you're done with this, change the variable name back to the form you want, and all its occurrences will change back again as well.

Choosing meaningful variable names helps document your program and makes the inevitable debugging process easier. Meaningful variable names are an excellent way to clarify the point of many kinds of program statements.

You can't use words reserved by Visual Basic for variable names: for example, Print is not acceptable as a variable name. However, you can embed reserved words within a variable's name. For example, PrintIt is a perfectly acceptable variable name. Visual Basic will present an error message if you try to use a reserved word as a variable name, usually immediately after you press ENTER.

Our convention for variable names is that capitals appear only at the beginning of the words that make up its parts (for example, MortgageInterest, not Mortgageinterest). Some people add underscores as well (for example, Mortgage_Interest); that style is not used in this book.

Variable Types

Visual Basic handles six standard types of variables. It is also possible to define your own variable types, as you will see in Chapter 9. The six standard variable types are described here.

Strings

String variables hold characters. One method to identify variables of this type is to place a dollar sign ($) at the end of the variable name: AStringVariable$. String variables can theoretically hold up to 32,767 characters, but its practical limits are smaller. In fact, the total number of characters you can assign to all the string variables attached to your form will be less than 65,535.

One of the most common uses of string variables is to pick up the information contained in a text box. For example, if you have a text box named Text1, then

```
ContentOfText1$ = Text1.Text
```

assigns the string contained in the text box to the variable named on the left-hand side.

Integers

Integer variables hold relatively small integer values (between –32,768 and 32,767). Integer arithmetic is very fast but is restricted to this range. The identifier used is the percent sign (%):

```
AnIntegerVariable% = 3
```

Long Integers

The *long integer variable* is a type that was introduced in QuickBasic. It holds integers between -2,147,483,648 and 2,147,483,647. The identifier used is the ampersand (&). Long integer arithmetic is also fast.

```
ALongIntegerVariable& = 123456789
```

Single-precision

Single-precision variables are the default type of numbers in Visual Basic. If you use a variable without specifying the type, Visual Basic assumes it will hold numbers of this type. (It is still a good idea to specify the type of a variable.) For single-precision numbers, the identifier is an exclamation point (!). These variables hold numbers that are approximations. They can be fractions, but you can be sure of the accuracy of only seven digits. For instance, if the number 87,654,321 is assigned to the variable Num!, then the last digit would be lost: Num! will be equivalent to 87,654,320. Although the accuracy is limited, the size (range) of these numbers is up to numbers as large as 3.4×10^{38}. Calculations will always be approximate for these types of variables. Moreover, arithmetic with these numbers is slower than with integer or long integer variables.

Double-precision

Double-precision variables hold numbers with 16 places of accuracy and allow numbers as large as 1.7×10^{308}. The identifier used is a sharp or pound sign (#). Calculations are also approximate for these variables. You can rely only on the first 16 digits. Calculations are relatively slow with double-precision numbers. Double precision variables are mainly used in scientific calculations in Visual Basic—because of the data type described next.

Currency

Currency variables are a type that will be new to all but users of the BASIC Professional Development System and Visual Basic for Windows. They are designed to avoid certain problems inherent in switching from binary fractions to decimal fractions. (It's impossible to make 1/10 out of combinations of 1/2, 1/4, 1/8, 1/16, and so on). The currency type can have 4 digits to the right of the decimal place and up to 15 to the left of the decimal point. Arithmetic will be exact within this range. The identifier is an "at" sign (@)—*not* the dollar sign, which identifies strings. Addition and subtraction are much faster with these variables than for double-precision numbers. And while multiplication and division is not faster, this is still the preferred type for financial calculations of reasonable size. (For those who are interested, this type of number uses very large integers, with 19 digits, which are then scaled by 10,000 to give four decimal places and 15 places to the left of the decimal point.)

Fine Points of Variables

You can use variables like A% and A!, which differ only in the type identifier, in the same program. Most programmers avoid this, however, since confusion can result when the variable is written without the identifier.

The first time you use a variable, Visual Basic gives it a *default value.* For strings, this is the null (empty) string—the one you get by assigning " " to a string variable. For numeric variables, the default value is zero. You should only rely on the default values if this is documented in your program. Otherwise you risk creating a breeding ground for hard-to-find bugs. It is quite common to use the first statements in a program or event procedure to initialize the variables.

Swapping

A common task is *swapping,* or interchanging the values of two variables. Suppose you have two variables, *X* and *Y,* of the same data type. The statement

```
SWAP X, Y
```

interchanges the values of the two variables. If you try to swap the values of two variables of different types, you get an error message as shown here:

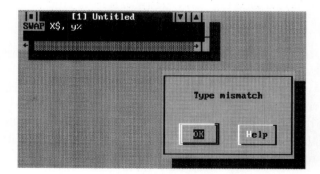

The DIM Statement for Types

Many people prefer not to use the identifiers to specify the type of variable. Instead they use the DIM statement. Here are some examples:

```
DIM I AS INTEGER
DIM TextBox AS STRING
DIM Interest AS CURRENCY
```

The technical term for these statements is *declarations.* You can combine multiple declarations on a single line:

```
DIM Year AS INTEGER, Rate AS CURRENCY, Name AS STRING
```

Declaring the types of variables before using them—and commenting as needed, of course—is a good programming habit. It can make your programs more readable than using single-character identifiers, which are easy to skip over. Many people prefer the following to using the variables Years%, Rate@, and Currency@:

```
SUB Calculate_Click
  'This procedure calculates mortgage interest

  DIM Years AS INTEGER
  DIM Rate AS CURRENCY
  DIM Amount AS CURRENCY
  .
  .
END SUB
```

You can also use DIM Years%, Rate@, and so on if you prefer using a type identifier.

 Note   If a variable is declared in a DIM statement, then trying to use variables with the same name but a different type identifier at the end of the variable will cause a "Duplicate definition" error when the program is run.

For example, if you use the statement DIM Count AS INTEGER to declare the integer variable Count, then the variables Count$, Count!, Count#, and Count@ may not be used. Count% may be used, however, and is recognized by Visual Basic as just another way of denoting the variable Count.

Changing the Default for Types

Sometimes you know a program will only (or primarily) use integer variables. In this case it is convenient to change the defaults built into Visual Basic. (Recall that undeclared variables are assumed to be single precision.) You change the defaults with what is called a DEF*type* statement. Here are some examples:

DEF*type* Statement	What It Does
DEFINT A-Z	Changes the default—all variables are assumed to be integers
DEFINT I	All variables beginning with I are assumed to be integers
DEFSTR S-Z	All variables beginning with the letters S through Z are assumed to hold strings

The general forms of the various DEF*type* statements are

DEFINT *letter range* (for integers)
DEFLNG *letter range* (for long integers)
DEFSNG *letter range* (for single precision)
DEFDBL *letter range* (for double precision)
DEFCUR *letter range* (for currency)
DEFSTR *letter range* (for strings)

The letters in the ranges are automatically converted to caps. For instance, the smart editor converts DEFstr s-Z to DEFSTR S-Z. You can always override the default settings by using an identifier or a DIM statement for a specific variable.

When a DEF*type* statement appears in an event procedure, it applies only to the variables following it in that procedure. Usually, you'll want your DEF*type* statements to apply to all the procedures attached to a form. To see how to do this, see the next section.

Leading Code for a Form

Leading code for a form (sometimes called *module level* or *form level* code) contains the DEF*type* statements and other non-executable code that you want to apply to all the event procedures attached to a form. To get to the leading code for the form:

1. Open the Code selection window.

2. Select the first item in the list. It appears as *FormName*.FRM and corresponds to the file name under which you saved the Form module.

Now you can enter the DEFtype statement—an example of this is shown in Figure 5-2.

The OPTION EXPLICIT Statement

One of the most common bugs in programs is the misspelled variable name. Most versions of BASIC have allowed you to create variables "on the fly" by merely using the variable's name in your program, and so made the misspelled variable name possible. But misspelled variable names will almost certainly lead to a default value that causes your program to behave incorrectly. These are among the most difficult bugs to eradicate—because you need to find the misspelled variable name.

One way around this is to force all variables to be declared, so you can be notified if you spelled the name of a variable incorrectly inside a procedure. Giving you this option (but not forcing you to use it) was the path chosen by the designers of Visual Basic.

To turn this feature on, add the command OPTION EXPLICIT in the leading code for your form. Once Visual Basic processes this command, it will no longer allow you to use a variable unless you declare it first. Trying to do so will lead to an error message that the variable was not declared, as shown here:

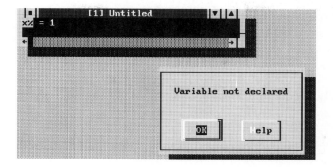

READing Values into Variables

So far, you only used the assignment statement to give a value to a variable. This task can also be accomplished via READ and DATA statements. DATA statements appear in the leading code of a form and

FIGURE
5-2

Leading code with DEF*type* statements

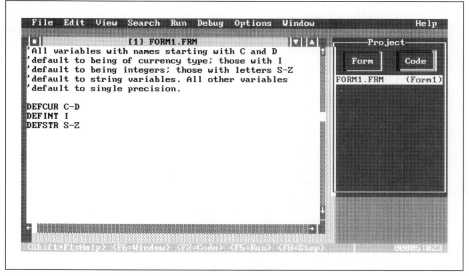

consist of sequences of values separated by commas that can be accessed, in order, by READ statements inside procedures. An example of a DATA statement is

```
DATA John Doe, 9.35, 39
```

When code such as

```
READ PersonName$, HourlyWage, HoursWorked
PRINT PersonName$; " earned"; HourlyWage * HoursWorked
```

is executed by Visual Basic, the variables PersonName$, HourlyWage, and HoursWorked are assigned the values John Doe, 9.35, and 39. The resulting output is

John Doe earned 364.65

In general, when a statement of the form

READ *var*

is encountered, Visual Basic looks for the first unused value in a DATA statement and assigns that value to var. Statements of the form

READ *var1, var2, ...*

have the same effect as the sequence of statements

READ *var1*
READ *var2*
.
.
.

Essentially what Visual Basic does is keep an invisible pointer at the last READ item. Each time it processes another item in a READ statement, it moves the pointer forward. DATA statements are read in the order they appear in the leading code.

In certain situations you need to manipulate this invisible pointer, most often to read the data in the DATA statements more than once. The statement

```
RESTORE
```

tells Visual Basic to begin anew with the first item of the first DATA statement when assigning values to variables in future READ statements.

(You can also restore to a specific line of DATA. See the RESTORE statement in Appendix C.)

The Scope of Variables

Programmers refer to the scope of variables when they want to talk about the availability of a variable used in one part of a program to the other parts of a program. In older programming languages, where *all* variables were available to *all* parts of the program, keeping variable names straight was always a problem. If, in a complicated program, you had two variables named Total, the values could (and would) contaminate each other. The solution in modern programming languages like Visual Basic is to isolate variables within procedures. Unless you specifically arrange it, changing the value of a variable named, for example, Total, in one procedure will not affect the variable named Total in another procedure. The technical explanation is that variables are *local* to procedures unless otherwise specified. An event procedure will not normally have access to the value of a variable in another event procedure.

As always, it is not a good programming practice to rely on defaults. If you want to be sure a variable is local within an event procedure, use the DIM statement inside the event procedure.

Sharing Values Among Procedures

Of course, occasionally you do want to share variables across procedures. If an application is designed to do a calculation involving one interest rate at a time, that rate should be available to all the procedures in the form. Variables that do this are called *form level variables*. Figure 5-3 gives the scope of variables for a Visual Basic project having one form only.

As with the DEF*type* statements, you put the DIM statements for form level variables in the leading code of the form, using the additional keyword SHARED. For example, if you enter

```
DIM SHARED InterestRate AS CURRENCY
```

in the leading code of the form, then the following is true:

☐ The value of the variable InterestRate will be visible to all the procedures attached to the form.

☐ Any changes made in one procedure will persist.

Obviously, the last point means you have to be careful when assigning values to form level variables. Any information passed between procedures is a potential breeding ground for programming bugs. Moreover, these errors are often hard to pinpoint.

Although most programmers don't think it is a good idea, you can use the same variable name as both a local and a form level variable. Any DIM statements contained in a procedure take precedence over form level

FIGURE 5-3   Scope of variables

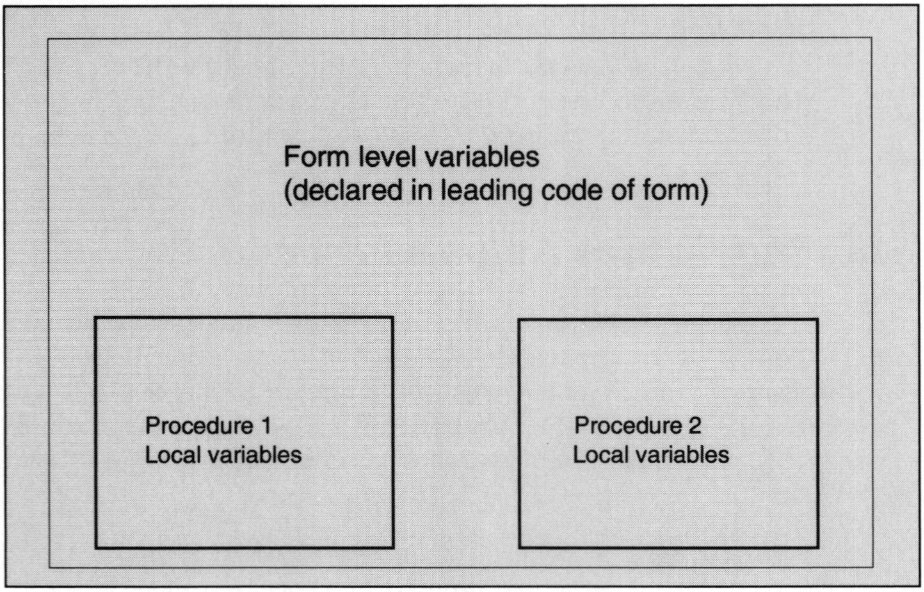

Form level variables
(declared in leading code of form)

Procedure 1
Local variables

Procedure 2
Local variables

declarations—they force a variable to be local. Therefore, you lose the ability to use the information contained in the form level variable (and so the scope of the variable would shrink). Duplicating the names makes the form level variable invisible to the procedure. Visual Basic doesn't tell you whether a form level variable has been defined with the same name as a local variable. This is one more reason to make sure that variables you want to be local really are local by declaring them with DIM inside the procedure. This forces the variable to be local to that procedure.

Having Values Persist

When Visual Basic invokes an event procedure, the old values of local variables are wiped out. They go back to their default values. (As mentioned before, you are usually better off if they are reinitialized.) Such variables are called *dynamic variables.* However, such variables are not enough for all programming situations. For example, suppose you need to keep track of how many times a command button has been clicked. If the counter is always set back to zero, you're in trouble. You *could* have the values persist by using a form level variable, but it is generally a good idea to reserve form level variables only for sharing information. Most programmers choose this method only if other event procedures need the count.

The solution is to use *static variables.* These variables are not reinitialized each time Visual Basic invokes a procedure. Besides being ideal for counters, they are ideal for making controls alternately visible or invisible (or for switching between any Boolean properties, for that matter) and as a debugging tool.

To make a variable static within a procedure, replace the keyword DIM with the keyword STATIC:

```
STATIC Counter AS INTEGER, IsVisible AS INTEGER
```

Here is an example of an event procedure for a command button that counts the clicks and displays the number:

```
SUB Command1_Click()
    'This procedure uses a static variable to count clicks
```

```
  STATIC Counter AS INTEGER
  Counter = Counter + 1
  PRINT Counter
END SUB
```

The first time you click, the counter starts out with its default value of zero. Visual Basic then adds 1 to it and prints the result. Notice that by placing the PRINT method after the addition, you are not off by 1 in the count.

Occasionally, you want all local variables within a procedure to be static. To do this, add the keyword STATIC before the word "SUB" that starts any procedure. For example:

```
STATIC SUB Command1_Click( )
```

Strings

Since information in Visual Basic forms is always displayed as text, strings are far more important in Visual Basic than in ordinary BASICs. To put two strings together (*concatenate* them), use a plus sign (+). For example, if

```
Title$ = "Queen "
Name$ = "Elizabeth "
WhichOne$ = "I"
```

then

Title\$ + Name\$ + WhichOne\$ is "Queen Elizabeth I"
Title\$ + Name\$ + WhichOne\$ + WhichOne\$ is "Queen Elizabeth II"

The + joins strings in the order you present them. Thus, unlike adding numbers together, order is important when you use the + sign to join two strings together. You can use the + sign to join together two strings before Visual Basic makes an assignment. For example, using the variables defined above:

```
CurrentQueen$ = Title$ + Name$ + WhichOne$ + WhichOne$
```

ASCII Codes

A computer doesn't have one kind of memory for text and another for numbers. Anything stored in a computer's memory is changed into numbers (actually, a binary representation of a number). The program keeps track of whether the memory patterns are codes for text or not. Usually, the code for translating text to numbers is called the ASCII code (American Standard Code for Information Interchange). The ASCII code associates each number from 0 through 255 with a displayable or control character (see Appendix A). The control characters and special keys such as TAB and LINE FEED have numbers less than 32. The value of the function CHR$(n) is the string consisting of the character with ASCII value n. The statement

```
PRINT CHR$(n)
```

either displays the character numbered n in the ASCII sequence or produces the specified effect that the control code will have on your screen, or both. For instance, the statement

```
PRINT CHR$(1)
```

displays a smiling face and the statement

```
PRINT CHR$(227)
```

prints the Greek letter pi (π) on the screen.

The following code uses the ASCII value for the quotation mark, 34, to display a sentence surrounded with quotation marks.

```
PRINT CHR$(34);
PRINT "Quoth the raven, nevermore.";
PRINT CHR$(34)
```

The output of this command looks like:

```
"Quoth the raven, nevermore."
```

The preceding output also can be produced by the statement

```
PRINT """Quoth the raven, nevermore."""
```

since Visual Basic—unlike other forms of DOS BASIC—treats " " as the literal quotation mark inside PRINT statements.

Visual Basic has a function that takes a string expression and returns the ASCII value of the first character: it is ASC. If the string is empty (the null string), using this function generates a run-time error.

As you'll see in Chapter 6, ASCII order is what Visual Basic uses to compare strings when you use relational operators like < or >. The most important use of the ASCII codes is for the KeyPress event procedure, which also is covered in Chapter 6.

The New Line Code

One of the most important uses of the CHR$ function is to set up a new line code for use in your programs. If you want to place separate lines in a multi-line text box or add breaks in a message box, you'll need this code.

As with old-fashioned typewriters, new lines are made up of two parts: a carriage return to bring the cursor to the first column and a line feed to move it to the next line. To set up a new line code, first define NewLine as a form level string variable and then define:

```
NewLine = CHR$(13) + CHR$(10)
```

in the Form_Load procedure. (CHR$(13) is the carriage return and CHR$(10) is the line feed.)

Now you can add line breaks in message boxes or multi-line text boxes by using the NewLine character. The fastest way to do this is to set up a string variable that includes the NewLine character:

```
TextString$ = "Visual Basic For DOS" + NewLine
TextString$ = TextString$ + "Osborne McGraw-Hill" + NewLIne
TextString$ = TextString$ + "Berkeley, CA"
Text1.Text = TextString$
```

Similarly, you can force a break in a message box by setting up a message string using the NewLine character.

Fixed-Length Strings

A fixed-length string is a special type of string that plays an important role in later chapters (Chapter 9 and 13). These variables are created with a DIM statement. For example:

```
DIM ShortString AS STRING * 10
```

sets up a string variable (in spite of not using the identifier). However, this variable will always hold strings of length 10. If you assign a longer string to ShortString, as shown here:

```
ShortString = "antidisestablishment"
```

what you get is the same thing as:

```
ShortString = "antidisest"
```

As you can see, the contents of the variable are changed because the right part of the string is cut off. Similarly, if you assign a shorter string to ShortString, like this:

```
ShortString = "a"
```

then you still get a string of length 10. Only this time the variable is padded on the right so that the string is really stored in the same way as:

```
ShortString = "a         "
```

Thus, fixed-length strings are "right padded" with spaces if necessary.

Chapter 13 explains how fixed-length strings are used with random-access files. People whose only experience is with the clumsy method of handling random-access files in interpreted BASIC are in for a very pleasant surprise.

Numbers

Numbers in Visual Basic cannot use commas. They *can* use a decimal point, unless they are integers or long integers. If you need to give a numeric value to a variable, place the number on the right-hand side of the assignment statement. If you assign a number with a decimal point to an integer variable, it is automatically rounded. If you assign a number larger than the limits for the given variable, Visual Basic gives you an error message at run time.

Here are some examples:

Number	Acceptable Variable Type
3001	Okay for all numeric variables
3000001	Okay for all but (short) integer variables
30000.01	Okay for all but integer variables (rounded for them)
3,001	Illegal because it uses a comma

To change a string of digits to a number, use the built-in function VAL:

VAL("3001") is 3001

The VAL function will be used extensively in all your Visual Basic applications. This is because all input received from text boxes is in the form of strings (text).

The VAL function reads through the string until it encounters a nonnumeric character (or a second period). The number you get from it is determined by where it stopped searching

VAL("30Something") = 30

Similarly, you will have to change a number back to a string of digits when you want to display it in a text box. There are many ways to do this, depending on the form you want the number to take. The function STR$ is the simplest. It converts a number to a string but doesn't clean it up in any way. It also leaves a space in front of positive numbers:

```
STR$(123)         = " 123"
STR$(123.4567)    = " 123.4567"
STR$(-987654321)  = "-987654321"
```

To polish the display, the STR$ function is often replaced by the FORMAT$ function. (See the section "The FORMAT$ Function" in Chapter 7.) The FORMAT$ function is very versatile. Among its many features, this function lets you cut off extraneous digits and display a (large) number with commas or a leading dollar sign.

Operations on Numbers

The following table gives the symbols for the five fundamental arithmetic operations:

Operator	Operation
+	Addition
–	Subtraction (and to denote negative numbers)
/	Division
*	Multiplication
^	Exponentiation

For integers and long integers, there is one symbol and one keyword for the arithmetic operations that are unique to numbers of these types:

Operator	Operation
\	Integer division (this symbol is a backslash)
MOD	The remainder after integer division

The ordinary division symbol (/) gives you a value that is a single-precision, double-precision, or currency answer, depending on the numbers involved. Integer division, which is represented by the backslash (\), is division that throws away the remainder in order to give you an integer. For example, 7 \ 3 = 2. Since a / gives either a single- or double-precision answer, use a \ (backslash) if you really want to work with integers or long integers. If you use the \ or MOD operator with non-integers, Visual

Basic throws away anything to the right of the decimal point before proceeding.

The MOD operator yields the remainder after integer division. For example, 7 MOD 3 is 1. When one integer perfectly divides another, there is no remainder, so the MOD operator gives zero: 8 MOD 4 is 0.

The usual term for a combination of numbers, variables, and operators from which Visual Basic can extract a value is a *numeric expression*.

Parentheses and Precedence

When you do calculations, you have two ways to indicate the order in which you want operations to occur. The first way is by using parentheses, and you may well prefer this method. Parentheses let you easily specify the order in which operations occur. Something like 3 + (4 * 5) gives 23 because Visual Basic does the operation within the parentheses (4 times 5) first and only then adds the 3. On the other hand, (3 + 4) * 5 gives 35 because Visual Basic adds the 3 and the 4 first to get 7 and only then multiplies by 5.

Here's another example:

((6 * 5) + 4) * 3

The innermost parentheses give 30, the second set of parentheses tells Visual Basic to add 4 to get 34, and then Visual Basic multiplies by 3 to get 102.

Visual Basic allows you to avoid parentheses, provided you carefully follow rules that determine the precedence of the mathematical operations. For example, multiplication has higher precedence than addition. This means 3 + 4 * 5 is 23 rather than 35 because the multiplication (4 * 5) is done before the addition.

The following list gives the order (hierarchy) of operations:

exponentiation (^)
negation (making a number negative)
multiplication and division
integer division
the remainder (MOD) operation
addition and subtraction

For example, –4 ^ 2 gives –16 because Visual Basic first does the exponentiation (4 ^ 2 = 4 * 4 = 16) and only then makes the number negative.

Think of these as being levels. Operations on the same level are done from left to right, so 96 / 4 * 2 is 48. Because division and multiplication are on the same level, first the division is done, giving 24, and then the multiplication is done. On the other hand, 96 / 4 ^ 2 is 6. This is because the exponentiation is done first, yielding 16, and only then is the division done.

To show you how obscure using the hierarchy of operations can make your programs, try to figure out what Visual Basic would do with this:

4*2 + 16/8 + 2^3^4

Here's what happens: first the exponentials (level 1) are computed left to right (2 ^ 3 = 8, 8 ^ 4 = 8 * 8 * 8 * 8 = 4096), then the multiplication and division from left to right (4 * 2 = 8, 16 / 8 = 2), and then the addition (8 + 2 + 4096 = 4106).

Examples like this one should convince you that a judicious use of parentheses will make your programs clearer and your life easier as a result.

More on Numbers in Visual Basic

If you've tried any calculations involving large numbers in Visual Basic, you've probably discovered that Visual Basic often doesn't bother printing out large numbers. Instead, it uses a variant on *scientific notation*. For example, if you ask Visual Basic to print a 1 followed by 25 zeros using a statement like PRINT 10^25, what you see is 1E+25 (the E stands for exponent).

If you are not familiar with this notation, think of the E+ as meaning: move the decimal place to the right, adding zeros if necessary. The number of places is exactly the number following the "E." If a negative number follows the "E," move the decimal point to the left. For example, 2.1E–5 gives you .000021. You can enter a number using the E notation if it's convenient; Visual Basic doesn't care whether you enter 1000, 1E3, or 1E+3. To make a number double precision, use a "D" instead of an "E."

If you assign the value of a single-precision variable to a double-precision variable, you do not suddenly increase its accuracy. The number may have more (or even different) digits, but only the first seven or eight can be trusted. When you assign a value of one type to a variable of a different type, Visual Basic does a type conversion if it can. If it cannot figure out a way to do this that makes sense, it generates an error at run time.

When you use numbers in your program, Visual Basic assumes the following:

☐   If a number has no decimal point and is in the range –32768 to 32767, it's an integer.

☐   If a number has no decimal point and is in the range for a long integer (–2,147,483,648 to 2,147,483,647), it's a long integer.

☐   If a number has a decimal point and is in the range for a single-precision number, it is assumed to be single precision.

☐   If a number has a decimal point and is outside the range for a single-precision number, it is assumed to be double precision.

These built-in assumptions occasionally lead to problems. This is because the type of an answer is determined by the types of the questions. If you start out with two integers, Visual Basic assumes the answer is also an integer. For example, a statement like

```
PRINT 12345 * 6789
```

starts with two integers, so the answer is assumed to also be an integer. But the answer is too large for the limits on Visual Basic's integers, so you would get an overflow error. The solution is to add the appropriate identifier to at least one of the numbers. Use the statement

```
PRINT 12345& * 6789
```

and Visual Basic treats both 12345 and the answer as long integers—so no error message results.

You can also use one of the built-in functions to force a type conversion:

Conversion Function	What It Does
CINT	Makes a numeric expression an integer by rounding
CLNG	Makes a numeric expression a long integer by rounding
CSNG	Makes a numeric expression single precision
CDBL	Makes a numeric expression double precision
CCUR	Makes a numeric expression of the currency type

You must do the conversion before the calculation: PRINT CLNG(12345 * 6789) still generates an error message. You need to use PRINT CLNG(12345) * 6789. Conversions will be done only if the numbers you're trying to convert are in the range of the new type; otherwise Visual Basic generates an error message. Using the conversion functions has the same effect as assigning the numeric expression to a variable of the type specified.

An Example Program: A Mortgage Calculator

You now have seen enough of Visual Basic to write a really useful program: a mortgage calculator. At this stage, what this program will do is allow a user to enter the amount of the mortgage, the interest rate, and the term in years in three text boxes. Then the program will calculate the monthly mortgage payment.

The first thing to do is design the form. Figure 5-4 shows the form. This form has two command buttons, four labels, and four text boxes. It uses the default sizes for all the controls. This lets you use the double-click method for generating them. You then need to drag the controls around until you are happy with the locations. Table 5-1 lists the controls in this project, following the tab order.

As you can see in Figure 5-4 or by looking at the ampersands in Table 5-1, this form has many access keys for the controls. There are even access keys for the labels. As you saw in Chapter 4, this gives quick access to the text boxes. For this to work, though, the text box must follow the label in tab order. The TabStop property for the MortgagePayment text box has been changed to False since there is no reason in this application to allow the user to move the focus to this box. (Another possibility is to set the Enabled property to False, but this has the side effect of graying the box. One other possibility is to use a label with the border style property set to 1—to give the appearance of a text box.)

Let's go over one way to code this application. All the code is attached to the two command buttons. The code for the Quit button is easy:

```
SUB Quit_Click ()
    END
END SUB
```

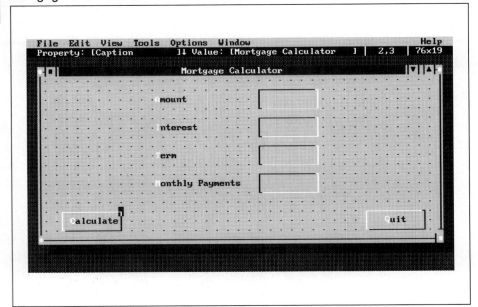

FIGURE 5-4
Mortgage calculator form

TABLE 5-1 The Controls for the Mortgage Calculator Program in Tab Order

Control	Control Name	Caption (or Text)
Form		Mortgage Calculator
1st label	Label1	&Amount
1st text box	MortgageAmount	
2nd label	Label2	&Interest
2nd text box	InterestRate	
3rd label	Label3	&Term
3rd text box	MortgageTerm	
4th label	Label4	Monthly Payment
4th text box	MortgagePayment	
Left command button	Calculate	Calculate
Right command button	Quit	Quit

The code to actually calculate the mortgage payment is a little more complicated. First, you need a formula for mortgage payments. The formula for monthly mortgage payments is

*Principal * MonthInt/(1 − (1/ (1 + MonthInt)) ^ (Years * 12))*

where *MonthInt* is the annual interest rate divided by 12. Here's the code that activates the calculation.

```
SUB Calculate_Click ()
  'Calculate the mortgage
  'using the formula  Payment =
  'Principal*MonthInt/(1-(1/(1+MonthInt))^(Years*12))

  'local variables
  DIM Years AS INTEGER, Payment AS CURRENCY
  DIM MonthInt AS SINGLE, Amount AS CURRENCY
  DIM Percent AS SINGLE, Principal AS CURRENCY
```

```
'Get info
Years = VAL(MortgageTerm.Text)
Principal = VAL(MortgageAmount.Text)
Percent = VAL(InterestRate.Text) / 100

MonthInt = Percent / 12
'compute payment
Payment = Principal * MonthInt / (1 - (1 / (1 + MonthInt)) ^_
(Years * 12))       'this and preceding line are one line
MortgagePayment.Text = STR$(Payment)
END SUB
```

For more accuracy, this program keeps the years in an integer variable, the interest rate and percent as a single-precision number, and all the others as currency variables. The program will run a little more quickly if it uses single-precision variables instead of currency variables. The next point to remember is that text boxes do not give numbers; you always need to convert the data inside them by using the VAL command. This program assumes that the user enters the interest rate as a percent. Because the VAL function stops when it encounters a nonnumeric character, the user may use a percent sign at the end of what he or she types. (Converting a percent to a decimal means dividing by 100.) To make the logic of the program clearer, there is a separate calculation for the monthly interest.

Finally, the program has to convert the data back to a string in order to assign it to the text property of the MortgagePayment text box.

Improvements to the Mortgage Calculator

There are lots of ways the mortgage calculator program can be improved. Probably the most important would be to make the program more "bulletproof." Inexperienced users often enter information in the wrong form or use the wrong kind of information. For example, they might use commas or dollar signs for the mortgage amounts. In the next chapter you'll see how to write the code to either allow or prevent this as you see fit.

For now, though, suppose you wanted to add two command buttons that either increase or decrease the interest rate (say by 1/8% = .00125) and then redo the calculations. Here's a simple way to write the code for a button to increase the interest rate:

```
SUB Increase_Click ()
  DIM NewRate AS SINGLE

  Percent = VAL(InterestRate.Text) / 100
  NewRate = (Percent + .00125) * 100
  InterestRate.Text = STR$(NewRate)
  CALL Calculate_Click
END SUB
```

Before getting to the question of why this program may not be the best solution, take a look at the key statement, CALL Calculate_Click. This is the first example you've seen of one event procedure using (the technical term is *calling*) another event procedure. Chapter 8 discusses this in depth.

As your programs become more sophisticated, event procedures will be more and more interrelated. In this case, when Visual Basic calls the Click procedure, it uses the current contents of the text boxes. Because the line

```
InterestRate.Text = STR$(NewRate)
```

changes the contents of the text box directly, the Click procedure has new data to work with.

Now why would some people think this version of the mortgage program is not the most efficient programming solution? The offending line is

```
Percent = VAL(InterestRate.Text) / 100
```

What this line does is recalculate something that has been calculated once already. While not a mistake, it is inefficient. In a more complicated program, these inefficiencies might grow until they really put a drag on the performance of your application. They also might become a breeding ground for bugs. A better solution is to make all the numeric information from the text boxes the values of form level variables. Add the following to the leading (module level) code of the form:

```
DIM SHARED Principle AS SINGLE
DIM SHARED Years AS INTEGER, Percent AS SINGLE
```

Now remove the corresponding declarations from the Calculate_Click event procedure and eliminate the recalculation of Percent in the Increase_Click event procedure.

Inefficiencies are common when you modify an old program for new uses. You end up forcing the original program into a frame in which it was never supposed to appear. You're likely to introduce bugs as well. Often you're better off rewriting the program from scratch.

Debugging a program will always be necessary, but it will never be fun. Programs rarely run perfectly the first time. One way to cut down on debugging time is to get into the habit of "thinking first and coding later" (sometimes described as "the sooner you start coding, the longer it takes"). If you think through the possibilities carefully first—for example, deciding which variables should be global and which should be local— you'll go a long way towards "bug proofing" your programs.

Constants

A program is easiest to debug when it's readable. You should prevent the MEGO (My Eyes Glaze Over) syndrome that is all too common when a program has lots of mysterious numbers sprinkled about. It's a lot easier to read lines of code like

```
Calculate.Visible = TRUE
Text1.CurrentY = PageLength
```

than one like

```
Calculate.Visible = -1
Text1.CurrentY = 66
```

Visual Basic's *named constant* feature allows you to use mnemonic names for values that never change. (Programs using constants instead of variables for the right hand of assignment statements will also run faster.) The rules for naming named constants are the same as for variables: 40 characters, first character a letter, and then any combination of letters, underscores, and numerals. The convention is to use all capitals for named constants.

You set up a named constant by using the keyword *CONST* followed by the name of the constant, an equal sign, and then the value:

```
CONST TRUE = -1
CONST FALSE = 0
CONST PI = 3.14159
```

You can set up string constants:

```
CONST USERNAME = "John Doe"
CONST LANGUAGE = "Visual Basic Version 1.0"
```

You can even use numeric expressions to assign values to named constants—or define new named constants in terms of previously defined named constants:

```
CONST PIOVER2 = PI / 2
```

What you can't do is define a named constant in terms of Visual Basic's built-in functions or the exponentiation operator. If you need the square root of ten in a program, you need to calculate it (for example in the Immediate window) before you can write

```
CONST SQUAREROOTOFTEN = 3.162278
```

You also can't use the + sign to join together two strings to define a string constant.

Visual Basic uses the simplest type it can for a constant, but you can override this by adding a type identifier to a constant. For example,

```
CONST THISWILLBEALONGINTEGER& = 37
```

forces Visual Basic to treat the number 37 as a long integer instead of an ordinary integer. (Named constants are not affected by any DEF*type* statements you set up.) Even if you use a type identifier at the end of the constant when you define it, you don't need to use the identifier in the program. Using the preceding example, all subsequent occurrences of this constant can be

THISWILLBEALONGINTEGER

As mentioned, the convention is to use all caps for constants, but this is not required. Moreover, references to constants don't depend on the case.

Usually you put constant definitions in the leading code for the form as you did with DEF*type* statements. You can also define a named constant within a procedure, but this is unusual, and only that procedure would have access to the constant. Finally, Visual Basic comes with a large number of pre-defined constants that you may find useful in your programs; for more on this file, see Chapter 7.

INPUT Boxes

Text boxes are the normal way for a Visual Basic application to accept data. (For those who know ordinary BASIC, the INPUT statement is not allowed when a form is showing.) There is one other technique that is occasionally useful. The INPUTBOX$ function displays a dialog box on the screen. The principal advantage of input boxes is that they insist that a user supply some necessary data before letting him or her move on in the application. The disadvantage is that the dimensions of the input box are fixed beforehand. Here is an example of an input box:

As you can see, input boxes have a title and four components, three of which are controls. The first is the prompt ("Please enter your name" in this case). There are always two command buttons labeled OK and Cancel. Finally, there is a text box at the bottom. Visual Basic always places the focus here when it processes a statement containing an InputBox$ function. The simplest syntax for the InputBox$ function is

StringVariable = INPUTBOX$(*prompt*$)

where the prompt is a string or string variable. This gives a dialog box that is roughly centered horizontally and one-third of the way down the screen.

Now the user types whatever he or she wants in the text box. Pressing ENTER or clicking the OK button causes whatever is in the text box to become the value of the string variable. Pressing ESC or clicking the Cancel button causes Visual Basic to assign the null string to the variable. The full syntax for the InputBox$ function is

Var$ = INPUTBOX$(*prompt*$ [,*title*$, *default*$, *xpos*%, *ypos*%])

Here are short descriptions of these items.

**prompt$**   The *prompt*$ is a string or string variable whose value Visual Basic displays in the dialog box. It is limited to 255 characters. If necessary, the prompt wraps around to additional lines. You may also explicitly add line separators if you wish. (See the section in this chapter on "The New Line Code" for how to do this.)

**title$**   The *title*$ is optional and gives the caption used in the title bar. There is no default value; if you leave this out, nothing is displayed in the title bar. Any string larger than 46 characters is cut off from the right.

**default$**   The *default*$ is also optional. It lets you display default text in the Edit box where the user will be entering information. If you leave this off, Visual Basic will use the empty string.

xpos%,ypos%   Also optional, both *xpos*% and *ypos*% are integer numeric expressions. *xpos*% is the distance in columns between the left edge of the input box and the left edge of the screen. *ypos*% gives the distance in rows between the top of the box and the top of the screen.

The notation just presented may seem cryptic at first, but it is a good idea to get used to it. It is the notation used in both the manual and the on-line documentation. With this notation, anything in square brackets is optional. In this case, the parentheses are outside the square brackets, so they are required. The commas separate the optional elements (the *arguments*) in this function. If you skip one of the arguments, you still have to use a comma as a separator. (How else would Visual Basic know which argument belongs where?) For example,

X$ = INPUTBOX$("Example",, *default$*, *xpos%*, *ypos%*)

leaves out the title of the dialog box.

Printing to Forms

The general syntax for the PRINT method applied to a form is

FormName.PRINT *expressions to print*

 Caution: Early versions of Visual Basic will crash a program with an "Overflow" error message if you try to print too many lines to a form. Since information on a form doesn't scroll anyway, you are better off using a multi-line text box with scroll bars in this situation.

Where Visual Basic displays the information depends on the current value of two properties of a form, called CurrentX and CurrentY. CurrentX refers to the horizontal position where Visual Basic will display information, and CurrentY refers to the vertical position where it will display information. The units used are columns and rows. As long as you are using a single form (see Chapter 14 for multiple form applications), or restrict yourself to procedures attached to a form, the form name is optional.

Whenever you use the CLS method to clear a form, Visual Basic resets the CurrentX and CurrentY values to zero, so that the next PRINT statement puts information in the top left-hand corner of the form.

You set CurrentX and CurrentY the same way you'd set any property:

CurrentX = *Value*
CurrentY = *Value*

The values may be any numeric expression resulting in a value from 0 to 254.

An Example of Centering Text Inside a Form

Suppose you wanted to display a message in the center of a form. Here is an outline of what you need to do to find the coordinates of the center of the form:

1. Find the current values of the ScaleHeight and ScaleWidth properties. This tells you the size of the internal area of the form (without the borders and title bar).

2. Divide these values in half.

The problem is that this doesn't quite finish the job. If you reset the values CurrentX and CurrentY to the results from step 2 of this outline, you would start printing at the center of the screen, but the message wouldn't be centered. What you also need to do is take into account the length of the message and then shift over by half the length of the message. The key to do this is the built-in method TEXTWIDTH. The syntax for the TEXTWIDTH method is

[*FormName.*]TEXTWIDTH(*string*)

Where, as usual, the brackets indicate that the form name is optional. After processing this statement, Visual Basic returns the value for the width in columns of the string inside the parentheses. In general, TEXTWIDTH is the amount of horizontal space you need to display a string. If the string contains any carriage returns, then this method returns the length of the longest single line.

3. Use the TEXTWIDTH method on the string you want to center. Now subtract one-half the value Visual Basic obtains from this method from the value in step 2, and make this the value of CurrentX.

Here is another example where these methods are useful. Suppose you want to display information at the beginning of the tenth line of text as it would appear in the ordinary coordinate system (0,0 as the top left). Use the following fragment:

```
CurrentY = 9
CurrentX = 0
```

You have to use 9 rather than 10 to take into account that Visual Basic numbers the rows of a form as 0, 1, 2, etc.

The TEXTHEIGHT Method

The counterpart to the TEXTWIDTH method used in the preceding section is the TEXTHEIGHT method, which returns one more than the number of carriage return/line feed sequences contained in the string.

The TEXTHEIGHT method lets you center text vertically on the form. For this all you have to do is to set CurrentY to be:

SCALEHEIGHT / 2 - TEXTHEIGHT(*string*) / 2

Tables

Although the CurrentX and CurrentY properties give you absolute control over the placement of text in a form, this is often too cumbersome a method to use. When you want to display a table on a blank form, you are often better off using the built-in *print zones*. Print zones are preset 14 columns apart.

Each time you use a comma in a PRINT method (statement), Visual Basic displays the data to the next print zone. For example, a statement like

```
PRINT FirstName$, MiddleInit$, LastName$
```

tries to have the value of the string variable FirstName$ printed in the first zone, the value of the variable MiddleInit$ at the beginning of the second zone, and the value of the variable LastName$ printed at the beginning of the third zone. However, if a previous expression runs over into the next print zone, Visual Basic moves to the beginning of the first unused print zone. (This may cause printing to resume on the line below.)

The TAB and SPC Commands and Semicolons

Normally, after Visual Basic processes a statement involving the PRINT method, it moves to the next line. You also use an empty PRINT statement to add a blank line. If you want to suppress the automatic carriage return/line feed, place a semicolon at the end of the statement. For example:

```
SUB Form_Click ()
  'Demonstrate the use of a semi-colon

  Form1.PRINT "This is a test "
  Form1.PRINT "of the PRINT method."
  Form1.PRINT                        'blank line
  Form1.PRINT "This is a test ";
  Form1.PRINT "of the PRINT method."
END SUB
```

The output of this click procedure looks like this:

This is a test
of the PRINT method.

This is a test of the PRINT method.

The TAB function lets you move to a specific column and start printing there. Its syntax is

PRINT TAB(*ColumnNumber*%);

ColumnNumber% is an integer expression. If the current column position is greater than its value, TAB skips to this column on the next line. If the value is less than 1, Visual Basic moves to the first column.

The SPC function has a similar syntax to the TAB function:

SPC(*Integer*%)

This function inserts the specified number of spaces into a line starting at the current print position. The value inside the parentheses can't be negative.

The Printer

You've already seen one method for sending information to a printer: the PRINTFORM method sends a screen dump of a form to the printer. Because this method does a character-by-character dump of the whole form (including captions and borders), it lacks flexibility.

The usual way to send information to a printer is the PRINT method, which also sends information to a form. Since Visual Basic methods only apply to Visual Basic objects, you need a built-in Visual Basic object corresponding to the printer. The object for printing is called, naturally enough, the Printer Object.

The syntax used to send text to the printer is

Printer.PRINT *text*

Semicolons and commas work the same way they do for forms. The semicolon suppresses the automatic carriage return/line feed; the comma moves to the next free print zone (still 14 columns apart). The TAB and SPC functions also work similarly.

Properties and Methods for the Printer

One property and two methods for the printer are available in Visual Basic.

ENDDOC   You use the ENDDOC method to indicate that a document is finished. The syntax is

Printer.ENDDOC

This releases whatever information there is about the page or pages still in memory and sends it to the printer.

NEWPAGE   The NEWPAGE method ends the current page and tells the printer to move to the next page; that is, it performs a form feed. The syntax is

Printer.NEWPAGE

Controlling Printers

Modern printers, whether dot matrix, ink jet, or laser, are quite versatile. You can usually control the size, positioning, and even the fonts used in printing text. Many printers let you control the placement of each dot on a page.

The codes that control the features of a printer usually vary from printer to printer, but the features are usually invoked by sending either a control code (an ASCII code less than 32) or a combination of control codes. For example, on most Epson dot-matrix printers, you would turn on the compressed mode (usually 132 characters to the standard line) by the following:

```
Printer.PRINT CHR$(15);
```

To turn off this feature, you need to have Visual Basic process a line of code like:

```
Printer.PRINT CHR$(18);
```

The other way to control a printer involves sending it more than one character code at a time. Most of these combination codes are preceded by the special code for the ESC key (ASCII 27). For example, to turn underline printing on for the EPSON class of printers, send:

```
Printer.PRINT CHR$(27) + "-1";
```

To turn it off, send:

```
Printer.PRINT CHR$(27) + "-0";
```

You should check the documentation that comes with any specific printer to find out the codes needed to control that particular printer.

CHAPTER

Controlling
Program Flow

*T*his chapter shows you how to make a program repeat operations (loops) or check if a condition is True or False (conditionals). The parts of a programming language that let you do this are *control structures.* This term has nothing to do with the controls you place on forms in Visual Basic. The control structures in Visual Basic are essentially the same ones that are in QuickBASIC; users familiar with QuickBASIC may need only to skim this chapter. If you are familiar only with GW-BASIC, you're in for a pleasant surprise. The control structures in Visual Basic are far richer and allow you far more flexibility than the ones in the older, interpreted BASICs.

Repeating Operations

Suppose you need to repeat an operation. You may want to repeat the operation a fixed number of times, continue until you reach a predetermined specific goal, or continue until certain initial conditions have finally changed. In programming, the first situation is called a *determinate loop* and the latter two are called *indeterminate loops.* Visual Basic allows all three kinds of loops, so there are three different control structures in Visual Basic for repeating operations.

Determinate Loops

Suppose you want to print the numbers 1 to 10 on the current form using code inside an event procedure. The simplest way to do this is to place the following lines of code inside the procedure:

```
FOR I% = 1 TO 10
  PRINT I%
NEXT I%
```

The line with the FOR and TO keywords above is shorthand, meaning "FOR every value of I% from 1 TO 10."

FOR and NEXT are keywords that must be used together. The statements between the FOR and the NEXT are usually called the body of the loop, and the whole control structure is called, naturally enough, a FOR-NEXT loop.

Think of a FOR-NEXT loop as winding up a wheel inside the computer so it will spin a fixed number of times. During each spin of the wheel, the computer can be told what it is you want it to do.

The keyword FOR sets up a *counter variable*. In the preceding example, it's an integer variable, I%. In this example, the starting value for the counter is set to 1. The ending value is set to 10. Visual Basic first sets the counter variable to the starting value. Then it checks that the value for the counter is less than the ending value. If it is greater than the starting value, nothing is done. If the starting value is less than the ending value, Visual Basic processes subsequent statements until it gets to the keyword NEXT. At that point it adds 1 to the counter variable and starts the process again. This process continues until the counter variable is larger than the ending value. At that point, the loop is finished and Visual Basic moves past it. A flow diagram for the FOR-NEXT loop is shown in Figure 6-1.

 Tip You can use any type of numeric variable for the counter; however, keep in mind that Visual Basic works quickest with integer variables on the arithmetic needed to change the counter.

Finally, you may have noticed that the body of the FOR-NEXT loop was indented. As always, the spacing within a program is there to make the program more readable and therefore easier to debug. The designers of Visual Basic made it easy to consistently indent code. The Visual Basic editor remembers the indentation of the previous line, and every time you press ENTER, the cursor returns to the spot directly below where the previous line started. To indent further, simply press TAB. Each TAB stop is set several spaces in from the previous one. To move the cursor back one unit of indentation when using the auto indent feature, press BACKSPACE. Or, if you have already begun typing on the new line, use the SHIFT+TAB combination to move the text left by one TAB stop. (The cursor itself will not move.) You may indent or unindent an entire block by selecting the block of text and then pressing TAB or SHIFT+TAB, respectively. (To select a block of text, place the cursor at the beginning of the text and hold down the shift key while moving the cursor with the arrow keys.)

FIGURE
6-1

Flow diagram for FOR-NEXT loop

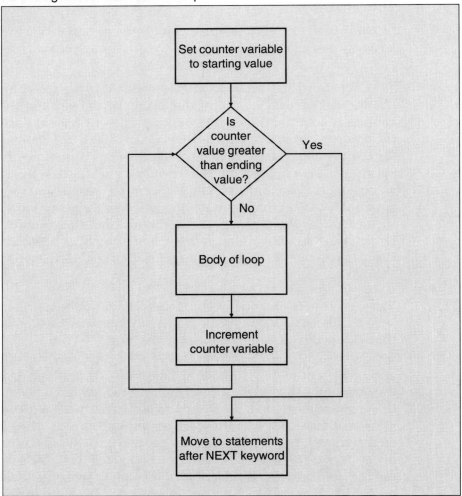

An Example: A Retirement Calculator

With a FOR-NEXT loop, you can compute many financial quantities without knowing a formula. For example, suppose you wanted to write a program that would allow users to enter the following:

- ☐ The fixed amount of money they think they can save for retirement each year

- ☐ The interest rate they expect to get each year

- ☐ The number of years until retirement

The program would then tell them how much money they will have when they retire. There are sophisticated formulas involving geometric progressions for this sort of calculation, but a simple FOR-NEXT loop suffices to calculate each year's interest and the total amount.

Assume that the interest is compounded annually. This program will need four text boxes, four labels, and two command buttons. The screen in Figure 6-2 shows the form. The control names for the controls in the program should be self-documenting: AmountPerYear, InterestRate, NumberOfYears, and NestEgg. The command buttons are named Calculate and Quit.

Here is the Calculate_Click procedure:

```
SUB Calculate_Click()
  'Calculate retirement value assuming fixed
  'deposit and fixed interest rate

  'local variables are
  DIM Amount AS CURRENCY, Total AS CURRENCY
  DIM Interest AS SINGLE
  DIM Years AS INTEGER, I AS INTEGER
  Total = 0
  Amount = VAL(AmountPerYear.Text)
  Interest = VAL(InterestRate.Text) / 100
  Years = VAL(NumberOfYears.Text)
  FOR I = 1 TO Years
    Total = Amount + Total + (Total * Interest)
  NEXT I
  NestEgg.Text = STR$(Total)
END SUB
```

The program calculates each year's total as the previous total plus interest earned. The final result appears to the user as the Nest Egg amount.

FIGURE
6-2

Form for retirement calculator

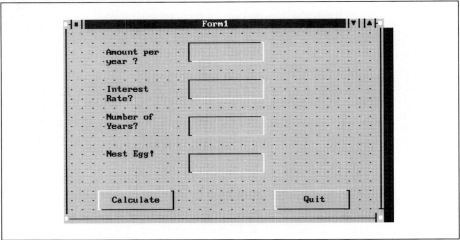

More on FOR-NEXT Loops

You don't always count by ones. Sometimes it's necessary to count by twos, by fractions, or backward. You do this by adding the STEP keyword to a FOR-NEXT loop. The STEP keyword tells Visual Basic to change the counter by the specified amount rather than by 1.

For example, a space simulation program would not be complete without the inclusion, somewhere in the program, of the fragment

```
FOR I = 10 TO 1 STEP -1
  PRINT "It's t minus"; I; "and counting."
NEXT I
PRINT "Blastoff!"
```

When you use a negative step, the body of the FOR-NEXT loop is bypassed if the starting value for the counter is smaller than the ending value.

For a more serious example, let's modify the mortgage program introduced in Chapter 5 to add a table showing the payments with varying interest rates. One way to do this is to allow the user to click a button that brings up a multi-line text box with a table showing the mortgage payments for a full percent range above and below the rate initially selected.

First, you have to add a command button and a multi-line text box with vertical scroll bars at design time. You can call this text box MortgageTable and include a label named TableLabel right above it to describe what the user will see. Since this form is becoming rather crowded, you might also consider making the text box fill the screen at run time when the user clicks the button (see Figure 6-3). You could move the controls around in the Form_Resize procedure. By setting the Visible property of the text box and label to be False at design time, you can make them visible only after the user clicks on the button.

The code for this example is surprisingly simple. Besides the code to make the label and text box visible, you need only to set the text property of the multi-line text box and enclose the original formula in a FOR-NEXT loop with a step of 1/8% = 1/800 = .00125.

```
SUB ShowTable_Click()
  'Calculates a mortgage table using original amounts
  'but having the interest rate move up by 1/8%
  'local variables and constants
  CONST TRUE = -1
  DIM NewLine AS STRING, MText$
  DIM Years AS INTEGER, Payment AS CURRENCY
  DIM MonthInt AS Single, Principal AS CURRENCY
  DIM Percent AS SINGLE, Interest  AS SINGLE
  DIM StartInterest AS SINGLE, EndInterest AS SINGLE

  NewLine = CHR$(13)+ CHR$(10)      'for multiline text box
  ' Get info
  Years = VAL(MortgageTerm.Text)
  Principal = VAL(MortgageAmount.Text)
  Percent = VAL(InterestRate.Text) / 100
  StartInterest = Percent - .01              '1% change
  EndInterest  =  Percent + .01

  'Make label and text box visible and maximize form
  ' and Print header for table using the label
  WindowState = 2
  Calculate.MOVE 0, 20
  ShowTable.MOVE 32, 20
  Quit.MOVE 64, 20
  MortgageTable.Visible = TRUE
  TabelLabel.Visible = TRUE
  TabelLabel.Caption = "Interest Rate" + SPACE$10()_
     + "Payment"
  FOR Interest = StartInterest TO EndInterest STEP .00125
```

```
      MonthInt = Interest / 12
      Payment = Principal * MonthInt / (1 - (1 / (1 + _
            MonthInt))^ (Years * 12))
      MText$ = MText$ + STR$(Interest) + _
            SPACE$(14) + STR$(Payment) + NewLine    'above &
            this one line
   NEXT Interest
   MortgageTable.Txt = MText$
END SUB
```

You might consider making the constant TRUE a form level constant as well as making the variables NewLine Years, Principal, and Percent form level variables.

Nested FOR-NEXT Loops

Suppose you wanted to allow not only a range of interest rates in the mortgage table but also a range of dollar amounts. And for each dollar amount you wanted to run through the entire range of interest rates. This is a typical situation; you have an inner loop that does something interesting in a particular case, and you want to redo the situation in a

FIGURE
6-3

Form for improved mortgage calculator

slightly different case. Placing one loop inside another is called *nesting* loops.

You'll see how to solve the mortgage table later in this section. For now, though, a simpler example to keep in mind is a multiplication table. A fragment like

```
FOR I = 2 TO 12
   PRINT 2 * I
NEXT I
```

gives you the "two's table." To get an entire multiplication table, you need to enclose this loop with another one that changes the 2 to a 3, the 3 to a 4, and so on. The loop looks like this:

```
FOR J = 2 TO 12
    FOR I = 2 TO 12
       PRINT I * J,
    NEXT I
 PRINT
NEXT J
```

Here's what is happening: The value of J starts out at 2, and then Visual Basic enters the inner loop. The value of I starts out at 2 as well. Now Visual Basic makes 11 passes through the loop before it finishes. Once it does this, it processes the extra PRINT statement before it processes the NEXT J statement. At this point Visual Basic changes the value of J to 3 and starts the process all over again.

Sometimes it's helpful to think of the inner loop in a nested FOR-NEXT loop as really doing one thing—it's a statement in Visual Basic a bit more complicated than the usual ones. If you keep in mind the idea of the inner loop of a nested FOR-NEXT loop as accomplishing one task, then an outline for the nested loops needed for the mortgage program given in the previous section is easy. Here it is:

FOR Principal = StartingAmount TO EndingAmount STEP 1/8%
    The original loop with new display statements and principal modified
NEXT Principal

Nested loops have a reputation for being hard to program, hard to understand, and a breeding ground for bugs. This doesn't have to be true. If you are careful about outlining the loops, they won't be hard to program. If you are careful about your indentation pattern, they won't be hard to understand (or, therefore, to debug).

The rule for nesting FOR-NEXT loops is simple: the inner loop must be completed before the NEXT statement for the outer loop is encountered. You can have triple-nested loops, quadruple-nested loops, or even more. You are limited only by how well you understand the concept, not by Visual Basic.

Indeterminate Loops

Going back to the retirement example from a few pages ago, suppose the problem changes a little bit. Now, instead of asking how much money the user would have at the end of a specified number of years, the question is how long it would take to get $1,000,000—again assuming the same amount of money is put in each year and the interest rate doesn't change. You could use the previous program and try trial and error, but that would not be very useful. You will soon see how to resolve this and many related problems.

These types of problems come up repeatedly in programming. These loops must either continue repeating an operation or stop, depending on the results obtained within the loop. Such loops are indeterminate—that is, not executed a fixed number of times. The way you write this type of loop in Visual Basic follows this pattern:

DO
   Visual Basic statements
UNTIL *condition is met*

Figure 6-4 shows a diagram of what Visual Basic does in a DO loop.

A simple example of this is a password fragment in a Form_Load() procedure that starts an application. If you compiled a program to a stand-alone file with a Form_Load procedure that looks like this:

```
SUB Form_Load()
  DO
    X$ = INPUTBOX$("Password please?")
  LOOP UNTIL X$ = "Vanilla Orange"
END SUB
```

it would be more difficult for anyone who didn't know the password to use this program. (It would not be impossible, however; a very experienced programmer could find the password by carefully examining the .EXE file, but it wouldn't be easy.)

It's important to remember that the test for equality is strict: typing **VANILLA OranGE** would not work, nor would **Vanilla orange**. Another point worth keeping in mind is that the test is done only at the end of the loop, when Visual Basic processes the UNTIL statement. If you change the fragment to

```
SUB Form_Load()
  'local variables
  DIM X$
```

Flow diagram for DO loop (test at end)

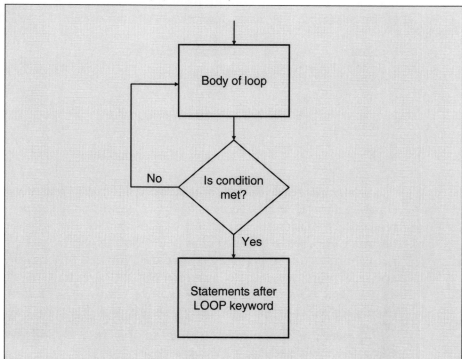

```
   DO
      X$ = "Vanilla Orange"
      X$ = INPUTBOX$("Password please?")
   LOOP UNTIL X$ = "Vanilla Orange"
END SUB
```

then, whether you break out of the loop still depends on what the user types in the input box. Initializing the variable to the correct value is irrelevant.

When you write an indeterminate loop, something must change; otherwise the test will always fail and you'll be stuck in an infinite loop. To stop an infinite loop, you can use the CTRL+BREAK combination. When the program is run as an EXE file away from the Visual Basic development environment, the CTRL+BREAK combination only works at the time an INPUT statement is reached unless you've checked off the Debug option in the MAKE EXE dialog box.

In more sophisticated programs involving indeterminate loops, you need ways to check for conditions besides equality. You do this by means of the *relational operators*. The relational operators are listed here:

Symbol	Checks (Tests for)
< >	Not equal to
<	Less than
<=	Less than or equal to
>	Greater than
>=	Greater than or equal to

For strings, these operators test for ASCII order. This means that "A" comes before "B" but "B" comes before "a" (and a space comes before any typewriter character). The string "aBCD" comes after the string "CDE" because uppercase letters come before lowercase letters. (The on-line help contains a complete ASCII table that you can find by opening HELP and selecting "Contents" followed by "ASCII Character Codes." The ASCII codes from 0 to 33 are for the control characters or keys, such as BACKSPACE, and ENTER. (See also Appendix A of this book.)

For example, suppose you wanted to prevent a "Divide by zero" error. Use a fragment like the following:

```
DO
  N$ = INPUTBOX$("Non-zero number Please!")
  Number = VAL(N$)
LOOP UNTIL Number <> 0
```

Or, to test that the first character of a string in a text box was not a space or a control code, use this:

```
DO
  Text$ = Text1.Text
LOOP UNTIL Text$ > CHR$(31)   'space = ASCII 32
```

These kinds of loops are the first steps for stopping a user from entering the wrong kind of data. Testing input data with an indeterminate loop, as in the example above, is the most common way to begin to bulletproof a program. In fact, a large part of bulletproofing programs (the jargon is "making them robust") requires making them tolerant of input errors. Instead of ending with an error message because of a typo, they check that the data entered is usable. If not, they warn the user. The more robust a program is, the less likely it is to behave strangely for an inexperienced user. (Chapter 7 has more on checking user input.)

You can even monitor keystrokes as they are made inside any control that accepts input. For this, see the section "An Example: The KeyPress Procedure" later in this chapter.

You now can write the program mentioned in the introduction to this section. Here is the Calculate_Click() procedure to determine how long it will take to accumulate $1,000,000:

```
SUB Calculate_Click()
  'Calculate retirement value assuming fixed
  'deposit and fixed interest rate

  ' local variables
  DIM Amount AS CURRENCY, Total AS CURRENCY
  DIM Interest AS SINGLE
  DIM Years AS INTEGER, I AS INTEGER

  Amount = VAL(AmountPerYear.Text)
  Interest = VAL(InterestRate.Text) / 100
  DO
    Total = Amount + Total + (Total * Interest)
    Years = Years + 1
  LOOP UNTIL Total >= 1000000
```

```
  NumberOfYears.Text = STR$(Years)
END SUB
```

The body of the loop is much like the one in the retirement program from the earlier section of this chapter: figure the yearly change and add it to the previous total to get a new total. This time, however, another counter (Years) was set up to keep track of the number of years. Finally, the loop continues as long as the value of the variable Total is less than 1,000,000. The moment the total equals or exceeds the target, the loop ends and Visual Basic reports the results.

You should be aware of a problem that frequently occurs with these kinds of loops. Consider this fragment:

```
Total = 0
PassNumber = 0
DO
  Total = Total + .1
  PassNumber = PassNumber + 1
  PRINT PassNumber, Total
LOOP UNTIL Total = 1
```

You might think this program would end after ten passes through the loop, but it doesn't. In fact, this fragment gives you an infinite loop, and you'll need the CTRL+BREAK combination to stop it. The reason this infinite loop occurred is subtle but important. In this fragment, all the numbers are defaulted to be values of single-precision variables, and, as discussed in Chapter 5, these numbers are only approximations. Visual Basic's internal characterization of .1 is off by a little in, say, the seventh place. As Visual Basic adds .1 to the total, tiny errors accumulate and the resulting total, while close to 1, never exactly equals 1. The point of this example is that you should test only integer variables and long integer variables for equality. (Chapter 11 on debugging techniques explains a couple of ways you could have isolated this problem.)

In any case, this program should be rewritten to allow for the tiny error by changing the test to read

```
LOOP UNTIL Total > .99999999
```

or, to be sure that the number is at least 1,

```
LOOP UNTIL Total >= 1
```

Changing the test to either case ensures that the program really will stop after ten passes through the loop. Single-precision, double-precision, and currency variables can be checked only to see if they are close (within a certain tolerance).

The most common type of error in using loops is called an *off-by-one error.* This means that instead of doing an operation 500 times as you planned, the program seems to do it 499 or 501 times. If your program suffers from this problem, the debugging techniques from Chapter 11 can help you pinpoint the fault in the loop that is causing the off-by-one error. Obviously, it's best to avoid off-by-one errors in the first place. The best policy for loops is to constantly keep in mind that the loop terminates only when the counter exceeds (not equals) the test value. If a program still is off by one, one useful technique is to check by hand how many times the loop cycles for a much smaller test value.

Sophisticated Indeterminate Loops

A common task is to read a list of names until the last one is encountered, keeping count at the same time. Suppose, for example, that while looking through the dictionary you notice the last entry is the name of an insect: the "zyzzyva." You decide to add up the number of different types of insects that exist in North America. You take out your entomology book and start running the following code:

```
InsectCount = 0
 DO
    InsectName$ = INPUTBOX$("The next insect name")
    InsectCount = InsectCount + 1
 LOOP UNTIL InsectName$ = "zyzzyva"
PRINT "The number of different types of insects is"; InsectCount
```

While this fragment may seem like a prototype for other programs that count the number of items on a list (or even in the DATA statements built into a program), you won't always know what the last entry of the list should be. A more general program that uses an indeterminate loop to keep count will need an ending string to test for, so you're likely to use a group of strange characters (like "ZZZ") to act as a flag. Instead of testing for the zyzzyva, you test for a flag. This is quite common when READing DATA. (When you are working with a form, you will also often use a command button to stop the count.)

It's easy to modify the "InsectCount" fragment to test for a flag. Here is a program that does this (but beware—this program has a subtle bug):

```
NameCount = 0
DO
  Entry$ = INPUTBOX$("Name - type ZZZ when done")
  NameCount = NameCount + 1
LOOP UNTIL Entry$ = "ZZZ"
PRINT "The total number of names is"; NameCount
```

The bug in this fragment is that it suffers from an off-by-one error. Imagine that the list consists of only one name besides the flag. What happens? Let's work through this program by hand. The user types the first name and the count increases to 1. Next the user types ZZZ. However, because the test is only done at the end of the loop, the count increases to 2 before the test is done. Therefore, when the loop ends, the count is 2 when it ought to be 1. One possible cure is to subtract 1 from the count once the loop ends. The trouble with this type of ad-hoc solution (in the jargon, a "kludge"—pronounced "klooge") is that the programmer ends up having to constantly figure out how far off the results of the loops are when they finish in order to move backward.

Moving backward, however, is unnecessary, because Visual Basic makes the cure for this so easy: move the test to the top. Consider this:

```
NameCount = 0
Entry$ = INPUTBOX$("Name - ZZZ to end")
DO UNTIL Entry$ = "ZZZ"
   NameCount = NameCount + 1
   Entry$ = INPUTBOX$("Name - ZZZ to end")
LOOP
```

Now the user types the first name before the loop starts. Once this is done, the program does an initial test. The loop is entered and 1 starts being added to the counter only if this test fails. (Notice that this kind of loop also works if there is nothing in the list except the flag.) Figure 6-5 shows a diagram of what Visual Basic does for this type of loop.

A good rule of thumb is that if you are going to use the flag, put the test at the end; if not, put it at the beginning. More precisely, with the test at the end, the loop is always executed at least once; with the test at the beginning, the loop may not be executed at all. Also remember that when the test is at the top, you obviously have to have something to test.

FIGURE
6-5 Flow diagram for DO loop (test at beginning)

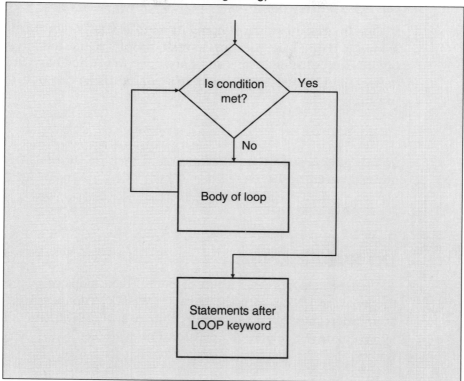

Therefore, when the test is done at the beginning, initialize all variables before the loop starts. Finally, don't forget that you usually have to have two assignment statements when the test is at the top—the first before the test and the second (to keep the process going) inside the loop.

You can also use the second (test at the beginning) kind of DO loop to replace the FOR-NEXT loop. Doing this is not just a good way to test your mastery of the DO loop. For example, suppose your loop has to be interrupted to go to another event procedure. If you want to return to exactly the same place in the loop that you left, you may need to use a static variable as a counter inside a DO loop.

You must follow a similar rule, when nesting DO loops together or when nesting them with FOR-NEXT loops, to the rules you follow for nesting FOR-NEXT loops alone: inner loops must be finished before the outer loops are tested. Choose a reasonable indenting pattern and you will not have any problems.

One final point worth keeping in mind is that Visual Basic is always asking a True-False question in a DO loop; it's just hidden sometimes. Luckily, all arithmetic operators are done first (they have higher precedence) than the relational operators. Visual Basic has no trouble interpreting

```
LOOP UNTIL Number * 5 > 10
```

as meaning first do the calculation and then do the test. Of course, as always, parentheses make this clearer:

```
LOOP UNTIL (Number * 5) > 10
```

DO WHILE Loops

Visual Basic has other kinds of loops. These loops consist of replacing the keyword UNTIL with the keyword WHILE. This new loop may seem superfluous since you can always change a DO UNTIL into a DO WHILE by reversing the relational operator. For example,

```
DO

LOOP UNTIL X$ <> " "
```

is the same as

```
DO

LOOP WHILE X$ = " "
```

and

```
DO UNTIL Number > 5
```

is the same as

```
DO WHILE Number <= 5
```

Given this, why bother learning this new type of loop? There are two reasons why the WHILE command is important. The first is that, as much as possible, you want to write a program conforming to the way your mind works. Sometimes you will think of an operation as going on *until* something happens, while other times you think of it as continuing *while*, as the saying goes, "the status is quo." The richness of Visual Basic's programming language makes the fit better between your thought patterns and the computer program you're trying to write. In fact, psychologists have found that tests with positive conditions are easier to understand. DO WHILE Number = 0 is easier to process than its counterpart, DO UNTIL Number <> 0.

DO Loops with AND, OR, NOT

The previous section gave you one reason to use both DO UNTIL and DO WHILE loops, but this is not the only reason. Probably the best reason to use both kinds of loops comes when you have to combine conditions. This is most commonly done with the OR and AND keywords. These two keywords work just like they do in English. You can continue a process as long as both conditions are True or stop it when one turns False. However, it becomes increasingly confusing to try to force combination of the AND, OR, and NOT operators into loops that they don't seem to fit. For example, suppose you want to continue a process while a number is greater than zero and a text box is empty. It is much easier to say

```
DO WHILE Number > 0 AND Text1.Text = ""
```

than to say

```
DO UNTIL Number <= 0 OR Text1.Text <> ""
```

The WHILE/WEND loop

There is one other loop possible in Visual Basic. To preserve compatibility with interpreted BASIC, Visual Basic allows a variant on the DO WHILE LOOP (that is, the test at the top). Instead of saying

```
DO WHILE X = 0

LOOP
```

you can simply omit the DO keyword and say

```
WHILE X = 0

WEND
```

Making Decisions

At this point, all your programs can do is to decide whether to repeat a group of statements or not. They can't, as yet, change which statements are processed depending on what the program has already done or what it has just encountered. The next few sections take care of this. All the commands in these sections deal with turning an outline containing a phrase like

IF *condition* THEN *do something...*

into Visual Basic code. Visual Basic uses the IF-THEN in much the same way that you do in normal English. For example, to warn a user that a number must be positive, use a line like this:

```
IF X < 0 THEN MSGBOX("Number must be positive!")
```

More generally, when Visual Basic encounters an IF-THEN statement, it checks the first clause (called, naturally enough, the IF clause) and checks whether it's True. If that clause is True, the computer does whatever follows (called the THEN clause). If the test fails, processing skips to the next statement.

Just as in the loops from the previous sections, you can use the IF-THEN to compare numbers or strings. For example, a statement like

```
IF A$ < B$  THEN PRINT A$;" comes before "; B$;"
```

tests for ASCII order, and

```
IF A <= B  THEN PRINT A; "is no more than"; B
```

tests for numerical order.

Suppose you need to write a social security calculator. The way this tax works is that you pay (in 1992) 6.20 percent of the amount you make up to 53,400. After that, whether you make 55,000 or 550,000,000 per year, you pay no more social security tax. To write code that would activate this type of calculator, you need to write

```
IF Wages < 53400 THEN SSTax=.062 * Wages ELSE SSTax=53400 * .062
```

When Visual Basic processes an IF-THEN-ELSE, if the test succeeds, Visual Basic processes the statement that follows the keyword THEN (the THEN clause). If the test fails, Visual Basic processes the statement that follows the keyword ELSE (called the ELSE clause). Figure 6-6 shows you what Visual Basic does with an IF-THEN-ELSE.

Here's another example. Some credit cards charge you 18 percent interest if your balance is less than $2000; otherwise (ELSE) they charge you 15 percent. This would translate into

```
IF Balance < 2000 THEN IntRate = .18 ELSE IntRate = .15
```

You can also use the keywords AND, OR, EQV, XOR, and NOT in an IF-THEN. These let you check two conditions at once. For example, suppose you have to check if a number is between zero and 9:

```
IF Digit >= 0 AND Digit <= 9 THEN PRINT "OK"
```

Flow diagram for IF-THEN-ELSE

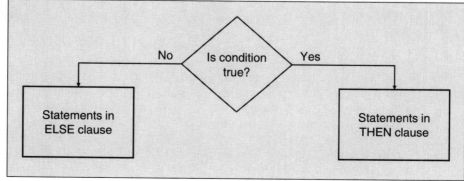

One word of caution. In both speaking and writing, we sometimes say, "If my average is greater than 80 and less than 90, then ...." Translating this sentence construction directly into code won't work. You must repeat the variable each time you want to test something. To do the translation from English to Visual Basic, say, "If my average is greater than 80 and my average is less than 90, then...."

A final note on AND: You do not have to use the same variable. A statement like

```
IF (Grade4 > Grade3) AND (Average > 60) THEN PRINT "Improving!"
```

is a perfectly good Visual Basic statement. (The parentheses are there only to improve readability; they are not needed. As you saw earlier, Visual Basic calculates relational operators before worrying about the logical connectors like AND.)

Using the keyword OR in an IF-THEN test is similar. The test is successful if either one of the conditions is True. Suppose you had to test if at least one of two numbers was nonzero:

```
IF (A <> 0) OR (B <> 0) THEN
```

There are other, somewhat less common ways of combining tests. For example, there's the EQV (equivalence) operator. This asks the question whether two conditions are both true or both false. For example:

IF (X = TRUE AND Y = TRUE) OR (X = FALSE AND Y = FALSE) ...

is the same as:

IF X EQV Y ...

Another useful operator (especially for graphics programs and file security programs is the XOR (exclusive OR). This corresponds to the English "If A or B but not both."

Similarly, you can also use the NOT operator. Choosing to use this operator depends a lot on personal taste (a lot like deciding between DO WHILE and DO UNTIL). Most people find it easier just to change the relational operators. For example,

```
IF NOT (A$ = "Big Blue")
```

is harder to understand than

```
IF A$ <> "BIG Blue"
```

Similarly,

```
IF (NOT A > 50)
```

is exactly the same as

```
IF A <= 50
```

If you prefer to use the NOT operator, you'll need parentheses; without them the program is apt to be unreadable.

Since Visual Basic is really testing for a Boolean (True-False) relation in the IF clause, you can actually have any Boolean property. For example, in the statement

```
IF Text1.Enabled THEN ...
```

Visual Basic processes the THEN clause only when the Text1 box is enabled. Finally, an extremely important use of the IF-THEN is to determine what button on a message box was clicked. For example, if

```
Continue = MSGBOX("Continue?",4)
```

then use an IF-THEN to test if the user pressed the Yes button (Continue = 6) or pressed the No button (Continue = 7).

The Block IF-THEN

More often than not, you will want to process multiple statements if a condition is True or False. For this you need the most powerful form of the IF-THEN-ELSE, called the block IF-THEN. This lets you process as many statements as you like in response to a True condition, as in this example:

IF I win the lottery THEN
 I'm happy
 My family is happy
 And, the tax man is happy.

There are three statements in response to something being True. To write this statement in Visual Basic, you use a slightly different format than the usual IF-THEN. The block IF-THEN looks like this:

IF *thing to test* THEN
  lots of statements
ELSE
  more statements
END IF

You do not put anything on the first line following the keyword THEN; press ENTER immediately after typing it. This bare THEN is how Visual Basic knows it's beginning a block. The ELSE is optional; placing it (again alone on a line) means that another block will follow, to be processed only if the IF clause is False. However, whether the ELSE is there or not, the IF block must end with the keywords END IF.

For an example of this, let's modify the original mortgage program in Chapter 5 so that the program checks whether the user wants to calculate the payment or the maximum he or she can borrow *depending on which text box is empty.* The comments in the following program give the formula you need for this. (You have to do a little algebra on the original formula.)

```
SUB Calculate_Click ()
  'This calculates the mortgage
  'using the formulas  Payment =
  'Principal * MonthInt / (1 - (1 / (1 + MonthInt))^ Years * 12)
  'and  Principal =
  'Payment /(MonthInt / (1 - (1 / (1 + MonthInt)) ^ (Years * 12)))

  'local variables
  DIM Years AS INTEGER, Payment AS CURRENCY
  DIM MonthInt AS SINGLE, Amount AS CURRENCY
  DIM Percent AS SINGLE

  'Get info
  Years = VAL(MortgageTerm.Text)
  Principal = VAL(MortgageAmount.Text)
```

```
Payment = VAL(MortgagePayment.Text)
Percent = VAL(InterestRate.Text) / 100
MonthInt = Percent / 12
IF Payment = 0 THEN
  Payment = Principal * MonthInt / (1 - (1 / (1 + _
  MonthInt)) ^ (Years * 12))  'above & this 1 line
  MortgagePayment.Text = STR$(Payment)
ELSE
  Principal =  Payment / (MonthInt / (1 - (1 / (1 + _
  MonthInt)) ^ (Years * 12)))  'above & this 1 line
  MortgageAmount.Text = STR$(Principal)
END IF
END SUB
```

Again, as usual, the indentation is there to make the program more readable; Visual Basic doesn't care.

An Example: The DIR$ Function

Another good example of where you'll need an IF-THEN-ELSE is when, during a program, you have to find out if a file or files exist with a specific extension. (You can use a file list box—see Chapter 13—but this is more often used to give the user the information, not the program.) Visual Basic has a built-in function called DIR$. The syntax for this function is

DIR$(*filespec*)

filespec is a string expression that contains the file name or file pattern. You can use the two DOS wildcards (? for a single character match and * to allow more characters). You can also include path name information. Each time Visual Basic encounters a DIR$ command with a filespec, it returns the first file name it finds that matches the pattern. When no file names match, Visual Basic returns the empty string. To continue searching for the same pattern, you call the DIR$ function with no pattern.

Here is a program fragment that checks if the current directory contains any .TXT files:

```
X$ = DIR$(*.TXT)
IF X$ = ""  THEN
  PRINT "No text files found"
```

```
ELSE
  PRINT "First file found is "; X$
END IF
```

To find all the files with a .TXT extension, use this:

```
X$ = DIR$(*.TXT)
DO WHILE X$ <> ""
   PRINT "First file found is "; X$
   X$ = DIR$                        'Don't reuse the file spec
LOOP
```

Combining the IF-THEN with Loops

Suppose you need to check that there is exactly one file with a .TXT extension in the current directory. To do this, you have to use the DIR$ function, but you need to allow two ways to leave the loop. Here is a fragment that does this:

```
NameOfFile$ = DIR$("*.TXT")
NumberOfFiles = 0
DO UNTIL (NameOfFile$ = "") OR (NumberOfFiles > 1)
   NumberOfFiles = NumberOfFiles + 1
   NameOfFile$ = DIR$
LOOP
IF NumberOfFiles = 0 THEN PRINT "No Files Found"
IF NumberOfFiles > 1 THEN PRINT "Too many Files"
```

Notice that Visual Basic enters the loop only if it finds a matching file. You have to allow for the loop never being entered at all. Once the loop is entered, you have Visual Basic add 1 to the file count.

These kinds of loops are so common that computer scientists gave them a special name, Eureka loops, after Archimedes' famous bathtub experience. You set up a loop to end if either one of two situations prevails. Then you follow the loop by a test for what actually took place.

Another example of this type of loop would occur if you modified the earlier program that calculated how long it would take to build up a $1,000,000 nest egg to end either if the number of years until you retired was exceeded or you reached the $1,000,000 goal.

You can use the IF-THEN to give you a way to write a loop that "tests in the middle." For this, you combine the IF-THEN with a new command: the EXIT DO. Whenever Visual Basic processes the EXIT DO statement, it pops you out of the loop, directly to the statement following the keyword LOOP.

More generally, Visual Basic allows you to set up a potentially infinite loop at any time; just leave off the tests in a DO loop (an unadorned DO at the top and an equally unadorned LOOP at the bottom). Once you've done this, the loop will end only when Visual Basic processes an EXIT DO statement. (During program development, you can always end the program prematurely using the CTRL+BREAK combination.) There is a version of the EXIT command for leaving a FOR-NEXT loop as well; in this case, it takes the form EXIT FOR.

Visual Basic places no restriction on the number of EXIT statements you place inside a loop, but loops that have 37 different ways to end are awfully hard to debug. As a general rule, most programmers aim for programs that have only "single entry/single exit" loops. They also find it easier to debug programs that have the loop test at the beginning or end of the loop. Most programmers use the EXIT DO (or EXIT FOR) only for abnormal exits from loops, such as when a program is about to divide by zero and leave the loop rather than generate a "divide by zero" error.

SELECT CASE

Suppose you were designing a program to compute grades based on the average of four exams. If the average was 90 or higher, the person should get an A, 80-89, a B, and so on. This is such a common situation that Visual Basic has another control structure designed exactly for it. It's called the SELECT CASE. To use this command, you start with something you want to test. For example, suppose you want to test if a character is a vowel. You could write

```
IF (Char$ = "A") OR (Char$ = "a") THEN PRINT "Vowel"
IF (Char$ = "I") OR (Char$ = "i") THEN PRINT "Vowel"
```

and so on.

Using the SELECT CASE control structure (combined with the UCASE$ command to turn the letter into uppercase), you can write

```
SELECT CASE UCASE$(Char$)
  CASE  "A"
    PRINT "Vowel"
  CASE  "E"
    PRINT "Vowel"
  CASE  "I"
    PRINT "Vowel"
  CASE  "O"
    PRINT "Vowel"
  CASE  "U"
    PRINT "Vowel"
  CASE  "Y"
    PRINT "Y is a problem - sorry"
END SELECT
```

The SELECT CASE command makes it clear that a program has reached a point with many branches; multiple IF-THENs do not. (And the clearer a program is, the easier it is to debug.)

What follows the keywords SELECT CASE is a variable or expression, and what Visual Basic is going to do depends on the value of the variable or expression. The keyword CASE is shorthand for "In the case that the variable (expression) is," and you usually follow it by a relational operator. For example, to begin to check that the value of the variable Char$ is a letter, you can add the CASE keyword:

```
CASE IS < "A"
  PRINT "Character is not a letter."
  PRINT "Meaningless question"
```

To eliminate all possible nonletter values, you have to consult, for example, the ASCII chart in Appendix A. By looking at that, you can see that you also need to eliminate those characters whose ASCII codes are between 91 and 96. You do this as follows:

```
CASE CHR$(91) TO CHR$(96)
   PRINT "Character is not a letter."
   PRINT "Meaningless question."
```

Here, the keyword TO allows you to give a range of values. Therefore, this statement is shorthand for "In the case that the variable is in the range from CHR$(91) TO CHR$(96) inclusive, do the following."

Having eliminated the case when the character was not a letter or was a vowel, you want to print out the message that it is a consonant. You do this with the CASE ELSE, which is shorthand for "Do this case if none of the other situations hold." (You could, of course, have used the LCASE$() function instead, which converts letters to lowercase.)

Finally, the SELECT CASE control structure allows you to combine many tests for equality on one line. You could write the following:

```
Case "A", "E", "I", "O", "U"
   Print "is a vowel"
```

Finishing Up with the IF-THEN

The SELECT CASE command allows you multiple branches, but allows you to test only one expression—ultimately one number or string. Suppose you have two numbers, A and B, and your outline looks like this:

```
If A  =  B  Do .....
If A  >  B  Do .....
If A  <  B  Do .....
```

One way to program this is to set up a variable:

```
Difference = A - B
```

and then select on whether the value of Difference was zero (when A = B), greater than zero (in which case A > B), or less than zero (A < B). But now suppose someone throws in one or two extra conditions:

```
IF (A > B) AND (A < 2 * B)
IF A > 2 * B
```

Now it's no longer obvious how to use the SELECT CASE command. You could write four block IF-THENs corresponding to each of the different conditions in the outline, and most of the time this wouldn't cause any problems. Problems may happen if (as in the preceding example) you have to do something to A or B in one of the blocks. From that point on you're in trouble; all further tests are off. More precisely, suppose the outline was to do one of the following:

If A = B
  Print A
If A < B
  Print A and add two to A
If A > B
  Print B and add two to B

Here is a translation of this outline:

```
IF A = B THEN PRINT A
IF A < B THEN
  PRINT A
  A = A + 2
END IF
IF A > B THEN
 PRINT B
 B = B + 2
END IF
```

Suppose the value of A was 4 and the value of B was 5. Then the second option is taken, and the program prints out 4 and makes A = 6. But now the third option is activated—contrary to the outline, which says do only one of the possibilities.

This situation is similar to when you first used the ELSE command. You need to continue testing within the confines of the original IF-THEN. This is done by adding another line to the IF-THEN in the form:

ELSEIF *condition* THEN

Here is the correct translation of the outline:

```
IF A = B THEN
  PRINT A
ELSEIF A < B THEN
  PRINT A
  A = A + 2
ELSEIF A > B THEN
```

```
    PRINT B
    B = B + 2
END IF
```

Now everything is tied together. And just like in the IF-THEN-ELSE or the SELECT command, Visual Basic activates, at most, one clause. In particular, if A < B, then Visual Basic processes only the second clause. And when Visual Basic is done doing that, it bypasses any other ELSEIFs that may be contained in the block; it goes immediately to the statement following the END IF. (By the way, you could replace the final ELSEIF with a simple ELSE; you've eliminated all the other possibilities.)

A block IF-THEN can have as many ELSEIFs as you like but only one ELSE (as the last clause). The limits are determined by how much you can process rather than what Visual Basic can do. (That's why it's often preferable to use SELECT CASE. Although any SELECT CASE can be transformed into an IF-THEN-ELSEIF, the latter can be much harder to read and hence to debug.)

The final point worth noting is that the block IF-THEN is extremely flexible. You can put any Visual Basic statement following the keyword THEN—in particular, another IF-THEN-ELSE. Consider the following, which a teacher might use if he or she regarded the final exam as being not all-important:

```
IF FinalExam < 65 THEN
   PRINT "You failed the final exam."
   IF Average > 70 THEN
      PRINT "You pass because your average is"
      PRINT "high enough to overcome failing the final."
   ELSE
      PRINT "I'm sorry failing the final and a marginal ";
      PRINT " passing average means failing the course."
   END IF
END IF
```

Is it clear (forgetting the indentation pattern for a moment) that the ELSE belongs to the inner IF-THEN? The way to see this is to "play computer." For the ELSE to belong to the outer IF-THEN, the inner IF-THEN must have already finished. But it hasn't because, to that point, no END IF has shown up. Therefore, the first END IF finishes the inner IF-THEN and the second finishes the outer one, and so the ELSE must belong to the inner IF-THEN. Of course, you should, as in the preceding example, use a consistent indentation pattern to make it obvious at a glance where nested IF-THENs belong.

An Example: The KeyPress Procedure

Almost all Visual Basic objects will recognize when a user presses and then releases a key. If the key that was pressed generates an ordinary ASCII code, it triggers the KeyPress event procedure. Not only can this procedure detect what the user types, but you can also use it to change or restrict what the control will accept.

The syntax for this event procedure is a little different than all the event procedures you've seen up to now. The template for the KeyPress event procedure looks like this:

SUB ControlName_KeyPress (KeyAscii AS INTEGER)

END SUB

Inside the parentheses is the first example of a *parameter*—the formal name for a placeholder. When Visual Basic detects the user pressing an ASCII key inside a control that recognizes this event, you get a call to this event procedure. Visual Basic replaces the parameter with the ASCII code of the key that generated the event.

For example, a form can detect the KeyPress event if there are no controls on it or all the controls on it are disabled or invisible. If you start a new project with a blank form and attach the following event procedure to it:

```
SUB Form_KeyPress (KeyAscii AS INTEGER)
  CLS
  PRINT "The ASCII code of the key you pressed is"; KeyAscii
  PRINT "The character itself is"; CHR$(KeyAscii)
END SUB
```

you'll be able to explore the ASCII codes for characters until you end the program.

On the other hand, if you want to cancel a keystroke, you need only reassign the variable KeyAscii to be zero. For example, use the following to force the user to type a digit between zero and 9:

```
SUB Form_KeyPress (KeyAscii AS INTEGER)
  IF (KeyAscii < ASC("0")) OR (KeyAscii > ASC("9")) THEN
     BEEP
     KeyAscii = 0
  END IF
END SUB
```

This event procedure absolutely prevents the user from typing anything but a digit inside the text box. The procedure blanks out any other character the user may have typed.

Since you can detect whether a user has typed a comma or more than one decimal point, you can use the KeyPress event procedure to check what he or she types in a text box. The next chapter shows you how to write a procedure that accepts a number but disregards commas, extraneous decimal points, and nonnumeric characters.

CHAPTER

The Built-in Functions

*T*his chapter covers Visual Basic's built–in functions. These commands transform raw data into the form you need. For example, there are functions that take strings apart as well as ones that put them together. You'll see how to control the look of your forms with format, date, and time functions and how to include Visual Basic's supplied constants file to make your programs cleaner. You'll also see how the pseudo–random number generator lets you build an element of indeterminacy (chance) into your programs, a necessary tool for programming games of chance or simulations.

As always, be prepared to check the on-line help window about specific functions. The examples given there complement the ones given in this chapter.

String Functions

Since information in Visual Basic is always displayed as text, string functions are far more important in Visual Basic than in ordinary BASICs. In Chapter 5 you learned how two strings can be joined together, or concatenated, using the plus sign (+). In this section you'll see the functions available in Visual Basic that let you examine the characters in a string, take strings apart, insert one string inside another, and much more.

There are two built-in functions that you often use when building up strings. The function

SPACE$(*NumberOfSpaces*)

gives you a string consisting of only spaces, with the number of spaces determined by the value inside the parentheses. And the function

STRING$(*Number, StringExpression$*)

gives you a string of repeated characters. The character repeated is the first character of the string expression in the second position of the function, and the number is determined by the value in the first position. You can also use the ASCII code in the second position. The following examples all give the same string of ten z's:

```
STRING$(10, "z")
STRING$(10, "zyzzyva")                'only first character is used
STRING$(10, 122)                      '122 = ASC("z")
```

You can use loops to build up useful strings as well. For example, suppose you need a string variable that contains the lowercase alphabet. Rather than doing the typing yourself, combining the + with a FOR-NEXT loop makes it easy:

```
Lowercase$ = ""
For I% = ASC("a") TO ASC("z")
  Lowercase$ = Lowercase$ + CHR$(I%)
Next I%
```

You can also look up the ASCII codes for "a" (97) and "z" (122) in Appendix A or in the help files.

Analyzing Strings

Suppose you want to examine an expression character by character. For example, you might want to check how many periods (decimal points) are in a string expression before you convert it to a number with the VAL function. The code for this calls for a FOR-NEXT loop with the ending value set to the length of the string. In Visual Basic, the function that gives the length is LEN, where the parentheses following the function hold a string expression. Unlike the TextWidth function, this function counts all spaces or nonprinting characters that may appear in the string and gives you the true size of the string.

Next, you need a function that lets you extract a copy of individual letters or larger chunks from a string. The most important of these functions is the MID$ function. The syntax for this function is

MID$(*StringExpression, start[, length]*)

or

MID$(*StringExpression, start*)

The first entry holds the string (or string expression) you want to analyze. Next comes the starting position of the characters you want extracted from the string. The optional last position specifies the number of characters you want to pull out. Both of these last two options can be either integers or long integers or an expression that Visual Basic can round to lie in this range. Here are some examples of this function:

```
MID$("computer", 1, 4) = "comp"
MID$("computer", 1, 5) = "compu"
MID$("computer", 6, 3) = "ter"
```

If you leave out the last entry (the one telling how many letters to pull out), as shown here:

```
MID$("computer", 6, 3) = MID$("computer", 6)= "ter"
```

Visual Basic retrieves the rest of the string—starting, of course, from the position determined by the second entry. You also get the rest of the string if the third entry is too large (greater than the number of characters remaining).

Programmers say that MID$ is a function of three (or occasionally two) parameters, or arguments. Both terms are borrowed from mathematics. Think of them as meaning "the number of pieces of information to be processed." In a function, each argument is separated from the next by commas. The MID$ function usually uses three pieces of information: a string in the first position and integers in the remaining two positions (of course, you can use expressions that evaluate to these as well).

For example, a fragment that would count the number of periods in a string expression might look like this:

```
PeriodCount% = 0    'just in case
FOR I% = 1 TO LEN(StringExpression$)
  IF MID$(StringExpression$, I%, 1) = "." THEN
    PeriodCount% = PeriodCount% + 1
  END IF
NEXT I%
```

On each pass through the loop, the position (the value of I%) where the MID$ function starts working increases. The number of characters pulled out remains the same (one).

The MID$ function has two cousins that are equally useful: LEFT$ and RIGHT$. As the names suggest, LEFT$ picks out characters from the beginning of a word and RIGHT$ picks them out from the end. Of the two, RIGHT$ is the more common. It avoids a subtraction inside the MID$ function and can work a bit faster as a result. For example, the following lines:

```
MID$(A$, LEN(A$) - 3, 4)
MID$(A$, LEN(A$) - 3)
RIGHT$(A$, 4)
```

all have the same effect.

LEFT$ works the same way but only saves you from putting a "1" in the second position in the MID$ function. If you want the first five characters in a string, use one of the following:

```
MID$ (A$, 1, 5)
LEFT$ (A$, 5)
```

MID$ has one other useful feature. You can use it as a statement rather than as a function to make changes inside a string. For example, if

```
BestBasic$ = "PowerBasic"
```

then the statement

```
MID$ (BestBasic$, 1, 5) = "Quick"
```

gives the string variable BestBasic$ the value "QuickBasic". When you use MID$ this way, the second position controls where the change will start and the third position controls how many letters to pull out from the string on the right-hand side. These are the letters that will be switched into the original string. For example,

```
MID$ (BestBasic$, 1, 5) = "QuickBasic by Microsoft"
```

gives the same result as before. If the right-hand side has fewer characters than the number given in the third position of the left-hand side demands, Visual Basic changes as many characters as occur on the right-hand side. Therefore,

```
MID$(BestBasic$, 1, 5) = "QB"
```

gives BestBasic$ the value "QBwerBasic".

More on the MID$ Statement

The MID$ statement makes changes within a string but never changes the length of the original string. If the number in the third position is too large relative to the number in the second position—that is, greater than the remaining number of characters—then only the characters remaining can change. Finally, just as with the MID$ function, you can leave out the last position. For example,

```
Phrase$ = "In the beginning "
MID$(Phrase$, 8) = "middle was"
```

changes the string to

```
"In the middle was"
```

In this case, there's just enough room to fit the string on the right-hand side into the string on the left, starting at the eighth position. Counting from the eighth position, there are ten characters left in the phrase "In the beginning was". (The space counts as a character.)

If you want to change the size of a string, the MID$ statement is of little use. Instead, you need to follow a procedure that's a bit like splicing tape. For example, suppose you want to change the string

```
"Fortran is the best programming language."
```

to read

```
"Visual Basic is the best programming language."
```

Since the string "Fortran" has 7 letters and the string "Visual Basic" has 12, you cannot use the MID$ statement. Instead, you must follow the splicing analogy:

1. Cut out the phrase "Fortran".

2. Hold the phrase "is the best programming language".

3. Splice in the phrase "QuickBasic" and reassemble.

Here's the fragment:

```
Phrase$ = "Fortran is the best programming language"
Begin$ = "Visual Basic"
EndPhrase$ = MID$(Phrase$, 8)
Phrase$ = Begin$ + EndPhrase$
```

Programming this kind of change can be a bit painful if you always have to go in and count characters in order to find the position where a character was located. As usual, this task is simplified by one of Visual Basic's built-in functions. Like the MID$ function, INSTR also works with three (and occasionally two) pieces of information; that is, it's a function of three (occasionally two) arguments.

INSTR tells you whether a string is contained within another string (the jargon is "is a substring of"). And if it is, INSTR tells you the position at which the substring starts. Using the same variable, Phrase$, as in the last example, in the line of code

```
x = INSTR(1, Phrase$, "the")
```

the value of x is 12 because the string "the" occurs in the phrase "Fortran is the best programming language", starting at the twelfth position.

In this case, Visual Basic searches the string starting from the first position until it finds the substring. If it doesn't find the substring, it gives back a value of zero. Therefore, if

```
x = INSTR(1, Phrase$, "THE")
```

then the value of x is zero because "THE" isn't a substring of the phrase "Fortran is the best programming language". Remember that case is important inside quotes; the INSTR function is case sensitive. You can search regardless of capitalization with the UCASE$ and the LCASE$ functions, which you saw in Chapter 6.

In the previous example, the INSTR function essentially translates the following outline into a single command:

1. Pull out characters 1 through 3.

2. Check if they are the searched-for substring. If so, return value = 1 and stop.

3. Now do it for characters 2 through 4. If successful, return value = 2 and stop.

4. Continue until no more substrings need to be checked. If totally unsuccessful, return a value of zero.

You can easily translate this outline into a program that, using MID$, would work for any string; it's a routine exercise. The program you end up with will, however, take much longer to do what INSTR does.

The general form of the INSTR function is

INSTR(*string to search*, *string to find*)

or

INSTR(*where to start*, *string to search*, *string to find*)

In this case, the optional first position specifies from which position to start the search. If you leave this entry out, the search automatically starts from the first position.

Since the INSTR function returns the value zero (that is, False) when Visual Basic doesn't find a character or a nonzero value (True) when it does, you will often find yourself writing IF-THEN statements in the form

```
IF INSTR(Expression$, ".") THEN
  PRINT "Decimal point found."
ELSE
  PRINT "No decimal point found."
END IF
```

rather than

```
IF INSTR(Expression$, ".") <> 0 THEN
  PRINT "Decimal point found"
ELSE
  PRINT "No decimal point found."
END IF
```

Parsing a String

Another good example of how to use the INSTR command is a program that *parses* a string, which means to take it apart into logical pieces and examine the components—for example, to break a name into its component parts. Suppose you had a string made up of individual words, each separated from the next by a single space. Here is a simple outline for pulling out the individual words:

1. Find the first occurrence of a space. Everything up to the first space is a word.

2. Find the second space. Everything between these two spaces is a word.

3. Find the third space. Everything between the second and third spaces is a word.

4. Continue until there are no more spaces.

Now everything between the last space and the end of the word is the last word.

Here is a fragment that implements this outline for the contents of a text box with a control name of Text1:

```
'This fragment uses INSTR to parse a phrase
'by searching for a space as the separator

'local variables
DIM LenPhrase AS INTEGER, BeforeSpace AS INTEGER
DIM AfterSpace AS INTEGER, SizeOfWord AS INTEGER

Phrase$ = Text1.Text
LenPhrase = LEN(Phrase$)
IF LenPhrase = 0 THEN
  MsgBox("No string entered!")
ELSE
  Separate$ = CHR$(32)              'space
  BeforeSpace = 0
  AfterSpace = INSTR(BeforeSpace + 1, Phrase$, Separate$)
  DO UNTIL AfterSpace = 0
    SizeOfWord = AfterSpace - BeforeSpace - 1
    NextWord$ = MID$(Phrase$, BeforeSpace + 1, SizeOfWord)
    PRINT NextWord$
```

```
    BeforeSpace = AfterSpace
    AfterSpace = INSTR(BeforeSpace + 1, Phrase$, Separate$)
  LOOP
END IF
PRINT MID$(Phrase$, BeforeSpace + 1)
```

This fragment of code would usually be inside an event procedure or a general procedure (see Chapter 8). The initialization makes it easy to start the process. Without this, the fragment would have to treat the first word separately.

The next space is found starting one position in from the previous space. At the beginning of the process, this must be the first position because the IF-THEN-ELSE ends if the string is not empty.

The DO loop stops when no more spaces are left. By testing at the top of the loop, you take care of the case when there is only a single word. If you are puzzled by why the size of the word is given by one more than the value of AfterSpace – BeforeSpace, it's easy to work out an example. Suppose spaces are at the fifth and ninth positions; this means the actual word takes up positions 6, 7, and 8 (that is, it is three characters long). Setting up a variable for the size of the word makes the MID$ statement cleaner. There's rarely a need to combine many statements into one.

Next, the program sets the new value of BeforeSpace to be the old value of AfterSpace, which moves you along to the position of the next space. This sets Visual Basic up to look for the next space. If it finds a space, the cycle continues; if not, Visual Basic moves to whatever is left since there are no more spaces. The rest of the string must be a word.

One problem with this program is that it doesn't handle multiple spaces within the phrase. The problem as usual stems from the outline, which assumed that a word is bound by no more than one space. How can you take care of the quite common possibility of a double space or even more? You need to change the outline for the previous program. The second step in the previous outline assumed that a word was always located between two spaces, one on either side of it. What you need to do is find the next space as you did before, but what is between these two spaces is a word *only if it is not empty space.*

But what really happens if there are two consecutive spaces? As always, an example helps. Suppose the string Phrase$ was given by the following line of code:

```
Phrase$ = "This" + SPACE$(2) + "is" + SPACE$(3) + "a test"
```

This puts two spaces between the first and second words in the phrase, three spaces between the second and third words in the phrase, and one space between the third and fourth words.

Let's "play computer." Especially when dealing with loops, this is often best done by setting up a little chart detailing the values the important variables are supposed to have on each pass, as shown here:

Pass Number	Value of (Key) Variables
0 (Before entering loop)	BeforeSpace = 0
	AfterSpace = 5
(start of) 1st pass through loop	SizeOfWord = 4
(end of) 1st pass through loop	BeforeSpace = 5
	AfterSpace = 6
(start of) 2nd pass	SizeOfWord = 0
(end of) 2nd pass	BeforeSpace = 6
	AfterSpace = 9
(start of) 3rd pass	SizeOfWord = 2
(end of) 3rd pass	BeforeSpace = 9
	AfterSpace = 10
(start of) 4th pass through loop	SizeOfWord = 0

You will often use a table like this when you debug a program. Watch the values of the variables in the Debug window statements (see Chapter 11) and then check the values Visual Basic displays against your table. Examining the value of variables is of little use unless you know what's supposed to happen.

As you can see, the table indicates that whenever you have two spaces together, the variable SizeOfWord has the value zero. Does this always have to be true? Yes, it does, because if you have two consecutive spaces, the value of AfterSpace is always one more than the value of BeforeSpace. And so the value of

AfterSpace – BeforeSpace – 1 = SizeOfWord

must be zero.

Knowing this makes it easy to modify the program. (Change the PRINT statements to read "IF SizeOfWord > 0 THEN..."). A version of this program that takes this into account and also checks for other word separators, like commas, periods, and question marks, can be found in Chapter 8.

Finally, although you need a bit of work to pull out extra spaces within a string, you don't have to do very much for spaces at the beginning or end of a string. Visual Basic comes with two built-in functions for this: LTRIM$ and RTRIM$. As the names suggest, these functions trim spaces from the left and right, respectively. For example, if

```
A$ = "     This has too many spaces on the left."
```

then

LTRIM$(A$) = "This has too many spaces on the left."

or if

```
A$ = "This has too many spaces on the right.     "
```

then

RTRIM$(A$) = "This has too many spaces on the right."

 Note   None of Visual Basic's string functions (except for the statement form of MID$) ever changes a string. They all make a copy and modify that copy.

As another example, suppose you need to decide on the number of digits before the decimal point in a number. This is easy to do if you combine the STR$ command with the INSTR command. Here's an outline for this:

1. Change the number to a string.

2. Find the decimal point using INSTR.

3. If the value from the previous step is zero, there's no decimal point and the number of digits is one less than the length of the converted number.

4. Otherwise, the number of digits in front of the decimal point is two less (because of the extra space that STR$ sticks on positive values and the decimal point) than the value given by the INSTR function.

Here's the Visual Basic fragment:

```
'Find the number of digits

'local variables
DIM Numeral$
DIM Digits AS INTEGER

Numeral$ = STR$(Number)
Digits = INSTR(Numeral$, ".")
IF Digits = 0 THEN
  NumOfDigits = LEN(Numeral$) - 1
ELSE
  NumOfDigits = Digits - 2
END IF
```

An Example: Checking Input

Probably the most important way to bulletproof a program is to check user input, which has already been discussed to some extent in Chapter 6. Check what the user enters before you start processing the data; don't wait until it's too late. This section shows you how to write the code that will accept a number but disregard commas, extraneous decimal points, and so on. The outline for this is

1. Examine a character.

2. If it's a digit, place it on the right.

3. If it's the first decimal point, accept that too and also place it on the right. Otherwise, disregard it.

4. All other characters are canceled.

As you saw in Chapter 6, the KeyPress event procedure lets you examine characters as they are entered, wiping out the extraneous characters.

The main issue you have to decide is how to store the information. The two most common possibilities are

☐   Set up a form level variable for the number.

☐   Leave the text as the (string) contents of the control and convert the text inside the control to a number inside whatever procedures need it.

The advantage of the first option is that you don't have to cancel out commas, which users might prefer. The advantage of the second is that you may not need to do the extra analysis at all.

The following fragment stores the information as the contents of a form level variable called Numeral$ and assumes you've set up named constants TRUE (= −1) and FALSE (= 0):

```
SUB Text1_KeyPress (KeyAscii AS INTEGER)

  'This fragment accepts only a number

  'local variables
  STATIC DecimalPointUsed AS INTEGER

  SELECT CASE KeyAscii
    CASE ASC("0") TO ASC("9")
      Numeral$ = Numeral$ + CHR$(KeyAscii)
    CASE ASC(".")
      IF DecimalPointUsed THEN
        KeyAscii = 0
        BEEP
      ELSE
        DecimalPointUsed = TRUE
        Numeral$ = Numeral$ + CHR$(KeyAscii)
      END IF
    CASE ASC(",")
      'Comma - do nothing to Numeral$
    CASE ELSE
      KeyAscii = 0
      Beep
  END SELECT
END SUB
```

Since DecimalPointUsed was set up as a static variable, this information is preserved by Visual Basic during each subsequent call to the KeyPress event procedure. On the other hand, if you wanted to allow more than one number to be entered in the control, the situation would be a bit more complicated. You could make this a form level variable and reset it back to False each time you wanted to reuse the information, or you could leave it as a static variable and set it to False whenever the Text box starts out blank.

If a character is in the range from zero to 9, then it's a digit. Therefore, it's concatenated at the right of the variable Numeral$. Next, the fragment moves to the case that accepts a single decimal point in the number. However, entering a decimal point flips the DecimalPointUsed flag to True.

The fragment leaves the commas intact in the display but, of course, doesn't add them to the Numeral$ variable, which will be turned into a number. Any other characters are canceled and the computer beeps to provide some feedback. You might also use a message box here.

Using FORMAT$, DATE$, and TIME$

If you've run the mortgage program presented in Chapters 5 and 6 or have been experimenting on your own with calculations displayed in text boxes, you have probably decided that the answers to simple calculations look strange. You may end up with 16 decimal digits when you really want the answer to look like 1.01, for example. You overcome this problem by replacing the STR$ function with a new function called the FORMAT$ function.

The FORMAT$ Function

The FORMAT$ function works with a number and a *template* (also called a *format string*). The syntax is

FORMAT$(*NumericExpression*, *FormatString*$)

For example, the statement

```
a$ = FORMAT$(123.456789, "###.##")
```

stores the string "123.46" in a$. Visual Basic rounds the number to have only two digits after the decimal point.

The FORMAT$ function, unlike the STR$ function, does not leave room for an implied + sign. This means that in a statement like

```
PRINT "The interest rate is "; FORMAT$(Payment, "####.##")
```

the extra space after the word "is" is essential.

In general, a # is the placeholder for a digit. However, leading and trailing zeros will not be included, and any excess places to the left and right of the decimal point are ignored. For example, executing the statement

```
a$ = FORMAT$(123.450, "####.####")
```

stores the string "123.45" in a$.

Unlike interpreted BASIC and QuickBASIC, Visual Basic will print all the digits to the left of the decimal point, so you don't have to worry about having too few #'s on the left of the decimal point in the format string. This way you can concentrate on deciding the number of decimals you want displayed and adjust the format string accordingly. For example, the statement

```
a$ = FORMAT$(123456.12345, "#.###")
```

stores "123456.123" in a$.

If you want to have Visual Basic display leading or trailing zeros, you use a 0 (zero) in place of the # in the format string. For example, the statement

```
a$ = FORMAT$(123.45,"#.000")
```

stores "123.450" in a$, while the statement

```
a$ = FORMAT$(123.45,"00000")
```

stores "00123" in a$.

You may want to display numbers with commas every three digits. To do this, place a comma between any two digit placeholders to the left of the decimal point. For example, the statement

```
a$ = FORMAT$(123456789.991, "#,#.##)
```

stores "123,456,789.99" in a$.

The comma may also be used to display output scaled in units of thousands, millions, billions, etc. If you place a comma immediately to the left of the decimal point, Visual Basic interprets this to mean it should scale the output in units of thousands. That is, Visual Basic displays the number divided by 1000. For example, the statement

```
a$ = FORMAT$(123456789.991, "#,.##")
```

stores "123456.79" in a$. If you place two adjacent commas anywhere to the left of the decimal point, Visual Basic displays the number divided by 1000*1000, that is, by one million. As an example, suppose your program is dealing with Japanese yen and you need to display one hundred million yen. If you want to write "100 million yen" rather than "100,000,000 yen," use two adjacent commas and no decimal point in the format string:

```
PRINT FORMAT$(100000000, "#,,");" million yen"
```

If you want to express a number as a percentage, place a percent sign at the end of the format string. Visual Basic will automatically multiply the expression by 100 before converting. For example, the statement

```
a$ = FORMAT$(1.234, "#.##%")
```

stores "123.4%" in a$.

If you need to display a −, +, $, (,), or spaces, use the appropriate symbol in the format string exactly in the place you want it to occur. For example, if you want to have a dollar sign in front of a value, use this:

```
PRINT FORMAT$(AmountOfMoney, "$#.##"")
```

The FORMAT$ function is very important, but because the number of options is so large, you have seen only a sample of the possibilities in this section. A detailed discussion and additional examples can be found in Appendix C and the on-line help.

One final point about the FORMAT$ function: it is often useful to set up string constants for the various format strings. Especially when you have to repeatedly format values, it's worth first setting up a constant like

```
CONST MONEY = "#,#.##"
```

From that point on you can write

```
FORMAT$(Amount, MONEY)
```

which is far more readable and less prone to typos.

Calendar Information

Visual Basic has many built-in functions that you can use to read the time, day, and year information contained in the system clock. If you combine this with built-in functions for converting dates to numbers, financial calculations become much easier.

The DATE$ Function

The DATE$ function returns a string of the form *Month-Day-Year* (*mm-dd-yyyy*). The month and day always use two digits; the year uses four (for example, 01-01-1992 for January 1, 1992). You can also use the statement form of DATE$ to reset the current date in the system. The least ambiguous way to do this is by assigning a string to DATE$ in one of the following forms:

```
DATE$ = "mm-dd-yyyy"
DATE$ = "mm/dd/yyyy"
```

where *mm* are numerals between 01 and 12, *dd* are days between 01 and 31, and *yyyy* are years between 1980 and 2099.

If you try to reset the date to an illegal date like 31 February, you get an "Illegal function call" message when you run the program. You may also use a two-digit year for the years 1980 to 1999, but this is not practical for forward-looking programs.

You can also read the time in the system clock or reset it with the TIME$ function. The TIME$ function returns an eight-character string of the form *hh:mm:ss* using a 24-hour clock. To reset it, assign a string of the correct form to TIME$:

Example of Time Command	Effect
TIME$ ="hh"	Sets the hour, minutes & seconds = 0
TIME$ ="hh:mm"	Sets the hours & minutes, seconds = 0
TIME$ ="hh:mm:ss"	Sets the hours, minutes, & seconds

The hours range between 00 for midnight and 23 for 11:00 P.M.

Note If your computer has a built in clock calender these functions may not change the time stored there. To do this you may need to use the setup program that came with your computer. TIME$ and DATE$ may only change the clock setting until the next time you reboot the computer.

The Numeric Calendar Functions

To do financial calculations accurately, your programs have to be able to calculate the number of days that have passed between two dates—taking leap years into account as well. Visual Basic usually stores this information in the form of a double-precision number where the digits to the left of the decimal point represent the date and the digits to the right of the decimal point represent the time. Midnight on December 30, 1899 is 0.000000, midnight on December 31, 1899 is 1.000000, and midnight on January 1, 1900 is 2.000000. Midnight on January 1, 2000, is 36526.00000 because 36,526 days have passed since December 30, 1899. In the Visual Basic documentation, numbers of this form are called *serial numbers*. Visual Basic makes the adjustment necessary for leap years when it does this calculation.

The most important function for applications that uses this information is DATEVALUE(*String*). This function gives a serial number representing the date defined by the string expression inside the parentheses. Besides accepting strings in the expected form of *mm-dd-yyyy*, this function can also accept the name of the month or any unambiguous abbreviation for the month. For example, all of the following return the value zero:

```
DATEVALUE("12-30-1899")
DATEVALUE("December 30, 1899")
DATEVALUE("Dec 30, 1899")
DATEVALUE("30 December 1899")
DATEVALUE("30-Dec-1899")
```

You cannot use this function if the date doesn't make sense. For example,

```
DATEVALUE("1992-2-30")
```

gives an "Illegal function call" message at run time.

Of course, you will usually need to know what serial number represents the current day and time. For this, Visual Basic has the built-in NOW function, as shown here:

```
PRINT "The serial number for today is "; NOW
```

This returns the information about the date and time in the system clock.

You will occasionally need the DATESERIAL function. Its syntax is

DATESERIAL(*Year*%, *Month*%, *Day*%)

Year% is an integer between 1753 and 2078, inclusive (or an integer expression that Visual Basic can reduce to this form). *Month*% is an integer (or integer expression) with a value between 1 and 12, and *Day*% must be between 1 and 31. Again, you may use this function only if the date makes sense. For example,

```
DATESERIAL(1992, 2, 30)
```

will also give an "Illegal function call" message at run time.

You can apply the FORMAT$ function to any serial number to display the information contained in the number. For example, if it is now 10:01 P.M. on January 1, 1992, the results are as follows:

Form	**Display**
FORMAT$(NOW,"m-d-yy")	1-1-92

Form	Display
FORMAT$(NOW,"hh:mm")	22:01
FORMAT$(NOW,"hh:mm am/pm")	10:01 pm
FORMAT$(NOW,"hh:mm AM/PM mm/dd/yy")	10:01 PM 01-01-92

There are many other possibilities for format strings attached to serial numbers. See the on-line help window for more details and examples.

An Example Using the DATEVALUE Function

Suppose you want to write an application that will tell the user how many days he or she has been alive. The screen for that application might look like the one shown in Figure 7-1, which has two labels, two text boxes, and two command buttons. The following table describes the properties of these controls:

Control	Control Name	Caption (Text)
Top text box	Birthdate	-
Bottom text box	Answer	-
Left button	Calculate	&Calculate
Right button	Quit	&Quit

FIGURE 7-1   Form for days alive program

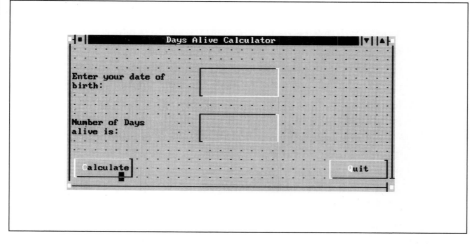

Notice that because of the ampersand in front of the "C" on the caption for the command button, a user can use the ALT+C combination as an access key to do the calculation. Similarly, the Quit button can be activated by pressing ALT-Q.

Besides the trivial code for the Quit button (the END command alone) that ends the application, all the code for this application is in the Calculate_Click event procedure:

```
SUB Calculate_Click ()
  DIM NumberOfDays AS LONG
  NumberOfDays = NOW - DATEVALUE(BirthDate.Text)
  Answer.Text = FORMAT$(NumberOfDays, "#,#")
END SUB
```

This procedure needs to use long integers because the limit on ordinary integers would be around 89 years. In addition, Visual Basic does the subtraction in double precision but rounds to an integer because you are assigning a double-precision value to a (long) integer variable. Finally, the FORMAT$ command displays the answer, using a comma.

The Other Numeric Calendar Functions

There is a handful of other functions that let you analyze the information contained in a serial number. These are occasionally useful when you need to write applications that work on a day-to-day or even a minute-to-minute basis.

TIMEVALUE(String)   The TIMEVALUE(*String*) function returns a serial number between 0 and 1 representing the time defined by the string expression. If n seconds have passed since midnight, then the serial number returned is n / 86400 (a day has 86,400 seconds). Acceptable formats for the string expression are hh:mm:ss, hh:mm:ss AM, and hh:mm:ss PM.

TIMESERIAL(hours%, minutes%, seconds%)   The function TIME-SERIAL (*hours%, minutes%, seconds%*) returns a serial number in the same manner as the TIMEVALUE function. TIMESERIAL differs from TIMEVALUE only in its parameters which must be three integer expressions giving the hours (0 to 23), minutes (0 to 59), and seconds (0 to 59) of the time to be converted to a serial number.

YEAR(SerialNumber)   The YEAR(*SerialNumber*) function gives an integer between 1753 and 2078 for the year determined by the serial number.

MONTH(SerialNumber)   The MONTH(*SerialNumber*) function gives an integer between 1 and 12 for the month.

DAY(SerialNumber)   The DAY(*SerialNumber*) function returns an integer between 1 and 31 that is the day of the month represented by the serial number inside the parentheses.

WEEKDAY(SerialNumber)   The WEEKDAY(*SerialNumber*) function gives you an integer between 1 (Sunday) and 7 (Saturday) for the day.

MINUTE(SerialNumber)   The MINUTE(*SerialNumber*) function gives an integer between zero and 59 for the number of minutes represented in the serial number.

SECOND(SerialNumber)   The SECOND(*SerialNumber*) function gives you the number of seconds between zero and 59.

The RND Function

In card games and most other games, the play is unpredictable. This is exactly what is meant by a game of chance. On the other hand, computers are machines, and the behavior of machines should be predictable. To write a program in Visual Basic that allows you, for example, to simulate the throwing of a die, you need a function that makes the behavior of the computer seem random. You do this by means of the RND function. For example, run the following Form_Click procedure on a blank form:

```
SUB Form_Click()
  CLS
  FOR I = 1 TO 5
    PRINT RND
  NEXT I
END SUB
```

FIGURE 7-2

Demonstration of the random number generator

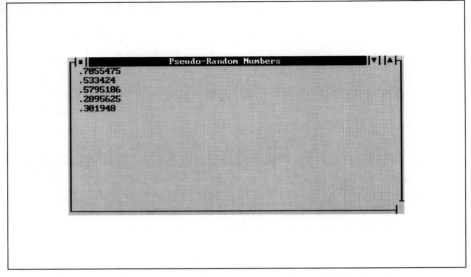

```
Pseudo-Random Numbers
.7055475
.533424
.5795186
.2895625
.301948
```

What you'll see will look like the screen in Figure 7-2. As you can see, five numbers between zero and 1, each having up to 7 digits, roll down the screen. These numbers seem to follow no pattern: that's what is usually meant by random. They'll also have many but not all of the sophisticated statistical properties that scientists expect of random numbers. Without some changes, for example, they would not be very useful in simulation programs. See Chapter 9 for how to modify the built-in random number generator for simulations.

Each time the computer processes a line containing the statement "PRINT RND", a different number between zero and 1 pops out. In theory, the number can be zero but can't ever be 1.

It's natural to wonder what a number with up to 7 decimal places is good for. Suppose, for example, you wanted to write a program that simulated a coin toss. There are three possibilities: it could be heads, it could be tails—or it could stand on edge. A fragment to simulate a coin toss might look like this:

```
'A coin toss simulator

CoinToss = RND
SELECT CASE CoinToss
```

```
    CASE IS < .5
      PRINT "Heads"
    CASE .5
      PRINT "Stood on edge!!!!"
    CASE ELSE
      PRINT "Tails"
END SELECT
```

Suppose you incorporate this fragment into a Form_Click procedure:

```
SUB Form_Click ()
  'A multiple coin toss simulator

  'local variables
  DIM Trials AS INTEGER, NumOfHeads AS INTEGER
  DIM NumOfTails AS INTEGER, I AS INTEGER
  DIM CoinToss AS SINGLE

  Trials = VAL(InputBox$("How many trials?"))
  NumOfHeads = 0
  NumOfTails = 0
  Unbelievable = 0

  FOR I = 1 TO Trials
    CoinToss = RND
    SELECT CASE CoinToss
      CASE IS < .5
        NumOfHeads = NumOfHeads + 1
      CASE .5
        PRINT "Stood on edge!!!!"   'maybe in a couple of years?
        BEEP: BEEP
        Unbelievable = Unbelievable + 1
      CASE ELSE
        NumOfTails = NumOfTails + 1
    END SELECT
  NEXT I
  CLS
  PRINT "Number of heads was"; NumOfHeads
  PRINT "Number of tails was"; NumOfTails
  IF Unbelievable > 0 THEN
    PRINT "The coin stood on edge!"
  END IF
END SUB
```

Try this program with a different number of trials. You should get roughly the same number of heads as tails and no "standing on edges."

(For a large number of trials, it would be very unlikely that you'd get equal numbers of heads and tails.) Now end the program and run it again, using the same number of trials each time. If you do, you'll notice that you will get exactly the same number of heads and tails. This would certainly be unusual behavior for an honest coin. What is happening?

Well, the numbers you get using the RND function are only *pseudo-random*. *Pseudo* generally means false, and you've just seen one of the problems of pseudo–random numbers. Every time you start a program anew, you will get the same sequence of pseudo–random numbers, as though the computer reads the same set of cards in the same order each time. The deck always starts out the same and therefore the results are fixed. You need a way to "shuffle the deck" each time the program starts up. You can do this in many ways. A slow but sure way is to start your program with something like this:

```
X$ = INPUTBOX$("Everyone who wants to play should press a number
key.")        'above and this are one line
Number% = VAL(X$)

FOR I% = 1 TO Number%
  X = RND
NEXT I%
```

Think of this fragment as advancing you to a place in the list of random numbers that no one can tell beforehand. The problem with this approach is that moving ahead in the list (generating all those pseudo-random numbers) takes time. You can modify the RND function to eliminate any wait by adding a parameter.

First, suppose you issue a RND(0). Then you get the last pseudo-random number generated. This is useful when trying to debug a program. RND(0) gives you a way of checking which pseudo-random number the machine just used. (Imagine trying to debug a program if an important number changes each time and you have no way of knowing its value.)

Suppose next there is a negative number inside the parentheses. Each time you give the command

RND(*negative number*)

you get the same pseudo-random number. This is another important debugging tool. It lets you rerun a program keeping the pseudo-random numbers temporarily stable. A good way to think about what a negative seed does is to imagine that there is a different list of pseudo-random numbers, each one corresponding to a different negative seed. You can think of the seed as the number from which the random numbers grow. This is done by transforming the seed using the *linear congruential method*, which transforms the number using the MOD function. The easiest way to understand what Visual Basic is doing for its random number generator is to imagine you are working only with integers. The random number generator would then use the built-in MOD function to generate the next pseudo-random number roughly as follows:

NextNumber = A * PreviousNumber + B MOD M

Here, A, B, and M are fixed integers. This method is very fast. But because A, B, and M are fixed by Visual Basic designers, this method can be unreliable if you need many random numbers for a simulation program. If you need thousands of random numbers for a program, see Chapter 9, which gives you one way of improving the built-in random number generator. The cost is that the program will run somewhat more slowly and need more memory.

Note   From this point on, this book will stop using the term "pseudo–random" and refer to the numbers coming from the RND function as being "random"; this follows the usual terminology in programming.

The easiest and fastest way to not stack the cards at the outset is to use the system clock to reseed the random number generator. You do this by using a new command: RANDOMIZE.

Numbers between zero and 1 may (with a little work) be good for imitating a coin toss, but the method used earlier would be cumbersome for, say, a dice simulation. The outline would be something like this:

- ☐   If the random number is less than 1/6, make it a 1.

- ☐   If more than 1/6 but less than 2/6 (= 1/3), make it a 2.

- ☐   If more than 2/6 but less than 3/6 (= 1/2), make it a 3.

and so on. Thinking about this outline leads to a simple trick called *scaling* that more or less automates this process. Suppose you take a number between zero and 1 and multiply it by 6. If it was less than 1/6 to start with, it will now be less than 1; if it was between 1/6 and 2/6 (1/3), it will now be between 1 and 2; and so on. All you need to do then is multiply the number by 6 and move up to the next integer. In general, if the number was between zero and 1 (but never quite getting to 1), the result of multiplying by 6 goes from zero not quite up to 6.

Unfortunately, there's no command in Visual Basic to move up to the next integer. Instead, the FIX function throws away the decimal part of a number. For example:

FIX(3.456) = 3   FIX(–7.9998) = –7   FIX(8) = 8

However, by adding 1 to the result of "fixing" a positive number, you will, in effect, move to the next highest positive integer. For example, look at the following fragment:

```
'A dice simulation using FIX

RANDOMIZE
CLS
Die% = FIX(6 * RND) + 1
PRINT "I rolled a"; DIE%
```

The key to the fragment is that the number inside the parentheses—6 * RND—is always between 0 and 6, but it can't be 6 because RND is never 1. Applying the FIX function gives you an integer between 0 and 5 (that is, 0, 1, 2, 3, 4, or 5), and now you only have to add 1 to make it a proper-looking die.

There's another function that works much the same way as FIX: INT. INT gives the *floor* of a number—the first integer that's smaller than or equal to the number. It's technically called the greatest integer function. However, thinking of it as the floor function makes it easy to remember what happens for negative numbers. With negative numbers, you move down. For example, INT(–3.5) is –4, INT(–4.1) is –5 but INT(–4) is still –4, and so on. You can see that FIX and INT work the same way for positive numbers but are different for negative ones. Using INT and adding 1 always moves to the next *largest* integer.

The INT and FIX functions have other uses. For example, the post office charges for first-class mail are 29 cents for the first ounce and 23 cents for each additional ounce (or fraction thereof). Suppose an item weighed

3.4 ounces. Then the cost would be 29 cents for the first ounce and 69 (3 * 23) for the additional ounces, counting the fraction. The cost is

.29 + INT(3.4) * .23

In general, it's given by the following fragment:

```
IF INT(WeightOfObject) = WeightOfObject THEN
  Cost = .29 + .23 * (WeightOfObject - 1)
ELSE
  Cost = .29 + 23 * INT(WeightOfObject)
END IF
```

An Example Using the Random Number Generator

Suppose you wanted to write a "jumble" program. This would take a string and shuffle the letters around. It's a prototype for many other types of operations—for example, shuffling a deck of cards. Here's an outline for one way to do it:

1. Start at the first character.

2. Swap it with a randomly chosen character.

3. Do the same for the second character until there are no more characters left.

The swapping can be done with the MID$ statement, since you are never changing the size of the string. The screen in Figure 7-3 shows what the form might look like. Suppose the command button is given a control name of JumbleIt, the top text box is called OriginalText, and the destination text box is called JumbledText. Then the click procedure looks like this:

```
SUB JumbleIt_Click ()
  'A Jumble program

  'local variables
  DIM Phrase$, HoldChar$
  DIM I AS INTEGER
  DIM LenPhrase AS INTEGER, INum AS INTEGER
```

```
RANDOMIZE
Phrase$ = OriginalText.Text
LenPhrase = LEN(Phrase$)
FOR I = 1 TO LenPhrase
   INum = INT(LenPhrase * RND) + 1
   HoldChar$ = MID$(Phrase$, I, 1)
   MID$(Phrase$, I, 1) = MID$(Phrase$, INum, 1)
   MID$(Phrase$, INum, 1) = HoldChar$
NEXT I
JumbleText.Text = Phrase$
END SUB
```

Since values inside the string commands start at 1 and range up to the length of the string, you need to add 1 to INT(LenPhrase * RND). Using this value gives you a random position within the string. Once you have the random character, you swap it with the current character in the string, as determined by the counter in the FOR-NEXT loop.

Since the SWAP statement can only swap variables, a statement like:

SWAP MID$(*Phrase$, INum, 1*), MID$(*Phrase$, I, 1*)

won't work.

FIGURE 7-3

Form for a jumble program

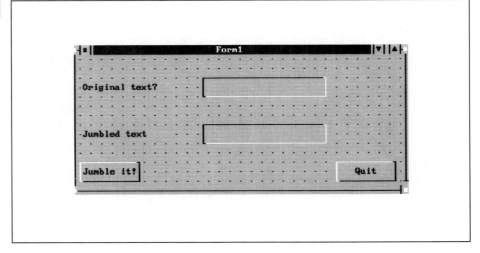

To make this program into a card shuffler, all you need to do is give Phrase$ the right value. You can do this by using the CHR$ command. You'll see how to do this in Chapter 8.

Up to this point, all the random integers you've used have started from zero or 1. Sometimes it's convenient to have random integers that span a range. For example, take a random four-letter combination; how likely is it to be a word in English? To try this out, you need to generate four random letters and string them together. An obvious way to do this is to apply the CHR$ command to a random integer between 65 and 90 (the range of ASCII codes for the uppercase alphabet). To get a random integer in this range:

1. Generate a random integer between 0 and 25.

2. Add it to 65 to get the ASCII value of a lowercase letter.

Here is a translation of this into code:

```
CharNum = INT(26 * RND) + 65
```

And here is a fragment that uses this code to continuously generate random four-letter combinations:

```
'Random 4 letter 'words'
'demonstrates RND for a range

'local variables
DIM I AS INTEGER, CharNum AS INTEGER

RANDOMIZE
CLS
DO
  Word$ = ""
  FOR I = 1 TO 4
    CharNum = INT(26 * RND) + 65
    Word$ = Word$ + CHR$(CharNum)
  NEXT I
  PRINT Word$
LOOP
```

The key, as explained in the outline above, is the statement defining the value of CharNum that gives you a random integer in the right range.

The next statement turns it into a random uppercase letter. As usual, these two statements could have been combined into one:

```
Word$ = Word$ + CHR$(INT(26 * RND) + 65)
```

but this is clearly less readable than the preceding code. Note, however, that because of a bug in early versions of Visual Basic, you would be better off printing to a multi-line text box.

Finally, this fragment is an infinite loop, since no way to end it was programmed. You can use the CTRL+BREAK combination to end it, but more in keeping with the spirit of Visual Basic is to make this a Form_Click procedure to start the process and add a Form_DblClick procedure to end it.

Bit Twiddling

Bit twiddling refers to looking at the individual bits that make up a number and resetting them if needed. You need to do this in order to use the KeyUp and KeyDown event procedures that let you detect the keys that do not correspond to standard keyboard characters, like the function and arrow keys. Knowing how the logical operators work on the bit level also makes it easy to program powerful systems for encrypting your data (see Chapter 13). To do this you first need to learn a little bit about how binary arithmetic works.

Counting in Base 2 and Base 16

A computer is ultimately a giant collection of on-off switches, and a disk is a collection of particles that can either be magnetized or not. Think of each memory location in your PC as being made up of eight on-off switches. This affects the internal representation of numbers inside a PC. For example, when you write 255, you mean two hundreds, five tens, and five ones. The digits are arranged in positional notation, with each place holding numbers ten times as large as the one to the right. (This is called *decimal notation*.) However, your computer would store this number in a single memory location as 11111111, meaning one 128, one 64, one 32, one 16, one 8, one 4, one 2, and one 1. Each of these switches is called a *bit* (for binary digit). When it stores a 1, the bit is said to be on, and the value stored in that position is twice what the value was in the place to the right (instead of ten times the value, as in decimal notation). Eight bits form a *byte* (which is one memory location), two bytes form a *word*, and half a byte is called a *nibble*.

The following table shows you how to count to 15 in binary.

Binary	Decimal
0	0
1	1
10	2
11	3
100	4
101	5
110	6
111	7
1000	8
1001	9
1010	10
1011	11
1100	12
1101	13
1110	14
1111	15

15 is the largest number that can be stored in a single nibble, and 255 is the largest number that can be stored in a byte. Bits are numbered with the leftmost bit called the *most significant* and the rightmost (or 0th) bit the *least significant*.

Binary numbers can be a bit difficult to handle. It's much easier if you use hexadecimal numbers (base 16). Each place in a hexadecimal numbering scheme is 16 times the previous place. So instead of saying "one's place, 10's place, 100's place," as you learned in grade school, in hexadecimal (hex) you say, "one's place, 16's place, 256's place," and so on. For example, a hexadecimal 10 is 16 in decimal. Hexadecimal notation uses A for decimal 10, B for decimal 11, C for decimal 12, D for decimal 13, E for decimal 14, and F for decimal 15. In Visual Basic programs, you prefix a number with &H to indicate that it is a hexadecimal number; for example, 49 = &H31. Each hexadecimal digit represents 4 binary digits, or 1 nibble. To convert binary numbers to hex, just group the digits from right to left in groups of four and convert.

For example, 11010111 (1101 0111, in two groups of four) is D7 in hex, because 1101 is 13 in decimal and is D in hex, and 0111 is 7 in both decimal and hex.

Visual Basic has built-in functions to convert a number to a string of hexadecimal (base 16) or octal (base 8) digits. They are

HEX$ for hexadecimal
OCT$ for octal

Surprisingly, Visual Basic does not have a built-in function for converting a number to binary. There are many ways to write such a program. As usual, it's best to take an example and work through it step by step. The easiest examples are, of course, zero and 1, which are the same in decimal and binary. What about 3? This is 11 in binary (1 * 2 + 1). In general, the rightmost (least significant) binary digit is given by looking at whether the number is even or odd. The built-in MOD function tells this. For example, the last binary digit is the number MOD 2.

To move to the next binary digit, you have to divide by 2 and throw away the remainder (which you just took into account by using the MOD function). You continue this process until there's nothing left to divide.

As a more serious example, suppose you want to convert a number like 43 to binary:

Last Binary Digit = 43 MOD 2 = 1

Now you divide by 2, using the integer division operation (the backslash) and continue the process:

Next binary digit = (43 \ 2) MOD 2 = 21 MOD 2 = 1

and then you continue this process:

Next binary digit = (21 \ 2) MOD 2 = 10 MOD 2 = 0)
Next binary digit = (10 \ 2) MOD 2 = 5 MOD 2 = 1
Next binary digit = (5 \ 2) MOD 2 = 2 MOD 2 = 0
Next binary digit = (2 \ 2) MOD 2 = 1 MOD 2 = 1

Since 1 \ 2 is zero, you stop here. Stringing these digits together from bottom to top gives you 101011.

Here's a program that implements this outline attached to a ConvertToBinary_Click event procedure. The program assumes there are two text boxes, Text1 for the number and Text2 for the string of binary digits.

```
SUB ConvertToBinary_Click ()

  'local variables
  DIM Number AS INTEGER
  DIM BinaryForm AS STRING

  Number = VAL(Text1.Text)
  BinaryForm = ""
  DO
    Digit = Number MOD 2
    IF Digit = 0 THEN
      BinaryForm = "0" + BinaryForm
    ELSE
      BinaryForm = "1" + BinaryForm
    END IF
    Number = Number \ 2
  LOOP UNTIL Number = 0
  Text2.Text = BinaryForm
END SUB
```

If the number to be converted was zero, you still need to start the loop. On the other hand, you do want to give the representation of zero in binary, as "0". The real work in this procedure is done in the ELSE clause. You could use a SELECT CASE statement inside the procedure, but with two options this seems like overkill. Finally, as the example shows, when integer division gives you zero, you stop.

The next section shows you another way to write a binary conversion routine.

The Logical Operators at the Bit Level

You may have thought that Visual Basic's use of zero for False made sense, but wondered about –1 for True. To understand this, you have to know that all the logical operators (NOT, AND, OR, and so on) are really functions that work on the bit level.

Suppose you are given two bits, *a* and *b*. The value of *a* AND *b* is 1 only if both binary digits are 1; otherwise, it is zero. If X and Y are integers, then X AND Y is determined by the ANDing of corresponding bits in their binary representations. For example, if

X = 7 in decimal   = 0111 in binary
Y = 12 in decimal   = 1100 in binary

then X AND Y = 0100 in binary (4 in decimal) because only in the third position are both bits 1. Because AND gives a 1 only in those bit positions where both digits are 1, ANDing with a number whose binary digit is a single 1 and whose remaining digits are all zero lets you isolate the binary digits of any integer. For example:

X AND 1	Tells you whether the least significant (rightmost) binary digit is on. You get a zero if it is not on.
X AND 2	Since 2 in decimal is 10 in binary, a zero tells you that the next significant (second from the right) binary digit is off.
X AND 4	Since 4 in decimal is 100 in binary, this tells you whether the next significant (third from the right) binary digit is on.

This process is called *masking* and is the key to using the KeyUp, KeyDown event procedures described in the next section. You can also easily adapt this process to write another binary conversion routine:

```
SUB ConvertToBinary_Click ()

   'local variables
   DIM BitPattern AS INTEGER, Number AS INTEGER
   DIM BinaryForm AS STRING
```

```
Number = VAL(Text1.Text)
BinaryForm = ""
BitPattern = 1
DO
  Digit = Number AND BitPattern
  IF Digit = 0 THEN
    BinaryForm = "0" + BinaryForm
  ELSE
    BinaryForm = "1" + BinaryForm
  END IF
  BitPattern = BitPattern * 2     'next bit
LOOP UNTIL BitPattern > Number
Text2.Text = BinaryForm
END SUB
```

Now consider the OR operator with bits *a* and *b* and integers X and Y. The value of *a* OR *b* is 1 if either or both binary digits are 1; otherwise, it is zero. X OR Y is determined by the ORing of corresponding bits in their binary representations. Therefore,

7 OR 12 = 15 (0111 OR 1100 = 1111 in binary)

Use OR to set specific bits to one (the on state). For example, X OR 4 makes sure that the third bit is on, X OR 64, the seventh bit, and so on.

One of the most interesting operators on the bit level is XOR (exclusive OR—*a* or *b* but not both). This gives a 1 in a specific position if exactly one of the bits is on. Here's an example:

7 XOR 12 = 11 (= 0111 XOR 1100 = 1011 in binary)

XORing has the useful property that XORing twice with the same number does nothing. For example,

(7 XOR 12) XOR 12 = 11 XOR 12 = 7

or, on the bit level,

0111 XOR 1100 = 1011
1011 XOR 1100 = 0111

A popular animation technique is based on the use of the XOR command twice to bring you back to where you started. This is because you can restore the previous display exactly as it was before (see Chapter 16). This property of the XOR operator is also the key to a popular method of encrypting information (see Chapter 13).

There are three other logical operators, IMP, EQV, and NOT. X IMP Y gives 1 except when X is 1 and Y is zero. X EQV Y is 1 only when both bits are the same—both 1 or both zero. The NOT operator, on the other hand, works on a number by reversing the bits—a 1 becomes a zero and a zero becomes a 1.

Finally, to answer the question posed at the beginning of this section, here's why –1 is True in Visual Basic. Each integer takes 16 bits. NOT 0 is then

NOT(0000 0000 0000 0000) = 1111 1111 1111 1111

You might expect this to be the largest integer representable in 16 bits (65,535 in decimal), but Visual Basic uses the leftmost bit for the sign. A 1 there means the number is negative. However, Visual Basic uses what is called *twos-complement notation* for negative numbers. In twos-complement notation, to represent a negative number you do the following:

1. Apply NOT to the 15 bits that represent the number.

2. Set the leftmost (16th) bit to 1.

3. Add 1 to the result.

Therefore, for –1, take the bit pattern for 1:

000 0000 0000 0001

Apply NOT:

111 1111 1111 1110

Add the leftmost bit as a 1:

1111 1111 1111 1110

Now add 1:

1111 1111 1111 1111

The result is that NOT(0) is −1!

For an explanation of why this system really is useful, consult any book on microcomputer architecture.

KeyUp and KeyDown

The KeyPress event reports on which ASCII-coded key a user pressed. The two event procedures described in this section report much lower-level information. They will tell exactly what the user did to the keyboard. If you need to determine whether he or she pressed CTRL, a function key, or the like, these are the event procedures to use. For example, if you want your application to supply context-sensitive help when the user presses the F1 key, these are the event procedures to use.

However, these event procedures are a bit more complicated to use because you must distinguish, for example, between lowercase and uppercase letters. The syntax for both of these event procedures is the same:

SUB Control_KeyUp(*KeyCode AS INTEGER, Shift AS INTEGER*)
SUB Control_KeyDown(*KeyCode AS INTEGER, Shift AS INTEGER*)

Only the control that has the focus can respond to keyboard events. The active form has the focus if no control on the form does.

First, you have to use bit masking on the Shift parameter to determine whether the SHIFT key, the CTRL key, or the ALT key (or some combination of the three) was pressed:

```
IF Shift AND 1 = 1 THEN PRINT "Shift key pressed"
IF Shift AND 2 = 2 THEN PRINT "Ctrl key pressed"
IF Shift AND 4 = 4 THEN PRINT "Alt key pressed"
```

This means there are eight possibilities. For example, set up a blank form and add the following event procedure:

```
SUB Form_KeyDown(KeyCode AS INTEGER, Shift AS INTEGER)
  SELECT CASE Shift
    CASE 0
      PRINT "Neither Ctrl, Alt or Shift key was pressed"
    CASE 1
      PRINT "Only Shift key pressed"
```

```
   CASE 2
     PRINT "Only Ctrl key pressed"
   CASE 3
     PRINT "Shift + Ctrl key pressed"
   CASE 4
     PRINT "Only Alt key pressed"
   CASE 5
     PRINT "Alt + Shift key pressed"
   CASE 6
     PRINT "Alt + Ctrl key pressed"
   CASE 7
     PRINT "Alt, Shift and Ctrl key pressed"
   END SELECT
END SUB
```

This procedure assumes that only the first three bits of the Shift parameter are used. Since Microsoft reserves the right to use the higher order bits, it may be preferable to start by setting the following:

```
LowerThreeBits = Shift AND 7        '7 = 0111 in binary
```

and using this new variable in the SELECT CASE statement.

The KeyCode integer parameter tells you what physical key was pressed. The code does not distinguish between the key and its shifted sibling. "A" and "a," "1" and "!" have the same codes. The codes for these integers follow the ASCII codes only for A through Z and 0 through 9 on the keyboard. The codes for a through z and ! through (are the same as those for A through Z and 0 through 9, respectively. The remaining codes, whether for the arrow keys, the function keys, or the numeric keypad, are given mnemonic devices in a special file called the CONSTANT.BI file that you can incorporate into your programs.

You almost certainly will want to include these mnemonic constants in your project when you start developing sophisticated projects. For example, suppose you want to detect if a user presses F1. The code for this turns out to be &H70. After including this file into your program, a statement inside a KeyDown event procedure like

```
IF KeyCode = Key_F1 THEN        'easier than &H70!
   ' perhaps put a MSGBOX with help information here
   'or show a form until the F1 key was released
   ' check this with KeyUp!
END IF
```

would be all that it takes. (As indicated in the remarks, you could use this to start context-sensitive help, for example.)

To use these constants, you'll first want to incorporate the CON-STANT.BI file into your leading code of the form. The easiest way to do this is with a new type of command—the meta-command. Unlike ordinary commands, meta-commands tell the Visual Basic compiler what to do with your program. All meta-commands must be placed in the leading code of the form, must be preceded by a comment symbol and a $ (dollar sign). The meta-command you need to include a file in your program is:

'$INCLUDE *filename*

For example, the statement:

```
'$INCLUDE "C:\VBDOS\CONSTANT.BI"
```

tells Visual Basic to look in the C:\VBDOS directory for the file name CONSTANT.BI and include the information contained in that file in your program. You can tell Visual Basic where to look for $INCLUDE files by using the Set Paths item on the Option menu (ALT+O P). It's best to only use $INCLUDE files for storing nonexecutable code.

For most purposes, using a $INCLUDE meta-command is as if you had entered all the information in your file by hand. However, to look at the lines in the $INCLUDE file, you'll need to choose the Included Lines option on the View menu (ALT+V L). To actually edit the contents of the $INCLUDE file, you must use the Included File option on the View menu (ALT+V I). The information used from the CONSTANT.BI file doesn't make the executable version of your program any larger, although it will use up some space in memory while you're developing the program.

Here are some sample codes taken from the CONSTANT.BI file:

```
CONST KEY_END = &H23
CONST KEY_HOME = &H24
CONST KEY_LEFT = &H25
CONST KEY_UP = &H26
CONST KEY_RIGHT = &H27
CONST KEY_DOWN = &H28

CONST KEY_NUMPAD0 = &H60
CONST KEY_NUMPAD1 = &H61
CONST KEY_NUMPAD2 = &H62
```

```
CONST KEY_NUMPAD3 = &H63
CONST KEY_NUMPAD4 = &H64
CONST KEY_NUMPAD5 = &H65
CONST KEY_NUMPAD6 = &H66
CONST KEY_NUMPAD7 = &H67
CONST KEY_NUMPAD8 = &H68
CONST KEY_NUMPAD9 = &H69

CONST KEY_F1 = &H70
CONST KEY_F2 = &H71
CONST KEY_F3 = &H72
CONST KEY_F4 = &H73
CONST KEY_F5 = &H74
CONST KEY_F6 = &H75
CONST KEY_F7 = &H76
CONST KEY_F8 = &H77
CONST KEY_F9 = &H78
CONST KEY_F10 = &H79
CONST KEY_F11 = &H7A
CONST KEY_F12 = &H7B
```

The Numeric Functions

If you don't do a lot of scientific work, you will not likely use the information in this section very much. (One surprising use of the numeric functions is to draw curves and various pictures.)

SGN(NumericExpression) The SGN(*NumericExpression*) function gives you a 1 if the number is positive, −1 if negative, and a zero if it's zero. A cute use of this for integers or long integers is a FOR-NEXT loop in the form

```
FOR I = a TO b STEP SGN(a - b)
```

which, as long as a <> b, runs through the FOR-NEXT loop the correct number of times, regardless of whether "a" was greater than "b."

ABS( ) The ABS function gives the absolute value of whatever is inside the parentheses. All this function does is remove minus signs:

```
ABS(-1) = 1 = ABS(1)
```

One common use of the absolute value function is ABS(B–A). This gives the distance between the numbers A and B. For example, suppose

A = 3 and B = 4

Then,

```
ABS(A - B) = ABS(B - A) = 1
```

because 3 and 4 are one unit apart. As another example,

```
ABS(ASC(A$) - ASC(B$))
```

gives the "distance" between the first two characters of the strings A$ and B$.

You often use the ABS function to set up a tolerance test in a DO loop.

SQR() The SQR function returns the square root of the numeric expression inside the parentheses, which must be nonnegative, or a run-time error follows.

EXP() The EXP function gives e (e is roughly 2.7182) to the power x where e is the base for natural logarithms. The answer is single precision if x is an integer or is itself a single-precision number; otherwise, the answer is a double-precision number.

LOG() The LOG function gives the natural logarithm of a number. To find the common log (log to base 10), use

```
LOG10( ) = LOG( ) / LOG(10)
```

which gives the common logarithm of the value (which must be positive) inside the parentheses. Another way to find the number of digits in a number is to use, for a number greater than 1,

INT(LOG10(x)) + 1

For example, LOG10(197) is between 2 and 3 because LOG10(100) is 2 and LOG10(1000) is 3.

As with the EXP function, the answer is single precision if *x* is an integer or is itself a single-precision number; otherwise, the answer is a double-precision number.

Trigonometric Functions()   Also for those who need them, Visual Basic has the built-in trigonometric functions SIN (sine), COS (cosine), and TAN (tangent). The only problem is that Visual Basic expects the angle inside the parentheses following the functions to be in radian measure. To convert from degrees to radians, you need the value of π. The formula is

radians = degrees * π / 180

To get the value of π, the easiest method is to set up, early on in your program, a form level variable called PI, and then use the ATN function in the Form_Load procedure to define an approximation to π.

```
PI = 4 * ATN(1#)
```

(This works because the arctangent of 1 is $\pi/4$.) You can also use the ATN function to get all the other inverse trigonometric functions. The following table summarizes this as well as some other useful constants and functions you may want to build from the built-in functions:

To Set or Define	Use
π	pi = 4 * ATN(1#) (double precision)
e (base of natural logs)	Exp(1#) (for double precision)
degrees to radians	radians = degrees * π / 180
radians to degrees	degrees = radians *180 / π
Sec(x)	1 / COS(x)
Csc(x)	1 / SIN(x)
Cot(x)	1 / TAN(x)
ArcCos(x)	ATN(x / SQR(–X * X + 1) + π / 2
ArcSin(x)	ATN(x / SQR(–X * X + 1))
ArcCot(x)	ATN(x) + π / 2

To Set or Define	Use
$\cosh(x)$	$(EXP(x) + EXP(-x)) / 2$
$\sinh(x)$	$(EXP(x) - EXP(-x)) / 2$
$\log_{10}(x)$	$LOG(x) / LOG(10)$
$\log_{a}(x)$	$LOG(x) / LOG(a)$

CHAPTER

Procedures and Error Trapping

You've already seen how to use many of Visual Basic's event procedures. Event procedures are the core of Visual Basic programming, but they shouldn't be made too complicated. If an event procedure is much longer than one page—or even one screen—it may be too long to easily debug. Consider doing some of the work in one or more of Visual Basic's general procedures. There are two kinds of general procedures in Visual Basic. The first, *Function procedures*, let you create new functions, thus extending the functions built into Visual Basic that you saw in Chapter 7. *Sub procedures*, on the other hand, are smaller "helper programs" that are used (called) as needed. You use Sub procedures to break down larger tasks into smaller ones or to automate repeated operations.

Function Procedures

Start thinking about defining your own functions when you use a complicated expression more than once in a project. For example, suppose you need a random integer between 1 and 10. You could write

```
INT(10 * RND) + 1
```

each time you needed it, although this would eventually grow tiresome. Now suppose the same program requires a random integer between 1 and 40, between 1 and 100, and so on. The statements needed for these are so similar to the preceding statement that one would hope there is a way to automate the process—that is, to have Visual Basic do some of the work. Suppose you want to attach this function to the current form. What you do is open the Edit window and choose New Function (ALT+E F), and the New Function dialog box pops up, as shown here:

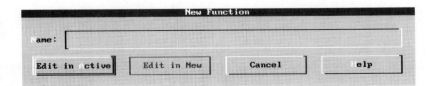

Now type a name. (The example uses RandomRange.) Press ENTER, and a function template like the one shown in Figure 8-1 pops up. Here's how the whole function will look:

```
FUNCTION RandomRange (X) AS INTEGER
   RandomRange = INT(X * RND) + 1
END FUNCTION
```

Now you can use RandomRange just like a built-in function for any procedure attached to the current form. If you need to display a random integer between 1 and 10, you can write

```
PRINT RandomRange(10)
```

The name of the function (in this case, RandomRange) must follow the same rules as for variables in Visual Basic. If you prefer, when defining a function you can add a type identifier at the end of the function name instead of using an AS *VarType* clause. For example, you could have written

```
FUNCTION RandomRange% (X)
```

For both methods of beginning the RandomRange function, Visual Basic knows that the function returns integer values.

Function template for the RandomRange function

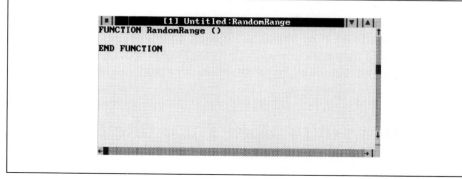

Note   Even if a function is defined using a type identifier, you do not need to include the type identifier when using the function. For example,

```
PRINT RandomRange(10)
```

will work with either designation

The key to the RandomRange function's smooth operation is the *X*. It's called a *parameter*, but it's easiest to think of it as a placeholder. You've seen parameters in the various Key event procedures, such as KeyUp. To use (or call) this random integer function, you replace the parameter (the placeholder) with a numeric expression (a variable, number, or calculation) called an *argument*. Visual Basic then replaces all occurrences of the parameter in the definition of the function with the value of the argument. In particular, Visual Basic does any calculations called for. Therefore, if

A = 3 and B = 2

then

```
N% = RandomRange(A * B + 37)
```

has the same effect as

```
N% = RandomRange(43)
```

which in turn is the same as writing

```
N% = INT(43 * RND) + 1
```

 Caution   You shouldn't expect to get an exceptionally large random integer with the RandomRange function. RandomRange, like any integer expression, can't be larger than 32,767.

Functions with More Than One Parameter

The function RandomRange works with one piece of information; that is, it's a function of one variable (or one argument). You frequently want the value of a function to depend on more than one piece of information. For example, suppose you want a range of random integers between *X* and *Y*. You can modify RandomRange as follows:

```
FUNCTION RandomRangeXToY (X, Y) AS INTEGER
   RandomRangeXToY = INT((Y - X + 1) * RND) + X
END FUNCTION
```

This may seem a little tricky. If so, try to see what happens when *X* = 5 and *Y* = 37. Multiplying RND by *Y* – *X* + 1 (33) and taking the integer part of the number gives a range between zero and 32 (= *Y* – *X*). Finally, add *X* to get the range wanted (5 through 37).

If you want to make sure the function uses only integer values, rewrite it as follows:

```
FUNCTION RandomRangeXToY (X AS INTEGER,Y AS INTEGER) AS INTEGER
   RandomRangeXToY = INT((Y - X + 1) * RND) + X
END FUNCTION
```

Now the placeholders can only have integer values. If you set

```
Number% = RandomRangeXToY(2.7, 39.2)
```

then 2.7 is rounded up to 3 and 39.2 is rounded down to 39 when Visual Basic substitutes their values into the function definition. If you wrote

```
Number% = RandomRangeXToY(3, 300000)
```

you'd get an overflow error.

Function Names and Function Types

Since the name of a function follows the same rules as the name of a variable, choose meaningful function names; they will make your program more readable and easier to debug. Keep in mind that unless you give it an explicit type identifier, the type of the function defaults to single precision, or it will be determined by the function's first letter if a corresponding DEFType statement is currently in effect.

For example, if you are writing a program that needs to calculate the cost of mailing a letter, you could use this function which identifies the types involved:

```
FUNCTION Postage% (Weight AS SINGLE)
   'Calculate the cost, in cents, of mailing
   'a first-class letter of Weight ounces

   Postage = 6 - 23 * INT(-Weight)
END FUNCTION
```

If you are confused as to why the previous function works, here's why: Using INT of *minus* the weight moves down one integer, then taking one more negative flips it back to the correct positive value.

Now executing the following Form_Click proceedure and responding to the input prompt by entering 4.7 will produce the output,

The cost is 121 cents

```
SUB Form_Click()
   'local variables:
   DIM WeightOfLetter AS SINGLE

   WeightOfLetter = VAL(INPUTBOX$("Enter the weight in ounces:")
   PRINT "The cost is"; Postage(WeightOfLetter); "cents."
END SUB
```

To make the program run smoothly, you need to check the information you send a function before you call the function. Otherwise, you risk a meaningless result. With the Postage % function, you need to check if the weight is a positive number. The following fragment does this:

```
IF WeightOFLetter > 0 THEN
   PRINT Postage%(WeightOfLetter)
ELSE
  BEEP
  MSGBOX "A letter must have positive weight."
END IF
```

The General Form of a Function

The general form of a function definition is

FUNCTION *FunctionName* (*parameter1, parameter2, ...*)
   statements
   FunctionName = *expression*
END FUNCTION

where *parameter1, parameter2,* and so on are variables which will be used only as place holders. These variables are referred to as the *parameters* of the function. The types of the parameters can be specified by type-declaration tags or with phrases of the form "AS type". Function names must begin with a letter and can consist of up to 40 characters consisting of letters, numbers, underscores, and decimal points.

If *FunctionName*(*argument1, argument2, ...*) appears in a Visual Basic statement, then the value of *argument1* is assigned to *parameter1,* the value of *argument2* is assigned to *parameter2,* and so on. After this, Visual Basic executes the statements in the function definition, and the last value assigned to *the FunctionName* inside the body of the function definition is the one used for the statement involving *FunctionName* (*argument1, argument2, ...*). The argument entries *argument1, argument2,* and so on can be either constants, variables, or expressions.

A Visual Basic statement using (or *accessing*) a function is said to *invoke* (or call) the function and to *pass* the arguments to the parameters. The function is said to *return* its value. For instance, in the previous example, the statement

```
PRINT "The cost is"; Postage%(WeightOfLetter); "cents."
```

calls the function Postage%, and passes the argument WeightOfLetter to the parameter Weight. The function returns the value 121. You can even have a statement like

```
PRINT "The cost is"; Postage%(Weight); "cents."
```

This time, however, Visual Basic looks for the variable named Weight and substitutes it for the parameter Weight. (Remember parameters are placeholders—they have no real existence outside of that role.)

The type of value returned by the function is specified with a type-declaration tag (%, !, &, #, or $) appended to the function name, an AS clause at the end of the FUNCTION line, or a DEFtype statement appearing above the FUNCTION definition. See Chapter 5 for a discussion on variable types and type declaration tags.

Lines in your programs cannot simply have a form such as

FunctionName(argument1, argument2, argument3)

The call to a function *must* be part of an expression or statement.

You can only call a function when you use the same number of arguments as parameters. Each variable argument can have the same name or a different name than its corresponding parameter, but it must be of the same type (integer, long integer, and so on). If an argument is not a variable, its value must be of a type that can be converted to that of its corresponding parameter. For instance, an integer variable argument can be passed to an integer parameter, but not to a long integer parameter. However, an integer constant can be passed to a long integer parameter.

Working with Multiple Functions

Each function definition is contained in a separate window. We have seen how to create a function by pressing ALT+E F. Another method is

1. Type FUNCTION *FunctionName* as a line in the Code window.

2. Press ENTER or move the cursor off the line. A special window containing a template will appear for the named function (see Figure 8-1). The window will contain two lines: the typed name followed by a pair of parentheses and the line END FUNCTION.

3. Type the parameters inside the parentheses and type the body of the function between the two lines.

To select a different part of the program, press F2. The code selection window containing a list of the different parts of the program will appear. Use the cursor-movement keys to highlight the part of the program with which to work next, and then press ENTER.

To delete a function, press F2 to open the code selection window, select the function to be removed, press the TAB key four times to reach the Delete box (or use the ALT+D shortcut), and press ENTER. (You can also use a mouse, of course.)

DECLARE Statements

When you save a program containing user-defined functions, Visual Basic adds DECLARE statements to the beginning of the leading code that identify all of the functions and their parameters. These DECLARE statements are used for housekeeping—they do not take up any room in your compiled program. For example, the leading code of the mailing cost program would begin with the line

```
DECLARE FUNCTION Postage% (Weight!)
```

In this book, function names begin with uppercase letters. However, like variable names, they can be written with any combination of uppercase and lowercase letters. To improve readability, the Visual Basic editor will automatically see to it that the capitalization of a function name is consistent throughout a program. For instance, if in the program above, you typed the function name as postage in the calling statement and as Postage in the FUNCTION statement, the editor would change the first name to match the second.

Advanced Use of Functions

Nothing prevents a function from calling another function. You'll find yourself doing this frequently in order to increase the power of your Function procedures. Visual Basic allows you to call as many functions as you want from within a given function. Functions can even call themselves. This is called *recursion*.

At this point, your functions in Visual Basic are manipulating the values of variables assigned to parameters; they haven't changed the values. As you saw in the KeyPress event in Chapter 6, it's possible for an event procedure to change the values of variables assigned to parameters. This is because the default for Visual Basic is that the memory locations for the variables assigned to parameters are passed. (See the section "Advanced Uses of Procedures and Functions: Passing by Reference/Passing by Value" later in this chapter for more on this subject.) In practice, however, you should rarely have to change the value of a parameter inside a function procedure. Generally, a function should simply manipulate existing values and return a new value.

As with event procedures, you can set up your own local variables inside Function procedures and have them be static or not, depending on the application. Static variables retain their values between successive function calls. Variables are specified as static with a statement of the form STATIC *variable1, variable2,....* You can make all the variables in a general procedure static by putting the keyword STATIC before the name of the function:

STATIC *FunctionName* ( )

Form level variables are visible to functions attached to that form. As you saw in Chapter 5 in the section on the scope of variables, the purpose of using local variables is to avoid inadvertent side effects. A *side effect* means that something done in the procedure affects the rest of the program. If you use the CLS method in a function attached to a form, then every time the function is used, the form will clear; this is clearly a side effect. Any time you change the value of a parameter or a form level variable, you cause side effects.

There's certainly nothing wrong with controlled side effects. The key, though, is the word "controlled." You must know exactly when they're going to happen and what the result will be for the rest of the project.

Finally, be aware that you don't have to give every function a value. Sometimes you are forced to exit a function prematurely:

```
FUNCTION BailOut (X)
  IF X < 0 THEN
    EXIT FUNCTION
  ELSE
    .
    .
    .
  END IF
  .
  .
  .
END FUNCTION
```

This function bails out if a negative value is sent to it. Now calling the function with a negative value gives the function the value zero—the default value of any numeric variable. A string function that you bail out of returns the null string " " as its value.

You should rarely find yourself needing the EXIT FUNCTION statement. And certainly don't use it as in the preceding example. Check out the information you want to send to a function before you call the function (possibly by another function). The EXIT FUNCTION statement should only be used if it makes the program clearer, or in emergencies.

Some Example String Functions

Suppose you want to write a function that would allow you to chop out any substring. You saw how to do this in Chapter 7; you use INSTR to find out where the string is and then use RIGHT$, LEFT$, and MID$ to do the cutting. Here's the function:

```
FUNCTION CutSmall$ (Big$, Small$)
  'local variables:
  DIM Place AS INTEGER, Length AS INTEGER

  Place = INSTR(Big$, Small$)
  Length = LEN(Small$)
  IF Place = 0 THEN
    CutSmall$ = Big$
  ELSE
    CutSmall$ = LEFT$(Big$, Place-1) + MID$(Big$, Place+Length)
  END IF
END FUNCTION
```

The local variables named Place and Length defined here will, of course, have no effect on any other variable named Place or Length that might occur elsewhere within the program. Once you've finished defining a function, you can also use the Immediate window to test it.

As another example, suppose you want to write a function that counts the number of times a character appears in a string. This would be a function of two string variables, and it should return an integer. Let's call it CharCount:

```
FUNCTION CharCount (X$, Y$) AS INTEGER
  'This function counts the number of times
  'the character Y$ is inside the string X$
  'If Y$ is not a single character or Y$ does not
```

```
'occur in X$, then this function returns zero

'local variables:
DIM Count AS INTEGER, I AS INTEGER

Count = 0
FOR I = 1 TO LEN(X$)
   IF MID$(X$, I, 1) = Y$ THEN Count = Count + 1
NEXT I
CharCount = Count
END FUNCTION
```

First, notice the extended remark section. In defining a complicated function, you're best off explaining what's supposed to happen. Explain what kind of information the function expects to deal with, which local variables it uses, and what it is supposed to send out. (If you know what the function expects, you're more likely to check what you send it before the program blows up.) Most of the example programs in this book have, up to this point, been sparsely commented, mostly because the surrounding text explained it. However, when you are hired to write a program, this is the way you would be expected to comment it. In fact, you might explain what the local variables are doing as well.

The CharCount function uses two local integer variables: Count and I. As you've seen, it's a good programming practice to DIM the local variables before going on to the main business of the function. Being local variables, they have no connection with any variables that might share the same name elsewhere in the program. The advantages this gives over the older DEF FN in interpreted BASICs can't be stressed enough. (A complicated string-handling program might have 17 different functions with 17 different variables named Count or I, and you don't want their values contaminating each other.)

Next, notice that the function initialized the Count variable to zero. This was done for the same reason that you would initialize a variable in the main part of a program: relying on default values is sloppy (and occasionally dangerous) unless you make it clear by a remark statement that you are doing so deliberately.

The FOR–NEXT loop runs through the string character by character, checking for a match and adding 1 to the value of the Count variable if it finds one. Finally, the value of the local variable Count is what this function will return. In this case, the body of the function ends with the assignment that defines the function. Using a variable like Count to accumulate information as a function works is quite common. When you're done, you use the "accumulator" in the final assignment that determines the value of the function.

As another example, let's return to the "find the next word program" from Chapter 7. Suppose you want to modify this program so it gives the next word, no matter what separator you use. Using a user-defined function makes this easy. All you have to do is replace the statement

```
AfterSpace = INSTR(BeforeSpace + 1, Phrase$, Separate$)
```

with a function that finds the next separator.

Before you look at an outline for this function, think about the information this function needs to *massage* (manipulate). Is it clear that it will work much like INSTR except that the separators will be built into the function? Once you convince yourself of this, you will be able to understand the following outline for the function:

☐ The function works with a string and a position number.

☐ The function should begin searching at the position after the position number and look character by character until it finds a separator.

☐ If successful, the function should return the position number of the separator.

☐ If not successful, the function should return zero.

Here's a function definition that follows this outline:

```
FUNCTION FindSeparator (Phrase$, Position%) AS INTEGER
  ' Local variables
  DIM AfterSpace AS INTEGER, Answer AS INTEGER
  DIM LenString AS INTEGER, NxtChar$

  AfterSpace = Position% + 1
  Answer = 0
  LenString = LEN(Phrase$)
  DO UNTIL (Answer <> 0) OR (AfterSpace > LenString)
    NxtChar$ = MID$(Phrase$, AfterSpace, 1)
    SELECT CASE NxtChar$
      CASE " ", "!", "?", ".", ";", ":", ","
        Answer = AfterSpace
      CASE ELSE
```

```
        AfterSpace = AfterSpace + 1
     END SELECT
  LOOP
  FindSeparator = Answer
END FUNCTION
```

This function starts by looking from one position farther along in the string than the position passed as an argument. This takes into account any previous uses of the function.

The local variable Answer plays a key role in the function. As Visual Basic moves through the loop, this variable accumulates information either by staying equal to zero (in which case no separator was found) or by becoming positive (in which case its value is the location of the separator).

The DO loop has to stop if either the value of Answer signals that the hunt was successful or there's no place else to look (the loop has finished searching all the characters in the string). Notice that instead of using a DO loop with two conditions, you could have used multiple EXIT LOOP commands.

Using a SELECT CASE statement makes it easy to add a separator to this function; you need only add the appropriate character to the list in the first CASE clause. If the character being checked is not a separator, the CASE ELSE clause moves the search on to the next character in the string.

Finally, the value of the accumulator variable Answer will be zero if no separator was found; otherwise, it will be the position of the separator. (You also could have written this as a function of three variables, much like INSTR itself.)

Parsing Text

Next, suppose you want to examine the contents of a text box and print out the words one by one in a second text box in response to each click on a command button. The screen might look like the one in Figure 8-2. You want each click to print the next word. Supposing the command button is called MoreWords, here's how the whole program might go. (Notice that this uses the FindSeparator function from the last section.)

```
SUB MoreWords_Click ()
  'This event program uses the function
  'FindSeparator to parse a phrase
  'by searching for the separators
  '. , : ? ; ! and the space.
  'It finds all words contained in the phrase.

  'local variables:
  STATIC BeforeSpace AS INTEGER, AfterSpace AS INTEGER
  DIM Phrase$, LenPhrase AS INTEGER, SizeOfWord AS INTEGER

  Phrase$ = Text1.Text
  LenPhrase = LEN(Phrase$)
  AfterSpace = FindSeparator(Phrase$, BeforeSpace)
  SizeOfWord = AfterSpace - BeforeSpace - 1
  DO UNTIL (SizeOfWord > 0) OR (AfterSpace = 0)
    BeforeSpace = AfterSpace
    AfterSpace = FindSeparator(Phrase$, BeforeSpace%)
    SizeOfWord = AfterSpace - BeforeSpace - 1
  LOOP
  IF SizeOfWord > 0 THEN
    NextWord$ = MID$(Phrase$, BeforeSpace + 1, SizeOfWord)
    BeforeSpace = AfterSpace
    Text2.Text = NextWord$
  ELSE
    Text2.Text = MID$(Phrase$, BeforeSpace + 1)
    MSGBOX "No more words!"
```

FIGURE 8-2 Form for MoreWords program

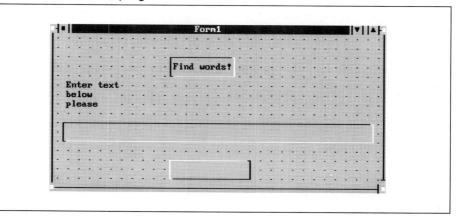

```
   Text1.Text = ""
   BeforeSpace = 0
  END IF
END SUB
```

First, notice that the variables BeforeSpace and AfterSpace must be static variables in order to preserve the information between clicks. If AfterSpace = 0, then you've finished the text and won't enter the DO loop at all. If SizeOfWord is also zero, then this small loop eliminates multiple spaces—another example of a eureka loop.

The IF clause changes the value of the static variables in preparation for the next function call and displays the word found in the second text box. The ELSE clause gives the last word and then a message box. Once the user clears the message box, the last line clears out the original text.

An Example: A Pig Latin Generator

This section shows you how to write a "Pig Latin converter" that shows off many of the techniques you've seen up to now. Pig Latin is a well-known variant on English that children often use: Ancay ouyay understandway isthay?

The rules are simple:

- ☐　All one-letter words stay the same.

- ☐　Words beginning with vowels get the suffix "way."

- ☐　Words beginning with a string of consonants have the consonants shifted to the end and the suffix "ay" added.

- ☐　Any "q" moved because of the preceding rule carries its "u" along with it.

- ☐　"Y" is a consonant.

- ☐　There are no more rules.

In its simplest form, an outline for a Pig Latin convertor is

While there are still words
"Pig Latinize" the next word

To "Pig Latinize" a word, follow the rules just given. You will need two (multi-line) text boxes labeled Source and Translation and a command button captioned Translate to start the process. Make the control names for these three objects the same as the label or caption. Here's the translator:

```
' A Pig Latin generator
' This program translates a phrase into
' Pig Latin. It modifies the 'Find word'
' program by adding a 'Latinize' function

' Form level Declarations
CONST TRUE = -1
CONST FALSE = 0

SUB Translate_Click()
  'local variables:
  DIM BeforeSpace AS INTEGER, AfterSpace AS INTEGER
  DIM SizeOfWord AS INTEGER
  DIM NextWord$, PigWord$, FinalWord$   'Guarantee local

  Translation.Text = ""
  Phrase$ = Source.Text
  IF Len(Phrase$) = 0 THEN EXIT SUB
  BeforeSpace = 0
  AfterSpace = FindSeparator(Phrase$, BeforeSpace)
  DO UNTIL AfterSpace = 0
    SizeOFWord = AfterSpace - BeforeSpace - 1
    NextWord$ = MID$(Phrase$, BeforeSpace + 1, SizeOFWord)
    IF SizeOFWord > 0 THEN
      PigWord$ = Latinfy$(NextWord$)
      Translation.Text = Translation.Text + PigWord$ + Space$(1)
    END IF
    BeforeSpace = AfterSpace
    AfterSpace = FindSeparator(Phrase$, BeforeSpace)
  LOOP
  FinalWord$ = MID$(Phrase$, BeforeSpace + 1)
  PigWord$ = Latinfy$(FinalWord$)
  Translation.Text = Translation.Text + PigWord$
END  SUB

FUNCTION FindSeparator (Phrase$, Position%) AS INTEGER
  'local variables:
```

```
    DIM AfterSpace AS INTEGER,Answer AS INTEGER,LenString AS INTEGER
    DIM NxtChar$

    AfterSpace  = Position%  + 1
    Answer = 0
    LenString = LEN(Phrase$)
    DO UNTIL (Answer <> 0) OR (AfterSpace > LenString)
      NxtChar$ = MID$(Phrase$, AfterSpace, 1)
      SELECT CASE NxtChar$
        CASE " ", "!", "?", ".", ";", ":", ","
          Answer  = AfterSpace
        CASE ELSE
          AfterSpace = AfterSpace  + 1
      END SELECT
    LOOP
    FindSeparator  = Answer
END FUNCTION

FUNCTION Latinfy$ (A$)
    'local variables:
    DIM FirstChar$

    IF LEN(A$) = 1 THEN
      Latinfy$ = A$
    ELSE
      FirstChar$ = UCASE$(LEFT$(A$, 1))
      SELECT CASE FirstChar$
        CASE "A", "E", "I", "O", "U"
          Latinfy$ = A$ + "way"
        CASE IS < "A"
          Latinfy$ = A$
        CASE IS > "Z"
          Latinfy$ = A$
        CASE ELSE
          Latinfy$ = ShiftCons$(A$) + "ay"
      END SELECT
    END IF
END FUNCTION

FUNCTION ShiftCons$ (A$)
    'local variables:
    DIM Count AS INTEGER, Done AS INTEGER
    DIM NextChar$

    Count = 1
    Done = FALSE
    DO
```

```
   NextChar$ = UCASE$(MID$(A$, Count, 1))
   SELECT CASE NextChar$
     CASE "A", "E", "I", "O", "U"
       Done = TRUE
     CASE "Q"
       Count = Count + 2
     CASE ELSE
       Count = Count + 1
   END SELECT
  LOOP UNTIL Done
  ShiftCons$ = MID$(A$, Count) + LEFT$(A$, Count - 1)
END FUNCTION
```

As mentioned earlier, all you have to do is change the "find next word" program to one that, instead of printing the next word, prints the converted form. (Along the way, this function strips out all punctuation and spaces. It is left to you to change the program so that the converted phrase retains the original punctuation.)

The Latinfy function starts out by dealing with the special case of one-letter words following the first rule: it does nothing to them. The first case in the SELECT CASE deals with vowels: words with a leading vowel add "way." The next case makes sure numbers and other special characters are not transformed. The ELSE case calls the most complicated function—the one that shifts consonants to the end.

The ShiftCons$ function works by using a flag to detect when, moving letter by letter, Visual Basic finally hits a vowel. By adding 2 to the count, you carry the "u" along with the "q" for this special case. The trick is that by starting with the count equal to one and incrementing the count every time a consonant shows up, LEFT$(A$, Count – 1) must, when the loop ends, contain the leading consonants.

This program is a good demonstration of how longer programs can be built from "building blocks." You'll see more about this later in the chapter in the section "Some General Words on Program Design."

Sub Procedures

Function procedures can be made to do almost anything, but should be used only when what you want to do is get an answer—a value—out of them. As mentioned before, although functions can change properties of a form or affect the value of form level variables, it's not a good idea to use them in this way unless the change is somehow related to what the function is designed to do. In any case, a function takes raw data, massages it, and then returns a single value. For example, although you can write a function that will work through a list and find the smallest or the largest value, it can't easily (or directly) return both at once. And though a function could be written to order (sort) a list, it could not return the list as its value. (You'll see ways to sort lists in Chapter 9.)

Function procedures are intended as an extension of built-in functions. Since function definitions can include many lines of code, you *could* use them as a subterfuge to execute a block of code. However, this purpose is better accomplished by a Sub procedure.

Suppose, for example, you want to print a song, one with many verses but only a single chorus. The outline is clear:

```
While there are verses left
    print the next verse
    print the single chorus
Loop
```

To translate this outline into a program using a function would require statements in the program like

```
X = Chorus()
```

even though the Chorus function would not have any value to return; its job would simply be to print. Unless you want to repeatedly type useless assignment statements (or the entire chorus) in the event procedure, you'll need a new structure: the Sub procedure.

The structure of the simplest kind of Sub procedure—although one powerful enough to translate the outline—looks like this:

```
SUB Chorus( )
 many PRINT statements
END SUB
```

The first line has the keyword SUB followed by the procedure's name. A procedure name can be up to 40 characters. Next comes the parameter list, enclosed in parentheses, for the information the procedure will use. In this case, the Sub procedure uses no parameters. After the parameter list come the statements that make up the procedure. Finally, there is the keyword END SUB, which you've seen to end all event procedures; it's used to indicate the end of general procedures as well. As with Function procedures, if you need to exit the Sub procedure prematurely, you can use the EXIT SUB command in the body of the procedure as often as necessary.

If you imagine an event procedure as the main verse and the Sub and Function procedures as the choruses, then thinking of a program as a song with many choruses would be a good metaphor for designing any program, except that it misses one key point: each time you need the procedure, it's likely to be in a different situation. The procedure must change to meet new requirements. You need a way to transfer information between the main program and the procedure. You do this in much the same way as you did for functions: by using the parameter list. This parameter list is used to communicate between the main program and the procedure. When you call the procedure, you follow the CALL keyword with the name of the procedure and a pair of parentheses surrounding the list of arguments. If there is more than one argument, the arguments are separated by commas.

CALL *NameOfProcedure (argument1, argument2, ...)*

Although the abbreviated version

NameOfProcedure Argument1, Argument2, ...

is also allowed in Visual Basic, the CALL keyword is more commonly used.

For example, suppose you want to print the first three verses of the song "100 Bottles of Beer on the Wall" on a blank form in response to a click:

100 bottle of beers on the wall,
100 bottles of beer,
If one of those bottles should happen to fall,
99 bottles of beer on the wall.

99 bottle of beers on the wall,
99 bottles of beer,
If one of those bottles should happen to fall,
98 bottles of beer on the wall.

98 bottle of beers on the wall,
98 bottles of beer,
If one of those bottles should happen to fall,
97 bottles of beer on the wall.

Here's what you can write in the event procedure:

```
SUB Form_Click ()
  'local variables:
  DIM I AS INTEGER

  FOR I = 100 TO 98 STEP -1
    CALL Chorus (I)
  NEXT I
END SUB
```

The chorus Sub procedure looks like this:

```
SUB Chorus (X AS INTEGER)
  PRINT X; "bottles of beers on the wall,"
  PRINT X; "bottles of beer,"
  PRINT " If one of those bottles should happen to fall,"
  PRINT X - 1; "bottles of beer on the wall."
  PRINT
END SUB
```

On each pass through the loop, the current value of the argument I is sent to the procedure, where it replaces the parameter *X*. Just as with functions, the names you choose for parameters are irrelevant. As before, they just serve as placeholders. Finally, note that you do not use a type identifier for a subprogram's name.

You may be thinking that this particular example seems a little forced; it's easy to rewrite the program using a FOR–NEXT loop. Of course this is true, but writing the program using a procedure (subprogram) changes the emphasis a little; it's a lot closer to the outline. Now think about a more complicated program. Imagine a FOR–NEXT loop that surrounds 50 lines of code. In this situation, it's too easy to forget what the loop is doing. Most programmers prefer loops to be "digestible"—the whole loop ideally should not be more than a single screen of code.

Notice how in this program most of the gritty details have been pushed under the rug. This is quite common when you use procedures. Your event procedures will often have a fairly clean look, containing directions and repeated procedure and function calls. (In fact, some people would even put the directions into procedure calls and so make an event procedure into one long sequence of procedure and function calls. This, too, is a matter of taste.) In any case, it's unlikely that any event procedure will need to be very long.

In general, a Sub procedure (subprogram) is a part of a program that performs one or more related tasks, has its own name, is written as a separate part of the program, and is accessed with a CALL statement.

A Sub procedure has the form

SUB *SubprogramName(parameter1, parameter2, ...)*
  statement(s)
END SUB

When Visual Basic executes a statement of the form

CALL *SubprogramName(argument1, argument2, ...)*

the values (actually the memory locations) of the arguments are passed to the corresponding parameters and the statements inside the subprogram are executed. When the END SUB statement is reached, execution continues with the line following the CALL statement. As with function procedures, you must use the same number of arguments as parameters and they must be of compatible types.

Procedures are created in a way analogous to functions; enter SUB *SubprogramName* as a line in the Code window or press ALT+E S to pop up a dialog window.

One final point: if you delete a control from a form, then any event procedures you may have written become general procedures for that form, using the same procedure name as before. For example, suppose you had a command button with a CtlName of Command1 and have written a Command1_Click procedure for it. If you delete the command button from the form, Command1_Click becomes a general procedure.

Some Useful Simple Procedures

A sophisticated program may need to beep at the user to provide feedback—the more beeps, perhaps the more feedback? Having a general procedure called ManyBeeps in a program is quite common:

```
SUB ManyBeeps(X AS INTEGER)
  'local variables:
  DIM I AS INTEGER

  FOR I = 1 TO X
    BEEP
  NEXT I
END SUB
```

Since I was dimensioned inside the procedure, it is a local variable. Now you can write

```
CALL ManyBeeps(10)
```

for 10 beeps and

```
CALL ManyBeeps(100)
```

for overkill.

Visual Basic lets you set up an event procedure that triggers itself after a set period of time has gone by (see the Timer event in Chapter 10). But you may need to write a timer loop inside a procedure that stops processing for a fixed length of time. (This is occasionally a useful debugging tool to use, rather than putting in a STOP command or breakpoint—see Chapter 11—that stops the program in its tracks.) To set up a timer loop to pause a fixed number of seconds in a Sub procedure, use the following:

```
SUB WasteTime (X AS SINGLE)
  'local variables:
  DIM StartTime AS SINGLE

  StartTime = TIMER
  DO UNTIL TIMER - StartTime >  X
  LOOP
END SUB
```

Since the TIMER function returns only the number of seconds since midnight, this procedure would run into problems near midnight. One way around this is to use the DateValue function. Another way uses the MOD function and the fact that there are 86400 seconds in a day. Just change the DO statement above to

```
DO UNTIL (TIMER - StartTime + 86400) MOD 86400 > X
```

To see how this works, assume that it is 2 seconds before midnight and that X is 3. StartTime will be 86398. Consider for now just the whole number values that TIMER will be taking on: 86399, 0(midnight), 1, 2, etc. For these values, the expression involving MOD will be:

(86399 - 86398 + 86400) MOD 86400 = 86401 MOD 86400 = 1;
(　　 0 - 86398 + 86400) MOD 86400 = 　　2 MOD 86400 = 2;
(　　 1 - 86398 + 86400) MOD 86400 = 　　3 MOD 86400 = 3;
(　　 2 - 86398 + 86400) MOD 86400 = 　　4 MOD 86400 = 4;

from which it can be seen that the expression involving MOD will equal X (3) after 3 seconds and exceed X after 3 seconds, thus ending the loop.

Actually, some people would prefer to have a short time interval between beeps in the ManyBeeps procedure rather than have them blend into one long beep. You can do this by combining the ManyBeeps procedure with a call to the waste time procedure.

Advanced Uses of Procedures and Functions: Passing by Reference/ Passing by Value

There are two ways to pass a variable argument to a procedure: *passing by value* and *passing by reference*. When an argument variable is passed by reference, any changes to the corresponding parameter inside the procedure will change the value of the original argument when the procedure finishes. When passed by value, the argument variable retains its original value after the procedure terminates—regardless of what was done to the corresponding parameter inside the procedure. Argument variables are always passed by reference *unless* surrounded by an extra pair of parentheses.

For example, the statement:

CALL Display(*variable1*, (*variable2*))

passes *variable1* by reference and *variable2* by value. That is, the compiler creates a temporary copy of *variable2*, passes that, and then abandons the copy after the routine finishes.

Consider the Sub procedure Triple, which triples the value of any argument passed to it:

```
SUB Triple (Num AS INTEGER)
  Num = 3 * Num
  PRINT Num
END SUB
```

(Notice the assignment to the parameter Num inside the procedure.) When the following lines of code are executed, the variable named Amt is passed by reference to the parameter Num.

```
SUB Form_Click ()
  'local variables:
  DIM Amt AS INTEGER

  Amt = 2
  PRINT Amt
  CALL Triple(Amt)
  PRINT Amt
END SUB
```

What you see is:

2
6
6

In this case, only one memory location is involved. Initially, the first line of code inside the Click procedure allocates a memory location to store the value of Amt. (See (a) in Figure 8-3.) When the Sub procedure is called, the parameter Num becomes the procedure's name for this memory location. (See (b) in Fig 8-3.) When the value of Num is tripled, the value in this memory location becomes 6. (See (c) in Fig 8-3.) After the completion of the procedure, the parameter Num is forgotten. However, its value lives on in Amt. (See (d) in Fig 8-3.)

Note Naming the parameter Amt produces the same result.

Now consider the same lines of code above with the CALL statement changed to CALL Triple((Amt)) so that the variable Amt is passed by value. The outcome of the revised code is:

2
6
2

This time two memory locations are involved. Initially, the first line of code allocates a memory location to store the value of Amt. (See (a) in Figure 8-4.) When the Sub procedure is called, a temporary second memory location for the parameter Num is set aside for the procedure's use, and the value of Amt is copied into this location. (See (b) in Figure 8-4.) When the value of Num is tripled, the value of Num becomes 6. (See (c) in Figure 8-4.) After the completion of the procedure, Num's memory location disappears. (See (d) in Figure 8-4.) Since only the value in the procedure's memory location is tripled, the value of the variable Amt remains the same. When the procedure is exited, the memory location for Num is released and the variable Num is forgotten.

Note The outcome of the program would be the same even if the parameter in the subprogram also was named Amt. There would still be two memory locations when the procedure was called, one for the argument Amt and the other for the parameter Amt.

FIGURE 8-3 Passing a variable to a procedure by reference

Amt	Amt	Amt	Amt
2	2	6	6
	Num	Num	
(a)	(b)	(c)	(d)

FIGURE
8-4

Passing a variable to a procedure by value

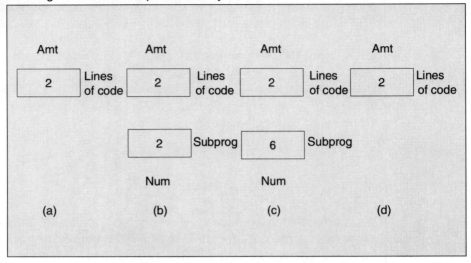

Here's another example. The following Form_Click event procedure and its associated general procedure use passing by reference to validate what was entered in an INPUTBOX. Here the value of the variable PhoneNum$ is changed.

```
SUB Form_Click ()
  'local variables:
  DIM PhoneNum$

  PhoneNum$ = INPUTBOX$("Enter phone number (xxx-xxx-xxxx):")
  CALL Validate(PhoneNum$)
  PRINT "Your phone number is "; PhoneNum$
END SUB

SUB Validate (Num$)
  DO WHILE LEN(Num$) <> 12
    MSGBOX "Don't forget your area code."
    Num$ = INPUTBOX$("Enter phone number (xxx-xxx-xxxx):")
  LOOP
END SUB
```

As another example, suppose you need to change a phrase by stripping out all the spaces inside a phrase—in other words, a more powerful version of the built-in function LTRIM$. The outline is clear:

Find out where the spaces are and remove them.

You can use the MID$ command to extract the nonspace characters in the string. The code that strips out spaces is easy:

```
FOR Count = 1 TO LenPhrase
  IF MID$(Phrase$, Count, 1) <> " " THEN
    Temp$ = Temp$ + MID$(Phrase$, Count, 1)
  END IF
NEXT Count
```

When this loop ends, the value of Temp$ is the original phrase stripped of all its spaces. Now you have to decide, do you want to change the phrase or set up a new phrase? If you want the original phrase to change, incorporate the preceding fragment into a procedure:

```
SUB StripSpaces(X$)
  'local variables:
  DIM Count AS INTEGER, LenPhrase AS INTEGER, Temp$

  LenPhrase = LEN(X$)
  FOR Count = 1 TO LenPhrase
    IF MID$(X$, Count, 1) <> " " THEN
      Temp$ = Temp$ + MID$(X$, Count, 1)
    END IF
  NEXT Count
  X$ = Temp$
END SUB
```

Now whenever you call the procedure StripSpaces(Phrase$), the original string Phrase$ changes. If you rewrote the preceding Sub procedure as a Function procedure, as in the following listing,

```
FUNCTION StripSpaces$(X$)
  'local variables:
  DIM Count AS INTEGER, LenPhrase AS INTEGER, Temp$

  LenPhrase = LEN(X$)
  FOR Count = 1 TO LenPhrase
    IF MID$(X$, Count, 1) <> " " THEN
      Temp$ = Temp$ + MID$(X$, Count, 1)
    END IF
  NEXT Count
  StripSpaces$ = Temp$
END FUNCTION
```

then the value of the function StripSpaces$(Phrase$) is the phrase stripped of all its internal spaces, but the original Phrase$ is still intact. Of course, you can add a line to the function to make it equivalent to the subprogram; all you need to do is add the statement X$ = Temp$ inside the function.

In the next code fragment and function, the variable Bal is passed by value to the function. The outcome is

8667.02 is the future value of 1000

How would removing the parentheses surrounding Bal affect the outcome?

```
' Calculate future value after Yrs years with interest rate
' IntRate when Bal dollars is deposited and AnnDep dollars
' is added to the account at the end of each year

Bal = 1000
IntRate = .05
Dep = 100
Yrs = 26
PRINT NewBal((Bal), IntRate, Yrs, Dep);
PRINT "is the future value of"; Bal

FUNCTION NewBal (Bal, IntRate, Yrs, Dep)
  'local variables:
  DIM I AS INTEGER

  FOR I = 1 TO Yrs
    Bal = Bal + IntRate * Bal + Dep
  NEXT I
  NewBal = Bal
END FUNCTION
```

If you know that variables sent to a procedure should never be passed by reference, you can specify that some or all of the parameters inside Function and Sub procedures are to be passed *only* by value. For this, add the BYVAL keyword before the parameter in the argument list. Here's an example of what the syntax would be:

FUNCTION *Example* (*X* AS INTEGER, BYVAL *Y* AS SINGLE)

In this example, an integer variable passed to *X* may be passed by reference (the default) or by value (when enclosed in parentheses), but a single-precision variable passed to *Y* will always be passed by value whether or not it is enclosed in parentheses.

An Example: Shuffling a Deck of Cards

Suppose you want to write a program to create and then shuffle a deck of cards. You can think of a deck of cards as being a string variable, as shown here:

```
DeckOfCard$ = "2C3C4C5C6C7C8C9C0CJCQCKCAC" + _
              "2D3D4D5D6D7D8D9D0DJDQDKDAD" + _
              "2H3H4H5H6H7H8H9H0HJHQHKHAH" + _
              "2S3S4S5S6S7S8S9S0SJSQSKSAS"
```

where a zero is used for the 10—to keep all the cards the same length— and a "C" is used for clubs, a "D" for diamonds, and so on. (You could also use the low-order ASCII codes, of course.) Obviously, since this string variable has 104 characters, it makes sense to let the computer do some of the work of creating the string.

In any case, since you want to change this variable when you shuffle the cards, you should write a SUB Shuffle (X$) Sub procedure, not a function. This procedure will be similar to the Jumble event procedure from Chapter 7. The only difference is that you have to move characters by twos. (That's why the zero was used for the 10.)

Here's the Jumble procedure rewritten as a procedure to do this:

```
SUB Shuffle (Phrase$)
  ' a Jumble program converted to a procedure
  ' jumbles by twos

  'local variables:
  DIM I AS INTEGER, LenPhrase AS INTEGER

  RANDOMIZE      'seed the random number generator
  LenPhrase = LEN(Phrase$) / 2
  FOR I = 1 TO LenPhrase
    INum = INT((LenPhrase * RND) + 1)
    NewChar$ = MID$(Phrase$, 2 * INum - 1, 2)
```

```
      OldChar$ = MID$(Phrase$, 2 * I - 1, 2)
      MID$(Phrase$, 2 * I - 1, 2) = NewChar$
      MID$(Phrase$, 2 * INum - 1, 1) = OldChar$
   NEXT I
END SUB
```

In this case, the number of cards is half the length of the phrase, so you set the limits of the FOR-NEXT loop by taking half the length of the card string. Since the cards are located starting in the 1, 3, 5, 7... positions, you need to move two characters at a time inside the phrase in order to move to the next card. Otherwise, the Jumble procedure works exactly as before.

Now suppose you want to deal the cards in the course of writing a card program. Obviously, you should make DeckOfCards$ a form-level variable:

```
SUB Deal ()
   'DeckOfCards$ assumed to be form-level variable

   'local variables:
   DIM Cards AS INTEGER

   CALL Shuffle(DeckOfCards$)
   FOR Cards = 1 TO 52
     PRINT MID$(DeckOfCards$, 2 * Cards - 1, 2)
   NEXT Cards
END SUB
```

Again, the point of the 2 as the last argument of the MID$ function call is that each card is specified by a string of two characters.

Passing Control and Form Information

You will often want to write a general procedure to manipulate properties of forms or controls or the forms and controls themselves. Properties of forms and controls can only be passed by value. For example, consider the following simple Sub procedure:

```
SUB ChangeText (BYVAL X AS STRING, Y AS STRING)
   Y = X
END SUB
```

If you call it using the following:

```
CALL ChangeText(Form1.Caption, Y$)
```

then the current value of Y$ is the caption for Form1.

On the other hand, you will often want to affect the properties of a form or control by using a general procedure. For this, you have to declare the argument to be of the form or control data type.

The following code toggles the visibility of a form:

```
SUB BackAndForth (X AS FORM)
   IF X.Visible THEN
      X.Visible  = 0                    'FALSE
   ELSE
      X.Visible = -1                    'TRUE
   END IF
END SUB
```

If the form is visible, the procedure hides it; otherwise, it makes the form visible.

Similarly, you can have a Sub or Function procedure that affects a property of a control. For example, a general procedure to change the caption on a control might look like this:

```
SUB ChangeCaption (X AS CONTROL, Y AS STRING)
   X.Caption = Y
END SUB
```

However, suppose you tried to use this procedure in the form of

CALL ChangeCaption(*Text1*, "New text")

where *Text1* was the name of a text box. Then Visual Basic would give you a run-time error because text boxes do not have a Caption property.

The solution for this is to use a variant on the IF-THEN-ELSE in Visual Basic that allows you to determine what type of control is being manipulated. This takes the following form:

IF TYPEOF *Control* IS *ControlType* THEN

  .

  .

  .

ELSE

  .

  .

  .

END IF

For example:

```
SUB ChangeCaptionOrText (X AS CONTROL, Y AS STRING)
  IF TYPEOF X IS Text THEN
    X.Text = Y
  ELSE
    X.Caption = Y
  END IF
END SUB
```

You cannot use the keyword NOT in this type of control structure, so you will often find yourself using an empty IF clause. Another way to write the ChangeCaption Sub procedure is

```
SUB ChangeCaption (X AS CONTROL, Y AS STRING)
  IF TYPEOF X IS Text THEN
    'Do Nothing
  ELSE
    X.Caption = Y
  END IF
END SUB
```

Another possibility is to use

```
IF TYPEOF X IS Text THEN EXIT SUB
```

Since there is also no version of the SELECT CASE for controls, you may need the IF-THEN-ELSEIF version of this control structure:

IF TYPEOF *Control1* IS *ControlType1* THEN

  .

  .

```
ELSEIF TYPEOF Control2 IS ControlType2 THEN
 .
 .
ELSEIF TYPEOF Control3 IS ControlType3 THEN
 .
 .
 .
ELSE
 .
 .
 .
END IF
```

 Tip: If you set the tag property of the form or control to contain information you will need at run time, you can utilize the techniques from this section to process information that would otherwise not be available.

Some General Words on Program Design

The usual improved methods for writing programs—often called modular, top down, structured program design—were developed in the 1970s and 1980s from rules of thumb that programmers learned through experience in using conventional programming languages. An event-driven language like Visual Basic requires some obvious shifts. For one thing, there is normally no "top" of the program. Nonetheless, when you have something hard to do, you first divide it into several smaller jobs. Moreover, with most jobs, the "subtasks" (the smaller jobs) have a natural order in which they should be done. (You dig a hole for the foundation before you call the cement truck.) Programs are written from the general to the particular. After you design the interface for your Visual Basic project, start with a conception of the big picture—what are the event procedures supposed to do?—and then, in stages, break that down. This lets you keep track of the forest even when there are lots of trees.

Your first outline should list the event procedures and the jobs they have to do. Keep on refining your outline by adding helper Sub and Function procedures for the jobs the event procedures are supposed to do, until the pieces to be coded for all the procedures are well within your limits. Stop breaking down the jobs when you can shut your eyes and visualize the code for the procedure to accomplish the task you set out for it.

Sometimes this "step-wise refinement" is described as "relentless massage." Since programmers often say "massage a problem" when they mean "chew it over and analyze it," the metaphor is striking—and useful.

Even if you can see how to program two completely separate jobs in one Sub or Function procedure, it's usually better not to do so. Sticking to one job per procedure makes it easier both to debug the procedure and to optimize the code in it.

Often, professional programmers are hired to modify programs written by other people. Imagine trying to modify a big program that wasn't written cleanly—if, for example, no distinction was made between local and global variables (all variables were global) and no attempt was made to write the program in digestible pieces with clear lines of communication between the pieces.

What happens? Because all variables are global, a little change you make in a small module could foul up the whole program. Because the pieces of the program aren't digestible and the way they communicate is unclear, you can't be sure how they relate. Anything you do, even to one line of code, may introduce side effects—possibly disastrous ones.

This kind of disaster was common until the late 1960s or early 1970s. Companies first spent millions of dollars having programs modified; then they spent more money trying to anticipate the potential side effects that the changes they just paid for might cause. And then they hoped that more time (and more money) would fix the side effects. No matter where they stopped, they could never be certain the programs were free of bugs. Modular design, when combined with programming languages that allow local and global variables, can stop side effects completely; programs still have bugs, but these bugs don't cause epidemics. If you fix a small module in a giant, well-designed program, then you know how the changes affect everything because how the parts of the program communicate with the other parts is clearly spelled out. Only global variables and parameters need to be checked.

Ultimately, you will develop your own style for writing Visual Basic programs, and what works for one person may not work for another. Still, just as artists benefit from knowing what techniques have worked in the past, programmers can learn from what programmers have done before them.

The first rule still has to be "Think first—code later." You have some idea of what needs to be done and so you design the interface and start writing code. When your first attempt doesn't work, you keep on modifying your project until it does work (or seems to). This is usually referred to (sometimes with pride, sometimes with disdain) as "hacking away at the keyboard."

Of course, you will occasionally write programs with little or no preparation (you may need a ten-line program to print out a label or somesuch); that's one of the virtues of any BASIC, and Visual Basic is no exception. Where do you draw the line? How long must a program be before it can benefit from some paper and pencil? The answer is to know your own limits. You may find it hard to write a program longer than one screen or with more than one event procedure without some sort of outline. If you try to do it without an outline, it might end up taking longer than if you had written an outline first.

Outlines don't have to be complicated. The complete outline for the Pig Latin program was

Two text boxes and a command button

text1 for text
text2 for translation

Command button starts process

While there are still words
  latinize the next word

To latinize a word
  one letter words stay the same
  beginning vowels -> add way
  beginning consonants (y, qu = conson) -> ROTATE and add ay
ROTATE
  find consonant(s)
  move it to end

This may be a little hard for others to use, but that's not the point of an outline. Write your outlines to fit your own internal shorthand. In particular, outlines should help you fix the concepts that you'll use in the program. You may find it a good rule that when it looks like a line in your outline will correspond to no more than ten lines of code, you've done enough outlining and should start writing. (Of course, only practice will let you see at a glance how long the coded version is likely to be.)

Some people like to expand their outlines to pseudocode. This is especially common if you are developing a program with or for someone else. *Pseudocode* is an ill-defined cross between a programming language and English. While everyone seems to have his or her own idea of what pseudocode should look like, most programmers do agree that a pseudocode description (unlike an outline) should be sufficiently clear and detailed that any competent programmer can translate it into a running program.

Here's a pseudocode version of part of the preceding outline:

```
FUNCTION latinize (NEXT WORD)
  IF Length(NEXT WORD) = 1 THEN do nothing
  IF FirstLetter(NEXT WORD) = a, i, e, o, u THEN
    LATINIZE(NEXT WORD)  = NEXT WORD + WAY
  ELSE
    Find(leading consonants of NEXT WORD)  '(qu y consonant)
    LATINIZE(NEXT WORD) = NEXT WORD - leading consonants + ay
```

The point is that, although a phrase like

LATINIZE(NEXT WORD) = NEXT WORD - leading consonants + ay

doesn't seem on the surface to be very close to Visual Basic code, it is for an experienced programmer.

Error Trapping

Regardless of how carefully you develop your own program, it will often seem impossible to anticipate all the crazy things an inexperienced user may do. If you want your program to degrade gracefully and not just roll over, you'll want to prevent fatal errors. The command that activates (*enables*) error trapping within a given procedure is

ON LOCAL ERROR GOTO *label*

where *label* is the label (line number) that defines the start of the error trap. The labeled code must be in the current procedure. You cannot jump out of a procedure using an ON LOCAL ERROR GOTO command. On the other hand, the code for the error trap will often use other Sub or Function procedures.

A label is any identifier ending with a colon that satisfies the rules for variables. The label identifies the island of code—the isolated lines of code that make up the error trap—starting on the next line. For example:

```
ErrorTrap:
  'error code goes here
```

Since you do not want Visual Basic to inadvertently "fall" into the error-trapping code, it is quite common to have an EXIT (SUB or FUNCTION) on the line immediately preceding the label for the error trap.

The ON LOCAL ERROR GOTO command can occur anywhere in an event, Sub, or Function procedure. Usually, the error-trapping code is inside that procedure. The only exception to this is when one procedure has been called by another. In this case, Visual Basic will look to see if an error trap was enabled in the earlier procedure.

Once you start error trapping with the ON LOCAL ERROR GOTO command, a run-time error will no longer bomb the program. The ON LOCAL ERROR GOTO command should transfer control to a piece of code that identifies the problem and, if possible, fixes it. (On the other hand, an active error handler can make the program harder to debug.)

If the error can be corrected, then the RESUME statement takes you back to the statement that caused the error in the first place. However, you can't correct an error if you don't know why it happened. You identify the problem by means of the ERR function. This gives you an integer that you can assign to a variable. For example, if you write

```
ErrorNumber = ERR
```

the value of the variable ErrorNumber can help you pick up the type of error.

Visual Basic can identify more than 100 run–time errors. The run-time error codes found under "Contents" in the on-line help gives you the current list of errors. If a run-time error occurs while you are working in the Visual Basic environment, you can obtain a short explanation of what might have caused any specific error by pressing the F1 key. As a simple example, start a new project and enter the single line

```
LPRINT "Print this on the printer"
```

Now, turn your printer on but set it off-line. Then run the program. A "Device fault" error results because the printer is not ready to receive output. Pressing the F1 key gives you help in identifying what has caused the "Device fault" error.

The information in the run-time error codes list is useful: Suppose, for example, an event procedure will be using the printer. Somewhere in the procedure, before the error can occur, place the statement

```
ON LOCAL ERROR GOTO PrinterCheck
```

Now, before the END SUB, add code that looks like this:

```
EXIT SUB
PrinterCheck:
  ErrorNumber = ERR
  BEEP
  SELECT CASE ErrorNumber
    CASE  25
      MSGBOX "Your printer may not be on-line."
    CASE 27
      MSGBOX "Is there a printer available?"
    CASE ELSE
      M$ = "Please tell the operator (= program author?) that"
      M$ = M$ + CHR$(10) + CHR$(13)    'New Line
      M$ = M$ + "error number"+ STR$(ErrorNumber) +" occurred."
      MSGBOX M$
      END
  END SELECT
  M$ = "If the error has been corrected click on OK."
  M$ = M$ + CHR$(10) + CHR$(13)
  M$ = M$ + "Otherwise click on Cancel."
```

```
Continue = MSGBOX(M$, 1)
IF Continue = 1 THEN RESUME ELSE END
```

The idea of this error trap is simple, and the SELECT CASE statement is ideal. Each case tries to give some indication of where the problem is and, if possible, how to correct it. If you reach the CASE ELSE, the error number has to be reported. In any case, the final message box gives the user the option of continuing or not continuing. By analyzing which button was pressed you can continue or end the program.

You might want to get into the habit of writing a general procedure that analyzes the error code. The error trap inside a procedure will then just send control to the general procedure. If you do this, you can reuse the general procedure in many different projects.

Caution: Error trapping isn't a cure-all. Obviously, very little can be done about a hard disk crash or the user's not having any paper around to jot down the error code to report.

A variant on the RESUME command lets you bypass the statement that may have caused the problem. If you use

```
RESUME NEXT
```

Visual Basic begins processing at the statement following the one that caused the error. You can also resume execution at any line of code in the procedure that has been previously identified with a label. For this, use a statement of the form

RESUME *label*

It is unusual to have labels in Visual Basic except in connection with error trapping. Nonetheless, for compatibility with older BASICs, Visual Basic does let you use the unconditional GOTO or GOSUB to transfer to the line of code following the label, but there is never any reason to use an unconditional GOTO, and GOSUBs are far less flexible than procedures. (See Appendix C.)

Both the RESUME and RESUME NEXT commands behave differently if Visual Basic has to move backward to find the error trap in a different procedure. Recall that this happens when one procedure invokes a second procedure, the second procedure doesn't have an error trap, and an error occurs in the second procedure. For the RESUME command, Visual Basic will reinvoke the second procedure, executing all of its statements again. You *cannot* go directly back to the statement which caused the error and resume execution. For the RESUME NEXT command, Visual Basic will execute the statement in the first procedure coming immediately after the statement which had called the second procedure. You *cannot* go back into the second procedure and begin execution with the statement following the statement which caused the error.

Suppose the chain of procedural calls goes back even further: Procedure1 calls Procedure2, which calls Function3. Now an error occurs in Function3, but the only error handler is in Procedure1. If there is a RESUME command in the error handler in Procedure1, Visual Basic actually goes to the statement that called Procedure2.

Because this is unwieldy and so prone to problems, it is probably better to rely only on error handlers that occur in a specific procedure. If one procedure calls another, you can turn off the error handler in the calling routine with the statement

```
ON LOCAL ERROR GOTO 0
```

Occasionally, when debugging a program, it's helpful to know what the error message for the last error was (for example, to place it in a message box). The function that does this is

ERROR$

You can also use

ERROR$(*ErrorNumber*)

to give the error message corresponding to a specific error number. Of course, Visual Basic gives the current error number as the value of the ERR function.

When developing a program, you may want to test how your error handler works. Visual Basic includes the statement

ERROR *ErrNum*

which, when processed, makes Visual Basic behave as if the error whose error number is the value of *ErrNum* has actually occurred. This makes it easier to develop the trap.

If you are confident that you will no longer need an error trap, you can disable error trapping with the statement

```
ON LOCAL ERROR GOTO 0
```

Similarly, you can change which error trap is in effect by using another ON LOCAL ERROR GOTO statement. Be sure to have an EXIT command between the error traps. Visual Basic uses the last ON LOCAL ERROR GOTO statement processed to decide where to go.

CHAPTER

Arrays and Records

Often your Visual Basic application will need to add controls to a form while the application is running. Suppose there was an easy way of doing this. The problem remains that controls on a Visual Basic form are most useful when they have event procedures attached to them. Therefore, whenever you add a new control to a form at run time, Visual Basic needs to know what event procedures to use for the new control. An obvious solution is to have the new control inherit the event procedures for an existing Visual Basic control. This was the path chosen by the designers of Visual Basic, using control arrays. A *control array* is a related group of controls that share common event procedures. You'll see how to handle them in the first part of this chapter.

Next, you'll see arrays for holding variables. You use a *variable array* when you need to store lists and tables. Once you have a list, of course, you'll need to have fast and effective ways to search and sort the contents. This chapter covers some of the many methods known for searching and sorting.

Finally, you'll see how to create records. *Records* let you construct variables that combine both numeric and string information.

Control Arrays

You may have inadvertently given two controls of the same type the same control name, or tried to copy a control using the Edit menu. If you did, then you saw a dialog box that looks like the one in Figure 9-1. Any time you use the same control name more than once while designing a Visual Basic application, Visual Basic asks you whether you really want to create a control array. Click the Yes button (or press ENTER), and you will be able to add more controls of the same type now or while the application is running. Each new control in a control array is called an *element* of the control array. (To more easily follow this discussion, you might want to create two text boxes with the control name of Money and set up the same control array as in Figure 9-1. Notice as well that the text box in Figure 9-1 has the caption "Text1".)

Since both controls now have the same name, Visual Basic needs a way to distinguish them. You do this with the Index property. When you

FIGURE
9-1
Message box to create a control array

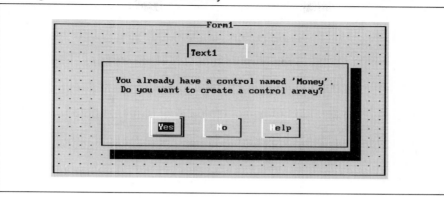

ask Visual Basic to create a control array, Visual Basic gives the first control an Index property of zero and the second control an Index property of 1. Like any properties of Visual Basic objects, you can change them at design time with the properties bar. In fact, if you assign any number to the Index property of a control at design time, Visual Basic automatically creates a control array. This lets you create a control array without having to use two controls at design time.

Suppose you want to work with the LostFocus procedure for the Money text box control array. Invoke the Event Procedures selection window (selected from the Edit menu or by pressing ALT+E V). Notice that two text boxes are not listed. Instead, there is the single entry Money(). Select the LostFocus event procedure for the Money() array. You'll see something like the screen in Figure 9-2. Notice that the LostFocus event procedure template looks a little different from anything you've seen up to now. Instead of having no parameters, as the LostFocus procedure ordinarily does, this event procedure now uses a new parameter, Index AS INTEGER.

This index parameter is the key to the smooth functioning of control arrays. If you want to use the LostFocus procedure for any element of the control array, call it with the appropriate index parameter:

```
CALL Money_LostFocus(0)        'applies to the original text box
CALL Money_LostFocus(1)        'applies to the second text box
```

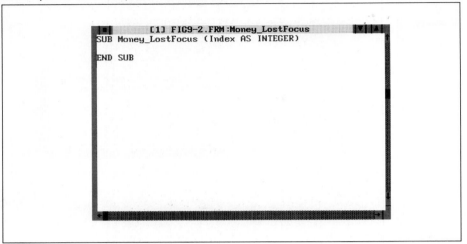

FIGURE
9-2

Event procedure template with index parameter

For example, add the following code to the event procedure shown in Figure 9-2:

```
SUB Money_LostFocus (Index AS INTEGER)
  IF Index = 0 THEN
    Money(0).Text = "Original box"
  ELSE
    Money(1).Text = "Next text box in control array"
  END IF
END SUB
```

Now, when you move the focus away from one of the text boxes, Visual Basic calls this event procedure *and* passes the index parameter to the procedure. In this way, the event procedure can use the index to determine what to do. When you move the focus away from the text box with the Index property of zero, Visual Basic activates the IF clause inside this event procedure. Otherwise, Visual Basic processes the ELSE clause. The IF-THEN-ELSE combined with the index parameter lets the event procedure reset the Text property for only the control that has lost the focus.

Any event procedure that would work for a single control can be used for a control array of that type while a program is running. Visual Basic adds an index parameter as the first item on the parameter list for the given event procedure. For example, the KeyPress event procedure for the control array of Money text boxes now starts out as

```
SUB Money_KeyPress (Index AS INTEGER, KeyAscii AS INTEGER)
```

instead of

```
SUB Money_KeyPress (KeyAscii AS INTEGER)
```

as it would for an ordinary text box named Money.

If you inadvertently added a control to a control array at design time, you can remove it by changing the control name or deleting the control. However, once Visual Basic creates a control array, you must change all the control names or delete all the controls that were in the array in order to eliminate the control array. After that, you can reuse the name.

Adding and Removing Controls in a Control Array

Once you've created a control array at design time, you can add controls while the application is running. To do this, you use the LOAD command. For example, suppose you want to add four new text boxes to the Money text box control array created in the previous section. To do this when the form loads, all you need to do is add the following code to the Form_Load event procedure for the form:

```
SUB Form_Load ()
  DIM I AS INTEGER

  FOR I = 2 TO 5
    LOAD Money(I)
    Money(I).Text = "Text box #" + STR$(I)
  NEXT I
END SUB
```

Whenever Visual Basic loads a new element of a control array, the new object is invisible—in other words, the Visible property is automatically set to False. All the other properties (except for TabIndex and the Control

Array Index) are copied from the object having the lowest index in the array. In particular, even if you modify the preceding Form_Load procedure to read

```
SUB Form_Load ()
  DIM I AS INTEGER

  FOR I = 2 TO 5
    LOAD Money(I)
    Money(I).Text = "Text Box #" + STR$(I)
    Money(I).Visible = -1                      'TRUE
  NEXT I
END SUB
```

you may have changed the Visible property to True, but all you will still see is the fifth text box. This is because the Left and Top properties start out the same for all the newly created controls. They are the same as Money(0).Left and Money(0).Top. This means that newly created controls in a control array default to being stacked one on top of the other. Because of this, you'll often find yourself applying the Move method to controls in a control array after you tell Visual Basic to load them. For example, suppose you want to place the new text boxes on the far left. Then, using the default size for the height of a text box, you might write

```
SUB Form_Load ()
  DIM I AS INTEGER

  FOR I = 2 TO 5
    LOAD Money(I)
    Money(I).Text = "Text Box #" + STR$(I)
    Money(I).MOVE 0, 3 * (I - 2)
    Money(I).Visible = -1                      'TRUE
  NEXT I
END SUB
```

The key line

```
Money(I).MOVE 0, 3 * (I - 2)
```

starts at the top left when I = 2, because the command is then

```
Money(I).MOVE = 0, 0
```

On each pass through the loop, the location for the top of the box moves down by the default height of a text box (3 rows), as shown in Figure 9-3.

You can use the UNLOAD statement to remove any element of a control array that you added at run time. You cannot use the UNLOAD statement to remove the original elements of the control array that you created at design time. For example, if you add the following Click procedure:

```
Form_Click ()
  STATIC I AS INTEGER

  IF I < 4 THEN
    UNLOAD Money(I + 2)
    I = I + 1
  ELSE
    EXIT SUB
  END IF
END SUB
```

each click on an empty place in the form removes the next control in the control array.

You must be careful, of course; you can only load or unload an element of a control array once. If you try to load or unload a control array element twice, Visual Basic gives a trappable run-time error (ERR = 360).

FIGURE 9-3

Demonstration of loading text boxes in a control array

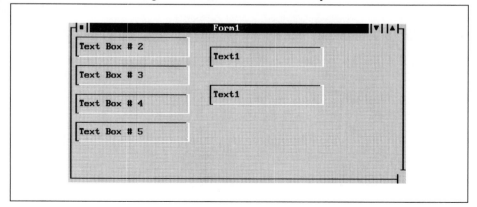

An Example: A Control Array of Labels

Later in this chapter, you'll see a program that creates magic squares, an example of which is shown in Figure 9-4. A *magic square* has rows, columns, and long diagonals of numbers that all add up to the same sum. For now, we'll create a control array of labels based on user input and display them sequentially numbered in a square on a form of maximal size. The method described later for filling the magic square requires that the number of rows and columns be odd, so we'll use that constraint here as well.

Here's the outline for the labels program:

1. Maximize the form.

2. Ask user for the number of rows and columns, making sure the response is an odd number less than or equal to 15. (Maximum number of controls per form is 255. To allow 17 rows and columns of labels would require 17*17 = 289 controls.) Store the response in the form level variable NumberOfDims.

FIGURE
9-4

7 × 7 magic square

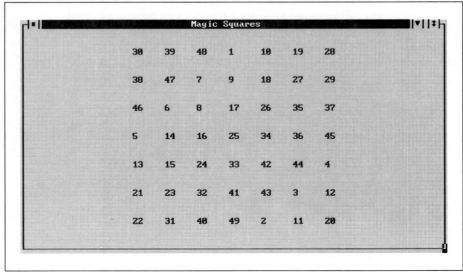

3. Ask user for the desired label height, making sure the response is at least 1. It is also necessary that (*label height*) * NumberOfDims <= Screen.Height so that all labels fit on the form. Store the response in the form level variable LabelHeight.

4. To make each label roughly square, set the width of a label equal to twice LabelHeight, but never less than 4. This lower limit guarantees that enough room exists to display a three digit number and still have a space between successive columns. Store the result in the form level variable LabelWidth.

5. Load the labels.

6. Arrange the labels in a square on the form.

Where should the labels be placed? Screen.Height \ 2 is the center of a vertical line and Screen.Width \ 2 is the center of a horizontal line, so start at

Screen.Height \ 2 – (NumberOfDims * LabelHeight) \ 2

for the vertical and

Screen.Width \ 2 – (NumberOfDims * LabelWidth) \ 2

for the horizontal.

Here's the code. First comes two form level constants:

```
CONST TRUE = -1

CONST FALSE = 0
```

Next, the Form_Load procedure invokes a procedure to obtain the number of rows and columns and the label height from the user. It then computes the label width and invokes two additional procedures to create the labels and display them in a square:

```
SUB Form_Load ()

  ' local variables:
  DIM NumberOfDims AS INTEGER
```

```
DIM LabelHeight AS INTEGER, LabelWidth AS INTEGER

' get # of rows & columns and label height from user
CALL AskUser(NumberOfDims, LabelHeight)

' compute label width, but always make it at least 4
LabelWidth = 2 * LabelHeight
IF LabelWidth < 4 THEN LabelWidth = 4

' create the array of labels
CALL MakeBoxes(NumberOfDims, LabelHeight, LabelWidth)

' arrange the array of labels in a square on the form
CALL LocateBoxes(NumberOfDims, LabelHeight, LabelWidth)
END SUB
```

The AskUser procedure obtains the needed information from the user, verifying that the data given is acceptable:

```
SUB AskUser (Dims AS INTEGER, BoxHeight AS INTEGER)
  ' local variables:
  DIM Temp$, Message$, Biggest$

  WindowState = 2                          'maximal
  'This loop makes sure the response given is an odd number
  'The upper bound of 15 is needed since the number of elements
  'in a controls per form is limited to 255
  DO
    Temp$ = INPUTBOX$("Number of rows and columns (1-15 odd)?")
    Dims = VAL(Temp$)
  LOOP UNTIL (Dims MOD 2 = 1) AND (Dims <= 15)

  'This loop makes sure labels aren't too large
  Biggest$ = LTRIM$(STR$(Screen.Height \ Dims))
  Message$ = "Height of Labels (1-" + Biggest$ + ")?"
  DO
    Temp$ = INPUTBOX$(Message$)
    BoxHeight = VAL(Temp$)
  LOOP UNTIL (BoxHeight >= 1) AND (BoxHeight <= VAL(Biggest$))
END SUB
```

The MakeBoxes procedure resizes the initial label in the control array, then creates the other needed labels:

```
SUB MakeBoxes (Dims AS INTEGER, BoxHeight AS INTEGER,_
                              BoxWidth AS INTEGER)

  'local variable:
```

```
DIM I AS INTEGER

  BoxLabel(0).Visible = FALSE       ' temp. hide original label
  BoxLabel(0).Height = BoxHeight    ' other labels will inherit
  BoxLabel(0).Width = BoxWidth      '     this height and width
  FOR I = 1 TO Dims * Dims - 1      'already have one label
    Boxlabel(0)
    LOAD BoxLabel(I)
  NEXT I
END SUB
```

Finally, the LocateBoxes procedure arranges the labels on the form:

```
SUB LocateBoxes (Dims AS INTEGER,BoxHeight AS INTEGER,
                                 BoxWidth AS INTEGER)
  'local variables
  DIM I AS INTEGER
  DIM StartC AS INTEGER, StartR AS INTEGER
  DIM BoxColumn AS INTEGER, BoxRow AS INTEGER
  DIM C AS INTEGER, R AS INTEGER

  'determine location of upper lefthand corner of magic square
  StartC = Screen.Width \ 2 - (Dims * BoxWidth \ 2)
  StartR = Screen.Height \ 2 - (Dims * BoxHeight \ 2)
  FOR I = 0 TO Dims * Dims - 1
    BoxColumn = I MOD Dims
    BoxRow = I \ Dims
    C = StartC + (BoxColumn * BoxWidth)
    R = StartR + (BoxRow * BoxHeight)
    Boxlabel(I).MOVE C, R
    Boxlabel(I).Caption = STR$(I + 1)
    Boxlabel(I).Visible = TRUE
  NEXT I
END SUB
```

Inside the LocateBoxes procedure, the starting column, StartC, and starting row, StartR, are set to the upper lefthand corner of the magic square, then the FOR-NEXT loop does all the work. The remainder (I MOD Dims) is used to find the column number of a given label, while integer division is used to determine the row number:

When I is 0, 1, ..., Dims–1, I MOD Dims (and thus BoxColumn) takes on the values 0, 1, ..., Dims–1, while I \ Dims (and thus BoxRow) is 0.

When I is Dims, Dims+1, ..., 2*Dims–1, I MOD Dims (and thus

BoxColumn) again takes on the values 0, 1, ..., Dims–1, while I \ Dims (and thus BoxRow) is 1.

And so on.

From the column and row numbers, an offset in screen columns and screen rows is computed and added to StartC and StartR to determine the screen location for the label. The line BoxLabel(I).Caption = STR$(I + 1) was put in to display the ordering of the boxes.

One nice point about these procedures is that you can easily adapt them to many situations. Minor changes allow you to use them whenever you need to load and position multiple controls on a form.

Lists: One-dimensional Arrays

Suppose you are writing a program that requires one variable with the value 1, a second with the value 2, a third with the value 3, and so on, for 100 different variables. The outline for this kind of program cries out for a FOR-NEXT loop something like this:

```
FOR I = 1 to 100
  Assign I to its variable
NEXT I
```

As another example, suppose you need data for a 12-month period. You would like to say something like this:

```
FOR I = 1 to 12
  MonthI = VAL(INPUTBOX$(Data for MonthI))
NEXT I
```

If this kind of loop were possible, the information entered would still be available in the various MonthI variables. Unfortunately, this is not quite correct. In Visual Basic, MonthI is a perfectly good variable name— for a single variable. Visual Basic cannot separate the I from the Month. After you see a systematic way to name variables, it's easy to take care of this problem.

To Visual Basic, a *list* (often called a *one-dimensional array*) is just a collection of variables, each one of which is identified by two things:

☐   The name of the list

☐   The position of the item in the list

For example, suppose you are writing a program that lets a user enter an "errand list" at the beginning of each day. You would probably choose to store the information in a list. The third errand might be stored as Errand$(3). The name of this list is Errand$. Notice the dollar sign ($) that indicates that the variables of this list will hold words (strings).

The number in the parentheses is usually called a *subscript, pointer,* or *index.* The term "subscript" comes from mathematics, where the item M(5) is more likely to be written M$_5$. The term "pointer" is used because the 5 "points" to the row holding the information. Finally, the term "index" reflects locating information, as in a book's index. To Visual Basic, M5 is the name of a single variable, but M(5) is the name of the fifth element in a list called M. By default, each list in Visual Basic has a zeroth entry, so the list M has an element M(0) as well.

Fixed Versus Dynamic Lists

Lists can't be open ended in Visual Basic. While the limits are quite large—you can have up to 32,768 items on certain kinds of lists—you must tell Visual Basic how much memory to set aside for the list before you use it.

There are two kinds of lists in Visual Basic: *fixed lists,* where the memory allocation never changes, and *dynamic lists,* where you can change size on the fly. The advantage of a fixed list is that memory is set aside at the beginning of the program; you run a much smaller risk of running out of memory while the program is running. The advantage of dynamic lists is the flexibility they provide. You can change the size in response to what the program has encountered.

Both kinds of lists may be made visible to all procedures associated with a specific form. To set up a fixed list in a form, place a statement like

```
DIM SHARED Errand(13) AS STRING
```

in the leading code of the form. This sets up a 14-element list for strings. The items would be stored in Errand(0) through Errand(13).

To set up a dynamic list in a form, place a statement like

```
DIM SHARED Errand() AS STRING
```

in the leading code of the form. You then use the REDIM statement inside a procedure to allocate the space:

```
SUB NameOfProcedure ()
  .
  .
  .
  REDIM Errand(Number) AS STRING
  .
  .
  .
END SUB
```

Each time Visual Basic processes a REDIM statement, any information in the array is lost. The advantage, though, is clear: you can calculate how much space you need before issuing the REDIM command. In the preceding example, the value of the variable Number can change depending on the circumstances.

A variation of the REDIM statement can be used to increase the size of a dynamic list while retaining any information already stored in the list. The statement

```
REDIM PRESERVE Errand(NewSize) AS STRING
```

could be placed in a procedure to increase the number of entries in the array Errand() to NewSize + 1 without losing data already stored in the list.

Finally, you can set up a local fixed list inside a procedure by declaring the array in a STATIC statement:

```
SUB ProcedureName()
   STATIC Errand() AS STRING, Dimmed AS INTEGER

   IF NOT Dimmed THEN
      DIM Errand(13) AS STRING
      Dimmed = -1
   ELSE
   .
   END IF
END SUB
```

Note that the size of the list cannot be given in the STATIC statement, but must be established in a subsequent DIM statement. If the procedure is to be called more than once (a reasonable assumption if you are going to the bother of setting up a local static list), precautions must be taken to guarantee that the DIM statement is executed only the first time that the procedure is called, otherwise a "Duplicate definition" error will occur. This is done in the example above by setting up the static integer variable Dimmed whose initial value defaults to False (0), and then using an IF statement to set up the list and set Dimmed to True (-1).

As with any static variable, the information you store in a static local list remains intact from one call of the procedure to another. Similarly, the information in a form-level dynamic list remains intact until *you* redimension it.

When you write code to dynamically dimension a list or array, Visual Basic sets aside space only when the dimensioning statement is executed. If the program is very large, it's possible that you won't have enough room. If this happens, you'll get the dreaded "Out of memory" error.

Some Examples of Using Lists

Values inside lists are most often assigned by using a FOR-NEXT loop or, since you often want to allow the user to stop before entering values in all the variables of a list, you can use a DO loop, as in the following fragment:

```
'in leading code:
CONST MaxListSize = 30
DIM SHARED Errand(MaxListSize) AS STRING
```

```
DIM SHARED NumberOfItems AS INTEGER

SUB GetErrands ()
  'local variables:
  DIM M$, NextErrand$

  NumberOfItems = 0
  DO
    M$ = "You've entered" + STR$(NumberOfItems) + " entries."
    M$ = M$ + " Enter the next errand - ZZZ when done."
    NextErrand$ = UCASE$(INPUTBOX$(M$))
    IF NextErrand$ <> "ZZZ" THEN
      NumberOfItems = NumberOfItems + 1
      Errand(NumberOfItems) = NextErrand$
    END IF
  LOOP UNTIL (NumberOfItems=MaxListSize) OR (NextErrand$="ZZZ")
END SUB
```

Notice that a temporary variable, NextErrand$, was set up to hold the user's response to the INPUTBOX$ request rather than placing the response directly in the list. Notice as well that the statements between IF and END IF are completely skipped when **"ZZZ"** is entered. Enter **"ZZZ"**, and the user moves immediately to the loop test and leaves. Using a temporary variable and testing it against the flag keeps the flag off the list.

Once you know that an entry is acceptable, you first move the pointer (add 1 to NumberOfItems) and then fill in the entry. If, instead, you move the pointer after filling an entry, then entry *n* would not be in Errand(*n*) and the value of the variable NumberofItems would always be one more than the number of items currently on the list. This latter fact is particularly undesirable since the purpose of the form level variable NumberOfItems is to record the number of items contained in the list for use by any other procedures that manipulate this list.

However, there are other ways to pass this information around than by using a variable like NumberOfItems. For this, recall that in Visual Basic all lists default to having a zeroth entry. In the example, when you wrote

```
DIM SHARED Errand(MaxListSize) AS STRING
```

Visual Basic actually set aside MaxListSize + 1 slots, the extra one being Errand(0). This zeroth slot is useful for things like the number of significant items in the list. What you might want to do (rather than using a form level variable) is

```
Errand(0) = STR$(NumberOfItems)
```

Now, to find the number of items (for example, to set up a FOR–NEXT loop), you can convert this entry back to a number by using the VAL function.

Another, perhaps even more popular, alternative is to keep a flag (like "ZZZ") as the last item in a list. This lets you use an indeterminate loop to manipulate the list. (This way you can test for the flag.) To do this, modify the previous fragment as follows:

```
' A simple list demo revisited and revised

'in leading code:
CONST MaxListSize = 30
DIM SHARED Errand(MaxListSize) AS STRING

SUB GetErrands ()
  'local variables:
  DIM Index AS INTEGER, M$

  Index = 0
  DO
    M$ = "You've entered" + STR$(Index) + " entries."
    M$ = M$ + " Enter the next errand - ZZZ when done."
    Index = Index + 1
    Errand(Index) = UCASE$(INPUTBOX$(M$))
  LOOP UNTIL (Index = MaxListSize) OR (Errand(Index) = "ZZZ")
END SUB
```

Notice that, here, the user's response is put directly in the list. Notice as well that the loop exits if the flag is placed in the list or the list reaches its maximum allowed length that you set with the MaxListSize constant in the above listing.

Of the two methods, the idea of keeping the number of items currently used in the zeroth entry (when possible) may be the most appealing, but this is clearly a matter of taste. You may find it comforting to always know how many entries are in a list. It makes debugging easier and, like most programmers, you may find FOR-NEXT loops easier to use than DO loops.

An Example: Improving the Built-in Random Number Generator

The built-in random number generator in Visual Basic that was introduced in Chapter 7 doesn't give good results for some types of simulations and is not a particularly good method for developing encryption programs (see Chapter 13). If you find that the random number generator is a problem, there is a simple method for improvement using arrays. This gives you a way to generate numbers that seem even more random. (Technically, what the method does is eliminate sequential correlations.) All you need to do is the following:

1. Set up an array of random numbers.

2. Use the built-in random number generator to pick one element of the array.

3. Replace the element chosen with a new random number generated by the built-in random number generator.

If you use this method instead of the built-in random number generator, you should eliminate most of the problems with very few performance penalties. Essentially, what these steps do is shuffle the cards one more time. An array of about 100 works very well. (Actually, 101 works a bit better because 101 is a *prime number*—you can't factor 101 like you can 100 = 4 * 25.) To implement the method outlined previously, first set up a form level array:

```
DIM SHARED RandomList(100)
```

Fill it with 101 random numbers in an Initialize procedure called by the Form_Load procedure. Now whenever you need a random number, use the following function:

```
FUNCTION NewRandom()
  'local variables:
  DIM Foo AS SINGLE, X AS INTEGER

  RANDOMIZE
  Foo = RND
  X = INT(101 * Foo)
```

```
   NewRandom = RandomList(X)
   RandomList(X) = Foo          'Replace used up entry
END FUNCTION
```

Lists with Subscript Ranges

Some people never use the zeroth entry of a list; they just find it confusing. (And if you are not going to use it in a program, it certainly wastes space.) For this reason, Visual Basic (to maintain compatibility with interpreted BASICs) has a command that eliminates the zeroth entry in all lists dimensioned in the form. It is the OPTION BASE 1 statement. This statement is used in the leading code of a form and affects all lists in the form. All new lists dimensioned in that form begin with item 1. After OPTION BASE 1, DIM Errand$(30), for example, sets aside 30 spots rather than 31.

As usual, Visual Basic goes one step beyond interpreted BASICs. Suppose you want to write the input routine for a bar graph program for sales in the years 1980 through 1989. You could write something like

```
DIM SalesInYear(9) AS SINGLE
DIM I AS INTEGER, Sales$
FOR I = 0 TO 9
   Sales$ = INPUTBOX$("Enter the sales in year" + STR$(1980 + I))
   SalesInYear(I) = VAL(Sales$)
NEXT I
```

This situation is so common that QuickBASIC and Visual Basic enhance the language by allowing subscript ranges. Instead of writing

```
DIM SalesInYear(9)
```

you can now write

```
DIM SalesInYear(1980 TO 1989)
```

The keyword TO marks the range, smaller number first (from 1980 to 1989, in this case), for this extension of the DIM and REDIM statements. Using this variant, you can rewrite the preceding fragment so that it is easier to read:

```
DIM SalesInYear(1980 TO 1989) AS SINGLE
DIM I AS INTEGER, Sales$

FOR I = 1980 TO 1989
  Sales$ = INPUTBOX$("Enter the sales in year"+ STR$(I))
  SalesInYear(I) = VAL(Sales$)
NEXT I
```

The ERASE Statement

As your programs grow longer, it will become more likely that you'll run out of space for new data. Visual Basic allows you to reclaim the space used by a dynamically dimensioned array. You do this with the ERASE command. For example, if the array Cities was dimensioned dynamically, then the statement

```
ERASE Cities
```

would erase the Cities array and free up the space it occupied. Notice that in an ERASE statement you do not follow the array name with parentheses.

If an array was not dimensioned dynamically, then the ERASE statement does not remove the array from memory, but simply resets all the entries to their default values (zero for numeric lists, the null string for lists of variable length strings, and a string of CHR$(0) for lists of fixed length strings). Thus, the ERASE statement provides a fast method to "zero out" the entries in static arrays. Only in the case of a static list of variable length strings will ERASEing the list also free up some memory.

Arrays with More Than One Dimension

You can also have arrays with more than one dimension; they're usually called *multidimensional arrays*. Just as lists of data lead to single subscripts (one-dimensional arrays), tables of data lead to double subscripts (multi-dimensional arrays). For example, suppose you want to store a multiplication table in memory—as a table. You could do this as

```
DIM MultTable(12, 12) AS INTEGER
DIM I AS INTEGER, J AS INTEGER

FOR I = 1 TO 12
 FOR J = 1 TO 12
  MultTable(I, J) = I * J
 NEXT J
NEXT I
```

To compute the number of items in a multidimensional array, multiply the number of entries. The dimension statement here sets aside one of the following:

☐   144 (12 * 12) entries if an Option Base 1 has been previously processed

☐   169 (13 * 13) entries if an Option Base 1 has not been processed.

So in this example, there are either 12 rows and 12 columns or 13 rows and 13 columns. In general, the number of entries in an array dimensioned with a statement of the form

DIM *ArrayName*(R, S, ..., Z)

is R*S*...*Z if Option Base 1 has been processed previously, otherwise the number of entries is (R+1)*(S+1)*...*(Z+1).

The convention is to refer to the first entry as giving the number of rows and the second the number of columns. Following this convention, you would describe the preceding fragment as filling an entire row, column by column, before moving to the next row.

As you can see, in arrays, the extra space taken up by the zeroth row and zeroth column can dramatically increase the space requirements for your arrays. For this reason, Visual Basic's range feature is even more welcome. A statement like

```
DIM Salary(1 TO 50, 1980 TO 1989)
```

sets aside 50 rows, numbered 1 through 50, and 10 columns, "numbered" 1980 through 1989. Therefore, this Salary array has 500 entries.

Visual Basic allows you up to 60 dimensions, but constraints on the maximum number of entries will usually limit you to a much smaller number of dimensions. For example, if we insist that the range of indices for each dimension include at least two values, then an example of an integer array with the maximum number of dimensions would be

```
OPTION BASE 1
DIM LargeArray%(2, 2, 2, 2, 2, 2, 2, 2, 2, 2, 2, 2, 2, 2, 2)
```

This area has only 15 dimensions but sets aside $2^{15} = 32768$ entries. In practice, you almost never see more than 4 dimensions in a program, and even a 3-dimensional array is uncommon.

An Example: Magic Squares

For a more involved example of a program using arrays, consider again the magic square, introduced earlier in this chapter. Remember that a magic square is one where all the rows, columns, and long diagonals add up to the same number. These squares were once thought to have magical properties. The most famous one is probably this:

16	3	2	13
5	10	11	8
9	6	7	12
4	15	14	1

taken from Albrecht Dürer's famous print "Melencolia I" engraved in 1514.

Many people have devised rules for constructing magic squares. The one used in this section is called Loubère's rule and works only for odd-order magic squares—those with an odd number of rows and columns. Here's the method:

1. Place a 1 in the center of the first row.

2. The numbers now go into the square in order by moving up on the diagonal to the right.

    Of course, you're immediately met with the problem of where to put the 2. If you've placed a 1 in the top row, going up takes you off the square. The solution is

3. If you go off the top, wrap around to the corresponding place in the bottom row.

Similarly, going to the right eventually drops you off the side. In this case, use

4. If you go off to the right end, wrap around to the left column.

5. Finally, if a square is already filled or the upper right-hand corner is reached, move down one row and continue applying these rules.

Here's a 5 × 5 magic square constructed with this rule:

```
17  24   1   8  15
23   5   7  14  16
 4   6  13  20  22
10  12  19  21   3
11  18  25   2   9
```

The method above is implemented in the procedure MakeMagic below. MakeMagic assumes you've created a form and set up a control array for labels using the code from the section "An Example: A Control Array of Labels" earlier this chapter. MakeMagic can be invoked by calling it at the end of the Form_Load procedure of the earlier label example, or from the Click event procedure of a command button that you add to the form.

```
SUB MakeMagic (Dimensions AS INTEGER)
  'local variables:
  DIM I AS INTEGER, Limit AS INTEGER
  DIM Row AS INTEGER, Col AS INTEGER
  DIM NewRow AS INTEGER, NewCol AS INTEGER

  Limit = Dimensions - 1
  REDIM Magic(Limit, Limit) AS INTEGER

  Row = 0
  Col = Dimensions \ 2

  Magic(Row, Col) = 1
  BoxLabel(Col+(Dimensions*Row)).caption=STR$(Magic(Row, Col))
```

```
FOR I = 2 TO Dimensions * Dimensions

  IF Row = 0 AND Col = Limit THEN
    NewRow = 1
    NewCol = Col
  ELSE
    NewRow = Row - 1
    NewCol = Col + 1
    IF NewRow < 0 THEN NewRow = NewRow + Dimensions
    IF NewCol > Limit THEN NewCol = NewCol - Dimensions
  END IF

  'find empty slot
  DO UNTIL Magic(NewRow, NewCol) = 0
    NewRow = Row + 1
    NewCol = Col
  LOOP

  Row = NewRow
  Col = NewCol
  Magic(Row, Col) = I
  BoxLabel(Col+(Dimensions*Row)).caption=STR$(Magic(Row, Col))

NEXT I

END SUB
```

The IF clause inside the FOR-NEXT loop corresponds to the special case of the upper right-hand corner. The two IF statements inside the ELSE clause correspond to the first rule, "up and to the right." Of course, this row may be off the square, and the IF-THENs take care of this.

The DO loop stops when you get to an unoccupied square. One of the nice properties of Loubère's method of constructing magic squares is that you know it will always work.

Using Lists and Arrays with Procedures

Visual Basic has an extraordinary facility to use lists and arrays in procedures. Unlike languages like Pascal, it's easy to send any size list or array to a procedure. One way to do this, of course, is to make the list or array a form level variable, as you saw in the section "An Example:

Improving the Built-in Random Number Generator" earlier in this chapter. However, using lists and arrays as parameters for procedures is much more common.

The reasons for doing this are similar to why one usually prefers parameters to shared variables—they increase your flexibility. To send an array parameter to a procedure, put the name of the array followed by ( ) in the parameter list. For example, assume that Array$ is a two-dimensional string array and BigArray% a three-dimensional array of integers. Then,

```
SUB Example (List#(), Array$(), BigArray%(), X%)
```

would allow this example procedure to use (and change) a list of double-precision variables, an array of strings, a three-dimensional array of integers, and a final integer variable. Note that just as with variable parameters, list and array parameters are placeholders; they have no independent existence. To call the procedure, you might have a fragment like this:

```
DIM PopChange#(50), CityState$(3, 10), TotalPop%(2, 2, 2)
```

Now,

```
CALL Example(PopChange#(), CityState$(), TotalPop%(), X%)
```

would call this procedure by sending it the current location (passed by reference) of the three arrays and the integer variable. And just as before, since the compiler knows where the variable, list, or array is located, it can change the contents.

Suppose you want to write a Function procedure that would take a list of numbers and return the maximum entry. Since you may want to do this for many different lists, you decide to write a procedure that follows this outline:

Function FindMax (List( ), Max)
  Set Max equal to first entry in list
  From the second entry to the end of the list
    Compare each entry to Max
    If an entry is bigger than the current Max,
      then change Max to this value

This kind of outline calls for a FOR-NEXT loop. But the problem with translating this outline to a program is, how do you know where the list starts or ends? You could arrange for every list to have a flag at the end, but then you would have trouble combining this with Visual Basic's range feature. Or you could use the trick of reserving one entry in the list for the number of items in the list.

Visual Basic makes this process easier with the functions LBOUND and UBOUND, which are not part of interpreted BASIC. LBOUND gives the lowest possible subscript and UBOUND the highest in a list. For example, you can easily translate the preceding outline to the following:

```
FUNCTION FindMax (A(), Max)
  'local variables
  DIM Start AS INTEGER, Finish AS INTEGER, I AS INTEGER

  Start = LBOUND(A)
  Finish = UBOUND(A)
  Max = A(Start)
  FOR I = Start + 1 TO Finish
    IF A(I) > Max THEN Max = A(I)
  NEXT I
  FindMax = Max
END FUNCTION
```

When this procedure is finished, the new value of Max would be the largest entry in the list of single-precision variables.

In general, the function LBOUND(NameOfArray, I) gives the lower bound for the I'th dimension. (For a list (for instance I = 1), using the dimension is optional, as in the preceding example.) Therefore,

```
DIM Test%(1 TO 5, 6 TO 10, 7 TO 12)
PRINT LBOUND(Test%, 2)
```

displays a 6 and

```
PRINT UBOUND(Test%, 3)
```

displays a 12.

Here's another example. Suppose you want to write a general procedure to copy one two-dimensional string array to another. The LBOUND and UBOUND commands allow you to copy lists or arrays with different ranges, provided the total number of rows and columns is the same. (Subtract the LBOUND from the UBOUND for each dimension and see if they match.)

It's hard to stress enough the flexibility that Visual Basic's method for handling lists and arrays within procedures gives, especially when combined with the LBOUND and UBOUND commands. For example, you may have learned about matrices in math or engineering courses. It is close to impossible to write a general matrix package in standard Pascal, yet it's almost trivial in Visual Basic. (One is contained in the professional edition of Visual Basic.)

You should be aware that you cannot pass a control array by reference to a procedure; you can only pass by value a specific entry in the array. To do this, give the entry. For example,

```
CALL Example(A(), BoxLabel(10))
```

would send a procedure a list named A and the value of the tenth entry in a control array named B. The actual procedure would look like this:

```
SUB Example (A(), X AS CONTROL)
  .
  .
  .
END SUB
```

One last point: using LBOUND and UBOUND is not a cure-all. If part of the list or array hasn't yet been filled, they may not help. Therefore, although adding the number of items in a list as the zeroth item in the list was a common programming trick for earlier BASICs (that didn't have UBOUND and LBOUND), it is still sometimes useful in Visual Basic. Also, you cannot use LBOUND and UBOUND with control arrays. One solution is to use the tag property to identify the number of items in the control array.

Searching

Suppose a long list of names is stored in the computer's memory. Now you want to find out if a certain name is in the list. You can do this easily: just write a program to compare the name you want with all the names in the list. Since a program like Visual Basic generates fast code, this method is quite effective for short lists. However, if the list had 5000 names and was already in alphabetical order, this would be a silly waste of time. If you are looking in a telephone book for a name beginning with "K," you don't start at page 1. You split the book roughly in half and proceed from there. When the information in the list you're searching is already ordered, you can speed things up by using an extension of this method. Each time, the program will look at a list that is only half the size of the previous list. This speeds things up almost beyond belief. Here's an outline for a program to search through a list that is already in alphabetical order:

1. Divide the list in half.

2. Have you gone too far? (Is the entry at the halfway mark before or after the name you're looking for?)

3. If you have gone too far, look at the first half; if not, look at the second half.

4. Go back to step 1 as long as there are names left to look at.

Suppose your list has 5000 names. Then, after doing step 4, you go back to step 1 with a list of 2500 names. Do it again, and you have only 1250 names, the third time only 625, and so on. By the 12th time there would be only two names to look for. This outline is called doing a *binary search*.

An extraordinary feature of the binary search is that it is almost as fast for large lists as for small. For example, suppose you are searching through the New York City telephone directory (with roughly 10,000,000 entries) and you have to find out if someone's name is there. Just by following this outline (and not doing any estimating of where the letters are), you would find out if the name was in the list of names in no more than 25 applications of step 4.

The procedure is a bit tricky, so it's worth spending time on. What follows is a first attempt. (It has a subtle bug.)

```
SUB BinarySearch (X$(), Target$)
  'form level variable: TargetPosition
  'local variables
  DIM Low AS INTEGER, High AS INTEGER, Middle AS INTEGER
```

```
      TargetPosition = 0
      Low = LBOUND(X$)
      High = UBOUND(X$)

      DO
        Middle = (Low + High) \ 2
        SELECT CASE X$(Middle)
          CASE IS = Target$
            TargetPosition = Middle
          CASE IS > Target$
            High = Middle - 1
          CASE IS < Target$
            Low = Middle + 1
        END SELECT
      LOOP UNTIL TargetPosition <> 0
      PRINT TargetPosition
END SUB
```

Setting the variable TargetPosition to zero initializes this form level variable at the beginning of the list. At the end of the procedure, it will contain the position of the target. (You also could set up another parameter for this information, and an even better idea would be to turn this into a Function procedure whose value was the location of the target.)

Notice that this procedure uses the UBOUND/LBOUND method of finding the limits. The method described earlier to store the number of entries in the list as the zeroth entry is not needed here since this procedure assumes the whole list is ordered.

The DO loop does the work. You first find the middle of the list by using the integer division operator. (List subscripts are always integers.) Since there are three possibilities in the search, it's a perfect candidate for the SELECT CASE command. (You can also use the IF-THEN-ELSEIF.) If the entry in the middle position is too large, you know that you should look at the first half of the list. Since the target can't be the middle entry (you eliminated that in the first CASE), you can move the "High" subscript down to one less than the current value of Middle. Similarly, if the entry in the middle position is too small, then the "Low" subscript can be set to one more than the current value of Middle so that the search continues in the second half of the list.

Now you get to the problem in this preliminary version of the binary search. The loop stops only if TargetPosition has a nonzero value—in other words, if you have found the entry. But suppose the entry wasn't in the list? The loop never stops in this situation; this program is stuck in an infinite loop.

How can you fix this procedure so it stops when there are no more entries left to check? As usual, a concrete example that you can "play computer" with helps. Suppose you are down to a list that consists of two names, say in the 42nd and 43rd positions. The 42nd entry is too small and the 43rd entry too large. What does this procedure do? The first time you're in this situation, the value of Middle is set to (42+43) \ 2 = 42. Since you're assuming the value in the 42nd position is too small, the value of Low is set to one more than Middle—that is, 43. The value of Low and High are now the same. What happens next? Since both Low and High are the same, the value of Middle is also the same. Now the entry in the middle position is too large, so the value of High shrinks by one. It's now 42—less than the value of Low. This gives you one way to end the loop. Change it to read

```
LOOP UNTIL (TargetPosition <> 0) OR (High < Low)
```

There's another way to write this loop that some people find easier to understand. It depends on realizing that something special happens for small lists when, say, the difference between High and Low is 1. Arrange to leave the loop when the list has size 1 and add a few lines to take care of this special case:

```
IF (High - Low) < = 1 THEN
   IF A$(High) = Target$ THEN TargetPosition = High
ELSE
   IF A$(Low) = Target$ THEN TargetPosition = Low
END IF
```

Notice that both these possibilities take care of the case when there is only one entry—or even no entries—in the list. Remember, it's the boundary cases that often cause the most subtle bugs in a program.

On the subject of finding bugs, how do you write a realistic test module for a binary search procedure? Obviously, you need a long, ordered list. One way to do this is to have the list consist of all possible two-letter strings:

AA,AB,AC,...BA,BB,...ZZ

There are 26 * 26 = 676 two-letter combinations. (Using three-letter combinations allows a list of 26^3 = 17576 entries.)

To create this list, you can use this fragment:

```
DIM A$(1 TO 676)
DIM Index AS INTEGER, I AS INTEGER

Index = 1
FOR I = 65 TO 90
  FOR J = 65 TO 90
    A$(Index) = CHR$(I) + CHR$(J)
    Index = Index + 1
  NEXT J
NEXT I
```

Now you can try the binary search procedure with various possibilities, such as testing it with a two-letter string that is in the list and one that is not in the list, or with the first entry and the last. You would have quickly discovered that the program was running too long in the second case!

Sorting

Programmers like ordered lists, just as people prefer alphabetized lists like dictionaries and telephone books, because techniques like the binary search work so quickly. Rearranging data—sorting, or ordering, it—is one of the most common demands placed on a computer. Unfortunately, sorting is also one of the most time-consuming tasks a computer can be asked to do. Because of this, computer scientists have developed literally hundreds of different ways to sort lists, and it's impossible to say which is best in all possible circumstances. In this section you'll see four methods. The first two are useful for short lists. The third is often the method of choice, even for lists having thousands of entries. The last sort you'll see is called the *bubble sort* and is the most common sort offered in elementary programming books. Unfortunately, the bubble sort has few, if any, redeeming features, and you may find it better not to use it even if you are adapting code already written. It is usually better to switch to one of the other three sorts given here.

Ripple Sort

When you sit down to write a program, it's always a good idea to ask yourself if there's anything you do in real life that's analogous to what you want the computer to do. Think about a game of cards and the hands dealt to different people. Some people will pick up all the cards at once and sort their hands, first finding the smallest card, then the next smallest, and so on; some will pick up one card at a time, scan what they have already sorted, and position the new card in the correct place. (For what it's worth, computer scientists have proved that these two methods take roughly the same amount of time, with the second method usually being a tiny bit faster.)

Each of these methods translates into a way to sort lists. The first is usually called *ripple sort,* while the second is called *insertion sort.* Here's an outline for ripple sort:

1. Start with the first entry.

2. Look at the remaining entries one by one. Whenever you find a smaller entry, swap it with the first.

3. Now shrink the list; start with the second entry and look at the remaining entries (3, 4, and so on).

4. Continue this until all items are worked through.

Notice that if, for example, the list has 50 entries, you only have to make 49 passes through the list. This is because by the time this procedure works it way to the last entry, enough switching has happened that it has to be the largest entry. Here's the procedure.

```
SUB RippleSort (A$())
  'local variables
  DIM NumOfEntries AS INTEGER, NumOfTimes AS INTEGER
  DIM I AS INTEGER, J AS INTEGER

  NumOfEntries = UBOUND(A$)
  NumOfTimes = NumOfEntries - 1
  FOR I = 1 TO NumOfTimes
    FOR J = I + 1 TO NumOfEntries
      IF A$(J) < A$(I) THEN SWAP A$(J), A$(I)
    NEXT J
```

```
    NEXT I
END SUB
```

This procedure assumes the list starts from one. An even more useful version (and a more elegant one) is to make this procedure depend on two more parameters, for example, Low and High, and use these to establish the bounds on the loops.

First Steps for Testing Sorts

How do you write a procedure to test a sort? Well, you need a way to create random lists of strings. Here's one way. Add the following lines to a Form_Click procedure:

```
DIM B$(100)
DIM I AS INTEGER, RndInt1 AS INTEGER, RndInt2 AS INTEGER

RANDOMIZE
FOR I = 1 TO 100
  RndInt1 = INT(26 * RND)
  RndInt2 = INT(26 * RND)
  B$(I) = CHR$(RndInt1 + 65) + CHR$(RndInt2 + 65)
NEXT I
```

At this point, of course, you have only one sort to test, although this method can be used to test any sort. To test ripple sort, use the following

```
CALL RippleSort(B$())
```

and print out the list to make sure it's been sorted:

```
FOR I = 1 TO 100
  PRINT B$(I);"    ";
NEXT I
```

Insertion Sort

The second method, usually called *insertion sort,* is no harder to program than a ripple sort. In this sort, at every stage you'll have an already sorted, smaller list. Look through the list, from the first entry to what is currently the last, until you find something larger than the new entry. Unfortunately, unlike the case of playing cards where you can force a card into its proper place, you have to move all the entries in the list down one position to make room for the new entry. Since you must move the entries anyway, you can "tweak" (computer jargon meaning "make a small change that improves performance") the original outline. The new version is even easier to program. Instead of moving forward from the front of the list, move backward from the back of the list and look for something smaller than the new entry. Now, each time the comparison fails, move the old entry down by one. If you do this, you'll be moving a "hole" along with you as you move through the list. When the comparison finally fails, you drop the new entry into the hole. Here's that procedure:

```
SUB InsertionSort (A$())
  'local variables
  DIM NumOfEntries AS INTEGER, I AS INTEGER, J AS INTEGER, Temp$

  NumOfEntries = UBOUND(A$)
  FOR I = 2 TO NumOfEntries
    Temp$ = A$(I)
    FOR J = I - 1 TO 1 Step -1
      IF Temp$ >= A$(J) THEN EXIT FOR
      A$(J + 1) = A$(J)
    NEXT J
    A$(J + 1) = Temp$
  NEXT I
END SUB
```

As with the ripple sort example given earlier, you might want to make this procedure depend on a Low and High parameter. The loop moves entries forward until conditions are ripe for the EXIT FOR statement. This occurs when you have located the position of the hole in preparation for the statement A$(J+1) = Temp$, which fills the hole. (Notice that the special case of a list with zero or one entry is handled correctly: the list is not modified since the outer FOR loop is never entered.)

Since these methods follow the playing card analogy closely, they are not hard to program. Moreover, for small lists, they are reasonably fast. Sorting 100 strings by using insertion sort or ripple sort takes about .5 seconds on a basic 16MHz 386SX. Unfortunately, sorting 200 entries takes about 2 seconds. Both these types of sorts have the unfortunate property that doubling the list quadruples the time. Sorting a list of 12,000 names (by no means a very large list) would take about three-quarters of an hour, so you can see that these are not the methods to use for lists much longer than 200 or so entries. You need to turn to a faster method. (Now you can see why the binary search is so nice—doubling the list adds only one step.)

The next section shows you one of the fastest all-purpose sorts.

Shell Sort

The fast *Shell sort* was discovered by Donald Shell around 30 years ago. Shell sort is unusual because while the procedure is simple and short, understanding what makes it work is not. In part, this is because nothing that you do in real life is analogous to Shell sort. In addition, even after you understand why it works, it's unclear why it's so much faster than the previous two methods.

To understand Shell sort, you should first determine the advantages and disadvantages of the two previous sorting methods. One obvious disadvantage of ripple sort is that most of the time the comparisons in the various loops are wasted. The disadvantage of insertion sort is that most of the time it moves objects inefficiently. Even when the list is mostly sorted, you still have to move the entries one by one to make the hole. The big advantage of ripple sort is that it moves objects efficiently. Once the smallest object gets to the top, it stays there.

In a sense, then, the insertion and ripple sorts are opposites. Shell decided to improve insertion sort by making comparisons over long distances, as is done in ripple sort. Consider the following list of numbers to sort:

57, 3, 12, 9, 1, 7, 8, 2, 5, 4, 97, 6

Suppose, instead of comparing the first entry to the second, you compare it with the seventh, and instead of comparing the second with the third, you compare it with the eight. In short, cut up the list into six different lists. Now use an insertion sort on these six small lists. After this, you have six lists, each of which is sorted, while the whole list is probably still not sorted. Merge the smaller lists and break up the result into three new lists (the first with the fourth, seventh, and so on, and the second with the fifth, eighth, and so on). Do an insertion sort on these three smaller lists and merge again. Now the resulting list is very close to being sorted. A final sort finishes the process. (Insertion sort is very efficient when it doesn't have much work to do.)

If the numbers are already stored in a list, you never have to break up the list into smaller lists. Instead, you shift your point of view by concentrating on the different sublists. Also, because the entries moved fairly long distances on the earlier passes, when you're down to the final step not many more moves are needed. Here's a version of Shell sort:

```
SUB ShellSort (A$())
  'local variables
  DIM NumOfEntries AS INTEGER, Increm AS INTEGER
  DIM I AS INTEGER, J AS INTEGER, Temp$

  NumOfEntries = UBOUND(A$)
  Increm = NumOfEntries \ 2
  DO UNTIL Increm < 1
    FOR I = Increm + 1 TO NumOfEntries
      Temp$ = A$(I)
      FOR J = I - Increm TO 1 Step - Increm
        IF Temp$ >= A$(J) THEN EXIT FOR
        A$(J + Increm) = A$(J)
      NEXT J
      A$(J + Increm) = Temp$
    NEXT I
    Increm = Increm \ 2
  LOOP
END SUB
```

The DO loop gives you the way of dividing the lists into smaller lists. Inside the DO loop, the inner FOR-NEXT loop does an insertion sort on the smaller lists. Since each entry on the smaller list differs from the next by the number given by the variable Increm, the STEP clause gives you a way of working with the smaller lists.

What's amazing about Shell sort is that it's so much faster than ripple or insertion sort, although, surprisingly enough, nobody yet knows how much faster it will be in general. (An easy way to get a PhD. would be to fully analyze Shell sort.) In any case, sorting a list of 3600 names will take only about 95 seconds using Shell sort on a basic PC.

The speed of Shell sort depends somewhat on the numbers you use to split the list into smaller ones. These are usually called the *increments* (the 6, 3, and 1 used in the preceding example), and they should be chosen with care. (Because the increments get smaller on each pass,

Shell sort is sometimes known as a "diminishing increment" sort.) The numbers used in the example (half the current size of the list) are Shell's original choice. Today we know you can obtain slightly better results with other increments. One of the simpler choices that gives slightly better results is

1, 4, 13, 40, 121, 364, 1093 ...

where each new number in the sequence is arrived at by multiplying the preceding number by 3 and adding 1. (You start with the largest increment that's smaller than the size of your list, so a list with 10,000 entries would start with an increment of 9841.) In any case, no one yet knows the best choice of increments. Try other sequences and see if you get better results.

How do you write a realistic test procedure for a fast sorting routine? In this case, unlike for a ripple sort or an insertion sort, you want to create a long list of random strings. This is not very difficult to do, but it can sometimes take longer than the sort. For a list of random four-letter strings for the Shell sort, use

```
DIM Test$(1 TO 3600)
DIM I AS INTEGER, J AS INTEGER, CNumber AS INTEGER

FOR I = 1 TO 3600
  FOR J = 1 TO 4
    CNumber =INT(26 * RND)
    Test$(I) = Test$(i) + CHR$(CNumber + 65)
  NEXT J
NEXT I
```

and call Shell sort. (We wouldn't recommend your trying a list of 3600 entries on an insertion or ripple sort.) Finally, add a routine to print out part of the transformed list. If the result is ordered, you might want to add a routine to time the various sorts on lists of varying size. (If you devise your own sort or want to test these, you might want to also test the sorts on the two "boundary cases." For a sorting routine, this is usually thought of when the list is either already ordered or completely in reverse order.)

A Common but Bad Sort: The Bubble Sort

Finally, you should be aware of (or may already be using) a sort called *bubble sort.* It's very common in elementary programming books. The idea of bubble sort is the easiest of all: you constantly compare an entry with the one below it. This way, the smallest one "bubbles" to the top. The code for this is almost trivial:

```
FOR I = 2 TO N
  FOR J = N TO I Step -1
    IF A$(J-1) > A$(J) THEN
      SWAP A$(J-1), A$(J)
    END IF
  NEXT J
NEXT I
```

The problem is that the bubble sort is almost always the slowest sort of all. Since it has few, if any, redeeming virtues, it should be replaced, at the very least, by a ripple sort (which is just as easy to program) for small lists and one of the faster sorts, such as Shell sort, for longer lists.

Records

Suppose you want to have a two-dimensional array for 100 employees in a company. The first column is to be for names, the second for salaries, and the third for social security numbers. This common situation can't be programmed in a multidimensional array except with a kludge (computer jargon meaning an awkward, ad hoc method of solving a problem). (Use the STR$ command.) You probably would prefer to set up three parallel lists—one for the names, the second for salaries, and the third for social security numbers (they are strings, to include the dashes), as shown here:

```
DIM Names(100) AS STRING * 50
DIM Salary(100) AS CURRENCY
DIM SocSecNumber(100) AS STRING * 11
```

Having done this, you now would use the same pointer (that is, the row number) to extract information from the three lists.

The way around using three separate arrays for this related data is to use a new structure called a *record*. Records are not part of traditional BASICs, although they are common in programming languages such as C and Pascal. Essentially, a record is a type of "mixed" variable that you create as needed. It usually mixes different kinds of numbers and strings. Visual Basic makes it easy to avoid maintaining parallel structures (as in the employee list example above).

Here's the first step: in the leading code of the form, enter

```
TYPE  VitalInfo

  Name AS STRING * 50
  Salary AS Currency
  SocSecNumber AS STRING * 11

END TYPE
```

This defines the type. From this point on in the program, it's just as good a variable type for variables as single precision or double precision.

Now, to make (set up) a single variable called YourName of "type" VitalInfo, use one of the following statements

```
DIM YourName AS VitalInfo
DIM SHARED YourName AS VitalInfo
STATIC YourName AS VitalInfo
```

Each of these statements sets up a single "mixed" variable. The jargon is to say, "YourName is a record variable (or type variable) of type VitalInfo." Now you use a dot (period) to isolate the parts of this record:

```
YourName.Name = "Howard"
Yourname.Salary = 100000
YourName.SocSecNumber = "036-78-9987"
```

You can also set up an array of these record variables:

```
DIM SHARED CompanyRecord(1 TO 75) AS VitalInfo
```

This sets up a list capable of holding 75 of these records. Now you can fill this array using the following event procedure. The form used for this input operation requires three labels, three text boxes, and a command button. Note that the labels for each of the three text boxes change to show the count of the current employee:

```
'leading code for form level variables:
DIM SHARED Count AS INTEGER

SUB Form_Load ()
  Count = 1
  'Initialize prompts and fields for first record
  CALL PrepCapsAndText
END SUB

SUB AddEmpData_Click ()
  CompanyRecord(Count).Name = Names.Text
  CompanyRecord(Count).Salary = VAL(Salary.Text)
  CompanyRecord(Count).SocSecNumber = SSNum.Text

  'Change prompts and reinitialize fields for next record
  Count = Count + 1
  CALL PrepCapsAndText
END SUB

SUB PrepCapsAndText ()
  NamesLabel.Caption = "Name of employee #" + STR$(Count)
  SalaryLabel.Caption = "Salary of employee #" + STR$(Count)
  SSNumLabel.Caption="Social Sec # of employee #"+STR$(Count)
  Names.Text = ""
  Salary.Text = ""
  SSNum.Text = ""
END SUB
```

Note the periods for each component, or element, of the record. You can even have a component of a record be a record itself. For example, you could make up a RecordOfSalary type to keep track of monthly earnings along with the previous year's salary:

```
TYPE RecordOfSalary

  SalInJan AS INTEGER
  SalInFeb AS INTEGER
  SalInMar AS INTEGER
  SalInApr AS INTEGER
  SalInMay AS INTEGER
  SalInJun AS INTEGER
  SalInJul AS INTEGER
  SalInAug AS INTEGER
```

```
SalInSep AS INTEGER
SalInOct AS INTEGER
SalInNov AS INTEGER
SalInDec AS INTEGER
SalInPrevYear AS LONG

END TYPE
```

Now you can set up a record of records:

```
TYPE  ExpandedVitalInfo

  Name AS STRING * 30
  Salary AS RecordOfSalary
  SocSecNumber AS STRING * 11

END TYPE
```

Of course, filling out all the information needed for a single record is now that much harder. Filling in the record RecordOfSalary for a single employee requires at least 13 lines of code, so filling in a record of type ExpandedVitalInfo requires at least 15. It also gets a little messy to refer to the information in ExpandedVitalInfo. You thread your way down by using more periods. After using

```
DIM GaryStats AS ExpandedVitalInfo
```

to set up a variable of this new type, use a statement like

```
PRINT GaryStats.Salary.SalInPrevYear
```

to display the information on the previous year's salary. You can have records as one of the parameters in procedures. For example, you might write a general procedure to analyze salary data. The first line in the procedure would look like this:

```
SUB AnalyzeSalary (X AS ExpandedVitalInfo)
```

This procedure allows (and in fact requires) that only variables of type ExpandedVitalInfo be passed to it. Now you can call it at any time by using a line of code like this:

```
CALL AnalyzeSalary(BillStats)
```

This would analyze Bill's salary information. You also can pass individual components of a record whenever they match the type of the parameter.

Visual Basic inherited the ability from the BASIC Professional Development System to use arrays in user-defined records. By setting up an array inside the record:

```
TYPE RecordOfSalary

  DIM Salaries(1 TO 12) AS INTEGERS
  SalInPrevYear AS LONG

END TYPE
```

You can then use a loop plus one individual statement to fill a record rather than using 13 statements.

You're probably wondering, why all the fuss about records? After all, parallel lists are not that difficult to manage. The short answer to this is that records are amazingly useful when dealing with random-access files (see Chapter 13).

CHAPTER

Finishing Up the Interface

*T*his chapter shows you how to use the remaining controls on the toolbox, except for the three controls that work with files and disks, which are discussed in Chapter 13. The controls covered in this chapter let you add check boxes, combo boxes, option buttons, and list boxes to forms. In addition, you'll learn how to use timers to make parts of your program spring to life at specified time intervals and how to use picture boxes and frames to group together sets of controls. You'll also see another method for creating multiple controls on a form at design time.

Menus are covered in the second half of this chapter. Think of menu items as specialized controls that you add to your forms. Menu items respond only to the Click event and, unlike all the other controls in Visual Basic, menus are not added to forms by using the toolbox. Instead, you use the Menu Design window, which is available from the Window menu on the main menu bar.

Finally, you will see how to customize the look of your forms, menus, and controls by working with the SCREEN object and its ControlPanel property.

The Toolbox Revisited

In Chapter 4 you saw the most important controls for a Visual Basic project: command buttons, text boxes, and labels. Figure 10-1 shows you the controls covered in this chapter. Following is a brief description of each control.

Frames   This control is mainly used to group other Visual Basic controls. Frames give you a way to visually separate parts of a form from other parts.

Picture Boxes   This control is similar to a frame but, in addition, it can receive the focus and have text displayed on it with the PRINT method.

Check Boxes   This control appears on your form as

[ ] *selection*

The toolbox revisited

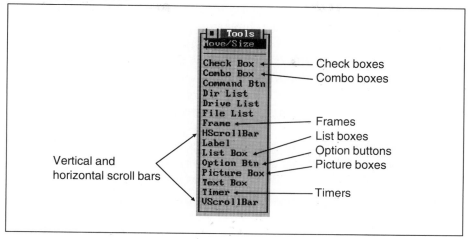

When your project is running, clicking on a check box, or pressing the SPACEBAR with the focus on a check box, toggles an "X" inside the brackets.

Option Buttons   Option buttons appear as a pair of parentheses with a caption:

( ) *selection1*
( ) *selection2*
( ) *selection3*

Option buttons work in groups. One button in a group is always on as signified by a dot between the parentheses. When the user chooses one button in the group, whichever other button was on is turned off. An option button is chosen by clicking on the button, or pressing the SPACEBAR with the focus on the button.

List Boxes   Use list boxes when you want to give users a list of items from which they must make a choice. List boxes often come with scroll bars, which are automatically added if there are too many items to display for the current size of the list box.

Combo Boxes   Combo boxes combine a list box and a text box. You use this control when you want to give users the option of entering their own choices in addition to those you provide on the list.

Vertical and Horizontal Scroll Bars   The controls for the vertical and horizontal scroll bars give you another way of getting user input. Another possibility is to use them to display how close you are to the beginning or end of a time-consuming process. They can also be attached to forms.

Timers   This control wakes up at specified time intervals. Unlike all other Visual Basic controls, timers are always invisible to the user. You can see them only during the design phase of your project.

Each of these controls is described more fully in the following sections.

Frames

You rarely write event procedures for frames. In fact, there are only two events that frames can respond to. These events tell you whether a control was dragged over or dropped onto the frame. (See Chapter 12 for these events). Instead, you use frames to group controls. The screen in Figure 10-2 is an example of a form with three frames used to divide the form functionally.

FIGURE
10-2

Form with frames

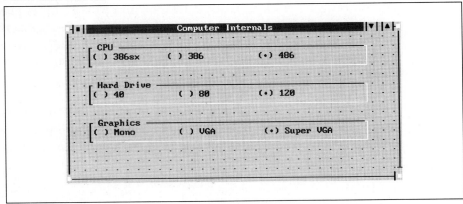

There are 21 properties for frames, and all of them are common to the controls you are already familiar with. For example, Top and Left are available to reposition the frame while your project is running, MousePointer is available to control how the mouse pointer appears, and so on. The only properties you haven't seen for frames are the ones for mouse activities, and they're covered in Chapter 12.

The most important point to keep in mind when using a frame is that you must draw the frame first and then create new controls directly on the frame. In this way, Visual Basic knows the controls are attached to the frame. (Otherwise, Visual Basic will not let the control respond to events that the frame can respond to.) One way to know that a control is attached to a frame is to look at the ASCII representation of the form (see Chapter 4). Controls attached to a frame are shown in the ASCII representation by the controls listing being indented from the frame's listing. In particular, do not use the DblClick method for creating a control when you want to attach a control to a frame. The DblClick method places the control in the center of the screen, but even if the frame was there, Visual Basic will not attach the control to the frame. Instead, use the StickyClick method described following the next section or select the control from the toolbox and position the mouse pointer inside the frame before dragging and dropping the control. (See Chapter 4 for more details on this method for creating controls.)

Picture Boxes

You can use picture boxes as a container for standard and graphics (ASCII codes $\geq$ 128) text. You can use the PRINT method along with the CurrentX and CurrentY properties to position and print text anywhere within a picture box. Because picture boxes respond to the Click and DblClick events, you can use them exactly as you would use a command button. Picture boxes can also be used like frames to group other controls. Unlike frames, picture boxes can receive the focus and respond to many different events.

Picture boxes have 23 properties and respond to 14 events, and you can use any one of 8 methods for them. Most of the properties are already familiar to you. For example, Enabled and Visible determine whether the control is responsive or even visible, TabStop determines whether or not

TAB can be used to move the focus to the picture box, and so on. Like text boxes, labels, and command buttons, the picture box can be resized by manipulating the sizing handles when you've selected the control at design time.

The picture box events that respond to mouse movements or clicks are covered in Chapter 12. All the remaining events are those like the Click, DblClick, or key events, which you've already seen.

The methods used with picture boxes are similar to those used with forms as a whole. The CLS method erases whatever text was placed on the picture box *while the program was running.* The MOVE method lets you move the picture box around at run time. The TEXTHEIGHT and TEXTWIDTH methods are used to size text in order to position it using the CurrentX and CurrentY properties.

Tip   Picture boxes are ideal if you do character-based graphics using the higher order ASCII characters.

The StickyClick Method for Creating Controls

Visual Basic provides another way to create controls on a form in addition to the "Drag-Drop" and "DblClick" approaches described in Chapter 4. This approach for creating controls is a cross between the two earlier methods, and is especially useful when working with frames and picture boxes. Using the *StickyClick method,* you can create, position, and size multiple copies of the same control with only one trip to the toolbox. (Recall that the Drag-Drop method requires you to make a selection from the toolbox each time you wish to position and size a new control, while the DblClick method always gives you similarly sized controls, stacked one on top of another in the center of the form.) To create controls using the StickyClick method, follow these steps:

1. Move to the toolbox and press CTRL while clicking the left mouse button.

2. Move to the form or frame and press the left mouse button. The upper-lefthand corner of the new control is "stuck" at this location.

3. Hold the left mouse button down and drag until you are happy with the size of the control.

4. Release the mouse button and repeat steps 2 and 3 until you have finished placing all the controls of that type on the form or picture box frame.

To change to another way of working with the toolbox, go back to the toolbox and click "Move/Size" or any control other than the one you were working with using the StickyClick method.

Option Buttons

Option buttons always work together. When the user chooses one button, the previously active button in the group is turned off. For this reason, any application that uses more than one group of option buttons on a form *must* use a frame or picture box to separate the groups. (See the section "Frames" or "Picture Boxes" earlier in this chapter.) You add option buttons to a form when you want the user to make one choice from a set of possibilities. For example, the screen in Figure 10-3 shows how a form for a database might look.

Form for possible database

```
┌──────────────────────Sample Data Form──────────────────────┐
│ · Title · · · · · · · · · · · · · · · · · · · · · · · · · · │
│                                                             │
│ ·( ) Mr.    ·( ) Ms.      (•) Mrs.   · · ( ) Other  · · ·   │
│                                                             │
│ ·First Name · · ┌───────────────────────────┐ · · · · · ·  │
│                 │                           │               │
│ ·Last Name  · · ┌───────────────────────────┐ · · · · · ·  │
│                 │                           │               │
└─────────────────────────────────────────────────────────────┘
```

The Value property of the option button tells you whether a button was selected by the user. If the Value property is True (–1), the user selected that button; otherwise, its Value property is False (0).

If you give control names to the option buttons in Figure 10-3 of "Mr", "Ms", "Mrs", and "Other", you could use code like the following to pick up the information:

```
IF Mr.Value THEN
  Title$ = "Mr."
ELSEIF Ms.Value THEN
  Title = "Ms."
ELSEIF Mrs.Value THEN
  Title = "Mrs."
ELSE
  Title$=InputBox$("Please enter the title you want us to use.")
END IF
```

This code works because of the Boolean (True/False) nature of the Value property. For example, the clause "Ms.Value" will be True only when the user has chosen the Ms option button.

Option buttons respond to the Click and DblClick events as well as to the key events. They can also detect if a button has received or lost the focus. Visual Basic generates the Click event when the user selects the button by clicking with the mouse or by moving to the button with the TAB key and pressing the SPACEBAR. If you reset the Value property of the option button to True (–1) inside code, then you also generate the Click event. This is occasionally useful for demonstration programs. You can also turn on one of the buttons at design time by setting its Value property to True via the properties bar.

Option buttons and command buttons have the same set of properties, except that option buttons have no "Cancel" property. They do have a "Value" property, and for example, you can temporarily disable the button by setting the Enabled property to False at design or run time as you see fit.

Check Boxes

Check boxes differ from option buttons in that, regardless of how many check boxes you place on a form, they can all be turned on and off independently. For this reason, placing check boxes in a frame or picture box is necessary only when you think it polishes the appearance of your form.

As with option buttons, whether a check box is on or off is determined by its Value property. If the user has selected a check box, the Value property switches to 1 (Checked). It becomes 0 again only when the user deselects that box. This is unlike the situation with option buttons, where selecting one of the buttons flips the value of all the others to 0 (False). If you want a check box to be on when the project starts up, set the Value property of the box to 1 (Checked) at design time or in the Form_Load procedure.

As an example of where you might want to use check boxes, consider the form in Figure 10-4.

Notice that several of the check boxes are already defaulted to be on. Most people *do* want color monitors for their computers, but the user can still switch to a monochrome monitor by deselecting the check box.

Another good example of check boxes is the Save dialog box on the Options menu:

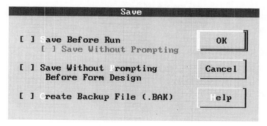

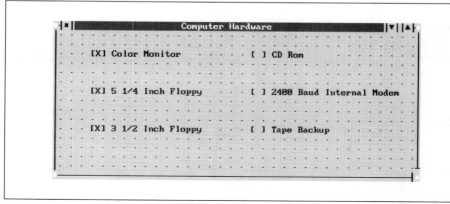

FIGURE 10-4

Sample form using check boxes

As with option buttons, check boxes will respond to the Click and DblClick events as well as to the key events. They will also detect if a box has received or lost the focus. As with option buttons, Visual Basic generates the Click event when the user selects the button by clicking with the mouse or by moving to the check box with the TAB key and pressing the SPACEBAR. If you reset the Value property of a check box to 1 (Checked) inside code, you also generate the Click event.

List and Combo Boxes

Use list boxes when you have a fixed list of choices. For example, suppose you are designing an application to provide information about the United States presidents. The form might look like the one in Figure 10-5. Note that (as in this figure) Visual Basic automatically adds vertical scroll bars whenever the list box is too small for all the items it contains.

On the other hand, you might want this application to let the user select a president by number rather than by scrolling through the list. To allow users to input data as well as make choices from a list, use a combo box, as shown in Figure 10-6. Notice that this form has a label near the combo box to identify what the user should type into the input area at the top of the combo box.

There are actually three types of combo boxes. Which one you get depends on the value of the Style property.

☐   If the value of the Style property is set to the default value of zero, the combo box appears as an input area (marked by a pair of

List box with presidents' names

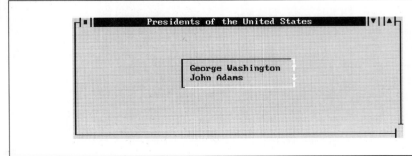

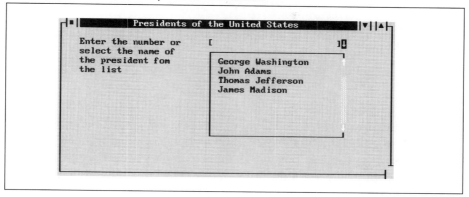

FIGURE
10-6
Combo box with label for presidents' names

brackets) followed by a down arrow. If the user clicks the arrow, a list box appears below the input area. After the user makes a choice from this list, the dropdown list disappears.

☐   If the value of the Style property of a combo box is 1, the combo box appears with the list already pulled down below the input area.

Here are examples of these two types of combo boxes. Notice that both combo boxes provide an input area for the entry of a choice not presented in the list:

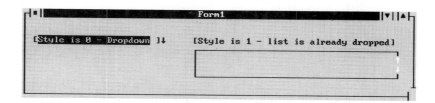

The third type of combo box, obtained by setting the Style property to 2, is more appropriately thought of as a variation of the list box and, in fact, is referred to as a dropdown list box. Only items in the list may be selected; no new choice may be given. To select an item, the user types the first character of the desired item and/or uses the cursor control keys to scroll through the list. Alternatively, the user clicks on the arrow to display the list and then makes a selection. The following illustration is an example of a dropdown list box.

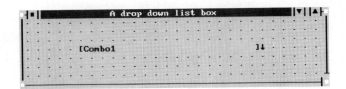

Thus, although you create a dropdown list box by selecting Combo Box from the toolbox, once you set the Style property to 2 (either via code or at design time), the input area becomes an alternate selection area, similar to a list box with room to display only a single item. On the other hand, the events that a dropdown list box will respond to are those of a combo box and not those of a list box.

Items in a list or combo box can be sorted in ASCII order. This depends on the value of the Sorted property. If you set the Sorted property to True, Visual Basic will order the items in ASCII order. Otherwise, the order of the items depends on the order in which you placed them in the list box. You may only set the Sorted property to True at design time.

Manipulating the Items on a List or Combo Box

You can add or remove items from a list or combo box only while the project is running. Use the ADDITEM method to add an item to a list or combo box. The syntax for this method is

ListName.ADDITEM *Item$*

where *ListName* is the control name of the list or combo box, and *Item$* is a string or string expression. If the Sorted property is True for the list or combo box, then the *Item$* goes where ASCII order places it. If the Sorted property is False, Visual Basic places *Item$* at the end of the list. An extension of the ADDITEM method

ListName.ADDITEM *Item$, Index*

inserts *Item$* at the position determined by the *Index* parameter. The *Index* parameter must be an integer or integral expression. An *Index* value of zero (not 1) means you are at the beginning of the list. If you use the

Index option when the Sorted property is True, Visual Basic may no longer be able to maintain the list in sorted order.

The most common place to use the ADDITEM statement is in the Form_Load procedure. For example, assume that the leading code of a form includes the statements

```
DIM SHARED PresidentsInfo$(1 to 41)
DATA George Washington, <none>
DATA John Adams, Harvard
DATA Thomas Jefferson, William and Mary
DATA James Madison, Princeton
.
.
.
DATA EOD, EOD
```

and that the form contains a list or combo box with the control name of Presidents. The code to build a list of presidents and a corresponding array holding the colleges each president attended might look like this:

```
SUB Form_Load ()
  'local variables
  DIM Name$, College$, I AS INTEGER

  I = 0
  READ Name$, College$
  DO WHILE Name$ <> "EOD"
    Presidents.ADDITEM Name$
    I = I + 1
    PresidentsInfo$(I) = College$
    READ Name$, College$
  LOOP
END SUB
```

You can also remove an item from a list while the program is running. The syntax for the REMOVEITEM method is

ListName.REMOVEITEM *Index*

where, as before, *ListName* is the control name for the list or combo box and *Index* is the position where the item to be removed is located.

The List and Combo Box Properties

Many of the properties of lists and combo boxes determine how the information should be displayed. These properties are the same as ones you've already seen. For example, the BackColor and ForeColor properties control what colors are used for the background and foreground, respectively. Similarly, properties like Height, Left, Top, and Width control the shape and location of the list or combo box.

The properties special to list and combo boxes let you get at the information in the box or what item the user has moved to within the box. For example, when a user moves the focus to a list or combo box, he or she can select an item on the list or combo box by using the arrow keys, PGUP, PGDN, END, and so on. Once the focus moves to the list or combo box, pressing a letter key moves to the first item on the list beginning with that letter. The item selected is always highlighted. All these details are handled automatically by Visual Basic. The item selected by the user is the value of the ListIndex property of the box.

Following are descriptions of the four list and combo box properties you'll use most often. These properties can only be accessed after items have been added to a list, and so are not available at design time.

ListIndex   The value of the ListIndex property gives the index number of the highlighted item, which is where the user has stopped in the list. If no item was selected, the value of this property is –1. For example, suppose you've stored information about the presidents in a string array named PresidentInfo$ and you need to get at the item that contains information about the president the user has selected. A statement like

```
IF Presidents.ListIndex = -1 THEN
  MSGBOX "No president selected!"
ELSE
  Info$ = PresidentInfo$(Presidents.ListIndex + 1)
END IF
```

makes the value of the Info$ string variable the information you'll need. The code also assumes you've stored the information about George Washington in the first position in the PresidentInfo$ string array. If the information about Washington is in the zeroth slot, you don't need to add 1 to the value of President.ListIndex.

Text   The Text property gives the currently selected item stored as a string. (If you need the numeric equivalent, apply the VAL function.)

List   The List property is a string array that contains all the items on the list. The value of the *BoxName*.Text property for a list or combo box is the same as that of *BoxName*.List(*ListIndex*).

ListCount   The ListCount property gives you the number of items on the list. Since the Index property starts at zero, to analyze the contents of the Presidents list using a FOR-NEXT loop, you would use ListCount-1 as the upper limit of the loop:

```
FOR I = 0 TO Presidents.ListCount - 1
  work with Presidents.List(I)
  .
  .
  .
NEXT I
```

The List Box Events

Lists respond to 12 events. The KeyUp, KeyDown, and KeyPress events work exactly as before. The mouse events are covered in Chapter 12. List boxes can also tell you whether they've received or lost the focus.

The two most important events for list boxes are the Click and DblClick events. An important convention is that clicking an item selects (highlights) the item but does not choose the item. By convention, choosing an item is reserved for double-clicking on the item. In general, therefore, you do not write code for the Click event procedure for a list box, but only for the DblClick event procedure.

Another reason not to write code for the Click event procedure is that each time the user moves through the list, Visual Basic generates the Click event. Landing on an item in a list box by using the keyboard is the functional equivalent of clicking the item. (There is no keyboard equivalent for double-clicking, although you can write your own for a specific list box by using the key events.)

The Combo Box Events

Combo boxes respond to many of the same events as list boxes. You can analyze which keys were pressed or whether the box has received or lost the focus.

The first event that is different is the Change event. The Change event occurs only for dropdown combo boxes and simple combo boxes (Style = 0 or 1). Visual Basic does not generate this event if you are using a dropdown list box (Style = 2). Visual Basic generates this event whenever the user enters data in the text area of the combo box or you change the Text property of the combo box from code.

As an example of where you might use this, suppose you've set up the list of presidents using a simple combo box (Style = 0, CtrlName = Presidents). Again, let's assume the information you want to display about that president is stored in the same string array as before: PresidentsInfo$. As the directions on the screen in Figure 10-6 indicate, you want to allow the user the possibility of entering the number of the president instead of scrolling through the list. Now, suppose someone typed a number in the text box. Then you might first try to use the following Change event procedure to supply the information the user might be looking for:

```
SUB Presidents_Change ()
  PresidentNum% = VAL(Presidents.Text)
  IF (PresidentNum%<1) OR (PresidentNum%>Presidents.ListCount)_
THEN
    MSGBOX "Only" + STR$(Presidents.ListCount) + _
    " presidents so far!"
  ELSE
    MSGBOX PresidentsInfo$(PresidentNum%)
  END IF
END SUB
```

The trouble with this is that the Change event procedure is *too* responsive for this particular task. Visual Basic calls this event procedure every time the user types a character in the text area of the combo box. This means that for all but the first nine presidents, the procedure is called twice. (For example, if the user entered **16**, information about both Washington and Lincoln would be displayed!) A better way to analyze the information is to put this code inside the KeyPress event procedure and add a check for the pressing of the ENTER key. You can do this with

```
SUB Presidents_KeyPress (KeyAscii AS INTEGER)
   IF KeyAscii = 13 THEN                        'the Enter key
     PresidentNumber% = VAL(Presidents.Text)
     SELECT CASE PresidentNumber%
       CASE IS < 0
         MSGBOX "No negative (numbered at least) presidents."
       CASE 0
         MSGBOX  "Please enter a number or double-click on an
                 entry."
       CASE IS > 41
         MSGBOX "Only 41 presidents so far!"
       CASE ELSE
         MSGBOX PresidentInfo$(PresidentNumber%)
     END SELECT
   END IF
END SUB
```

You can easily modify this procedure to let the user select an item by scrolling through the list and pressing ENTER. (Change the CASE 0 clause.)

Since simple combo boxes (Style = 1) recognize the DblClick event, another possibility is to code this in the DblClick event procedure. However, since there is no keyboard equivalent for double-clicking, you still might want to write a KeyPress event procedure to add keyboard equivalents for the user.

Visual Basic calls the DropDown event procedure right after the user clicks the detached arrow to drop the list box down or presses ALT+DOWN ARROW when the combo box has the focus—before the list drops down. For this reason, this event procedure is mostly used to update a combo box before the list appears. Since only when the Style property is 0 or 2 can you have a dropdown list, this event is not invoked for simple combo boxes (Style = 1).

Scroll Bars

Scroll bars are used to get input or display output when you don't care about the exact value of an object, but you do care whether the change is small or large. A good example of scroll bars is found in the Visual Basic editor, where they are available to scroll up and down through your program code. Vertical scroll bars and horizontal scroll bars work exactly the same way. Scroll bars span a range of values; the scroll box (or elevator) shows where the value is relative to the two extremes. Scroll bars work with 8 events and 19 properties. The event that is the key to using scroll bars is the Change event. This is activated whenever the user manipulates the scroll bar.

You can also attach scroll bars to the border of a form by changing the Attached property of the scroll bar to True. When you do this the border of the form itself becomes a scroll bar. Moreover, you can no longer set the Left, Height, Width, and Top properties when you've attached a scroll bar. However, by writing code, you would be able to let users scroll through the form—much like they do through a text box.

Only 5 of the 19 properties are special to scroll bars. What follows is a short description of those special properties.

Min and Max   The Min property is an integer that defines the smallest value for a scroll bar. The Max property is an integer that defines the largest value for a scroll bar. Both Min and Max take integer values, so the possible settings are from –32,768 to 32,767. You can set the Max value to be less than the Min value. This causes the maximum value of the scroll bar to be reached at the left end of a horizontal scroll bar or the top of a vertical scroll bar rather than at the right end or bottom. Both Max and Min are usually set at design time, but you can change them with code while a project is running.

Value   The Value property tells you where the scroll bar is. It is always an integer. The range is determined by the Min property and the Max property. The Value property can be as small as the Min value or as large as the Max value.

SmallChange   The SmallChange setting determines how Visual Basic changes the Value property of the scroll bar in response to a user's clicking one of the scroll arrows. If the user clicks the up scroll arrow, the Value property of the scroll bar increases by the amount of SmallChange until the Value property reaches the value of the Max property. If the user clicks the down scroll arrow, Visual Basic decreases the Value property similarly. The default value of SmallChange is 1, and it can be set to be any integer between 1 and 32,767. As with Min and Max, this property is usually set at design time but can be changed in code as well.

LargeChange　The LargeChange setting determines how Visual Basic changes the Value property of the scroll bar in response to a user's clicking between the elevator and the scroll arrow. The default LargeChange value is also 1 but is usually set to be a multiple of the SmallChange value. It too is an integer between 1 and 32,767. As with Min, Max, and SmallChange, this property is usually set at design time but can also be changed at run time.

An Example: Adjusting Tones via Scroll Bars

You have two statements in Visual Basic for producing sound from the computer's speaker. The statement

SOUND *frequency, duration*

produces a sound at *frequency* Hertz (cycles per second) that lasts for *duration* / 18.2 seconds. The statement

PLAY "N" + STR$(*n*)

plays the *n*th note on the piano, where *n* = 1 corresponds to the lowest C and *n* = 84 to the highest B. The PLAY statement has many other features, which are discussed in Chapter 16 and Appendix C.

The following program uses horizontal scroll bars and the SOUND and PLAY statements to allow the user to produce tones corresponding to notes from a piano or tones from a continuous range of frequencies. The form used is shown in Figure 10-7. It consists of two horizontal scroll bars and two labels to identify the function of each scroll bar. The control names used for the two scroll bars are Note and Frequency. The properties of the scroll bars are set in the Form_Load procedure, but could also have been set at design time.

Here's the code for this project:

```
SUB Form_Load ()
  Note.Min = 1
  Note.Max = 84
  Note.SmallChange = 1
  Note.LargeChange = 12   ' one octave

  Frequency.Min = 40      '   37 is smallest allowed by SOUND
```

```
   Frequency.Max = 4000    '32767 is largest allowed by SOUND
   Frequency.SmallChange = 4    '1 is too small to hear any change
   Frequency.LargeChange = 50   'arbitrary, results in 79 "notes"
END SUB

SUB Frequency_Change ()
   SOUND Frequency.Value, .5    'tone last about a quarter second
END SUB

SUB Note_Change ()
   PLAY "N" + STR$(Note.Value)
END SUB
```

Timers

Use a timer control whenever you want something to happen period-ically. You might want to have a program that wakes up periodically and checks stock prices. Or, on a more prosaic level, if you want to display a "clock" on a form, you might want to update the clock's display every minute or even every second. Timers are not visible to the user; the control appears only at design time. For this reason, where you place the timer control at design time is not important. Although timers are an important tool for Visual Basic programmers, they shouldn't be overused because they can cause your program to run slowly. In fact, a maximum of 16 timers may be active (enabled) at any one time.

FIGURE 10-7

Form to adjust sound using scroll bars

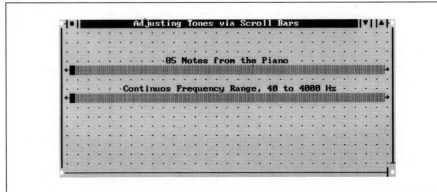

The screen in Figure 10-8 shows an example of a form at design time with a label and a timer control that you can use to develop a simple clock (see the "Timer Event and Some Sample Uses" section).

Besides the control name of the timer (the defaults are Timer1, Timer2, and so on), there are two important properties of timer controls: Enabled and Interval.

Enabled

Enabled is a Boolean (True/False) property that determines if the timer should start ticking or not. If you set this to True at design time, the clock starts ticking when the form loads. "Ticking" is meant metaphorically; there's no noise unless you program one. Also, timer controls are invisible to the user, who may well be unaware that a timer has been enabled. For this reason, you may want to notify the user that a timer is working by means of a message box.

If you set the Enabled property to False at design time, the timer control starts working only when you switch this property to True (–1) in code. Similarly, you can disable a timer inside code by setting its Enabled property to False (0).

Interval

The Interval property determines how much time Visual Basic waits before calling the Timer event procedure (see the next section). The interval is measured in milliseconds, and the theoretical limits are

FIGURE 10-8

Form for a simple clock

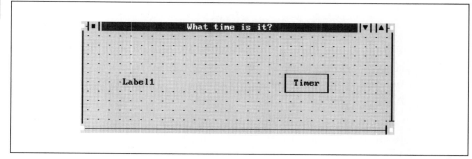

between 1 millisecond and 65,535 milliseconds (a little more than one minute and five seconds). These limits are theoretical because the underlying operating system reports the passage of only 18 clock ticks per second. Since this is a little less than 56 milliseconds per clock tick, you can't really use an Interval property any less than 56, and intervals that don't differ by at least this amount may give the same results.

The smaller you set the Interval property, the more CPU time is spent waking up the Timer event procedure. Set the Interval property too small, and your system performance may slow to a crawl.

Finally, since the CPU may be doing something else when the interval time elapses, you cannot be guaranteed that Visual Basic will call the Timer event procedure exactly when you want it. If the interval has elapsed, Visual Basic will call the Timer event procedure as soon as it is free to do so. The next section explains how to deal with this problem.

The Timer Event and Some Sample Uses

Suppose you want to develop a project with a clock that will update itself every second, following the form shown in Figure 10-8. To design the form, follow these steps:

1. Add a label and a timer to a blank form.

2. Set the Interval property of the timer control to be 1000 (1000 milliseconds = 1 second).

Now write the following code in the Timer event procedure for the Timer1 control:

```
SUB Timer1_Timer ()
  Label1.Caption = "The time is " + FORMAT$(NOW, "hh:mm:ss")
END SUB
```

Visual Basic will call this event procedure and update the clock's time roughly every second because the Interval property was 1000. It would be easy enough to add an option button to let the user switch to an AM/PM display

Here is another example. One of the problems with computer screens is that they may be left on too long. This causes an image to be burned into the screen, its ghostly presence interfering with efficient use of the monitor forever after. Screen-blanking programs work by constantly drawing a different image in a different color. This prevents burn-in. It is very simple to use a timer control to write a screen-blanking program. While commercial programs provide beautiful images and can even be made to run within other programs, the following program simply gives you a randomly colored, randomly placed "Press any key to end!" message.

For this, start up a new project and create a form. To the form, add a timer control and set the Interval property to 2000 (two seconds). Next, make the BackColor property black. You can do this either by using the color palette or by directly setting the BackColor property color code to the color code for black (0). Finally, since you want to have this screen take over the whole screen, set the Border property to None (0) and the WindowState property to Maximized (2).

Here's the code for the Timer1_Timer event procedure:

```
SUB Timer1_Timer ()
  CLS
  CurrentX = RND * ScaleWidth
  CurrentY = RND * ScaleHeight
  ForeColor = 16 * RND
  PRINT "Press any key to end!"
END SUB
```

This program first clears the screen. Next, it calculates a random location on the screen and sets the ForeColor randomly. Of course, since you are taking a percentage of the screen width, this may occasionally not give the program enough room to display the full message. If this bothers you, you can easily add code by using the TEXTWIDTH method to make sure the text is always on the screen.

Now, having the program end when the user presses a key requires only a simple KeyDown event procedure:

```
SUB Form_KeyDown (KeyCode AS INTEGER, Shift AS INTEGER)
  END
END SUB
```

This procedure is invoked by Visual Basic whenever the user presses any key, thus ending the application.

Next, suppose you want to have a Timer event procedure do something even less frequently than the maximum setting for the Interval property—much more slowly than once per minute. The trick is to add a static variable to the Timer event procedure. For example, suppose you want to have a Timer event procedure wake up only once an hour. Set the Interval property to 60,000 (one minute):

```
SUB Timer1_Timer ()
  'local variables
   STATIC TimerTimes AS INTEGER

  TimerTimes = TimerTimes + 1
  IF TimerTimes MOD 60 = 0 THEN
    TimerTimes = 0              'reset counter
    'Here's where the once an hour code would go
  ELSE
    EXIT SUB
  END IF
END SUB
```

The MOD function is zero only when the counter TimerTimes is divisible by 60. But this happens only when the Timer event procedure has been called 60 times, because TimerTimes is a static variable. Now, put whatever code you want inside the IF clause. That code will be processed only once an hour.

Finally, to take into account the possibility that Visual Basic was doing something else exactly when the timer elapsed, you can add code inside the Timer event procedure to check the system clock if you feel this is necessary. (See Chapter 7 or Appendix C for the functions that check the clock.)

Menus

Designing the right kind of menus will make your applications much more user friendly. Visual Basic lets you build up to five levels of menus. The screen in Figure 10-9 shows you a menu with four of the possible five levels. Menus that contain submenus are usually called *hierarchical menus*. Of course, using too many levels of menus can make the application confusing to the user. Four is almost certainly too many, and two or three levels are the most you will usually see. The user knows that a submenu lurks below a given menu item when a little right-pointing arrow (→) follows the menu item.

Notice in the following illustration that each of the three items in the first level of menus has the arrow (→) symbol and so conceals a submenu:

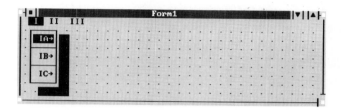

You can open a submenu by using the standard conventions: press ENTER, click the item with the mouse, or press RIGHT ARROW.

 Tip Rather than use many levels of submenus, consider designing a dialog box form (see Chapter 14).

You create menus in Visual Basic when you design the form. This is done using the Menu Design window available from the Window menu on the Form Designer main menu bar. If you open the Window menu or press the Alt+W M access key, you'll see a dialog box that looks like the

FIGURE 10-9

Hierarchical menus

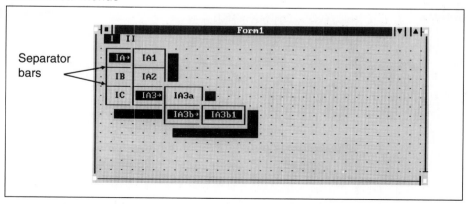

Separator bars

one in Figure 10-10. What follows is a short description of each of the components of this dialog box.

Caption   What you type in the Caption text box is what the user sees. The caption also shows up in the text area, the rectangle at the bottom of the dialog box. Unlike other Visual Basic controls, menu items do not have default captions. ALT+P is the access key for the Caption text box in the Menu Design window.

CtlName   Each menu item must have a control name. (Control arrays are available for menu items, so that a single name plus an index can be used to refer to different items in a menu.) What you enter in the CtlName text box becomes the control name that is used by Visual Basic for the Click event procedure for the menu item. Visual Basic will not let you leave the Menu Design window until you give each menu item a control name. The access key is ALT+M.

Tag   Menu items, like other controls, have a Tag property which may be assigned a string value. The value of the Tag property is most often used in identifying which specific menu item (by name) has been passed to a procedure. The access key is ALT+G.

Menu Design window

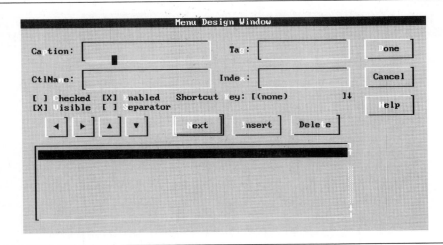

The Index Box   Use the Index box if you want to make a menu item part of a control array. As you saw in Chapter 9, control arrays let you add new instances of the control at run time. In the case of menu items, this would let you have the menu enlarge or shrink while the program was running. Once you've set a menu item to be part of a control array at run time, you add new menu items with the LOAD method you saw in Chapter 9. Similarly, you remove menu items from a control array by using the UNLOAD method. The Caption property for the first menu item in a control array is often left blank since the caption is inherited by each additional menu item LOADED into the control array. The access key is ALT+X.

The Checked Check Box   The Checked check box determines whether a check mark shows up in front of the menu item. As you'd expect, this box controls the setting of the Checked property of the menu item. The default is off. It is much more common to switch the Checked property to True when a user selects the item while the program is running than to set it at design time. The access key is ALT+C.

The Visible Check Box   The Visible check box determines the value of the Visible property of the menu item. If a menu item is made invisible, all its submenus are also invisible. The access key is ALT+V.

The Enabled Check Box   The Enabled check box determines the value of the Enabled property of the menu item. A menu item that is Enabled will respond to the Click event. If this property has been changed to False either at design time (by toggling this box off) or at run time via code, the menu item shows up grayed. The access key is ALT+E.

The Separator Check Box   The Separator check box determines the value of the Separator property of the menu item. When a menu item's Separator property is True (checked), the item is not selectable by the user, but instead serves to separate the menu into different sections. When the user displays the menu, such an item will appear as a horizontal line regardless of the value of its caption property. No caption is needed for a separator, but a control name is required. Also, if a caption consisting of a single hyphen (-) is specified, then Visual Basic automatically checks the Separator check box. The access key is ALT+S.

Tip Separator bars are a good choice for the first item in a menu control array. This is because you can then reduce the menu to appear as if it has no items on it.

The Shortcut Key Box The Shortcut Key box lets you add shortcut keys to your menu items. Recall that shortcut keys are either function keys or CTRL key combinations that activate a menu item without the user needing to open the menu at all. If you click the down arrow to the right of the Shortcut Key box, a list box drops down with the choices for shortcut keys. You need only click the key you want. The access key is ALT+K.

The Arrow Buttons The arrow buttons work with the current menu item. The menu item you're currently working with is highlighted in the large text window below the arrow buttons. Submenus are indicated by the indentation level in this text window, as you'll see in the next section. The left arrow and right arrow buttons control the indentation level. Clicking the left arrow button moves the highlighted item out one indentation level; clicking the right arrow button moves it in one level deeper. You cannot indent an item more than one level deeper than the item above it. If you try, Visual Basic will not let you leave the Menu Design window until you fix it.

Clicking the up arrow button interchanges the highlighted menu item with the item above it; clicking the down arrow button interchanges the highlighted item with the item below it. The up arrow and down arrow do not change the indentation pattern of an item.

The Next Button Clicking the Next button moves you to the next menu item or inserts a new item if you are at the end of the menu. The indentation of the new item is the same as the indentation of the previous item. ALT+N is the access key. You can also use the mouse to move among items.

The Insert Button Clicking the Insert button inserts a menu item above the currently highlighted menu item. ALT+I is the access key.

The Delete Button Clicking the Delete button removes the currently highlighted item. The access key is ALT+T. You cannot use the DEL key to remove menu items.

The Done and Cancel Buttons   Click the Done button (or use the Alt+D access key) when you are finished designing the menu. Click the Cancel button if you decided not to build the menu at all. Even after you've finished designing a menu and clicked the Done button, you can return to the Menu Design window and make changes.

A Sample Menu Design Window

Part of the Menu Design window that led to the hierarchical menu in Figure 10-9 looks like the screen in Figure 10-11. Menu items that are not indented appear on the main menu bar. Menu items that are indented once (preceded by two dots) appear as a menu item below the main menu bar. Items indented twice (four dots) are submenus, items indented three times (six dots) are sub-submenus, and so on. You can always determine the main menu bar by looking for items that appear flush left in the text window of the Menu Design window. Next, notice the hyphens (-) in the Menu Design window. These correspond to the separator bars that showed up in Figure 10-9. Unlike other menu items, separator bars do not respond to the Click event (but you still must give them a control name).

FIGURE
10-11
Menu Design window for Figure 10-9

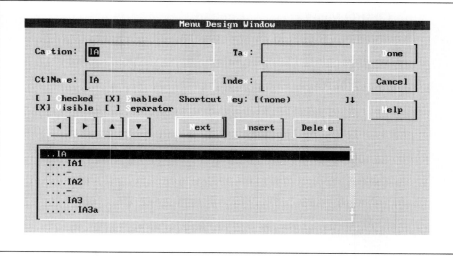

FIGURE
10-12

Form for conversion program

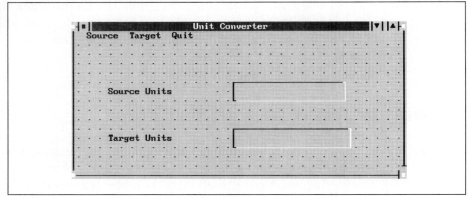

Working with Menus at Run Time

Suppose you want to write a program that would convert between various kinds of units—for example, between inches, centimeters, meters, and feet. A form for this application might look like the one in Figure 10-12. Notice that this form has three items on the menu bar: Target, Source, and Quit. The Menu Design window for this form looks like the one in Figure 10-13.

The control names and captions for the menu items and the controls are given in the following table:

Control Name	Caption
Source	Source
Target	Target
FromInches	Inches
FromFeet	Feet
FromCentimeters	Centimeters
FromMeters	Meters
ToInches	Inches
ToFeet	Feet
ToCentimeters	Centimeters
ToMeters	Meters
Text1	-

Label1	-
Label2	Source Units
Label3	Target Units

Notice that the Caption properties are the same for the items on the Target and Source menus; only the control names are different. A text box is provided for the user to specify the source value, but a label with BorderStyle property set to 1 (so that it resembles a text box) should be used to display the converted value. By using a label rather than a text box, the user is prevented from erroneously specifying a target value.

Whenever you write a conversion program, it's easiest to establish one unit as the basic unit, then convert all the units using the basic unit as an intermediary. For our conversion program, we will use centimeters as our basic unit. For this, set up the form level variable

```
DIM SHARED BasicLength AS SINGLE
```

in the leading code of the form. Next we write a general procedure to convert any source unit into centimeters:

```
SUB ConvertToCentimeters ()
   IF FromInches.Checked THEN
```

FIGURE 10-13 Menu Design window for conversion program

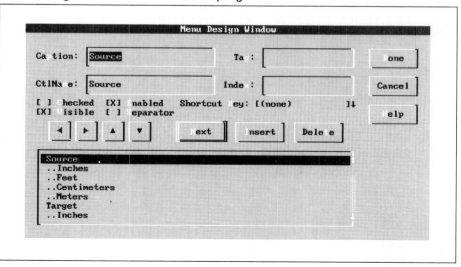

```
      BasicLength = VAL(Text1.Text) * 2.54   '2.54 Centimeters/inch
   ELSEIF FromFeet.Checked THEN
      BasicLength = VAL(Text1.Text) * 2.54 * 12
   ELSEIF FromMeters.Checked THEN
      BasicLength = VAL(Text1.Text) * 100
   ELSEIF FromCentimeters.Checked THEN
      BasicLength = VAL(Text1.Text)
   END IF
END SUB
```

Now, suppose the user clicks the menu item marked Inches in the Source menu. The code should do the following:

☐   Put a check mark next to the Inches item and remove check marks from all other items.

☐   Disable the Inches item in the Target menu and enable all the other items.

Here's the code for the Click procedure that implements this outline for one of the menu items. (The others work the same.)

```
SUB FromInches_Click()
   FromInches.Checked = -1                  'TRUE
   FromFeet.Checked = 0
   FromCentimeters.Checked = 0
   FromMeters.Checked = 0
   'change items on Target menu
   ToInches.Enabled = 0
   ToFeet.Enabled = -1
   ToCentimeters.Enabled = -1
   ToMeters.Enabled = - 1
   'set the caption for units
   Label2.Caption = "Inches"
END SUB
```

Now suppose the user clicks an item in the Target menu. You need to call the ConvertToCentimeters procedure to convert the value in the text box to centimeters, then display the new units and value. Suppose, for example, the user clicked the Meters item, indicating he or she wanted to convert from inches to meters. Here's the code that does this:

```
SUB ToMeters_Click()
   CALL ConvertToCentimeters
```

```
   Label3.Caption = "Meters"
   Label1.Caption = STR$(BasicLength / 100)
END SUB
```

This procedure uses the fact that clicking an item in the Target menu changes the Checked property to False for all but the unit to be converted. If you add some directions to the Form_Load procedure, you can see the result shown in Figure 10-14.

The SCREEN Object and the ControlPanel

By now you can design the interface of almost any Visual Basic program—you've seen all the controls but those specific to handling disks and files. Visual Basic lets you jazz up your displays by setting the ControlPanel property of the SCREEN object directly.

The syntax for this is:

SCREEN.ControlPanel(*CharacteristicNum*) = *Setting*

There are 18 different characteristics you can change. They are numbered from 0 to 17, and you can replace the values with symbolic

FIGURE 10-14

Results of running the conversion program

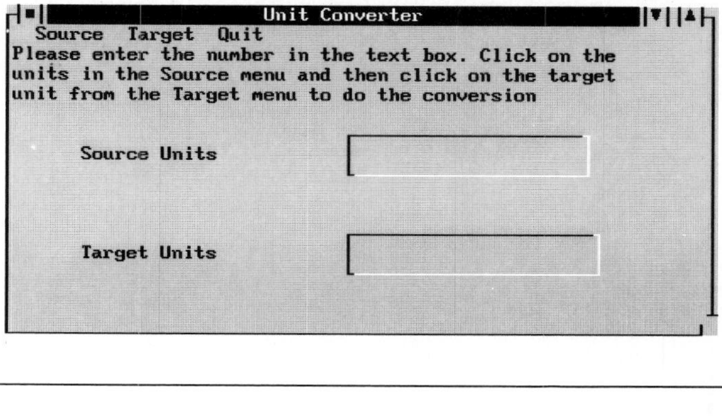

constants (found in the CONSTANT.BI file, see the section in Chapter 7 on this). The following table summarizes this information:

CharacteristicNum	Symbolic Constant
0	ACCESSKEY_FORECOLOR
1	ACTIVE_BORDER_BACKCOLOR
2	ACTIVE_BORDER_FORECOLOR
3	ACTIVE_WINDOW_SHADOW
4	COMBUTTON_FORECOLOR
5	DESKTOP_BACKCOLOR
6	DESKTOP_FORECOLOR
7	DESKTOP_PATTERN
8	DISABLED_ITEM_FORECOLOR
9	MENU_BACKCOLOR
10	MENU_FORECOLOR
11	MENU_SELECTED_BACKCOLOR
12	MENU_SELECTED_FORECOLOR
13	SCROLLBAR_BACKCOLOR
14	SCROLLBAR_FORECOLOR
15	THREE_D
16	TITLEBAR_BACKCOLOR
17	TITLEBAR_FORECOLOR

The uses of these controls are in most cases self-evident, as is the range of possible values. Color codes range from 0 to 15 and use the usual Visual Basic conventions (see Appendix C). The most interesting and only nonobvious property is the one for DESKTOP_PATTERN. This determines the fill pattern used for the background screen where forms sit. (This is usually called the *desktop*.) You can set this pattern to any ASCII code, and then you'll see that pattern repeated endlessly. The

FIGURE
10-15

Results of changing the ControlPanel

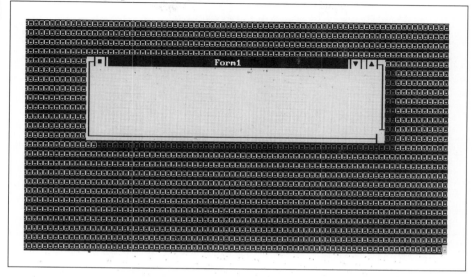

default value is ASCII 176 (▒). For example, the following Form_Click procedure, results in Figure 10-15.

```
SUB Form_Click()
  SCREEN.ControlPanel(7) = 1    'or use $INCLUDE CONSTANT_BI
END SUB                         'and DESKTOP_PATTERN
```

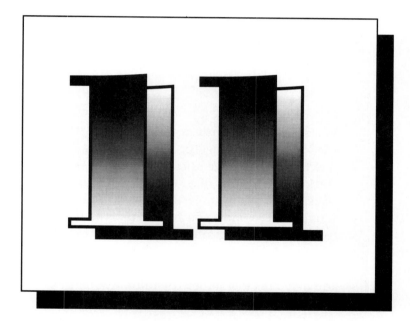

Tools and Techniques for Testing and Debugging

Once a program becomes in any way complicated, no matter how carefully you outline your program, how carefully you think about it, and how much you are convinced that it will do what you expect—it probably won't. At first. This is one lesson programmers are forced to painfully relearn over and over again. It seems that no matter how robust you try to make a program, someone, somehow, will find a way to crash it. A realistic goal is not a perfect program but one that is as bulletproof (robust) as possible. In particular, a program that, even while crashing, tries to save the user's work before fading away. So you might make it your goal to write programs that conform to a sign the authors once saw. Slightly paraphrased, it said,

> Our goal is a program
> THAT SPUTTERS OUT AND DOESN'T BLOW UP!

The technical term for this is to *degrade gracefully*.

So, after you write a program, you will still need to test it for *bugs*. Testing and debugging programs take place only in the debugging environment. Once the testing process convinces you that there are lurking bugs, you need to find them so you can eradicate them. Visual Basic has many tools that assist with this task—the purpose of this chapter is to show you how to use them. Of course, before trying to test and debug a program, you're always best off with a hard copy that gives the program source code. You might also want to have a copy of the specifications of the forms in ASCII format (see Chapter 4), so you can quickly check whether the initial properties of the form and its controls match what you expect.

Testing Programs

Testing programs is the first step in debugging because you cannot correct errors until you determine that they are there. Some people's idea of testing a program consists of running the program a few times, each time using slightly different inputs to see what happens. This can work out well when you have a short program, but it's not effective (or convincing) for a long program or even a short program that is in any way subtle. In any case, even for the simplest programs, the choice of test data (sometimes dignified with the fancy term *the testing suite*) is all important.

Testing programs is an art, not a science. There's no rule that always works. If your program is so long and complicated that you can't test all the possibilities, you have to be content with testing the reasonable ones.

The key is the word "reasonable," and the following story explains how subtle this concept can be. A utility company had a complicated but, they thought, carefully checked program to send out bills, follow up bills, and finally automatically cut off service if no response was received. One day, the story goes, someone went on vacation and shut off the electricity. The computer sent out a bill for $0.00, which, understandably, wasn't paid. After the requisite number of follow–up requests, the computer finally issued a termination notice saying that if this unfortunate person didn't pay $0.00 by Thursday, his electricity would be automatically cut off.

A frantic call might have succeeded in stopping the shut–off; the story doesn't say. If this story is true, the programmer forgot to test what the program would do if the bill was $0.00. This wasn't a "reasonable" possibility. (Of course, all the programmer had to do was change a > to a >= somewhere in the program...)

The moral of this story is that you must always test your programs using the boundary values (the extreme values that mark the limits of the problem, like the $0.00 that the programmer in the story forgot). For example, for sorting routines, a completely ordered or reverse-ordered list are good candidates for testing. In programs that require input, the empty string (or 0) is always a good candidate for testing.

 Tip   Having an active error trap (ON ERROR GOTO), can prevent your tests from doing their job. You often will need to temporarily disable any active error traps before starting the testing process. For more on error traps, see Chapter 8.

On the other hand, since errors are often caused by bugs, error trapping can help you isolate what portion of a procedure caused the bug. To do this, you'll need to use a version of the binary search technique (successive divisions in two) that you saw in Chapter 9. Divide the program in two and place a label at the beginning and at the half-way point of the program. Then use the ERL statement to tell you in which half of the program Visual Basic found the error. Continue this process until you've found the line that seems to be causing the error (bug). For more on ERL, see Chapter 8 or Appendix C.

Designing Programs to Make Testing Easier

Long and complicated programs are never easy to test, but writing the programs in certain ways will make your job easier. (They also make programming in general easier!) By breaking the program down into manageable pieces (*modularity*, in the jargon), each of which ideally does one task alone, you can make testing your programs much, much easier. After you finish each procedure or function, you can test it thoroughly (test that it can deal with all possible parameters that may be passed to it).

Next, combine the procedure with the pieces you've already checked, and test everything again. In some cases, a procedure or function may need results from a piece not yet written in order to run. In this case, the best technique, often called "stub programming," substitutes constants, where necessary, for the results of as yet unwritten procedures or functions. Define the Sub procedure or Function procedure, but fill it with constants instead of having it do anything. The procedure calls will still work the same, but they get only these constants back from the stubs. You can then change the constants to vary the tests.

The Immediate Window

Although the Immediate window can be used to do quick calculations (ALT+W I is the shortcut), its primary function is in debugging. (Unlike Visual Basic for Windows 1.0, the Immediate window is available at all times from the Window menu.) The Immediate window can hold no more than 10 lines of code at any one time.

Lines in the Immediate window can use the colon separator and up to 255 characters. Because of these restrictions, you can write loops in the Immediate window, although they'll look strange:

```
FOR I% = 10 TO 1 STEP -1:Form1.Text1.Text = STR$(I)+CHR$(13)+_
CHR$(10): NEXT I
```

is a perfectly acceptable line of code for the Immediate Window. (Don't type the underscore that we're using to indicate that the line is running over the printed page. The line must fit on one line in the Immediate window.) To see the output of this, use the F4 toggle to move to the output screen. You can also use ordinary Visual Basic cutting and pasting editing techniques (see Chapter 2) to copy code from the Code window to the Immediate window. As the example indicates, testing requires rapid shifts between the Code window, Immediate window, and Output screen. You can have the Code window, the Immediate window, and the Output screen on the screen simultaneously when you need to look at the results of your calculations, although the screen will sometimes be too crowded to work effectively.

The Immediate window keeps up to 10 lines of code. When you enter the 11th line, the first line entered disappears. Keep in mind that you can always reexecute any lines that are currently appearing in the Immediate window by moving the cursor anywhere on the line and hitting ENTER. (Use the arrow keys or mouse to move around the Immediate window.)

The most common use for the Immediate window is to examine the values of variables and properties when a program is suspended during the debugging process. Please see the section on "Breakpoints" later in this chapter.

Debugging

Now suppose you have eliminated the obvious syntax errors and can get the program to run—after a fashion. But testing the program has told you that it doesn't work as it's supposed to. There are bugs to isolate and eradicate. Don't be surprised or dismayed; bugs come with the territory. You have to find them and determine what kind they are.

There are actually two kinds of bugs: grammatical and logical. An example of a grammatical error is a misspelled variable name, which leads to a default value that ruins the program. Surprisingly enough, they are often the most difficult kind of bug to detect. Probably the best choice in Visual Basic is preventative: use the OPTION EXPLICIT command (see Chapter 5) to force you to declare all variables.

Another useful tool for understanding how the variables are used in your programs is a programmer's tool called a cross-reference (or XREF) program. This program works through the source code of a program and then lists the names of all the variables that occur and where they occur. A cross-referencing program is especially useful if you have made the common error of using the wrong variable in an assignment statement. While meaningful variable names can help to a certain extent, the mistake of using the variable called ThisWeeksSales when you really meant the variable called ThisMonthsSales is still all too common. (The OPTION EXPLICIT command doesn't help if the wrong variable was already dimensioned.)

Note One company that has an XREF program available is Crescent Software, 11 Bailey Ave., Richfield, CT 06877 (1-800-35-BASIC).

One useful point worth remembering is that Visual Basic has a primitive form of variable and constant help built-in.

Tip If you press F1 when the cursor is on a variable or constant, Visual Basic displays a message box telling you what type of variable and where it is defined or the value of the constant.

Here, for example, is what you see for the variable named Op1 in the Calculator application supplied with Visual Basic:

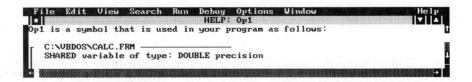

As you can see, this message box tells what kind of variable Op1 is: it's a form level, double-precision variable. To close this message box, press ESC.

Logical Bugs

To get rid of subtle logical bugs, you have to isolate them—that is, find the part of the program that's causing the problem. If you've followed the modular approach, your task is a lot easier. The pieces are more manageable, so finding the bug means the haystack isn't *too* big.

If you've been testing the program as you develop it, then it's clear in what procedure or function the problem lies. Pinpointing the problematic procedure or function is usually easier if it's your program, mostly because you start off with a good idea of the logic of the program. If the program is not yours or you've waited until the program is "finished," you can use the following techniques to check the pieces one at a time.

Let's assume that you've chosen the procedure or function to test. There are only three possibilities:

☐ What's going in is wrong—what you've fed to the procedure or function is confusing it

☐ What's going out is wrong—it's sending incorrect information to other parts of the program

☐ There's something wrong inside the procedure or function (for example, it's doing an operation too many times, or it may even be something as simple as not clearing the screen at the right time)

In the first two cases, the fault can be traced to any or all of the following: the parameters you send to the procedure or function; what you've assigned to the parameters; or the form level variables that are modified within the function or procedure.

How do you decide which situation you're dealing with? First, it's hard to imagine a correctly written short procedure or function that you couldn't analyze on a piece of paper and determine what should happen in many cases. Work through the procedure or function by hand, "playing computer" (this means: don't make any assumptions other than what the computer would know at that point; don't assume variables have certain values unless you can convince yourself that they do).

Single Stepping

Often, when you have worked through a program by hand, you want to have the computer walk through the same example, one line of code at a time. Visual Basic lets you execute one statement in your program at a time—single stepping—by repeatedly pressing F8. (Of course, if Visual Basic is waiting for an event to happen, there won't be any statements to execute.)

When F8 is first pressed, the first executable statement of the program is highlighted in the code window. (Usually, this will be in the Form_Load procedure, if there is one.) Each subsequent press of F8 executes the highlighted statement and highlights the next statement to be executed. As you can imagine, single stepping through a program is ideal for tracing the logical flow of a program through decision structures and procedures.

While you're single stepping through the program, press F4 at any time to view the contents of the output screen. Another possibility is to use the Immediate window to check the values of constants, variables, or conditions by using PRINT statements. You also might want to consider having the Immediate window and code window simultaneously on the screen. You can do this by resizing and relocating them as needed.

Whenever a procedure is called during single stepping, the procedure code fills the code window. After its statements have been highlighted and executed (one at a time), the routine that called it reappears in the code window.

Besides the F8 key, you can also use the F10 key to single step through a program. However, when the F10 key is used, each procedure is processed as if it were a single statement. In many cases, this is preferable to tracing through a complex function that you know works.

Single stepping through a program will probably take you to the place where you know a problem lurks. Now you want to place a break at that point before continuing the debugging process. This can be done with the STOP statement or more commonly by using a *breakpoint*, one of the tools available from the Debug menu (see the section following).

The Debug Menu

Most of the debugging tools you'll use are accessed from the Debug menu. (Use your mouse to open the Debug menu and select options, or use the key shortcuts offered for each item.) As you can see in Figure 11-1 there are 11 items on this menu. The individual items in this menu will be covered extensively in the sections that follow.

Breakpoints

Breakpoints have already been discussed in this chapter as a useful debugging tool. To set up a line as a breakpoint, move the cursor to that line using the arrow keys or the mouse, and then press ALT+D B (Toggle Breakpoint option on the Debug menu) or F9. When you run the program, it will stop when it reaches that line and the line will be highlighted.

Once a program is suspended (either with a breakpoint or the STOP command), you can open up the Immediate window using the Window menu. The Immediate window can then be used to display the value of all variables, expressions, or conditions appearing in the procedure

FIGURE 11-1   The Debug menu

```
 Debug
┌──────────────────────────────┐
│ Add Watch...                 │
│ Instant Watch...    Shift+F9 │
│  atchpoint...                │
│ Delete Watch...              │
│ Delete All Watch             │
├──────────────────────────────┤
│  race On                     │
│  istory On                   │
├──────────────────────────────┤
│ Toggle Breakpoint         F9 │
│  lear All Breakpoints        │
│ Break on  rrors              │
│ Set Next Statement           │
└──────────────────────────────┘
```

where the program is stopped. You can also look at any form level variables or property settings, but you *cannot* look at the value of local variables in any other procedures in the program. You can also reset properties or make changes in the values of variables inside the current procedure or form level variables at this point—and continue the program with the new values. Certain changes may prevent you from continuing the program; if so, Visual Basic will notify you with the following message box:

If you do not choose to Restart the program when presented with this dialog box, any changes you made to the code will be lost.

While a program is temporarily stopped, you can call any Sub procedure or Function procedure that is attached to the current form.

When you've completed examining the variables or making changes, you can continue running the program by pressing F5, start single stepping by pressing F8, or rerun it from the beginning by pressing SHIFT+F5.

You can set multiple breakpoints. To remove a breakpoint, position the cursor on the breakpoint and press ALT+D B (or press F9). To clear all breakpoints from a program, press ALT+D C (Clear All Breakpoints option on the Debug menu).

Using Breakpoints to Test Programs

Now suppose you want to test a procedure. Put a breakpoint right before the call to the procedure or function you want to test. Once the program stops at the breakpoint, open up the Immediate window, if necessary, and write a driver program. A *driver* is a program fragment that calls a function or procedure with specific values. For example, suppose you know that with the parameter

Variable1 = 10

and the parameter

Variable2 = 20

the result of a procedure of two parameters (a form level variable, say named FormLevel1) has the value 97. When you want to test how this procedure or function behaves at a particular place in a program, add the breakpoint at the appropriate point and use the Immediate window to enter

```
CALL WhateverYouAreTesting(10, 20)
PRINT "The value of the variable FormLevel1 is: "; FormLevel1
```

See what happens. If the value of the variable FormLevel1 isn't right, then you can begin to suspect that there's something wrong inside this procedure. To confirm it, you'll need to check that no other form level variable is causing the problem. You can add PRINT statements inside the Immediate window to check this. (Another possibility is to use Watch Variables—see the section on them that follows.) Examine the values of the relevant variables. These are the ones whose values affect the value of the variable FormLevel1. This may quickly tell you if there is something wrong inside the procedure or function. If the value of the variable FormLevel1 is right, then determine, again by hand, what happens for some other values. Always remember to try the boundary values (the strange values, like the $0.00 that the programmer in the story forgot). If you always match up with what you expect, there's probably nothing wrong with the procedure or function.

Of course, in practice, you have to make sure your driver fragment sends all the information needed by the procedure or function. And that's not likely to be only the values of two variables. You can do all the assignments needed in the Immediate window while the program is stopped, before issuing the CALL statement.

You've tested the procedure and know that the problem seems to be coming from outside it. Check each procedure that calls this procedure or function. Apply the same techniques for them: check what goes in and out of these procedures or functions.

 Tip Use F10 to treat a call to a Sub procedure or Function procedure as one step.

This way, you don't have to step through all the lines in all the functions and procedures in your program when you don't need to.

Sometimes, when testing a program with an error handler (see Chapter 8) (after all, you do need to test error handlers as well), you'll want to use the Break on Errors option on the Debug Menu (ALT+D E). This causes Visual Basic to stop at the first statement in the currently activated error handler.

Instant Watch

In every case, you eventually wind your way down to a procedure or function that just doesn't work. You now know that you have an error internal to a procedure or function. Although the Immediate window can be used to examine the values of expressions while single stepping through a program, using Visual Basic's *Instant Watch* provides a more efficient mechanism.

The Instant Watch item on the Debug menu lets you look at the value of any variable whenever a program is stopped. It complements your ability in Visual Basic to use the Immediate Window to look at the value of any variables inside a procedure when a program is stopped inside it.

To use Instant Watch:

1. Select the variable or expression you want to watch by moving the cursor to the item or highlighting the expression using SHIFT+ Arrow combinations.

2. Choose Instant watch from the Debug Menu (ALT+D I or SHIFT+F9).

A dialog box appears that looks like this:

```
╔══════════════════ Instant Watch ══════════════════╗
║                                                     ║
║  ┌Expression───────────────────────┐  ┌─────────┐  ║
║  │Op1                               │  │Add Watch│  ║
║  └──────────────────────────────────┘  └─────────┘  ║
║                                                     ║
║  ┌Value─────────────────────────────┐  ┌─────────┐  ║
║  │<Not available>                   │  │ Cancel  │  ║
║  └──────────────────────────────────┘  └─────────┘  ║
║                                         ┌─────────┐  ║
║                                         │  Help   │  ║
║                                         └─────────┘  ║
╚═════════════════════════════════════════════════════╝
```

If the value isn't currently available, Visual Basic will tell you, as shown in the previous illustration. At this point, you can close the box with the ESC key or choose to add this variable as a Watch item.

Watch Items

Watch items are variables, expressions, or conditions that are displayed in a special window, called the Debug window (see Figure 11-2). You choose the watch items you want to examine either before you start the program or while the program is running and you have temporarily stopped it. Visual Basic executes the program, and the values of these items appear in the Debug window. To create a watch item, press ALT+D A (Add Watch option on the Debug menu). A dialog box will appear with the request "Enter expression to add to Debug window." Any variable, expression, or condition can be typed into the dialog box. When you press ENTER, the item will appear in the Debug window. To remove an item from the Debug window, press ALT+D D (Delete Watch), use the DOWN ARROW key to highlight the item, and then press ENTER. To remove all items from the Debug window, press ALT+D L (Delete All Watch).

The Debug window

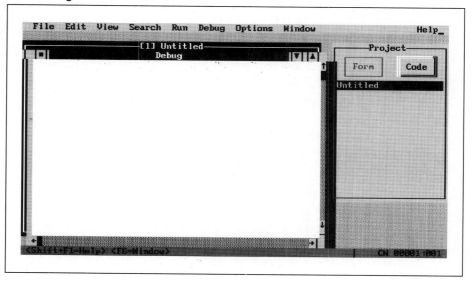

Tip If you have to watch a string variable, use an expression like:

"{" + NameOfStringVariable + "}"

That way you can quickly detect if the string is the empty string because all you'll see is { } in the Debug window.

There is one fine point in the use of watch items. Each watch item is considered as belonging to the part of the program that occupied the code window when the watch item was created. That is, each item belongs to either the leading code of a form (form level variables) or to one of the procedures. (Watch items belonging to the leading code of a form are automatically preceded in the Debug window by the name of the program. Watch items belonging to a procedure are preceded by the name of the procedure.) While a particular part of a program is being single-stepped through, only the items that belong to that part can be watched. Other items are followed by the phrase "<not watchable.>".

Watchpoints

As mentioned above, sometimes the problem with a program appears to be tied to a variable or expression whose value falls outside some anticipated range, yet the line at which this is happening is unclear. In this case, setting a breakpoint at a specific line is not appropriate and watching the variable and single stepping may be too time consuming. What is needed instead is the ability to suspend the program at whichever line causes the variable or expression to reach or exceed some value. In Visual Basic, this debugging tool is referred to as setting a watchpoint. Pressing ALT+D W (Watchpoint on the Debug menu) displays the Watchpoint dialog box and requests that you enter a logical expression (logical expressions are expressions like: Total > 100 or Name$ <> "Bob").

When the program is run, Visual Basic stops the program as soon as a watchpoint expression is True, and it highlights the line that caused the expression to become True. Here's an example of the dialog box:

Trace and History

Setting the Trace option to ON (ALT+D T) runs your project in slow motion. A bullet appears next to this option. Each statement is highlighted as Visual Basic executes it. You can combine breakpoints and watchpoints with the Trace On facility to have the program stop at any point. Once a program is stopped, you can move forward by single stepping through the program using F8 (or F10 to treat procedure calls as a single step).

More exciting however, is that with this option set and the program temporarily suspended, you can move *backwards* through the last 20 lines of code that Visual Basic has just executed. This lets you examine the "context" of any statement. You can use SHIFT+F8 or SHIFT+F10 to move backward (F8 or F10 still moves you forward), so you can move back and forth through those previous 20 lines of code.

Setting History On (ALT+D H) on the other hand, runs the program at normal speed but tells Visual Basic to keep the last 20 lines of code it executed constantly around. As with the Trace On option, you can use a combination of F8/SHIFT+F8 or F10/SHIFT+F10 to move back and forth through those previous 20 lines of code. A bullet appears next to this item when you've selected it.

Setting the Next Statement

Set Next Statement on the Debug menu lets you bypass part of a program while you are stepping through it. Sometimes (especially when using the "stub programming" technique described earlier) you'll want to start a program other than at the beginning of a procedure or function.

Or, you may, while single stepping, want to skip to another place in the program. To use this option, you need to be in a running program (usually one you are stepping through). To set this option, while in the code window, move the cursor to the line where you want to restart execution. Press ALT+D S. When you tell Visual Basic to continue, Visual Basic starts executing at the line you just set.

 Note This is equivalent to using GOTO (see Appendix C), and if you jump forward, the intervening statements are not executed as they would be otherwise.

Final Remarks on Debugging

Feeding a procedure or function specific numbers and using these techniques is not a cure–all. No technique can help unless you have a good grip on what the procedure or function should do. If you use an IF–THEN, are you testing for the right quantity? Should a >= be a >? Use watch items to check the value (true or false) of any Boolean relations that seem to be off (it is perfectly legal to enter X=19 as a watch value). Check any loops that are inside the routine; loops are a common source of problems. Are counters initialized correctly (do you have an off–by–one error)? Are you testing your indeterminate loops at the top when you should do it at the bottom?

Event Driven Bugs and Problems

When you debug an event-driven program you have to be aware of certain problems that could never come up in older programming languages. "Event cascades" are perhaps the most common. These are bugs that are caused by an infinite regress of one event procedure calling itself or another event procedure, with no way to break out of the infinite chain of events. The most likely place for this to happen is if you make a change in the Change event procedure for a control. The change procedure is called again, which in turn is called again, and so on—theoretically forever, but in practice you'll get an "Out of Stack Space" error message.

Other special problems occur when you stop a program during a MouseDown or KeyDown event procedure. In both situations, during the debugging process you'll naturally release the mouse button or lift the key that invoked the event procedure. However, when Visual Basic resumes the program it assumes the mouse button or key is still down, and so the relevant MouseUp and KeyUp procedures will never be called. The usual solution is to call the MouseUp or KeyUp procedure from the Immediate window as needed.

Debugging Examples

The following examples use the debugging tools with the programming structures you've already seen.

Stepping Through an Elementary Program

Start up a new project, add a blank form in the form designer, then enter the following Form_Click procedure in the programming environment.

```
SUB Form_Click()
  PRINT "Hello World"
  CLS
  Num$ = INPUTBOX$("Enter a number")
  Number = VAL(Num$)
  Number = Number + 1
  Number = Number + 2
  PRINT Number
END SUB
```

Now use F8 to single step through the program. Visual Basic presents the form, but nothing will happen until you click on the form. Do that. Visual Basic immediately brings you to the code window as shown in Figure 11-3.

Notice that the PRINT statement is highlighted, but if you press F4 to switch back to the output screen you'll see that nothing has happened. That's because the PRINT statement is the *next* line to be executed. Press

FIGURE 11-3 Single stepping through a program

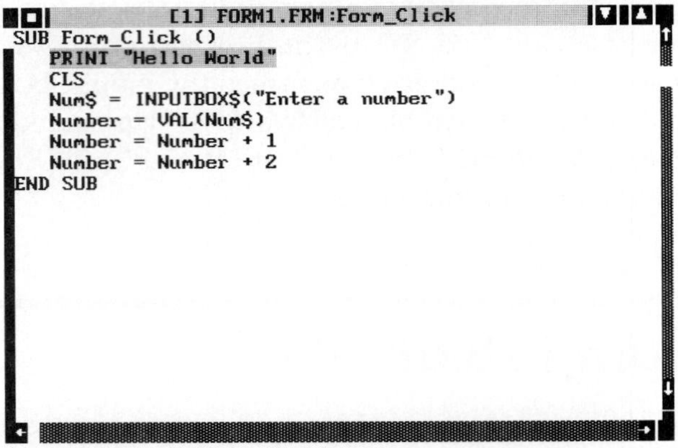
[1] FORM1.FRM:Form_Click
SUB Form_Click ()
PRINT "Hello World"
CLS
Num$ = INPUTBOX$("Enter a number")
Number = VAL(Num$)
Number = Number + 1
Number = Number + 2
END SUB

F4 to toggle back to the code window, and press F8 to execute the statement and move to the next step. To see that the PRINT statement now was executed, you should be able to see something in the output screen, again via F4. Back in the code window, the CLS statement is now highlighted to indicate that it is the next statement to be executed. Press F8 twice to execute the INPUTBOX$ statement. Type a number (for this example, 37) and hit ENTER. The VAL statement converting the string to a number is highlighted.

Now press F8 four more times to execute the rest of the program and then press any key to return to the Code window. Move the cursor to the line Number = Number + 2. Press F9 to highlight the line and set it as a breakpoint.

Rerun the program by pressing SHIFT+F5. Click on the form so that the program executes the first three lines and stops for the INPUTBOX; enter 37 as before. After you enter a value, the program will continue until it stops at the breakpoint just set. The breakpoint line is not executed.

Now open the Immediate window and enter

```
PRINT "Number ="; Number
```

The appearance of 38 in the form window shows you that the breakpoint line was not yet executed.

Place a breakpoint at the first statement in the program and restart the program by pressing SHIFT+F5. Run the program, and then when you are in the code window, move the cursor to the line Number = Number + 1 and then press ALT+D S to specify that line as the next line to be executed. Press F8 to execute the selected line. Use the Immediate window to confirm that the value of Number is now 1, and then return to the code window. (The value is 1 because the variable never received a value from the INPUTBOX$ statement.)

Stepping Through a Program That Calls a Procedure

The following walkthrough uses the single-stepping feature of Visual Basic to trace the flow through a program and a call to a Sub procedure. First, start up a new project with a blank form in the form designer, return to the programming environment and enter the following program:

```
'Form level variables Principal, Balance
DIM SHARED Principal AS SINGLE
DIM SHARED Balance AS SINGLE

SUB Form_Load
  Principal = 1000
  Balance = 0
END SUB

SUB Form_Click()
  CALL GetBalance(Principal, Balance)
  PRINT "The balance is"; Balance
END SUB
```

Now enter the following general Sub procedure, which is supposed to calculate the balance you'll have in your account after one year at 5%.

```
SUB GetBalance (Prin, Bal)
 'Calculate the balance at 5% interest rate
  DIM Interest AS Single

  Interest = .05 * Prin
  Bal = Prin + Interest
END SUB
```

What you discover when you click two times is that the program always gives you the same answer. You will see the following:

The balance is 1050
The balance is 1050

Restart the program using the Restart option on the Run menu (ALT+R R). The first form level declaration is highlighted. Press F8 until the form load procedure is finished. Visual Basic now shows you the blank form. Click anywhere inside the form. The CALL statement is now highlighted. Now press F8 once and observe that the Sub procedure GetBalance is now displayed on the screen with its first executable statement highlighted. (The procedure heading and remark statement have been skipped.) Press F8 three times to execute the assignment statements and to highlight the END SUB statement. When you press F8 you'll notice that the Form_Click event procedure code is again displayed in the code window with the highlight on the statement immediately following the CALL statement. Use the Immediate window to check that the value of the variable Principal wasn't updated. It now is clear that we didn't need the extra variable in this procedure or at the very least we should have changed the parameter variable Prin inside the GetBalance general procedure so that the changes would persist.

Debugging a Buggy Loop

Recall in Chapter 6 we mentioned that a loop that looks like this:

```
Total = 0
PassNumber = 0
DO
  PassNumber = PassNumber + 1
  Total = Total + .1
LOOP UNTIL TOTAL = 1
```

would continue forever. Suppose you had a loop like this inside a procedure, forgetting that you should never test single-precision numbers for equality. How can you use the Debug menu to find this bug?

Whenever you have a loop that is running amok, you'll need to either watch the loop variable, set up a watchpoint involving it, or both. In this case, what you might first do is watch the value of Total. You would quickly discover that it is growing without bound. Knowing this, you need only set a watchpoint with the expression:

PassNumber > 10

Once the program stops, you can examine the value of Total to discover it isn't quite equal to 1—and that is the root of your problem.

 Tip When a DO LOOP seems to be running too long, add a temporary counter in a DO LOOP. Then use the counter in a watchpoint. When the program stops, examine the state of the expression tested in the loop to help you find out why your loops are running too long.

Documentation, Managing Procedures, and Program Style

Although you can remember the logic of a complicated program for a while, you can't remember it forever. Good documentation is the key that can open the lock. Some people include the pseudocode or outline for the program as multiple remark statements. Along with meaningful variable names, this is obviously the best form of documentation. Try to avoid tricky code; if you need to do something extraordinarily clever, make sure it's extensively commented. (Most of the time, you'll find that the clever piece of code wasn't really needed.) Nothing is harder to change six months down the line than "cute" code. Cute code often comes from a misplaced attempt to get a program to run more quickly. While this is sometimes necessary, Visual Basic is usually fast enough that it's really not necessary. The authors once saw a sign that made this point clearly:

> Rules for program optimization:
>   1. Don't do it.
>   2. (For expert programmers only) DON'T DO IT!

The point is that when you start thinking of tricks to speed up your programs, you can all too easily lose sight of the fundamental issue:

making sure they run robustly in the first place. In fact, dramatic speedups usually come from shifts in the algorithms in the program, not from little "tweaks." (Roughly speaking, an *algorithm* is the method you use to solve a problem.) For example, in problems like sorting a list, it's the method you choose that determines how fast the sort is. As you saw in Chapter 9, choosing the right sorting technique can speed up a program many-fold. This is more than any minor tweak can ever hope to accomplish. Discovering new (and, with luck, faster) algorithms is one of the main tasks of computer scientists and mathematicians.

This is not to say that after a program is running robustly, you might not want to consider ways of making it run faster. Making sure that variables are Integers whenever possible is an obvious and not dangerous change. However some ways that are known to make Visual Basic programs run faster (like using global variables instead of parameters) are usually more dangerous than the speedups are worth.

In any case, it's extremely difficult to modify or debug a program (even one that you, long ago, wrote yourself) that has few or no remark statements, little accompanying documentation, and noninformative variable names. A procedure called MakeMartini(Shaken,ButNot,Stirred) should be in a program about James Bond (and perhaps not even there), not in a program about trig functions. In addition, since Visual Basic allows long variable names, don't make your programs a morass of variables named X, X13, X17, X39, and so on. If you strive for clarity in your programs rather than worry about efficiency at first, you'll be a lot better off.

Finally, if a procedure or function works well, remember to save it for reuse in other programs. Complicated programs will often have many procedures and functions. These procedures and functions may often have come up before in a slightly different context. This means that after you design the interface, sometimes all you have to do is modify and connect parts of a thoroughly debugged library of subprograms and functions to the event procedures for the interface. (This is one reason why commercial toolkits for Visual Basic are so useful. The time saved is worth the small cost.)

CHAPTER

Monitoring Mouse Activity

Visual Basic constantly monitors what the user is doing with the mouse. Up to this point, all you have used are the Click and Double Click events. These detect whether the user clicked the mouse once or twice in a form or control. This chapter shows you how to obtain more subtle information. Was a mouse button pressed? Which button was it? Is the mouse pointer over a control? Did the user release a button and, if so, which one? Did the user move the mouse out of one form and into another? Exactly where inside the form is the mouse? Visual Basic can detect all these events. Of course, as with all Visual Basic operations, you must write the event procedures that determine how Visual Basic will respond to the event.

Finally, just as designing a Visual Basic application involves dragging controls around a blank form, Visual Basic lets you write applications that let the user move controls around by dragging and dropping. The last section of this chapter shows you how.

The Mouse Event Procedures

There are three mouse event procedures:

Name	Event That Caused It
MouseDown	User clicks one of the mouse buttons
MouseUp	User releases a mouse button
MouseMove	User moves the mouse pointer

In many ways, these procedures are analogous to the KeyUp and KeyDown event procedures that you saw in Chapter 7. For example, as with those event procedures, Visual Basic lets you use bit masking to determine if the user was holding down the SHIFT, ALT, or CTRL key at the same time he or she pressed or released a mouse button.

Only forms, labels, picture boxes, and the list controls recognize the mouse events. Controls recognize a mouse event only when the mouse pointer is inside the control; the underlying form recognizes the mouse event in all other cases. However, if a mouse button is pressed *and held* while the mouse pointer is inside a control or form, that object *captures the mouse*. This means that no other Visual Basic object can react to mouse events until the user releases the mouse button, regardless of where the user moves the mouse.

All mouse event procedures take the same form and use the same parameters:

Object_MouseEvent(*Button* AS INTEGER, *Shift* AS INTEGER, _
        X AS SINGLE, *Y* AS SINGLE)

(As usual, the underscore would not appear on your Visual Basic screen).

If the object were part of a control array then, as usual, the parameter list starts with an *Index* parameter:

Object_MouseEvent(*Index* AS INTEGER, *Button* AS INTEGER, _
        Shift AS INTEGER, *X* AS SINGLE, *Y* AS SINGLE)

As the next sections shows, bit masking lets you use the *Button* parameter to determine which mouse button was pressed. Similarly, you can find out if the user was holding down any combination of the SHIFT, CTRL, or ALT keys by bit masking, using the *Shift* parameter. Finally, *X* and *Y* give the column and row of the mouse pointer relative to the upper left corner of the object that has captured the mouse.

The MouseUp/MouseDown Events

To see the event procedures given in this section at work, you will create a program for drawing rectangles and filling them with smiling faces. Figure 12-1 shows an example of what you get when you create a single rectangle.

First, start up a new project and create a blank form. Return to the code window with ALT+F4 and enter the following form level variables in the leading code for the form:

```
DIM SHARED FirstCol AS SINGLE, FirstRow AS SINGLE
DIM SHARED UpperLeft AS STRING * 1, UpperRight AS STRING * 1
DIM SHARED LowerLeft AS STRING * 1, LowerRight AS STRING * 1
DIM SHARED Horizontal  AS STRING * 1, Vertical AS STRING * 1
```

FIGURE
12-1

Demonstration of MouseUp and MouseDown event procedures

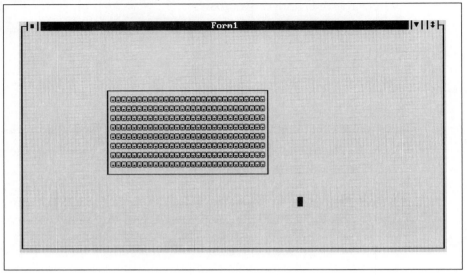

Now, press ALT+E V to edit event procedures, and then select the Form_Load event procedure. Now enter the following:

```
SUB Form_Load ()
  WindowState = 2
  'assign names to the box drawing characters
  UpperLeft = CHR$(218): UpperRight = CHR$(191)
  LowerLeft = CHR$(192): LowerRight = CHR$(217)
  Horizontal = CHR$(196): Vertical = CHR$(179)
END SUB
```

Here are the ASCII characters appearing in this procedure along with characters for a double-lined rectangle:

Again, press ALT+E V to edit event procedures, and then select the MouseDown event procedure. Now enter the following:

```
SUB Form_MouseDown (Button AS INTEGER, Shift AS INTEGER, _
                                    X AS SINGLE, Y AS SINGLE)
    'record location of upper-lefthand corner
    FirstCol = X
    FirstRow = Y
    'display location of starting corner
    CurrentX = FirstCol: CurrentY = FirstRow
    PRINT UpperLeft
END SUB
```

This event procedure uses the positioning information passed by *X* and *Y* to mark the location of the upper-lefthand corner of the rectangle. Each time you press a mouse button, the symbol "⌐" is displayed where you clicked—namely, at CurrentX = *X* and CurrentY = *Y*. If you add a MouseUp event procedure that looks like this:

```
SUB Form_MouseUp (Button AS INTEGER, Shift AS INTEGER, _
                                    X AS SINGLE, Y AS SINGLE)
    'local variables:
    DIM SecondCol AS SINGLE, SecondRow AS SINGLE
    DIM FillChar AS STRING * 1, NumberBetween AS INTEGER
    DIM I AS INTEGER

    'determine coordinates of opposite corners in rectangle
    SecondCol = X
    SecondRow = Y
    IF SecondCol < FirstCol THEN SWAP SecondCol, FirstCol
    IF SecondRow < FirstRow THEN SWAP SecondRow, FirstRow
    'sides of rectangle cannot overlap
    IF SecondCol = FirstCol THEN SecondCol = FirstCol + 1
    IF SecondRow = FirstRow THEN SecondRow = FirstRow + 1
    FillChar = CHR$(1)   'smiling face
    'record number of characters between left edge and right edge
    NumberBetween = SecondCol - FirstCol - 1
    'draw rectangle row by row, using appropriate fill character
    CurrentX = FirstCol: CurrentY = FirstRow:
    PRINT UpperLeft;STRING$(NumberBetween, Horizontal);UpperRight
    FOR I = FirstRow + 1 TO SecondRow - 1
      CurrentX = FirstCol: CurrentY = I
      PRINT Vertical; STRING$(NumberBetween, FillChar); Vertical
    NEXT I
    CurrentX = FirstCol: CurrentY = SecondRow:
```

```
PRINT LowerLeft;STRING$(NumberBetween, Horizontal);LowerRight
END SUB
```

then each time you release the same button, the position of the mouse determines the location of the lower right corner of the rectangle, and with this information, a rectangle is drawn and filled with smiling faces (see Figure 12-1).

Note Even though you may have two or even three mouse buttons, Visual Basic will not generate another MouseDown event until you release the original mouse button.

Suppose you wanted to allow the user to draw double-lined as well as single-lined rectangles. One way to do this is to use the added information given by the *Button* parameter. The *Button* parameter uses the lowest two bits of the value of the integer, as shown here:

Button	Value of Button Parameter
Left	1
Right	2

Visual Basic will tell you about only one button for the MouseUp/MouseDown combination. You cannot detect if both the left and right buttons are down simultaneously.

Suppose the user has a two-button mouse. You can easily write code so that if the user presses the right mouse button, he or she gets a double-lined rectangle, and otherwise gets a single-lined rectangle. To do this, remove from the Form_Load event procedure the statements that assign names to the box drawing characters and place the following IF block at the beginning of the MouseDown event procedure:

```
IF Button = 1 THEN
  UpperLeft = CHR$(218): UpperRight = CHR$(191)
  LowerLeft = CHR$(192): LowerRight = CHR$(217)
  Horizontal = CHR$(196): Vertical = CHR$(179)
ELSE
  UpperLeft = CHR$(201): UpperRight = CHR$(187)
  LowerLeft = CHR$(200): LowerRight = CHR$(188)
  Horizontal = CHR$(205): Vertical = CHR$(186)
END IF
```

You can also let the user combine the keyboard with a mouse. The value of the *Shift* parameter in the MouseUp or MouseDown event procedures is used to determine which "shift" keys (SHIFT, ALT, and CTRL) were being pressed at the time of the mouse event. Here's a table of the possible values for the lower three bits of the *Shift* parameter:

Action	Bit Set	Value
SHIFT key down	Bit 0:	Value = 1
CTRL key down	Bit 1:	Value = 2
ALT key down	Bit 2:	Value = 4
SHIFT+CTRL	Bits 0 and 1:	Value = 3
SHIFT+ALT	Bits 0 and 2:	Value = 5
CTRL+ALT	Bits 1 and 2:	Value = 6
SHIFT+CTRL+ALT	Bits 0, 1, and 2:	Value = 7

Microsoft reserves the right to use the other five bits in the *Shift* parameter for other purposes in the future. It's preferable, then, to use the AND operator to isolate the first three bits before proceeding. Thus, for example, a SELECT CASE statement involving the *Shift* parameter would begin with

```
SELECT CASE Shift AND 7
```

rather than

```
SELECT CASE Shift
```

By ANDing with 7 (binary pattern = 111), you eliminate any information that may eventually be contained in the higher order bits, letting the program concentrate on the information contained in the lowest three bits. You might also want to apply the same preventative measure to guard against future problems with the *Button* parameter.

The rectangle drawing program can be further enhanced so that the fill character is determined by the value of the *Shift* parameter. To do this, replace the statement

```
FillChar = CHR$(1)
```

in the MouseUp event procedure with statements like

```
'assign fill character based on which "shift" keys were
'being pressed when the button was released
SELECT CASE (Shift AND 7)
  CASE 0: FillChar = " "         'blank if none
  CASE 1: FillChar = CHR$(1)     'smiling face
  CASE 2: FillChar = CHR$(3)     'hearts
  CASE 3: FillChar = CHR$(15)    'star burst
  CASE 4: FillChar = CHR$(176)   'light "gray"
  CASE 5: FillChar = CHR$(177)   'medium "gray"
  CASE 6: FillChar = CHR$(178)   'dark "gray"
  CASE 7: FillChar = CHR$(219)   'solid
END SELECT
```

The MouseUp and MouseDown event procedures work similarly for picture boxes as for forms, the only difference being that, as you've seen, you must use the control name of the picture box (and the index if the picture box is part of a control array), as shown here:

SUB *CtrlName_MouseDown* (*Button* AS INTEGER, *Shift* AS _
    INTEGER, *X* AS SINGLE, *Y* AS SINGLE)

The MouseMove Event

Visual Basic calls the MouseMove event procedure whenever the user moves the mouse. This is the most powerful of the mouse event procedures because, unlike the MouseUp/MouseDown event pair, you can use it to analyze completely the state of the mouse buttons. For this event procedure, the *Button* parameters tell you whether some, all, or none of the mouse buttons are down.

On the other hand, as you'll see in the demonstration program that follows, it is a little misleading to claim that Visual Basic generates the MouseMove event continuously as the mouse pointer moves across objects. Visual Basic does not necessarily generate a MouseMove event for every character position that the mouse moves over.

To see the problem, start up a new project and enter the following MouseMove event procedure:

```
SUB Form_MouseMove (Button AS INTEGER, Shift AS INTEGER, _
                            X AS SINGLE, Y AS SINGLE)
  CurrentX = X
```

```
    CurrentY = Y
    PRINT ".";
END SUB
```

Now run the project and move your mouse around the form at different speeds. Figure 12-2 shows an example of what is obtained as you decrease your speed, moving from left to right in a vaguely rectangular motion. As you can see, the dots are more tightly packed when you move the mouse slowly than when you move it rapidly. This happens because Visual Basic relies on the underlying operating system to report mouse events, and such events are generated frequently but not continuously. Because the MouseMove event procedure is *not* called continuously, the dots are relatively sparse when the mouse is moved rapidly.

 Tip Tighten code inside MouseMove event procedures as much as possible.

Tightening code is important because the MouseMove event procedure will be called relatively frequently, and so any code inside this event procedure will be executed often. For example, use integer variables for counters and do not recompute the value of variables inside this procedure unless the new value depends on the parameters for the event.

 Demonstration of MouseMove response time

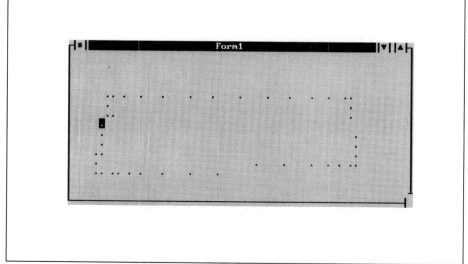

As mentioned in the introduction to this section, the MouseMove event uses the two lower bits of the value of the *Button* parameter to tell you the complete state of the mouse buttons, as shown here:

Button	Value
Left button	1
Right button	2
Left + right	3

As with the *Shift* parameter in the MouseUp/MouseDown event procedures, you are safest masking out all but the lowest two bits before using this information:

```
SELECT CASE Shift AND 3
  CASE 1
    PRINT "The left mouse button is down."
  CASE 2
    PRINT "The right mouse button is down."
  CASE 3
    PRINT "The left and right mouse buttons are down."
END SELECT
```

Dragging and Dropping Operations

To move a control as you are designing the interface in your Visual Basic project, you hold down a mouse button (the left one) and then move the mouse pointer to where you want the control to end up. An outline of the control moves with the mouse pointer. When you are happy with the location, you release the mouse button. Moving an object with the mouse button depressed is called *dragging* and releasing the mouse button is called *dropping*. Visual Basic makes it easy to program this potential into your projects.

Controls permit two types of dragging. These correspond to two different values of the DragMode property. The default is to not allow you to drag controls around except under special circumstances. (As always, you'll need to write the code for these special circumstances; see the next section.) This is called *manual dragging,* and the DragMode property will have the value zero. Changing this property to 1, *automatic dragging,* means that the user may drag the control around the project. Regardless of the setting for the DragMode property, the control will actually move only if you write the code using the Move method to reposition it, as shown in the next example.

For this example, start up a new project and create a form with a single command button. Set the DragMode property of that command button to 1 (automatic). The event that recognizes dragging and dropping operations is called the *DragDrop* event, and it is associated with the control or form where the "drop" occurs. Thus, if you want to drag a control to a new location on a form, you write code for the form's DragDrop event procedure. For example, to allow dragging and dropping to move the single command button around the form in this example, use the following:

```
SUB Form_DragDrop (Source AS CONTROL, X AS SINGLE, Y AS SINGLE)
  Source.Move X, Y
END SUB
```

Since the type of the *Source* parameter is a control, you can refer to its properties and methods by using the dot notation, as in the preceding example. If you need to know more information about what type of control is being dragged before applying a method or setting a property, use the IF TYPEOF *Source* IS... statement you saw in Chapter 8.

If you run this example, you will notice that the object remains visible in its original location while the outline moves. You cannot use the DragDrop event to make a control invisible while the dragging/dropping operation takes place. This is because this event procedure is called only after the user drops the object.

The following table summarizes the events, methods, and properties used for dragging and dropping:

Item	Description
DragMode property	Allows automatic dragging (value = 1) or manual dragging (value = 0)
DragDrop event	Associated with the target of the operation; generated when the source object is dropped on the target

Item	Description
DragOver event	Associated with any control that the source passes over; generated during a DragDrop operation
Drag method	Starts or stops dragging when DragMode is set to manual

Manual Dragging

If you have left the value of the DragMode property at its default value of zero, you must use the DRAG method to allow dragging of the control. The syntax for this method is

*Control.*DRAG *TypeOfAction*

The *TypeOfAction* is an integer value from 0 to 2, as shown here:

*Control.*DRAG 0	Cancel dragging
*Control.*DRAG 1	Begin dragging
*Control.*DRAG 2	Drop the control

If you omit the *TypeOfAction* argument, the method has the same effect as the statement Control.DRAG 1. That is, Visual Basic initiates the dragging operation for the control.

With the flexibility of this method, expert users could be allowed to drag and drop controls, while the inability to do so would be the default for other users. For example, use the CTRL+MouseDown combination to allow dragging to take place. In the case of a form, for example, you can do this by beginning the MouseDown event procedure with the following:

```
SUB Form_MouseDown (Button AS INTEGER, Shift AS INTEGER, _
                    X AS SINGLE, Y AS SINGLE)
  IF (Shift AND 7) = 2 THEN    'or CTRL_MASK
    Form.DragMode = 1
    .
    .
    .
```

```
      .
   END IF
END SUB
```

You might also want to use this method in self-running demonstration programs. You can use a value of 1 to start the dragging operation and a value of 2 to drop the control. This lets you show off dragging and dropping operations.

The DragOver Event

All Visual Basic objects but menus and timers will detect if a control is passing over them. You can use the DragOver event to allow even greater flexibility for your projects. This event lets you monitor the path a control takes while being dragged. You might consider changing the background color of the control being passed over. The syntax for this event procedure is

SUB *Object_DragOver* (*Source* AS CONTROL, *X* AS SINGLE, _
       Y AS SINGLE, *State* AS INTEGER)

As is usual when the object is a control array, an *Index* parameter is added:

SUB *CtrlName*_DragOver (*Index* AS INTEGER, *Source* AS CONTROL,_
     X AS SINGLE, *Y* AS SINGLE, *State* AS INTEGER)

The *Source* is the control being dragged, but the event procedure is associated with the control being passed over. The *X* and *Y* parameters give you the column and row of the mouse pointer. The *State* parameter has three possible values:

Value of State Parameter	Description
0	Source has just come in contact with target
1	Source is not in contact with target
2	Source has moved while in contact with target

An Example: Deleting Items via Drag/Drop

The process of dragging a symbol for an object to another symbol representing a disposal unit provides a good example of using mouse controls. By placing appropriate captions on a control array of labels and constructing a representation of a trash can on another label, we can allow the user to drag an item to the trash. Figure 12-3 shows an example of what the screen might look like. The project in this section allows the user to drag one of the displayed items into the disposal unit, at which point (after a warning, of course) the named item is deleted.

To follow this discussion, start up a new project and create a new form. Add a label in the lower-right corner of the form and give it the control name Garbage and set the border style property to 1. Next, set up a control array of labels using the control name Item. Now enter the following in the form's leading code:

```
CONST True = -1
CONST False = 0
DATA Carrots, Squash, Broccoli, Spinach, Zucchini, EOD
```

Next, enter the following Form_Load routine:

```
SUB Form_Load ()
  'maximize form
  WindowState = 2

  'draw a "trash can" on the garbage label and position it
  DIM CrLf AS STRING * 2
  CrLf = CHR$(13) + CHR$(10)   'needed to start new line
  Garbage.Caption="|      |"+CrLf+"|       |"+CrLf+"|____|"
  Garbage.Height = TEXTHEIGHT(Garbage.Caption)
  Garbage.Width = TEXTWIDTH(Garbage.Caption)
  Garbage.Top = ScaleHeight - Garbage.Height - 1
  Garbage.Left = ScaleWidth - Garbage.Width - 3

  'set desired default values for all item labels
  Item(0).Caption = ""
  Item(0).AutoSize = True
  Item(0).DragMode = 1
  Item(0).Left = 1

  CALL GetItems
END SUB
```

FIGURE 12-3   Form for drag and drop demo

After maximizing the form, Form_Load "draws" the trash can on the Garbage label then sizes and positions it. Next, Form_Load sets appropriate default values for the properties of the initial element of the control array of labels, then calls the following general procedure, which sets up an array of labels with appropriate captions. As always, all subsequent elements in the control array inherit the properties set for the initial element.

```
SUB GetItems()
  'local variables:
  DIM Index AS INTEGER, Vegetable AS STRING

  Index = 0
  READ Vegetable
  DO WHILE Vegetable <> "EOD"
    IF Index > 0 THEN LOAD Item(Index)
    Item(Index).Caption = Vegetable
    Item(Index).Top = 2 * Index
    Item(Index).Visible = True
    Index = Index + 1
    READ Vegetable
```

```
   LOOP
END SUB
```

For simplicity, the labels are displayed on every other row in a column along the left edge of the form. (If more than 11 items are to be displayed, then a fancier positioning algorithm will be required.) As with any new element in a control array, the labels remain invisible until the Visible property is set to True.

Most of the work in this project is in the following simple DragDrop event procedure:

```
SUB Garbage_DragDrop(Source AS CONTROL,X AS SINGLE,Y AS SINGLE)
   'local variables:
   DIM Msg AS STRING
   DIM ControlIndex AS INTEGER, YesNo AS INTEGER

   ControlIndex = Source.Index
   Form1.Item(ControlIndex).Visible = False

   Msg = "Do you really want to delete "
   Msg = Msg + Form1.Item(ControlIndex).Caption + "?"
   YesNo = MSGBOX(Msg, 4, "Confirmation Box")

   IF YesNo = 6 THEN
     IF ControlIndex > 0 THEN
       UNLOAD Form1.Item(ControlIndex)
     END IF
   ELSE
     Form1.Item(ControlIndex).Visible = True
   END IF
END SUB
```

The ControlIndex line in this event procedure extracts the index array of the control being dragged. The next two lines make the label temporarily invisible after the drop operation. The ControlIndex variable lets Visual Basic extract the caption (which will be the name of the item) from the label. The message box has type = 4 so it's a Yes/No message box. The title is Confirmation Box. If the user clicks "Yes," then the program unloads the label from the control array to recover memory. The program could also carry out any other tasks appropriate to deleting an item. If the user has made a mistake and clicks on "No," then the original label is simply made visible again.

CHAPTER

Working with Files

This chapter shows you how to handle disks and disk files within Visual Basic. The first section explains the commands in Visual Basic that interact with DOS. For example, you can tell DOS to rename files, change the logged drive, or switch directories. Next you'll see how to use the file system controls on the toolbox. Finally, there's an extensive introduction to file handling in Visual Basic, including a discussion on how to keep file information confidential by encrypting the information in the files.

Interacting with DOS

Visual Basic has six commands that interact directly with DOS by mimicking usual operating system commands. The following table summarizes these commands.

Command	Function
CHDRIVE	Changes the logged drive for DOS
CHDIR	Changes the default directory
MKDIR	Makes a new directory
RMDIR	Removes a directory
NAME	Changes the name of a file or moves a file from one directory to another
KILL	Deletes a file from a disk

You use these commands by following them with a string or string variable. For example,

```
MKDIR "TESTDIR"
```

adds a subdirectory called TESTDIR to the current directory, while the line

```
MKDIR "C:\TESTDIR"
```

adds it to the root directory of the C drive.

The commands that handle files also accept the normal DOS wildcards. For example,

```
KILL "*.*"
```

deletes all the files in the current directory (not to be done casually—unlike with DOS, this gives no warning!). As the preceding table indicates, the NAME command can actually do a bit more than the DOS REN command; with release 3.3 or later it can copy files from one directory in the current drive to another. To do this, give the full path name. For example,

```
NAME "C:\VBDOS\TEST.BAS" AS "C:\EXAMPLES\TEST.BAS"
```

moves the TEST.BAS file from the VBDOS directory to one named EXAMPLES. Of course, the file cannot be moved from one drive to another, or between multiple partitions of a single drive.

In addition, the function CURDIR$ returns the current drive and directory, and the function DIR$ returns the names of files matching a specified pattern. See Appendix C for details.

The SHELL Command

Although a few of DOS' utility programs are built into Visual Basic commands—usually with slightly different names, such as KILL for DEL)—most are not. However, with the SHELL command, you can run any .COM, .EXE, or .BAT file from within a Visual Basic program. For example, if you want to allow a user to format a disk, add a line like this:

```
SHELL "FORMAT A:"
```

For this to work, of course, DOS must know where the FORMAT.COM file is located.

The general form for the SHELL command is

SHELL *string*

where the *string* contains the path and name of the stand-alone program (or batch file) that you want to execute. (The string is not case sensitive.)

The SHELL command has to be used with care, especially while you're developing the program from within Visual Basic. To successfully execute a SHELL command, you must have enough memory for Visual Basic, a new copy of DOS, and the program you're "shelling to" all to be simultaneously in memory.

Command-line Information

Most professional programs allow (or require) the user to type in additional information when he or she invokes the program. This extra information is usually called *command-line information*. For example, when you write

```
COPY A:*.* B:
```

the command-line information is the string "A:*.* B:". COPY uses this information to decide what to do. Unlike interpreted BASICs, Visual Basic makes it easy to read this information. When you run a Visual Basic program directly from DOS (having compiled the program to an executable form) and use the form

FileExeName info1 info2 info3. . .

then the value of the function Command$ is the string "*info1 info2. . . .*" To access the individual pieces of information in this string, use the techniques for parsing a string that were presented in Chapter 7.

Obviously, you need a way to create sample pieces of command-line information while developing the program; otherwise, you wouldn't have any test data to debug the program with. You do this with the Modify COMMAND$ option from the Run menu (ALT R C is the shortcut). This opens the dialog box shown here:

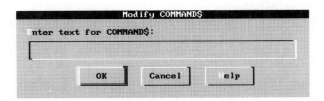

In this dialog box you can place a string to be returned by the COMMAND$ function when the program is run from within the Visual Basic environment.

You can also pass command-line information to Visual Basic itself when Visual Basic starts up. For this, start Visual Basic from DOS using the form

VBDOS /CMD *COMMANDLINEINFO*

Now, anything after the /CMD switch (except leading spaces) is sent to Visual Basic as command-line information.

The File System Controls

The file system controls in Visual Basic allow users to select a new drive, see the hierarchical directory structure of a disk, or see the names of the files in a given directory. As with all Visual Basic controls, you need to write code to take full advantage of the power of the file system controls. In addition, if you want to tell DOS to change drives or directories as the result of a mouse click, you need to write code using the commands listed in the first section in this chapter.

Figure 13-1 shows the toolbox with the file system controls marked. The file system controls are designed to work together. Your code checks what the user has done to the drive list box and passes this information on to the directory list box. The changes in the directory list box are passed on to the file list box. (See the section "Tying All the File Controls Together" a little later in this chapter.)

File List Boxes

A file list box defaults to displaying the files in the current directory. As with any list box, you can control the position, size, and color at design time or via code. Figure 13-2 shows a typical example of a file list box:

Most of the properties of a file list box are identical to those of ordinary list boxes. For example, as with all list boxes, when the number of items can't fit the current size of the control, Visual Basic automatically adds vertical scroll bars. This lets the user move through the list of files using the scroll bars. You can set the size or position of file list boxes with the

FIGURE
13-1

The toolbox with the file system controls marked

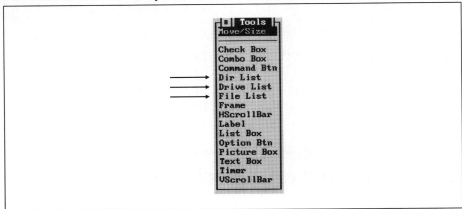

Properties bar or with code as needed. Similarly, file list boxes can respond to all the events that list boxes can detect. In addition, you can write event procedures for a key press or a mouse movement. One point is particularly worth remembering, though: the standard convention is that double-clicking a file, not single-clicking, chooses the file. This is especially important when using a file list box because using an arrow key to move through a file list box would call any Click procedure that you have written. (Recall that arrow movements are functionally equivalent to a single mouse click for a list box.)

FIGURE
13-2

Sample File List box

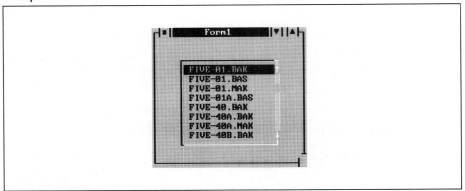

It is quite common to use the List, ListCount, and ListIndex properties to analyze the information contained in a file list box rather than to use the DIR$ command. For example, suppose the file list box has the default name of File1 and you have already set up a string array for the information contained in the box. Then a fragment like

```
FOR I% = 0 TO File1.ListCount - 1
  FileNames$(I%) = File1.List(I%)
NEXT I%
```

fills a string array with the information contained in the file list box named File1. If you need to find out the name of the file that a user selects, you can use File1.List(ListIndex) or the new FileName property which, when read, has the same function.

One reason you might choose to use code such as that just given rather than the DIR$ command is that file list boxes can be used to show more subtle file information. For example, you can look at files that are ordinarily hidden. Similarly, you can have a file list box display only files that are read only (good for novice users) or those that have the archive bit turned on or off (indicating whether or not the files have been backed up since the last change). There are five Boolean properties (True, False) that control what type of files are shown in a file list box: Archive, Hidden, Normal, ReadOnly, and System. The default setting is True for Archive, Normal, and ReadOnly, and False for Hidden and System.

As an example of this, consider the code to activate the form shown in Figure 13-3, which has a single file list box and five check boxes to specify the type of files the file list box shows. For example, if the file list box is named File1 and one of the check boxes is named ShowHidden, a line of code like

```
File1.Hidden = ShowHidden.Value
```

would tell the file list box to display (or not display) hidden files depending on whether or not the box was checked.

Pattern and Path

The most important properties for file list boxes are Pattern and Path. The Pattern property determines which files are displayed in the file list

FIGURE
13-3

A form with a single file list box and five check boxes

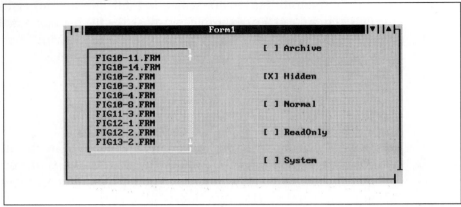

box. The Pattern property accepts the ordinary DOS wildcards: the *
(match any) and the ? (match a single character). The default pattern is
set to *.* to display all files. (Of course, the Pattern property checks the
attribute properties discussed earlier before Visual Basic displays the
files.) When you change the Pattern property, Visual Basic looks to see
if you have written a PatternChange event procedure for the file list box
and, if so, activates it.

The Path property, which is only available at run time, sets or returns
the current path for the file list box, but not for DOS. To tell DOS to
change the current path from within Visual Basic, you need the CHDIR
command. It may be that you just need to accumulate this information
for use by your program without disturbing the default path. When you
change the Path property, Visual Basic looks to see if you have written a
PathChange event procedure for the file list box and, if so, activates it.

Changing the FileName property activates the PathChange event or
the PatternChange event (or both), depending on how you change the
FileName property. For example, suppose you are in the C: root directory.
The setting

```
File1.FileName ="C:\DOS\*.COM"
```

activates both the PathChange and PatternChange events.

Directory List Boxes

A directory list box displays the directory structure of the current drive. The current directory is highlighted. Immediate subdirectories of the current directory are shown below the current directory, while all parent directories back to the root directory (\) are shown above. The root directory is displayed flush left while each successive directory level is indented a space. Here's a picture of a typical directory list box:

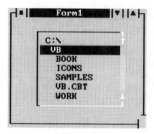

The List property for a directory list box works a little differently than it does for file list boxes. While subdirectories of the current directory are numbered from zero to ListCount–1, Visual Basic uses negative indexes for the current directory and its parent and grandparent directories. For example, –1 is the index for the current directory, –2 for its parent directory, and so on. Unfortunately, you cannot use the LBOUND function to determine the number of directories above a given directory list box. You must either count the number of backslashes in the Path property or move backward through the items in the directory list box until you get to the root.

As an example of how powerful the file system controls can be when they begin to work together, put a directory list box and a file list box together on a new project, as shown in Figure 13-4. Now suppose you want a change by the user in the Dir1 list box to tell Visual Basic to update the file list box immediately. All you have to do is enter one line of code in the Dir1_Change event procedure:

```
SUB Dir1_Change ()
  File1.Path = Dir1.Path
END SUB
```

This is all it takes to update the file list box whenever a user changes the current directory. To activate this event procedure, the user must

FIGURE
13-4

A project with a directory list box and a file list box

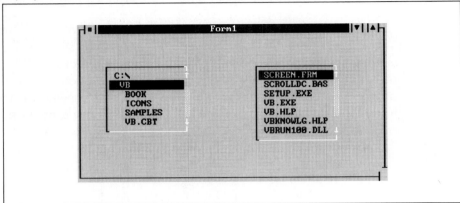

double-click a new directory in the Dir1 list box. (Directory list boxes do not recognize the DblClick event; instead they call the Change procedure in response to a double-click.) Again, Visual Basic cannot use a single click to activate the Change event, because users then could not use the arrow keys to move through the list box. In order to have pressing ENTER update the file list box as well, use the Dir1_KeyPress event procedure as follows:

```
SUB Dir1_KeyPress (KeyAscii AS INTEGER)
  IF KeyAscii = 13 THEN      'Enter key = ASC(13)
    Dir1.Path = Dir1.List(Dir1.ListIndex)
  END IF
END SUB
```

Whereas double-clicking automatically updates the Dir1.Path property, pressing ENTER doesn't. Visual Basic calls the Change event procedure for a directory list box whenever you change the value of the Path property. This procedure directly changes Dir1.Path and as a result invokes the Dir1_Change procedure.

Finally, keep in mind that while the meaning of the Path property for file list boxes is similar to that for directory lists boxes, they are not identical. For directory list boxes, the Path property specifies which directory was selected; for file list boxes, the Path property specifies where to look for files to display.

Drive List Boxes

Unlike file and directory list boxes, drive list boxes are pull-down boxes. Drive list boxes begin by displaying the current drive and then, when the user clicks on the arrow, Visual Basic pulls down a list of all valid drives. Figure 13-5 shows an example of a typical drive list box.

The key property for a drive list box is the Drive property, which can be used to return or reset the current drive. For example, to synchronize a drive list box with a directory list box, all you need is code that looks like this:

```
SUB Drive1_Change ()
   Dir1.Path = Drive1.Drive
END SUB
```

On the other hand, if you also want to change the logged drive that DOS is using, write

```
SUB Drive1_Change ()
   Dir1.Path = Drive1.Drive
   CHDRIVE Drive1.Drive
END SUB
```

FIGURE 13-5   An example of a drive list box

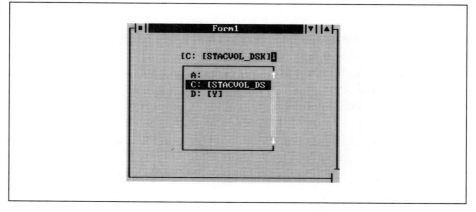

Tying All the File Controls Together

When you have all three file system controls on a form, you have to communicate the changes among the controls in order to have Visual Basic show what the user wants to see. For example, if the user selects a new drive, the Drive1_Change event procedure is activated. Then the following occurs:

1. The Drive1_Change event procedure assigns the Drive1_Drive property to the Dir1.Path property.

2. This changes the display in the directory list box by activating the Dir1_Change event procedure.

3. Inside the Drive1_Change event procedure, you assign the Dir1.Path property to the File1.Path property. This updates the File1 list box.

It is easy to add a text box for a file pattern (assign it to the File1.Pattern property) and check boxes to allow the user to choose what type of files to view in the file list box, as shown in Figure 13-6. Including all this information gives you something close to the usual Visual Basic file control box with the added advantage of allowing the user to choose what type of files to display.

FIGURE 13-6

A form with a text box and check boxes for file viewing

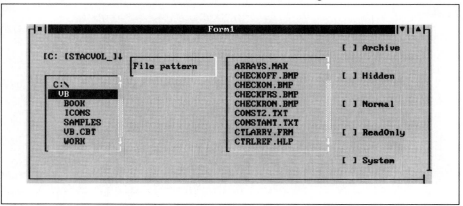

Sequential Files

Sequential files are analogous in Visual Basic to recording information on a cassette tape. The analogy is a particularly useful one to keep in mind. For example, easy operations on a cassette recorder, such as recording an album on a blank tape, are analogous to easy operations on a sequential file. Likewise, more difficult operations on a cassette recorder, such as splicing tapes together or making a change within a tape, are analogous to more difficult operations on a sequential file.

To avoid unnecessary work, it is useful to keep in mind that a sequential file is best when you know that you will

☐   Rarely make changes within the file

☐   Massage (process) the information the file contains from start to finish, without needing to constantly jump around

☐   Add to the file only at the end of the file

It's not that you can't make changes within the file, jump around when processing information, or add to the file other than at the end; it's just that these procedures are a bit painful.

Here's a table of some common operations on a cassette tape and the analogous operations on a sequential text file called TEST in the currently active directory:

Operation	Visual Basic Equivalent
Put the machine in playback and pause	OPEN "TEST" FOR INPUT AS #1
Put the machine in record and pause	OPEN "TEST" FOR OUTPUT AS #1
Push stop	CLOSE #1

Each time Visual Basic sees the OPEN command, it gets ready to send information into or take information out of the file. (The jargon is that it "sets up a channel" to communicate with the file.) What follows the OPEN command is the name of the file you are working with. The file name must be a string variable or enclosed in quotes, and unless it is in the current directory, you have to provide sufficient information to identify its path. (The value of a string variable must be a legal file name.) The rules for file names are the rules that DOS imposes:

☐   The file name can be at most eight characters with an optional three-character extension following the period.

☐   The characters you can use are

A-Z 0-9 ( ) { } @ # $ % & ! - _ ' / ~

☐   Lowercase letters are automatically converted to uppercase.

☐   You need a file identifier. This is a number between 1 and 255 optionally preceded by the # sign that you will use to identify the file. Although you can't change this number until you close the file, the next time you need the file you can open it with a different ID number. The number of possible files you can have open at once is limited by DOS to eight unless you change your CONFIG.SYS file.

When Visual Basic processes an OPEN command, it also reserves a file buffer in the computer's memory. Without a buffer, each piece of information sent to (or from) the disk would be recorded (or read back) separately. Since mechanical operations like writing to a disk are much slower than writing to RAM, this would waste a lot of time. Instead, when a file buffer fills up, Visual Basic tells DOS to activate the appropriate drive, and a whole packet of information is sent in a continuous stream to the disk. The number of buffers can also be changed from your CONFIG.SYS file.

The CLOSE command empties the buffer and tells DOS to update the FAT (file allocation table). For this reason, a sudden power outage when you have a file open almost inevitably leads to lost information and occasionally even to a corrupted disk.

The PRINT command sends information to the screen. A variant, the PRINT # command, is one way to send information to a file. Here is an example of a fragment that sends one piece of information to a file named TEST:

```
' Writing to a file
OPEN "TEST" FOR OUTPUT AS #1
```

```
PRINT #1, "TESTING, 1 2 3"
CLOSE #1
```

After the usual remark statement, the first executable statement tells Visual Basic that you are going to set up a file named TEST having file identifier #1.

Caution If a file in the current directory already exists with the name TEST, it is erased by this statement. Opening a file for output starts a new file; the contents of a previous file with the same name are lost.

Next comes the statement that actually sends the information to the file. The comma following the file identifier #1 is necessary, but what follows the comma can be anything that might occur in an ordinary PRINT statement. And what appears in the file is the same as what would have occurred on the screen. More precisely, the file will contain the word TESTING, followed by a comma, followed by a space, followed by the numeral 1, followed by a space, followed by the numeral 2, followed by a space, followed by the numeral 3, and then, although you may not have thought of it, the characters that define a carriage return/line feed combination—a CHR$(13) (carriage return) and a CHR$(10) (line feed). Note that the file does not contain any quotation marks, nor, of course, would an ordinary PRINT statement put any on the screen.

It is extremely important that you keep in mind that the PRINT # command works exactly like the PRINT command. By now you know of the automatic carriage return/line feed combination that follows an ordinary PRINT statement. More precisely, if the line read

```
PRINT #1, "TESTING, 1 2 3";
```

then the file would contain two fewer characters. The CHR$(13) and CHR$(10) would no longer be there because the semicolon (just as for an ordinary PRINT statement) suppresses the carriage return/line feed combination. This is important because the cardinal rule of file handling is that you must know the exact structure of a file if you want to be able to efficiently reuse the information it contains.

As a third example, suppose you change the line to read

```
PRINT #1, "TESTING", 1, 2, 3
```

Now the file contains many spaces (occurrences of CHR$(32)) that were not there before. To see why this must be true, just recall that a comma in a PRINT statement moves the cursor to the next print zone by inserting spaces. Use a comma in a PRINT # statement, and the same spaces are placed in your file.

Finally, the CLOSE command (followed by a file identifier) *flushes*, or moves, whatever is in the appropriate file buffer to the disk. The CLOSE command without a file ID flushes all open buffers—that is, it closes all open files.

Once a file is open, Visual Basic has a command LOF( ) (Length Of File) to tell you how large a file is. To use this command, place the appropriate file identifier number within the parentheses. To see this command at work (and to confirm what was said earlier about the sizes of the various versions of the TEST file), try the following Click procedure in a new project:

```
SUB Form_Click ()
' a file tester
' demonstrates the identical image property of PRINT #
  OPEN "TEST1" FOR OUTPUT AS #1
  OPEN "TEST2" FOR OUTPUT AS #2
  OPEN "TEST3" FOR OUTPUT AS #3
  PRINT #1, "TESTING, 1, 2, 3"
  PRINT #2, "TESTING, 1, 2, 3";
  PRINT #3, "TESTING", 1, 2, 3
  PRINT LOF(1)
  PRINT LOF(2)
  PRINT LOF(3)
  CLOSE
END SUB
```

If you run this program, you'll see

```
18
16
47
```

As you can see, the first file does contain 2 more characters (bytes) than the second (to account for the carriage return/line feed combination). And the third contains far more than the 14 characters (bytes) in the phrase "TESTING, 1 2 3". The extra characters, as you'll soon see, are indeed spaces (CHR$(32)) (see the section, "General Sequential Files," later in this chapter).

Reading Back Information from a File

To read information back from a file, you must open the file for input using its name (again, the full or partial path name if it's not in the currently active directory) and give it a file identifier that is not currently being used within the program. (It doesn't have to be the same identifier that it was written with originally.) The easiest way to find an unused file identifier is with the command FREEFILE. The value of FREEFILE is always the next unused file ID number. Therefore, you merely have statements of the form

FreeFileNumber% = FREEFILE
OPEN "*filename*" FOR INPUT AS #*FreeFileNumber*%

at the appropriate point in your program.

Caution   Never use OPEN "*filename*" FOR INPUT AS #*FREEFILE*.

Next, you choose a variant on the INPUT command to retrieve the information. For example, suppose you want to read back the file TEST1. This contains the word "TESTING", followed by a comma, followed by the numbers. It ends with the carriage return/line feed combination. For those who know some form of PC-BASIC, to choose how to read this information back from this file, pretend for a second that you were going to enter this information into the computer via the keyboard in the older version of BASIC. You could not say INPUT A$ because that would pick up only the word "TESTING". (The INPUT command would read information only up to the first comma.) So you would likely use LINE INPUT A$ because the LINE INPUT command disregards any spaces or commas that may have been typed; it accepts all the information typed until ENTER is pressed. (The carriage return/line feed combination corresponds to the ENTER key.) In general, you use the LINE INPUT # statement to read information from a sequential file one line at a time. Here is a fragment that reads back and displays the contents of the file named TEST1:

```
' Reading back a file
OPEN "TEST1" FOR INPUT AS #1
LINE INPUT #1, A$
PRINT A$
CLOSE #1
```

As an alternative you could have used

```
OPEN "TEST1" FOR INPUT AS #1
INPUT #1, A$, B$, C$, D$
PRINT A$; ", "; B$; ", "; C$; ", "; D$
CLOSE #1
```

or

```
OPEN "TEST1" FOR INPUT AS #1
INPUT #1, A$, B, C, D
PRINT A$; ","; STR$(B); ","; STR$(C); ","; STR$(D)
CLOSE #1
```

both of which seem clumsier but let Visual Basic do the work of parsing. Of course, the last program has recovered the numbers as numbers (values of numeric variables) rather than as strings of numerals (part of a larger string). If you have stored numbers in a file, this is often the method to choose to retrieve them.

If you know how many entries there are in a file, a FOR–NEXT loop is often the easiest way to read the information back. For example, suppose you're a teacher with a class of 25 students. You know the currently active disk contains a file called CLASS that stores the information about the class in the following form:

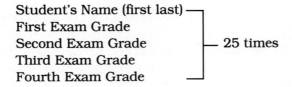

Two useful terms that recur often in file handling are "fields" and "records." Think of this file as being made up of 25 records and each record as consisting of five fields. Usually, a program that manipulates this file will read back the information by records—that is, five fields at a time. And each field can be picked up by a single INPUT # rather than needing the LINE INPUT# command. The similarity with user-defined records (see Chapter 9) is not a coincidence. You'll often find yourself filling in the components of a record from a file.

Knowing the exact format of this file means you can easily write a procedure that will retrieve this information. First set up a record.

```
TYPE StudentRecord
   Name AS STRING * 20
   FirstExam AS INTEGER
   SecondExam AS INTEGER
   ThirdExam AS INTEGER
   FourthExam AS INTEGER
END TYPE
```

Now declare a one-dimensional array with entries of type StudentRecord as a form level variable:

```
DIM SHARED StudentGrades() AS StudentRecord
```

and then use the following general procedure:

```
SUB RetrieveGrade ()
   DIM I AS INTEGER, FileNum AS INTEGER

   REDIM StudentGrades(1 TO 25)
   FileNum = FREEFILE
   OPEN "Grades" FOR INPUT AS #FileNum
   FOR I = 1 TO 25
     INPUT #FileNum, StudentGrades(I).Name
     INPUT #FileNum, StudentGrades(I).FirstExam
     INPUT #FileNum, StudentGrades(I).SecondExam
     INPUT #FileNum, StudentGrades(I).ThirdExam
     INPUT #FileNum, StudentGrades(I).FourthExam
   NEXT I
   CLOSE #FileNum
END SUB
```

Now each entry of the array StudentGrades contains a record with the name and grades of a student. You could easily incorporate this type of general SUB procedure into a program that analyzes the grades.

This file has a simple structure because the cardinal rule remains: You can't do anything with a file until you bring into memory the information you need from it.

The more complicated the structure of the file, the harder it is to work with. If you can keep the structure of your files simple, then filling up an array is often the method of choice. The reason is that once the information contained in the file is stored in the array, massaging it is easy, usually requiring only a few FOR-NEXT loops to run through the array.

For example, suppose you want to write a procedure that can return the average and number absent on each exam. In this case, if you chose to store the grade information in an array of strings rather than in the array of records given earlier, you could write a SUB that would take a parameter for the exam number, as in the following listing:

```
SUB AnalysisOfExams (ExamNumber)
  DIM NumAbsent AS INTEGER, Total AS INTEGER
  DIM I AS INTEGER

  ' StudentGrades$() is a form level variable
  NumAbsent = 0
  Total = 0
  FOR I = 1 TO 25
    IF StudentGrades$(I,ExamNumber) = "absent" THEN
      NumAbsent = NumAbsent + 1
    ELSE
      Total = Total + VAL(StudentGrades$(I, ExamNumber))
    END IF
  NEXT I
  PRINT "The number absent was"; NumAbsent
  PRINT "The class average was"; Total / (25 - NumAbsent)
END SUB
```

This procedure is straightforward. The parameter tells the procedure what exam number (column of the array) to look at, and the FOR-NEXT loop runs through each row. (The VAL command is needed because the exam grades are stored in a string array.)

Adding to an Existing File

The GRADE file contains each student's name followed by a list of his or her grades. This is a bit unnatural. A different, more natural, kind of file structure would occur if the teacher entered everything in steps: first the student's name and then, after a while, the results of the first exam, and so on. To write a program to do this, you need a command that lets you add information to the end of an already existing file. The statement

OPEN "*filename*" FOR APPEND AS #*filenum*

causes three things to occur at once:

☐   Visual Basic opens the file (if the file doesn't exist, it creates it) and sets up the appropriate buffer.

☐   Visual Basic locates the end of the file on the disk.

☐   Visual Basic prepares to output to the file at its end.

Recall that if you open an existing file for output, you erase it. Only by using the APPEND keyword can you add to an existing file.

If you are writing this type of program for yourself, for a single class' records, you might want to update this file, using a short fragment that reads the students' names and stores them in an array before the appending:

```
REDIM StudentNames$(25)
OPEN "StudentGrades" FOR INPUT AS # 1
FOR I = 1 TO 25
  INPUT #1, StudentNames$(I)
NEXT I
CLOSE #1
OPEN "StudentGrades" FOR APPEND AS #1
FOR I = 1 TO 25
  M$ = "The grade for" + StudentNames$(I) + " is?"
  StudentGrades$ = InputBox$(M$)
  PRINT #1, StudentGrades$
NEXT I
CLOSE
```

This fragment assumes the file was already created and contains the names of the students. The point of the CLOSE command is that to change a sequential file's status from reading to writing, it must first be closed. Once the file is closed, the APPEND keyword lets you add to it.

You will probably find yourself writing lots of these "quick and dirty" programs as you become more familiar with file-handling techniques. Although they're never very robust, they do get the job done. (You need special techniques to make file-handling programs robust; see the next section of this chapter.)

Suppose, however, you were teaching five classes, each with a different number of students. Then the "quick and dirty" approach is not worthwhile. It's possible to get the classes mixed up, leading to an error message or even to losing a student's grades. To prevent this kind of mishap, write a header to all your files. Use this header to put standard information about the file at the beginning of the file.

To write a usable grade book program, you can use the first few entries in the file for the name of the class, the semester, the number of exams, and the number of students. This kind of information isn't likely to change. (If you want to change it, see the section "Binary files" later in this chapter). Also, it has the added advantage that you can use it to set up the bounds on the loops that will read and process the information contained in the file. The following table shows you the form that lets the user fill in this header information inside various text boxes:

Type Of Object	Control (Form) Name	Caption (Text)
Form	HeaderForm	General Information
Label	Label1	File Name
Label	Label2	Class Name
Text box	NameOfFile	-
Text box	NameOfClass	-
Text box	NumberOfExams	-
Text box	NumberOfStudents	-
Command button	SetUp	Set Up File

Now you could have the following general procedure that sets up a grade book on a disk in the currently active directory:

```
SUB SetUpClick ()
  ' local variables:
  DIM ExamNum AS INTEGER, StuNum AS INTEGER, FileNum AS INTEGER

  FileNum = FREEFILE
  OPEN NameOfFile.Text FOR OUTPUT AS #FileNum
  PRINT #FileNum, NameOfClass.Text
  PRINT #FileNum, VAL(NumberOfExams.Text)
  PRINT #FileNum, VAL(NumberOfStudents.Text)
  CLOSE #FileNum
END SUB
```

General Sequential Files

Although FOR-NEXT loops are a convenient way to read back information contained in a file, obviously there are times when they are not practical. There may be too much information in the file, or you may not know what limits to use. You need a way to implement the following outline:

While there's information left in the file
  Get next piece of INFO
  Process it
Loop

To do this, you need a way to test when you're at the end of a file. The statement in Visual Basic that lets you do this is mnemonic: it's called EOF( ) (End Of File), where the parentheses hold the file ID number. A quite general program to read back the information contained in a file set up with PRINT # statements looks like this:

```
FileNum = FREEFILE
OPEN FileName$ FOR INPUT AS #FileNum
DO UNTIL EOF(FileNum)
  LINE INPUT #FileNum, A$
  ' process line - this would probably be a
  ' procedure call or function call
LOOP
CLOSE #FileNum
```

You use a loop that tests at the top to take into account the unlikely possibility that the file exists but doesn't contain any information—that is, it was opened for output but nothing was actually sent to the file. This fragment is a more or less direct translation of the outline. It picks up a line of data (that is, all the data up to a carriage return/line feed pair), and it continues doing this until it gets to the end of the file.

This kind of fragment is how you write a simple print formatter for text files. All you need to know is that you can LINE INPUT# each line (that is, that the lines are not too long or too short) and then add the lines to the current value of a string variable. When you're done, make them the Text property of a multiline text box with vertical scroll bars. (It's much faster in Visual Basic to make the string first and then assign it to the Text property when you're finished retrieving the information than to repeatedly change the Text property itself.)

By the way, a lot of people use the DO WHILE form of these loops. They prefer

```
DO WHILE NOT EOF(1)
    .
    .
    .
LOOP
```

or

```
WHILE NOT EOF(1)
    .
    .
    .
WEND
```

Since all three forms are equivalent, which you choose is a matter of taste.

One common use of the EOF statement is to read back the information contained in a file character by character. The analogy to keep in mind if you know PC-BASIC is that you read a file as if it were the keyboard. The command that picks individual characters from the keyboard is INPUT$. In Visual Basic, you pick up individual characters from a file with a statement of the form

```
A$ = INPUT$(NumberOfChars, FileNum)
```

where the first entry holds the number of characters to be read in and the second holds the file ID. Therefore,

```
SixChar$ = INPUT$(6, #2)
```

picks up six characters from a file opened for input with file ID #2 and assigns them to a string variable named SixChar$.

Here is a fragment that reads the contents of a file named FILENAME$ character by character and prints both the ASCII code and the character on the same line:

```
' A 'semi' master file reader
FileNum = FREEFILE
OPEN FileName$ FOR INPUT AS #FileNum
DO UNTIL EOF(FileNum)
   A$ = INPUT$(1, #FileNum)
   PRINT  A$, ASC(A$)
LOOP
CLOSE FileNum
```

If you use this program on the files TEST1, TEST2, and TEST3 created earlier, you can easily check that the spaces and carriage return/line feed combinations PRINT # sends to a file (as stated earlier) are, in fact, there.

Although the INPUT$ function lets you examine the structure of many files character by character, it shouldn't be overused. For example, it's much slower than using the LINE INPUT # or even the INPUT # statement. Moreover, it's possible for files created by word processors and spreadsheet programs not to be readable by these methods. This is because Visual Basic stops reading a file when it encounters ASCII character 26 (also known as CTRL+Z), the traditional end-of-file character. Some files created by word processors contain CHR$(26)s internally. You can see this by trying to use the previous program to read back the file created with the following fragment:

```
'demonstrates CTRL+Z = ^Z = CHR$(26) as EOF
FileNum = FREEFILE
OPEN "TEST" FOR OUTPUT AS #FileNum
PRINT #FileNum, CHR$(26)
FOR I = 1 TO 10
```

```
   PRINT #FileNum, "The previous program can't ever read this"
NEXT I
CLOSE #FileNum
```

 Note This is a simple and effective way to keep casual snoopers out of your files.

Since it can be very important to massage non-ASCII files (like Lotus 1-2-3 files), Visual Basic has another method of reading back files that, among its other powers, gets around this CTRL+Z problem. (See the section "Binary Files" later in this chapter.)

In any case, even if a file is readable by using the INPUT$ function, it's usually better to think of a file as being made up of fields, possibly grouped into records. Each field is separated from the next by a delimiter—that is, a comma or carriage return/line feed combination. The delimiter is what lets you use a single INPUT # to pick up the field. This is much faster than doing it character by character.

Sending Special Characters to a File

Since you send information to a file as if it were the screen, you again have to solve the following problems:

❑   How do you send special characters to the file?

❑   How do you nicely format a file?

Visual Basic uses the WRITE # statement to send items to a file separated by commas and with quotes around strings. For example,

```
WRITE #3, "Testing", 1, 2, 3
```

sends everything (including the quotes and the commas) to the output (or append) file with ID #3. This is exactly the same as (and of course less cumbersome than) writing

```
PRINT #3, CHR$(34);
PRINT #3, "Testing";
```

```
PRINT #3, CHR$(34);
PRINT #3, "1,2,3"
```

(Note the three semicolons to prevent inadvertent carriage return/line feed combinations.)

As long as you send individual pieces of information to a file, the PRINT # and WRITE # command can be used interchangeably. For example,

```
PRINT #FileNum, "Hello"
```

and

```
WRITE #FileNum, "Hello"
```

both put a single piece of information into a file. In either case, you can read back the information by using the INPUT # command. (Although the files won't be the same size, the WRITE# command adds two quotation marks (CHR$(34)) to the file.) It's only when you send more than one piece of information at a time that the differences really emerge. For example, to send three numbers to a file using

```
PRINT #FileNum, 1; 2; 3
```

records the three numbers in the file with no quotes or commas to mark the separate pieces of information. On the other hand, the command

```
WRITE #FileNum, 1, 2, 3
```

sends the appropriate commas to the file, making it easier to read back the individual pieces of information. It's equivalent to the cumbersome

```
PRINT #FileNum, 1; ","; 2; ","; 3
```

Simply put, use WRITE # together with INPUT # and PRINT # with LINE INPUT #.

Making Changes Inside a Sequential File

The information inside a sequential file is packed tight and is hard to change, but that doesn't mean you can't do it. If the changes you're making don't alter the size of the file, then the methods described in the section on "Binary Files" in this chapter are your best bet. This section explains some other ways that do not use these techniques.

The OPEN *FileName* FOR APPEND AS *#FileNum* command lets you add information to the end of a sequential file. Suppose you now want to add information to the beginning of a file. Proceed as follows:

1. OPEN a temporary file FOR OUTPUT.

2. Use PRINT # or WRITE # to place the new information in the temporary file.

3. Close the temporary file.

4. Append the information from the original file onto the end of the temporary file. Two techniques are available to perform this task:

   The first technique involves reopening the temporary file FOR APPEND. The original file is then opened FOR INPUT and information is read from the original file and appended to the temporary file. Finally, the temporary file is closed again.

   The second technique is much faster when the original file is large. Visual Basic's SHELL command is used to execute DOS's COPY command. The DOS command

   COPY *file1+file2*

   appends the file named *file2* onto the file named *file1*. Thus the SHELL command would take the form

   SHELL "COPY *TempFileName+OriginalFileName*"

   or alternately

   SHELL "COPY" + *TempFileName$* + "+" + *OriginalFileName$*

5. Delete the original file using the KILL command.

6. Rename the temporary file to the original file's name using the NAME command.

Suppose the information does not go right at the beginning of the file or you want to remove or replace information already in the file. To do this, imagine what you might do if these modifications were to be done to a cassette tape. First, you'd record the words to be added on a separate tape with a little bit of leader, which means you leave some blank tape so you can cut and paste. Then you'd find where on the tape the new information is to go and splice (or cut) the tapes.

For example, suppose you want to change all occurrences of the word "QuickBASIC" in a file to "Visual Basic" (or, more generally, to write your own search and replace function). Follow these steps:

1. Read the information in the file into a temporary file, stopping the parade whenever you get to the string "QuickBASIC".

2. Write "Visual Basic" into the temporary file

3. Move past the occurrence of the word "QuickBASIC" and continue repeating steps 1 and 2 until EOF.

4. Now kill the original file and rename the temporary file back to the original file's name.

Since you have to read the information back character by character, a program that implements this outline can run for quite a bit of time. The program will run a lot more quickly (and is actually much simpler) if you know that each occurrence of the string you're searching for is in a separate field. If this is true, you can use a loop that in pseudo code is

```
OPEN Original File
OPEN Temp File
INPUT Field from Original File
DO UNTIL EOF(Original File)
  IF field <>"QuickBASIC" THEN
    WRITE It to Temp File
  ELSE
    WRITE "Visual Basic" to Temp File
  END IF
  INPUT next field
LOOP
KILL Original File
ReNAME Temp File as Original File
```

Making a File Program Robust: Error Trapping

Usually, when you're testing a program, you don't care if you get a run-time error and your program crashes. However, when an open file is around, then after a crash, strange things may get written into your files or information you need may never get there. Even if you've thoroughly debugged the program, someone may try to send information to a full disk or try to access a file that doesn't exist. To solve these problems, you must stop the program when, for example, it faces a full disk. The command that activates error trapping, as you saw in Chapter 8, is

```
ON LOCAL ERROR GOTO...
```

where the three dots are for the label (line number) that defines the error trap. Now you need to transfer control to a part of the procedure that identifies the problem and, if possible, fixes it.

If the error can be corrected, you can use the RESUME statement to pick up where you left off. However, you can't correct an error if you don't know why it happened. Table 13-1 gives the error codes most common to file-handling programs, and you would use this information just as was outlined in Chapter 8. For example, place the following statement somewhere in the program before the error can occur:

```
ON LOCAL ERROR GOTO DiskCheck
```

Now add code to your event procedure like the fragment given here:

```
Diskcheck:
  ErrorNumber = ERR
  BEEP

  SELECT CASE ErrorNumber
    CASE  53
      PRINT "Your file was not found. Please check on the "
      PRINT "spelling or call your operator for assistance."
```

```
      CASE 61
         PRINT "The disk is full. Please replace with a slightly"
         PRINT "less used model"   'could SHELL to FORMAT.COM here
      CASE 71
         PRINT "I think the drive door is open - please check"
      CASE 72
         PRINT "Possibly big problems on your hard disk. You'd"
         PRINT "better pray that a low level re-format can help - "
         PRINT "definitely time to call for assistance"
      CASE 57
         PRINT "Possibly big problems on your hardware. You"
         PRINT "definitely should call for assistance"
      CASE ELSE
         PRINT "Please tell the operator (= program author?) that"
         PRINT " error number "; ErrorNumber; "occurred."
   END SELECT
   M$ = "If the error has been corrected click on retry."
   M$ = M$ + "Otherwise click on cancel."
   YN% = MsgBox(M$, 5)        'retry/cancel message box
   IF YN% = 4 THEN RESUME ELSE END
```

The idea of this error trap is simple and straightforward thanks to the SELECT CASE statement. Each CASE tries to give some indication of where the problem is and, if possible, how to correct it. If you reach the CASE ELSE, the error number has to be reported. In any case, the final block gives you the option of continuing or not, using a Retry/Cancel message box (Type = 5). (Depending on the situation, you may prefer to replace the PRINT statements with message boxes.)

Error trapping isn't a cure-all. Obviously, very little can be done about a hard disk crash. On the other hand, if you can "shell" to the FORMAT command, then not having a formatted (empty) floppy around is not a crisis for the novice user.

A complete DiskCheck fragment in each of your file-handling programs is the only way to make them robust. Even better, write one general procedure to do all the work and pass the error code to it as a parameter. In any case, writing a serious file-handling program without an error trap is an awful idea.

TABLE	The Most Common Error Codes in File-handling Programs

13-1

Error Code	Explanation
53	File not found (probably a typo)
55	File already open (You obviously can't open again what is already open unless you use a different identification number.)
57	Device I/O error (Big problems! Your hardware is acting up. I/O stands for Input/Output, but check the disk drive anyway.)
61	Disk full (not enough room to do what you want)
62	Input past end of file (You put the test for EOF in the wrong place.)
64	Bad file name (You didn't follow the DOS naming conventions for a file name.)
67	Too many files (maximum number of open files is determined by CONFIG.SYS)
70	Permission denied (The disk you're writing to has the write-protect notch covered.)
71	Disk not ready (The disk drive door is opened, or where's the floppy?)
72	Disk media error (Time to throw out the floppy or start thinking about the state of your hard disk.)
76	Path not found (Probably a typo—you asked to open a file on a nonexistent path.)

Random-access Files

Suppose you are tired of having to search through entire cassettes for certain songs. To avoid this, you decide to put songs that you want instant access to on individual cassettes. The advantages of doing this are obvious, but there are disadvantages as well. First, to gain more or less instant access to an individual song, you're going to waste a considerable amount of blank tape on each cassette. If, to prevent this, you decide to create a standard size tape—one that holds, say, four minutes—you're sure to have at least a couple of songs that run more than four minutes.

It's clear that no matter what you do, you'll either waste space or have a few songs that won't fit. Also, if you single out too many songs for separate tapes, you increase the number of cassettes you have to store. If you have hundreds of tapes, each containing an individual song, then you're almost back where you started. It can't possibly be easy to find an individual song if you have to search through a hundred tapes. At this point you would probably choose to alphabetize the tapes by some key feature (such as singer or title), set up an index, or both.

Random-access files are stored on a disk in such a way that they have much the same advantages and disadvantages as the song collector's tapes. You gain instant access to individual pieces of information, but only at some cost. You must standardize the packets of information involved, which means that some things may not fit or that space is not efficiently used, and if the file grows too big—with too many pieces of information—you'll have to set up another file to index the first.

When setting up a sequential file, it's occasionally useful to think of a group of fields as forming a single record. For example, grouping the fields by fives gave a logical and convenient way to read back the information contained in the grade book program. It's worth stressing that this particular grouping was not intrinsic to the file—it's only one of many ways to look at the file. The only intrinsic divisions within a sequential file are those created by the delimiters (commas or carriage return/line feed combinations). When you read back information, you read it field by field, with the delimiters acting as barriers.

In a random-access file, however, the notion of a record is built in. A *random-access file* is a special disk file arranged by records. This lets you immediately move to the 15th record without having to pass through the 14 before it, which saves a considerable amount of time.

When you first set up a random-access file, you specify the maximum length for each record. And when you go to fill up an individual record, you may, of course, put in less information than this preset limit, but you may never put in more. So just like the song collector, you might need to prepare for the worst possible situation.

The command that sets up a random-access file is analogous to the one for opening a sequential file. For example,

```
OPEN "Sample.Rnd" AS #5 LEN = 100
```

opens a random-access file called SAMPLE.RND on the current directory with a file ID of 5, and each record can hold 100 bytes (characters). Note that unlike the situation for sequential files, you don't have to specify whether you're opening the file for input, output, or appending. As you'll soon see, this distinction is taken care of in the commands that manipulate a random-access file; an open random-access file can be read from and written to essentially simultaneously. You can have any mixture of random-access and sequential files open at the same time. The only restrictions are set by DOS (the FILES command in your CONFIG.SYS file). To prevent confusion between file types, many programmers use an extension like .RND for all random-access files, as in the preceding example.

Similarly, you close a file opened for random access by using the CLOSE command followed by the file ID number. As before, the CLOSE command alone closes all open files, regardless of whether they were opened for sequential or random access. This is especially useful because a sophisticated program for random files often has many files open simultaneously—both sequential and random.

Suppose you want to write a random-access file that would keep track of someone's library. You start by designing the form. You decide on five categories—AUTHOR, TITLE, SUBJECT, PUBLISHER, and MISCELLANEOUS, and after looking over your library, you decide on the following limits for the categories:

Category	Size
AUTHOR	20
TITLE	30
SUBJECT	15
PUBLISHER	20
MISCELLANEOUS	13

Therefore, the total for each record is 98. A random-access file to fit this form is set up (via FileNum = FREEFILE, as always):

```
OPEN "MYLIB.RND" AS #FileNum LEN = 98
```

Just as each file has an ID number, each record within a random-access file has a record number. A single random-access file can hold from

1 to 16,777,216 records. Moreover, you don't have to fill the records in order. As you'll see, you can place information in the 15th record without ever having touched the first 14. The disadvantage of doing this, however, is that Visual Basic would automatically set aside enough space for the first 14 records on the disk, even if nothing was in them. Worse, you could get a bunch of junk (or old deleted stuff)!

The word "record" has been used frequently in this chapter. This is no coincidence. One of the main reasons QuickBASIC and then Visual Basic implemented record types was to simplify working with random-access files. First, set up a type:

```
TYPE BookInfo
  Author AS STRING * 20
  Title AS STRING * 30
  Subject AS STRING * 15
  Publisher AS STRING * 20
  Miscellaneous AS STRING * 13
END TYPE
```

Next, suppose ExampleOfBook has been declared by the statement

```
DIM ExampleOfBook AS BookInfo
```

Then the command

```
GET #FileNum, 10, ExampleOfBook
```

would transfer the contents of the 10th record from the random-access file into the record variable ExampleOfBook, automatically filling in the correct components of ExampleOfBook.

The command

```
PUT #FileNum, 37, ExampleOfBook
```

would send the components of ExampleofBook to the 37th record of file #FileNum.

This method of sending information to a random-access file is unique to QuickBASIC and Visual Basic, and it's a very valuable improvement over older PC-BASIC.

The record types you create determine the size of the random-access file. Since records can hold numbers as well as character strings, it's a bit messy to compute the length of a record variable of a given record type. (You have to remember that an integer takes 2 bytes, a long integer 4, and so on.) Visual Basic will do all the work for you, however, because the LEN command not only gives the length of a string, it gives you the length of a record as well. Take any variable of the given type—for example,

```
DIM ExampleOfRecord AS ThisType
LenOfRecord = LEN(ExampleOfRecord)
```

and use this to set the length for the OPEN command used to create the random-access file.

Headers and Indexes for Random-access Files

If you have the information you want to transfer to a newly created random-access file stored in an array of records, you can use a loop to transfer the information. The loop counter determines where to put the record. Usually, however, you set up a variable whose value is the number of the next record you want to read from or write to.

Similarly, you could read back all the information in a random-access file by using the EOF function:

```
' Records is declared by a statement of the form
' DIM Records(1 TO 1000) AS RecordType
DO UNTIL EOF(FileNum)
  I = I + 1
  GET #FileNum, I, Records(I)
LOOP
```

There are many problems with doing this. For one, you're unlikely to want all the information contained in the file at once, and it may not fit anyway—suppose you have 1,000,000 records. Also, go back to square one: how do you even know what length to use to open the random-access file? While there are many ways to determine this, a common practice is to set up another file that contains this (and other) vital information about the random-access file. At the very least, this sequential file will contain information about the sizes and types of the fields, possibly names for the fields, and the number of records stored to date. In fact, it may even contain an index of certain keys and the numbers of the records that contain those keys.

Indexes are vital to a random-access file. A data base manager is nothing more than an elaborate program to manage random-access files. Its speed depends on how the program finds the record containing keyed information. This can only be done effectively through indexes. (The alternative is to examine the relevant component of each record one by one.)

An index can be as simple as a sequential file containing a list of keys followed by a record number, or it can be a more elaborately ordered one.

Note For heavy duty database management, we recommend using Visual Basic Professional, whose ISAM (Indexed Sequential Access Method) feature automatically creates and manages indexes.

Binary Files

Binary files are not a new type of file but a new way of manipulating any kind of file. Binary file techniques let you read or change any byte of a file. Among other features, binary file techniques do not care about any embedded EOFs (CTRL+Z = CHR$(26)) that the file may have. (Recall that it was impossible to read back the file created earlier in the chapter using sequential file techniques because of the presence of CTRL+Z characters in the file.) A command of the form

OPEN "*FileName*" FOR BINARY AS #*FileNum*

sets up a file to be read with these new techniques.

Just as with random-access files, you can now both read and write to the file. For example, one way to pick up the information from a file open in binary file mode is with the INPUT$ function you saw earlier. This command works the same way for binary file techniques. The first slot still holds the number of characters and the second the file ID number. For example, the following listing gives a procedure that prints the contents of any file, regardless of any embedded control characters:

```
SUB PrintAFile (A$)
DIM I AS INTEGER, FileNum AS INTEGER
DIM Char$

' example of binary input
FileNum = FREEFILE            ' get free file i.d.
OPEN A$ FOR BINARY AS #FileNum

FOR I = 1 TO LOF(FileNum)
  Char$ = INPUT$(1, #FileNum)
  PRINT Char$;
NEXT I
CLOSE #FileNum
END SUB
```

More often than not, however, you'll want to modify this procedure by adding some filtering lines—for example, to make it strip out characters where the high-order bit is set (ASCII codes greater than 127) or all the control characters (ASCII values less than 32) except for the carriage return/line feed pair CHR$(13)+CHR$(10). Once you strip such a file, it can be displayed with the DOS TYPE command or more easily sent by a modem.

For example, the WordStar word processing program normally stores a file in such a way that when you use the DOS TYPE command, you would have trouble reading the file. Stated simply, here's what Wordstar does:

❑   It uses certain control codes inside the file (such as CTRL+B for bold).

❑   Each word-wrapped line ends with CHR$(141)+CHR$(10). Note that 141 = 13 + 128, thus 141 corresponds to a carriage return with the high-order bit set. Also, the first letter of each word in a word-wrapped line may have its high-order bit set.

❑   Wordstar uses the carriage return/line feed combination (CHR$(13)+CHR$(10)) for hard returns. This means that someone pressed ENTER rather than that the program did a word wrap.

It's easy to modify the procedure given earlier to strip out all formatting (control) codes and convert back characters with their high-order bits set. (For those who do use Wordstar, the procedure will not strip out dot

commands; the changes needed for that are left to you.) Here's how to
modify the procedure:

```
SUB StripAFile (A$)
DIM FileNum AS INTEGER, I AS INTEGER
DIM Char$

' example of binary input
  FileNum = FREEFILE                    ' get free file i.d.
  OPEN A$ FOR BINARY AS #FileNum
  FOR I = 1 TO LOF(FileNum)
    Char$ = INPUT$(1, #FileNum)
    ' strip high-order bit, if any
    IF ASC(Char$) > 127 THEN
      CharCode = ASC(Char$)
      Char$ = CHR$(CharCode - 128)
    END IF
    ' ignore all control codes except line feed
    IF Char$ >= CHR$(32) THEN
      PRINT Char$
    ELSEIF Char$ = CHR$(10) THEN
      'issue a CHR$(13) and a CHR$(10)
      PRINT
    END IF
  NEXT I
END SUB
```

Of course, in a more general program, you'd probably want to do
something more than print the character.

Visual Basic maintains a file pointer within a file opened for binary
access. Each time you use INPUT$(*CharCount, #FileNum*) the file pointer
moves *CharCount* positions farther ahead in the file. The SEEK command
is a fast forward command and a rewind command combined into one.
More precisely,

SEEK #*FileNum, PositionNum*

moves the file pointer for the file with ID *FileNum* directly to the byte at
position *PositionNum*. (The beginning of the file corresponds to a position
number of 1.) Any INPUT$ would start picking up characters from this
location.

SEEK has another use. The function SEEK(*filenum*) tells you the
position number for the last byte read for either a binary or sequential

file. You can also use the SEEK function with random-access files, in which case it will return the record number of the next record.

To place information into a file opened for binary access, use a modification of the PUT command. For example,

```
PUT #1, 100, A$
```

would place the contents of the string value directly into the file with file ID #1 starting at the 100th byte. The number of characters sent to this file is, of course, given by LEN(A$). The PUT command overwrites whatever was there. If you leave a space for the byte position but don't specify it in the PUT command, like this:

```
PUT #1, , A$
```

then the information is placed wherever the file pointer is currently located. If the file was just opened this is byte number 1.

The GET command also works with a binary file. Here, though, you are best off dimensioning the variable as a fixed-length string. This is because the command

GET *FileNum, Position,* A$

picks up only as many characters as is the current length of A$. (You could use normal string variables if you were careful to initialize them to have the correct length.)

Now that you know the commands for working on the byte level for a file, you're in a position to write any file utility you like. You also now can use the information contained in a book like *File Formats for Popular PC Software, second edition,* by Jeff Walden (New York: John Wiley & Sons, 1991). The manual to your favorite program probably contains this information as well. Now you can massage the output of any application program.

Tip   Binary file techniques work much faster if you do not read a single character in at a time. The optimum setting seems to be in 4096 character "chunks". Then analyze the characters in the string after they've picked up the information contained in the file.

Keeping File Information Secret

Since a simple utility program using binary file techniques can read back the information contained in any file, the data contained in your files is readily available to anyone with a compatible computer, a little programming skill, and a copy of your disk. In the next few sections you'll see how to encode a file so that only people having the right key can easily read your file. The methods here aren't perfect, but considering how easy they are to implement, they are surprisingly secure.

First, a little history. All the earliest ciphers that we know about use simple substitutions. For example, Julius Caesar kept his messages secret by taking each letter in the message and replacing it with the one three letters further on; the letter "A" would be replaced by "D," "B" by "E," and so on, until you got to the letters after "X." Since "X" is the 24th letter of the alphabet, you have to wrap around to the beginning of the alphabet, and "X" becomes "A," "Y" becomes "B," and "Z" becomes "C." Here is a normal alphabet and below it a complete Caesar alphabet:

```
ABCDEFGHIJKLMNOPQRSTUVWXYZ
DEFGHIJKLMNOPQRSTUVWXYZABC
```

(Actually, in Caesar's time, the alphabet had fewer letters—23 instead of 26. For example, "U" and "V" developed out of "V" around a thousand years ago, and "J" came around 500 years after that.) For example, the sentence, "Can you read this" becomes

```
FDQ BRX UHDG WKLV
```

Shift ciphers go back further than Caesar; one occurs in the Old Testament. In Jeremiah 25-26, the prophet conceals his prophecy by changing the name of Babylon using a cipher that splits the Hebrew alphabet in half and replaces the first letter with the middle letter, the second by the middle + 1, and so on.

Here is a general procedure that shifts any character by any number of characters, wrapping around if necessary.

```
SUB CaesarShift (A$, Shift%)
  DIM CharNum AS INTEGER
```

```
   CharNum = (ASC(A$) + Shift%) MOD 256
   A$ = CHR$(CharNum)
END SUB
```

It wouldn't be hard to incorporate this procedure into a file encrypter; just pass the procedure the contents of the file character by character. The trouble is that a shift cipher is easy to break; you can even do it by hand. Look at the coded message and run back down the alphabet by steps, shifting the letters back step by step. After, at most, 25 steps, you're done. Here's what you get at each step in the example:

```
FDQ BRX UHDG WKLV
ECP AQW TGCF VJKU
DBO ZPV SFBE UIJT
CAN YOU READ THIS
```

Note that it's better to work with the whole message than with individual words because occasionally English words (*clear text*) show up by mistake. For example, the word "HTQI" backs up to the word "FROG" on the second try and to the word "COLD" on the fifth.

Decoding a Caesar cipher, simple as it is, stresses the usefulness of the computer and its limitations. It can do the drudgery, but you have to recognize when to stop. For the more complicated ciphers described in what follows, this division of labor is essential.

More Complicated Ciphers

Since a shift cipher provides virtually no security, the next step is to change the letters in a more random manner. Write down the alphabet and below it write all the letters in some arbitrary order:

```
ABCDEFGHIJKLMNOPQRSTUVWXYZ
QAZXSWEDCVFRBGTYHNUJMIKOPL
```

Now, every time you see an "A" in your original message, replace it with a "Q", replace each "B" with an "A," each "C" with a "Z," and so on. This cipher can't be broken by the techniques used for shift ciphers, but it's extremely hard to remember the random alphabet used for the code. Around 1600, in an attempt to combine the virtues of this method with the ease of shift codes, people began to use a keyword cipher. The idea is to replace the letters of the alphabet with the letters in the key phrase, using the order in which they occur there. For example, suppose the key is THE RAY GUN ZAPPED ME QUICKLY. Now look at the following:

```
ABCDEFGHIJKLMNOPQRSTUVWXYZ
THERAYGUNZPDMQICKLBFJOSVWX
```

What this does is take the individual letters from the key phrase, avoiding duplicates as needed, and place them below the normal alphabet. Since the phrase contains only 18 different letters, the unused letters went at the end. To encipher a message using this code, replace the letters in the original message with the ones directly below them—"A" with "T", "B" with "H," and so on.

Here's one possible outline for a procedure that takes a key phrase and creates the code:

```
Get keyphrase
  Run through each letter in key phrase
  Check if already used
    if not used:
    store in next place in 'cipher' list
    mark that letter as used
  Until no more letters are in the keyphrase
Now store unused letters from normal alphabet into key
```

However, this outline turns out to not quite be the best way of proceeding. For example, suppose you want to decipher a message enciphered this way. Say you see an "A" in the coded message; then, because an "A" is below an "E" in the alphabets just given, the original letter must have been an E.

To set up the two lists to be used for encoding and decoding, start with two ordinary alphabets, Now, since "T" replaces "A," you swap the "A" in the first alphabet with the "T" in the second. Next, you swap the "B" and the "H." How can you tell if a letter is already used? Just look at that letter's position in the second alphabet. If the letter is still in its original position, that letter has not been used. When you are done with the letters in the key phrase, any remaining letters should be swapped out of the first alphabet into the second one.

To actually write this program, set up two lists. To make life easier, use two form level arrays of integers dimensioned to run from 65 to 90 (the ASCII codes for A-Z):

```
DIM SHARED EncodeAlph() AS INTEGER, DecodeAlph() AS INTEGER
```

Now call an initialize procedure:

```
SUB Initialize ()
  DIM I AS INTEGER
  REDIM EncodeAlph(65 TO 90) AS INTEGER
  REDIM DecodeAlph(65 TO 90) AS INTEGER

  FOR I = 65 TO 90
    EncodeAlph(I) = I
    DecodeAlph(I) = I
  NEXT I
END SUB
```

Now you can write the SUB that makes both lists by translating the preceding outline. To do that, you need to keep track of where you are in the original alphabet because that determines where the letter will go. Suppose you call this variable PosOfLet. Each time you use a letter from the key, swap the letter determined by this position number with its counterpart in the other alphabet, determined from the key, and increase PosOfLet by one. The tricky part comes when you've used up all the letters in the key. Then you have to decide where to put the remaining letters from the first alphabet. The problems come because there is no convenient pointer to the unused letters in the second alphabet. To take care of this, set the letters you use to the negative of their ASCII values. For example, if "X", "Y," and "Z" were the only letters not used in the key, then they would be the only ones that were still positive in the Decode alphabet.

```
SUB Makelists (Key$)
  'Uses global variables EncodeAlph(), DecodeAlph()
  'local variables
  DIM LenKey AS INTEGER, PosOfLetUsed AS INTEGER
  DIM I AS INTEGER, A AS INTEGER
  DIM A1$

  LenKey = LEN(Key$)
  PosOfLetUsed = 65                       'start with ASC("A")
```

```
FOR I = 1 TO LenKey
   A1$ = MID$(Key$, I, 1): A1$ = UCASE$(A1$)
   SELECT CASE A$
    CASE "A" TO "Z"
      A = ASC(A$)
      IF DecodeAlph(A) = A THEN          'character not yet used
         EncodeAlph(PosOfLetUsed) = A
         DecodeAlph(A) = -PosOfLetUsed 'swap the encode/decode
                                        'and flag a used char
         PosOfLetUsed = PosOfLetUsed + 1
      END IF
    CASE ELSE
      ' not a letter - of course you can
      ' do something with these too
   END SELECT
NEXT I
' Now throw in unused letters
' This loop should end if you've used up all 26 letters or
' you can't find any new letters to swap
FOR I = 65 TO 90                 ' start looking in second alph
                                 ' here.
   IF DecodeAlph(I) = I THEN
      EncodeAlph(PosOfLetUsed) = I
      DecodeAlph(I) = -PosOfLetUsed     'swap the encode / decode
      PosOfLetUsed = PosOfLetUsed + 1
   END IF
NEXT I
END SUB
```

Now, encoding or decoding a letter is almost a trivial task. Suppose you wanted to encode a "C" (ASCII code 67). Then you have to look at the value of Encode(67) to find the ASCII for the coded version. Similarly (and this is the nice part), to decode a "C" you just have to look at the absolute value of the entry in Decode(67). Thus, you can pass the appropriate array as a parameter and use the following listing:

```
SUB EncodeDecode (A(), X$)
DIM X1 AS INTEGER, Y$
  X1 = ASC(UCASE$(X$))
  X  = CHR$(ABS(A(X)))
END SUB
```

A More Practical Cipher

Having spent all of the previous section on a fairly subtle program to create a keyword cipher, you might expect it to be secure—or at least difficult to break. (It does work quickly, though.) Unfortunately, any substitution cipher can be broken, given enough text. In fact, assuming the encoded text was originally written in standard, everyday English, it's pretty easy if you have, say, a thousand words of encoded text. The key to breaking a substitution code is that letters do not exist in isolation. "E" is almost certainly the most common letter, "T" is likely to be the next most common, and "A" is likely to be third highest. Over the years, cryptographers have examined thousands of pages of texts to determine the frequency of letters in standard English. The problem with a simple substitution cipher is that if you always replace a letter with the same symbol, someone can break it by using frequency analysis.

One way to avoid this method of breaking a code is to change the substitution. Instead of always replacing, say, an "E" with the letter "T," use a "T" the first time and a "Z" the next. This way, each time an "E" occurs, it is replaced with another letter. This method is called a *multi-alphabet substitution cipher.* It's much more difficult to break this cipher, but it's also much more difficult to set up. After all, you have to devise a way of getting these multiple alphabets.

However, you can use the built-in random number generator in Visual Basic to generate the alphabets. Recall that the command

```
X = RND
```

gives you a different random number between zero and 1. However—and this is the key to breaking the cipher—given enough data, a professional cryptographer (or a good amateur) can find out the next number in the sequence. Cryptographers would say the random number generator in Visual Basic isn't "cryptographically secure." Finding (and then proving that you have) a cryptographically secure random number generator is probably the most important problem in cryptography.

The idea for the cipher that follows is that you scale this number and use it to determine the "Caesar shift." Now, instead of using the same shift for the next letter, use the random number generator to get a different shift for each letter. Each time you encode a letter, it's transformed differently.

Unfortunately, this method won't quite work. Since the patterns don't obviously repeat (that's what is meant by "random"), there isn't any reasonable method of decoding the message. You would never know what to shift back by. You have to modify this idea slightly. The first idea that might come to mind is that the RND function when given a negative number as an argument is supposed to give a repeatable sequence. This means if you precede all other uses of RND with a statement of the form

A = RANDOMIZE *Seed*

where *Seed* is a negative number, then Visual Basic is always supposed to give you the same sequence of random numbers. Each seed is *supposed* to gives a different, repeatable sequence of random numbers. *Unfortunately, because of a bug in the current version of Visual Basic this won't work.* You need to modify this somewhat. To get a repeatable sequence of random numbers, you must have Visual Basic process the following statement before generating the next random number in the sequence:

X = RND(the negative number)

To use random Caesar shifts you need only ask the user for a key—say, a four-digit number. Use this to reseed the random number generator:

```
A = RND(-Key)
```

Now you can generate a list of shifts, one for each character in the file:

```
NextShift = INT(256 * RND)
```

Use these shifts just like in a Caesar cipher—call this shift generator for each letter in the message.

Now the question is how to decode. The whole point of repeatability is that if you process the command

```
X = RND(-Key)
```

again, then when you generate Caesar shifts, you get the same series of numbers you did before. And just as before, if you know what the original shift was, you can reverse it just as easily.

However rather than using this idea as is, there's a more elegant and faster way to proceed. For this recall from the bit twiddling section of Chapter 7 that the XOR operator has the nice property that if

```
B = A XOR Shift
```

and you do it again:

```
C = B XOR Shift
```

then the value of C is the same as the original value of A. Thus, by XORing twice, you get back to where you started. This means you can use the same procedure to both encode and decode. Here's the procedure to do that:

```
SUB EncodeDecode (FileName$, KeyValue)
  ' local variables:
  DIM FileNum AS INTEGER, X AS SINGLE, I AS INTEGER
  DIM CharNum AS INTEGER, RandomInteger AS INTEGER
  DIM SingleChar As STRING * 1             'for use in GET and PUT

  X = RND(-KeyValue)
  FileNum = FREEFILE
  OPEN FileName$ FOR BINARY AS #FileNum
    FOR I = 1 TO LOF(FileNum)
    GET #FileNum, I, SingleChar
    CharNum = ASC(SingleChar)
    RandomInteger = INT(256 * RND)
    CharNum = CharNum XOR RandomInteger 'this is it
    SingleChar = CHR$(CharNum)
    PUT #FileNum, I, SingleChar
  NEXT I
  CLOSE FileNum
  END SUB
```

As mentioned before you will find that the program works faster if you read the information from the file in larger (4096 character) chunks. You may also choose the improved version of the random number generator given in Chapter 9 to make this even more secure.

CHAPTER

Advanced Topics

The purpose of this chapter is to show you some advanced topics that, for one reason or another, didn't find a home elsewhere in the book. This chapter will also give you the tools to understand (and so be able to write) sophisticated multiple-form programs, such as the finance program discussed in the next chapter.

Learning About Multiple Forms

When you start working with sophisticated programs, you won't want to restrict yourself to applications that use only one form. Being limited to only one form presents problems that are over and above those you saw in Chapter 4—problems such as controls blocking out text that you might want to display on a form.

A single form, along with its procedures, is called a *form module*. When you use the ALT+F S (Save Form) option, Visual Basic assigns the extension .FRM to a single file name. On the other hand, as you've already seen, if you use the ALT+F V (Save Project) option, Visual Basic produces an additional file whose name includes the extension .MAK. The .MAK (*make*) file, in this case, contains just the name of the .FRM file.

Programs can contain several forms. In multiple-form programs, each form is saved in its own .FRM file and its name is added to the .MAK file when you use the Save Project option. The .MAK file keeps the path names of all the files so that Visual Basic can reconstruct the project later on unless the form files are stored in the current directory.

You create multiple forms from the File menu in the same way that you create a program that uses only one form: choose NewForm from the file menu and specify the name of the form file. When you load a project that uses multiple forms, the Project window lists all the forms in the file. Figure 14-1 shows the list for a project with three forms. (As you can see, the files were saved under the names FORM1.FRM, FORM2.FRM, and FORM3.FRM—these are the names that appear in the Project window.)

The easiest way to move to the form designer and work with a form in a program that uses multiple forms is to double-click the appropriate form name in the Project window. Another method is to use the View Form option and to choose the name of the form from the Forms dialog box that pops up.

FIGURE
14-1

A sample project window

Writing Code for Programs That Contain Multiple Forms

Although a form does not have a control name that you use for writing code for event procedures, it does have a FormName property that serves the same role. If you use the properties bar to give forms meaningful names, understanding references to different properties or methods that apply to a form will be easier.

The default value for this property starts at Form1 for the first form, Form2 for the second form, and so on. Using the default value means that it is more obscure when you have to refer to properties when you code. For example:

```
Form3.Height = 10    'set height to 10 lines high
```

If Form3 is your "Help Form," the code will be a lot easier to read if you set the form name to HelpForm and enter

```
HelpForm.Height = 10  'set help height to 10 lines
```

Form names are used only in code to refer to properties and methods; they are not used for event procedures. For example, to apply the CLS (clear screen) method to the preceding form in code belonging to that form, you can enter either

```
HelpForm.CLS
```

or

```
CLS
```

On the other hand, regardless of how you name a form, the Click procedure template for the form itself will always look like this in the Code window:

```
SUB Form_Click ()

END SUB
```

This rarely causes problems, since event procedures for a form are attached to the form.

It is possible to have code in one form refer to properties and controls in another form. To do this, you must use the form's name. In any case, even in event procedures, using the form name can make your code cleaner. For example, suppose your HelpForm had a Quit button you wanted to disable via code within an event procedure attached to the HelpForm. Even in event procedures attached to the HelpForm, the code

```
HelpForm.Quit.Enabled = 0        ' or FALSE
```

is clearer and, therefore, easier to debug than

```
Quit.Enabled = 0
```

although both have the same effect if used in code of the HelpForm module. The general syntax is

FormName.ControlName.Property = Value

Coding for Multiple Forms

The four keywords that pertain to the handling of forms are SHOW, LOAD, HIDE, and UNLOAD.

SHOW   The SHOW keyword causes the form to appear on the screen. To do this, Visual Basic first checks that the form is loaded into memory. If it is not, it loads the form. The basic syntax for the SHOW method is

FormName.SHOW

The SHOW method also moves the form to the top of the desktop if the form was covered by another form.

LOAD   The LOAD keyword places the form into memory but does not display it. Visual Basic also loads the form into memory whenever you refer to its properties or controls in code. Because of this, the main reason to load a form prior to showing it is to speed up response time. The trade-off is that using LOAD takes more memory. The syntax for using the keyword is

LOAD *FormName*

When Visual Basic loads a form, it sets all the properties of the form according to the decisions you made at design time. You can use the Form_Load, Form_Paint, or Form_Resize procedure as needed to modify properties.

HIDE   The HIDE keyword removes the form from the screen but doesn't unload it from memory. The controls are not available to the user, but you can still refer to them in code. The values of the form-level variables do not disappear. As with loading a form, hiding a form speeds response and uses memory. The syntax is

FormName.HIDE

UNLOAD   The UNLOAD keyword removes the form from memory and destroys all information in form-level variables. The syntax for this command is

UNLOAD *FormName*

The $FORM Metacommand

When you refer to one form in the event procedures attached to another form, Visual Basic needs to know that the reference is a form name and not a variable name. The $FORM metacommand allows Visual Baasic to make this distinction. The program uses $FORM much as it uses DECLARE statements for Function procedures.

Putting in the $FORM metacommands manually is usually unnecessary. Just as Visual Basic adds DECLARE statements automatically, it automatically adds $FORM metacommands to each module that refers to other forms in the current project. Usually, you need to worry about a $FORM metacommand only if you write Visual Basic code away from the programming environment. In such a situation, you can avoid problems by creating an include file that contains all the nonexecutable statements—including the $FORM metacommands.

The StartUp Form

When you work with an application that uses multiple forms, one form must be specified as the startup form. This is the form invoked when the program is first executed. By default, the startup form is the first form you create for the specific project. You can change this by pressing ALT+R F (Set Start-up File). This opens up a dialog box, as shown in Figure 14-2.

FIGURE 14-2   The dialog box that appears after choosing Set Start-up File

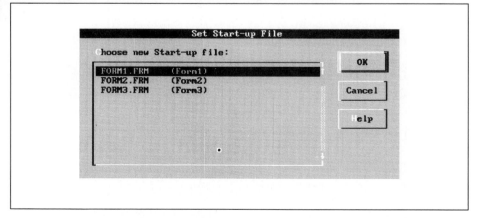

You can now reset the StartUp form by making the appropriate selections from this dialog box. The startup form is listed first in the project window.

An Application with Multiple Forms: An Example

To see an example of an application with multiple forms, create a project with two forms and add a command button to each form. The command button on the first form should move the second form to the left and bring it to the forefront. The command button on the second form should bring the first form back to the top, without moving it from its original place. For illustration purposes, do not change the default names for objects.

To make the command button for the first form work, you need to enter the following code:

```
SUB Command1_Click ()
  ' Moves the second form around and displays it
  Form2.SHOW
  Form2.Left = Form2.Left - 5
END SUB
```

Because the control name is deliberately not meaningful, the event procedure for the second command button starts off just like the first:

```
SUB Command1_Click ()
  ' Show original form
  Form1.SHOW
END SUB
```

The control names were unchanged to make the point that this is sloppy programming. Although Visual Basic would know which Command1_Click procedure belonged where, in a more sophisticated program, such a practice would create an obvious breeding ground for confusion. Even if the form names are mnemonic, use a control name like Form2Shift for the first command button and Form1ToTop for the second. (You will probably want to set the caption properties to explain the actions of the buttons, as well.)

Keeping the Focus in a Form (Modality)

Message boxes have a property that requires users to close them before they can work with a form. The Visual Basic documentation calls this property *modality.* Modality is often useful for a form as well as a message box. For example, you may want to make sure a user has digested the information contained in a form before he or she shifts the focus to another form in the application. A form with the property of modality is often called a *dialog box.* To make a form modal, add an option to the SHOW method that displays the form. For example, the procedure code

```
FormName.SHOW 1
```

causes Visual Basic to display the form "rigidly," or as a modal form. No user input to any other form in the application will be accepted until the modal form is hidden or unloaded. In particular, neither mouse clicks nor keypresses will register in any other form. Usually, the screen offers a cancel command button that the user can click to hide or unload the form. In any case, you must provide some way for the user to close the modal form; otherwise, the application just sits there, inert.

Forms are nonmodal by default, but you can use the following code to force them to be nonmodal:

```
FormName.SHOW 0
```

The convention is that modal forms (dialog boxes) are neither movable nor sizable. For this reason, you will generally use the following settings for them:

Property Setting	Effect
BorderStyle = 1,3,5	The border is fixed single, fixed double, or fixed solid, so the box isn't sizable.
Border style = 0	The box has no border, so it isn't movable. (Use a frame or picture box that fills up the form to give the effect of a border.)
MaxButton = False	The form can't be maximized.
MinButton = False	The form can't be minimized.

Property Setting	Effect
ControlBox = False	The form doesn't have a control box. (Note: you must provide a way for keyboard users to get rid of the form!)

Visual Basic comes supplied with many standard dialog boxes (forms). See the section called "Common Dialog Boxes," later in this chapter.

Learning About MDI Forms

MDI stands for *multiple document interface*, which is Microsoft's term for a "windowing" environment (that is, an environment like Visual Basic), where one window contains many other windows. The windows within the larger window are usually called *child windows*. The surrounding window is usually called the *MDI container form*. For example, you can use MDI container forms to allow a user to work with two separate windows in the same application.

An MDI container form takes up the whole screen. The user can't resize the container form, although he or she can minimize the form so that an icon appears as a representation of it. Each project can have only one MDI container form, and that form must, naturally enough, be the startup form. On the MDI container form, you cannot place any controls except menu controls.

To make a form an MDI container form, set the form's FormType property to 1 (= MDI) from the properties bar in the form designer. From that point, any forms you add to the project become child forms to the MDI container form. You will have to use the SHOW method to explicitly load and display the child forms. If you use the LOAD method to unload the container form, all the child forms are also unloaded; you can hide, show, or unload child forms independently of each other, however.

One of the nicest features of working with Visual Basic MDI forms is that menus change according to which child form the user is focusing on. The menus for the relevant child form appear on the menu bar of the MDI container form, replacing whatever menu was there previously. The user sees only the menu for the child form he or she is working with.

Creating Code Modules

As you have learned, a single form and the procedures that relate to it are called a form module. There is another type of module called a *code module.* Other names for a code module are *.BAS module* and *BASIC module.* The most common code modules consist of several procedures that may contain nonexecuting statements (such as DIM SHARED statements) in the leading code. Of course, the procedures are activated with CALL statements rather than events. To create a code module, go to the code environment and press ALT+F M for New Module. Previously created modules saved on a disk can be added from the File menu by selecting Add File (ALT+F D).

Code modules *can* contain executable statements in their leading code. However, these statements will only be executed if the code module is specified as the startup module. You can also place the older-style DEF FN functions or error handlers in the leading code of a code module.

When a project is saved, the .MAK file holds the path names of the .FRM files and the .BAS files. The collection of files is called a *project.* You open an existing project by pressing ALT+F O and then selecting the .MAK file.

Understanding the Scope of Procedures

Where you put a procedure determines which parts of the project can use it. If you attach a general procedure to a form, the procedure will be usable only by procedures attached to the form. However, if you put the procedure in a code module, the procedure will be available to the whole project.

When you use a Sub or Function procedure inside another procedure, Visual Basic follows very simple steps to determine where to look for it:

1. Visual Basic first looks at procedures attached to the current module.

2. If the procedure is not found in the current module, Visual Basic looks at all code modules attached to the project.

The second of these steps explains why the name of a procedure must be unique throughout all code modules. On the other hand, the same procedure name can certainly be attached to two different forms; otherwise, forms could not have their own Form_Load() procedures.

Sharing Variables Among Modules

We have regularly used the declaration statement DIM SHARED to make a variable available to all the procedures of a form. An analogous statement, the COMMON SHARED statement, permits the sharing of variables among different modules. If the leading code of each module contains a declaration statement of the form

COMMON SHARED *var1, var2, . . .*

then these *global* variables can be used jointly by all the modules in the project. That is, changes in the values of these variables while one module is executing will be recorded in the other modules. The COMMON SHARED statement passes variables among modules in much the same way procedures pass values by reference. An example of a COMMON SHARED statement is

```
COMMON SHARED Num AS INTEGER, Name$
```

Figure 14-3 shows the scope of variables in Visual Basic projects.

Selecting a Part of a Module

When F2 is pressed, all the parts of the current project are displayed in the code selection window. Below the name of each module is an indented list of its procedures. To place a particular part of a code module or form module in a code window, double-click its name. (Double-clicking the name of a module displays the leading code of the module or form.) To remove a particular part of a module, highlight its name and then activate the Delete button.

FIGURE
14-3

The scope of variables

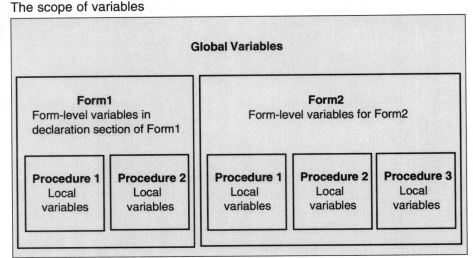

Adding Modules or Code

You can add to your project procedural modules that are stored on a disk. This lets you share code between projects (and often means you won't have to reinvent the wheel). On the other hand, code from one module may conflict with that from another module, especially if you are incorporating other people's code. (For example, if you introduce code written by someone else, you may inadvertently introduce a procedure name that has already been used. Names of procedures in modules must be unique, regardless of how many modules you may have.)

To add an existing module or form, open the File menu and choose the Add File option. A dialog box appears, asking for the name of the file. The convention is that module names include the extension .BAS, which signifies that the modules contain BASIC code. With relatively little work, you can reuse a great deal of Visual Basic code by incorporating the BASIC code into procedural modules.

You can merge a file into your current project if it was saved in text (ASCII) form. To do this:

1. Move to the code window where you want the merged text to be.

2. Choose Load text from the File Menu (ALT+F L).

3. Enter, in the dialog box, the name of the text file.

4. Choose the Merge button.

Removing a Module or Replacing Code

Occasionally, you will need to remove a module from a project. To do this:

1. Open the Project window by clicking any part that's visible or by choosing Project Window from the Window menu (ALT+W P).

2. Select the module or form you want to remove.

3. From the File menu, choose Remove File (ALT+F R).

To replace text in a code window, follow the steps for merging text, which were given in the previous section. This time, however, choose the Replace option rather than the Merge option.

Saving a Module

Once you create a procedural module, saving it to disk is easy. When you are working with the module, open the File menu and choose Save File As (use ALT+F A). You'll be presented with a dialog box. Type the path name for the module and press ENTER; Visual Basic will do the work. However, as in all the File menu operations, Visual Basic will save the code in a binary format not usually readable by other programs. To save the code for the entire module in ASCII form, choose the Save Text option. Or choose the Print option on the File menu, but print to a file rather than the printer.

Making Include Files

The $INCLUDE metacommand tells Visual Basic to treat statements in an external file as if they were part of the program. The names of include files usually contain the extension .BI (which stands for "BASIC include"). Typically, include files are used for storing declarations and COMMON statements. To create a .BI file, open a new .BAS module, type the statements you want to be part of the include file, and use ALT+F A to save them as a text file whose name contains the extension .BI.

Visual Basic looks for include files in the current directory as well as in the directory set from the Options menu Set Paths item.

Form Activation from a Startup Code Module

Instead of choosing a form as the startup module, suppose you use a code module. To show a form and activate its events, you must execute a statement such as

FormName.SHOW 1

in your code module. Execution of the code module will continue only when the form is hidden or unloaded.

Note If a QuickBasic program adheres to Visual Basic's naming conventions and has been saved in ASCII format, you can open it in the Visual Basic environment. This code module will run just as it would in the QuickBasic environment.

Common Dialog Boxes: An Example

By adding one code module, or BASIC module, and one form module to your projects, you can use Visual Basic's kit of common dialog boxes. Visual Basic includes pre-defined dialog boxes for seven common operations in a file called CMNDLGF.FRM:

☐ Opening files

☐ Saving files

- ☐   Printing files

- ☐   Finding text

- ☐   Changing text

- ☐   Using the color palette

- ☐   Using a generic About box

Note   Although the procedures that create pre-defined dialog boxes supply the user interface and return user input, you must still supply code to perform the actual operations desired. Visual Basic does supply code samples, however, and these samples are easy to modify.

   If you load the file CMNDLGF.FRM in the form designer, you'll see that the form it creates contains multiple picture boxes. Each picture box contains the controls needed for that dialog box. When you use the correct Sub procedure to create and display a specific common dialog box, Visual Basic makes the picture box for that dialog box visible. Moreover, the form is automatically centered and resized to match the dialog box (the picture box container).

FileOpen   Figure 14-4 shows the dialog box that FileOpen creates. As with all the common dialog boxes, you create this box by using CALL to call a special Sub procedure contained in the CMNDLG.BAS module. The syntax for this Sub is

CALL FileOpen (*FileName* AS STRING, *PathName* AS STRING, *DefaultExt* AS STRING, *DialogTitle* AS STRING, *ForeColor* AS INTEGER, *BackColor* AS INTEGER, *Flags* AS INTEGER, *Cancel* AS INTEGER)

   When you call this Sub procedure, the FileName parameter returns the name (without a path) of the file the user wants to open. You can supply a default file name in the dialog box by giving a specific value to the FileName parameter, then passing it to this procedure.

   The PathName returns the path (without a file name) of the file the user wants to open. As with FileName, you can supply a default path. (Be careful not to assign an invalid path name or use a file name or pattern here.)

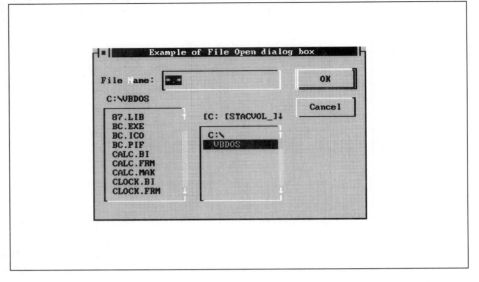

FIGURE 14-4 The File Open dialog box

The DefaultExt parameter sets the default search pattern for the FileList box. When DefaultExt is the null string, the default pattern is "*.*" (all files). Assigning new values (such as ".FRM") to DefaultExt lets you specify a search pattern (such as "*.FRM").

The parameter DialogTitle sets the title bar of the dialog box. The default title is Open. To specify a different title, assign a new value to the DialogTitle parameter.

The ForeColor parameter sets the foreground color; the BackColor parameter sets the background color.

You use the Flags parameter to determine the type of files listed in the dialog box (based on file attributes). The table that follows explains the relationships between values and the listing.

Flag Value	Meaning of the Flag Value
1	Don't list archive files. (The default is to list them.)
2	List hidden files. (The default is not to list them.)
4	Don't list ordinary files. (The default is to list them.)
8	Don't list ReadOnly files. (The default is to list them.)
16	List system files. (The default is not to list them.)

To change the type of files listed, change the value of the Flag parameter.

The Cancel parameter tells you whether the user pressed the dialog's Cancel button. If the Cancel parameter contains the value -1 (True) after the call, then the user pressed ESC or clicked the Cancel button.

Again, all this information is simply provided to the programmer; what the programmer makes of it is up to him or her. (The files supplied with Visual Basic give good examples of how to apply this information.)

FileSave   Figure 14-5 shows the dialog box that FileSave creates. The syntax and parameters for the associated Sub procedure are the same as those used with FileOpen:

CALL FileSave (*FileName* AS STRING, *PathName* AS STRING, *DefaultExt* AS STRING, *DialogTitle* AS STRING, *ForeColor* AS INTEGER, *BackColor* AS INTEGER, *Flags* AS INTEGER, *Cancel* AS INTEGER)

FilePrint   Figure 14-6 shows the dialog box that FilePrint creates. The syntax and parameters for this Sub procedure are

SUB FilePrint (*Copies* AS INTEGER, *ForeColor* AS INTEGER, *BackColor* AS INTEGER, *Cancel* AS INTEGER)

The Copies parameter returns the number of copies (1 to 99) the user wants to print. You can supply a default value by assigning a default value to the Copies parameter and then passing it to this procedure. (Amusingly enough, if you use the default value 0, the user sees a "1".)

ForeColor and BackColor set the dialog foreground and background colors, respectively. The Cancel parameter works as discussed earlier.

FindText   Figure 14-7 shows the dialog box that FindText creates. The syntax and parameters for this Sub procedure are

SUB FindText (*FindText* AS STRING, *ForeColor* AS INTEGER, *BackColor* AS INTEGER, *Options* AS INTEGER, *Flags* AS INTEGER, *Cancel* AS INTEGER)

The FindText parameter returns a string—the text the user wants to change. You can supply a default value for the string by assigning the value to the parameter before calling the procedure.

FIGURE 14-5   The File Save dialog box

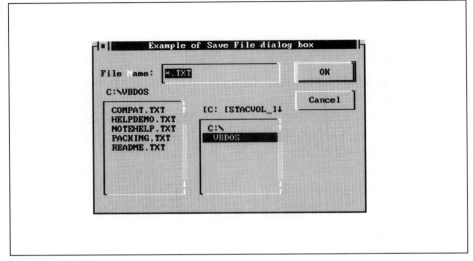

The ForeColor and BackColor parameters work as before, as does the Cancel parameter. Reading the bits in the returned value of the Options parameter tells you what the user wants to do.

Value of Options Parameter	The User Wants to
1	Match case (The default is not to match case.)
2	Match the whole word (The default is not to match the whole word.)
4	Set the search direction to up (The default is down.)

FIGURE 14-6   The Print dialog box

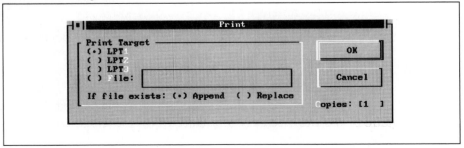

FIGURE
14-7

The Find dialog box

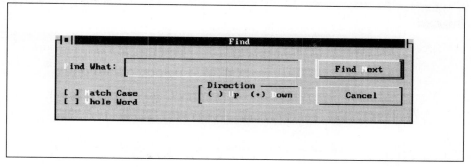

The Flags parameter is also a bit field. It determines which dialog options the user can work with.

Value of Flags Parameter	The Programmer Wants to
1	Not display the Match Case check box (The default is to display the check box.)
2	Not display the Whole Word check box (The default is to display the check box.)
4	Not display the Direction option button (The default is to display the button.)

As always, you change what's available to the user by setting the bit and then passing it to the SUB procedure.

ChangeText   Figure 14-8 shows the dialog box that ChangeText creates. The syntax and parameters for this SUB are

SUB ChangeText (*FindText* AS STRING, *ChangeText* AS STRING, *ForeColor* AS INTEGER, *BackColor* AS INTEGER, *Options* AS INTEGER, *Flags* AS INTEGER, *Cancel* AS INTEGER)

The FindText parameter returns a string—the text the user wants to change. You can supply a default value for the string by assigning the value to the parameter before calling the procedure.

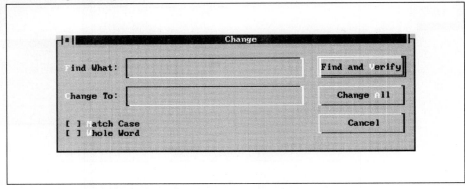

FIGURE 14-8

The Change dialog box

The ChangeText parameter returns the desired replacement text for FindText. You can supply a default value.

The ForeColor and BackColor parameters work as before, as does the Cancel parameter.

Reading the bits in the returned value of the Options parameter tells you what the user wants to do:

Value of Options Parameter	The User Wants to
1	Match case (The default is not to match case.)
2	Match the whole word (The default is not to match the whole word.)
4	Replace all occurrences of FindText with ChangeText (The default is to find and verify occurrences.)

The Flags parameter is also a bit field. It determines which dialog options the user can work with.

Value of Flags Parameter	The Programmer Wants to
1	Not display the Match Case check box (The default is to display the check box.)

Value of Flags Parameter	The Programmer Wants to
2	Not display the Whole Word check box (The default is to display the check box.)
4	Not display the Change All command button (The default is to display the button.)

You change what's available to the user by setting the bit and then passing it to the SUB procedure.

ColorPalette Figure 14-9 shows the dialog box that ColorPalette creates. The syntax and parameters for this SUB are

SUB ColorPalette (*ColorNum* AS INTEGER, *ForeColor* AS INTEGER, *Back-Color* AS INTEGER, *Cancel* AS INTEGER)

The only new parameter is ColorNum, which returns the Visual Basic color number (0 through 15) that the user selected. As with all common dialog boxes, you can supply a default value.

About Figure 14-10 shows the dialog box that About creates. The About dialog box contains a picture box and text is centered and sized around the picture. You'll need to pass, as an argument, the text to be displayed and create the picture with the supplied DrawAboutPicture routine.

FIGURE
14-9

The Color Palette dialog box

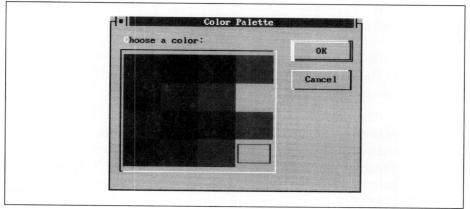

FIGURE
14-10
The About dialog box

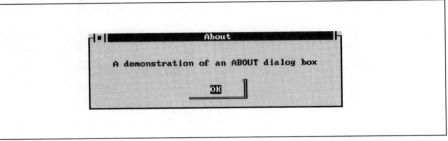

The syntax and parameters for this SUB are

SUB About (*AboutText* AS STRING, *ForeColor* AS INTEGER, *BackColor* AS INTEGER, *Flags* AS INTEGER)

The Flags parameter determines if the picture is displayed. The default is no picture. (Of course, only ASCII character can be used for the picture.)

The DoEvents Function

Usually you want Visual Basic to constantly monitor the environment for events to respond to. On the other hand, in the time the program spends monitoring, it could be doing many other tasks—time-consuming numeric calculations or sorts, for example. However, you don't want a Visual Basic application to stop responding to events completely. Obviously, you need a way to tell Visual Basic to respond periodically to events in the environment and to return to the other tasks when nothing else needs to be done.

The function that does this is called DoEvents. Whenever Visual Basic processes a statement containing this function, it suspends execution of the current procedure and processes all the events that have occurred. Obviously, you should not use the DoEvents function inside an event procedure if it is possible to reenter the same event procedure. For example, the user can call a click event procedure again by pressing the mouse button. If you forget about this possibility, your program may be caught in an infinite regress.

A loop that is processed only when no events are occurring is called an *idle loop*. Idle loops are normally written in SUB procedures inside a code module. The format of an idle loop looks like this:

```
SUB IdleLoop1 ()
  DO WHILE DoEvents()
    'Code you want to be processed during idle time
  LOOP
END SUB
```

Having written one or more idle loop procedures, you must add, to the leading code of the code module, appropriate CALL statements to invoke these procedures. Finally, you must designate the module containing the idle loop procedure(s) as the startup module. To do this, go to the Run menu and choose Set Start-up File (ALT+R F). In the dialog box that Visual Basic presents, choose the code module containing the idle loop procedure(s). Once you've set a code module as the startup file, Visual Basic does not load any forms automatically. You will have to write the code for this yourself (in the leading code of the startup code module or in a procedure called by this leading code).

To see a very simple example of an idle loop at work, start up a new project and in the leading code place the statements

```
COMMON SHARED Count AS LONG
CALL Main
```

This sets up a global variable Count as a long integer and invokes the procedure Main. Next, add the Main procedure to the module:

```
SUB Main ()
  Form1.SHOW
  DO WHILE DoEvents()
    Count = Count + 1
  LOOP
END SUB
```

Add a form called Form1 and enter the following leading code and event procedure:

```
COMMON SHARED Count AS LONG

SUB Form_Click ()
  PRINT Count
END SUB
```

When you run this program, you'll notice that the number gets larger each time you click in the form. The reason is that, during the idle time (when you are not clicking), Visual Basic moves to the Main procedure and keeps adding 1 to the count. Since Count is a global variable, Visual Basic preserves the value for each call.

The DoEvents function actually gives you the number of forms loaded. Idle loops constructed using the statement DO WHILE DOEVENTS() stop when all forms are unloaded (or when Visual Basic processes an END statement).

The DoEvents function is often used inside a Function procedure that is making a time-consuming numeric computation. Set up a timing loop so that Visual Basic periodically processes a DoEvents function to check what events may have taken place while it was calculating. The gains the application can make by alternately processing and checking are well worth the little extra time that Visual Basic uses to manage the timing loop inside the function.

Peeking and Poking

Would you like to have the program tell you if the CAPS LOCK key has been pressed to lock capping? Would you like the program to be able to control whether capping is locked? These tasks and many more are easily accomplished by using PEEK to look into a memory location and using POKE to place a number into a memory location. To work with PEEK and POKE, you have to learn a bit about how memory in a PC is organized.

Understanding PC Memory Organization

The abbreviation K (for the word "kilobyte") represents the number 1024. Therefore, 64K is 65,536 and K * K is 1,048,576. Theoretically, the

IBM PC can contain 1,048,576 memory locations numbered from 0 to 1,048,575. Normally, 640K locations—at most—will consist of random-access memory, which is sometimes called lower memory. The remainder will be read-only memory, memory assigned to hold the contents of the monitor or memory for future applications. Memory managers such as the one in DOS 5.0 can use some of this so-called higher memory.

A *segment* is a 64K portion of memory beginning at a location that is a multiple of 16. Segment 0 consists of memory locations 0, 1, 2, 3, . . . , 65535. Segment 1 consists of memory locations 16, 17, 18, . . . , 65551. Segment 2 consists of memory locations 32, 33, 34, . . . , 65567. In general, segment m consists of memory locations $16 * m$, $(16 * m) + 1$, $(16 * m) + 2$, . . . , $(16 * m) + 65{,}535$.

Within each segment, the first memory location is said to have offset 0, the second memory location is said to have offset 1, and so on. The last memory location is said to have offset 65535. Memory locations are specified by giving a segment containing the location and the offset of the location in that segment. Most memory locations can be specified in many ways. For instance, the designations "segment 0:offset 34," "segment 1:offset 18," and "segment 2:offset 2" specify the same location.

Each memory location holds a number from 0 to 255. To read the number in the memory location segment m:offset n, execute the code that follows.

```
DEF SEG = m
Contents = PEEK(n)
```

The DEF SEG statement specifies the mth segment as the current segment, and the value of PEEK(n) is the number contained in the byte-sized memory location of offset n in the current segment. To place the number r into the memory location segment m:offset n, execute this code:

```
DEF SEG = m
POKE n, r
```

The POKE statement places the number r into the memory location of offset n in the current segment.

Using Locations in Lower Memory

DOS uses the first segment to store various types of useful information. The subsequent PEEK and POKE statements, each of which should be preceded by DEF SEG = 0, give you ways of accessing this information.

Keyboard Peeks and Pokes

The following statements set and determine the status of the keyboard toggle keys.

The CAPS LOCK Key   PEEK(1047) AND 64 has value 0 if the keyboard is in lowercase mode. If in uppercase mode, the value is 64.

☐   To specify lowercase, use POKE 1047, PEEK(1047) AND 191

☐   To specify uppercase, use POKE 1047, PEEK(1047) OR 64

☐   To toggle the mode, use POKE 1047, PEEK(1047) XOR 64

PEEK(1048) AND 64 has value 64 if CAPS LOCK is pressed; otherwise, the value is 0.

The NUM LOCK Key   PEEK(1047) AND 32 has value 0 in the cursor-control mode and value 32 in the numeric-keypad mode.

☐   To specify the cursor-control mode, use POKE 1047, PEEK(1047) AND 223

☐   To specify the numeric-keypad mode, use POKE 1047, PEEK(1047) OR 32

☐   To toggle the mode, use POKE 1047, PEEK(1047) XOR 32

PEEK(1048) AND 32 has value 32 if NUM LOCK is pressed; otherwise, the value is 0.

The INS Key   PEEK(1047) AND 128 has value 128 in the insert mode; otherwise, the value is 0.

☐   To specify the insert mode, use POKE 1047, PEEK(1047) OR 128

❑   To specify the noninsert mode, use POKE 1047, PEEK(1047) AND 127

❑   To toggle the mode: POKE 1047, PEEK(1047) XOR 128

   PEEK(1048) AND 128 has value 128 if INS is pressed; otherwise, the value is 0.

The SCROLL LOCK Key   PEEK(1047) AND 16 has value 16 in the scroll-lock mode; otherwise, the value is 0.

❑   To specify the scroll-lock mode, use POKE 1047, PEEK(1047) OR 16

❑   To specify the unlocked mode, use POKE 1047, PEEK(1047) AND 239

❑   To toggle the mode, use POKE 1047, PEEK(1047) XOR 16

   PEEK(1048) AND 16 has value 16 if SCROLL LOCK is pressed; otherwise, the value is 0.

Some Special Keys   The statements that follow test the status of some special keys.

❑   PEEK(1047) AND 8 has value 8 if ALT is pressed; otherwise, the value is 0.

❑   PEEK(1047) AND 4 has value 4 if CTRL is pressed; otherwise, the value is 0.

❑   PEEK(1047) AND 2 has value 2 if the left SHIFT key is pressed; otherwise, the value is 0.

❑   PEEK(1047) AND 1 has value 1 if the right SHIFT key is pressed; otherwise, the value is 0.

❑   PEEK(1047) AND 3 has value 0 if neither of the SHIFT keys is pressed.

The Status of Monitors

   The table that follows lists the meanings of the values that represent monitor status.

Value of PEEK(1040) AND 48	Monitor Status
0	No monitors
16	40×25 graphics monitor
32	80×25 graphics monitor
48	Monochrome display

Screen Mode Status

The table that follows lists the meanings of the values that represent screen mode status.

Value of PEEK(1097)	Mode Type
0	Text mode, WIDTH 40, color disabled
1	Text mode, WIDTH 40, color enabled
2	Text mode, WIDTH 80, color disabled
3	Text mode, WIDTH 80, color enabled
4	SCREEN 1, color enabled
5	SCREEN 1, color disabled
6	SCREEN 2
7	Hercules or MDPA, text mode
8	Hercules, SCREEN 3
13	SCREEN 7
14	SCREEN 8
15	SCREEN 10
16	SCREEN 9
17	SCREEN 11
18	SCREEN 12
19	SCREEN 13
48	3270 graphics

PEEK(1098) + 256 * PEEK(1099) gives the width in columns.

The Graphics Card

The contents of the graphics screen are stored in a buffer of size PEEK(1100) + 256& * PEEK(1101).

When using text mode with a graphics monitor, there are several "pages" at the programmer's disposal. Think of the cursor locations for the various pages as being given in this form: Let CR(n) and CC(n) be the Cursor Row and Cursor Column for page n. Then PEEK(1105+2*n) has value CR(n) – 1, and PEEK(1104+2*n) has value CC(n) – 1.

The shape of the cursor can be set with a statement of the form LOCATE ,,,I,J. PEEK(1121) AND 31 has value I and PEEK(1120) AND 31 has value J. If (PEEK(1121) AND 32) = 32, then the cursor is not displayed.

The visual page (that is, the page currently displayed) is PEEK(1122).

In medium-resolution graphics, background color and palette are selected by the statement COLOR b,p. The statement PEEK(1126) AND 15 has the value b and (PEEK(1126) AND 32)/32 has the value p. In text mode with a color monitor, the value of PEEK(1126) MOD 16 is the border color, and (PEEK(1126) AND 16) is 16 if the current color was specified by a statement of the form COLOR f,b with b >7.

In graphics mode, where n is a number from 128 to 254, the statement PRINT CHR\$(n) causes the computer to display a rectangle of pixels that forms a character. Each character is described by a sequence of 8 bytes. The 8 bytes describing CHR\$(128) are contained in the eight successive memory locations beginning with the location of offset PEEK(124) + 256& * PEEK(125) in segment PEEK(126) + 256& * PEEK(127). The pattern for CHR\$(129) is contained in the next eight locations, and so on. Creating a character set for ASCII values 128 through 254 requires three steps:

1. Set aside a portion of memory to hold the bytes describing the characters.

2. Poke the pattern for character 128 into the first eight memory locations, the pattern for character 129 into the next eight locations, and so on.

3. Poke the offset and segment of the first byte into locations 124 through 127.

One way to place the pattern for CHR$(129) in the proper locations is to dimension an integer array with DIM A%(1 TO 512) and execute DEF SEG = VARSEG(A%(1)) to finish the process.

The Printer

The number of printer adapters is (PEEK(1041) AND 192)/64. There are several ports associated with each printer. The code that determines the first port associated with LPT*n* is

PEEK(1030 + 2 * *n*) + 256& * PEEK(1031 + 2 * *n*)

If this number is 0, then LPT*n* is not available. (To swap two printers, interchange their first port numbers.)

The parallel printer timeout values can be read and set. The timeout value for LPT*n* is about 1.6 * PEEK(1143+*n*) seconds. Use POKE 1143 + *n*,.64 * S to set the timeout value for LPT*n* to S seconds.

Disk Drives

The number of diskette drives is

```
(PEEK(1040) AND 1) * (1 + PEEK(1040) \ 64)
```

The number of hard disks is PEEK(1141).

In the event that there is only one disk drive, it plays the role of both drives A and B. The current role is CHR$(65 + PEEK(1284)).

The RS-232 (Serial) Interface

The number of RS-232 cards attached is (PEEK(1041) AND 14)/2. To determine the first of the seven ports associated with COM*n*, use

PEEK(1022 + 2 * *n*) + 256& * PEEK(1023 + 2 * *n*)

If this number is 0, then COMn is not available. (To swap two RS-232 interfaces, interchange their first port numbers.)

Miscellaneous Peeks and Pokes

The number of game adapters is

```
(PEEK(1041) AND 16) / 16
```

The size of initial RAM, in kilobytes (up to 640), is

```
PEEK(1043) + 256& * PEEK(1044)
```

The internal clock ticks 18.20648 times per second. The number of ticks that have occurred since midnight is given by PEEK(1132) + 256& * PEEK(1133) + 65536 * PEEK(1134). The value increases until it reaches 1,533,039 (an instant before midnight). At midnight, it is reset to 0. The value of PEEK(1136) is increased by 1 as a result of resetting. Executing either TIME$ or DATE$ changes the value of PEEK(1136) back to 0. To determine the date N days from now, execute the code that follows.

```
FOR I = 1 TO N
  POKE 1136,1
  A$ = DATE$
NEXT I
PRINT DATE$
```

Disk Storage for Numeric Arrays

Arrays consume valuable memory space, and a program with too many arrays can easily run out of memory. One way to solve this problem for a dynamic array is to store the contents of the array in a disk file, erase the array, and then reload the array when it is needed. The program that follows creates an integer array, places values into the array, saves the array in a disk file, deletes the array, and then restores the values into the array. When you need to save and later restore any numeric array, these are the steps you will have to perform. The number 200 in the sixth line is the number of bytes needed to store an integer multiplied by the number of subscripts in the array (2 * 100).

```
REDIM A%(1 TO 100)
FOR I = 1 TO 100
  A%(I) = I
NEXT I
DEF SEG = VARSEG(A%(1))  '1 is the lowest subscript of the array
BSAVE "ARRAY" , VARPTR(A%(1)), 200    '200 = 2x100
ERASE A%                      'remove the array from memory
REDIM A%(1 TO 100)
DEF SEG = VARSEG(A%(1))
BLOAD "ARRAY", VARPTR(A%(1))
```

 Note   This program will not work with regular string arrays or with huge arrays. For more about this program, see Appendix C and the discussions of BSAVE, BLOAD, VARSEG, and VARPTR.

The number of bytes needed to store each type of numeric variable varies, as the table that follows shows.

Type of Numeric Variable	Number of Bytes Needed
Integer	2
Long integer	4
Single precision	4
Double precision	8
Currency	8

Learning About Quick Libraries

A *quick library* is best thought of as commands that you are temporarily adding to the Visual Basic programming environment. Such a library is made up of pre-compiled procedures and functions (possibly created in another programming language) that you can use like any other Visual Basic statement. Since quick libraries are not readable, they give you a way to protect your source code from other people's eyes. Also, a quick library loads faster and is usually smaller than the equivalent .BAS module.

You tell Visual Basic to load a library by invoking Visual Basic with the /L option followed by the name of the library. The custom is to use .QLB as the extension for the names of quick libraries. If you don't specify a library but do use the /L option, then Visual Basic loads the default library VBDOS.QLB, which comes with Visual Basic. The VBDOS.QLB library contains three pre–compiled assembly language programs that let you, for example, find the amount of free space on a disk in an efficient way (see the next section of this chapter).

The easiest way to create a quick library made from Visual Basic source code is from within Visual Basic. Use the editing facilities of Visual Basic to remove any procedures or modules that you do not want as part of the library. (However, be careful: unlike a module, a library can use only procedures and functions that are defined within itself.) Also, it's best to strip out any inessential module-level code before creating the library. If you want your library to contain another library, then you must invoke Visual Basic with the /L option, giving it the name of the smaller library. To actually create the library, choose the Make Library option from the Run menu. This opens a dialog box that lets you supply the name of the library. If you don't provide a file name extension, Visual Basic automatically provides .QLB. (For more on creating libraries by using LINK and the stand-alone BC compiler, see Chapter 19 of *The Programmers Guide.* In addition, that chapter in the guide explains what's necessary for creating mixed-language libraries.)

Tip   Because quick libraries cannot be placed in expanded memory, the only reason to make a quick library from Visual Basic's source code is to keep the code a secret.

Quick libraries are basically stand-alone programs without support routines. As such, they run very fast. However, you can't tell at a glance the names of the procedures and functions that are included in the library. Since you can't use the same procedure name twice, you'll occasionally want to examine a quick library with the program QLBVIEW that is supplied with Visual Basic. This program can analyze any quick library and list all the procedures, functions, and data in the binary file that constitutes it.

Finally, commercial developers can supply you with libraries that improve Visual Basic—they'll give you new functions or faster versions of functions that you wrote yourself. Check out *BASIC Pro* or one of the other PC magazines for details.

Learning About DOS Interrupts

Recall the bit-level operations you saw in Chapter 7. In Visual Basic, one of the most important uses for these operations is to prescribe DOS interrupts. An *interrupt* forces Visual Basic to suspend what it's doing and it cues DOS to tell the central processing unit (CPU) to do something else. To use a DOS interrupt, you invoke Visual Basic with the /L option to load the default Visual Basic .QLB library. Next, you set up a user-defined type of the following form:

```
TYPE CPURegisters
   AX AS INTEGER
   BX AS INTEGER
   CX AS INTEGER
   DX AS INTEGER
   BP AS INTEGER
   SI AS INTEGER
   DI AS INTEGER
   Flags AS INTEGER
END TYPE
```

The components of the TYPE in the preceding code correspond to the eight registers inside the CPU. Now use DIM to define two variables as being of the type CPURegisters. The code that follows shows how to do this.

```
DIM InReg AS CPURegisters, OutReg AS CPURegisters
```

Each register is divided into two bytes (half words). And the reason you'll need binary operations is that you'll need to read and turn on or turn off individual bytes inside individual registers. For example, the AX (accumulator) register, like some of the registers, is divided into two bytes usually called AH (A high) and AL (A low). To put a number (say, decimal 54) in the AH component of InReg.AX, use

```
InReg.AX = 54*256
```

The 256 shifts the bits to the high-order byte. (You could also use hex notation to perform the same task. Using hex, you would make the low-order byte 0 and, by setting Inreg.AX to &H3600, make the high-order byte decimal 54 (&H36).

Roughly speaking, what you now have to do is put certain numbers in the components of the variable InReg and read off the results from the components of OutReg. More precisely, assuming you have loaded the VBDOS.QLB library, you use the

CALL Interrupt(*interrupt number,inreg, outreg*)

command, which VBDOS.QLB adds to Visual Basic. Then you must read the results from OutReg.

The most important interrupt number is decimal 33 (&H21). Among its many other powers, it can efficiently find the amount of free disk space. To determine free disk space, complete these three steps:

1. Place the number of the drive in the InReg.DX component (0 is the current drive, 1 is A, 2 is B, and so on).

2. Place decimal 54 in the AH part of InReg.AX. (Do this because 54 (&H36) is the DOS function that means "Get free disk space.")

3. Use CALL to call Interrupt (33,InReg,OutReg). Or, use an equivalent call, CALL Interrupt (&H21,InReg,OutReg).

Now you can calculate the amount of free disk space by multiplying the AX, BX, and CX components of OutReg. (If there's an error—if the computer says the disk drive doesn't exist, for example—then OutReg.AX = &HFFFF.)

Consider another example. Suppose you want to hide a file—that is, to prevent it from displaying when the DIR command is used. This requires use of the &H43 function of interrupt &H21. First, you need to tell DOS the name of the file. DOS doesn't use ordinary ASCII strings for file names; instead, it uses what are called ASCIIZ strings. An ASCIIZ string is an ordinary ASCII string with CHR$(0) attached at the end. Next, you need to tell the &H21 interrupt where in memory it can find this name. (After all, registers contain numbers only using the VARPTR function [see Appendix C].)

Here are some of the other common functions available through the &H21 interrupt.

Function &H0E   This function sets the default drive. To use this function, set AH equal to &H0E. Then place the appropriate integer in DL, using 0 for A, 1 for B, and so on.

Function &H19   This function gets the default drive. On return, AL contains the code for the drive. The codes are the same as those for function &H0E.

Function &H21   This function determines the version of DOS being used. On return, AL contains the major version number (that is, the number 3 would represent DOS 3.3); AH contains the decimal part of the version name.

Interrupt &H0F

This interrupt gives the current display type. (Refer to the error handler you will learn about in Chapter 16. Except for the problem with Hercules cards, using an interrupt would be a better way than using the error handler.) After you set AH equal to &H0F and call this function, the value of the AH byte indicates the type of display card detected. The table that follows tells what each value means.

Value of AH Byte	Type of Card
&H01	40×25 color text for CGA
&H02	80×25 monochrome text for CGA
&H03	80×25 color text for CGA
&H04	320×200 4-color graphics
&H05	As in &H04 with color burst off
&H06	640×200 2-color graphics
&H07	Monochrome text only
&H08-&H0A	The type found in the late unlamented PCjr.
&H0D	320×200; 16 colors, EGA
&H0E	640×200; 16 colors, EGA
&H0F	640×350 monochrome graphics, EGA
&H10	640×350, either 4 or 16 colors, EGA
&H11	Monochrome graphics (MCGA, VGA)

Value of AH Byte	Type of Card
&H12	640×480; 16 colors, VGA
&H13	320×200; 256 colors, MCGA or VGA

Learning About the Clipboard

Visual Basic lets you exchange text between different text boxes and combo boxes. The clipboard can hold only one piece of text at a time. If you send new information to it, you wipe out what was there before. Therefore, sometimes you will want to make sure the clipboard is completely free before working with it. To do this, add the following line of code inside your project:

```
Clipboard.CLEAR
```

As you might expect, this applies the CLEAR method to the pre-defined clipboard object.

If you need to send text to and from the clipboard, use the SETTEXT and GETTEXT methods, which the next sections describe.

Clipboard.SETTEXT   The SETTEXT method is usually used in the following form:

Clipboard.SETTEXT *StringData*

This sends the string information contained in the variable or string expression StringData to the clipboard, wiping out whatever text was there.

Clipboard.GETTEXT   The Clipboard.GETTEXT method takes a copy of the text currently stored in the clipboard. Because the text contents of the clipboard remain intact until you explicitly clear the clipboard or send new text to it, you can do multiple pasting operations.

You use this method like a function. The general form is

Destination = Clipboard.GETTEXT( )

Selecting Text in Visual Basic

When you use a text box or a combo box on a Visual Basic form, users can select text by the usual Visual Basic (and Microsoft) means: by pressing SHIFT and using an arrow key or by pressing PGUP or PGDN. In many cases when working with selected text, you will want to add cut-and-paste functions to your project—especially when working with multiline text boxes. To do this within Visual Basic, you will refer to selected text by three properties: SelStart, SelLength, and SelText. Two of these contain long integer values; the third contains a string.

SelStart   The SelStart long integer specifies the place where the selected text starts. If the value is 0, the user has started selecting text from the beginning of the text or combo box. If the value is equal to the length of the text string—LEN(Text1.Text), for example—the user wants to start after all the text that's currently in the box. You can specify where selected text starts (say, in a demonstration program) by setting the value of this property from code. For example, for a text box named Text1, the code

```
Text1.SelStart = LEN(Text1.Text)/2
```

starts the selected text in midstream.

SelLength   SelLength gives you the number of characters the user has selected. If SelLength is equal to 0, no text was selected. If SelLength is equal to the length of the text string, all the characters in the control were selected. To highlight the first half of the contents of a text box, you would use code like this:

```
Text1.SelStart = 0
Text1.SelLength = LEN(Text1.Text)/2
```

SelText   SelText is the actual string the user has selected. If the user hasn't selected any text, this is the empty (null) string. If, to the fragment just given, you add

```
FirstHalfOfText$ = Text1.SelText
```

then the value of the string variable FirstHalfOfText is the selected string.

If you assign a new string value to the SelText property, Visual Basic replaces the selected string with the new value. To allow users to copy selected text, combine these properties with the SetText method. For a menu item named Copy and a text box named Text1, all you need to do is use

```
SUB Copy_Click()
   Clipboard.SETTEXT Text1.SelText
END SUB
```

To change this to a procedure that cuts out the selected text, use the following code:

```
SUB Cut_Click()
   Clipboard.SETTEXT Text1.SelText
   Text1.SelText = ""
END SUB
```

By adding the line that resets the value of SelText to the empty string, you have cut the selected text out of the text box.

For example, to implement a Paste_Click procedure at the place where the user has set the insertion point inside a text box named Text1, use the following code:

```
SUB Paste_Click ()
   Text1.SelText = Clipboard.GETTEXT()
END SUB
```

Notice that, if the user hasn't selected any text, this code acts as an insertion method. Otherwise, it replaces the selected text.

Using the Clipboard: An Example

As an example of how to use the clipboard methods, start up a new project and add two multiline text boxes with vertical scroll bars and a menu with two items: Edit and Quit. The Edit menu contains four items: Copy, Cut, Paste, and Quit. The screen in Figure 14-11 shows you what the Menu Design Window looks like. Figure 14-12 shows you what the form looks like. The control names for these items are CutText, CopyText,

FIGURE
14-11

The Menu Design Window, for copying

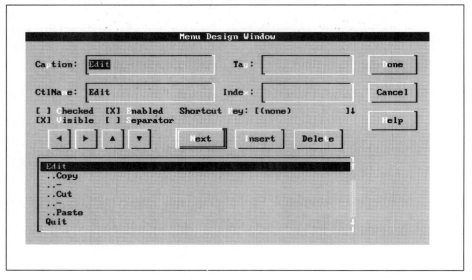

FIGURE
14-12

The form for copying

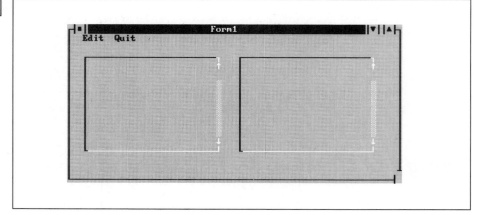

and PasteText. In this case, the code that activates the click procedures for the CopyText click event is

```
SUB CopyText_Click ()
  IF Text1.Text = "" THEN
    MSGBOX ("No text to copy.")
  ELSE
    Clipboard.CLEAR
    Clipboard.SETTEXT Text1.Text
  END IF
END SUB
```

This code checks the contents of the Text1 text box. If there is nothing there, it tells Visual Basic to inform the user. Otherwise, it clears the clipboard and sends the text contained in the box to the clipboard. (Strictly speaking, the CLEAR method isn't needed except in unusual circumstances; sending new text to the clipboard wipes out whatever text was there.)

To retrieve text from the clipboard, you first have to make sure the clipboard contains text. The IF clause in the following procedure does this by using the GetText statement:

```
SUB PasteText_Click ()
IF Clipboard.GetText() = "" THEN
  MsgBox("No text to paste.")
ELSE
  Text2.Text = Clipboard.GETTEXT()
END SUB
```

See the Notepad application that came with Visual Basic for more on cutting and pasting.

CHAPTER

A Checkbook
Management Program

T he purpose of this chapter is to take you through the design and implementation of a professional-quality program for personal checkbook management. This program will be far longer than any you've seen in this book. The complete code is available, of course, on the optional companion disk.

The length of the program not withstanding, the program contains few techniques that will be new to you. However, many people find the jump from small one-objective programs to multiple-objective programs daunting. This chapter should make the transition easier.

In our opinion, nothing in this book shows off the power of Visual Basic better than the program in this chapter. That a user-friendly checkbook management program can be written by designing eight forms and creating only 12 pages of code clearly shows Visual Basic's ability to improve the productivity of programmers. It is easy to imagine an entire finance program, similar to programs that have generated millions of dollars of sales, being written in only a few weeks by using Visual Basic!

The Design of the Program

Though there are many commercial programs available for personal financial management, they include so many bells and whistles that their original purpose—keeping track of checks and reporting amounts spent by category—has become obscured. The program in this chapter was designed specifically as a checkbook program. It keeps track of deposits and expenditures and reports totals by categories. Adding a reconciliation feature would be easy enough, although we did not include one.

The program is supposed to be user friendly. Therefore, it showcases many of the techniques and tools available in Visual Basic. It uses most of the tools available in the Visual Basic toolbox.

The general design goals for the program included the abilities to

☐   Handle multiple accounts

☐   Categorize each check as well as specify tax-deductible expenditures

☐   Categorize the source of each deposit

❏   Provide, at all times, the account statistics

As developed, the report facility can

❏   Report on either checks or deposits

❏   Specify the dates to be included

❏   Include, exclude, or ignore tax status

❏   Pick one specific category or all categories for totals

❏   Send reports to the screen, printer, or both

The User Interface

To achieve the design goals, the user interface includes

❏   A main menu-driven form

❏   A form to allow work with existing accounts or to create a new account

❏   A form, for working with new or existing accounts, that permits modification or entry of account data

❏   A form, visible almost all the time, that gives current statistics about the active account

❏   A form to record checks

❏   A form to record deposits

❏   A form to specify the kind of reports

❏   A form to display the reports

This chapter will present screens of the various forms, and it will discuss the most important event procedures that must be attached to them. Tables summarizing the forms are given at the end of the chapter, in individual sections with appropriate headings. The complete code attached to each form is given at the end of the chapter as well.

The General Code for the Program

First, here's the .MAK file that lists the names of the forms and modules:

FINANCE.FRM
CHECKS.FRM
REPORTS.FRM
DEPOSITS.FRM
ESTATS.FRM
GENPROCS.BAS
STATS.FRM
RESULTS.FRM
ACCOUNTS.FRM

We used a global include file, GLOBAL.BI, which looks like this:

```
'global variables and constants
COMMON SHARED AccountName$, AccountId$
COMMON SHARED Balance AS CURRENCY
COMMON SHARED NextChk AS INTEGER, NextDep AS INTEGER
CONST True = -1
CONST False = 0
CONST MaxAcctNameLen = 30
```

As you can see, the preceding code sets up five global variables. These are used to identify the account name, an id number (actually a string of digits) used by the program to identify the account the user is working with, the current balance, the number of the next check, and the number of the next deposit. Since this sort of information really needs to be available to the whole program, using COMMON SHARED in an include file to define these variables was the obvious way to proceed.

We needed four SUB procedures and one Function procedure that were accessible to the entire program. As with all modules, we began with the nonexecutable statements that declare the functions, identify the names of the forms referred to, and specify use of the include files. (Since the project was built in the Visual Basic programming environment, Visual Basic added the DECLARE and '$FORM statements automatically.)

```
DECLARE SUB EditStats ()
DECLARE FUNCTION ValidDate (D$) AS INTEGER
'$FORM EStats
'$FORM Accounts
'$FORM Checks
'$FORM Deposits
'$FORM Stats
'$INCLUDE: 'GLOBAL.BI'
```

Since adding a category to the various combo and list boxes is such a common operation, we used a general SUB procedure to accomplish it. By using the same control name (Category) for all the combo boxes, we simplified the code a little. The program doesn't need to pass the name of the combo box—passing the form name is enough.

In the AddCat procedure that follows, the loop runs through the items in the combo box on the active form and checks whether the category is included. (The function UCASE$ enables the procedure to ignore case.) If the category doesn't exist, the application presents the user with a message box giving the option to add the category. The program appends a new category to the sequential file named by the CatFile$ string variable; the category name is added to the combo box as well.

```
SUB AddCat (NewItem$, Op AS FORM, CatFile$)
  'local variables:
  DIM I AS INTEGER, TempNewItem$

  TempNewItem$ = UCASE$ (NewItem$)
  'check to see if category is already listed
  FOR I = 0 TO Op.Category.ListCount
    IF UCASE$(Op.Category.List(I)) = TempNewItem$ THEN
      EXIT FOR
    END IF
  NEXT I
  'if category not listed, confirm and add to list and file
  IF I = Op.Category.ListCount + 1 THEN
    I = MSGBOX("Add new category " + NewItem$ + " to list?", 1)
    IF I = 1 THEN
      Op.Category.ADDITEM NewItem$
      OPEN CatFile$ FOR APPEND AS 1
      WRITE #1, NewItem$
      CLOSE 1
    ELSE
      NewItem$ = ""
      Op.Category.Text = ""
```

```
     END IF
    END IF
END SUB
```

The general procedures that edit and update the statistics forms have only one task: to format the current values of the global variables—that is, those variables created by COMMON SHARED.

```
SUB EditStats ()
  EStats.AcctName.Text = AccountName$
  EStats.AcctBalance.Text = FORMAT$(Balance, "0.00")
  EStats.AcctNextChk.Text = FORMAT$(NextChk, "0")
  EStats.AcctNextDep.Text = FORMAT$(NextDep, "0")
  EStats.SHOW 1
END SUB

SUB UpDateStats ()
  Stats.AcctName.Caption = AccountName$
  Stats.AcctBalance.Caption = FORMAT$(Balance, "0.00")
  Stats.AcctNextChk.Caption = FORMAT$(NextChk, "0")
  Stats.AcctNextDep.Caption = FORMAT$(NextDep, "0")
END SUB
```

The procedure that creates an account sets up, in the current directory, a sequential file called ACCOUNTS. (It would be easy to change the code so that the user could use an arbitrary directory.) This file contains the user's name for the account (his or her name or the account name) and the id number string that is passed to the procedure. This procedure also creates the basic data file, list of checks, and list of deposits. The names of these files are distinguished by the extensions .DAT, .CHK, and .DEP, respectively.

```
SUB CreateAccount (Id$)
  'add account name and id to ACCOUNTS file
  OPEN "ACCOUNTS" FOR APPEND AS #1
  AccountName$ = "Account " + Id$
  AccountId$ = Id$
  WRITE #1, AccountName$, AccountId$
  CLOSE #1
  'create ACCT#.DAT, ACCT#.CHK, and ACCT#.DEP
  OPEN "ACCT" + AccountId$ + ".DAT" FOR OUTPUT AS #1
  Balance = 0
  NextChk = 1
  NextDep = 1
  WRITE #1, Balance, NextChk, NextDep
```

```
    CLOSE #1
    OPEN "ACCT" + AccountId$ + ".CHK" FOR OUTPUT AS #1
    CLOSE #1
    OPEN "ACCT" + AccountId$ + ".DEP" FOR OUTPUT AS #1
    CLOSE #1
    'mark new account as the last account accessed
    OPEN "LASTACCT" FOR OUTPUT AS 1
    WRITE #1, AccountName$, AccountId$
    CLOSE #1
    'add account name (and id) to AccountNames list
    Accounts.AccountNames.ADDITEM AccountName$ + _
SPACE$(MaxAcctNameLen - LEN(AccountName$)) + AccountId$
    CALL EditStats
END SUB
```

Finally, the function that checks whether a date is valid uses the trick of holding the current date for reassignment, attempting to assign the trimmed value of the string to the DATE$ function, and seeing if an error results. If no error results, then the date is correct. The function passes either True or False back to the calling procedure.

```
FUNCTION ValidDate (D$) AS INTEGER
    'local variables:
    DIM Hold$

    ON LOCAL ERROR GOTO notgood
    ValidDate = True
    Hold$ = DATE$
    DATE$ = RTRIM$(D$)  'try to make given date the current date
    D$ = DATE$          'work with all dates in the format
                        'returned by DATE$

    DATE$ = Hold$
    EXIT FUNCTION
notgood:
    ValidDate = False
    RESUME NEXT
END FUNCTION
```

The Startup Form

We decided to set Finance as the FormName property for this form and to have it fill 80 percent of the screen. For simplicity, we designed the form in the location where we wanted it to appear. Figure 15-1 is a picture of the form. This version of the program has one submenu attached to the Account main menu item; each menu item has an access key. Figure 15-2 is the Menu Design Window for this program.

Besides the usual nonexecutable code that specifies the forms referred to and the include file, the code for all the click procedures attached to each of the menu items is straightforward. Each procedure cites the appropriate form and initializes the various objects in it. Here, for example, is the Check_Click procedure that the user activates to write a check.

```
SUB Check_Click ()
   Checks.Number.Text = FORMAT$(NextChk, "0")
   Checks.Date.Text = ""
   Checks.Payto.Text = ""
   Checks.Amount.Text = ""
   Checks.Memo.Text = ""
   Checks.Category.Text = ""
   Checks.Tax.Value = False
   Checks.SHOW 1
   Finance.SHOW
END SUB
```

FIGURE 15-1   The startup form, with menu names

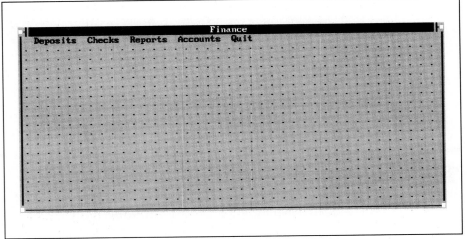

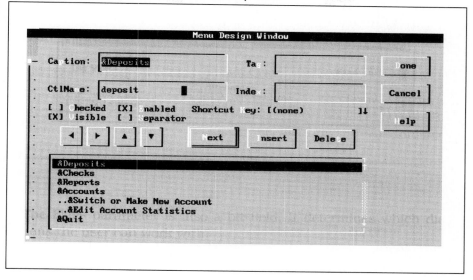

FIGURE
15-2 The Menu Design Window for the startup form

This resets the values of almost all the text boxes, which are now empty as a result. The exception is the Number text box. The preceding code adds the current check number—that is, the value of the global variable NextChk—to the Number text box.

When the user clicks the Quit button, the application updates the account statistics by using the value of the global variable AccountId$. (AccountId$ plus the .DAT suffix and ACCT prefix yields the filename used to record account data.) In addition, the application, in a tiny sequential file called LASTACCT, keeps track of the last account accessed. That account becomes the default account.

```
SUB Quit_Click ()
  'record final stats on account
  OPEN "ACCT" + AccountId$ + ".DAT" FOR OUTPUT AS 1
  WRITE #1, Balance, NextChk, NextDep
  CLOSE #1
  'record last account accessed so it can be the
  'default account next time
  OPEN "LASTACCT" FOR OUTPUT AS 1
  WRITE #1, AccountName$, AccountId$
  CLOSE #1
```

```
'clear screen and exit
Stats.HIDE
Finance.HIDE
CLS
END
END SUB
```

The Form_Load procedure displays a message box that contains the copyright information and loads the categories for expenses and income. These are hard-wired by name into the program and so are not associated to the individual accounts. (If you want to associate them, you can easily make the changes needed to do so.) If no account exists, Visual Basic creates a new one. The default name of the new account is Account 1, and its id string is 1. If one or more accounts exist, then the account name and other information needed are loaded into the combo box displayed on the EStats form (the name is derived from "Edit Statistics").

The Accounts Form

When the user chooses the Account option on the main menu bar, two options appear. Figure 15-3 shows the form that appears as a result of choosing the first option, Switch or Make New Accounts. As the figure shows, the form is a modal dialog box superimposed on the main screen. (Notice that the screen shown in Figure 15-3 presents no means for storing the path of file information—the current version uses the current directory. You can easily add a path feature yourself.) Suppose the user now chooses the <Create New Account> option. After the application completes some internal bookkeeping through which it creates a new id string for the account, the user sees the form shown in Figure 15-4. (The same form appears if the user chooses Edit Account Statistics.) The next section discusses this form further.

Because DOS does not allow more than eight characters in a file name, we had to use a common programming trick to set up account names with more than eight characters. Internally, the accounts are named ACCT1, ACCT2, and so on. A separate sequential file translates these internal file names (determined according to the id number string—1, 2, and so on) to the names the user specifies. Associated to each account are three files: one for the account statistics, one for the checks, and one for the deposits. Internally, as far as the program is concerned, the files

FIGURE
15-3

The form for choosing an existing account or setting up a new account

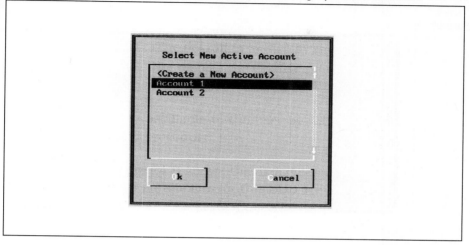

are called ACCT1.DAT, ACCT1.CHK, and ACCT1.DEP, and so on. The values of the global variable AccountId$, which was created by using COMMON SHARED, is the digit string that identifies the account. In the examples given, the digits are 1, 2, and so on.

The list box shows all the account names, and the first option in the box allows the user to create a new account. If necessary, the application pads or trims account names so each has a length of 30 (the value of the global constant MaxAcctNameLen). The id string is then added at the far right of the string. If you use the right arrow key to scroll through the items in the list box at design time, then you can actually see the internal id string the program uses.

When the user clicks the OK button, the click procedure calls the ChangeName procedure to check the name. The click procedure assigns the account name to its internal account id string, then it updates the sequential file that contains the user's version of the account name.

Since the Form_Load procedure for the startup form loads this information into the list box on this form, the whole procedure is completely transparent to the user. Form_Load also loads the data for the account that was last used. Or, if this is the first time the user has used the program in the current directory, Form_Load sets up an account and causes the EditStats form to pop up on the screen. The user can, of

FIGURE
15-4   The EStats form

course, click the Accounts main menu option and choose the Switch or Make New Accounts option to choose another account or add a new account.

There are two interesting procedures attached to the startup form: GetNextId and OK_Click. The GetNextId procedure is simple; it looks at the master account file (ACCOUNTS) and finds out how many accounts exist. The procedure does this so it can create the next id number string.

Clicking the OK button activates the OK_Click procedure. This procedure records current account statistics by using the internal id string given by the variable Id$. Then OK_Click checks whether the user clicked the Switch or Make New Accounts menu option. If so, the application asks the user to confirm the choice. If the choice is confirmed, OK_Click generates a new id string by using the CreateAccountId SUB procedure. If the user does not confirm the choice, the program finds the account id by looking to the far right of the items in the list where account id information is stored.

The Edit Statistics (EStats) Form

Figure 15-4 shows the Edit Statistics (EStats) form, which the user accesses by choosing Accounts from the main menu bar and then choosing Edit Account Statistics. If no accounts exist or if the user wants to create a new account, the EStats form appears with the default name Account 1 showing. In the appropriate text box, the user can enter a new balance, the next check number, or the next deposit number.

After the user enters an account name or changes the account statistics and clicks the OK button, the OK_Click procedure checks if the name in the first text box has changed. If it has and the user hasn't tried to create a new account (by choosing the appropriate option from the appropriate menu), then the program rewrites the ACCOUNTS file and includes the new information. Otherwise, the program uses the id string created in the Accounts form and adds that account name and id string to the list box and the ACCOUNTS file.

```
SUB OK_Click ()
  'local variables:
  DIM NewName$

  NewName$ = LTRIM$(LEFT$(AcctName.Text, MaxAcctNameLen))
  IF NewName$ <> AccountName$ THEN
    'adjust the account name in the ACCOUNTS file &
    'AccountNames list
    CALL ChangeName(NewName$)
    AccountName$ = NewName$
  END IF
  Balance = VAL(AcctBalance.Text)
  NextChk = VAL(AcctNextChk.Text)
  NextDep = VAL(AcctNextDep.Text)
  CALL UpDateStats
  EStats.HIDE
END SUB

SUB ChangeName (NewName$)
  'local variables:
  DIM N$, Id$, I AS INTEGER

  OPEN "ACCOUNTS" FOR INPUT AS #1
  OPEN "_t_e_m_p" FOR OUTPUT AS #2
  DO WHILE NOT EOF(1)
    INPUT #1, N$, Id$
    IF Id$ = AccountId$ THEN N$ = NewName$
    WRITE #2, N$, Id$
  LOOP
  CLOSE #1, #2
  KILL "ACCOUNTS"
```

```
NAME "_t_e_m_p" AS "ACCOUNTS"
FOR I = 0 TO Accounts.AccountNames.ListCount - 1
  IF MID$(Accounts.AccountNames.List(I), MaxAcctNameLen + 1)_
= AccountId$ THEN
    Accounts.AccountNames.List(I) = NewName$ + _
SPACE$(MaxAcctNameLen - LEN(NewName$)) + AccountId$
    EXIT FOR
  END IF
NEXT I
END SUB
```

The Forms for Entering Checks and Deposits

Figures 15-5 and 15-6 show the forms that allow the user to enter check data and deposit data. As the figures show, we used a frame to set off deposit and check data from the combo box, which lists categories and the command buttons that activate the event procedures. Both of these forms have a default Cancel button. In other words, the user can press the ESC (Escape) key to go back to the main screen (the Finance form).

As an example of user friendliness, which is easy to add using Visual Basic, we decided to have the application print the current date if the

FIGURE 15-5

The form for entering check data

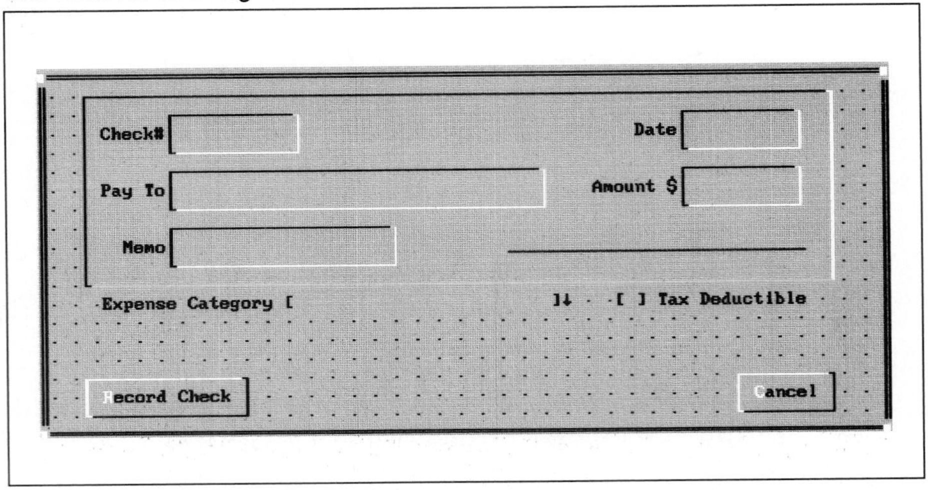

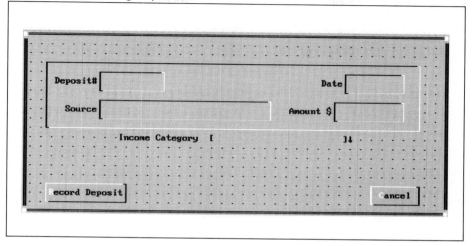

FIGURE
15-6

The form for entering deposit data

user moves the focus away from the Date box without entering a date. This feature required only two lines of code, in the LostFocus event procedure:

```
SUB Date_LostFocus ()
  Date.Text = RTRIM$(Date.Text)
  IF LEN(Date.Text) = 0 THEN Date.Text = DATE$
END SUB
```

(We assumed that, if nothing but blanks are entered, then the user wants the current date.)

The forms shown in Figures 15-5 and 15-6 use a similar Function procedure to validate the data entered, before writing it to disk. For example, if the user hasn't entered a numeric string for a value, the application notifies him or her. In writing the program, we did not require that the string be composed of only digits and commas—although you saw techniques for doing so in Chapters 6 and 7, which presented ways of bulletproofing programs. Just as we used a general function to validate the date, we could have used a general function to validate values. Whenever a check is written or a deposit made, the sequential file (identified by the AccountName$ id string) is immediately updated—no buffering is ever done, so data is unlikely to be lost.

The Reports form

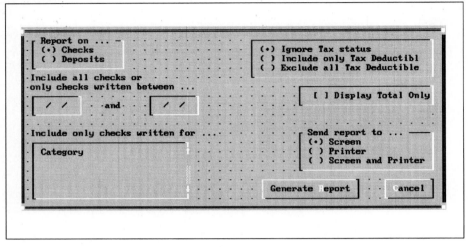

The Reports Form

Most of the hard work in this program is contained in the procedures and functions attached to the form that gives reports. The Reports form (shown in Figure 15-7) is quite complicated. It contains four framed areas. As you can see in Figure 15-7, some of these are for visual effect, but three are absolutely necessary because they contain independent groups of option buttons. For example, the frame in the top left-hand corner asks the user whether he or she wants a report on checks or deposits. The one near the bottom right corner asks whether the report is to go to the screen, the printer, or both.

To understand how the procedures work, suppose the user wants to know what checks were written in a specific category during a specific time. The user chooses the appropriate option buttons, selects the relevant category from the list box, and clicks the Generate Report command button.

Here's the GenReport_Click procedure:

```
SUB GenReport_Click ()
    'local variables:
    DIM Total AS CURRENCY, SubTotal AS CURRENCY
    DIM DoAll AS INTEGER, Index AS INTEGER
```

```
   DIM StartDate AS STRING, StopDate AS STRING
   DIM TaxVal AS INTEGER, SearchCat AS STRING
   Reports.RepTotal.Visible = False
@list =    IF ReportOptionsOk(DoAll, Index, StartDate, StopDate,
TaxVal)_ THEN
     CALL TitleReport(StartDate, StopDate)
     Total = 0
     DO
        SearchCat = RTRIM$(Reports.Category.List(Index))
        SubTotal = 0
        CALL ReportOnOneCategory(SearchCat, SubTotal, StartDate,_
StopDate, TaxVal)
        IF DoAll THEN
           CALL ReportSubTotal(SearchCat, SubTotal)
        END IF

        Index = Index + 1
        Total = Total + SubTotal
     LOOP UNTIL (NOT DoAll) OR (Index >
Reports.Category.ListCount - 1)
     Reports.CheckReport.SETFOCUS
     CALL ReportTotal(Total)
  END IF
END SUB
```

This procedure first calls the ReportOptionsOk function to check whether the user's request is acceptable. Because this function passes the key variable DoAll by reference, it can modify DoAll to be True or False. The result depends on whether the first option (which specifies all categories) or a specific category (any of those in the list box) was selected. The function also checks the start date and stop date to see if they are valid. If no date was selected, the values are set to 00000000 and 99999999, respectively. Since these values are trimmed by the YMD function, the defaults specify all checks.

Suppose the user has chosen a single category and specific dates. The key variable DoAll is set to False in the ReportOptionsOk function. At this point, at the bottom of the click procedure, the DO loop is tested. Review the code to see how this works. The positioning of the test ensures that the application always passes through the loop at least once. If DoAll is False, then the application passes through the loop *only* once. Otherwise, the DO LOOP continues until the application runs out of categories.

What happens inside this loop? The loop calls a procedure that displays the title of the report. Next, the line of code that follows identifies the category to be analyzed.

```
SearchCat = RTRIM$(Reports.Category.List(Index))
```

This procedure then calls the ReportOnOneCategory Sub procedure. To identify the acceptable data, this Sub procedure analyzes the contents of the sequential file. It examines, in the appropriate account, the checks or deposits that pertain to the cited category.

The Results Form

As Figure 15-8 shows, the Results form is fairly simple. It consists of a large multiline text box with vertical scroll bars. Other elements include a label to identify the type of report and a command button that allows the user to return to the main form. To allow use of the arrow keys as well as the scroll bars, the KeyPress event procedure filters out actions involving all the ordinary "typewriter" keys.

FIGURE 15-8   The Results form

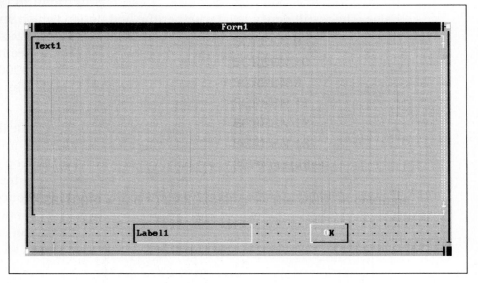

FIGURE 15-9 The Account Statistics form

The Account Statistics Form

This form (see Figure 15-9) holds account information. The Account Statistics form should be available at all times except when the user is in the Accounts form. Moreover, the Account Statistics form is not sizable or movable, so the enabled property is set to False. The Account Statistics form contains eight labels. Four are used for identification; the other four are used to show the data.

The Full Code for the Project

What follows is the full code for the program—except for the general procedures, which were given and discussed earlier in this chapter. Each section includes a table which lists the controls with their control names and their caption or text properties, followed by the code for the event procedures attached to the form. The form information in ASCII form was very long, so we chose to summarize the information in tabular format rather than give the 30 pages needed for the ASCII description. You might also want to refer to the figures for each form given in the previous sections in this chapter for more information. (The complete ASCII version is provided on the optional companion disk to this book.)

The Main Form

As you can see in Figure 15-1, the main form has only menu controls. The control names for these menu items are given in the following table.

Control	Control Name	Caption (or Text) Property
Form	Finance	Finance
Menu Item	Deposit	&Deposits
Menu Item	Check	&Checks
Menu Item	Report	&Reports
Menu Item	Accts	&Accounts
Menu Item	Switch	&Switch or Make New Account
Menu Item	EditStats	&Edit Account Statistics
Menu Item	Quit	&Quit

Here's the code:

```
DECLARE SUB LoadCatLists ()
DECLARE SUB OpenAccount ()
DECLARE SUB CreateAccount (Id$)
DECLARE SUB EditStats ()
DECLARE SUB UpDateStats ()
'$FORM Accounts
'$FORM Stats
'$FORM Deposits
'$FORM EStats
'$FORM Reports
'$FORM Results
'$FORM Checks
'$INCLUDE: 'GLOBAL.BI'

SUB Check_Click ()
  Checks.Number.Text = FORMAT$(NextChk, "0")
  Checks.Date.Text = ""
  Checks.Payto.Text = ""
  Checks.Amount.Text = ""
  Checks.Memo.Text = ""
  Checks.Category.Text = ""
  Checks.Tax.Value = False
  Checks.SHOW 1
  Finance.SHOW
END SUB

SUB Deposit_Click ()
  Deposits.Number.Text = FORMAT$(NextDep, "0")
  Deposits.Date.Text = ""
  Deposits.Source.Text = ""
```

```
      Deposits.Amount.Text = ""
      Deposits.Category.Text = ""
      Deposits.SHOW 1
      Finance.SHOW
   END SUB

   SUB EditStats_Click ()
      CALL EditStats
      Finance.SHOW
   END SUB

   SUB Form_Load ()
      DIM M$, CR$
      CR$ = CHR$(13)+CHR$(10)
      M$ = "This program is from Visual Basic for DOS Inside"
      M$ = M$ + CR$ +"& Out by David Schneider and Gary Cornell."
      M$ = M$ + CR$ + "You have the right to use this code for"
      M$ = M$ + CR$ +"personal use, but you may not give it away"
      M$ = M$ + CR$ + "or sell it."
      MsgBox(M$)
      CALL OpenAccount
      CALL LoadCatLists
      CALL UpDateStats
      Stats.SHOW
      Finance.SHOW
   END SUB

   SUB LoadCatLists ()
      'load list of expense categories
      IF DIR$("EXPCATS") = "EXPCATS" THEN
        OPEN "EXPCATS" FOR INPUT AS 1
        DO WHILE NOT EOF(1)
           INPUT #1, catname$
           Checks.Category.ADDITEM catname$
        LOOP
        CLOSE 1
      END IF
      'load list of income categories
      IF DIR$("INCCATS") = "INCCATS" THEN
        OPEN "INCCATS" FOR INPUT AS 1
        DO WHILE NOT EOF(1)
           INPUT #1, catname$
           Deposits.Category.ADDITEM catname$
        LOOP
        CLOSE 1
      END IF
   END SUB
```

```
SUB OpenAccount ()
  IF NOT (DIR$("ACCOUNTS") = "ACCOUNTS") THEN
    'setup initial account files the first time program is run
    CALL CreateAccount("1")
  ELSE
    'load list of account names into Accounts combo box
    OPEN "ACCOUNTS" FOR INPUT AS #1
    DO WHILE NOT EOF(1)
      INPUT #1, AccountName$, AccountId$
      Accounts.AccountNames.ADDITEM AccountName$ + _
SPACE$(MaxAcctNameLen - LEN(AccountName$)) + AccountId$
    LOOP
    CLOSE #1
    'open last account accessed as the default account
    OPEN "LASTACCT" FOR INPUT AS #1
    INPUT #1, AccountName$, AccountId$
    CLOSE #1
    OPEN "ACCT" + AccountId$ + ".DAT" FOR INPUT AS #1
    INPUT #1, Balance, NextChk, NextDep
    CLOSE #1
  END IF
  'add an entry for the user to select when a new account
  'is to be created
  Accounts.AccountNames.ADDITEM "<Create a New Account>"
  'make the first account created the default when switching
  'accounts the first time
  Accounts.AccountNames.ListIndex = 1
END SUB

SUB Quit_Click ()
  'record final stats on account
  OPEN "ACCT" + AccountId$ + ".DAT" FOR OUTPUT AS 1
  WRITE #1, Balance, NextChk, NextDep
  CLOSE #1
  'record last account accessed so it can be the default
  'account next time
  OPEN "LASTACCT" FOR OUTPUT AS 1
  WRITE #1, AccountName$, AccountId$
  CLOSE #1
  'clear screen and exit
  Stats.HIDE
  Finance.HIDE
  CLS
  END
END SUB
```

```
SUB Report_Click ()
  Reports.Date1.Text = ""
  Reports.Date2.Text = ""
  Reports.Category.ListIndex = -1
  Reports.SHOW 1
  Finance.SHOW
END SUB

SUB Switch_Click ()
  Accounts.SHOW 1
  Finance.SHOW
END SUB
```

The Form for Recording Checks

As you can see in Figure 15-5, this form has 17 controls. They are described in the following table.

Control	Control Name	Caption (or Text) Property
Form	Checks	
CheckBox	Tax	Tax Deductble
ComboBox	Category	
Label	Label7	Expense Category
Frame	Frame1	
TextBox	Number	
Label	Label1	Check#
Label	Label2	Date
TextBox	Date	
Label	Label3	Pay To
TextBox	PayTo	
Label	Label4	Amount $
TextBox	Amount	
Label	Label5	Memo
TextBox	Memo	
Label	Label6	----------------------------
CommandButton	Record	&Record Check
CommandButton	Cancel	&Cancel

Here's the code attached to this form:

```
DECLARE SUB AddCat (NewItem$, Op AS FORM, CatFile$)
DECLARE SUB UpDateStats ()
DECLARE FUNCTION CheckDataOk (ExpCat$) AS INTEGER
DECLARE FUNCTION ValidDate (D$) AS INTEGER
'$FORM Finance
'$INCLUDE: 'GLOBAL.BI'

SUB Amount_LostFocus ()
  Amount.Text = FORMAT$(VAL(Amount.Text), "0.00")
END SUB

SUB Cancel_Click ()
  Number.SETFOCUS
  Checks.HIDE
END SUB

FUNCTION CheckDataOk (ExpCat$) AS INTEGER
  'local variables:
  DIM D$@LIST =  'verify that all needed check information has
been given
  CheckDataOk = False
  IF VAL(Number.Text) = 0 THEN
    MSGBOX "Check Number must be indicated"
    Number.SETFOCUS
    EXIT FUNCTION
  END IF
  D$ = Date.Text
  IF NOT ValidDate(D$) THEN
    MSGBOX "A valid date must be given"
    Date.SETFOCUS
    EXIT FUNCTION
  END IF
  IF LEN(Payto.Text) = 0 THEN
    MSGBOX "A Payee must be indicated"
    Payto.SETFOCUS
    EXIT FUNCTION
  END IF
  IF VAL(Amount.Text) = 0 THEN
    MSGBOX "An amount must be indicated"
    Amount.SETFOCUS
    EXIT FUNCTION
  END IF
  IF LEN(ExpCat$) = 0 THEN
    MSGBOX "An expense category must be chosen"
```

```
      Category.SETFOCUS
      EXIT FUNCTION
   END IF
   CheckDataOk = True
END FUNCTION


SUB Date_LostFocus ()
   Date.Text = RTRIM$(Date.Text)
   IF LEN(Date.Text) = 0 THEN Date.Text = DATE$
END SUB@LIST = SUB Record_Click ()
   'local variables:
   DIM ExpCat$, CNumber AS INTEGER, CAmount AS CURRENCY

   'if a new expense category is given, add it to the list
   ExpCat$ = LTRIM$(Category.Text)
   IF LEN(ExpCat$) <> 0 THEN
      CALL AddCat(ExpCat$, Checks, "EXPCATS")
   ELSE
      ExpCat$ = Category.List(Category.ListIndex)
   END IF
   IF CheckDataOk(ExpCat$) THEN
      'record new check and update account statistics
      OPEN "ACCT" + AccountId$ + ".CHK" FOR APPEND AS 1
      CNumber = VAL(Number.Text)
      CAmount = VAL(Amount.Text)
      WRITE #1, CNumber, Date.Text, Payto.Text, CAmount, _
Memo.Text, ExpCat$, Tax.Value
      CLOSE 1
      Balance = Balance - CAmount
      NextChk = NextChk + 1
      CALL UpDateStats
      Checks.Number.SETFOCUS
      Checks.HIDE
   END IF
END SUB
```

The Form for Recording Deposits

As you can see in Figure 15-6, this form has 13 controls. They are described in the following table.

Control	Control Name	Caption (or Text) Property
Form	Deposits	

Control	Control Name	Caption (or Text) Property
ComboBox	Category	
Label	Label5	Income Category
Frame	Frame1	
TextBox	Number	
Label	Label1	Deposit#
Label	Label2	Date
TextBox	Date	
Label	Label3	Source
TextBox	Source	
Label	Label4	Amount$
TextBox	Amount	
CommandButton	Record	&Record Deposit
CommandButton	Cancel	&Cancel

Here's the code attached to this form:

```
DECLARE SUB AddCat (NewItem$, Op AS FORM, CatFile$)
DECLARE SUB UpDateStats ()
DECLARE FUNCTION DepositDataOk (IncCat$) AS INTEGER
DECLARE FUNCTION ValidDate (D AS STRING) AS INTEGER
'$FORM Finance
'$INCLUDE: 'GLOBAL.BI'

SUB Amount_LostFocus ()
  Amount.Text = FORMAT$(VAL(Amount.Text), "0.00")
END SUB

SUB Cancel_Click ()
  Number.SETFOCUS
  Deposits.HIDE
END SUB

SUB Date_LostFocus ()
  Date.Text = RTRIM$(Date.Text)
  IF LEN(Date.Text) = 0 THEN Date.Text = DATE$
END SUB
```

```
FUNCTION DepositDataOk (IncCat$) AS INTEGER
  'local variables:
  DIM D$

  'verify that all needed information has been given
  DepositDataOk = False
  IF VAL(Number.Text) = 0 THEN
    MSGBOX "Deposit Number must be indicated"
    Number.SETFOCUS
    EXIT FUNCTION
  END IF
  D$ = Date.Text
  IF NOT ValidDate(D$) THEN
    MSGBOX "A valid date must be given"
    Date.SETFOCUS
    EXIT FUNCTION
  END IF
  IF LEN(Source.Text) = 0 THEN
    MSGBOX "A Source must be indicated"
    Source.SETFOCUS
    EXIT FUNCTION
  END IF
  IF VAL(Amount.Text) = 0 THEN
    MSGBOX "An amount must be indicated"
    Amount.SETFOCUS
    EXIT FUNCTION
  END IF
  IF LEN(IncCat$) = 0 THEN
    MSGBOX "An income category must be chosen"
    Category.SETFOCUS
    EXIT FUNCTION
  END IF
  DepositDataOk = True
END FUNCTION

SUB Record_Click ()
  'local variables:
  DIM IncCat$, DNumber AS INTEGER, DAmount AS CURRENCY

  'if a new income category is given, add it to the list
  IncCat$ = LTRIM$(Category.Text)
  IF LEN(IncCat$) <> 0 THEN
    CALL AddCat(IncCat$, Deposits, "INCCATS")
  ELSE
    IncCat$ = Category.List(Category.ListIndex)
  END IF
  IF DepositDataOk(IncCat$) THEN
```

```
        'record new deposit and update account statistics
        OPEN "ACCT" + AccountId$ + ".DEP" FOR APPEND AS 1
        DNumber = VAL(Number.Text)
        DAmount = VAL(Amount.Text)
        WRITE #1, DNumber, Date.Text, Source.Text, DAmount, IncCat$
        CLOSE 1
        Balance = Balance + DAmount
        NextDep = NextDep + 1
        CALL UpDateStats
        Deposits.Number.SETFOCUS
        Deposits.HIDE
    END IF
END SUB
```

The Form for Account Statistics

This form (see Figure 15-9) has no code attached to it, but eight labels are on it. The control names are described in the table that follows.

Control	Control Name	Caption (or Text) Property
Form	Stats	Stats
Label	Label1	Account Name
Label	AcctName	Label2
Label	Label3	Balance
Label	AcctBalance	Label4
Label	Label5	Next Check
Label	AcctNextChk	Label6
Label	Label7	Next Deposit
Label	AcctNextDep	Label8

The Form for Selecting an Account

As you can see in Figure 15-3, this form has nine controls. They are described in the following table.

Control	Control Name	Caption (or Text) Property
Form	Accounts	

Control	Control Name	Caption (or Text) Property
ListBox	AccountNames	
CommandButton	Ok	&OK
CommandButton	Cancel	&Cancel
Label	Label1	Select New Active Account

Here's the code attached to this form:

```
DECLARE SUB ChangeName (NewName$)
DECLARE SUB UpDateStats ()
'$FORM Accounts
'$FORM Finance
'$INCLUDE: 'GLOBAL.BI'

SUB Cancel_Click ()
  AcctName.SETFOCUS
  EStats.HIDE
END SUB

SUB ChangeName (NewName$)
  'local variables:
  DIM N$, Id$, I AS INTEGER

  OPEN "ACCOUNTS" FOR INPUT AS #1
  OPEN "_t_e_m_p" FOR OUTPUT AS #2
  DO WHILE NOT EOF(1)
    INPUT #1, N$, Id$
    IF Id$ = AccountId$ THEN N$ = NewName$
    WRITE #2, N$, Id$
  LOOP
  CLOSE #1, #2
  KILL "ACCOUNTS"
  NAME "_t_e_m_p" AS "ACCOUNTS"
  FOR I = 0 TO Accounts.AccountNames.ListCount - 1
    IF MID$(Accounts.AccountNames.List(I), MaxAcctNameLen + 1)
= AccountId$ THEN
      Accounts.AccountNames.List(I) = NewName$ + _
SPACE$(MaxAcctNameLen - LEN(NewName$)) + AccountId$
      EXIT FOR
    END IF
  NEXT I
END SUB@list = SUB OK_Click ()
  'local variables:
  DIM NewName$
```

```
NewName$ = LTRIM$(LEFT$(AcctName.Text, MaxAcctNameLen))
IF NewName$ <> AccountName$ THEN
   'adjust the account name in the ACCOUNTS file &
   'AccountNames list
   CALL ChangeName(NewName$)
   AccountName$ = NewName$
END IF
Balance = VAL(AcctBalance.Text)
NextChk = VAL(AcctNextChk.Text)
NextDep = VAL(AcctNextDep.Text)
CALL UpDateStats
EStats.HIDE
END SUB
```

The Form for Modifying Account Statistics

As you can see in Figure 15-4, this form has nine controls. They are
described in the following table.

Control	Control Name	Caption (or Text) Property
Form	EStats	
Label	Label2	Balance
Label	Label3	Next Check#
Label	Label4	Next Deposit#
TextBox	AcctName	
TextBox	AcctBalance	
TextBox	AcctNextChk	
CommandButton	OK	&OK
TextBox	AcctNextDep	
Label	Label1	Account Name

Here's the code attached to this form:

```
DECLARE SUB CreateAccount (Id$)
DECLARE SUB UpDateStats ()
DECLARE SUB GetNextId (Id$)
'$FORM Finance
'$INCLUDE: 'GLOBAL.BI'
```

```
SUB Cancel_Click ()
  Accounts.HIDE
END SUB

SUB GetNextId (Id$)
  'local variables
  DIM NextId AS INTEGER, N$

  NextId = 1
  OPEN "ACCOUNTS" FOR INPUT AS #1
  DO WHILE NOT EOF(1)
    INPUT #1, N$, Id$
    IF VAL(Id$) >= NextId THEN NextId = VAL(Id$) + 1
  LOOP
  CLOSE #1
  Id$ = FORMAT$(NextId, "#")
END SUB

SUB OK_Click ()
  'local variables:
  DIM Id$, Index AS INTEGER

  'record stats on current account
  OPEN "ACCT" + AccountId$ + ".DAT" FOR OUTPUT AS 1
  WRITE #1, Balance, NextChk, NextDep
  CLOSE #1
  Index = AccountNames.ListIndex
  IF LEFT$(AccountNames.List(Index), 1) = "<" THEN
    'user has asked to create a new account
    IF MSGBOX("Please confirm: Create a New Account", 4) <> 6 _
THEN EXIT SUB
    Accounts.HIDE
    CALL GetNextId(Id$)
    CALL CreateAccount(Id$)
  ELSE
    'switch to new account
    Accounts.HIDE
    AccountName$ = RTRIM$(LEFT$(AccountNames.List(Index),_
 MaxAcctNameLen))
    AccountId$ = MID$(AccountNames.List(Index), MaxAcctNameLen_
+ 1)
    OPEN "ACCT" + AccountId$ + ".DAT" FOR INPUT AS #1
    INPUT #1, Balance, NextChk, NextDep
    CLOSE #1
  END IF
  CALL UpDateStats
END SUB
```

The Form for Generating Reports

As you can see in Figure 15-7, this form is the most complicated. It has 22 controls, which are described in the following table.

Control	Control Name	Caption (or Text) Property
Form	Reports	
ListBox	Category	
Label	CatLabel	Include only checks written for ...
Frame	Frame4	Send Reports to ...
OptionButton	OnScreen	Screen
OptionButton	OnPrinter	Printer
OptionButton	OnBoth	Screen and Printer
TextBox	Date1	/ /
TextBox	Date2	/ /
Frame	Frame1	Report On ...
OptionButton	CheckReport	Checks
OptionButton	DepositReport	Deposits
CommandButton	GenReport	Generate &Report
Label	DateLabel	Include all checks or only checks written between ...
Label	Label1	and
Frame	Frame3	
CheckBox	TotalOnly	Display Total Only
CommandButton	Cancel	&Cancel
Label	RepTotal	
Frame	Frame2	
OptionButton	IgnoreTax	Ignore Tax Status
OptionButton	TaxOnly	Include only Tax Deductible
OptionButton	NonTaxOnly	Exclude all Tax Deductible

Here's the code attached to this form:

```
DECLARE SUB CheckReport_Click ()
DECLARE SUB ReportOnOneCategory (SearchCat AS STRING, _
SubTotal AS CURRENCY, StartDate AS STRING, StopDate AS STRING, _
```

```
  TaxVal AS INTEGER)
DECLARE SUB ReportSubTotal (SearchCat AS STRING, SubTotal AS_
CURRENCY)
DECLARE SUB ReportTotal (Total AS CURRENCY)
DECLARE SUB TitleReport (StartDate AS STRING, StopDate AS_
STRING)
DECLARE FUNCTION ReportOptionsOk (DoAll AS INTEGER, Index AS_
INTEGER, StartDate AS STRING, StopDate AS STRING,_
TaxVal AS INTEGER) AS INTEGER
DECLARE FUNCTION ValidDate (D AS STRING) AS INTEGER
DECLARE FUNCTION YMD (D$) AS STRING
'$FORM Finance
'$FORM Results
'$FORM Deposits
'$FORM Checks
'$INCLUDE: 'GLOBAL.BI'

SUB Cancel_Click ()
  Reports.CheckReport.SETFOCUS
  Reports.HIDE
END SUB

SUB CheckReport_Click ()
  'local variables:
  DIM I AS INTEGER, CR$, C$
  CR$ = CHR$(13) + CHR$(10)
  DO WHILE Reports.Category.ListCount > 0
    Reports.Category.REMOVEITEM 0
  LOOP
  Reports.Category.ADDITEM " <Include All Categories>"
  FOR I = 0 TO Checks.Category.ListCount - 1
    Reports.Category.ADDITEM Checks.Category.List(I)
  NEXT I
  CatLabel.Caption = "Include only checks written for ..."
  C$ = "Include all checks or " + CR$
  C$ = C$ + "all checks written between ..."
  DateLabel.Caption = C$
  IgnoreTax.Enabled = True
  TaxOnly.Enabled = True
  NonTaxOnly.Enabled = True
END SUB

SUB DepositReport_Click ()
  'local variables:
  DIM I AS INTEGER, CR$, C$
  CR$ = CHR$(13) + CHR$(10)
  DO WHILE Reports.Category.ListCount > 0
```

```
      Reports.Category.REMOVEITEM 0
   LOOP
   Reports.Category.ADDITEM " <Include All Categories>"
   FOR I = 0 TO Deposits.Category.ListCount - 1
      Reports.Category.ADDITEM Deposits.Category.List(I)
   NEXT I
   CatLabel.Caption = "Include only deposits written for ..."
   C$ = "Include all deposits or " + CR$
   C$ = C$ + "all deposits between ..."
   DateLabel.Caption = C$
   IgnoreTax.Enabled = False
   TaxOnly.Enabled = False
   NonTaxOnly.Enabled = False
END SUB@list = SUB Form_Load ()
   CALL CheckReport_Click
END SUB

SUB GenReport_Click ()
   'local variables:
   DIM Total AS CURRENCY, SubTotal AS CURRENCY
   DIM DoAll AS INTEGER, Index AS INTEGER
   DIM StartDate AS STRING, StopDate AS STRING
   DIM TaxVal AS INTEGER, SearchCat AS STRING

   Reports.RepTotal.Visible = False
   IF ReportOptionsOk(DoAll, Index, StartDate, StopDate, TaxVal)_
THEN
      CALL TitleReport(StartDate, StopDate)
      Total = 0
      DO
         SearchCat = RTRIM$(Reports.Category.List(Index))
         SubTotal = 0
         CALL ReportOnOneCategory(SearchCat, SubTotal, StartDate, _
StopDate, TaxVal)
         IF DoAll THEN
            CALL ReportSubTotal(SearchCat, SubTotal)
         END IF

         Index = Index + 1
         Total = Total + SubTotal
      LOOP UNTIL (NOT DoAll) OR (Index >_
Reports.Category.ListCount - 1)
      Reports.CheckReport.SETFOCUS
      CALL ReportTotal(Total)
   END IF
END SUB
```

```
SUB ReportOnOneCategory (SearchCat AS STRING, SubTotal AS_
CURRENCY, StartDate AS STRING, StopDate AS STRING,_
TaxVal AS INTEGER)
  'local variables:
  DIM N$, D$, W$, A$, Number AS INTEGER, ItemDate$
  DIM Amount AS CURRENCY, Memo$, ItemCat$, Tax AS INTEGER
  DIM UCat$
  'allocate space for items appearing in each line of report
  N$ = SPACE$(6)
  D$ = SPACE$(10)
  W$ = SPACE$(20)
  A$ = SPACE$(10)
  UCat$ = UCASE$(SearchCat)
  'open appropriate database
  IF CheckReport.Value THEN
     OPEN "ACCT" + AccountId$ + ".CHK" FOR INPUT AS 1
  ELSE
     OPEN "ACCT" + AccountId$ + ".DEP" FOR INPUT AS 1
  END IF
  DO WHILE NOT EOF(1)
     IF CheckReport.Value THEN
        INPUT #1, Number, ItemDate$, Who$, Amount, Memo$,_
ItemCat$, Tax
     ELSE
        INPUT #1, Number, ItemDate$, Who$, Amount, ItemCat$
     END IF
     'only process items which meet search criteria
     IF UCASE$(RTRIM$(ItemCat$)) = UCat$) AND (YMD(ItemDate$) _
>= StartDate) AND (YMD(ItemDate$) <= StopDate) AND (TaxVal = _
99 OR TaxVal = Tax) THEN
        SubTotal = SubTotal + Amount
        IF TotalOnly.Value = 0 THEN
           RSET N$ = STR$(Number)
           LSET D$ = ItemDate$
           LSET W$ = Who$
           RSET A$ = FORMAT$(Amount, "0.00")
           IF OnScreen.Value OR OnBoth.Value THEN
              Results.Info.Text = Results.Info.Text + CHR$(13) + _
CHR$(10) + N$ + "   " + D$ + "   " + A$ + "   " + W$
           END IF
           IF OnPrinter.Value OR OnBoth.Value THEN
              LPRINT N$ + "   " + D$ + "   " + A$ + "   " + W$
           END IF
        END IF
     END IF
  LOOP
```

```
   CLOSE 1
END SUB

FUNCTION ReportOptionsOk (DoAll AS INTEGER, Index AS INTEGER, _
StartDate AS STRING, StopDate AS STRING, TaxVal AS INTEGER) AS_
INTEGER
  'local variables:
  DIM D$

  ReportOptionsOk = False
  IF Reports.Category.ListIndex = 0 THEN
    DoAll = True
    Index = 1
  ELSEIF Reports.Category.ListIndex > 0 THEN
    DoAll = False
    Index = Reports.Category.ListIndex
  ELSE
    MSGBOX "Category must be selected"
    EXIT FUNCTION
  END IF
  D$ = Reports.Date1.Text
  IF LEN(RTRIM$(D$)) = 0 THEN
    StartDate = "00000000"
  ELSEIF ValidDate(D$) THEN
    StartDate = YMD(D$)
  ELSE
    MSGBOX "Starting date is not a valid date"
    EXIT FUNCTION
  END IF
  D$ = Reports.Date2.Text
  IF LEN(RTRIM$(D$)) = 0 THEN
    StopDate = "99999999"
  ELSEIF ValidDate(D$) THEN
    StopDate = YMD(D$)
  ELSE
    MSGBOX "Ending date is not a valid date"
    EXIT FUNCTION
  END IF
  IF CheckReport.Value THEN
    IF IgnoreTax.Value THEN
      TaxVal = 99
    ELSEIF TaxOnly.Value THEN
      TaxVal = 1
    ELSEIF NonTaxOnly.Value THEN
      TaxVal = 0
    END IF
  ELSE
```

```
      TaxVal = 99
    END IF
    ReportOptionsOk = True
END FUNCTION


SUB ReportSubTotal (SearchCat AS STRING, SubTotal AS CURRENCY)
    IF OnPrinter.Value OR OnBoth.Value THEN
      LPRINT
      LPRINT "Subtotal for " + SearchCat + ": " +
FORMAT$(SubTotal, "$0.00")
      LPRINT
      LPRINT
    END IF
    IF OnScreen.Value OR OnBoth.Value THEN
      Results.Info.Text = Results.Info.Text + CHR$(13) + CHR$(10)
      Results.Info.Text = Results.Info.Text + CHR$(13)+CHR$(10)+_
  "Subtotal for " + SearchCat + ": " + FORMAT$(SubTotal, "$0.00")
      Results.Info.Text = Results.Info.Text + CHR$(13) + CHR$(10)
      Results.Info.Text = Results.Info.Text + CHR$(13) + CHR$(10)
    END IF
END SUB


SUB ReportTotal (Total AS CURRENCY)
    IF OnPrinter.Value OR OnBoth.Value THEN
      LPRINT
      LPRINT "Total: " + FORMAT$(Total, "$0.00")
      LPRINT CHR$(12);    'form feed
    END IF
    IF OnScreen.Value OR OnBoth.Value THEN
      IF TotalOnly.Value = 0 THEN
        Results.RepTotal.Caption = "Total: " + FORMAT$(Total,_
"$0.00")
        Reports.HIDE
        Results.SHOW 1
      ELSE
        Reports.RepTotal.Caption = "Total: " + FORMAT$(Total,_
"$0.00")
        Reports.RepTotal.Visible = True
      END IF
    END IF
END SUB


SUB TitleReport (StartDate AS STRING, StopDate AS STRING)
    DIM ReportTitle AS STRING, Header1 AS STRING, Header2 AS_
STRING
```

```
IF CheckReport.Value THEN
   ReportTitle = "Report on checks "
   Header1 = "Number    Date          Amount  Paid to"
ELSE
   ReportTitle = "Report on deposits "
   Header1 = "Number    Date          Amount  Received from"
END IF
Header2 = "======  ==========  ==========  ===================="
IF StartDate <> "00000000" AND StopDate = "99999999" THEN
   ReportTitle = ReportTitle + "written on or after " + d1$
ELSEIF StartDate = "00000000" AND StopDate <> "99999999" THEN
   ReportTitle = ReportTitle + "written on or before " + d2$
ELSEIF StartDate <> "00000000" AND StopDate <> "99999999" THEN
   ReportTitle = ReportTitle + "written " + d1$ + " to " + d2$
END IF
IF OnPrinter.Value OR OnBoth.Value THEN
   LPRINT ReportTitle
   LPRINT
   LPRINT Header1
   LPRINT Header2
END IF
IF OnScreen.Value OR OnBoth.Value THEN
   Results.Caption = ReportTitle
   Results.Info.Text = Header1 + CHR$(13) + CHR$(10) + Header2
END IF
END SUB

FUNCTION YMD (D$) AS STRING
   YMD = RIGHT$(D$, 4) + LEFT$(D$, 2) + MID$(D$, 4, 2)
END FUNCTION
```

The Form for Displaying the Reports

As you can see in Figure 15-8, this form has three controls. They are described in the following table.

Control	Control Name	Caption (or Text) Property
Form	Results	Form1
Label	RepTotal	Label1
CommandButton	OK	&OK
TextBox	Info	Text1

Here's the code attached to this form:

```
'$FORM Finance
'$INCLUDE: 'GLOBAL.BI'

SUB Info_KeyPress (KeyAscii AS INTEGER)
  KeyAscii = 0
END SUB

SUB OK_Click ()
  Results.HIDE
END SUB
```

CHAPTER

An Introduction to Graphics and Sound

*M*ost of this chapter is about graphics—picture drawing by a computer. With suitable hardware, the graphics power of PCs unleashed by Visual Basic are astounding. Figure 16-1 is an example of what you can draw with a short (24-line) program.

You should be aware that the on-line help files for the graphics statements are particularly good. It's worth consulting them, as well as the graphics chapter of the Visual Basic *Programmer's Guide* and Appendix C of this book, if you need more information on any of the statements covered here. (The *Programmer's Guide* also covers a few topics not discussed here.)

Finally, this chapter ends with a short section on sound. Unfortunately, while Visual Basic's statements for sound effects are in theory quite powerful, in practice they are limited by the tinny speaker that most PCs have. For that reason, not much time will be spent on them here (consult the *Programmer's Guide* or Appendix C for more details).

FIGURE 16-1 Rotating squares

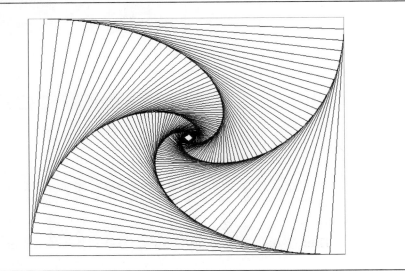

Getting Started

You can only use Visual Basic's graphics statements if you have the appropriate hardware (usually called a graphics board). Visual Basic allows you to control a CGA (color graphics adapter), an EGA (enhanced graphics adaptor), or a VGA (video graphics array). (The PS/2 25 and 30 almost have a VGA adapter; IBM calls it an MCGA and it's slightly less powerful.) Visual Basic also supports the Hercules graphics card and ATT's proprietary graphics card. Both of these—unlike the CGA, EGA, and VGA—allow you to draw in only two colors, usually green and white. (If you have a Hercules card, you have to run a program called MSHERC.COM before using Visual Basic graphics.)

Having the right kind of board is not enough, however. You also need the appropriate monitor. You can use four kinds of monitors: monochrome monitors (which in spite of the name use two colors) and three kinds of color monitors. Getting graphics on a monochrome monitor usually requires a Hercules or Hercules-compatible card, but they will work with EGA and VGA boards as well. As for color monitors, the most primitive (and the cheapest) are called composite monitors (TV sets equipped with an "RF modulator" work like composite monitors). These are usually attached to a CGA. Next up on the scale is an RGB monitor, which can be attached to all three types of boards. However, to take full advantage of a VGA board, you need a special analog monitor (a good way to think of an analog monitor is that with one you can easily adjust the exact amount of red, blue, and green in the signal).

Since the statements that control a CGA will work with any color card, the CGA will be used here to illustrate most of the ideas in this chapter. (Keep in mind that the results may be slightly different with the various combinations of hardware.) EGA and VGA boards recognize some specialized statements that will be described later.

It is possible to write a program that determines what kind of graphics board a computer has and adjusts itself accordingly. You'll see one way to do this in the section titled "Other SCREEN Modes" later in this chapter.

There's one more thing you should know before getting started with graphics. As you learned in Chapter 3, Visual Basic forms are created and manipulated in *text* mode. In text mode, the screen is divided into rows and columns of characters, and only ASCII characters may be displayed; graphics such as points, lines, and circles cannot be displayed. Therefore, before a graphics routine can be executed, you should first include code to hide all forms (see Chapter 14).

Here's one possible code fragment to use in invoking graphics (note that the form called Form1 is first hidden):

```
SUB Form_Click ()
  Form1.HIDE
  CALL GraphicsRoutine
  SCREEN 0
  WIDTH 80
  Form1.SHOW
END SUB
```

Another approach, particularly in projects that require only graphics, is to omit forms and use a .BAS startup module (see Chapter 14).

Graphics Modes and Coordinates

The two graphics modes that work with all graphics boards are usually called medium resolution and high resolution. Medium resolution allows up to four colors on the screen, whereas high resolution allows only two. The tradeoff is that the dots (*pixels*) that form graphics images are much larger in medium resolution than in high resolution mode, while the pictures are much finer in high resolution.

Medium resolution divides the screen into 64,000 pixels, each of which you can control individually. Executing the statement SCREEN 1 clears the screen and enables (turns on) medium resolution graphics. In this mode, Visual Basic uses a grid that's 320 (graphics) columns across and 200 (graphics) rows down. You identify each of the 64,000 pixels by means of its coordinates, an ordered pair giving the column and the row. Both are numbered starting with 0—so the columns are numbered from 0 to 319 and the rows from 0 to 199. For example,

(0,0)	is the top left corner
(319,0)	is the top right corner
(0,199)	is the bottom left corner

(319,199)   is the bottom right corner

(160,100)   is roughly in the center.

If two points have the same first coordinate, they're on the same vertical line; if they have the same second coordinate, they're on the same horizontal line.

High resolution graphics are turned on by the statement SCREEN 2. This erases the screen and sets up a grid 640 across and (same as medium resolution) 200 down. The row positions remain at 0 to 199 and the column positions are now numbered 0 to 639. Thus, (0,0) remain the coordinates of the top left corner, but now (320,100) is roughly the center and (639,199) is the bottom right corner.

 Note   If you have a Hercules card, then your only graphics mode is the high resolution mode obtained by using the statement SCREEN 3. This mode gives you a 720 by 348 grid. For simplicity, the discussions of high resolution graphics in this chapter assumes a resolution of 640 x 200.

Positioning Text

Graphics screens normally display 25 rows and 40 or 80 columns of text. Text is positioned on the graphics screen in much the same way as on a form. However, the CurrentX and CurrentY properties are replaced by a single LOCATE statement. After the statement

LOCATE *r, c*

is executed, subsequent text will be displayed starting in (text) row *r* and (text) column *c*. Rows and columns are numbered beginning with 1. So, for example, the statement

```
SCREEN 1
LOCATE 2, 6
PRINT "Hello"
```

displays the word Hello on the second row of the screen indented 5 spaces.

Labeling graphics with text is a common task. To do this, you must know how to determine the graphics coordinates at which a LOCATE statement will place a character. In SCREEN 1 and SCREEN 2, each character is 8 pixels high and 8 pixels wide. Thus, to calculate in which (graphics) column and row the upper-left corner of a letter will appear, start with the (text) row and column in the LOCATE statement, subtract 1 from each number (since LOCATE uses the numbers 1,2,3,... while graphics uses the numbers 0,1,2,...), and then multiply each number by 8. Finally, reverse the order of the numbers, since the LOCATE statement has rows first while graphics coordinates have columns first. For example, the following code

```
SCREEN 1
LOCATE 5, 9
PRINT "Hello world!"
```

puts you in medium resolution graphics mode (SCREEN 1) and displays the message starting at graphics position (64, 32).

Colors

The next step is to decide what colors you want. This is done via the COLOR statement, which takes two integer arguments:

COLOR *X, Y*

The first position specifies the background color, and here you have the most leeway. You can choose any one of 16 colors as the background color, and they are the same for character (text) graphics. (But, if you have an EGA or VGA, then a later section will show you how to change these colors.)

Here's the list:

0	black		5	magenta
1	blue		6	brown
2	green		7	white
3	cyan		8	gray
4	red		9	light blue

10	light green	13	light magenta
11	light cyan	14	yellow
12	light red	15	high intensity white

See the on-line help for how these are interpreted on monochrome monitors.

The COLOR statement can be used to switch the background color, as the following fragment demonstrates:

```
SCREEN 1
LOCATE 1, 1
PRINT "Press Any Key For The Next Color"
FOR CNumber = 0 TO 15
   LOCATE 12, 1
   COLOR CNumber, 0
   PRINT "This is color #"; CNumber
   SLEEP        'pause until a key is pressed
NEXT CNumber
```

The second position in the COLOR statement (for example, the 0 in the above fragment) is a bit less powerful. This controls what is usually called the palette. And, just as an artist's palette holds the colors he or she has available, this second entry controls what colors you have available for the foreground. Two palettes are available, Palette 0 and Palette 1. They each contain the following four colors (more or less—depending on your monitor):

Palette 0

0. background color
1. green
2. red
3. brown

Palette 1

0. background color
1. cyan
2. magenta
3. white

For example, the statement COLOR 5, 0 means that the screen will be able to display magenta (the background color), green, red, and brown (the colors available in Palette 0). Similarly, the statement COLOR 14, 1 gives you brown (the background color), cyan, magenta, and white. For example, the statements

```
SCREEN 1
COLOR 3, 0
PRINT "Hello world!"
```

put you in medium resolution, turn the background color to cyan, and display the message in brown letters (text always appears in the third color of the current palette).

The colors contained in a palette are usually called the attributes of that palette. As you will see shortly, the attribute number preceding each color in the table above is what you use in Visual Basic's graphics statements to specify the color in which an image is to be drawn. Think of the attribute number as identifying a location on an artist's palette. An artist could put whatever color paint he or she wished at each of these numbered locations. In SCREEN 1, unlike an artist, you must choose between two predefined palettes, each of which holds only four colors. Your only freedom is the choice of the color placed at the location numbered 0.

In summary, to get started in medium resolution graphics, issue two statements:

SCREEN 1
COLOR *background, palette number*

(Even integers in the second entry give palette zero and odd numbers give palette one.)

One important characteristic worth noting about medium resolution graphics mode is that text appears twice as wide as in text mode. As a result, there are 40 characters to a line instead of 80. The statement SCREEN 0, which you use to return to text mode, does not return you to 80 characters per line; the additional statement WIDTH 80 is required. Thus, to exit graphics mode and prepare to display forms, issue the two statements:

```
SCREEN 0
WIDTH 80
```

 Note   The wide characters of medium resolution graphics mode can also be used in text mode by issuing the statement WIDTH 40. The statement WIDTH 80 brings things back to normal. The screen is erased when the WIDTH statement is executed, so you can't combine the two sizes.

When working with high resolution graphics mode, you only have two colors available and text always appears in its normal (WIDTH 80) size. In SCREEN 2, in graphics statements that allow a color attribute, you will only be able to use 0 (to draw in the background color) or 1 (to draw in the foreground color). The background color is the lowest color in the current palette and the foreground color is the highest.

Pixel Control

Now you know about the two basic graphics modes and about the colors available. How do you turn a pixel on? You use the statement

PSET(*x, y*)

where *x* is the column and *y* is the row of the point you wish to turn on. After Visual Basic processes this statement, the pixel at the indicated coordinates lights up. Where that point is depends on whether you've previously issued a SCREEN 1 or SCREEN 2 statement. After a SCREEN 1 statement

PSET(319, 0)

would turn on the top right corner pixel, but after a SCREEN 2 statement it would be in the center of the first row. It's possible to PSET outside the limits of the screen, for example: PSET(2000, 1000)—no error message results.

```
'use PSET to draw line down center of screen
SCREEN 1
COLOR 1, 0
FOR I = 0 TO 199
  PSET (160, I)
NEXT I
END
```

The color used by PSET defaults to the one with the highest attribute number in the current palette. In high resolution, this is your one and only foreground color. In medium resolution, this is the color associated with attribute 3 in the current palette (brown or white). For example, in the preceding program the statement COLOR 1, 0 chooses blue as the background and palette 0. Thus you'll get a brown line on a blue screen. In medium resolution you can also choose among the colors in the current palette by a modification of the PSET statement. For example, if you wanted to get a red line (color 2 of palette 0), change the PSET statement above to PSET(160, I), 2. Using PSET(160, I), 0 in the program above would "turn on" pixels in the background color and so the line would be invisible.

Your color preference follows the PSET statement like this:

PSET(*x, y*), *ColorCode*

Suppose you wanted to erase every other pixel in the line of the program above. Although there are many ways to do this, at this point the simplest is to notice that redrawing a point in the background color erases it:

```
FOR I = 0 TO 199 STEP 2
  PSET (160, I), 0
NEXT I
```

Another possibility is a variant on the PSET statement, PRESET. PRESET(*x, y*) "turns off" the pixel at the coordinates given in the parentheses.

Lines

Obviously, if you had to draw everything by plotting individual points, graphics programming would be too time-consuming. Instead, Visual Basic comes with a rich supply of graphics statements (in computerese, graphics primitives) that allow you to plot such geometric figures as lines, boxes, circles, ellipses, or wedges with a single statement.

For example, the statement:

LINE (160, 0)-(160, 199)

draws a line identical to the one produced using PSET at the beginning of this section. More generally the statement:

LINE (*StartColumn, StartRow*)-(*EndCol, EndRow*), *ColorCode* gives you a line connecting the two points with the given coordinates using the color specified by ColorCode. The parameter ColorCode is optional. For example, the listing that follows gives you a "starburst" by drawing random lines in random colors from the center of the screen:

```
'random lines in random colors
RANDOMIZE
SCREEN 1
COLOR 0, 0
FOR I = 1 TO 100
   Col = INT(320 * RND)
   Row = INT(200 * RND)
   ColorCode = 1 + INT(3 * RND)
   LINE (160, 100)-(Col, Row), ColorCode
NEXT I
SLEEP          'pause until a key is pressed
```

The body of the FOR-NEXT loop calculates a random point and color code on each pass. Next, it draws a line from the center of the screen to that point. It's good to have a SLEEP statement like this at the end of a graphics program that you're developing, because the ubiquitous "Press any key to continue" that appears when a Visual Basic program finishes often wipes out a portion of the painted screen.

Suppose you wanted to draw a rocket ship as in Figure 16-2.

Since you can read off the coordinates from the diagram, it's easy (if a bit tedious) to write the program as shown here:

```
' A rocket ship
SCREEN 1
COLOR 0, 0
LINE (120, 199)-(200, 199)
LINE (200, 199)-(180, 179)
LINE (180, 179)-(180, 79)
LINE (180, 79)-(160, 59)
LINE (160, 59)-(140, 79)
LINE (140, 79)-(140, 179)
LINE (140, 179)-(120, 199)
SLEEP
```

It's possible to draw almost anything by outlining it using graph paper—just mimic what was done above. Obviously, as the object becomes more complicated, it becomes less and less practical. (One of the reasons why mathematics is needed for computer graphics is to give formulas for various complicated objects. The formulas then shorten the length of the program because they themselves incorporate an enormous amount of information. Formulas make writing a program practical, whereas writing a few thousand PSET statements does not.)

A modification of the LINE statement lets you draw a rectangle using the B (for Box) option. The statement:

LINE (*FirstCol, FirstRow*)-(*SecCol, SecRow*), *ColorCode*, B

draws a rectangle in the given color code (ColorCode) whose opposite corners are given by (FirstCol, FirstRow) and (SecCol, SecRow). For

**FIGURE
16-2**

A rocket ship

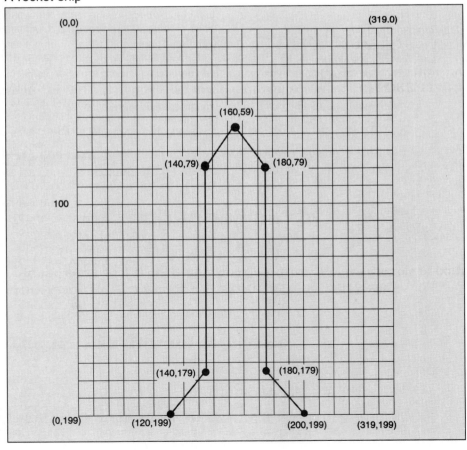

example, the following fragment gives you "nested boxes" in the high resolution screen mode.

```
SCREEN 2
FOR I = 1 TO 65 STEP 5
  LINE (5 * I, I)-(639 - 5 * I, 199 - I), , B
NEXT I
```

Notice that the color code has been left off—but the comma remains to separate out the B. Without this comma Visual Basic would think the B was the name of a variable rather than the "box" clause. Leave out the comma, and Visual Basic would think you're asking for a line connecting (5 * I, I)-(639-5 * I, 199-I) with color code the current value of B (probably 0 so you'd get nothing!). You also could have entered a 1, 2, or 3 for the color code.

Say "BF" rather than "B" and you get a "filled" box, so:

LINE (*FirstCol, FirstRow*)-(*SecCol, SecRow*), *ColorCode*, BF

yields a solid rectangle whose opposite corners are given by (FirstCol, FirstRow) and (SecCol, SecRow). For example, change the fragment to read:

```
DIM I AS INTEGER, ColorCode AS INTEGER
SCREEN 1
COLOR 0, 0
FOR I = 1 TO 32 STEP 3
  ColorCode = I MOD 4
  LINE (5 * I, I)-(320 - 5 * I, 199 - I), ColorCode, BF
NEXT I
```

and you get a rather dramatic nesting of colored frames. This happens for two reasons. The first is that the MOD function lets you cycle through the color codes in order, and the second is that when Visual Basic draws each smaller rectangle it overdraws part of the previous one using the new color.

Visual Basic has a feature called *line clipping*. Consider a statement of the form LINE (*a,b*)-(*c,d*) where one or both of the points (*a,b*) and (*c,d*) are off the screen. Visual Basic locates the points in a fictitious coordinate system larger than the screen but containing the two points. Visual Basic then "imagines" the line connecting the two points in the large coordinate system and displays the portion of the line lying on the screen. That is, it clips off any imaginary portion of the line.

Simple Animation

Although Visual Basic has many powerful tools to create animation (see Chapter 18 of the Visual Basic *Programmer's Guide*), you have the tools available now to simulate one kind: a so-called drunkard's walk (or a random walk, as it's more technically called). All this involves is an object whose movements over time can be plotted. If it seems to move randomly (like some people say the stock market does—or did, until October 19, 1987), then you have a random walk. To simulate this movement, put a tiny square in the middle of the screen and move it around, erasing the previous square each time. However, instead of moving the square a fixed amount, have it move up and down and left and right randomly. As you'll see, the square will spend most of it's time in a narrow range around the center.

```
' moving squares to imitate a 'random walk'
RANDOMIZE
SCREEN 1
COLOR 0
DIM X AS INTEGER, Y AS INTEGER, I AS INTEGER
DIM XMove AS INTEGER, YMove AS INTEGER, T AS INTEGER
X = 160: Y = 100
FOR I = 0 TO 500
  XMove = 6 * RND
  YMove = 5 * RND
  IF RND < .5 THEN X = X + XMOVE ELSE X = X - XMOVE
  IF RND < .5 THEN Y = Y + YMOVE ELSE Y = Y - YMOVE
  IF (X < 0) OR (X > 293) OR (Y < 0) OR (Y > 194) THEN
  'DO NOTHING
  ELSE
    LINE (X, Y)-(X + 6, Y + 5), 2, BF
    FOR T = 1 TO 1000: NEXT    'a slight delay
    LINE (X, Y)-(X + 6, Y + 5), 0, BF
  END IF
NEXT I
SLEEP
```

Here's the random motion: the box moves up or down and left or right depending on whether the random number generator delivers a number less than one half. By redrawing the rectangle in the background color, it's erased, producing the animation. If you remove the second line statement, then the animation is lost but is replaced by a visible trace of where the box has been. Change the ELSE clause to read:

```
ColorCode = 1 + 3 * RND
LINE (X, Y)-(X + 6, Y + 5), ColorCode, BF
```

and the results are (usually) a quite attractive random pattern.

Last Point Referenced

Visual Basic keeps track of where it stopped plotting. This is usually called the *last point referenced* (LPR). If you are continuing a line from the last point referenced, Visual Basic allows you to omit it in the LINE statement. For example:

```
LINE -(160, 90)
```

draws a line from the last point referenced to the point with coordinates (160, 90). When you start any graphics mode with a SCREEN statement, then the last point referenced is the center of the screen. After a LINE statement, the last point referenced is the end point of the line (the second coordinate pair).

Up to now you've been using absolute coordinates. Each point is associated with a unique row and column. It's occasionally useful to use relative coordinates, where each point is defined by how far away it is from the last point referenced. For example,

PSET(12, 100) or PRESET(12, 100)

makes (12, 100) the last point referenced. Then,

```
PSET STEP(50, 10)
```

turns on the point in column 62 (50 + 12) and row 110 (10 + 100). In general, when Visual Basic sees the statement:

STEP(*x, y*)

in a graphics statement it uses the point whose coordinates are *x* units to the right or left and *y* units up or down from the last point referenced. (Depending on whether *x* and *y* are positive or not.)

Circles, Ellipses and Pie Charts

Normally, to describe a circle in Visual Basic, you give its center and radius. For example, after a SCREEN 1 statement,

```
CIRCLE (160, 100), 60
```

draws a circle of radius 60 in the default foreground color (the third color of the current palette). The last point referenced after a CIRCLE statement is always the center of the circle: (160, 100) in the example above. On the other hand:

```
CIRCLE (160, 100), 60, ColorCode
```

would draw a circle of radius 60 in the color code indicated by the variable ColorCode. The following program shows off this use of the circle statement:

```
' nested circles
DIM I AS INTEGER, ColorCode AS INTEGER
SCREEN 1
COLOR 1, 1
FOR I = 59 TO 259 STEP 4
  ColorCode = 1 + (I MOD 3)
  CIRCLE (I, 100), 60, ColorCode
NEXT I
SLEEP
```

These circles are a bit jagged because the resolution in SCREEN 1 is minimal. If you don't mind the loss of color, you can smooth the circles considerably by using high resolution (SCREEN 2) graphics.

You may be wondering what the radius figure exactly means—60 columns, or 60 rows, or both 60 columns and 60 rows, as a mathematical radius would be. The CIRCLE statement usually counts pixels by columns to determine the radius. It then scales the number of rows by dividing by 1.2. So a circle of width 60 would take 60 columns and only 50 rows, in medium resolution mode. In high resolution it divides the number of columns by 2.4 to get the number of rows. So the CIRCLE statement in this program had Visual Basic plot what it hopes will be a circle, assuming that your monitor has the width-to-height ratio of 4 to 3. Obviously, if you have a monitor that has a different aspect ratio, you must override Visual Basic's assumption, using a variant on the CIRCLE statement that you'll see shortly.

You may have seen pie charts used to display data. Visual Basic sets up a pie chart with a modification of the circle statement. First, some terminology: a sector is a pie-shaped region of a circle, and an arc is the curved boundary of a sector. See Figure 16-3.

To draw a sector or arc you have to tell Visual Basic at which angles to start and finish. This is done using radian measure—which you may have seen in school (and is used in the trigonometric functions in Visual Basic). Radian measure isn't very difficult: it measures angles by the percentage of the circumference of a circle of radius one. All the way around is called 2π radians because 2π is the length of the circumference of this circle. So 360° is 2π or approximately 6.28 radians, 1/2 a circle (180°) is π radians, 1/4 circle (90°) is $\pi/2$ radians, and so on. To go from degrees to radians multiply by $\pi/180$, to go back multiply by $180/\pi$. In any case, the statement:

CIRCLE (*XRad, YRad*), *radius, ColorCode, StartAngle, EndAngle*

draws an arc of the circle starting at the angle (in radians) StartAngle and ending at Endangle. To draw a sector, use negative signs. So,

FIGURE 16-3 Sector and arc

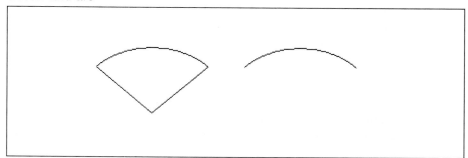

assuming that you're in SCREEN 2 and have set up a variable called Pi = 3.14159 (or 4 * ATN(1) ¶) then:

```
CIRCLE (150, 100), 160, 1, -Pi / 4, -3 * Pi / 4
```

gives you the sector in Figure 16-3. And:

```
CIRCLE (150, 100), 160, 1, Pi / 4, 3 * Pi / 4
```

gives you the arc.

There are a few peculiarities of these statements that should be mentioned: the first is that, although mathematics allows negative angles, Visual Basic does not. The negative sign only serves to indicate: "Draw a sector rather than an arc." The second is that if you want your arc to start with a horizontal line pointed due east (in other words, 0 degrees = 0 radians), you shouldn't use -0 for the StartAngle or EndAngle. Instead, use -2 * π (= -6.28...). The final peculiarity is that angles in the CIRCLE statement can only have values between -2π (-6.28...) and 2π (6.28..).

Suppose you wanted to write a general "pie making program," meaning a program that takes positive numbers (stored in an array) and sets up a pie chart using the numbers. Essentially, what you need to do is to determine what percentage of the total each number represents, and set up an arc using that percentage. Here's the procedure:

```
SUB MakePie(A(), SizeOfCircle)
  ' This procedure takes an array of positive entries and
  ' creates a pie chart using proportions determined by the
  ' array.
  ' local variables: I, First, Last, Total, StartAngle, EndAngle
  DIM I AS INTEGER, First AS INTEGER, Last AS INTEGER
  DIM TwoPi AS SINGLE, Total AS SINGLE
  DIM StartAngle AS SINGLE, EndAngle AS SINGLE

  TwoPi = 8 * ATN(1)
  First = LBOUND(A)
  Last = UBOUND(A)
  Total = 0
  FOR I = First TO Last
    Total = Total + A(I)
  NEXT I
  SCREEN 2
```

```
    StartAngle = -TwoPi
    FOR I = First TO Last
       EndAngle = ((A(I)/ Total) * TwoPi) + StartAngle
       CIRCLE (320, 100), SizeOfCircle, 1, StartAngle, EndAngle
       StartAngle = EndAngle
    NEXT I
 END SUB
```

The value of A(I)/Total yields the fraction of the total a particular entry is. Multiplying by TwoPi (= 2*3.14159..) results in the radian equivalent. Since the StartAngle is -2 * π, adding this angle gives the necessary negative number for the size of the sector—starting due east and going counter-clockwise.

How can you test this procedure? Simply create some random arrays of random sizes with random positive entries and CALL the procedure.

The CIRCLE statement allows you to adjust the aspect ratio by adding one more option:

CIRCLE (*XCenter*, *YCenter*), *radius*, , , , *aspect*

The four commas must be there even if you are not using the color code and angle options that you saw earlier. This version of the CIRCLE statement lets you change the default ratio of columns to rows. (It's really an ELLIPSE statement.)

Aspect ratios such as 2 or 3 give narrow, tall ellipses, while aspect ratios such as .4 or .5 give wide, short ellipses. Here's a program that demonstrates this:

```
' Aspect ratio test for ellipses
SCREEN 2
PRINT "Press any key to continue"
SLEEP
FOR I = .1 TO 2 STEP .1
  CIRCLE (320, 100), 75, , , , I
  LOCATE 24, 10
  PRINT "This is aspect ratio"; I;
  PRINT "Press any key to continue";
  SLEEP
  CLS
NEXT I
SLEEP
```

Although this program stops when the aspect ratio reaches 2, you could continue making it bigger. As the aspect ratio gets larger, the ellipses get closer and closer to a vertical line.

You also can fill in enclosed areas using the PAINT statement. The statement

PAINT *x, y, PaintColor, BorderColor*

begins filling in the area about the point (*x, y*) and stops whenever it gets to a pixel of the color given by BorderColor. If you leave BorderColor out, then Visual Basic stops "painting" only when it encounters a pixel whose color is the same as PaintColor.

How the PAINT statement will actually work in practice is a bit subtle, but a good analogy to keep in mind is a spreading paint slick. A slick will stop whenever it hits a boundary point. On the other hand, it could continue "forever" if there's a hole in the boundary, however small, as the following two fragments will show. First, paint a circle:

```
SCREEN 1
COLOR 0, 0
CIRCLE (160, 100), 75
PAINT (160, 100)
```

This gives you a white circle. Now insert a PRESET statement to turn one pixel on the boundary of the circle off:

```
SCREEN 1
COLOR 0, 0
CIRCLE (160, 100),75
PRESET (235, 100)
PAINT (160, 100)
```

and rerun the fragment. What you'll see is the whole screen gradually turning white. The moral is to make sure your boundaries are solid. (You should be aware that the whole concept of boundary is a subtle one in mathematics, as is finding an inside point. In this case the only points on the boundary that are easy to calculate are the ones horizontal with the center.)

Usually, lines are solid and paint fills with a solid color. It's possible to change this. (See Chapter 18 of the Visual Basic *Programmer's Guide.*)

The DRAW Statement

The rocket ship program demonstrated earlier was short but tedious. The DRAW statement gives you a much more powerful way to create any graphics figures that you can sketch. Essentially, the DRAW statement gives you the control of a pen that you can move and lift as needed. Moreover, once an object is drawn you can store it, rotate it, scale it, or move it with a single statement.

For example, the statement DRAW "U10" draws a 10-pixel line directly up from the last point referenced. In general, the DRAW statement uses certain combinations of command letters and numerals. Here are a few more DRAW commands:

DRAW Command	What it does
U	up
D	down
L	left
R	right
E	diagonally up and to the right
H	diagonally up and to the left
F	diagonally down and to the right
G	diagonally down and to the left

These statements alone are enough to let you imitate the famous Etch-A-Sketch toy, and this is a standard, but still fun, programming problem. See the section "Using a Mouse in Graphics" for a mouse-driven version. For another example, the following fragment redraws the rocket ship again. First, invoke medium resolution graphics and make (120, 199) the last point referenced:

```
SCREEN 1
COLOR 0, 0
PSET (120, 199)        'There are other ways to do this
```

Now enter:

```
DRAW "R80 H20 U100 H20 G20 D100 G20"
```

This statement draws a line to the right 80 pixels, then diagonally up and to the left 20 pixels, then straight up 100 pixels, etc. Here, as in any DRAW statement, the spaces improve readability but Visual Basic doesn't require them.

However, you can do much more. Set up a string:

```
RocketShip$ = "R80 H20 U100 H20 G20 D100 G20"
```

Now, to have two rocket ships on the screen:

```
PSET (50,199)        'set LPR
DRAW RocketShip$
PSET (200, 199)      'reset LPR
DRAW RocketShip$
```

Most of the power of the DRAW statement comes after you've set up string variables that will draw the figures you're interested in. This is because you can add statements before you issue a DRAW statement (or inside a DRAW statement) that scale, rotate, change color, or paint the object. For example:

DRAW "S*Number*"

enlarges the object by a factor given of *Number*/4. This means that the statements:

```
RocketShip$ = "R80 H20 U100 H20 G20 D100 G20"
SCREEN 1
COLOR 0,0
PSET (50,199)
DRAW "S8"
DRAW RocketShip$
```

give you a rocket ship that is twice as large as the ones drawn by the earlier code fragments. The scaling number must be between 1 and 255. (You'll soon see how to incorporate a numeric variable.) Scaling can easily lead to a clipped image. A statement like DRAW "S64" enlarges your figure by a factor of 16—very few figures will fit in their entirety after this.

For an example of scaling, try the following:

```
Rocket$ = "R80 H20 U100 H20 G20 D100 G20"
SCREEN 1
COLOR 0, 0
PSET (20, 199)
DRAW "S1"
DRAW Rocket$
```

Now try the following program called "armada":

```
' An armada
DIM Rocket$, I AS INTEGER, Scale$, NewPos AS INTEGER

Rocket$ = "R80 H20 U100 H20 G20 D100 G20"
SCREEN 1
COLOR 0, 0
LOCATE 1, 10
PRINT "Buck Rogers revisited"
FOR I = 1 TO 4
  Scale$ = "S" + STR$(I)
  DRAW Scale$
  NewPos = NewPos + 5 + (20 * I)
  PSET (NewPos, 199)
  DRAW Rocket$
NEXT I
SLEEP
```

The line with the SCALE command is the most interesting line. Although there are other ways to incorporate numeric variables into a DRAW statement, by far the simplest is shown in the example just given: use STR$ to convert the value of the numeric variable to a string value, and concatenate this onto the appropriate command letter.

The position of the next rocket has to take into account the size of the rocket. S1 is one-quarter size, S2 half-size, etc. The rockets would be 20, 40, 60, and 80 pixels across.

Now go back to the analogy of pen plotting. The DRAW "B_" command "lifts the pen" for the next movement command. So a statement like:

DRAW "B U10 L8"

moves the last point referenced 10 points up without plotting any points, and then plots 8 points to the left.

Instead of moving a certain number of pixels in a given direction, you can move to a specific point with the DRAW "M_" command. The statement:

DRAW "M x, y"

moves to the point (x, y), plotting points as it goes. This has the same effect as: LINE -(x, y). If a plus or minus sign proceeds x or y, then the movement is relative to the LPR. For example, the statement DRAW "M +x, -y" would work like:

LINE -STEP (x, -y)

The statement

DRAW "B M x, y"

makes (x, y) the last point referenced without plotting the point. For example, you could use it in place of the PSET statements in the armada program above.

The DRAW "N_" command allows you to plot without changing the last point referenced:

DRAW "N D10"

draws a line 10 pixels long but doesn't change the LPR. As with the DRAW "B_" command, the DRAW "N_" command only applies to the next movement command.

Suppose you wanted to make the rocket ship move. Here's one way to do this:

DRAW Rocket$
Change to the background color, wait a bit
DRAW Rocket$ again
Change the LPR
reDRAW Rocket$

The command to set the drawing color is DRAW "C_", as you'll see in the following program to move the rocket. (The conversion of the outline is complicated by the fact that a statement like SLEEP .1 isn't yet possible):

```
'another way to animate
DIM Rocket$, I AS INTEGER, Row$

SCREEN 1
COLOR 0, 0
Rocket$ = "R80 H20 U100 H20 G20 D100 G20"
DRAW "S1"
FOR I = 199 TO 50 STEP -10
  Row$ = STR$(I)
  DRAW "B M 140," + Row$
  DRAW "C3" + Rocket$
  CALL Delay(.1)
  DRAW "C0" + Rocket$
NEXT I

SUB Delay (x AS SINGLE)
  'local variables:
  DIM StartTime AS SINGLE

  StartTime = TIMER
  DO UNTIL (TIMER - StartTime) >= x
  LOOP
END SUB
```

Notice how this program again creates a string using concatenation.

The DRAW statement also lets you rotate a figure a certain number of degrees (not radians!). The DRAW "TA_" command followed by the number of degrees rotates the figure to be plotted. For example:

```
DRAW "B M 100, 160"
DRAW "TA 45"
DRAW Rocket$
```

gives you the original-sized rocket at a 45° angle (counter-clockwise).

Finally, the statement DRAW "P x, y" works exactly like the statement PAINT (x, y) using whatever color has been set by the previous DRAW "C_" command.

Other SCREEN Modes—Some Powers of EGA and VGA Cards

EGA and VGA cards give you enormous powers. The help files that explain how to control them are about 20 pages long and can be a bit intimidating. Hopefully, after reading this section, the help files won't seem quite so formidable.

So far you've seen SCREEN 1 and 2 (as mentioned before, SCREEN 3 for Hercules cards works like SCREEN 2 except the resolution is higher). Here's a brief explanation of what the other screen modes can do:

❑ SCREEN 4: Is for ATT and Olivetti computers only. In this mode you have 640 columns and 400 rows (640 x 400), text is 80 characters/line, and any one of 16 foreground colors may be selected through the COLOR statement (the background is always black).

All the other screen modes require at least an EGA card.

❑ SCREEN 7: EGA or VGA. 320 x 200 graphics—text is 40 characters/line with 25 lines/screen. A palette of 16 colors is available. Any one of these colors may be selected as the background color. The remaining 15 colors may be used simultaneously as foreground colors.

❑ SCREEN 8: EGA or VGA. 640 x 200 graphics—text is 80 characters/line with 25 lines/screen. Has the same color capabilities as SCREEN 7.

❑ SCREEN 9: EGA or VGA. 640 x 350 graphics. 80 characters/line for either 25 or 43 lines/screen. 64 colors are available. Depending on the memory on your graphics card, you can choose either 4 or 16 of these colors for simultaneous display as foreground colors; all 64 colors are available for the background.

❑ SCREEN 10: EGA or VGA with a monochrome monitor only. 640 x 350 graphics. 80 characters/line for either 25 or 43 lines/screen.

❑ SCREEN 11: VGA (or a PS/2 25-30's MCGA, the "semi VGA"), 640 x 480, 80 characters/line for either 30 or 60 lines/screen. One foreground and one background color chosen from among (honestly) 262,144 (256k) colors. (Expect the differences to be subtle.)

☐   SCREEN 12: VGA only. 640 x 480, 80 characters/line for either 30 or 60 lines/screen. This time there will be one background and 15 foreground colors chosen from the same 262,144 colors as in SCREEN 11.

☐   SCREEN 13: VGA (or the "semi VGA" of a PS/2 30). 320 x 200 resolution, 40 characters/line for 25 lines/screen. Allows one background color and up to 255 foreground colors chosen from the same 262,144 colors.

Whenever you are allowed more than 25 lines, then the WIDTH statement is used to do so. For example, WIDTH , 43 sets the number of lines to 43 after a SCREEN 10 statement.

Finding the SCREEN Mode

Finally, the easiest way to determine what kind of video card a machine has is to use error trapping. For example, if SCREEN 12 is not allowed but SCREEN 11 is, then you have an MCGA. Similarly, if SCREEN 7 is allowed but not SCREEN 11, you have an EGA, and so on.

The actual programming is a bit tricky. What you can do is set up an array for the possible modes. Next, set up a loop that stops either when you've tried all the modes or have managed to use the SCREEN statement without going to the error handler. The easiest way to do this is to use a variable called Found. In each pass of the loop, Found is set back to TRUE but the error handler, if invoked, always switches it back to FALSE. This works because your loop is only tested at the top. Here is the module:

```
'find out acceptable SCREEN modes via error handler
CONST FALSE = 0, TRUE = NOT (FALSE)
DIM Modes(1 TO 7) AS INTEGER,I AS INTEGER,ModeToTry AS INTEGER
ON ERROR GOTO VideoHandler
FOR I = 1 TO 7
  READ Modes(I)
NEXT I
ModeToTry = 1
Found = FALSE
DO UNTIL ModeToTry = 6 OR Found
  Found = TRUE
```

```
    SCREEN Modes(ModeToTry)
LOOP
PRINT "The screen mode you can use is"; Modes(ModeToTry)
DATA  12,11,7,4,3,2,0

VideoHandler:
ModeToTry = ModeToTry + 1
Found = FALSE
RESUME NEXT
```

Graphics Screen Dumps

If you want to print a graphics screen, execute the DOS program GRAPHICS.COM before you invoke Visual Basic. Then pressing SHIFT+PRINTSCREEN may produce the desired screen dump. Whether you are successful or not depends on the screen mode you're in, the version of DOS you have, and your printer. As an alternative, the companion diskette for this book contains several procedures that print a graphics screen from within a Visual Basic program without requiring either the execution of GRAPHICS.COM or a specific version of DOS.

Working with Palettes

Suppose you are in SCREEN 1. Recall that in SCREEN 1 you had two palettes each with four fixed colors. These "tubes of paint" are, as mentioned earlier, usually called attributes. The numbers used in coloring pixels via any graphics statement are therefore called attribute numbers.

Now suppose you have an EGA or VGA card. You can change these previously fixed colors—that is, change the colors assigned to the different attribute numbers. For example, the statement

```
PALETTE 1, 14
```

would change the color in tube one (attribute one) to the color with code 14—which happens to be yellow. The 16 colors that you can use to replace the default colors are exactly those for the background colors given in the table in the "Colors" section earlier in this chapter. A PALETTE statement with no other entries restores the default colors.

In general, the PALETTE statement chooses the colors available for display by assigning a color (number) to an attribute (the number of attributes depending on the screen mode). Attributes are then used in statements like DRAW "C_", LINE, and CIRCLE to draw objects. For example, the statement:

LINE (*x*1, *y*1)-(*x*2, *y*2), *attribute*

would give you a LINE in the color specified by the current value of *attribute*.

Moreover, the PALETTE statement will change the screen instantaneously. If a part of the screen appears in attribute 2, and you were allowed, say, 64 colors, then the statement PALETTE 2, 53 would recolor that part of the screen in the fifty-third color. Because there are 15 attributes possible in text mode when you have an EGA or VGA card, you also can use the PALETTE statement to change the colors for TEXT (SCREEN 0) as well.

One place to show off the PALETTE statement is in SCREEN 9. In this mode, if you have enough memory on your graphics board, then you can have 16 attributes (colors) on the screen at any one time chosen from the 64 background colors.

Recall from earlier in this chapter that text is displayed in the color of the highest numbered attribute in a given palette, and the background is the color assigned to attribute 0. The following is a program that changes the text colors using the PALETTE statement:

```
' A demonstration of the PALETTE statement in SCREEN 9
DIM BGColor AS INTEGER, TextColor AS INTEGER
SCREEN 9
FOR BGColor = 0 TO 63
   PALETTE 0, BGColor
   CLS
   TextColor = (BGColor + 1) MOD 64
   PALETTE 15, TextColor
   LOCATE 1, 1
   PRINT "The background color is"; BGColor;
   PRINT "while the text appears in color number"; TextColor
   SLEEP 2
NEXT BGColor
```

Since the PALETTE statement works instantaneously, this changes the background color on each pass. As mentioned earlier in this chapter, text appears in the highest number attribute of the palette, which for SCREEN 9 is attribute 15. You are always using the color numbered one higher than the background color for the text. The MOD statement is just to wrap around when BGColor gets to 64.

Of course a more dramatic demonstration would be to change all the colors in a palette simultaneously. This is done using the PALETTE USING statement. The statement:

PALETTE USING *array*

where array is an array of integers or long integers, changes the colors in the palette by using the integers (long integers) stored in the array for the color attributes. You must DIMension the array to have at least as many entries as there are attributes. For example, suppose you have:

```
DIM A%(0 TO 31)
A%(0) = 12
A%(1) = 15
A%(2) = 37
```

then PALETTE USING A% would change the first (zeroth) attribute to color number 12, the second to color number 15, and so on. If an entry is -1 in the array, then the attribute stays its original color. Any other negative entry in A%, or one too large, would give an error message.

The above list was dimensioned at 31 (= 32 entries) to show off an optional feature of PALETTE USING. For example,

```
PALETTE USING A%(16)
```

uses colors starting from the sixteenth and going to the thirty-first entry. The general form is:

PALETTE USING *arrayname(index)*

where index determines where to start. You must have DIMensioned the array so there's enough room starting from the index to fill all the attributes.

Next is a program that changes all 16 colors in SCREEN 9's palette simultaneously. Because you can only display 16 colors at any one time, it shows them in four groups (colors 0-15, 16-31 etc.).

```
' A demonstration of the PALETTE USING statement in SCREEN 9
DIM Attrib(0 TO 63) AS INTEGER, I AS INTEGER, J AS INTEGER
SCREEN 9
FOR I = 0 TO 3
  FOR J = 0 TO 15
    Attrib((16 * I) + J) = (16 * I) + J
  NEXT J
  CALL Demo(Attrib(), I)
NEXT I

SUB Demo (A%(), ColorGroup AS INTEGER)
  'This SUB demonstrates the PALETTE USING statement
  'local variables:
  DIM Count AS INTEGER, I$

  CLS
  PALETTE USING A%(16 * ColorGroup)
  FOR Count = 0 TO 14
    LINE (0, 22 * Count)-(640, (22 * Count) + 21), Count, BF
  NEXT Count
  LINE (0, 330)-(640, 350), 15, BF
  LOCATE 1, 10
  PRINT "This shows off colors "; 16 * ColorGroup;
  PRINT " to"; (16 * ColorGroup) + 15;
  PRINT " Press any key to continue.";
  I$ = INPUT$(1)
END SUB
```

The inner FOR-NEXT loop fills an array with the integers from 0 to 63 in groups of 4 (indexed by I). Then use the counter I in the call to the subprogram.

The starting index in the PALETTE USING statement is computed using the parameter ColorGroup. On the first call start with 0, on the second with 16, and so on. The loop with the counter Count draws colored boxes 22 lines high, except for the last box, which is only 20 lines high.

As mentioned earlier, you might need a long integer array for the PALETTE USING statement. This is because in SCREEN 11-13 the color numbers can be as large as 4,144,959. For the analog monitors that are needed in these modes, colors are determined by explicitly setting the intensity of the blue, green, and red signal according to the formula:

(65536*Blue Intensity)+(256*Green Intensity)+Red Intensity

where the intensity for all the colors is a number between 0 (essentially don't use that color) and 63 (maximize that color component). A color code of:

(65536*63)

gives the bluest color possible, (256*63) the greenest, and 63 the reddest. 4144959 gives the one closest to white, and 0 is closest to black. By varying the blue, green, and red intensity, you can customize colors to your heart's content.

The WINDOW Statement

The screen is normally numbered with (0,0) as the upper-left corner. This is obviously inconvenient for doing mathematics, which uses an "X-Y" system with X measuring how far across you are from a central point, the origin, and Y measuring how far up or down from the center you are. For example, Figure 16-4 plots a few points on the plane.

The WINDOW statement, available in all graphics modes, sets up a new coordinate system that mimics the coordinates in the plane. For example:

```
WINDOW (-320, -100)-(320, 100)
```

sets up a new coordinate system with the coordinates of the lower-left corner as (-320, -100) and the upper-right corner as (320, 100). After this WINDOW statement is executed, the statements

```
PSET (-320, 100)
PSET (320, 100)
PSET (320, -100)
PSET (-320, -100)
PSET (0, 0)
```

FIGURE
16-4

X-Y plane with points

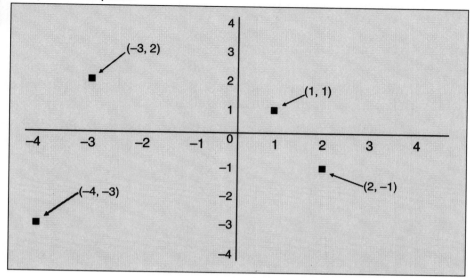

illuminate the four corners in a clockwise order, starting from the upper-left, and then illuminates the center of the screen. Whenever you issue a WINDOW statement followed by a graphics statement, Visual Basic automatically finds the pixel that corresponds to your coordinates, rounding if necessary.

Note Another important feature of the Windows statement is that it lets you draw without regard to the screen mode, because the actual number of pixels displayed on the screen is no longer relevant.

In general the WINDOW statement looks like this:

WINDOW (*LeftX, BottomY*)-(*RightX, TopY*)

where *LeftX* is a single-precision real number that will represent the smallest X coordinate (leftmost), *TopY* a single-precision number for the largest Y (top), etc. WINDOW (–1E38, –1E38)-(1E38, 1E38) gives you the largest possible scale, which means the smallest amount of detail—large

X and Y changes will be needed just to light up adjacent pixels! On the other hand, in SCREEN 2, the statement

```
WINDOW (-319, -99)-(320, 100)
```

sets up a coordinate system where each pixel corresponds to a pair of integer coordinates, and adjacent pixels have coordinates that differ by exactly one in either the X or Y direction.

The next program sets up an X-Y axis in SCREEN 2 that allows numbers on the axes satisfying:

$-5 \le X \le 5, -5 \le Y \le 5$

```
SCREEN 2
WINDOW (-5, -5)-(5, 5)
LINE (-5, 0)-(5, 0)            'X Axis
LINE (0, 5)-(0, -5)           'Y Axis
' Now to label the axes add:
LOCATE 12,1: PRINT "X -Axis";
FOR I = 1 TO 6
  LOCATE I, 42
  PRINT MID$("Y Axis", I , 1);
NEXT I
```

LOCATE on the twelfth text line and forty-second column in order to be a bit away from the center. Finally, you might want to add little lines as tick marks.

```
FOR I = -5 TO 5
  LINE (I, .2)-(I, -.2)
  LINE (-.1, I)-(.1, I)
NEXT I
```

This fragment is actually the most interesting. It takes into account that, with this WINDOW setting, a horizontal line as long as a vertical one needs roughly twice the vertical distance. In terms of pixels, in this window, a line from -.2 TO .2 takes up .4/10 (= 1/25) of the rows (= 8 pixels = one text line). A line from -.1 to .1 takes up .2/10 (= 1/50) of the columns (= 13 pixels or a little less than 2 text columns.)

Labeling objects after a WINDOW statement is made easier with two statements: PMAP and POINT. After a WINDOW statement, PMAP(X,0) gives the ordinary pixel column coordinate for the point X, and PMAP(Y,1) gives you the ordinary row coordinate corresponding to Y. As you can imagine, these statements make captioning graphics easier. If you want to mark a specific place on the screen after a WINDOW statement, go to the Immediate window, issue two PMAP statements to find its ordinary coordinates, and then convert these to text rows and columns by dividing by the appropriate number (8 for rows, 8 or 16 for columns). Finally, use LOCATE to put the text where you want it.

Similarly, you can go the other way: PMAP(ColumnCoord, 3) gives you the X coordinate and PMAP(RowCoord, 4) gives the Y coordinate of points in the window in their ordinary coordinates.

POINT works with the last point referenced (LPR). POINT(0) gives you the ordinary column coordinate of the LPR, POINT(1) the ordinary row coordinate. On the other hand, after a WINDOW statement, POINT(2) gives you the X coordinate and POINT(3) the Y coordinate using the WINDOW statement's X-Y coordinates.

The WINDOW statement makes graphing any mathematical function easy. The only problems come in deciding the maximum and minimum values to use for the statement—which often takes Calculus. However, as before, Visual Basic will clip any figure that is off the screen, so no problems result from setting the wrong scale.

Here's a program for a Cosine graph:

```
DIM TwoPi AS SINGLE, I AS SINGLE
TwoPi = 8 * ATN(1)
SCREEN 2
WINDOW (-TwoPi, -1)-(TwoPi, 1)
FOR I = -TwoPi TO TwoPi STEP .01
  PSET (I, COS(I))
NEXT I
```

You can put in the axes and mark them. Experiment with the other functions—the ones that you may need for school or work.

Using a Mouse in Graphics

The following program, which allows the user to draw on the screen, illustrates the use of a mouse in connection with graphics. To run this program, you must start up Visual Basic with VBDOS / L. After entering the following code, press ALT+F D and add the module MOUSE.BAS to your project. This module contains several procedures for manipulating the mouse on a graphics screen. The mouse procedures used in the following program are described by REM statements.

The program displays a rectangle and allows you to draw a figure within this rectangle by moving the mouse with the left button pressed.

```
DIM Row AS INTEGER, Col AS INTEGER
DIM lButton AS INTEGER, rButton AS INTEGER
DIM sMode AS INTEGER, sWidth AS INTEGER, Drawing AS INTEGER
DIM r1 AS INTEGER, r2 AS INTEGER, c1 AS INTEGER, c2 AS INTEGER
DIM MaxX AS INTEGER, MaxY AS INTEGER

' Change to highest resolution graphics mode available.
CALL SetHigh
' Check if mouse driver is installed.
CALL MouseInit
' Display mouse pointer.
CALL MouseShow
' Determine the screen mode which resulted from SetHigh
CALL ScrSettings(sMode, sWidth)
' Set background color to bright red
SELECT CASE sMode
  CASE 12, 11
    PALETTE 0, 63
  CASE 10, 9, 8, 7
    COLOR , 4
  CASE 1
    COLOR 4
END SELECT
' Determine the width and height of the screen in pixels
SELECT CASE sMode
  CASE 12, 11:
    MaxX = 640
    MaxY = 480
  CASE 10, 9
    MaxX = 640
    MaxY = 350
  CASE 8, 2
    MaxX = 640
    MaxY = 200
  CASE 7, 1
    MaxX = 320
    MaxY = 200
```

```
      CASE 3
         MaxX = 720
         MaxY = 348
   END SELECT
   c1 = .1 * MaxX
   c2 = .9 * MaxX
   r1 = .1 * MaxY
   r2 = .9 * MaxY
   ' Restrict the mouse to the rectangle with
   ' opposite vertices (r1, c1) and (r2, c2)
   CALL MouseBorder(r1, c1, r2, c2)
   LINE (c1, r1)-(c2, r2), , B
   PRINT "Hold down left button to draw."
   PRINT "Press right button to exit."
   DO UNTIL rButton
      ' Get mouse location and button status.
      CALL MousePoll(Row, Col, lButton, rButton)
      IF lButton THEN
         CALL MouseHide
         IF Drawing THEN
            LINE -(Col, Row)
         ELSE
            PSET (Col, Row)
            Drawing = NOT Drawing
         END IF
      ELSE
         MouseShow
         Drawing = 0
      END IF
   LOOP
   END
```

Sound

Sound is measured in Hertz (Hz is the abbreviation). 1 Hz equals 1 cycle per second. Ideally, but rarely in practice, humans can hear sounds between 20Hz and 20,000Hz. The BEEP statement gives a sound at 800Hz for about 1/4 of a second. The SOUND statement lets you, theoretically, play a given pure tone for a given amount of time. It's used as follows:

SOUND *frequency in Hz, duration*

The duration is measured in clock ticks, which are about 1/18 of a second (1/18.2 to be precise). So the statement:

```
SOUND 800, 18
```

produces a BEEP which lasts nearly one second. The statement SOUND 523, 18 would play a sound close to a middle C (523.25 is the frequency of middle C, but frequencies in Visual Basic must be integers.)

Combining the SOUND statement with a FOR-NEXT loop gives you an easy way to incorporate sound effects into your programs:

```
FOR I = 100 TO 5000 STEP 10
  SOUND I, 1
NEXT I
```

SOUNDs beyond 5,000 Hz are not likely to be audible on a PC's speaker.

Visual Basic can also use the PLAY statement to generate music. To use this facility, you have to know how music is scored. If you do and are interested in having the computer play tunes, you might want to refer to the on-line help as well as the write-up in Appendix C, which both give detailed discussions of the PLAY statement.

It's possible to write a program that can automate the process of entering notes, and anyone who reads Appendix C and knows enough about music shouldn't have much of a problem doing so. But in all honesty, IBM PCs are not known for their musical abilities.

As a sampling, however, of what you have to do, here is how to play something that sounds like the first few notes of "Auld Lang Syne":

```
PLAY "O3 C8 F8. F4 F4 A4 G4. F4 G4 A4 F4"
```

ISAM and Other Features of Visual Basic Professional

*I*SAM (Indexed Sequential Access Methods) is a powerful database management system that is one of the most exciting parts of the Professional Edition of Visual Basic. Random-access files are useful and are a valuable part of both the standard and professional edition of Visual Basic. But sometimes you might find yourself working with large data files, a task that is challenging and sometimes difficult. For example, in what order should records be placed so they can easily be retrieved? How should a file be searched for all records containing a certain value in one of its fields? If the file is too large to fit all the index keys in an array, how should (can) the index be handled? ISAM takes care of these tasks automatically—without you writing the thousands of lines of code that might otherwise be necessary.

After a detailed discussion of ISAM, this chapter ends with a short discussion of the other features of the Professional Edition. These features add capabilities to Visual Basic that can make your programming jobs easier and your projects more impressive. If you need any of the features of the Professional Edition, you will probably find the extra expense more than compensated by the time you save.

 Note   ISAM supplied with Visual Basic Pro currently does not work very well on networks. Some companies sell add-ons that will let you use ISAM on networks.

Getting the Feel of ISAM

Here's a paper-and-pencil example to get the idea of an ISAM table. Suppose you are interested in storing the following information about cities: name, state, and population. You could draw vertical lines on the top sheet of a pad of paper to create three columns, give each column a name, and enter data on the various cities, as shown in Table 17-1. Each line of the table is called a *record*, and each item of data in a record is called a *field*. So far, your table looks like a random-access file.

By placing a piece of carbon paper under the top sheet of paper, a second copy of the table is produced at the same time as the original table. Suppose you had a magical piece of carbon paper with the following properties:

1. The carbon paper has a name of its own and the name of one of the columns on it.

2. Inserting the carbon paper before a blank page reproduces the entire table on that page.

3. The new copy of the table is ordered by the entries in the column whose name appears on the carbon paper.

4. Any changes made to a record in the original table or in the copy are automatically made to all copies. (A change might be an addition, alteration, or deletion.)

For example, if you write "CityName" on a piece of carbon paper and place it in the pad, then the new copy of the table appears as in Table 17-2. Notice how the city names are now alphabetized. If you write "Population" on another piece of carbon paper and place it in the pad, the new copy appears ordered by population size, as in Table 17-3. Each copy has its advantages. If you are searching for a specific city, the "CityName" copy is more helpful. If you are looking for all cities with populations between 400,000 and 700,000, the "Population" copy works better.

This magic carbon paper sounds too good to be true. Yet, for all practical purposes, the ISAM statements and functions provide the same capabilities.

TABLE 17-1 Initial Population Data Table

CityName	State	Population
Detroit	MI	1027974
Atlanta	GA	394017
Concord	MA	17076
Chicago	IL	3005072
Boston	MA	574283
Ann Arbor	MI	109592

TABLE
17-2

The Table Ordered by City Name

CityName	State	Population
Ann Arbor	MI	109592
Atlanta	GA	394017
Boston	MA	574283
Chicago	IL	3005072
Concord	MA	17076
Detroit	MI	1027974

The original table is called simply the *table* (or the *NULL index*), and each copy of the table is called an *index*. A single table can have many different indexes.

You can think of an ISAM database as a collection of one or more tables and their associated indexes. This chapter will illustrate ISAM with a database consisting of just one table, the table of Table 17-1. The entire database is called "PLACES" and the table (NULL index) is named "Cities."

An Overview of Using ISAM

Before you can use ISAM, you must load the program PROISAMD.EXE from the operating system prompt into memory. This creates a memory-resident program used by Visual Basic Pro to carry out ISAM operations.

TABLE
17-3

The Table Ordered by Population

CityName	State	Population
Concord	MA	17076
Ann Arbor	MI	109592
Atlanta	GA	394017
Boston	MA	574283
Detroit	MI	1027974
Chicago	IL	3005072

Once you've loaded PROISAMD.EXE, then start up Visual Basic Professional.

 Caution   You must run PROISAMD.EXE before entering Visual Basic. Do not shell to DOS from Visual Basic and try to run this program.

You create a table in much the same way as a random-access file. First, a TYPE statement specifies the names and data types for each column. An appropriate TYPE statement for the Cities table is

```
TYPE CityType
   CityName AS STRING * 12
   State AS STRING * 2
   Population AS LONG
END TYPE
```

Then use a variant of the OPEN statement that you saw in Chapter 13:

```
OPEN "PLACES" FOR ISAM CityType "Cities" AS #1
```

creates the table, names the columns with the fields of the TYPE statement, and assigns file identifier number 1 to the file.

You place a record into the table by assigning the field values to a variable of type CityType and then using the INSERT statement. For instance, the following code places Detroit's record into the table.

```
DIM City AS CityType
City.CityName = "Detroit"
City.State = "MI"
City.Population = 1027974
INSERT #1, City
```

The indexes (other tables) "Name" and "Size" are created with the statements

```
CREATEINDEX #1, "Name", 0, "CityName"
CREATEINDEX #1, "Size", 0, "Population"
```

that give a name to each index and specify the key column for the index. (Actually, a CREATEINDEX statement can list several columns. If so, the records are ordered by these columns with the columns given precedence by their position in the list.)

Names of tables, indexes, and columns must satisfy special ISAM naming conventions. They must begin with a letter, consist only of letters and digits, be no longer than 30 characters, and not be a Visual Basic reserved word.

 Tip   Follow the same rules as required for an ordinary TYPE statement (see Chapter 9). This guarantees that every field can be used to create an index.

At any time, there is a *current index* and a place in that index called the *current position*. Initially, the current index is the original table (that is, the NULL index). However, the statement:

```
SETINDEX #1, "Name"
```

makes "Name" the current index and the statement:

```
SETINDEX #1, "Size"
```

makes "Size" the current index.

When an index first becomes the current index, the current position inside the index is always the first record of the index. For instance, after the statement SETINDEX #1, "Size", Concord's record is located at the current position. The current position of the current index can be changed with the statements MOVE*dest* and SEEK*operand* (see the sections on those commands that follow).

In addition to the positions occupied by actual records, there are two special positions. Think of the *beginning position* and *ending position* as preceding and following all the records, respectively. The functions BOF (Beginning Of File) and EOF (End Of File) are used to determine if the current position is one of these special positions. If a table is empty, then the current position will be both the beginning and ending position.

The record in the current position is called the *current record*. The statements UPDATE, DELETE, and RETRIEVE revise, remove, and read the current record. The statements MOVEFIRST and MOVELAST change the current record to the first or last record of the index. The statements MOVENEXT and MOVEPREVIOUS move the current position forward or backward one position. The statements SEEKEQ, SEEKGT, and SEEKGE search the key column of the index for the first entry equal to, greater than, or greater than or equal to a specified value and change the current position to the record found. The functions TEXTCOMP, BOF, EOF, and LOF are used in conjunction with the MOVE*dest* and SEEK*operand* statements to examine the new position. The TEXTCOMP function tells whether two strings are the same. The LOF function gives the number of records in the index. The following table summarizes the basic ISAM commands:

Command	Action
DELETE	Removes current record
RETRIEVE	Retrieves current record
UPDATE	Revises current record
MOVEFIRST	Moves to first record
MOVELAST	Moves to last record
MOVENEXT	Moves to next record
MOVEPREVIOUS	Moves to previous record
SEEKEQ	Finds first entry with key equal to specific value
SEEKGT	Finds first entry with key greater than specific value
SEEKGE	Finds first entry with key greater than or equal to specific value
TEXTCOMP	Compares two strings using ISAM conventions
BOF	Finds out if you are at the beginning of the file
EOF	Finds out if you are at the end of the file
LOF	Tells how many records are in the file

An innovative feature of ISAM is its capability to undo changes made to a database. The statements BEGINTRANS and COMMITTRANS begin and terminate the recording of alterations to a database. The SAVEPOINT statement records the status of the database for the possibility that a ROLLBACK will have to throw away all changes made since the SAVEPOINT statement was executed. (See the sections on these statements.)

As a precaution against the loss of data, the CHECKPOINT statement can be used at any time to write all open database buffers to disk. The current index is returned by the GETINDEX$ function and removed with the DELETEINDEX statement. Entire tables are closed with the CLOSE statement and deleted with the DELETETABLE statement. When you are finished using ISAM, you can remove the memory-resident program by entering PROISAMD.EXE /D from the operating system prompt.

 Tip The memory-resident program established by PROISAMD.EXE must be present when a database is first created and whenever new tables or indexes are added to a database. However, for modifying existing tables and indexes, a smaller version (one that requires less of the PC's memory), PROISAM.EXE, can be substituted for PROISAMD.EXE.

Finer Points of the ISAM Statements

Now consider some examples of the ISAM statements mentioned in the preceding section. The following examples assume that you've created the table shown in Table 17-1, and the table was opened with identifier number 1. Also, the examples assume that the leading code of the module contains the TYPE statement for CityType created in the previous example and the statement DIM SHARED City AS CityType. This section will go over each statement, demonstrating its use with the table given in Table 17-1.

First, TYPE statements used with ISAM tables must not contain fields of type SINGLE. Although static array fields are allowed in ISAM TYPE statements, the columns they create cannot be used in indexes.

You create the database initially, along with its first table, with a statement of the form:

OPEN *database$* FOR ISAM *tableType tableName$* AS #*n*

where the string *database$* is the name of the database, *tableType* is the user-defined record type that assigns a name and data type to each column, the string *tableName$* is the name of the table, and *n* is the file identifier number for the table.

 Note A string identifies the database and a number identifies the table.

You can then proceed to write to and read from the database. The statement CLOSE #*n* should be executed when you are finished working with the table. From the time the table is opened until the table is closed, you refer to it not by *tableName$* but by the file identifier number *n* given in the OPEN statement—just like you access regular files. After the table is closed, it can be referred to only by the *tableName$*; the file identifier number *n* was temporary and no longer identifies the table. For the examples given here, reopen the table with the same OPEN statement given above. You can also use any other file identifier (for example, one obtained with the FREEFILE function) by making the appropriate changes in the examples given below.

Working with Multiple Tables

Several different tables can be defined for the same database. The entire database is saved on disk in a single file. When a table is reopened, all records will be intact and every index that was active when the table was saved will be reactivated.

The following statements create two tables for the same database:

```
OPEN "PLACES" FOR ISAM CityType "Towns" AS #1
OPEN "PLACES" FOR ISAM CityType "Boroughs" AS #2
CLOSE
```

Putting Records in a File with the INSERT Command

Suppose an ISAM table has been opened with file identifier number *n* and the user-defined record type *RecType*. *RecVar* is a record variable declared to be of type *RecType*. The statement

INSERT #*n*, *RecVar*

places the contents of *RecVar* into the table and updates each of its indexes. The value in each field of *RecVar* is placed in the corresponding column of the table. The new record will be the last record in the original table and will appear in its proper location in each index.

Suppose the current index is the one shown in Table 17-2. After Visual Basic Pro executes the following code,

```
City.CityName = "Baltimore"
City.State = "MD"
City.Population = 736014
INSERT #1, City
```

the index in Table 17-2 will hold the record for Baltimore between the records for Atlanta and Boston.

Executing an INSERT statement has no effect on the current position. That is, the current position either remains one of the two special positions (beginning or ending) or contains the same record as before.

Making New Indexes with CREATEINDEX

Suppose an ISAM table has been opened with file identifier number *n*. If *columnName* is the name of one of the columns of the table, then a statement of the form

CREATEINDEX #*n*, *indexName$*, *t*, *columnName*

creates an index (named *indexName$*) associated with the named column. This index can be thought of as a copy of the original table ordered by the entries in the specified column. If the value of the number *t* is nonzero, then each item in the column must be unique. If the value of *t* is zero, then the items in the columns needn't be unique. If *columnName1* and *columnName2* are the names of two columns of the table, then a statement of the form

CREATEINDEX #*n*, *indexName$*, *t*, *columnName1*, *columnName2*

creates a combined index associated with the two columns. This index can be thought of as a copy of the original table ordered first by the entries of *columnName1* and any duplications ordered by the entries of *columnName2*. A nonzero value of *t* specifies that there be no duplications of item pairs. Actually, any number of distinct columns can be listed in the CREATEINDEX statement. If so, the copy will be ordered successively by the listed columns, beginning with the first.

Note When two strings are ordered in an index, trailing spaces are ignored and all letters are treated as having lowercase. (See the discussion of TEXTCOMP later in this chapter for a precise explanation of the comparison method used.)

The index created by the statement:

```
CREATEINDEX #1, "StateNpop", 0, "State", "Population"
```

appears in Table 17-4.

```
CREATEINDEX #1, "Name", 1, "CityName"
```

can be thought of as the table text shown in Table 17-2. (Assume that for the group of names under consideration there will be no duplication.)

Once an index has been created, it is saved along with the table in the database when the database is closed. Therefore, when the table is reopened, there is no need to recreate the index. Actually, doing so generates the error message "Duplicate definition."

When a nonzero value of t is used in a CREATEINDEX statement, the presence of duplicate items in the column (or sequence of columns) produces the run-time error message "Duplicate value for unique index." Also, after an index has been created with a nonzero value of t, the insertion of a duplicate item generates the same error message. An error-trapping routine should be written to handle these situations.

The width of a column is the number of bytes required to store each item of the column. For instance, in the examples, the column CityName has width 12 and the column State has width 2. If the width of a column exceeds 255, then the column cannot be used to create an index. Also, the sum of the widths of the columns in a combined index cannot exceed 255. (Actually, the maximum sum of the widths must be a little below 255 due to some overhead requirements.)

If the type of variable in a column is an array or a user-defined record type, then the column cannot be used to create an index.

TABLE 17-4   The Index Created by State and Population

Atlanta	GA	394017
Chicago	IL	3005072
Concord	MA	17076
Boston	MA	574283
Ann Arbor	MI	109592
Detroit	MI	1027974

At any time, one index is identified as the *current index*. The CREATEINDEX statement merely creates the index. The statement does not make the created index the current index. Specifying the current index is the responsibility of the SETINDEX statement.

Two indexes with different names can be created for the same column. A table can have at most 28 indexes. Indexes should be created only as needed. An unused index slows record operations unnecessarily, because every index is modified when the table is modified.

Using Different Indexes with SETINDEX

Suppose an ISAM table has been opened with file identifier number *n*. If *indexName$* is the name of one of the indexes of the table, then the statement

SETINDEX #*n*, *indexName$*

makes *indexName$* the current index and sets the current position to the first record of the index. The statement

SETINDEX #*n*

makes the NULL index (the original table) the current index.

Attempting to set an index that is not in the table corresponding to the file identifier number *n* produces the error message "Index not found."

Getting New Records with UPDATE

Suppose an ISAM table has been opened with file identifier number *n* and the user-defined record type *RecType*, and that the current position is not one of the two special positions, beginning or ending. If *RecVar* is a record variable of type *RecType*, the statement

UPDATE #*n*, *RecVar*

replaces the current record with the values in *RecVar*. That is, the entry in each field of *RecVar* will be placed in the corresponding column of the current record. In the NULL index, the record will appear in the same position as before. In other indexes, the record may move to another location. If so, the current position is changed to this new location.

Suppose the current index is the one in Table 17-2 and the current record is Boston. After Visual Basic Pro executes the statements

```
RETRIEVE #1, City
City.CityName = "Arlington"
City.Population = 44630
UPDATE #1, City
```

the first four records will be

Ann Arbor	MI	109592
Arlington	MA	44630
Atlanta	GA	394017
Chicago	IL	3005072

If the current position is the beginning or ending position, the UPDATE statement produces the run-time error message "No current record."

Removing Records with DELETE

Suppose an ISAM table has been opened with file identifier number n and the current position is not the beginning or ending position. The statement

DELETE #n

removes the record in the current position from the table (and from every index) and makes the next record (in the order of the index) the new current record.

Suppose the current index is shown in Table 17-2 and the current record is Atlanta. Then, after Visual Basic Pro executes the statement

```
DELETE #1
```

the first two records will be Ann Arbor and Boston.

If the current position is the beginning or ending position, then the statement DELETE #*n* produces the run-time error message "No current record."

Getting Records with RETRIEVE

Suppose an ISAM table has been opened with file identifier number *n* and the user-defined record type *RecType*, and that the current position is not the beginning or ending position. If *RecVar* is a record variable of type *RecType*, the statement

RETRIEVE #*n*, *RecVar*

places the contents of the record at the current position into *RecVar*. That is, the entry in each column of the record will be assigned to the corresponding field of *RecVar*.

Suppose the current index is shown in Table 17-2 and the current record is Atlanta. Then, the statements

```
RETRIEVE #1, City
PRINT City.State; City.Population
```

display:

GA 394017

Note Executing a RETRIEVE statement has no effect on the current position.

If the current position is the beginning or ending position, then the RETRIEVE statement produces the run-time error message "No current record."

After a table has been initially created (for example, with user-defined record type RecType1) and closed, it can be reopened with a different user-defined record type (call it RecType2). The fields of RecType2 must be a subset of the fields of RecType1. That is, each field of RecType2 must have the name of one of the columns of the table and be of the same type as the values in that column. If RecVar2 has type RecType2, then the statement

RETRIEVE #*n*, RecVar2

assigns to each field of RecVar2 corresponding items from the current record of the table. Of course, some of the items in the record might not be retrieved.

The statement INSERT #*n*, RecVar2 places the value in each field of RecVar2 into the corresponding item of the current record. If a column has no corresponding field in RecVar2, then it is assigned a default value, either 0 or the empty string. The statement UPDATE #*n*, RecVar2 places the value in each field of RecVar2 into the corresponding item of the current record. Of course, some of the items in the record might have no chance of being altered. If each field of RecType2 is not identical to one of the fields of RecType1, the run-time error "Type mismatch" is generated by the second OPEN statement.

Moving Through an ISAM File with MOVEdest

Suppose an ISAM table has been opened with file identifier number *n*. The statement

MOVEFIRST #*n*

sets the current position to the first record of the current index. The statement

MOVELAST #*n*

sets the current position to the last record of the current index. If the current position is not the ending position, then the statement

MOVENEXT #*n*

specifies the position following the current position as the new current position. If the current position is not the beginning position, then the statement

MOVEPREVIOUS #*n*

sets the current position to the preceding position.

Suppose the current index is shown in Table 17-2 and the current record is Boston. Then, the statements

```
RETRIEVE #1, City
PRINT City.CityName; City.State
MOVELAST #1
RETRIEVE #1, City
PRINT City.CityName; City.State
MOVEPREVIOUS #1
RETRIEVE #1, City
PRINT City.CityName; City.State
MOVEFIRST #1
RETRIEVE #1, City
PRINT City.CityName; City.State
MOVENEXT #1
RETRIEVE #1, City
PRINT City.CityName; City.State
CLOSE #1
```

display the following five cities

Boston	MA
Detroit	MI
Concord	MA
Ann Arbor	MI
Atlanta	GA

If the current position is the beginning position and you execute the statement MOVEPREVIOUS #n, then the current position is not changed. This also happens if the current position is the ending position and you execute the statement MOVENEXT #n.

How to Find Records with SEEK Operations

The commands SEEKEQ, SEEKGE, and SEEKGT are used to find records in an index. The suffixes EQ, GE, and GT are abbreviations for "EQual to," "Greater than or Equal to," and "Greater Than."

Suppose an ISAM table has been opened with file identifier number n and the current index (not the NULL index) was created with statement CREATEINDEX #n, indexName$, t, columnName$. Let the key value *keyVal* have a type compatible with the items in *columnName$*. The statement

SEEKEQ #*n*, *keyVal*

searches *columnName$* for the first item equal to *keyVal*. If an item is found, the current position is set to the record containing that item. Otherwise, the ending position becomes the current position. Similarly, the statements

SEEKGE #*n*, *keyVal*

and

SEEKGT #*n*, *keyVal*

search for the first item greater than or equal to *keyVal* and greater than *keyVal*, respectively. These three statements are not case sensitive. Also, trailing spaces are ignored. (See the following section on COMPTEXT for a precise explanation of the comparison algorithm.)

Suppose the current index is shown in Table 17-2. The statements

```
keyVal$ = "Boston"
SEEKEQ #1, keyVal$
CALL DisplayCurrentRecord
SEEKGE #1, "ATLANTA"
CALL DisplayCurrentRecord
SEEKGT #1, "Chicago"
CALL DisplayCurrentRecord
SEEKEQ #1, "Denver"
CALL DisplayCurrentRecord

SUB DisplayCurrentRecord
   IF NOT EOF(1) THEN        'Test for ending position
      RETRIEVE #1, City
      PRINT City.CityName; City.State
   ELSE
      PRINT "No match found."
   END IF
END SUB
```

display the following

Boston	MA
Atlanta	GA
Concord	MA

No match found.

The SEEK*operand* statements also can be applied when the current index is a combined index created with a statement of the form

CREATEINDEX #*n*, *indexName$*, *t*, *colName1$*, *colName2$*, ...

This index can be thought of as a copy of the original table ordered first by the entries of *colName1$* and any duplications ordered by the entries of *colName2$*, and so on. If *keyVal1* and *keyVal2* have values compatible with the items in *colName1$* and *colName2$*, then the statement

SEEKEQ #*n*, *keyVal1*, *keyVal2*

searches the columns *colName1$* and *colName2$* for the first record in which the value of the item in *colName1$* is *keyVal1* and the value of the item in *colName2$* is *keyVal2*. If such a record is found, the current position is set to the record containing that sequence. Otherwise, the ending position becomes the current position. The statements

SEEKGE #*n*, *keyVal1*, *keyVal2*, ...

and

SEEKGT #*n*, *keyVal1*, *keyVal2*, ...

perform the analogous operations for "greater than or equal" and "greater than."

In SEEK*operand* statements, an integer key can be used with a long integer column and vice versa. However, attempting to use a single-precision, double-precision, or currency key value with an integer or long integer column produces the error message "Type mismatch." If an integer or long integer key value is used with a double-precision or currency column, no error message results. However, the SEEK*operand* statements will fail and the current position will be the ending position. Only single- or double-precision key values can be used accurately with a double-precision column. Only currency key values can be used accurately with a currency column.

The maximum length of a key value is 255 characters. If the current index is a combined index and the number of key values exceeds the number of indexed columns, an error message results.

When the current index is a combined index, the number of key values may be less than the number of indexed columns. Although Visual Basic Pro does its best, sometimes the search fails. SEEKEQ always fails. SEEKGE and SEEKGT ignore the excess columns.

If the NULL index is the current index, then a SEEK*operand* statement generates the error message "Invalid operation on NULL index." The current position can also be changed by one of the MOVE*dest* statements, which can be applied to *any* index, even the NULL index.

Assume the current index contains the records in Table 17-4. The code

```
SEEKEQ #1, "mi", 109592
CALL DisplayCurrentRecord
SEEKGT #1, "MA", 500000
CALL DisplayCurrentRecord
SEEKGT #1, "IL"
CALL DisplayCurrentRecord
SEEKGE #1, "IL"
CALL DisplayCurrentRecord

SUB DisplayCurrentRecord
   IF NOT EOF(1) THEN        'Test for ending position
       RETRIEVE #1, City
       PRINT City.CityName; City.State
     ELSE
       PRINT "No match found."
   END IF
END SUB
```

produces the following output

Ann Arbor	MI
Boston	MA
Concord	MA
Chicago	IL

Using the Beginning of File (BOF) Function

Suppose an ISAM table has been opened with file identifier number *n*. The value of the function

BOF(*n*)

is −1 (True) if the beginning position is the current position and is 0 (False) otherwise.

In the following code segment, the table is empty when "Name" is the current index, so the default position is the beginning position. However, when the index "Commonwealth" becomes the current index, the table contains a record, and this becomes the current record.

```
OPEN "PLACES" FOR ISAM CityType "Towns" AS #1
CREATEINDEX #1, "Name", 0, "CityName"
SETINDEX #1, "Name"        'Make "Name" the current index
PRINT BOF(1);
City.CityName = "Boston"
City.State = "MA"
City.Population = 574283
INSERT #1, City
CREATEINDEX #1, "Commonwealth", 0, "State"
SETINDEX #1, "Commonwealth"
PRINT BOF(1)
CLOSE #1
```

The output is:

```
−1
0
```

Suppose many cities are added to the table in the example above. The following code displays the cities in reverse alphabetical order.

```
OPEN "PLACES" FOR ISAM CityType "Towns" AS #1
SETINDEX #1, "Name"
MOVELAST #1
DO UNTIL BOF(1)
  RETRIEVE #1, City
  PRINT City.CityName; City.State
  MOVEPREVIOUS #1
LOOP
```

Using the EOF (End of File) Function

Suppose an ISAM table has been OPENed with ID number *n*. The value of the function

EOF(*n*)

is −1 (True) if the ending position is the current position and is 0 (False) otherwise.

In the following code, the table is empty when "Name" becomes the current index and so the default position is the beginning (and ending) position. However, when the index "Commonwealth" becomes the current index, the table contains a record and so this record is the current record.

```
OPEN "PLACES" FOR ISAM CityType "Towns" AS #1
CREATEINDEX #1, "Name", 0, "CityName"
SETINDEX #1, "Name"   'Make "Name" the current index
PRINT EOF(1);
City.CityName = "Boston"
City.State = "MA"
City.Population = 574283
INSERT #1, City
CREATEINDEX #1, "Commonwealth", 0, "State"
SETINDEX #1, "Commonwealth"
PRINT EOF(1)
CLOSE #1
```

The output is:

```
−1
0
```

Suppose many cities are added to the table in the example above. The following program displays the cities in alphabetical order.

```
OPEN "PLACES" FOR ISAM CityType "Towns" AS #1
SETINDEX #1, "Name"
DO UNTIL EOF(1)
  RETRIEVE #1, City
  PRINT City.CityName; City.State
  MOVENEXT #1
LOOP
CLOSE #1
```

Determining Which String is Larger with TEXTCOMP

The ISAM function TEXTCOMP determines the relative order of two strings. The relational operators (such as < and =) rely on the ASCII table to determine the order of strings. Two strings are compared working from left to right, character by character, to determine which one should precede the other. However, the rules for comparing two strings when being ordered in an ISAM index are somewhat different than for ordinary ASCII order as seen in Chapter 5 and Appendix A. For strings consisting entirely of letters and digits, digits precede letters and the ordering of letters is case insensitive. Discussion will be limited to strings containing characters with ASCII values from 0 through 127.

ISAM indexes strings according to the following rules:

1. All trailing spaces are removed.

2. All letters from the English alphabet are considered lowercase. For instance, "Abc" equals "abc."

3. All characters are ordered with respect to their ASCII values with the following exceptions.

   a. The space character, CHR$(32) is the first character.

   b. The characters with ASCII values 20, 21, and 123 through 127 are moved and placed in between "`" and "a" [that is, in between CHR$(96) and CHR$(97)] in the following order: 123, 124, 125, 126, 127, 21, 20.

Note   As a result of rule 3b, letters come after all other characters in a TEXTCOMP comparison.

If a$ and b$ are strings, then the value of the function

TEXTCOMP(a$, b$)

is –1, 0, or 1 depending upon whether a$ precedes, equals, or follows b$. That is,

TEXTCOMP(a\$, b\$) = –1 if a\$ < b\$
TEXTCOMP(a\$, b\$) = 0 if a\$ = b\$
TEXTCOMP(a\$, b\$) = 1 if a\$ > b\$

Note   If either of the two strings a\$ and b\$ in a TEXTCOMP function have more than 255 characters, only the first 255 characters are considered.

The code

```
a$ = "abc   "
b$ = "Abc"
c$ = " abc"
PRINT TEXTCOMP(a$, b$);
PRINT TEXTCOMP(a$, c$)
```

produces the output: 0 1.

The code

```
PRINT TEXTCOMP("a1", "AB")
PRINT TEXTCOMP("[]", "ABC")
PRINT TEXTCOMP("", " ")
```

produces the output: –1 –1 0.

Finding Out the Current Index with GETINDEX\$

Suppose an ISAM table has been opened with file identifier number n. At any time, the value of the function

GETINDEX\$(n)

is the name of the current index. If the current index is the NULL index, then the value of GETINDEX\$(n) is the NULL string, the string with no characters.

Consider the following code:

```
OPEN "PLACES" FOR ISAM CityType "Capitals" AS #2
CREATEINDEX #2, "Municipality", 0, "Name"
CREATEINDEX #2, "CompleteName", 0, "State", "Name"
```

```
PRINT GETINDEX$(2); LEN(GETINDEX$(2))
SETINDEX #2, "Municipality"
PRINT GETINDEX$(2); LEN(GETINDEX$(2))
SETINDEX #2, "CompleteName"
PRINT GETINDEX$(2); LEN(GETINDEX$(2))
CLOSE #2
```

The output is

```
0
Municipality 12
CompleteName 12
```

Removing an Index with DELETEINDEX

Suppose an ISAM table has been opened with file identifier number *n*. If *indexName$* is the name of one of the indexes of the table, then the statement

DELETEINDEX #*n, indexName$*

removes the named index from the database.

Suppose a table has been opened with the statement

```
OPEN "PLACES" FOR ISAM CityType "Cities" AS #1
```

and the table "Cities" contains an index named "Name." The statement

```
DELETEINDEX #1, "Name"
```

removes the Name index from the database.

 Note Attempting to remove an index that is not in the table corresponding to the file identifier number produces the error message "Index not found."

Removing Tables with DELETETABLE

Several different tables can be defined in the same database, each with its own file identifier number and collection of indexes. The entire database is saved on disk in a single file. If *tableName$* is one of the closed tables in the database called *database$*, then the statement

DELETETABLE *database$*, *tableName$*

removes the table (and its indexes) from the database.

The DELETETABLE statement will cause Visual Basic Pro to stop executing the following lines of code when it reaches the RETRIEVE statement, and the error message "No current record" will appear.

```
OPEN "PLACES" FOR ISAM CityType "Towns" AS #1
City.CityName = "Boston"
City.State = "MA"
City.Population = 574283
INSERT #1, City
CREATEINDEX #1, "Commonwealths", 0, "State"
CLOSE #1
DELETETABLE "PLACES", "Towns"
OPEN "PLACES" FOR ISAM CityType "Towns" AS #1
RETRIEVE #1, City
PRINT City.CityName; City.State
CLOSE #1
```

Attempting to delete an open table generates the error message "File already open." Even if all the tables for a database are deleted, a sizable file with the name of the database will remain on disk. This file can be removed with Visual Basic's KILL statement or the DOS ERASE statement.

Clearing Buffers with CHECKPOINT

To increase efficiency, ISAM does not execute separate disk reads and writes for individual records in a table. Instead, ISAM reads many records at once from the disk and stores them in a memory location called a *buffer*. Periodically, ISAM writes the buffer back onto disk. The statement

CHECKPOINT

instructs ISAM to write the current database buffers to disk.

Tip   At some cost in time, using CHECKPOINT after altering the database ensures that changes will not be lost due to a loss of power. On the other hand, placing the CHECKPOINT statement in loops that do not alter the database reduces the efficiency of ISAM's buffered database scheme. Thus, CHECKPOINT should not be used in such loops.

The following code transfers each record to disk as soon as it is entered into the database.

```
OPEN "PLACES" FOR ISAM CityType "Capitals" AS #2
City.CityName = INPUTBOX$("Enter name of city.")
DO WHILE City.CityName <> ""
  City.State = INPUTBOX$("Enter State.")
  INSERT #2, City
  CHECKPOINT
  City.CityName = INPUTBOX$("Enter name of city.")
LOOP
CLOSE #2
```

Rolling Back (if Necessary)

With most database managers, changes are irrevocable. However, with ISAM transaction capability, the statements BEGINTRANS, COMMITTRANS, SAVEPOINT, and ROLLBACK can be used to undo alterations to the database even after many subsequent operations.

The statement

BEGINTRANS

starts the ISAM transaction log. After executing BEGINTRANS, the log will record all changes to tables in a database. While the log is recording, it may be used in conjunction with the ROLLBACK statement to undo changes made in the database.

A database *transaction* is a sequence of alterations made to tables in the database. For instance, operations involving UPDATE, INSERT, and DELETE are included in a transaction. However, setting an index, creating an index, and moving to a record are not included because they do not change a table in the database.

The log opened by BEGINTRANS is a temporary file stored on the current directory. The file remains open, recording the transaction, until a COMMITTRANS statement is executed or a table is closed, at which time the file is erased. Once the log file is erased, the transaction is said to be "committed," because the changes to the database can no longer be reversed.

Executing a BEGINTRANS statement when a transaction is already in progress or a COMMITTRANS statement when no transaction is in progress causes an "Illegal function call" error.

Tip   Although closing a table automatically commits the current transaction, COMMITTRANS should be used to explicitly commit the transaction before closing the table. It is a good practice to begin a transaction only after all tables are open and to commit a transaction before any table is closed.

Keeping Track of Where You Were with SAVEPOINT

The SAVEPOINT function is used to "remember" a particular status in a database transaction. When the SAVEPOINT function is called, the current condition of the database is marked in the transaction log. Even after many subsequent changes, the status of the database that existed at the time SAVEPOINT was called can be restored with a ROLLBACK statement. SAVEPOINT is valid only when a transaction is being recorded.

SAVEPOINT marks the status at a particular point in a transaction by returning an integer associated with that place. The mark is called a *savepoint*. The first time SAVEPOINT is executed, 1 is returned. The second time, 2 is returned, and so on. At a subsequent point in the transaction, the statement ROLLBACK *n* restores the database to the state that existed when SAVEPOINT returned *n*.

For instance, suppose a table is open and a large number of records are to be deleted. Before deleting all the records, you might execute the following statement,

```
Mark% = SAVEPOINT
```

to mark the current state of the database. After deleting the records, you might have second thoughts and want to restore them. Executing ROLLBACK Mark% would rescind every change made after the SAVEPOINT statement, thereby restoring the database to its original condition.

In some situations, marking several related database states is desirable. For instance, in the situation above, you might wish to mark the status of the database after each deletion. This would leave open the possibility of restoring the database to its condition before any one of the deletions. In this case, a convenient way to store the savepoints is with an array such as

```
DIM Marks(1 TO 100) AS INTEGER
```

Then including program statements such as

```
Num = Num + 1
Marks(Num) = SAVEPOINT
```

inside the loop that performs the deletions would mark each deletion for a possible ROLLBACK.

The beginning and end of a transaction are marked by the BEGINTRANS and COMMITTRANS statements, so SAVEPOINT can appear only in blocks of code bracketed by these two statements. If not, the error "Illegal function call" will be generated.

A savepoint is only valid within a single transaction. Once COMMITTRANS is executed, all previous savepoints become meaningless.

Undoing Changes with ROLLBACK

As explained in the previous SAVEPOINT function, executing

ROLLBACK *n*

during a transaction restores the database to the state that existed when the SAVEPOINT function was called and cancels all savepoints with associated values *n* or greater. The statement

ROLLBACK

restores the database to the state specified by the savepoint with the highest value, or, in the absence of savepoints, to the state existing when BEGINTRANS was executed. Executing the statement

ROLLBACK ALL

during a transaction restores the database to its condition at the time BEGINTRANS started the transaction and annuls all savepoints. Once a transaction is committed, either by closing a table or by executing COMMITTRANS, ROLLBACK cannot be used.

The following code creates a new table in the database "PLACES" and illustrates the four ISAM transaction statements.

```
OPEN "PLACES" FOR ISAM CityType "Capitals" AS #2
City.CityName = "Annapolis"
City.State = "MD"
City.Population = 33187
INSERT #2, City
BEGINTRANS
City.CityName = "Bismark"
City.State = "ND"
City.Population = 49256
INSERT #2, City
MOVELAST #2
mark% = SAVEPOINT      '1st savepoint
City.CityName = "Columbia"
City.State = "SC"
City.Population = 98052
UPDATE #2, City       'Change Bismark to Columbia
mark% = SAVEPOINT      '2nd savepoint
City.CityName = "Denver"
City.State = "CO"
City.Population = 467610
UPDATE #2, City       'Change Columbia to Denver
mark% = SAVEPOINT      '3rd savepoint
City.CityName = "Frankfort"
City.State = "KY"
City.Population = 25968
UPDATE #2, City       'Change Denver to Frankfort
mark% = SAVEPOINT      '4th savepoint
CALL Display(City)
ROLLBACK 3
CALL Display(City)
ROLLBACK
CALL Display(City)
```

```
ROLLBACK ALL
CALL Display(City)
COMMITTRANS
CLOSE #2

SUB Display (City AS CityType)
  MOVEFIRST #2
  DO UNTIL EOF(2)
    RETRIEVE #2, City
    PRINT City.CityName; City.State; City.Population
    MOVENEXT #2
  LOOP
  PRINT
END SUB
```

The output is

Annapolis	MD 33187
Frankfort	KY 25968
Annapolis	MD 33187
Denver	CO 467610
Annapolis	MD 33187
Columbia	SC 98052
Annapolis	MD 33187

An Overview of Other Features of the Professional Edition

Once you have the Professional Edition of Visual Basic:

☐   You can use overlays. This lets you build very large programs by having Microsoft's new MOVE (Microsoft's Overlay Virtual Environment) handle the loading.

❑   You can add a help system to your projects that works much like the ordinary Visual Basic Help system.

❑   You can write automated setup programs. (Moreover, you can use the functions supplied with this feature to make many routine file tasks, like copying files, a snap.)

❑   If you know even a tiny bit of assembly language, you can add custom controls to Visual Basic.

❑   Finally, there are many pages of printed documentation, and most of the information contained there is also available on line. This includes extensive documentation on mixed language programming. (Combining Visual Basic with C or assembly language, for example.)

Custom Controls

Custom controls let you build your own special purpose controls. For example, suppose you want a text box that can accept only correctly formatted number strings, or you want a text box that will accept only a fixed number of characters. How about a control to toggle on and off the various keyboard options such as NUM LOCK. All these are possible with custom controls. (Commercial developers also have many custom controls available to you.)

Custom controls are put into Quick libraries. Once created and loaded via the /L switch, they are available to you like any other controls in Visual Basic. You need an assembler that is compatible with Microsoft's MASM 5.1 or greater to create a custom control, although no real knowledge of assembly language is needed. The professional edition comes with a sample custom control, the code in which you can often mimic to meet your needs.

The Presentation Graphics Toolkit

This toolkit adds a professional-quality graphing facility to Visual Basic. However, because graphs are not drawn in text mode, you can't display them on forms. If you use a lot of graphs and don't want to spend the many hours needed to write the Visual Basic programs to create them, this control alone is worth the cost of the Professional Edition.

The graphing toolkit lets you construct four types of graphs:

☐   Pie charts (either exploded or not), as shown in Figure 17-1.

☐   Bar charts, as shown in Figure 17-2.

☐   Line charts, as shown in Figure 17-3.

☐   Scatter charts, as shown in Figure 17-4.

Although you design the graphs when you're building your project, you're not restricted to that. In fact, the reason the graphing facility is so useful is because you can easily write code that allows the user to do the following while the project is running:

☐   Change or add to the data used for the graph. Given new data, the graph control will redraw the graph automatically.

FIGURE 17-1   Pie chart

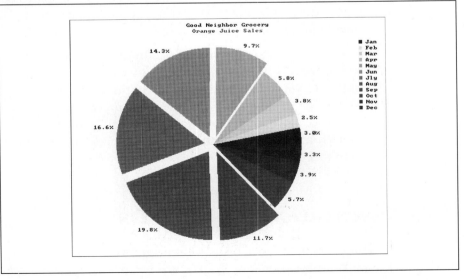

Bar chart

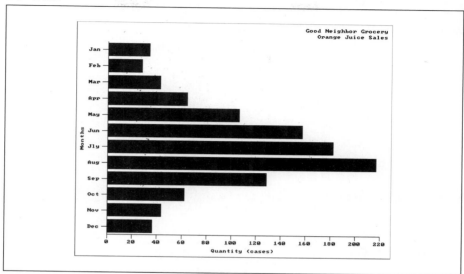

Line chart

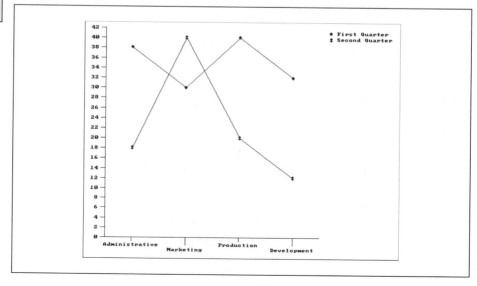

FIGURE
17-4 Scatter chart

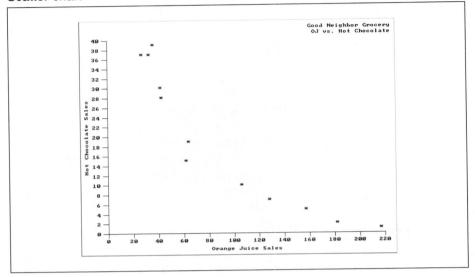

☐   Rescale the graph, change labels, or switch to a new kind of graph
    that displays the data from a different point of view.

You release all these features by using the supplied Functions and
Procedures and changing the values of the various parameters.

The Financial Toolkit

This toolkit adds 13 financial functions to Visual Basic. As it happens,
these functions and many other useful functions with source code are
contained in the optional companion disk for this book—so this feature
is not really a very good reason to buy the Professional Edition. (Having
the source code is sometimes very useful, since you can see how the
routines are written and learn from them—or maybe even make im-
provements and add new features.)

The functions supplied are divided into four groups:

Depreciation   These functions determine double declining, straight line, and sum of years depreciation.

Present and Future Value   These functions determine net present value, present value, and future value of an investment.

Rate of Return   These functions determine rate of return both with and without reinvestment of proceeds.

Payment Functions   These functions determine number of payments for an investment, payment on principal for a given period, and payments, including both principal and interest.

The Matrix Toolkit

This toolkit adds the standard matrix functions. These may be of some interests to engineers and economists. The functions included are addition, subtraction, determinants and inverses. However, there is no attempt to worry about ill-conditioned matrices and so the Inverse functions cannot be recommended for demanding use. They include different versions of these functions for the five different types of numbers in Visual Basic and you can only add matrices of entries of the same type.

The Help Program

A professional Visual Basic project needs a help system that does what users expect. If your on-line help doesn't have the look and feel of the one built into Visual Basic itself, users may have to relearn too much (and you'll probably be working too hard to provide this feature).

The Professional Edition Toolkit comes with two forms for the help system, one .BAS module containing the routines and a .BI file for the needed constants.

The way you use the help program is simple: You write a text file containing certain formatting codes that the help program translates into topics and hyperlinks within topics. Any word processor or ASCII editor will work.

Topics are indicated by placing the all caps TOPIC on a line by itself. The word TOPIC is preceded by a period and followed by a colon. The period *must* be in the first column and the name of the topic must be immediately below the period in the .TOPIC: statement.

```
.TOPIC:
First Topic
This is an example of a topic in a help file
.TOPIC
Second Topic

.

.

.
```

As the example above indicates, the next topic should begin immediately after the last line of the current topic.

Only spaces are allowed after the colon. The help toolkit will not wordwrap text. Use the ENTER key to break text into different lines. (64 characters/line is a good choice because the help window defaults to 66 characters wide.)

Jumps are indicated by surrounding the topic to be jumped to by ASCII 16 (▶) and ASCII 17 (◀) respectively:

```
.TOPIC:
First Topic
This is an example of a topic in a help file
Clicking ▶here◀ would let you jump to the "here" topic some place else
.TOPIC
Second Topic
This would be the second topic.

.
.TOPIC
Name of topic here
```
Both topics and hyperlinks must have exactly the same name or the program won't be able to find the jump!

To use the help toolkit in your programs, you have to include the files HELP.BAS, HELPF.FRM, HELPUTIL.FRM, and HELP.BI in your program—the help toolkit is written entirely in Visual Basic and can be modified freely.

The file HELP.BAS contains all the procedures used. HELPF.FRM is the main help form. Besides the form itself, HELPF.FRM contains the code to allow displaying and scrolling through the various help topics. It also has the code used to detect mouse clicks (at the hyperlinks) and keyboard support for jumps as well. The HELPUTIL.FRM form is used for the various dialog boxes: the Search dialog box, the History dialog box, and the Copy dialog box.

You can also use the supplied library versions (HELP.LIB or HELPA.LIB, which uses the older version of the math package) and the Quick library (HELP.QLB).

Next, you have to call the different routines to load and display your help topics. The actual routines (all are contained in HELP.BAS) are:

Routine	Purpose
HelpRegister	Initializes the help system and loads Help file
HelpShowTopic	Displays the specified help topic
HelpClose	Closes the Help file
HelpSetOptions	Sets the display options for help screens
HelpSearch	Calls the Help Search dialog box to let users search for specific topics

Figure 17-5 shows a typical example of what the text file for a help topic looks like. Figure 17-6 is the corresponding help screen.

To use the help system after you've written the text file with the topics and jumps indicated as above, all you need to do is:

1. Initialize the help system by calling the HelpRegister procedure with the name of the file.

   CALL HelpRegister(*HelpFileName*)

   Do this when your application starts (in the Form_Load of the startup form, for example).

FIGURE 17-5
How a help text file appears in a word processor

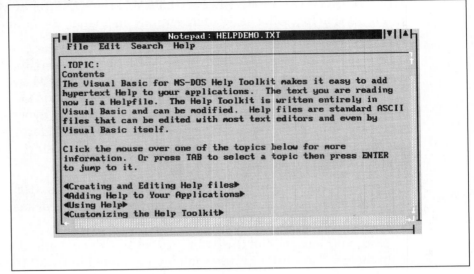

2. Display the various help topics or the table of contents by calling the procedure HelpShowTopic.

CALL HelpShowTopic(TopicName$)

FIGURE 17-6
The corresponding help screen

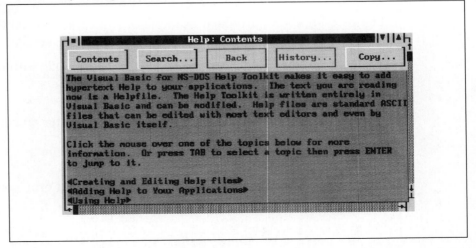

(Logically, the topic should be called "Contents" to show the table of contents.)

3. Call the HelpClose procedure before your application ends. This is especially important if your program ends by unloading all forms rather than by Visual Basic processing an END statement. Then you must call HelpClose during a Form_Unload event, because a help form is still LOADED although invisible.

You can also set the colors and show or hide specific Help buttons after you initialize the program by the call to HelpSetOptions.

In addition, you can call the HelpSearch procedure to open the Help Search dialog box. (As with Visual Basic itself, many applications have a Search item in their Help menu.)

(For more on the help system, see the comments and example code supplied with Visual Basic.)

The Setup Kit

If you want to write a professional-looking installation program for your Visual Basic projects, turn to the setup kit part of the Professional Edition. The setup kit makes it easy to produce a customized setup program with the look and feel of the one supplied with Visual Basic itself, or you can customize it as you see fit.

APPENDIX

ASCII and Extended ASCII Character Sets

Dec	Hex	ASCII Symbol	Control Code	Ctrl Key		Dec	Hex	ASCII Symbol
0	00		NUL	^@		32	20	
1	01	☺	SOH	^A		33	21	!
2	02	☻	STX	^B		34	22	"
3	03	♥	ETX	^C		35	23	#
4	04	♦	EOT	^D		36	24	$
5	05	♣	ENQ	^E		37	25	%
6	06	♠	ACK	^F		38	26	&
7	07	•	BEL	^G		39	27	'
8	08	◘	BS	^H		40	28	(
9	09	○	HT	^I		41	29	)
10	0A	◙	LF	^J		42	2A	*
11	0B	♂	VT	^K		43	2B	+
12	0C	♀	FF	^L		44	2C	,
13	0D	♪	CR	^M		45	2D	-
14	0E	♫	SO	^N		46	2E	.
15	0F	☼	SI	^O		47	2F	/
16	10	►	DLE	^P		48	30	0
17	11	◄	DC1	^Q		49	31	1
18	12	↕	DC2	^R		50	32	2
19	13	‼	DC3	^S		51	33	3
20	14	¶	DC4	^T		52	34	4
21	15	§	NAK	^U		53	35	5
22	16	▬	SYN	^V		54	36	6
23	17	↨	ETB	^W		55	37	7
24	18	↑	CAN	^X		56	38	8
25	19	↓	EM	^Y		57	39	9
26	1A	→	SUB	^Z		58	3A	:
27	1B	←	ESC	^[		59	3B	;
28	1C	∟	FS	^\		60	3C	<
29	1D	↔	GS	^]		61	3D	=
30	1E	▲	RS	^^		62	3E	>
31	1F	▼	US	^_		63	3F	?
						64	40	@

Dec	Hex	ASCII Symbol	Dec	Hex	ASCII Symbol
65	41	A	98	62	b
66	42	B	99	63	c
67	43	C	100	64	d
68	44	D	101	65	e
69	45	E	102	66	f
70	46	F	103	67	g
71	47	G	104	68	h
72	48	H	105	69	i
73	49	I	106	6A	j
74	4A	J	107	6B	k
75	4B	K	108	6C	l
76	4C	L	109	6D	m
77	4D	M	110	6E	n
78	4E	N	111	6F	o
79	4F	O	112	70	p
80	50	P	113	71	q
81	51	Q	114	72	r
82	52	R	115	73	s
83	53	S	116	74	t
84	54	T	117	75	u
85	55	U	118	76	v
86	56	V	119	77	w
87	57	W	120	78	x
88	58	X	121	79	y
89	59	Y	122	7A	z
90	5A	Z	123	7B	{
91	5B	[	124	7C	|
92	5C	\	125	7D	}
93	5D	]	126	7E	~
94	5E	^	127	7F	⌂
95	5F	_	128	80	Ç
96	60	`	129	81	ü
97	61	a	130	82	é

Dec	Hex	ASCII Symbol	Dec	Hex	ASCII Symbol
131	83	â	168	A8	¿
132	84	ä	169	A9	⌐
133	85	à	170	AA	¬
134	86	å	171	AB	½
135	87	ç	172	AC	¼
136	88	ê	173	AD	¡
137	89	ë	174	AE	<<
138	8A	è	175	AF	>>
139	8B	ï	176	B0	▒
140	8C	î	177	B1	▓
141	8D	ì	178	B2	▓
142	8E	Ä	179	B3	│
143	8F	Å	180	B4	┤
144	90	É	181	B5	╡
145	91	æ	182	B6	╢
146	92	Æ	183	B7	╖
147	93	ô	184	B8	╕
148	94	ö	185	B9	╣
149	95	ò	186	BA	║
150	96	û	187	BB	╗
151	97	ù	188	BC	╝
152	98	ÿ	189	BD	╜
153	99	Ö	190	BE	╛
154	9A	Ü	191	BF	┐
155	9B	¢	192	C0	└
156	9C	£	193	C1	┴
157	9D	¥	194	C2	┬
158	9E	Pt	195	C3	├
159	9F	ƒ	196	C4	─
160	A0	á	197	C5	┼
161	A1	í	198	C6	╞
162	A2	ó	199	C7	╟
163	A3	ú	200	C8	╚
164	A4	ñ	201	C9	╔
165	A5	Ñ	202	CA	╩
166	A6	ª	203	CB	╦
167	A7	º	204	CC	╠

Dec	Hex	ASCII Symbol	Dec	Hex	ASCII Symbol
205	CD	=	231	E7	τ
206	CE	╬	232	E8	φ
207	CF	╧	233	E9	θ
208	D0	╨	234	EA	Ω
209	D1	╤	235	EB	δ
210	D2	╥	236	EC	∞
211	D3	╙	237	ED	∅
212	D4	╘	238	EE	∈
213	D5	╒	239	EF	∩
214	D6	╓	240	F0	≡
215	D7	╫	241	F1	±
216	D8	╪	242	F2	≥
217	D9	┘	243	F3	≤
218	DA	┌	244	F4	⌠
219	DB	█	245	F5	⌡
220	DC	▄	246	F6	÷
221	DD	▌	247	F7	≈
222	DE	▐	248	F8	°
223	DF	▀	249	F9	•
224	E0	α	250	FA	·
225	E1	β	251	FB	√
226	E2	Γ	252	FC	η
227	E3	π	253	FD	2
228	E4	Σ	254	FE	■
229	E5	σ	255	FF	
230	E6	μ			

APPENDIX

Keyboard Shortcuts

Many common operations in Visual Basic can be done quickly using certain keystrokes or keystroke combinations. This appendix summarizes these shortcuts.

The Programming Environment

This section is divided into tables summarizing the keys that work in the code window and the keys that work for editing code.

Code Navigation Keys

Function	Key or Key Combination
To view, move, or remove project modules and sub or function procedures	F2
To start up a new code window	ALT+W+N
To edit an event procedure	F12
To display the next procedure	SHIFT+F2
To display the previous procedure	CTRL+F2
To move to the form designer to modify a form via Form selection window	SHIFT+F12
To move to the main menu bar	ALT
To highlight the main menu bar	F11

The Editing Keys

Many of the common editing functions, such as deleting to the end of the line, have keyboard equivalents that you may find easier to use.

Function	Key or Key Combination
Edit Undo	ALT+BACKSPACE or CTRL+Z
Character Left	CTRL+S or LEFT ARROW
Character Right	CTRL+D or RIGHT ARROW

Function	Key or Key Combination
Word Left	CTRL+A or CTRL+LEFT ARROW
Word Right	CTRL+F or CTRL+RIGHT ARROW
Go to beginning of file	CTRL+HOME or CTRL+Q,R
Go to beginning of line	HOME or CTRL+Q,S
Go to end of line	END or CTRL+Q,D
Go to end of program	CTRL+END or CTRL+Q,C
Go to end of screen	CTRL+Q,X
Page Down	PGDN
Page Left	CTRL+PGUP
Page Right	CTRL+PGDN
Page Up	PGUP or CTRL+R
Scroll Down	CTRL+Z or CTRL+DOWN ARROW
Scroll Up	CTRL+W or CTRL+UP ARROW
Get to change text dialog box	ALT+S,C or CTRL+Q,A
Get to find text dialog box	CTRL+\ or CTRL+Q,F
Copy selected text onto the clipboard	CTRL+C or CTRL+INS
Cut selected text onto the clipboard	CTRL+X or SHIFT+DEL
Cut current line onto the clipboard	CTRL+Q,L or CTRL+Y
Cut from cursor to end of line onto the clipboard	CTRL+Q,Y
Paste clipboard contents at cursor location	CTRL+V or SHIFT+INS
Delete character to left of cursor	CTRL+H or BACKSPACE
Delete character to the right of cursor	DEL or CTRL+G
Delete selected text	DEL
Delete word	CTRL+T
Move to home position on screen	CTRL+Q,E
Insert Mode (toggle)	INS
Line Down	DOWN ARROW
Line Up	CTRL+E or UP ARROW
Move the text one tab stop to the left	SHIFT+TAB
Move the text one tab stop to the right	TAB
Insert new line	CTRL+M or ENTER

Function	Key or Key Combination
Next Line	CTRL+J or CTRL+ENTER
Split Line	CTRL+N or ENTER
Set book mark 0	CTRL+K, 0
Set book mark 1	CTRL+K, 1
Set book mark 2	CTRL+K, 2
Set book mark 3	CTRL+K, 3
Go to book mark 0	CTRL+Q, 0
Go to book mark 1	CTRL+Q, 1
Go to book mark 2	CTRL+Q, 2
Go to book mark 3	CTRL+Q, 3

Function Keys

Key	Function
F1	Context sensitive help on item where cursor is located
F2	Open code selection window to view, move, or remove project modules and sub or function procedures
F3	Repeat the last find
F4	Toggle between viewing the output screen and the programming environment
F5	Continue program execution from current statement
F6	Move forward through open windows
F7	Execute program to cursor position
F8	Execute next program statement as a single step
F9	Set breakpoint (toggle)
F10	Procedure Step (execute next procedure call as a single step)
F11	Activate menu bar
F12	Open event procedures selection window
ALT+F1	Previous Help hyperlink topic (up to 20 back)

Key	Function
ALT+F4	Exit or close MDI container form or Visual Basic itself
CTRL+F1	Next Help topic in the Help file
CTRL+F2	Display the previous procedure
CTRL+F4	Close active window
CTRL+F5	Restore window size
CTRL+F6	Next window
CTRL+F7	Move window
CTRL+F8	Size window
CTRL+F9	Minimize window
CTRL+F10	Maximize window
SHIFT+CTRL+F1	Previous topic in the Help file
SHIFT+F1	Help on Help (how to use Visual Basic Help)
SHIFT+F2	Display the next procedure
SHIFT+F5	Start program execution from beginning
SHIFT+F6	Cycle backward through open windows
SHIFT+F8	Trace backwards
SHIFT+F9	Instant Watch
SHIFT+F10	Trace forward
SHIFT+F12	Opens form selection window to modify forms

The Form Designer Keys

Although many of the keys work similarly in the form designer and programming environment, there are differences. This section covers what the key combinations do in the form designer.

The Form Designer Function Keys

The following table summarizes the function keys that work differently between the form designer and the programming environment.

Key	Function
F2	Move the cursor to the properties bar
F4	Open or close the list
F10	Menu bar/properties bar display (toggle)
F11	Activate menu bar
F12	Edit event procedures (moves to programming environment)
ALT+F4	Exit or close MDI container or leave Form designer

Keys to Use When on the Properties Bar

Function	Key or Key Combination
To undo the last editing action	ESC
To cycle backward through the items in the list	UP ARROW or LEFT ARROW
To cycle focus between Value box and Properties list box	TAB
To cycle forward through the items in the list	DOWN ARROW or RIGHT ARROW
To move the focus to the Properties list box	TAB
To move to the first item displayed in the list	PGUP
To move to the first item in the list	HOME
To move to the last item displayed in the list	PGDN
To move to the last item in the list	END
To toggle between properties bar and menu bar	F10
To select a highlighted item from list	ENTER
To select item from list	Enter the item # if the list is enumerated or press the first letter of the item if not

APPENDIX

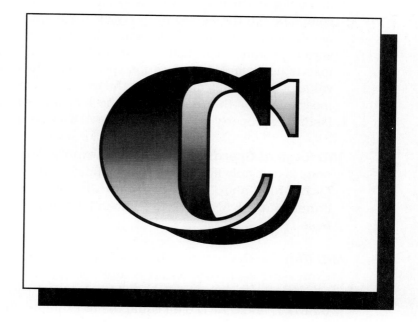

Visual Basic Reference

Th「his appendix presents a glossary of Visual Basic statements, functions, methods, data types, operators, and metacommands. Note that some of the entries refer you to specific topics in the "Supporting Topics" section, which can be found at the end of this appendix.

ABS   The function ABS strips the minus sign from negative numbers while leaving positive numbers unchanged—thus making all nonzero numbers positive. If *x* is any number, then the value of ABS(*x*) is the absolute value of *x*.

ADDITEM   The method *controlName*.ADDITEM *newItem$* adds the string *newItem$* to the list of items associated with the *controlName* list box or combo box. If the Sorted property for the list is false (the default), then *newItem$* is added to the end of the list, otherwise it is placed in its proper sorted position. The method *controlName*.ADDITEM *newItem$*, *index* inserts *newItem$* at the location specified by the number *index*, where a value of 0 indicates insertion at the top of the list, a value of 1 indicates insertion after the first item in the list, and so on. The value of the ListIndex property is set to –1 by the ADDITEM method.

AND (Logical Operator)   The logical expression *condition1* AND *condition2* is true only if both *condition1* and *condition2* are true. For example, (3<7) AND ("abc">"a") is true since 3<7 is true as is "abc">"a", while ("apple">"ape") AND ("earth">"moon") is false since "earth">"moon" is false.

AND (Bitwise Operator)   The expression *byte1* AND *byte2* is evaluated by expressing each byte as an 8-tuple binary number and then ANDing together corresponding digits, where 1 AND 1 equals 1, while 1 AND 0, 0 AND 1, and 0 AND 0 all equal 0. For example, the expression 37 AND 157 translated to binary 8-tuples becomes 00100101 AND 10011101. ANDing together corresponding digits gives the binary 8-tuple 00000101 or decimal 5. Thus 37 AND 157 is 5.

ASC   The extended ASCII table associates a number (from 0 to 255) with each of the characters available to the computer. The value of ASC(*a$*) is the ASCII value of the first character of the string *a$*.

ATN   The trigonometric function ATN, or *arctangent*, is the inverse of the tangent function. For any number *x*, ATN(*x*) is the angle in radians between $-\pi/2$ and $\pi/2$ whose tangent is x. See also Radian measure in the "Supporting Topics" section.

BEEP   The statement BEEP produces a sound of frequency 800 Hz that lasts a fraction of a second.

BEGINTRANS   The ISAM statement BEGINTRANS starts the ISAM transaction log, which records all changes made to open ISAM tables. Recording continues until either the statement COMMITTRANS is executed or any ISAM table is closed. Alterations to ISAM tables made after executing BEGINTRANS and before executing COMMITTRANS (or closing a table) may by undone with the ROLLBACK command. See also ISAM statements in the "Supporting Topics" section.

BLOAD   The statement BLOAD *filespec*, m places the bytes contained in the file *filespec* into successive memory locations beginning at offset m in the current segment of memory set using DEF SEG. If the contents of successive memory locations are saved in a file with the BSAVE statement, then they can later be restored with the statement BLOAD *filespec*. (This process is commonly used to save and later restore the contents of the screen.) See also Filespec, Memory in the "Supporting Topics" section.

BOF   Suppose an ISAM table has been opened with reference number n. The value of the function BOF(n) will be -1 (true) if the current position in the table is before the beginning position of the current index and 0 (false) otherwise. BOF will be true either when a table contains no records or after the MOVEPREVIOUS statement is executed from the beginning position of the current index. See also ISAM statements in the "Supporting Topics" section.

BSAVE   The statement BSAVE *filespec*, n, m stores in the file *filespec* the contents of the m consecutive memory locations beginning at offset n in the current segment of memory that was set with DEF SEG. See also Filespec, Memory in the "Supporting Topics" section.

CALL   A statement of the form CALL *SubprocedureName(argList)* is used to execute the named Sub procedure, passing to it the variables and values in the list of arguments. Arrays appearing in the list of arguments must be specified by the array name followed by empty parentheses. The value of a variable argument may be altered by the procedure unless the variable is surrounded by parentheses. After the statements in the procedure have been executed, program execution continues with the statement following CALL.

Note The keyword CALL may be omitted if the procedure is declared. In this case, the parentheses are omitted and the statement is written *SubprogramName argList*.

CALL ABSOLUTE The CALL ABSOLUTE statement passes control to a machine language subprogram in much the same way that CALL passes control to a procedure. The statement CALL ABSOLUTE (*argList, offvar*) passes control to the machine language program beginning at the memory location whose offset in the current segment of memory (set using DEF SEG) is the value of the numeric variable *offvar*. The arguments are used by the machine language subprogram. The statement CALLS ABSOLUTE works like CALL ABSOLUTE except that both segment and offset are passed for each of the arguments. See also Memory, Library routines in the "Supporting Topics" section.

CALL INT86OLD This statement is included in Visual Basic to maintain compatibility with early versions of QuickBASIC. The statement CALL INTERRUPT performs the same tasks as CALL INT86OLD and is more readable. The statement CALL INT86OLD (*n,inr(),outr()*) is the equivalent of causing system interrupt *n* to occur. The array variables *inr()* and *outr()*, which contain the register values used during and after the interrupt, must be declared in a DIM statement as eight-element integer arrays. For example, the pair of statements DIM inr(7) AS INTEGER, outr(7) AS INTEGER: CALL INT86OLD(5, inr(), outr()) activate a screen dump. See also Library routines in the "Supporting Topics" section.

CALL INT86XOLD The CALL INT86XOLD statement is identical to the CALL INT86OLD statement in syntax and use except that it makes use of the values of two additional registers. Therefore, the array variables *inr()* and *outr()* must be declared in a DIM statement as 10-element integer arrays. See also Library routines in the "Supporting Topics" section.

CALL INTERRUPT The statement CALL INTERRUPT (*n,inr,outr*) is the equivalent of causing system interrupt *n* to occur. The variables *inr* and *outr*, which contain the register values used during and after the interrupt, must be declared as the user-defined type RegType. For example, the pair of statements DIM inr AS RegType, outr AS RegType: CALL INTERRUPT(5,inr,outr) activate a screen dump. See also Library routines in the "Supporting Topics" section.

CALL INTERRUPTX   The CALL INTERRUPTX statement is identical to the CALL INTERRUPT statement in syntax and use except that it makes use of the values of two additional registers, and therefore it requires that *inr* and *outr* be declared as the user-defined type RegTypeX.

CCUR   The function CCUR converts integer, long integer, single-precision, and double-precision numbers (assuming they fit into the range for currency variables) to currency numbers. If x is any number, then the value of CCUR(x) is the currency number determined by x.

CDBL   The function CDBL converts integer, long integer, single-precision, and currency numbers to double-precision numbers. If x is any number, then the value of CDBL(x) is the double-precision number determined by x.

CHAIN   The CHAIN statement passes control from the current program to another program contained on disk. The CHAIN *filespec* statement will load and execute the source code program contained in *filespec* (appending the .BAS or .EXE extension if none was specified). Placing COMMON statements in the two programs allows the first program to pass the values of the variables appearing in its COMMON statement to corresponding variables in the second program's COMMON statement.

CHDIR   The statement CHDIR *path* changes the current directory on the specified disk drive to the subdirectory specified by *path* (although the default drive is unaffected). For example, CHDIR "C:\" specifies the root directory of the C drive as the current directory on C. Omitting a drive letter in *path* causes the default drive to be used. See also Directories in the "Supporting Topics" section.

CHDRIVE   The statement CHDRIVE *drive$* changes the default drive to the drive specified by *drive$*. For example, CHDRIVE "A" specifies the A drive as the new default drive. See also Directories in the "Supporting Topics" section.

CHECKPOINT   To increase efficiency, ISAM does not execute separate disk reads and writes for individual records or transactions, but instead reads and writes large blocks of data to and from a portion of memory referred to as a buffer. Closing a table or using the ISAM statement CHECKPOINT forces all changes to be written to disk. Changes made to ISAM tables that have not been written to disk would be lost in a power failure or system reboot. Overuse of CHECKPOINT will slow ISAM operation. See also ISAM statements in the "Supporting Topics" section.

CHR\$ If *n* is a number from 0 to 255, then CHR\$(*n*) is the character in the ASCII table associated with *n*.

CINT   The function CINT converts long integer, single-precision, double-precision, and currency numbers to integer numbers. If *x* is any number from -32768 to 32767, then the value of CINT(*x*) is the (possibly rounded) integer constant that *x* determines; otherwise an overflow error occurs.

CIRCLE   The graphics statement CIRCLE (*x,y*),*r,c,r1,r2,a* draws a portion, or all, of an ellipse. The center of the ellipse is the point (*x,y*) and the longer radius is *r*. The color of the ellipse is determined by *c*. If *r1* and *r2* are present, then the computer draws only the portion of the ellipse that extends from the radius line at an angle of ABS(*r1*) radians with the horizontal radius to the radius line at an angle of ABS(*r2*) radians with the horizontal radius line in a counterclockwise direction. If either *r1* or *r2* is negative, then the computer also draws its radius line. The ratio of the length of the vertical diameter to the length of the horizontal diameter will be *a*. If *a* is missing, the figure drawn will be a circle. See also Radian measure, Colors for CGA monitors, Palettes, Graphics coordinate systems in the "Supporting Topics" section.

CLEAR (Statement)   The statement CLEAR resets all variables and elements of static arrays to their default values, closes all files, deletes all dynamic arrays from memory, and reinitializes the stack. Also, if ,,*s* is added after the CLEAR statement, the stack size is set to *s*. See also Default values, Static vs. dynamic in the "Supporting Topics" section.

CLEAR (Method)   The method CLIPBOARD.CLEAR clears the clipboard, setting its contents to the null string.

CLNG   The function CLNG tries to convert integer, single-precision, double-precision, and currency numbers to long integer numbers. If x is any number from $-2,147,483,648$ to $2,147,483,647$, then the value of CLNG(x) is the (possibly rounded) long integer constant that x determines; otherwise an overflow error occurs.

CLOSE   The statement CLOSE #n closes the file that has been opened with reference number n. By itself, CLOSE closes all open files.

CLS (Statement)   The statement CLS clears the screen and positions the cursor at the upper-left of the screen. If a graphics viewport is active (see VIEW), then the statement CLS clears the viewport. The statement CLS 0 clears the entire screen. The statement CLS 1 clears the active graphics viewport if one exists; otherwise, it clears the entire screen. The statement CLS 2 clears only the text viewport (see VIEW PRINT). The CLS statement is not available when forms are visible.

CLS (Method)   The method *formName*.CLS clears the form *formName* of text placed on the form using the method *formName*.PRINT. The method *pictureBox*.CLS clears the named picture box. The CLS method resets the CurrentX and CurrentY properties of the cleared object to 0.

COLOR   In text-only mode (SCREEN 0), the COLOR statement produces either special effects (such as underlined text) or colors, depending on the type of monitor. The statement COLOR f, b, bd sets the foreground color to f, the background color to b, and the border color to bd, where f ranges from 0 to 15 and b from 0 to 7. The statement COLOR $f+16$, b, bd selects the same colors as the statement just given, but with a blinking foreground.

In screen mode 1, two palettes of four colors each are available. The statement COLOR b, p specifies b as the background color and p as the palette. Text will appear in color 3 of the selected palette and graphics may be displayed in any color of that palette.

In EGA and VGA modes 7, 8, and 9, a palette of 16 colors is available for text and graphics. The statement COLOR f, b sets the foreground color to the color assigned to palette entry f and the background color to the color assigned to palette entry b, where f and b range from 0 to 15.

In the VGA and MCGA modes 12 and 13, the statement COLOR *f* sets the foreground color to the color assigned to palette entry *f*. (The background is set to color *c* with the statement PALETTE 0, *c*.)

The COLOR statement is not available when forms are visible. See also Colors for CGA monitors, Palettes in the "Supporting Topics" section.

COM(n)   The statement COM(*n*) enables, disables, or defers trapping of the *n*th communications port depending on whether it is followed by ON, OFF, or STOP, respectively. See also Devices, Event trapping in the "Supporting Topics" section.

**COMMAND$**   The value of the function COMMAND$ is a string containing the command line information used to start Visual Basic or the application that was developed using Visual Basic. For example, in VBDOS /RUN CALC.MAK, the string "/RUN CALC.MAK" is the command line information.

COMMITTRANS   The ISAM statement COMMITTRANS closes the ISAM transaction log and causes all changes recorded there to be made to the appropriate ISAM tables. Alterations to ISAM tables made after executing the statement BEGINTRANS and before executing COMMITTRANS (or closing a table) may by undone with the ROLLBACK command. See also ISAM statements in the "Supporting Topics" section.

COMMON   The COMMON statement allows selected variables from a form or .BAS module to be shared with another form or module. If a statement of the form COMMON *AVar1*, *AVar2*, ..., *AVarN* appears in the leading code of one form or .BAS module, and a statement of the form COMMON *BVar1*, *BVar2*, ..., *BVarN* appears in the leading code of a second form or .BAS module in the same or a chained-to program, then *AVar1* and *BVar1* will always have the same value, *AVar2* and *BVar2* will always have the same value (and in fact refer to the same memory location), and so on. Although the names of corresponding COMMON variables need not be the same, corresponding variables must be of the same type: string, integer, long integer, single-precision, double-precision, currency, or user-defined record type. The type of each variable is determined either by a type-declaration tag or by inserting words of the form AS *type*. If the keyword SHARED is included in the COMMON statement, as in COM-MON SHARED *var1*, *var2*, ..., then the specified variables will be shared with all procedures in the form or .BAS module. COMMON statements must appear in the leading code before any executable statements. COMMON statements may not appear inside a procedure.

Visual Basic also allows you to use named COMMON blocks, which permit you to break up your global variables into named groupings. If you place just the appropriate named COMMON statements in the leading code of a module, the module is given access to just those global variables it requires. This provides further protection against inadvertent side effects. The syntax is COMMON SHARED /*NameOfBlock*/*var1*,*var2*,....

CONST The statement CONST *constantName* = *expression* causes Visual Basic to replace every subsequent occurrence of *constantName* with the value of the expression. This replacement takes place before any lines of the program are executed. Unlike LET, CONST does not set up a location in the program's memory for a variable. A *constantName* may appear in only one CONST statement and may not appear on the left side of an assignment statement. We call *constantName* a "symbolic constant" or "named constant." The expression may consist of explicit values (25 or "Diamonds", for example) and previously defined named numeric constants joined by the operators +, −, *, /, \, AND, OR, NOT, XOR, EQV, and IMP. (String constants can't use the + operator.)

CONTROL The CONTROL data type may be used in the parameter list of a SUB or FUNCTION definition to allow the passing of control names to the procedure.

COS The value of the trigonometric function COS(*x*) is the cosine of an angle of *x* radians. See also Radian measure in the "Supporting Topics" section.

CREATEINDEX Suppose an ISAM table has been opened with reference number *n*. If *columnName* is the name of one of the columns of the table, then the statement CREATEINDEX #*n*, *indexName$*, *t*, *columnName* creates the *indexName$* index associated with the named column. If *t* is nonzero, then each item in the column must be unique. If *columnName1* and *columnName2* are the names of two columns of the table, then the CREATEINDEX #*n*, *indexName$*, *t*, *columnName1*, *columnName2* statement creates a combined index associated with the two named columns. Combined indexes are ordered by the values of *columnName1* first, and then, when these are the same, by the values of *columnName2*. If *t* is nonzero, then each pair of items must be unique. Combined indexes for three or more columns are also allowed. See also ISAM statements in the "Supporting Topics" section.

CSNG The function CSNG converts integer, long integer, double-precision, and currency numbers to single-precision numbers. If *x* is any number, then the value of CSNG(*x*) is the single-precision number that *x* determines provided *x* is in the range for a single-precision number.

CSRLIN At any time, the value of the function CSRLIN is the number (1, 2, 3, ...) of the line of the screen on which the cursor is located. The CSRLIN statement is not available when forms are visible.

**CURDIR$** The value of the function CURDIR$(*drive$*) is a string specifying the current directory on the drive specified by *drive$*. The value of CURDIR$("") or CURDIR$ is a string specifying the current directory on the default drive. See also Directories in the "Supporting Topics" section.

CURRENCY The CURRENCY data type is extremely useful for calculations involving money. A variable of type CURRENCY requires 8 bytes of memory and can hold any number from -922,337,203,685,477.5808 to 922,337,203,685,477.5807, with at most four decimal places. CURRENCY values and variables are indicated by the type tag @: 21436587.01@, Balance@.

CVI, CVL, CVS, CVD, CVC With the buffer method of working with random-access files, numbers to be recorded in files by Visual Basic's LSET and PUT statements must first be transformed into strings. They are transferred back by these five functions. If an integer was transformed into the string *a$* of length 2, then the value of CVI(*a$*) will be the original integer. Similarly, CVL(*a$*), CVS(*a$*), CVD(*a$*), or CVC(*a$*) will be the long integer, single-precision, double-precision, or currency numbers that were transformed by Visual Basic into *a$*, a string of length 4, 4, 8, or 8. See also Random-access files in the "Supporting Topics" section.

CVSMBF, CVDMBF Random-access files created in Microsoft BASIC, GW-BASIC, BASICA, or early versions of QuickBasic use a method different from Visual Basic's for storing numbers as strings. Single- and double-precision numbers that have been converted to strings by one of these earlier versions of BASIC and entered into random-access files can be converted to Visual Basic's numeric format by these two functions. See also Random-access files in the "Supporting Topics" section.

DATA   The statement DATA *const1*, *const2*, ... holds constants. READ statements read these constants and assign them to variables. DATA statements must be placed in the leading code and are only accessible to READ statements within the same form or .BAS module.

**DATE$**   The value of the function DATE$ is the current date returned as a string of the form mm-dd-yyyy. If *d$* is a string of this form, then the statement DATE$ = *d$* resets the date as specified by *d$*.

DECLARE   The statement DECLARE SUB *SubprocedureName* (*par1*, *par2*,...) or the statement DECLARE FUNCTION *FunctionName* (*par1*, *par2*,...) placed in the leading code of a form or .BAS module indicates that the specified procedure is called by the form or module. Visual Basic uses the DECLARE statements to check that procedure calls use the proper number and types of arguments. DECLARE statements for each procedure (other than event procedures or code in a .QLB library) in a given form or module are automatically inserted at the top of the leading code whenever the form or module is saved. A DECLARE statement must be placed manually in the leading code of a form or .BAS module for each Function procedure which is used in that form or module but is defined in another form, quick library, or module. DECLARE statements may not appear inside procedures.

     The type of each parameter in a DECLARE statement is determined either by a type-declaration tag or by words of the form AS *type*. The parameters must match the types of the corresponding parameters in the procedure definition. A parameterless procedure should appear in a DECLARE statement with an empty pair of parentheses.

DEF FN/END DEF   DEF FN user-defined functions are created in one of two ways: by a single-line definition of the form DEF FN*name*(*parList*) = *expression*, or by a multiline block that begins with a statement of the form DEF FN*name*(*parList*), which is followed by one or more statements that calculate the value of the function, and ends with the statement END DEF. The items appearing in the list of variables *parList* constitute the input for the function. If one of the statements in the block has the form FN*name* = *expression*, then the output of the function is *expression*.

DEF FN functions must be defined in the leading code of each form or .BAS module in which they are used. This definition must be positioned earlier in the leading code than any use of the function. Variables inside a multiline block are global (that is, shared throughout the form or module) unless they are declared early in the block to be static by a statement of the form STATIC var1, var2,.... Static variables are not accessible outside of the block; however, they retain their values between subsequent calls to the function. This method of creating user-defined functions has, perhaps, been made obsolete with the introduction of the FUNCTION statement, which supports recursion and may take arrays and records as arguments.

DEFINT, DEFLNG, DEFSNG, DEFDBL, DEFSTR, DEFCUR   A variable can be assigned a type by either a type-declaration tag or an AS clause. A statement of the form DEFINT *letter* specifies that any "untyped" variable whose name begins with the specified letter will have integer type. A statement of the form DEFINT *letter1-letter2* specifies that all "untyped" variables whose names begin with a letter in the range *letter1* through *letter2* will have integer type. The statements DEFLNG, DEFSNG, DEFDBL, DEFSTR, and DEFCUR specify the corresponding types for long integer, single-precision, double-precision, string, and currency variables, respectively. A DEFtype statement is automatically displayed above procedures created after the DEFtype statement is placed in the leading code of a form or .BAS module.

DEF SEG   The statement DEF SEG = *n* specifies that the *current segment of memory* consists of memory locations 16*n through 16*n + 65535. Subsequently, all statements that access memory directly—like PEEK, POKE, BLOAD, and BSAVE—will refer to memory locations in this range. See also Memory in the "Supporting Topics" section.

DELETE   Suppose an ISAM table has been opened with reference number *n* and that both BOF(*n*) and EOF(*n*) are false. Then the statement DELETE #*n* removes the record in the current position from the table (and from every index) and makes the next position the new current position. See also ISAM statements in the "Supporting Topics" section.

DELETEINDEX Suppose an ISAM table has been opened with reference number *n*. If *indexName$* is the name of one of the indexes of the table, then the statement DELETEINDEX #*n*, *indexName$* removes the named index. See also ISAM statements in the "Supporting Topics" section.

DELETETABLE Suppose the ISAM database *database$* contains the table *tableName$* and that this table is currently closed. Then the statement DELETETABLE *database$*, *tableName$* removes the table and all its indexes from the named database. See also ISAM statements in the "Supporting Topics" section.

DIM The statement DIM *arrayName*(*m* TO *n*) declares an array with subscripts ranging from *m* to *n*, inclusive, where *m* and *n* are in the normal integer range of −32768 to 32767. A statement of the form DIM *arrayName*(*m* TO *n*,*p* TO *q*) declares a doubly subscripted, or two-dimensional, array. Three dimensional and higher arrays are declared similarly. If *m* and *p* are zero, the DIM statements above may be changed to DIM *arrayName*(*n*) and DIM *arrayName*(*n*,*q*). The statement DIM *variableName* AS *variableType*, where *variableType* is INTEGER, LONG, SINGLE, DOUBLE, CURRENCY, STRING, STRING*n, or a user-defined type, specifies the type of the variable. Inserting SHARED after the word DIM in the leading code of a form or .BAS module allows all procedures to access the array or variable. See also Static vs. dynamic in the "Supporting Topics" section.

**DIR$** The value of the function DIR$(*filespec$*) is a string specifying the first file that matches the pattern specified by *filespec$*. If this value is not the null string, then the next value returned by DIR$ is the next file that matches the previously specified pattern. For example, the value of DIR$("*.BAS") will be a string specifying the first file in the current directory of the default drive whose name has the .BAS extension. The next call to DIR$ would give the next file with a .BAS extension.

DO/LOOP A statement of the form DO, DO WHILE *cond*, or DO UNTIL *cond* is used to mark the beginning of a block of statements that will be repeated. A statement of the form LOOP, LOOP WHILE *cond*, or LOOP UNTIL *cond* is used to mark the end of the block. Each time a statement containing WHILE or UNTIL followed by a condition is encountered, the truth value of the condition determines whether the block should be repeated or whether the program should jump to the statement immediately following the block. A DO loop may also be exited at any point with an EXIT DO statement.

DOEVENTS   The value of the function DOEVENTS( ) is the number of forms currently loaded. Executing the DOEVENTS function permits Visual Basic to act upon any events that may have occurred while the current procedure has been executing. When the start-up module of a program is not a form, the DOEVENTS function must be used to process any form events.

DOUBLE   A variable of type DOUBLE requires 8 bytes of memory and can hold 0, the numbers from 4.94065×10^{-324} to $1.797693134862316 \times 10^{308}$ with at most 17 significant digits, and the negative of these numbers. DOUBLE values and variables are indicated by the type tag #: 2.718281828459045#, Pi#.

DRAG   The method *objectName*.DRAG *opt%* is used to control dragging and dropping of a form or control whose DragMode property is set to Manual (0). Dragging of a form or control is initiated by the statement *objectName*.DRAG or *objectName*.DRAG 1 and terminated by the statement *objectName*.DRAG 2. The statement *objectName*.DRAG 0 cancels the dragging operation.

DRAW   The graphics statement DRAW *a$*, where *a$* is a string of directions and arguments, is used to draw figures on the screen in much the same way figures are drawn with pencil and paper. The rich and varied command strings constitute a miniature graphics language. The DRAW statement can be used to produce straight lines beginning at the last point referenced and extending in several directions. After each line is drawn, the end point of that line becomes the "last point referenced" for the next DRAW statement. The possible directions are: U (up), D (down), L (left), R (right), E (northeast), F (southeast), G (southwest), H (northwest). If *Y* is one of these directions and *n* is a number, then the statement DRAW "*Yn*" draws a line of *n* units in the specified direction. If a direction is preceded by N, the last point referenced will not change after the line is drawn. If a direction is preceded by B, an invisible line will be drawn and the last point referenced will change to the endpoint of that line. Several such statements may be combined into a statement of the form DRAW "*Yn Zm* ...". Some other variations of the DRAW statement are

DRAW "An"	Draws subsequent lines rotated by n*90 degrees.
DRAW "Cn"	Draws subsequent lines in color n of the current palette.
DRAW "M x, y"	Draws a line from the last point referenced to (x,y). [Preceding x or y with a plus sign or minus sign causes relative coordinates to be used.]
DRAW "P c, b"	Fills in the closed region of boundary color b containing the last point referenced with the color c of the current palette.
DRAW "Sn"	Changes the unit scale to n/4 of the original scale.
DRAW "TAn"	Draws subsequent lines rotated by n degrees.

DRAW statements can use numeric variables to provide the numeric arguments of commands by employing the STR$ function. For instance, the statement DRAW "M 100,25" may be written as x=100: y=25: DRAW "M" + STR$(x) + "," + STR$(y). See also Palettes, Last point referenced, Graphics coordinate systems in the "Supporting Topics" section.

$DYNAMIC   The metacommand REM $DYNAMIC specifies that any array dimensioned after this point in the form or .BAS module should have its memory allocated dynamically at run-time. Dynamic arrays have the advantage that you may ERASE them to free up memory or REDIMension them to change their size. Dynamic arrays are stored in far memory so memory is conserved but access is a bit slower. Array memory allocation is automatically dynamic if the array is local to a non-STATIC procedure, the array is DIMensioned using a variable, or the array is declared in a COMMON or REDIM statement. See also Metacommands, Static vs. dynamic in the "Supporting Topics" section.

END   The statement END terminates the execution of the program and closes all files. Also, the statements END DEF, END FUNCTION, END IF, END SELECT, END SUB, and END TYPE are used to denote the conclusion of multiline function definitions, function blocks, IF blocks, SELECT CASE blocks, subprograms, and user-defined record type declarations.

ENDDOC   The method PRINTER.ENDDOC is used most often in a networked environment to indicate that the document currently being printed is complete and should be released to the printer.

ENVIRON   Visual Basic has an environment table consisting of equations of the form "*name=value*" that is inherited from DOS when Visual Basic is invoked. The ENVIRON statement is used to alter this table. The statement ENVIRON "*name=;*" removes any equation whose left side is *name*. The statement ENVIRON "*name=value*" places the equation in quotes in the table. Unless you have enlarged your environment from DOS' defaults you probably won't have room to add anything unless you delete something first.

ENVIRON\$ If *name* is the left side of an equation in Visual Basic's environment table, then the value of the function ENVIRON\$("*name*") will be the string consisting of the right side of the equation. The value of ENVIRON\$(*n*) is the *n*th equation in DOS' environment table.

EOF   Suppose a file has been opened for input with reference number *n*. The value of the function EOF(*n*) will be -1 (true) if the end of the file has been reached and 0 (false) otherwise.

Note   The logical condition NOT EOF(*n*) is true until the end of the file opened with file identifier *n* is reached.

When used with a communications file in binary mode, EOF(*n*) will be true if the communications buffer is empty and false if the buffer contains data.

EQV   The logical expression *condition1* EQV *condition2* is true only if *condition1* and *condition2* are both true or both false. For example, (1>2) EQV ("xyz"<"a") is true since both 1>2 and "xyz"<"a" are false, while ("apple">"ape") EQV ("earth">"moon") is false since "apple">"ape" is true but "earth">"moon" is false.

ERASE   For static arrays, the statement ERASE *arrayName* resets each array element to its default value. For dynamic arrays, the statement ERASE *arrayName* deletes the array from memory.

Note   After a dynamic array has been ERASEd, it may be dimensioned again to a different size if need be. However, the number of dimensions must be the same as before. See also Default values, Static vs. dynamic in the "Supporting Topics" section.

***ERDEV and ERDEV$*** After a device error occurs, the value of ERDEV provides information about the type of error and gives certain attributes of the device. The value of ERDEV$ is the name of the device. These functions are used in error-handling routines. See also Devices, Event trapping in the "Supporting Topics" section.

ERR and ERL (Functions) After an error occurs during the execution of a program, the value of the function ERR will be a number identifying the type of error, and the value of the function ERL will be the line number of the program statement in which the error occurred. (If the statement containing the error has no line number, then the nearest line number preceding it is returned. If no line number precedes it, a value of 0 is returned.) These functions are used in error-trapping routines. See also Event trapping in the "Supporting Topics" section.

ERR (Statement) The statement ERR = *errnum* changes the value returned by the ERR function to *errnum*.

ERROR The statement ERROR *n* simulates the occurrence of the run-time error identified by the number *n*, where *n* may range from 1 to 32767. It is a useful debugging tool.

***ERROR$*** The value of the function ERROR$ is the error message corresponding to the run-time error that has most recently occurred. The value of the function ERROR$(*errnum*) is the error message corresponding to run-time error designated by *errnum*.

EVENT The statement EVENT OFF suspends any and all event trapping that has been initiated by ON KEY, ON PLAY, ON TIMER, ON STRIG, ON PEN, ON COM, and ON UEVENT statements. The statement EVENT ON reenables all event trapping. If an event occurs while EVENT OFF is in effect, no action is taken, but the event is remembered and the appropriate event-trapping routine is executed once the EVENT ON statement is reached. EVENT is not used when forms are showing.

EXIT The EXIT statement may be used in any of the five forms EXIT FOR, EXIT SUB, EXIT FUNCTION, EXIT DEF, and EXIT DO. The EXIT statement causes program execution to jump out of the specified structure prematurely: EXIT FOR jumps out of a FOR/NEXT loop to the statement following NEXT, EXIT SUB jumps out of a Sub procedure to the statement following the CALL statement, and so on.

EXP   The value of the function EXP(x) is e^x, where e (about 2.71828) is the base of the natural logarithm function.

FIELD   With the buffer method of handling random-access files, a statement of the form FIELD #n, $w1$ AS *strvar1*, $w2$ AS *strvar2*, ... partitions each record of the file with reference number n into fields of widths $w1$, $w2$,... and names *strvar1*, *strvar2*, ... The sum $w1 + w2 + ...$ usually equals (but must not exceed) the record length specified when the file was opened. The GET statement assigns values directly to the string variables *strvar1*, *strvar2*, ...

FILEATTR   After a file has been opened with reference number n, the value of the function FILEATTR (n,1) is 1, 2, 4, 8, 32, or 64, depending upon whether the file was opened for INPUT, OUTPUT, RANDOM, APPEND, BINARY, or ISAM, respectively. The value of the function FILEATTR (n,2) is the file's DOS file handle, a number that uniquely identifies the file and is used in assembly language programming or with CALL INTERRUPT.

FILES   The statement FILES *path* produces a listing of the files in the directory specified by *path*. Variations of the statement produce selected sublistings. If *path* is not included, FILES produces a listing of all the files in the current directory of the default drive. The FILES statement is not available when forms are visible. See also Directories in the "Supporting Topics" section.

FIX   The value of the function FIX(x) is the whole number obtained by discarding the decimal part of the number x.

FOR/NEXT   The statement FOR *index* = a TO b STEP s sets the value of the variable *index* to a and repeatedly executes the statements between itself and the statement NEXT *index*. Each time the NEXT statement is reached, s is added to the value of *index*. This process continues until the value of *index* passes b. Although the numbers a, b, and s may have any numeric type, integers work the fastest. The statement FOR *index* = a TO b is equivalent to the statement FOR *index* = a TO b STEP 1. The variable name (*index*) following the word NEXT is optional.

FORM   The FORM data type may be used in the parameter list of a SUB or FUNCTION definition to allow the passing of form names to the procedure.

$FORM   The metacommand REM $FORM *formName* is used in a form or .BAS module to gain access to the controls and properties of the *formName* form. This metacommand must be placed in the leading code before any executable statements.

**FORMAT$**   The function FORMAT$(*n*, *a$*) converts the number *n* to a string using the rules given in *a$*. The function is used when numeric data needs to be assigned to the Text property of an object. The resulting string can be formated with commas, leading and trailing zeros, preceding or trailing signs (+ or -), and exponential notation. The special formatting characters used in *a$* are #, 0, decimal point (period), comma, %, E–, and E+.

The symbol # designates a place for a digit. If the number being formatted does not need all the places provided by the #'s given in *a$*, then the extra #'s are ignored (they do not become spaces as in PRINT USING).

The symbol 0, like #, designates a place for a digit. However, if the number being formatted does not need all the places provided by the 0's given in *a$*, then the character 0 is displayed in the extra places.

If the number being converted has more whole part digits than there is space reserved by #'s and 0's, then additional space is used as if the format string had more #'s at its beginning.

```
PRINT "x" + FORMAT$(56, "####") + "x" displays x56x
PRINT "x" + FORMAT$(56, "#") + "x" displays x56x
PRINT "x" + FORMAT$(0, "#") + "x" displays xx
PRINT "x" + FORMAT$(56, "0000") + "x" displays x0056x
PRINT "x" + FORMAT$(56, "0") + "x" displays x56x
PRINT "x" + FORMAT$(0, "0") + "x" displays x0x
```

The decimal point symbol (.) marks the location of the decimal place. It separates the format rules into two sections, one applying to the whole part of the number and the other to the decimal part. When included in the format string, a decimal point will always appear in the resulting string.

```
PRINT "x" + FORMAT$(56.246, "#.##") + "x" displays x56.25x
PRINT "x" + FORMAT$(.246, "#.##") + "x" displays x.25x
PRINT "x" + FORMAT$(.246, "0.##") + "x" displays x0.25x
PRINT "x" + FORMAT$(56.2, "0.00") + "x" displays x52.20x
```

The comma symbol (,) placed to the left of the decimal point between #'s and/or 0's causes commas to be displayed to the left of every third digit to the left of the decimal point, as appropriate. If commas are placed to the immediate left of the decimal point (or to the right of all #'s and 0's when the decimal point symbol is not used), then before the number is formatted, it is divided by 1000 for each comma, but commas will not appear in the result. In order to divide by 1000s and display commas in the result, use format strings like "#,#,.00", which displays the number with commas in units of thousands, and "#,#,,.00", which displays the number with commas in units of millions.

```
PRINT "x" + FORMAT$(1234000, "#,#") + "x" displays x1,234,000x
PRINT "x" + FORMAT$(1234000, "#,") + "x" displays x1234x
PRINT "x" + FORMAT$(1234000, "#,.") + "x" displays x1234x
PRINT "x" + FORMAT$(1234000, "#,,.0") + "x" displays x1.2x
PRINT "x" + FORMAT$(1234000, "#,0,.0") + "x" displays x1,234.0x
```

The percent symbol (%) placed to the right of all #'s, 0's, and any decimal point causes the number to be converted to a percentage (multiplied by 100) before formatting and the symbol % to be displayed.

```
PRINT "x" + FORMAT$(.05624,"#.##%")  + "x" displays x5.62%x
PRINT "x" + FORMAT$(1.23,"#%")  + "x" displays x123%x
```

The symbols E+ and E- placed to the right of all #'s, 0's, and any decimal point cause the number to be displayed in scientific notation. Places for the digits in the exponent must be reserved to the right of E+ or E- with #'s or 0's. When E+ is used and the exponent is positive, a plus sign appears in front of the exponent in the result. When E- is used and the exponent is positive, no sign or space precedes the exponent. When scientific notation is used, each position reserved by #'s to the left of the decimal point is used whenever possible.

```
PRINT "x" + FORMAT$(1234.56,"#.##E+##") + "x" displays x1.23E+3x
PRINT "x" + FORMAT$(1234.56,"##.##E-##")+"x" displays x12.34E2x
PRINT "x" + FORMAT$(1234,"###.00E+##")+"x" displays x123.40E+1x
PRINT "x" + FORMAT$(123,"###E+00") + "x" displays x123E+00x
```

FRE   At any time, the value of the function FRE("") is the amount of memory available for storing new (constant) string data. The value of the function FRE(–1) is the number of memory locations available for new numeric arrays. This function is useful in determining whether or not sufficient memory remains to declare a new type, new numeric array, or fixed length string. The value of FRE(–2) is the smallest amount of space on the stack that has existed at any time during the execution of the program. The value of FRE(–3) is the number of memory locations available in expanded memory. For values of *n* other than –1, –2, or –3, invoking FRE(*n*) causes a run-time error.

FREEFILE   When files are opened, they are assigned a reference number from 1 to 255. At any time, the value of the function FREEFILE is the next available reference number.

FUNCTION   A function is a multistatement block beginning with a statement of the form FUNCTION *FunctionName(parList) or FUNCTION FunctionName(parList)* AS *type*, followed on subsequent lines by one or more statements for carrying out the task of the function, and ending with the statement END FUNCTION. The parameter list, *parList*, is a list of variables through which values will be passed to the function when the function is called. Parameter types may be numeric, (variable-length) string, user-defined record type, or array. The types of the parameters may be specified with type-declaration tags, DEFtype statements, or AS clauses. Array names appearing in the parameter list must be followed by an empty pair of parentheses. Functions are named with the same conventions as variables, except that the name may not begin with FN. The value of a variable argument used in calling a function may be altered by the function unless the variable is enclosed by parentheses. Variables are local to the function unless declared as SHARED within the function or declared as DIM SHARED in the leading code. A statement of the form STATIC FUNCTION *FunctionName(parList)* specifies that all variables local to the function be treated as static by default; that is, they are invisible outside of the function but retain their values between function calls. Functions may invoke themselves (called *recursion*) or other procedures. However, no procedure may be defined inside of a function. (STATIC may prevent recursion from working as expected.)

GET (Files)   User-defined record types provide an efficient means of working with random-access files. After a user-defined record type is defined and a variable of that type, call it *recVar*, is declared, the file is opened with a length equal to LEN (*recVar*). The *r*th record of the random-access file is retrieved and assigned to *recVar* with the statement GET #*n,r,recVar*.

The GET statement is also used to retrieve data from a binary file and assign it to any type of variable. Suppose *var* is a variable that holds a value consisting of *b* bytes. (For instance, if *var* is an integer variable, then *b* is 2. If *var* is an ordinary string variable, then *b* will equal the length of the string currently assigned to it.) The statement GET #*n,p,var* assigns to the variable *var* the *b* consecutive bytes beginning with the byte in position *p* of the binary file having reference number *n*. The positions for the GET statement are numbered 1, 2, 3, and so on.

If *p* is omitted, then the current file position is used as the beginning position.

With the buffer method of working with random-access files, the statement GET #*n,r* retrieves record number *r* from the random-access file having reference number *n* and assigns the record's values to the variables appearing in the most recently executed FIELD statement for the file with reference number *n*. (If *r* is omitted, the record after the one most recently accessed by a GET or PUT statement is retrieved.) See also Random-access files, Binary files in the "Supporting Topics" section.

GET (Graphics) A graphics statement of the form GET (*x1,y1*)-(*x2,y2*), *arrayName* stores a description of the rectangular portion of the screen having upper-left corner (*x1,y1*) and lower-right corner (*x2,y2*) in the array *arrayName*. The rectangular region can then be duplicated at another location of the screen with a PUT statement. GET and PUT statements are the key tools for animation. See also Graphics coordinate systems in the "Supporting Topics" section.

**GETINDEX$** The value of the ISAM function GETINDEX$(*n*) is the name of the current index in the table opened with reference number *n*. See also ISAM statements in the "Supporting Topics" section.

GETTEXT The value of the method CLIPBOARD.GETTEXT is a string containing a copy of the data currently stored in the clipboard.

GOSUB A statement of the form GOSUB *label* causes a jump to the statement beginning at *label*. When the statement RETURN is reached, the program jumps back to the statement following the GOSUB statement.

Note Both the GOSUB statement and its target must be in the same part of the program, either both in the leading code of a .BAS module or both in a single procedure. See also Labels, Subroutines in the "Supporting Topics" section.

GOTO The statement GOTO *label* causes an unconditional jump to the first statement after the specified label.

Note The GOTO statement and its target must be in the same part of the program, either both in the leading code of a .BAS module or both in a single procedure. See also Labels in the "Supporting Topics" section.

HIDE The method *formName*.HIDE makes the form *formName* invisible, preventing the user (but not other program statements) from accessing the form in any manner. If a form is not loaded when the HIDE method is applied, then the form will be loaded but not displayed. The method SCREEN.HIDE makes all forms invisible, which is the required state before any graphics may be displayed.

HEX$ If *n* is a whole number from 0 to 2,147,483,647, then the value of the function HEX$(*n*) is the string consisting of the hexadecimal representation of *n*.

IF (single line) A statement of the form IF *condition* THEN *action* causes the program to take the specified action if *condition* is true. Otherwise, execution continues at the next line. A statement of the form IF *condition* THEN *action1* ELSE *action2* causes the program to take *action1* if *condition* is true and *action2* if *condition* is false.

IF (block) A block of statements beginning with a statement of the form IF *condition* THEN and ending with the statement END IF, indicates that the group of statements between IF and END IF are to be executed only when *condition* is true. If the group of statements is separated into two parts by an ELSE statement, then the first part will be executed when *condition* is true and the second part when *condition* is false. Statements of the form ELSEIF *condition* may also appear and define groups of statements to be executed when alternate conditions are true.

IF TYPEOF   To test for the type of a control when the control name is passed to a procedure, use IF TYPEOF *controlName* IS *controlType* THEN ... in either the single line or block form of the IF statement. ELSEIF TYPEOF is also permitted. For *controlType*, use one of the 16 control names that appear in the Form Design ToolBox (CheckBox, ComboBox, CommandButton, and so on). For example, IF TYPEOF *objectPassed* IS Label THEN ....

IMP   The logical expression *condition1* IMP *condition2* is true except when *condition1* is true and *condition2* is false. For example, (3<7) IMP ("abc">"a") is true since both 3<7 and "abc">"a" are true, while ("apple">"ape") IMP ("earth">"moon") is false since "apple">"ape" is true but "earth">"moon" is false.

$INCLUDE   The metacommand REM $INCLUDE: '*filespec*' directs the compiler to compile the program segment contained in the specified disk file as if that program segment appeared in the original program at the location of the $INCLUDE statement. The $INCLUDE metacommand is commonly used to insert a library's COMMON and DECLARE statements into a program.

**INKEY$**   The statement *a$* = INKEY$ assigns to the variable *a$* the one or two character string that identifies the next keystroke waiting in the keyboard buffer. Numbers, letters, and symbols are identified by a single character. Keys such as F1, HOME, and INS, are identified by two characters: CHR$(0) followed by CHR$(*n*), where *n* is the "scan code" for the key. If no keystroke is waiting, the null string, "", is assigned to *a$*. The INKEY$ function is not available when forms are visible.

INP   The value of the function INP(n) is the value of the byte read from port *n*. See also Devices in the "Supporting Topics" section.

INPUT   A statement of the form INPUT *var* causes the computer to display a question mark and to pause until the user enters a response. This response is then assigned to the variable *var*. Statements of the form INPUT "*prompt*"; *var* insert a prompting message before the question mark, statements of the form INPUT "*prompt*", *var* display the prompt without the question mark, and statements of the form INPUT; *var* suppress a carriage return following the entering of the response. In each of the above statements, *var* may be replaced by a number of variables separated by commas. After the user responds with the proper number of values (separated by commas) and presses ENTER, each of the values is assigned to the corresponding variable. The INPUT statement is not available when forms are visible.

INPUT# The statement INPUT #*n*, *var* reads the next item of data from a sequential file that has been opened for INPUT with reference number *n* and assigns the item to the variable *var*. The statement INPUT #*n*, *var1*, *var2*, ... reads a sequence of values and assigns them to the variables.

**INPUT$** A statement of the form *a$* = INPUT$(*n*) causes the program to pause until the user types *n* characters. The string consisting of these *n* characters is then assigned to *a$*. This form of the INPUT$ statement is not available when forms are visible. The statement *a$* = INPUT$(*n,m*) assigns the next *n* characters from the file with reference number *m* to *a$*.

**INPUTBOX$** The value of the function INPUTBOX$(*prompt$*) is the string entered by the user in response to the prompt given by *prompt$*. The INPUTBOX$ function automatically displays the prompt, a text box for user input, an OK button, and a CANCEL button in a dialog box in the center of the screen. If the user selects CANCEL, the value of the function is the null string (""). For greater control, use the function IN-PUTBOX$(*prompt$*, *title$*, *default$*, *column*, *row*), which titles the dialog box with *title$*, displays *default$* as the default value in the text box, and positions the upper-left corner of the dialog box at *column* and *row* of the screen. The INPUTBOX$ function may only be used in text mode (SCREEN 0).

INSERT The ISAM statement INSERT #*n*, *recVar* places the contents of *recVar* into the table opened with reference number *n*. The value in each field of *recVar* is placed in the corresponding column of the table. Any indexes associated with this table are also updated. The new record will be the last record in the original table and will appear in its proper location in each index. See also ISAM statements in the "Supporting Topics" section.

INSTR The value of the function INSTR(*a$,b$*) is the position of the string *b$* in the string *a$*. The value of INSTR(*n,a$,b$*) is the first position at or after the *n*th character of *a$* where the string *b$* occurs. If *b$* does not appear as a substring of *a$*, then the value is 0.

INT The value of the function INT(*x*) is the greatest whole number that is less than or equal to *x*.

INTEGER A variable of type INTEGER requires 2 bytes of memory and can hold the whole numbers from -32,768 to 32,767. INTEGER values and variables are indicated by the type tag %: 345%, Count%.

IOCTL and IOCTL$ After a device has been opened with reference number *n*, the value of the function IOCTL$(*n*) is a control string read from the device driver, and a statement of the form IOCTL #*n*, *a$* sends the string *a$* to the driver. See also Devices in the "Supporting Topics" section.

KEY The statement KEY *n*, *a$* assigns the string *a$* to function key F*n*. The string *a$* must have a length of 15 or less and *n* may be any number from 1 to 10 (and also 30 and 31 for function keys F11 and F12 on the 101-key keyboards). After KEY *n*, *a$* is executed, pressing the key F*n* has the same effect as typing the characters in *a$*. The statement KEY ON may be used to display the first six characters of the assigned strings on the last row of the Output window. The statement KEY OFF turns this display off. The statement KEY LIST displays all the assigned strings in their entirety. The KEY ON and KEY LIST statements are not available when forms are visible.

KEY(n) The statement ON KEY(*n*) GOSUB *label* sets up the trapping of function key *n*. After KEY(*n*) ON is executed, pressing F*n* at any time causes program control to transfer to the subroutine beginning at *label*. Trapping is disabled with KEY(*n*) OFF and deferred with KEY(*n*) STOP. The subroutine at *label* must be in the leading code of the .BAS module containing the KEY (*n*) statement. The KEY(*n*) statement is not available when forms are visible. See also Labels, Subroutines, Event trapping in the "Supporting Topics" section.

KILL The statement KILL *filespec* erases the specified disk file or files. You may use the ordinary DOS wildcards of ? and *. See also Filespec in the "Supporting Topics" section.

LBOUND   For a one-dimensional array *arrayName*, the value of the function LBOUND(*arrayName*) is the smallest subscript value that may be used. For any array *arrayName*, the value of the function LBOUND(*arrayName*, *n*) is the smallest subscript value that may be used for the *n*th subscript of the array. For example, after the statement DIM example(1 TO 31,1 TO 12,1990 TO 1999) is executed, the value of LBOUND(example, 3) is the smallest value allowed for the third subscript of example(), which is 1990. LBOUND cannot be used for control arrays.

**LCASE$**   The value of the string function LCASE$(*a$*) is a string identical to *a$* except that all uppercase letters are changed to lowercase.

**LEFT$**   The value of the function LEFT$(*a$*,*n*) is the string consisting of the leftmost *n* characters of *a$*. If *n* is greater than the number of characters in *a$*, then the value of the function is *a$*.

LEN   The value of LEN(*a$*) is the number of characters in the string *a$*. If *var* is not a variable-length string variable, then the value of LEN(*var*) is the number of bytes needed to hold the value of the variable in memory. That is, LEN(*var*) is 2, 4, 4, 8 or 8 for integer, long integer, single-precision, double-precision, and currency variables. LEN(*var*), when *var* is a variable with a user-defined record type, is the number of bytes of memory needed to store the value of the variable.

LET   The statement LET *var* = *expr* assigns the value of the expression to the variable. If *var* is a fixed-length string variable with length *n* and LEN(*expr*) is greater than *n*, then just the first *n* characters of *expr* are assigned to *var*. If LEN(*expr*) is less than *n*, then *expr* is padded on the right with spaces and assigned to *var*. If *var* has a user-defined type, then *expr* must be of the same type. The statement *var* = *expr* is equivalent to LET *var* = *expr*.

LINE   The graphics statement LINE (*x1*,*y1*)-(*x2*,*y2*) draws a line connecting the two points. (If the first point is omitted, then the line is drawn from the last point referenced to the specified point.) The line is in color *c* of the current palette if LINE (*x1*,*y1*)-(*x2*,*y2*),*c* is executed. The statement LINE (*x1*,*y1*)-(*x2*,*y2*),,B draws a rectangle with the two points as opposite vertices. (If B is replaced by BF, a solid rectangle is drawn.) If *s* is a number in hexadecimal notation from 0 to &HFFFF, then LINE (*x1*,*y1*)-(*x2*,*y2*),,,*s* draws a styled line (with the pattern determined by *s*) connecting the two points. See also Palettes, Last point referenced, Graphics coordinate systems in the "Supporting Topics" section.

LINE INPUT The statements LINE INPUT *a$*, LINE INPUT "*prompt*"; *a$*, and LINE INPUT "*prompt*", *a$* are similar to the corresponding INPUT statements. However, the user may respond with *any* string, even one containing commas, leading spaces, and quotation marks. The entire string is assigned to the string variable *a$*. The LINE INPUT statement is not available when forms are visible.

LINE INPUT# After a file has been opened as a sequential file for INPUT with reference number *n*, the statement LINE INPUT #*n*, *a$* assigns to the string variable *a$* the string of characters from the current location in the file up to the next pair of carriage return/line feed characters.

LOAD The method *formName*.LOAD loads the named form into memory, executes any Form_Load event procedure for this form, and displays the form if its Visible property is true. If the *formName* form is already loaded, the attempt to reload it is ignored. In general, the LOAD method is not needed since any reference to a form associated with a project automatically causes the form to be loaded into memory. Use the LOAD method to speed up later display of a form when forms are being loaded from slow floppy disk systems.

LOC This function gives the current location in a sequential, random-access, or binary file. For a sequential file with reference number *n*, LOC(*n*) is one more than the number MOD 128 of blocks of 128 characters read from or written to the file since it was opened. For a random-access file, LOC(*n*) is the current record (either the last record read or written, or the record identified in a SEEK statement). For a binary file, LOC(*n*) is the number of bytes from the beginning of the file to the last byte read or written. For communications, the value of LOC(*n*) is the number of bytes waiting in the communications buffer with reference number *n*. See also Binary files in the "Supporting Topics" section.

LOCATE The statement LOCATE *r,c* positions the cursor at row *r*, column *c* of the screen. The statement LOCATE,,0 turns the display of the cursor off, while the statement LOCATE,,1 turns the display back on. If *m* and *n* are whole numbers between 0 and 31, then the statement LOCATE,,,*m,n* will change the size of the cursor. The LOCATE statement is not available when forms are visible.

LOCK   The LOCK command is intended for use in programs that operate on a network. The DOS TSR program SHARE enables file sharing and must be executed from DOS prior to using the LOCK statement. After a file has been opened with reference number *n*, the statement LOCK #*n* denies access to the file by any other process. For a random-access file, the statement LOCK #*n*, *r1* TO *r2* denies access to records *r1* through *r2* by any other process. For a binary file, this statement denies access to bytes *r1* through *r2*. The statement LOCK #*n*, *r1* locks only record (or byte) *r1*. For a sequential file, all forms of the LOCK statement have the same effect as LOCK #*n*. The UNLOCK statement is used to remove locks from files. All locks should be removed before a file is closed or the program is terminated. See also Random-access files, Binary files in the "Supporting Topics" section.

LOF   After a file has been opened with reference number *n*, the number of characters in the file (that is, the length of the file) is given by LOF(*n*). For communications, the value of LOF(*n*) equals the number of bytes waiting in the communications buffer with reference number *n*.

LOG   If *x* is a positive number, then the value of LOG(*x*) is the natural logarithm (base e) of *x*.

LONG   A variable of type LONG requires 4 bytes of memory and can hold the whole numbers from -2,147,483,648 to 2,147,483,647. LONG values and variables are indicated by the type tag &: 12345678&, Population&.

LPOS   Printers have buffers that hold characters until they are ready to be printed. The value of LPOS(1) is the current position in the buffer of the first printer (LPT1) and LPOS(2) is the current position for the second printer (LPT2).

LPRINT and LPRINT USING   These statements print data on the printer in the same way PRINT and PRINT USING display data on the screen. In addition, LPRINT may be used to set various print modes, such as the width of the characters and the vertical spacing. The statements are not available when forms are showing.

LSET   If *af$* is a field variable of a random-access file, then the statement LSET *af$* = *B$* assigns the string *b$*, possibly truncated or padded on the right with spaces, to *af$*. If *a$* is an ordinary variable, then the statement LSET *a$* = *b$* replaces the value of *a$* with a string of the same length consisting of *b$* truncated or padded on the right with spaces. LSET also can be used to assign a record of one user-defined type to a record of a different user-defined type. See also Random-access files in the "Supporting Topics" section.

**LTRIM$**   The value of the function LTRIM$(*a$*) is the string obtained by removing all the spaces from the beginning of the string *a$*. The string *a$* may be of either fixed or variable length. This function does not remove the blank bytes in an unassigned fixed-length string.

**MID$**   The value of the function MID$(*a$,m,n*) is the substring of *a$* beginning with the *m*th character of *a$* and containing up to *n* characters. If the parameter *n* is omitted, MID$(*a$,m*) is all the characters of *a$* from the *m*th character on. The statement MID$(*a$,m,n*) = *b$* replaces the characters of *a$*, beginning with the *m*th character, by the first *n* characters of the string *b$*.

MKDIR   The statement MKDIR *path\dirName* creates a subdirectory named *dirName* in the directory specified by *path*. (You can specify a drive in the pathname as well.) See also Directories in the "Supporting Topics" section.

MKI$, MKL$, MKS$, MKD$, MKC$ These functions convert integer, long integer, single-precision, double-precision, and currency numbers into strings of lengths 2, 4, 4, 8, and 8, respectively. This conversion is needed with the buffer method of working with random-access files. See also Random-access files in the "Supporting Topics" section.

MKSMBF$, MKDMBF$ With the buffer method of working with random-access files, these functions convert single-precision and double-precision numbers into strings of lengths 4 and 8, respectively, in the Microsoft Binary Format. This conversion is necessary before placing these numbers into random-access files that will be read with Microsoft BASIC, GW-BASIC, BASICA, or early versions of QuickBasic. See also Random-access files in the "Supporting Topics" section.

MOD   The value of the expression *num1* MOD *num2* is the whole number remainder when *num1* is divided by *num2*. If either *num1* or *num2* is not a whole number, then it is rounded to a whole number before the MOD operation is performed. If one or both of *num1* and *num2* are negative, the result of the MOD operation will have the same sign as *num1*. For example, 25 MOD 7 is 4, 18.7 MOD 3.2 is 1, -35 MOD -4 is -3, and 27 MOD -6 is 3.

MOVE   The method *objectName*.

MOVE *column, row* moves the named form or control so that its upper-left corner is at *column* and *row*. For forms, positioning is relative to the upper-left corner of the screen. For controls, positioning is relative to the upper-left corner of the form, frame, or picture box to which the control is attached. The method *objectName*.MOVE *column, row, width, height* also resizes the named form or control to be *width* columns wide and *height* rows high. The MOVE method may be used whether or not a form or control is visible. If you wish to specify just a new width for an object, you CANNOT use *objectName*.MOVE ,,*width*. Instead, use *objectName*.MOVE *objectName*.Left, *objectName*.Top, *width*. Similar considerations apply for changing just the row, the height, the width and height, and so forth.

MOVEFIRST   Suppose an ISAM table has been opened with reference number *n*. The ISAM statement MOVEFIRST #*n* makes the current position in the table the beginning record in the current index of that table. See also ISAM statements in the "Supporting Topics" section.

MOVELAST   Suppose an ISAM table has been opened with reference number *n*. The ISAM statement MOVELAST #*n* makes the current position in the table the end record in the current index of that table. See also ISAM statements in the "Supporting Topics" section.

MOVENEXT   Suppose an ISAM table has been opened with reference number *n*. The ISAM statement MOVENEXT #*n* makes the current position in the table the record following the current record according to the order established by the current index of that table. If the current position was the end record, then EOF(*n*) becomes true. See also ISAM statements in the "Supporting Topics" section.

MOVEPREVIOUS   Suppose an ISAM table has been opened with reference number *n*. The ISAM statement MOVEPREVIOUS #*n* makes the current position in the table the record preceding the current record according to the order established by the current index of that table. If the current position was the beginning record, then BOF(*n*) becomes true. See also ISAM statements in the "Supporting Topics" section.

MSGBOX (Statement and Function)   The statement MSGBOX(*message$*) displays *message$* in a dialog box with an OK button. Multiline messages can be displayed by including a carriage return and linefeed (CHR$(13)+CHR$(10)) at the appropriate points in *message$*. The more general statement MSGBOX(*message$, buttons, title$*) displays *message$* in a dialog box titled with *title$* and containing from one to three buttons as determined by the value of *buttons*. The value of *buttons* also determines which button is the default (has the focus):

Value for First Button as Default	Value for Second Button as Default	Value for Third Button as Default	Buttons Displayed
0			OK
1	257		OK, Cancel
2	258	514	Abort, Retry, Ignore
3	259	515	Yes, No, Cancel
4	260		Yes, No
5	261		Retry, Cancel

The value of the function MSGBOX(*message$, buttons, title$*) indicates which of the displayed buttons the user pressed/clicked; in all other aspects the MSGBOX statement and function act in the same manner. The values returned for each of the possible buttons pressed are 1 for OK, 2 for Cancel (or Esc), 3 for Abort, 4 for Retry, 5 for Ignore, 6 for Yes, and 7 for No.

NAME   The statement NAME *filespec1* AS *filespec2* is used to change the name and/or the directory of *filespec1* to the name and/or directory specified by *filespec2*. The two filespecs must refer to the same drive if a drive or full pathname is used for *filespec2*. See also Filespec in the "Supporting Topics" section.

NEWPAGE The method PRINTER.NEWPAGE issues a formfeed (CHR$(12)) to the printer to cause the paper to advance to the top of a new page.

NOT (Logical Operator) The logical expression NOT *condition1* is true if *condition1* is false and false if *condition1* is true. For example, NOT (3<7) is false since 3<7 is true, while NOT ("earth">"moon") is true since "earth">"moon" is false.

NOT (Bitwise Operator) The expression NOT *byte1* is evaluated by expressing the byte as an 8-tuple binary number and then NOTing each individual digit, where NOT 1 is equal to 0, while NOT 0 is equal to 1.

OCT$ If *n* is a whole number between 0 and 2,147,483,647, then OCT$(*n*) is the octal (that is, base 8) representation of *n*.

ON COM(n) If *n* is the number 1 or 2, then the statement ON COM(*n*) GOSUB *label* sets up the trapping of the *n*th communications port. After COM(*n*) ON is executed, information coming into the port causes a GOSUB to *label*. The subroutine at *label* must be in the leading code of the .BAS module containing the ON COM (*n*) statement. See also Devices, Labels, Subroutines, Event trapping in the "Supporting Topics" section.

ON ERROR The statement ON ERROR GOTO *label* sets up error trapping. An error then causes a jump to an error-handling routine beginning at *label*. The label, and thus the associated error handler, must be in the leading code of the .BAS module containing the ON ERROR statement. To place an error-handling routine within a procedure to deal with errors which occur while that procedure is executing, use the statement ON LOCAL ERROR GOTO *label*. There's also an ON ERROR RESUME NEXT statement that sends execution to the statement following the one that caused the error. See the discussion of RESUME for further details. See also Labels, Event trapping in the "Supporting Topics" section.

ON...GOSUB and ON...GOTO The statement ON *expression* GOSUB *label1*, *label2*, ... causes a GOSUB to *label1*, *label2*, ... depending upon whether the value of the expression is 1, 2, ... Similarly, the GOTO variation causes an unconditional jump to the appropriate label. The GOSUB or GOTO statement and its target must be in the same part of the program, either both in the leading code of a .BAS module or both in the same procedure. See also Labels in the "Supporting Topics" section.

ON KEY(n)   The statement ON KEY(n) GOSUB *label* sets up trapping of the function key F*n*. After KEY(n) ON is executed, pressing F*n* causes a GOSUB to *label*. The subroutine at *label* must be in the leading code of the .BAS module containing the ON KEY(n) statement. The ON KEY(n) statement is not available when forms are visible. See also Labels, Subroutines, Event trapping in the "Supporting Topics" section.

ON PEN   The statement ON PEN GOSUB *label* sets up trapping of a light pen. After PEN ON is executed, pressing the metal clip on the light pen or pressing the light pen to the screen, as appropriate, causes a GOSUB to *label*. The subroutine at *label* must be in the leading code of the .BAS module containing the ON PEN statement. See also Labels, Subroutines, Event trapping in the "Supporting Topics" section.

ON PLAY(n)   The music background buffer holds notes that have been specified by PLAY statements and are waiting to be played. If *n* is a whole number, then the statement ON PLAY(n) GOSUB *label* sets up trapping of the music buffer. After PLAY ON is executed, as soon as the number of notes in the buffer falls below *n*, the program GOSUBs to *label*. The capacity of the music background buffer is 32 notes, counting pauses between notes as notes. The subroutine at *label* must be in the leading code of the .BAS module containing the ON PLAY(n) statement. See also Labels, Subroutines, Event trapping in the "Supporting Topics" section.

ON STRIG(n)   If *n* is 0, 2, 4, or 6, the statement ON STRIG(n) GOSUB *label* sets up trapping of one of the joystick buttons. The numbers 0 and 4 are associated with the lower and upper buttons of the first joystick, and the numbers 2 and 6 are associated with the lower and upper buttons of the second joystick. After STRIG(n) ON is executed, pressing the button associated with *n* causes a GOSUB to *label*. The subroutine at *label* must be in the leading code of the .BAS module containing the ON STRIG(n) statement. See also Labels, Subroutines, Event trapping in the "Supporting Topics" section.

ON TIMER   If *n* is an integer from 1 to 86400 (1 second to 24 hours), the statement ON TIMER(n) GOSUB *label* sets up trapping of the computer's internal clock. After TIMER ON is executed, every *n* seconds the program

GOSUBs to the subroutine beginning at *label*. The subroutine at *label* must be in the leading code of the .BAS module containing the ON TIMER statement. The ON TIMER statement is not available when forms are visible. See also Labels, Subroutines, Event trapping in the "Supporting Topics" section.

ON UEVENT The statement ON UEVENT GOSUB *label* sets up trapping of a user-defined event. After UEVENT ON is executed, an occurrence of the user-defined event causes a GOSUB to *label*. The subroutine at *label* must be in the leading code of the .BAS module containing the ON UEVENT statement. See also Labels, Subroutines, Event trapping in the "Supporting Topics" section.

OPEN The statement OPEN *filespec* FOR *mode* AS #*n* allows access to the file *filespec* in one of the following modes: INPUT (information can be read sequentially from the file), OUTPUT (a new file is created and information can be written sequentially to it), APPEND (information can be added sequentially to the end of a file), or BINARY (information can be read or written in an arbitrary fashion). The statement OPEN *filespec* FOR RANDOM AS #*n* LEN = *g* allows random access to the file *filespec* in which each record has length *g*. Throughout the program, the file is referred to by the reference number *n* (from 1 through 255). Some other variations of the OPEN statement are OPEN "SCRN" FOR OUTPUT AS #*n*, OPEN "LPT1" FOR OUTPUT AS #*n*, and OPEN "KYBD" FOR INPUT AS #*n*, which allow access to the screen, printer, and keyboard as if they were sequential files. See also Filespec, Binary files in the "Supporting Topics" section.

DOS 3.0 and later versions support networking and make possible two enhancements to the OPEN statement. (The DOS TSR program SHARE enables file sharing and must be executed from DOS prior to the use of the enhanced variations of the OPEN statement.) Visual Basic accesses data files in two ways; it reads from them or writes to them. When several processes may utilize a file at the same time, accurate file handling requires that certain types of access be denied to anyone but the person who has opened the file. The statement OPEN *filespec* FOR *mode* LOCK READ AS #*n* or OPEN *filespec* FOR RANDOM LOCK READ AS #*n* LEN = *g* opens the specified file and forbids any other process from reading the file as long as the file is open. LOCK WRITE forbids any other process from writing to the file as long as the file is open. LOCK READ WRITE forbids any other process from reading or writing to the file as long as the file is open. LOCK SHARED grants full access to any other process. Except with LOCK SHARED, if a file is currently opened and locked by a process for a certain access mode, then another process attempting to open the file for the same mode will receive the message "Permission denied" and be denied access.

OPEN "COM...   If *n* is 1 or 2, then the statement OPEN "COM*n:b,p,d,s,L*" AS #*m* LEN=*g* provides access to the *n*th serial port using reference number *m* and specifies the block size (*g*), the speed of transmission (*b*), the parity (*p*), the number of data bits to be used in transmitting each character (*d*), the number of stop bits (*s*), and the line parameters (*L*).

OPTION BASE   After the statement OPTION BASE *m* is executed, where *m* is 0 or 1, a statement of the form DIM *arrayName(n)* defines an array with subscripts ranging from *m* to *n*. Visual Basic's extended DIM statement, which permits both lower and upper subscript bounds to be specified for each array, achieves a wider range of results, making its use preferable to OPTION BASE.

OPTION EXPLICIT   If the statement OPTION EXPLICIT appears in the leading code of a form or .BAS module, then each variable appearing in the form or module must be declared before it is used. A variable is declared by appearing in a COMMON, CONST, DIM, REDIM, SHARED, or STATIC statement, or by appearing as a parameter in a SUB, FUNC-TION, or DEF FN definition. The OPTION EXPLICIT statement must be placed before any executable statement in the leading code.

OR (Logical Operator)   The logical expression *condition1* OR *condition2* is true except when both *condition1* and *condition2* are false. For example, ("apple">"ape") OR ("earth">"moon") is true since "apple">"ape" is true, while (1>2) OR ("moon"<"earth") is false since both (1>2) and ("moon"<"earth") are false.

OR (Bitwise Operator)   The expression *byte1* OR *byte2* is evaluated by expressing each byte as an 8-bit binary number and then ORing together corresponding digits, where 1 OR 1, 1 OR 0, and 0 OR 1 are all equal to 1, while 0 AND 0 is equal to 0. For example, the expression 37 OR 157 translated to 8-bit binary becomes 00100101 OR 10011101. ORing together corresponding digits gives the binary 8-tuple 10111101 or decimal 189. Thus 37 OR 157 is 189.

OUT   The statement OUT *n,m* sends the byte *m* to port *n*. See also Devices in the "Supporting Topics" section.

PAINT   If (*x,y*) is an unlit interior point of a region of the screen, then the graphics statement PAINT (*x,y*) fills the region. In medium-resolution graphics mode, if the boundary has color *b* of the current palette and *c* is one of the colors of the current palette, then the statement PAINT (*x,y*),*c,b* fills the bounded region with the color *c*. If *t$* is a string with a length of at most 64 characters, then the statement PAINT (*x,y*), *t$* fills the region with a repeating pattern based on a tile determined by *t$*. See also Palettes, Graphics coordinate systems in the "Supporting Topics" section.

PALETTE and PALETTE USING   When a graphics monitor is attached to an EGA, VGA, or MCGA display card, the PALETTE statement loads colors into the palette "jars" whose numbers range from 0 to 3, 0 to 15, 0 to 63, or 0 to 255. The statement PALETTE *m, n* assigns the *n*th color to the *m*th palette jar. The statement PALETTE USING *array(0)* specifies that each palette jar be filled with the corresponding color number stored in the array element: *array(0)* in jar 0, *array(1)* in jar 1, and so on. See also Colors for CGA monitors, Palettes in the "Supporting Topics" section.

PCOPY   Depending upon the screen mode in use, the video adapter card may have extra memory locations that give it the capability of working with several screens, called *pages*. (See the discussion of the SCREEN statement for details.) For instance, with an 80-character-per-line text mode screen, the Color Graphics Adapter has four pages. The statement PCOPY *m,n* copies the contents of page *m* onto page *n*. The PCOPY statement is not available when forms are visible.

PEEK   Each memory location contains a number from 0 to 255. If *n* is a number from 0 to 65535, then the value of PEEK(*n*) is the number stored at offset *n* in the current segment of memory (set with DEF SEG). See also Memory in the "Supporting Topics" section.

PEN   The statements PEN ON, PEN OFF, and PEN STOP respectively enable, disable, and defer the reading of the status of the light pen. For each *n* from 0 to 9, the value of the function PEN(*n*) gives information about the status of the light pen.

PLAY (function)   The music background buffer holds notes that have been specified by PLAY statements and are waiting to be played. The value of the function PLAY(0) is the number of notes currently in the music background buffer waiting to be played.

PLAY (statement)   The statement PLAY *a$*, where *a$* is a string of notes and parameters, produces musical notes with most of the embellishments indicated by sheet music. The rich and varied strings constitute a miniature music language. A note can be identified by one of the letters A through G, with a following plus or minus sign to indicate a sharp or a flat. A 1/*n*th note pause is specified by P *n*. The parameters O, L, T, MF, MB, ML, MS, and MN specify attributes of subsequent notes and are sometimes combined with a number giving a magnitude for the attribute. The parameter O *n*, where *n* ranges from 0 through 6, specifies the octave of subsequent notes. The parameter L *n*, where *n* ranges from 1 to 64, causes subsequent notes to be 1/*n*th notes. (For instance, *n* = 4 produces quarter notes.) The parameter T *n*, where *n* ranges from 32 to 255, sets the tempo of subsequent notes to *n* quarter notes per minute. The default values for the parameters O, L, and T are 4, 4, and 120, respectively. The parameter MF (music foreground) causes all notes to be played before the computer executes additional statements, while MB (music background) places up to 32 notes in a buffer that plays the notes while the program continues to execute. The parameters ML (music legato) and MS (music staccato) respectively decrease and increase the durations of notes; MN returns the durations to normal articulation. PLAY statements can give the numeric argument of a command as the value of a numeric variable by using the STR$ function. For instance, the statement PLAY "D8" may be written as n = 8: PLAY "D" + STR$(n).

PMAP   The graphics function PMAP converts the natural coordinates of a point to the physical coordinates and vice versa, as shown in Table C-1. See also Graphics coordinate systems in the "Supporting Topics" section.

TABLE C-1   The PMAP Function

n	c	Value of PMAP(c,n)
0	natural x-coordinate	physical x-coordinate
1	natural y-coordinate	physical y-coordinate
2	physical x-coordinate	natural x-coordinate
3	physical y-coordinate	natural y-coordinate

POINT   In graphics mode, the value of the graphics function POINT(x,y) is the number of the color of the point with coordinates (x,y). (With an EGA or VGA graphics card, POINT(x,y) gives the palette number assigned to the point.) The values of the functions POINT(0) and POINT(1) are the first and second physical coordinates of the last point referenced, and the values of POINT(2) and POINT(3) are the first and second natural coordinates of the last point referenced. See also Colors for CGA monitors, Palettes, Last point referenced, Graphics coordinate systems in the "Supporting Topics" section.

POKE   Each memory location contains a number from 0 to 255. If n is a number from 0 to 65535, then the statement POKE n,m stores the number m at offset n in the current segment of memory (set with DEF SEG). See also Memory in the "Supporting Topics" section.

POS   The value of the function POS(0) is the column number of the current position of the cursor. The POS function is not available when forms are visible.

PRESET   (See PSET and PRESET.)

PRINT (Statement & Method)   The PRINT statement is used to display data on the screen (when not working with forms). The statement PRINT *expression* displays the value of the expression at the current position of the cursor and moves the cursor to the beginning of the next row of the screen. The PRINT method displays data on forms and picture boxes. The method *objectName*.PRINT *expression* displays the value of the expression on the named form or picture box at the location specified by the values of *objectName*.CurrentX and *objectName*.CurrentY and moves the cursor to the beginning of the next row of the form or picture box.

Both the PRINT statement and the PRINT method display numbers with a trailing space and positive numbers with a leading space. In both cases, if *expression* is followed by a semicolon or comma, then the cursor will not move to the beginning of the next row, but rather will move to the next position or print zone, respectively. Several expressions may be placed in the same PRINT statement/method if separated by semicolons (to display them adjacent to one another) or by commas (to display them in successive zones).

PRINT USING (Statement & Method) Both the statement PRINT USING *a$*; *list of expressions* and the method *objectName*.PRINT USING *a$*; *list of expressions* (where *objectName* is a form or picture box) display the values of the expressions (possibly interspersed with text from *a$*) in formats specified by *a$*. The statement can be used to align and display financial quantities with dollar signs, commas, asterisks, two decimal places, and preceding or trailing signs (+ or -). Numbers are formatted with the symbols #, +, $, $$, *, **, ^^^^, comma, and period. Strings are formatted with the symbols &, !, and \ \. See Tables C-2 and C-3.

Note If you wish to use one of the above special symbols for text in a format string, you must precede it with an underscore (_).

PRINT# and PRINT# USING After a file has been opened as a sequential file for output or append with reference number *n*, the statements PRINT #*n*,*expression* and PRINT #*n*,USING *a$*;*expression* place the value of the expression into the file in the same way PRINT and PRINT USING display it on the screen.

PRINTER The PRINTER object provides access to the system printer. Methods available are PRINT to send text to the printer, NEWPAGE to execute a form feed to begin a new page, and ENDDOC to terminate the printing process. Properties which can be set are PrintTarget to specify which port (LPT1, LPT2, or LPT3) the printer is attached to or which DOS file is to receive redirected output.

PRINTFORM The method *formName*.PRINTFORM prints on the printer an image of the named form and all its contents.

Results Obtained by Executing PRINT USING *a$*; *x$*

TABLE C-2

a$	Meaning	x$	Result
&	Displays entire string.	"Nebraska"	Nebraska
!	Displays first letter of string.	"Nebraska"	N
\ \	Displays first *n* letters of string (where there are *n*-2 spaces between the slashes). Here demonstrated with n=4.	"Nebraska"	Nebr

TABLE C-3 Results Obtained from Executing PRINT USING *a$; n*

Symbol	Meaning	*n*	*a$*	Result
#	Each pound sign stands for one digit in a numeric field.	1234.6 123 123.4 12345	"########" "########" "########" "####"	1235 123 123 %12345
.	Denotes the placement of the decimal point.	123.4	"######.#"	123.4
,	Causes commas to be displayed to the left of every third digit to the left of the decimal point, as appropriate.	12345	"#######,"	12,345
$	Displays a $ sign as the first character of the field.	23.45	"$####.##"	$ 23.45
$$	Displays a $ sign immediatly before the first digit displayed.	23.45	"$$###.##"	$23.45
**	Inserts asterisks in place of leading blanks.	23.45	"**######"	******23
*	Displays an asterisk as the first character of the field.	23.45	"*#######"	* 23
^^^^	(at end) Displays the number in exponential notation.	12345 −12	"##.#^^^^" "#.##^^^^"	1.2E+04 −.12E+01
^^^^^	(at end) Displays the number in expanded exponential notation.	12345	"#.#^^^^^"	1.2E+004
+	Reserves a space for the sign of the variable.	12 −12	"+#######" "#######+"	+12 12−

PSET and PRESET   In graphics modes, the graphics statement PSET *(x,y)* displays the point with coordinates *(x,y)* in the foreground color and the statement PRESET *(x,y)* displays it in the background color. The statement PSET *(x,y),c* or the statement PRESET*(x,y),c* causes the point

(x,y) to be displayed in color c of the current palette. See also Colors for CGA monitors, Palettes, Last point referenced, Graphics coordinate systems in the "Supporting Topics" section.

PUT (Files)   With the buffer method of working with random-access files, after the file has been opened with reference number n and values have been assigned to the field variables, the statement PUT #n,r places these values in the rth record of the file. (If r is omitted, the record after the one most recently accessed by a GET or PUT statement will be filled.)

Suppose $recVar$ is a variable of a user-defined record type and that a file has been opened with a statement of the form OPEN $fileName$ FOR RANDOM AS #n LEN = LEN($recVar$). The statement PUT #$n,r,recVar$ places the value of $recVar$ in the rth record of the file.

The PUT statement is also used to place data into a file opened as a binary file. Suppose var is a variable that holds a value consisting of b bytes. (For instance, if var is an integer variable, then b is 2. If var is an ordinary string variable, then b will equal the length of the string currently assigned to it.) The statement PUT #n,p,var writes the successive bytes of var into the b consecutive locations beginning with position p in the binary file with reference number n. (*Note:* The positions are numbered 1, 2, 3, ...) If p is omitted, then the current file position is used as the beginning position. See also Random-access files, Binary files in the "Supporting Topics" section.

PUT (Graphics)   After a rectangular region of the screen has been stored in the array $arrayName$ by a GET statement, the graphics statement PUT $(x,y),arrayName$,PSET places an exact image of the rectangular region on the screen positioned with its upper-left corner at the point (x,y). The following list shows the possible alternatives to PSET in the statement and the conditions in which points on the high-resolution graphics screen will be white after PUT is executed for each alternative. See also Last point referenced, Graphics coordinate systems in the "Supporting Topics" section.

The point in the resulting graphic image will be white when using

XOR   if the corresponding point is white in either the stored image or the original screen image, but not both (default).

AND   if the corresponding point is white in the stored image and also in the original screen image.

OR   if the corresponding point is white in either the stored image or the original screen image or both.

PRESET   if the corresponding point is black in the stored image.

QBCOLOR   The value of the function QBCOLOR(*colorAttrib*) is *colorAttrib*, where *colorAttrib* is a whole number from 0 to 15. This function is included in Visual Basic for DOS for compatibility with Visual Basic for Windows.

RANDOMIZE   The statement RANDOMIZE automatically uses the computer's clock to seed the random number generator. The statement RANDOMIZE *n* seeds the generator with a number determined by *n*. If the random number generator is not seeded, the same list of numbers will be generated by RND each time a program is executed.

READ   The statement READ *var1*, *var2*, ... assigns to *var1* the first unused constant stored in a DATA statement, to *var2* the next unused constant, and so on. Use RESTORE to adjust where data is read from.

REDIM   The statement REDIM *arrayName*(...) erases the array from memory and recreates it. The information inside the parentheses has the same form and produces the same result as that in a DIM statement. After the REDIMensioning, all elements have their default values. Although the ranges of the subscripts may be changed, the number of dimensions must be the same as in the original DIMensioning of the array. The statement REDIM PRESERVE *arrayName*(...) may be used to increase (or decrease) the upper bound on the rightmost dimension of the array while preserving the values of all current elements in the array. Inserting SHARED right after REDIM in a REDIM statement in the leading code of the form or .BAS module allows all procedures in the form or module to share the array. Only dynamic arrays may be redimensioned. See also Default values, Static vs. dynamic in the "Supporting Topics" section.

REFRESH   The method *objectName*.REFRESH causes the named form or control to be refreshed, that is, redrawn reflecting any changes made to its properties. Generally, refreshing occurs automatically, but may be forced immediately to reflect changes such as a new list of files in a file list box due to a change in directories.

REM   The statement REM allows documentation to be placed in a program. A line of the form REM *comment* is ignored during execution. The REM statement is also used to place metacommands into the program. The REM statement may be abbreviated as an apostrophe.

REMOVEITEM   The method *controlName*.REMOVEITEM *index* removes the item specified by *index* from the *controlName* list box or combo box. A value of 0 for *index* causes deletion of the first item in the list, a value of 1 for *index* causes deletion of the second item in the list, and so on. If *index* is less than 0 or greater than *controlName*.ListCount, a run-time error occurs. The value of the ListIndex property is set to -1 by the REMOVEITEM method.

RESET   The statement RESET closes all open files. Using RESET is equivalent to using CLOSE with no file reference numbers.

RESTORE   The statement RESTORE *label* causes the next request to READ an item of data to take the first item in the DATA statement following the indicated label. If the *label* parameter is omitted, the first DATA statement in the leading code will be accessed. Subsequent READ statements will continue selecting data from that point on. See also Labels in the "Supporting Topics" section.

RESUME   When the statement RESUME is encountered at the end of an error-handling routine, the program branches back to the statement in which the error was encountered. The variations RESUME *label* and RESUME NEXT cause the program to branch to the statement at the indicated label or to the statement following the statement in which the error occurred, respectively. (The combination of ON ERROR and RESUME NEXT is similar to the combination GOSUB and RETURN.) See also Labels in the "Supporting Topics" section.

RETRIEVE   Suppose an ISAM table has been opened with reference number *n* and that both BOF(*n*) and EOF(*n*) are false. Then the statement RETRIEVE #*n*, *recVar* places the contents of the record at the current position into *recVar*. That is, the entry in each column of the record is assigned to the corresponding field of *recVar*. See also ISAM statements in the "Supporting Topics" section.

RETURN   When the statement RETURN is encountered at the end of a subroutine, the program branches back to the statement following the one containing the most recently executed GOSUB. The variation RE-TURN *label* causes the program to branch back to the statement at or following the indicated label. See also Labels, Subroutines in the "Supporting Topics" section.

RGB   The value of the function RGB(*red, green, blue*) is the color value from 0 to 15 that most closely approximates the RGB color which would be generated in Visual Basic for Windows for the given value of red, green, and blue. This function is included in Visual Basic for Dos to provide compatibility with Visual Basic for Windows.

**RIGHT$**   The value of the function RIGHT$(*a$,n*) is the string consisting of the rightmost *n* characters of *a$*. If *n* is greater than the number of characters of *a$*, then the value of the function is *a$*.

RMDIR   If *path* specifies a directory containing no files or subdirectories, then the statement RMDIR *path* removes the directory. (You can also specify a drive.) See also Directories in the "Supporting Topics" section.

RND   The value of the function RND is a single number from 0 to 1, not including 1, that has many of the properties one would expect from random choices. The convention is to refer to these as "random numbers." The value of INT(*n**RND)+1 is a random whole number from 1 to *n*.

ROLLBACK   The ISAM statement ROLLBACK *n* restores all tables (and indexes) to the state which existed when the value *n* was returned from an invocation of the SAVEPOINT function. If *n* is omitted, then all tables (and indexes) are restored to the state that existed when the most recent invocation of SAVEPOINT occurred. If SAVEPOINT has not been invoked during the current set of transactions or the statement ROLLBACK ALL is executed, then all tables (and indexes) are restored to the state that existed when the BEGINTRANS statement was executed to mark the beginning of the current group of transactions. ROLLBACK cannot be executed once the COMMITTRANS statement is executed or any table is closed. See also ISAM statements in the "Supporting Topics" section.

RSET   If *af$* is a field variable of a random-access file, then the statement RSET *af$* = *b$* assigns the string *b$* to *af$*, possibly truncated or padded on the left with spaces. If *a$* is an ordinary variable, then the statement RSET *a$* = *b$* replaces the value of *a$* with a string of the same length consisting of *b$* truncated or padded on the left with spaces. See also Random-access files in the "Supporting Topics" section.

**RTRIM$**   The value of the function RTRIM$(*a$*) is the string obtained by removing all the spaces from the end of the string *a$*. The string *a$* may be either fixed-length or variable-length.

RUN   The statement RUN restarts the currently executing program. All values previously assigned to variables are deleted. The variation RUN *filespec* loads the specified program from a disk and executes it. The specified program must be a Visual Basic program. The statement RUN *label* restarts the current program at the point referenced. See also Filespec, Labels in the "Supporting Topics" section.

SADD   The value of the function SADD(*stringVar$*) is the offset of the start of *stringVar$* in memory. The memory segment in which this offset is being measured is that returned by the function SSEG(*stringVar$*). The argument *stringVar$* must be a variable-length string. See also Memory in the "Supporting Topics" section.

SAVEPOINT   The value of the ISAM function SAVEPOINT is an integer indicating the number of times SAVEPOINT has been invoked since the BEGINTRANS statement was executed. Each time SAVEPOINT is invoked, the current state of all tables (and indexes) is noted in the transaction log. This permits the integer returned by SAVEPOINT to be used in a subsequent ROLLBACK command to restore all tables (and indexes) to the state which existed when a particular invocation of the SAVEPOINT function occurred. See also ISAM statements in the "Supporting Topics" section.

SCREEN (Function)   The value of the function SCREEN(*r,c*) is the ASCII value of the character in the *r*th row, *c*th column of the screen. The value of SCREEN(*r,c,*1) is the number of the palette jar used to color the character. The SCREEN function is not available when forms are visible. See also Palettes in the "Supporting Topics" section.

SCREEN (Statement)   If no forms are showing, a monitor can be placed in the desired graphics screen mode by one of the statements in Table C-4. Before forms can be displayed, the monitor must be returned to text mode by using the statement SCREEN 0.

When a graphics adapter is used in text mode, the computer can store the contents of several different screens, called *pages*. The number of pages allowed, call it *n*, depends on the graphics adapter and selected mode. The page currently displayed is called the *visual* page, and the page currently being written to is called the *active* page. If *a* and *v* are numbers from 0 to *n-1*, then the statement SCREEN ,,*a*,*v* designates page *a* as the active page and page *v* as the visual page. See also Colors for CGA monitors in the "Supporting Topics" section.

SEEK   The statement SEEK #*n*,*p* sets the current file position in the binary or random-access file referenced by *n* to the *p*th byte or record of the file, respectively. After the statement is executed, the next GET or PUT statement will read or write bytes, respectively, beginning with the *p*th byte or record. The value of the function SEEK(*n*) is the current file position either in bytes or by record number. After a PUT or GET statement is executed, the value of SEEK(*n*) is the number of the next byte or record. See also Binary files in the "Supporting Topics" section.

TABLE
C-4

The SCREEN Statement

SCREEN 0	text mode
SCREEN 1	medium-resolution graphics mode
SCREEN 2	high-resolution graphics mode
SCREEN 3	720x348 Hercules graphics mode, two colors
SCREEN 4	640x400 Olivetti/AT&T 6300 graphics mode, two colors
SCREEN 7	320x200 16 color EGA, VGA adapters
SCREEN 8	640x200 16 color EGA, VGA adapters
SCREEN 9	640x350 4 to 16 color EGA, VGA adapters
SCREEN 10	640x350 monochrome EGA adapters
SCREEN 11	640x480 2-color MCGA, VGA adapters
SCREEN 12	640x480 16-color VGA only
SCREEN 13	320x200 256-color MCGA, VGA adapters

SEEKEQ, SEEKGE, SEEKGT   Suppose an ISAM table has been opened with reference number *n* and that the current index was created with the statement CREATEINDEX #*n*, *indexName$*, *t*, *columnName$*. The statement SEEKEQ #*n*, *keyVal* moves the current position to the first record where the value in the *columnName$* column is equal to *keyVal*. The statement SEEKGE #*n*, *keyVal* moves the current position to the first record where the value in the *columnName$* column is greater than or equal to *keyVal*. The statement SEEKGT #*n*, *keyVal* moves the current position to the first record where the value in the *columnName$* column is greater than *keyVal*. If no match is found, the current position is after the end record of the current index and EOF(*n*) is true. See also ISAM statements in the "Supporting Topics" section.

SELECT CASE   The SELECT CASE statement provides a compact method of selecting for execution one of several blocks of statements based on the value of an expression. The SELECT CASE block begins with a line of the form SELECT CASE *expression* and ends with the statement END SELECT. In between are statements of the form CASE *valueList* and perhaps the statement CASE ELSE. The items in the *valueList* may be individual values, or ranges of values such as "*a* TO *b*" or "IS < *a*." Each of these CASE statements is followed by a block of one or more statements. The block of statements following the first CASE *valueList* statement for which *valueList* includes the value of *expression* is the only block of statements executed. If none of the value lists include the value of *expression* and a CASE ELSE statement is present, then the block of statements following the CASE ELSE statement is executed.

SETFOCUS   The method *objectName*.SETFOCUS moves the focus to the named form or control. Only the object with the focus can receive user input from the keyboard or the mouse. If *objectName* is a form, the form's default control, if any, receives the focus. Disabled and invisible objects cannot receive the focus. If an attempt is made to set focus to a control that cannot receive the focus, the next control in tab order receives the focus.

SETINDEX   The ISAM statement SETINDEX #*n*, *indexName$* makes the *indexName$* index the current index in the table opened with reference number *n*. The statement SETINDEX #*n* makes the null index the current index, that is, the table is ordered by the order in which items were inserted. See also ISAM statements in the "Supporting Topics" section.

SETMEM   The far heap is the area of memory where variables outside the default data segment are stored. The function SETMEM(n) both alters and returns the size of the far heap. The numeric expression n specifies the number of bytes by which to increase or decrease the far heap; the heap size is increased if n is positive or decreased if n is negative. The value of the function SETMEM(n) is the amount of memory in the far heap after the change. SETMEM is used with C and assembly language programs that need to allocate memory.

SETTEXT   The method CLIPBOARD.SETTEXT *info$* replaces the contents of the clipboard with the string *info$*.

SGN   The value of the function SGN(x) is 1, 0, or –1, depending upon whether x is positive, zero, or negative, respectively.

SHARED   A statement of the form SHARED *var1,var2,...* can be used at the beginning of a procedure to give variables *var1, var2, ...* access to form or module variables. The type of each variable is determined either by a type-declaration tag, a DEFtype statement, or an AS clause. If an AS clause is used in the SHARED statement, then an AS clause must be used to declare the type of the variable in the leading code. Any change made to a shared variable by the procedure will change the variable of the same name in the leading code, and vice versa. Declaring a variable as SHARED in a procedure allows form or module level variables to be used by the procedure without passing them as an argument. Arrays dimensioned in the leading code may be shared with procedures by listing their names followed by empty parentheses in a SHARED statement. (See the DIM statement with the SHARED keyword to share variables with all procedures in a given form or module. See the COMMON and COMMON SHARED statements to share variables between forms and modules.)

SHELL   If *c$* is a DOS command, then the statement SHELL *c$* suspends execution of the Visual Basic program, executes the DOS command specified by *c$*, and then resumes execution of the Visual Basic program. The statement SHELL by itself suspends program execution and invokes a copy of DOS. Entering the command EXIT resumes execution of the Visual Basic program after the SHELL statement.

SHOW   The method *formName*.SHOW displays the named form and gives it the focus. If necessary, SHOW first loads the form into memory. The method *formName*.SHOW 1 displays the named form and in addition puts it in a modal state. Before switching to other forms or dialog boxes, the user must first activate an event procedure that causes the form to be hidden. The method SCREEN.SHOW displays all forms that have been hidden by the method SCREEN.HIDE.

SIN   For any number x, the value of the trigonometric function SIN(x) is the sine of the angle of x radians. See also Radian measure in the "Supporting Topics" section.

SINGLE   A variable of type SINGLE requires 4 bytes of memory and can hold 0, the numbers from 1.40129×10^{-45} to 3.402823×10^{38} with at most seven significant digits, and the negative of these numbers. SINGLE values and variables are indicated by the type tag !: 32.156!, Meters!.

SLEEP   The statement SLEEP n suspends execution of a program until either n seconds elapse, a key is pressed, or an event enabled with *EVENT* ON occurs. (If a key is pressed, sleeping ends but the keystroke remains in the keyboard buffer.) The SLEEP statement is not available when forms are visible, and SLEEP alone pauses indefinitely (until a key is pressed).

SOUND   The statement SOUND f,d generates a sound of pitch f Hz for a duration of $d*$.055 seconds. The value of f must be at least 37.

Note   The keys of the piano have frequencies ranging from 55 to 8372 Hz.

SPACE$ If n is an integer from 0 to 32767, then the value of the function SPACE$($n$) is the string consisting of n spaces.

SPC   The function SPC is used in PRINT, LPRINT, and PRINT# statements to generate spaces. For instance, the statement PRINT a; SPC(n); b\$ skips n spaces between the displays of the two strings.

SQR   For any non-negative number x, the value of the square root function SQR(x) is the non-negative number whose square is x.

SSEG   The value of the function SSEG(*stringVar$*) is the number of the memory segment holding the variable-length string *stringVar$*. The value of the function SADD(*stringVar$*) is the offset of the start of *stringVar$*

within this segment. The argument *stringVar$* must be a variable-length string. See also Memory in the "Supporting Topics" section.

SSEGADD   The value of the function SSEGADD(*stringVar$*) is a long integer giving both the segment of memory in which *stringVar$* lies and the offset of the start of *stringVar$* within that segment. If *longVal* is the value of SSEGADD, then in hexadecimal notation the segment is LEFT$(HEX$(*longVal*),4) and the offset is RIGHT$(HEX$(*longVal*),4).

STACK (Function)   The value of the function STACK is the maximum allowable size of the stack in bytes.

STACK (Statement)   The stack is a special portion of memory used to hold certain temporary values, including the parameters and return addresses for SUB and FUNCTION procedures. Programs that involve recursive calls to procedures may require a larger than normal stack. The statement STACK *n* sets the size of the stack to the number of bytes specified by *n*, but is rarely necessary and may cause your program to run out of memory for other purposes. The statement STACK resets the stack to its default size.

STATIC   A statement of the form STATIC *var1,var2,...* can be used at the beginning of the definition of a procedure to specify that the variables *var1, var2, ...* are static local variables in the procedure. Memory for static variables is permanently set aside by Visual Basic, allowing static variables to retain their values between successive calls of the procedure. The type of each variable is determined either by a DEFtype statement, a type-declaration tag, or an AS clause. Static variables have no connection to variables of the same name outside the procedure, and so may be named without regard to "outside" variables. Arrays may be declared static by listing their names followed by empty parentheses in a STATIC statement, and then dimensioning them in a subsequent DIM statement. If STATIC precedes the word Sub or Function then all variables inside the procedure are static by default.

$STATIC   The metacommand REM $STATIC tells Visual Basic to use a static, or permanent, allocation of memory for arrays appearing in subsequent DIM statements, if possible. Effectively, the $STATIC metacommand reverses the effect of any previous $DYNAMIC metacommand by allowing arrays that are normally static by default to be allocated as static. An array is static by default if it is DIMensioned with constant upper and lower bounds, implicitly dimensioned by appearing in a statement without first being declared in a DIM statement, or is DIMensioned within a STATIC procedure. See also Metacommands, Static vs. dynamic in the "Supporting Topics" section.

STICK   For $n = 0$ or 1, the value of the function STICK(n) is the x- or y-coordinate, respectively, of the first joystick lever. For $n = 2$ or 3, the function gives the corresponding information for the second joystick.

STOP   The statement STOP suspends the execution of a program. Execution within the programming environment can be resumed beginning with the first statement after the STOP statement by pressing F5.

**STR$**   The STR$ function converts numbers to strings. The value of the function STR$($n$) is the string consisting of the number n in the form normally displayed by a print statement.

STRIG   The statements STRIG ON and STRIG OFF respectively enable and disable the reading of the status of the joystick buttons. For each n from 0 to 7, the value of the function STRIG(n) gives information about the status of the joystick button.

STRIG(n)   The statement ON STRIG(n) GOSUB *label* sets up the trapping of one of the joystick buttons. The numbers $n = 0$ and $n = 4$ are associated with the first joystick's lower and upper buttons, respectively, and the numbers $n = 2$ and $n = 6$ are associated with the second joystick's lower and upper buttons. The pressing of the corresponding button anytime after STRIG(n) ON is executed causes a GOSUB to the subroutine at *label*. See also Labels, Subroutines, Event trapping in the "Supporting Topics" section.

STRING   A variable of type STRING can hold a string of up to 32,767 characters. STRING values are enclosed in quotes: "January 1, 2001". STRING variables are indicated by the type tag $: FirstName$. A variable of type STRING*n holds a string of n characters, where n is a whole number from 1 to 32,767. Variables of this type have no type tag and must be declared in a COMMON, DIM, SHARED, or STATIC statement. Until assigned a value, these variables contain a string of n CHR$(0)'s.

STRING$ If n is a whole number from 0 to 32767, then the value of STRING$($n,a\$$) is the string consisting of the first character of $a\$$ repeated n times. If m is a whole number from 0 to 255, then the value of the function STRING$($n,m$) is the string consisting of the character with ASCII value m repeated n times. (Using an integer for the second argument is slightly more efficient.)

SUB/END SUB   A Sub procedure is a multistatement block beginning with a statement of the form SUB *SubprocedureName(parList)*, followed on subsequent lines by one or more statements for carrying out the task of the procedure, and ending with the statement END SUB. The parameter list *parList* is a list of variables through which values will be passed to the procedure whenever it is called. (See the discussion of CALL.) Parameters may be numeric or (variable-length) string variables as well as arrays.

SWAP   If *var1* and *var2* are two variables of the same type, then the statement SWAP *var1*, *var2* exchanges the values of the two variables.

SYSTEM   The statement SYSTEM terminates program execution, closes all files, and returns control to the Visual Basic environment (or DOS for EXE's).

TAB   The function TAB(n) is used in PRINT, LPRINT, and PRINT# statements to move the cursor to position n and place spaces in all skipped-over positions. If n is less than the cursor position, then the cursor is moved to the nth position of the next line. If n is greater than the screen width, the cursor moves to a position determined by n MOD screenwidth.

TAN   For any number x (except for $x=\pi/2$, $-\pi/2$, $3*\pi/2$, $-3*\pi/2$, and so on), the value of the trigonometric function TAN(x) is the tangent of the angle of x radians. See also Radian measure in the "Supporting Topics" section.

TEXTCOMP   The value of the ISAM function TEXTCOMP($a\$$, $b\$$) is -1 if $a\$$ precedes $b\$$ according to ISAM ordering rules, is 0 if $a\$$ equals $b\$$ according to ISAM ordering rules, or is 1 if $a\$$ follows $b\$$ according to ISAM ordering rules. In ISAM ordering rules, ASCII order is followed except that all trailing spaces are ignored, the uppercase letters are treated is if they were lowercase, the space character (CHR$(32)) is treated as if it precedes all other characters, and the characters with

ASCII values 123, 124, 125, 126, 127, 21, and 20 are treated as though they occur in that order between ASCII values 96 and 97. See also ISAM statements in the "Supporting Topics" section.

TEXTHEIGHT   The value of the function TEXTHEIGHT(*strVar$*) is 1 plus the number of carriage return/line feed pairs (CHR$(13)+CHR$(10)) contained in *strVar$*.

TEXTWIDTH   The value of the function TEXTWIDTH(*strVar$*) is the number of characters in the longest "line" contained in *strVar$*. Carriage return/line feed pairs (CHR$(13)+CHR$(10)), if any, separate successive "lines" in *strVar$*. If *strVar$* does not contain any carriage return/line feed pairs, then TEXTWIDTH(*strVar$*) = LEN(*strVar$*).

**TIME$**   The value of the function TIME$ is the current time expressed as a string of the form hh:mm:ss. (The hours range from 0 to 23, as in military time.) If *t$* is such a string, then the statement TIME$ = *t$* sets the computer's internal clock to the corresponding time.

TIMER   The value of the function TIMER is the number of seconds from midnight to the time currently stored in the computer's internal clock.

TRON and TROFF   These statements, which are abbreviations of "trace on" and "trace off," are used to debug programs. The statement TRON causes the program to execute more slowly than normal and for each statement to be highlighted on the screen as it executes. The statement TROFF terminates this tracing. The TRON and TROFF statements are not available when forms are visible.

TYPE/END TYPE   A multistatement block beginning with TYPE *typeName* and ending with END TYPE creates a user-defined record type. Each statement inside the block has the form *elt* AS *type*, where *elt* is a variable (simple or array without a type-declaration tag) and *type* is either INTEGER, LONG, SINGLE, DOUBLE, CURRENCY, STRING*n (that is, fixed-length string), or another user-defined record type. After a statement of the form DIM *var* AS *typeName* appears, the element corresponding to the statement *elt* AS *type* is referred to as *var.elt*. Visual Basic allows arrays inside TYPEs. TYPE statements may not appear inside procedures.

UBOUND   For a one-dimensional array *arrayName*, the value of the function UBOUND(*arrayName*) is the largest subscript value that may be used. For any array *arrayName*, the value of the function UBOUND(*arrayName*, *n*) is the largest subscript value that may be used for the *n*th subscript of the array. For example, after the statement DIM Example(1 TO 31,1 TO 12,1990 TO 1999) is executed, the value of UBOUND(example, 3) is the largest value allowed for the third subscript of Example( ), which is 1999.

**UCASE$**   The value of the string function UCASE$(*a$*) is a string identical to *a$* except that all lowercase letters are changed to uppercase.

UEVENT   User-defined events are defined through an assembly language routine. The statements UEVENT ON and UEVENT OFF respectively enable and disable trapping of a user-defined event. The statement UEVENT STOP suspends trapping of a user-defined event until trapping is resumed by a UEVENT ON statement.

UNLOAD   The statement UNLOAD *formName* removes the named form from memory. Any future reference to the form will cause the form to be reloaded using the property values set at design time. The statement UNLOAD *controlName* [*index*] frees up memory as it removes the control with index value *index* from the named control array.

UNLOCK   The UNLOCK command is intended for use in programs that operate on a network. The DOS TSR program SHARE enables file sharing and must be executed from DOS prior to using the LOCK and UNLOCK statements. After a LOCK statement has been used to deny access to all or part of a file (see the discussion of LOCK for details), a corresponding UNLOCK statement can be used to restore access. Suppose a data file has been opened as reference number *n*. The locks established by the statements LOCK #n; LOCK #n, *r1*; and LOCK #n, *r1* TO *r2* are undone by the statements UNLOCK #n; UNLOCK #n, *r1*; and UNLOCK #n, *r1* TO *r2*, respectively. There must be an exact correspondence between the locking and the unlocking statements used in a program, that is, each set of paired statements must refer to the same range of record numbers or bytes.

UPDATE   Suppose an ISAM table has been opened with reference number *n* and that both BOF(*n*) and EOF(*n*) are false. Then the statement UPDATE

#*n*, *recVar* replaces the current record with the values in *recVar*. That is, the entry in each field of *recVar* is placed in the corresponding column of the current record. In the null index, the record will appear in the same position as before. In other indexes, the record may move to another location. If so, the current position is changed to this new location. See also ISAM statements in the "Supporting Topics" section.

VAL   The VAL function is used to convert strings to numbers. If the leading characters of the string *a$* corresponds to a number, then VAL(*a$*) will be the number represented by these characters. For any number *n*, VAL(STR$(*n*)) is *n*.

VARPTR and VARSEG   The values of the functions VARSEG(*var*) and VARPTR(*var*) are the segment of memory and the offset in that segment where the *var* (if it is a numeric, array element, or fixed-length string) or of the descriptor of *var* (if it is a variable-length string or an array variable) is located. See also Memory in the "Supporting Topics" section.

**VARPTR$**   The value of the function VARPTR$(*var*) is a five-character string whose first character identifies the type of the variable and whose last four characters specify the location of the variable in memory. This function can be used in conjunction with DRAW and PLAY.

VIEW   The graphics statement VIEW establishes a rectangular portion of the screen as a *graphics viewport* that will contain all subsequent figures drawn by graphics statements. There are three variations of the VIEW statement.

In medium-resolution graphics mode, the pair of statements WINDOW SCREEN (0,0)-(319,199): VIEW (*x1,y1*)-(*x2,y2*),*c*,*b* establish a viewport with upper-left corner at physical coordinates (*x1,y1*) and lower-right corner at physical coordinates (*x2,y2*). The rectangle will have background color *c* and a boundary of color *b*, where *b* and *c* are two colors of the current palette. Subsequent graphics statements will scale their displays and place them into the viewport as if it were the entire screen. For the other graphics modes, the numbers 319 and 199 should be replaced by the physical x- and y-coordinates of the point in the lower-right corner of the screen.

If no WINDOW statement is active, the statement VIEW (*x1,y1*)–(*x2,y2*),*c*,*b* establishes a viewport at the same location and with the same colors as above. However, instead of forcing a future drawing to fit inside the viewport, subsequent graphics statements do no scaling, but simply translate the drawing $x1$ points to the right and $y1$ points down, and clip the drawing at the edge of the viewport; only that portion of the translated drawing that falls inside the viewport is displayed.

If no WINDOW statement is active, the statement VIEW SCREEN $(x1,y1)$-$(x2,y2)$,c,b establishes a viewport at the same location and with the same colors as in the first example. However, instead of scaling down or translating a future drawing, subsequent graphics statements simply clip the drawing at the edge of the viewport; only that portion of the drawing that falls within the viewport is displayed. See also Colors for CGA monitors, Palettes, Graphics coordinate systems in the "Supporting Topics" section.

VIEW PRINT Normally, the screen holds 25 lines of text numbered 1 through 25. However, only lines 1 through 24 scroll. These lines are called the "text viewport." The statement VIEW PRINT *lineA* TO *lineB* causes the text viewport to consist of lines *lineA* through *lineB*. After its execution, all text displayed with PRINT statements will appear in the viewport and only the lines in the viewport will scroll. The LOCATE statement is only valid if the line number specified is within the current text viewport, and the CLS statement affects only the viewport. Text lying outside of the text viewport stays fixed. The statement VIEW PRINT by itself allows the entire screen to scroll. It has the same effect as VIEW PRINT 1 TO h, where h is the number of text lines on the screen. The VIEW PRINT statement is not available when forms are visible.

WAIT If p is a port number, q is the value of a byte to be received at port p, and n and m are integers from 0 to 255, then the statement WAIT p, n, m suspends the execution of the program until the condition $((q\ \text{XOR}\ m)\ \text{AND}\ n) <> 0$ is true for the byte with value q received at port p. Bits in the result are set only if the source bits are different. See also Devices in the "Supporting Topics" section.

WHILE/WEND A WHILE ... WEND loop is a sequence of statements beginning with a statement of the form WHILE *condition* and ending with the statement WEND. After the WHILE statement is executed, the computer repeatedly executes the entire sequence of statements inside the loop as long as the condition is true.

WIDTH   When used with a monitor other than a monochrome display, the statement WIDTH 40 causes text to be displayed in wide characters with 40 characters per line. (The first PRINT zone contains 14 positions and the second 26 positions.) The standard 80-character-per-line format is restored with the statement WIDTH 80. (The first four PRINT zones consist of 14 positions, and the fifth consists of 24 positions.) In graphics modes, the WIDTH statement either has no effect or alters the mode to one that features the indicated number of characters per line.

The EGA, VGA, and the MCGA video adapter cards are capable of displaying 25, 30, 43, 50, or 60 lines of text depending on the type of adapter, the type of monitor, and the screen mode. When *t* is a valid length for the video adapter, the statement WIDTH ,*t* sets the number of lines of text to *t*. The WIDTH statement for changing the number of characters per line or number of lines per page is not available when forms are visible.

If *s* is an integer less than 255, the statement WIDTH "LPT1",*s* causes Visual Basic to permit a maximum of *s* characters to be printed on a single line by LPRINT statements. Visual Basic will send a carriage return/line feed pair to the printer after *s* characters have been printed on a line, even if LPRINT would not otherwise start a new line at that point. The statement WIDTH "LPT1",255 specifies infinite width; that is, a carriage return/line feed pair will be sent to the printer only when requested by LPRINT. The same effects can be obtained with the statement WIDTH LPRINT *s*.

WINDOW   The graphics statement WINDOW (*x1*,*y1*)-(*x2*,*y2*) imposes a standard (right-hand) coordinate system on the screen with the *x*-coordinates of points ranging from *x1* to *x2* and *y*-coordinates ranging from *y1* to *y2*. Subsequent graphics statements place figures on the screen scaled in accordance with this coordinate system. If the statement WINDOW is replaced by WINDOW SCREEN, then a left-hand coordinate system is imposed. That is, the y-coordinates of points are lower in the higher areas on the screen. See also Graphics coordinate systems in the "Supporting Topics" section.

WRITE   The statement WRITE *exp1*,*exp2*,... displays the values of the expressions one after the other on the screen. Strings appear surrounded by quotation marks and numbers do not have leading or trailing spaces. All commas are displayed and do not induce jumps to successive print zones. After all the values are displayed, the cursor moves to the beginning of the next line. The WRITE statement is not available when forms are visible.

WRITE#   After a sequential file is opened for output or append with reference number n, the statement WRITE #n, $exp1,exp2,...$ records the values of the expressions one after the other into the file. Strings appear surrounded by quotation marks, numbers do not have leading or trailing spaces, all commas in the expressions are recorded, and the characters for carriage return and line feed are placed following the data.

XOR (Logical Operator)   The logical expression *condition1* XOR *condition2* is true if *condition1* is true or *condition2* is true but not if both are true. For example, (3<7) XOR ("abc">"a") is false since both 3<7 and "abc">"a" are true, while ("apple">"ape") XOR ("earth">"moon") is true since "apple">"ape" is true and "earth">"moon" is false.

XOR (Bitwise Operator)   The expression *byte1* XOR *byte2* is evaluated by expressing each byte as an 8-tuple binary number and then XORing together corresponding digits, where 1 XOR 0 and 0 XOR 1 both equal 1, while 1 XOR 1 and 0 XOR 0 both equal 0. For example, the expression 37 XOR 157 translated to binary 8-tuples becomes 00100101 XOR 10011101. XORing together corresponding digits gives the binary 8-tuple 10111000 or decimal 184. Thus 37 XOR 157 is 184.

Supporting Topics

Binary files   A file that has been opened with a statement of the form OPEN *filespec* FOR BINARY AS #n is regarded simply as a sequence of characters occupying positions 1, 2, 3, ... At any time, a specific location in the file is designated as the "current position." The SEEK statement can be is used to set the current position. Collections of consecutive characters are written to and read from the file beginning at the current position with PUT and GET statements, respectively. After a PUT or GET statement is executed, the position following the last position accessed becomes the new current position.

Colors for CGA monitors   Sixteen different colors, identified by the numbers 0 through 15, are available on standard color monitors (that is, monitors that can be attached to the Color Graphics Adapter card).

0 Black	4 Red	8 Gray	12 Light Red
1 Blue	5 Magenta	9 Light Blue	13 Light Magenta
2 Green	6 Brown	10 Light Green	14 Yellow
3 Cyan	7 White	11 Light Cyan	15 Intense White

In text mode (invoked with the statement SCREEN 0), any of the colors are available as foreground colors and the first eight are also available as background colors. Forms also use these color codes to set the ForeColor and BackColor properties. In medium-resolution graphics mode, which is invoked with the statement SCREEN 1, two palettes of four colors each are available.

Palette 0

0. Background color
1. Green
2. Red
3. Brown

Palette 1

0. Background color
1. Cyan
2. Magenta
3. White

In high-resolution graphics mode, invoked with the statement SCREEN 2, only two colors, black (0) and white (1), are available. See the discussion of SCREEN for the ranges of colors available in the higher graphics modes.

Default values   Before a numeric, variable-length string, array element, or fixed-length string variable of length n has been assigned a value by the program, its value is 0, the null string (""), or a string of n CHR$(0) characters, respectively.

Devices   Some examples of devices are the video screen, keyboard, printer, modem, and diskette drives. The computer's microprocessor receives data from and sends data to the various devices of the computer through what are called *ports*. Each port is identified by a number from 0 to 65535. A *byte* of data consists of a number from 0 to 255.

Directories   Think of a disk as a master folder holding other folders, each of which might hold yet other folders. Each folder, other than the master folder, has a name. Each folder is identified by a *path*: a string beginning with a drive letter, followed by a colon and a backslash character, ending with the name of the folder to be identified, and listing the names of the intermediate folders (in order) separated by backslashes. For instance the path "C:\DAVID\GAMES" identifies the folder GAMES, which is contained in the folder DAVID, which in turn is contained in the master folder of drive C.

Each folder is called a *directory* and the master folder is called the *root directory*. When a folder is opened, the revealed folders are referred to as its *subdirectories*. Think of a file as a piece of paper inside one of the folders. Thus, each directory contains files and subdirectories.

At any time, one of the directories is said to be the *current directory*. Initially the root directory is the current directory. The current directory can be changed from DOS with the CD command or from Visual Basic with the CHDIR command. DOS and Visual Basic statements that access files, such as DIR and FILES, act on the files in the current directory unless otherwise directed.

The *default drive* is the drive whose letter appeared in the DOS prompt when Visual Basic was invoked. If a drive is missing from a path, then the drive is assumed to be the default drive.

Event trapping   Special events, such as the pressing of a function key or the occurrence of an error, can be set to trigger a jump to a subroutine. These events are specified by statements of the general form *Event* ON and ON *Event* GOSUB *label*, which cause the computer to check for the event after the execution of each statement. If the event has occurred, the computer then performs a GOSUB to the subroutine at *label*. Trapping is disabled with *Event* OFF and deferred with *Event* STOP.

Filespec   The filespec of a file on disk is a string consisting of the letter of the drive, a colon, and the name of the file. (The drive is optional). If directories are being used, then the file name is preceded by the identifying path.

Graphics coordinate systems   All graphics statements require that a graphics coordinate system be established using the SCREEN statement. Note, however, that before any graphics coordinate system can be set up, all forms must be unloaded or hidden (see the UNLOAD statement and HIDE method). The standard graphics coordinate system is called the *physical* coordinate system. For the CGA screen modes (SCREEN 1 or SCREEN 2), the y-coordinates range from 0 to 199 moving from the top to the bottom of the screen, and the x-coordinates range from 0 to 319 in medium-resolution graphics mode and from 0 to 639 in high-resolution graphics mode, moving from the left to the right side of the screen. See the discussion of SCREEN for the ranges in the higher graphics screen modes. The WINDOW statement can be used to specify a different coordinate system, called a *natural* or *logical* coordinate system. Points can also be specified in terms of *relative coordinates*. The phrase STEP (*X,Y*) refers to the point obtained by starting at the last point referenced and moving *x* units in the horizontal direction and *y* units in the vertical direction. Relative coordinates can be used in all statements that produce graphics.

ISAM statements   Indexed Sequential Access Method files and the statements for manipulating them are only available in the Professional Edition of Visual Basic for DOS. To use ISAM statements in the Professional Edition, the program PROISAMD.EXE must be run at the DOS prompt prior to invoking Visual Basic.

Labels   Visual Basic supports two mechanisms for identifying program lines that are the destinations of statements such as GOTO and GOSUB: line numbers and descriptive labels. Descriptive labels are named using the same rules as variables and are followed by a colon. This book uses the word *label* to refer to either a descriptive label or a line number.

When Visual Basic encounters a statement such as GOTO *label*, GOSUB *label*, or RESUME *label*, execution jumps to the statement immediately following *label* (which may be on the next line). Jumps cannot be made between forms or .BAS modules; *label* must be located in the same form or .BAS module as the statement causing the jump.

Last point referenced   At any time, one point on the screen is designated as the "last point referenced." Initially it is the point in the center of the graphics screen. After a graphics statement is executed, the point changes to one of the points used in the statement. For instance, after a circle is drawn, the center of the circle becomes the last point referenced.

After a line is drawn, the right point named in the LINE statement becomes the last point referenced.

Library routines   The library VBDOS.LIB contains the five routines Absolute, Int86Old, Int86XOld, Interrupt, and InterruptX. The include file VBDOS.BI contains the declarations for these five routines as well as for the user-defined data types RegType and RegTypeX. RegType consists of the eight integer elements AX, BX, CX, DX, BP, SI, DI, and FLAGS. RegTypeX contains the additional integer elements DS and ES. If a form or .BAS module requires the use of a routine from VBDOS.LIB, the statement REM $INCLUDE: 'VBDOS.BI' must appear in the leading code of that form or module. If the program is to be run within the Visual Basic environment, Visual Basic must be invoked with the /L parameter. If the program is compiled to an executable (.EXE) file, the VBDOS.LIB library must be linked into the program.

Memory   Each memory location holds an integer from 0 to 255. This unit of data or memory is called a *byte*. The computer's memory is divided into blocks of memory locations called *segments*. Each segment is 65,536 bytes in size. Within a segment, a particular memory location can be specified by giving its *offset* (a number from 0 to 65,535) from the beginning of the segment. Thus, to locate an item in memory, both its segment and offset within that segment must be known, although in many cases just the offset is sufficient. Segments overlap, that is, the same portion of memory may be considered to be within different segments. Segment 0 extends from location 0 to location 65535. Segment 1 extends from location 16 to location 65551. Segment 2 extends from location 32 to 65567, and so on. As a result of this overlap, the 34th memory location can, for instance, be identified as segment 0: offset 34, segment 1: offset 18, or segment 2: offset 2. Visual Basic reserves a special segment, called the *Default Data Segment* or DGROUP, where it stores special values such as the current row and column of the cursor, and the value of the random seed. The *current segment of memory* is used in conjunction with the offsets given in BLOAD, BSAVE, PEEK, and POKE statements. At the start of program execution, the current segment of memory is the Default Data Segment. It can be changed at any time by the DEF SEG statement.

Metacommands   The statements $STATIC, and $DYNAMIC are called metacommands. Metacommands instruct the interpreter and compiler to insert certain code into the program or to treat certain Visual Basic statements in a particular way. Because metacommands are not executed, they are preceded by the reserved word REM (or an apostrophe). For instance, the statement REM $STATIC or '$STATIC tells the interpreter to store arrays in a special way.

Palettes   A palette can be thought of as a collection of numbered jars that can hold paint. The number of jars available varies with the screen mode. Although the jars hold specified default colors, EGA, MCGA, and VGA adapters allow the colors to be changed with the PALETTE statement. Statements of the form PSET $(x,y),c$ and CIRCLE $(x,y),r,c$ use the color in the cth paint jar. In the absence of a COLOR statement, the PRINT statement displays characters with the color in jar 0 as the background color and the color in the highest numbered jar as the foreground color.

Radian measure   The radian system of measurement measures angles in terms of a distance around the circumference of the circle of radius 1. If the vertex of an angle between 0 and 360 degrees is placed at the center of the circle, then the length of the arc of the circle contained between the two sides of the angle is the radian measure of the angle. An angle of d degrees has a radian measure of $(\pi/180)$ *d radians.

Random-access files   The two methods for writing records to and reading records from random-access files are the "record variable method" and the "buffer method." The record variable method is discussed in Chapter 13. With the buffer method, a portion of memory referred to as a buffer is set aside for the file. A FIELD statement specifies fixed-length string field variables of the correct length whose values are held in the buffer. LSET and RSET statements assign values to the field variables, and PUT and GET statements move the contents of the buffer into a record of the file, and vice versa, respectively. The functions MKI$, MKL$, MKC$, MKS$, and MKD$ are used to convert numbers to fixed-length strings prior to placement into the buffer by LSET and RSET statements. After a GET statement places a record in the buffer, the functions CVI, CVL, CVC, CVS, and CVD are used to convert the strings back into numbers of the appropriate type.

Static vs. dynamic   Visual Basic uses two methods of storing arrays, dynamic and static. The memory locations for a static array are set aside at compile-time, and this portion of memory may not be freed for any other purpose. The memory locations for a dynamic array are assigned at run-time and *can* be freed for other purposes. Although dynamic arrays are more flexible, static arrays can be accessed faster. Visual Basic uses the dynamic allocation of arrays if either the range in a DIM statement is specified by a variable or the programmer insists on dynamic allocation with a $DYNAMIC metacommand.

Subroutines   A subroutine is a sequence of statements beginning with a label and ending with a RETURN statement. A subroutine is meant to be branched to by a GOSUB statement and is usually placed so that it cannot be entered inadvertently.

APPENDIX

Using a Mouse

Preliminaries

To use a mouse with Visual Basic, the mouse must be compatible with the Microsoft mouse, and the special driver program (often called MOUSE.COM) must be executed before loading Visual Basic

Although most mice have two buttons, only the left button is used in the following discussion. If a compatible mouse driver and mouse are installed, then a small rectangle should appear on the screen. This is the *mouse cursor* or *mouse pointer*, and its movement around the screen should correspond to the motion of the mouse on the desktop. People often say "move the mouse until it's at the left corner" as shorthand for: "Move the mouse so the mouse pointer is in the left corner." No confusion should result since the actual mouse and the mouse cursor on the screen move together.

If the mouse is not visible when Visual Basic is first invoked, then it possibly is the same color as the screen background. Try moving the mouse around the screen. If the mouse becomes visible in non-background regions of the screen, move the mouse to the Options menu, click the (left) button to get a pull-down menu, and then click on Display. Press the TAB key and then select a background color that makes the mouse visible by pressing the DOWN ARROW and UP ARROW keys to change the color until the mouse becomes visible in the background region.

Clicking

If the mouse is visible, move it to a menu name (such as File or Help) and press and release the left button. Moving the mouse to an item and pressing the button in this way is called "clicking the item." The menu should pull down, and its options should appear. These options in turn can be selected by clicking the desired option, that is, by moving the mouse to the desired option and pressing and releasing the left button. To remove a pull-down menu, move the mouse cursor to a blank area of the screen and click nothing.

Double Clicking

This refers to pressing and releasing the mouse button twice in quick succession. How fast you have to do this is usually set by a control program that comes with your mouse (like Microsoft's CPANEL.COM). The convention is that double clicking an item should correspond to activating the item (and be equivalent to moving to the item and pressing ENTER).

Dragging

Another way to use the mouse is called "dragging." Dragging refers to holding down the mouse button while moving the mouse. Dragging can be used to select an option from a menu by moving the cursor to the menu name, dragging the mouse until the desired option is highlighted, and then releasing the button.

Index

A

UNLOAD keyword, 443
UNLOAD method, for removing menu
    items, 343
UNLOAD statement, 281, 665
UNLOCK command, 639, 665
Unlocked mode, specifying, 465
Unlocking statements, 665
UPDATE ISAM command, 565, 570, 573,
    665-666
Uppercase, specifying, 464
Uppercase letters
        changing lowercase to, 665
        changing to lowercase, 637
User input, checking, 197-199
User interface, 2
        for the checkbook management
            program, 483
User-defined data types, 673
User-defined events, trapping, 645, 665
User-defined record type, creating, 664
User-defined records, arrays in, 316
Using Help option, on the Help menu, 25

V

VAL function, 130, 666
Value box, 45
Value property
        of check boxes, 325
        of option buttons, 324
        with scroll bars, 334
Values
        giving to variables, 110
        mnemonic names for, 140
        persisting, 125-126
        READing into variables, 121-123
        sharing among procedures, 123-125
Variable arrays, 276
Variable help, 358
Variable names, 113, 114
Variable types, changing the defaults for,
    119
Variables, 113-119
        assigning types to, 622

bytes needed to store numeric, 470
charting for each pass, 195
creating mixed, 313
declaring, 120-121
declaring types of, 118-119
form level, 240
giving values to, 110
global, 266
initializing, 117
initializing in functions, 242
interchanging the values of, 117
isolating, 123
local, 240
locations of in memory, 666
passing by reference, 257
passing by value, 258
READing values into, 121-123
scope of, 123-126, 449, 450
sharing, 618
sharing among modules, 449
specifying the type of, 623
types of, 114-116
VARPTR function, 666
VARPTR$ function, 666
VARSEG function, 666
VBDOS.QLB library, 471
VBDOS directory, 7, 10
VBDOS.BI file, 673
VBDOS.LIB library, 673
VBDRT10.EXE file, 70
Vertical scroll bars, 95, 320, 333
VGA screen mode, 546-547
VGA (video graphics array), 523
Video adapter cards, extra memory
    locations in, 647
VIEW graphics statement, 666-667
View menu, 17-18
        in the form designer, 43
VIEW PRINT statement, 667
Viewport, establishing, 666-667
Visible check box, 343
Visible property, 54-55
        for command buttons, 86
        for labels, 96
        with text boxes, 95

W

X

Y

Z